The Anthology of Social Studies

Issues and Strategies for
Elementary Teachers

UPDATED EDITION

The Anthology

of Social Studies

Issues and Strategies for Elementary Teachers

UPDATED EDITION

Roland Case

Penney Clark

Editors

Pacific Educational Press
Vancouver, Canada

Copyright © 2013 Roland Case and Penney Clark
ISBN 978-1-926966-31-1

Published by Pacific Educational Press
Faculty of Education
University of British Columbia
411 – 2389 Health Sciences Mall
Vancouver, Canada V6T 1Z3
Telephone: 604-822-5385
Fax: 604-822-6603
E-mail: pep.admin@ubc.ca

We acknowledge the financial support of the Government of Canada through the Canada Book Fund (CBF) for our publishing activities.

Library and Archives Canada Cataloguing in Publication Data

The anthology of social studies : issues and strategies for elementary teachers / Roland Case, Penney Clark, editors.

Updated ed. of: Issues and strategies for elementary teachers.
Includes bibliographical references and index.
Issued also in electronic format.
ISBN 978-1-926966-31-1

1. Social sciences—Study and teaching (Elementary).
2. Education, Elementary—Curricula.
3. Educational innovations.
          I. Case, Roland, 1951–
          II. Clark, Penney, 1950–
          III. Title: Issues and strategies for elementary.
          IV. Title: Issues and strategies for elementary teachers.

LB1584.A54 2012   372.83'044   C2012-907229-X

Cover Illustration: Genie MacLeod. Used with permission.
Design: Five Seventeen
Editing: Barbara Kuhne and Nancy Wilson
Proofreading: Patricia Wolfe
Indexing: Stephen Ullstrom

Printed in Canada
17   16   15   14   13   1   2   3   4   5   6

In memory of our parents
Warren and Mary Case
Hugh and Mildred Clark

Contents

PART 4: ACCESSING LEARNING RESOURCES   149

PART 5: INVESTIGATING PERSPECTIVES   225

PART 6: PLANNING AND ASSESSING FOR INSTRUCTION   277

Preface

It has been fifteen years since we first published a collection of readings for social studies educators. At the time, we sought out articles that would explain the "big ideas" that underpin the enduring practices and issues facing the field, while grounding these discussions in sound practical advice and illustrating them with powerful examples. Since then our book has undergone revision and expansion, but we have tried to stay true to our original purposes. In this updated version, we hope to make the collection more accessible by shortening the length of many of the articles and by eliminating those chapters that were least selected by instructors for use with their students. This volume has a stronger focus on elementary examples, a greater emphasis on the use of new technologies in social studies, updated sources, and more references to digital resources. You may notice that we have altered the chapter titles to distinguish them from the versions found in the previous edition. As well, we have added a new article on teaching geography. Notwithstanding the modifications reflected in this updated volume, we have retained, in fact enhanced, what we and others saw to be the strengths of its predecessors.

This work is in a true sense an anthology that marries the best of theory and practice in social studies. The word "anthology" originally meant a collection of flowers. It subsequently came to refer to a collection of the "flowers" of verse and, by extension, to the "flowers" of professional and scholarly thinking. Like a bouquet, this anthology of twenty-seven chapters by teachers and teacher educators from across Canada has the diversity and richness that comes only from a multiplicity of viewpoints and experiences. Like a carefully arranged bouquet, the different perspectives—rather than competing with others in the volume—complement and accentuate the features of the other chapters. In this respect, we are especially proud of both the harmony and the diversity of ideas in this volume. Collectively, they speak of a powerful and exciting vision of social studies. As well, they blend in countless very specific, practical suggestions with important discussions of the foundational issues at the heart of social studies teaching. We believe this new book will be of even greater value as a methods text for beginning teachers in teacher education programs and as a professional resource for experienced teachers and other educators working in social studies.

In a project of this undertaking, many individuals deserve thanks for the crucial contributions they have made. We especially appreciate the authors of the works found in this anthology. We believe they are among the finest educators and teacher educators in Canadian social studies and their writings reflect this expertise. The guidance and editorial support from our publisher, Catherine Edwards, and her staff at Pacific Educational Press have greatly enhanced the book. We acknowledge the contributions of our editor, Barbara Kuhne, designer, Five Seventeen, assistant editor, Nancy Wilson, and production manager, Nadine Pedersen. We would also like to acknowledge the able assistance of Andrea Webb in locating pertinent references.

Finally, we acknowledge the contributions of the two organizations that have occupied much of our professional and academic efforts over the past number of years: The History Education Network (THEN/HiER) (www.thenhier.ca) and The Critical Thinking Consortium (www.tc2.ca).

Roland Case
Penney Clark

PART 1 Exploring Priorities and Purposes

1

Meeting Challenges and Making Choices

Neil Smith

The challenges and choices facing social studies teachers are neither new nor simple. What goals should we emphasize? What methods could we employ to achieve these goals? How might we engage students in their own learning? This chapter invites social studies teachers to think in broad terms about what is needed to make social studies a valuable and interesting educational experience for students.

Whether we love social studies or reluctantly teach this subject, all of us can benefit from looking afresh at what social studies means to us and to our students. We may need to reconcile our personal orientation and predisposition to teach social studies in a particular way with new possibilities that may appear foreign or daunting. In some respects, this is because of our past socialization to the subject. Each of us comes to the role of "social studies teacher" having already experienced many hours of "teacher training" while attending social studies classes as a student in elementary and secondary school. During this time, ideas about the purpose of social studies and how it is supposed to be taught have been etched on our minds. These past experiences will likely profoundly shape our approach to teaching the subject. As the old adage goes, "We teach as we were taught."

Take a moment to think back over your own experiences as a social studies student in elementary and secondary school. What were your best experiences? What were your worst experiences? What do you need to learn so that your own teaching will reflect more of your positive experiences and fewer of your negative experiences?

Reassured by our own social studies experiences, many of us may ask: "Surely these established patterns of teaching social studies are still adequate?" I believe they are not. Even if we personally enjoyed social studies in school, the subject as a whole has been largely unsuccessful both in achieving its aims and in motivating students. According to John Goodlad's seminal study of over a thousand North American classrooms (1984/2004), social studies is one of the least popular of all the commonly taught subjects. Upper elementary students liked it less than any other subject (210–212). At the secondary level, Goodlad observed that:

> The topics commonly included in the social sciences appear as though they would be of great human interest. But something strange seems to have happened to them on the way to the classroom. The topics of study become removed from their intrinsically human character, reduced to the dates and places readers will recall memorizing for tests. (212)

It is also disturbing that students generally perceive social studies to be one of the most difficult subjects, largely because of the volume of information they must remember and not because of the amount of thinking required. Studies of British Columbia social studies teachers, for example, found that the importance they attach to critical thinking is not adequately reflected in the teaching strategies they use in their classrooms (Bognar, Cassidy, and Clarke 1997; Case 1993).

FINDING THE FACTS

"Okay, let's turn to page 83 in the text, please." James quietly groans and slouches a little lower in his seat. Glancing to the front, he recognizes the predictable signals. Ms. Knowles is about to launch into today's discussion. James' slight anxiety about not having read the assigned chapter on Canadian pioneers for homework is balanced by his confidence that most of his friends are probably in the same boat.

He opens the textbook and begins to flip through the pages. With a quick glance up at Knowles, James is reminded that she is an okay teacher. In fact, most kids quite like her. She is sincere and always keen about the subject. But in spite of her own enthusiasm, she isn't able to excite most students about this material. For most of them, the definition of social studies is "a school way to talk about the dead."

Knowles' first question dislodges James from his musings. "What jobs did pioneers in Canada perform?" Her eyes scan the room. James hasn't a clue. He mentally replays his survival strategy. If Knowles looks in his direction for an answer, he will first avert his eyes; if she asks him for the answer directly, he will look up politely with a shy, vacant look on his face, fumble through the pages, and mutter that he doesn't remember that part of the chapter. Be polite and uninformed. That usually suffices. He will stay in Knowles' good books, and she probably won't bother him

again for the rest of the lesson.

The teacher-directed questioning now begins in earnest. Page by page, the information emerges from the memories of the "regulars," those five students who always seem to appreciate the discussion and who recall the information well enough to offer intelligent comments. Slowly, relentlessly, Knowles extracts the desired facts and painfully constructs a picture from them, as if they were pieces of a jigsaw puzzle. Finally, she proclaims that the chapter has been "covered." James muses that this chapter, like the others before it, has been "buried"—but it will be resurrected very briefly at test time.

A writing assignment is then written on the board: "Describe how early pioneers contributed to the development of Canada." James spends the next fifteen minutes summarizing a few key ideas he remembers from the discussion: that many pioneers became hard-working farmers, while others worked on the construction of the railroad. He receives some help from Alex, an "A" student sitting beside him. He then scans the text, finds one or two other ideas, and copies them verbatim into his assignment. Enough to hold up the A– average, he thinks to himself. After staring dreamily into the pages of the text for a few minutes, then taking a drink at the water fountain, James sighs deeply and heads off to the library, where he is expected to continue his research project on Canadian pioneers.

The challenge—and it is a difficult one—is for each of us to recognize and understand both the strengths and the limitations of our inherited visions of social studies and then to build upon and beyond these experiences to enliven social studies for more of our students. I offer three typical vignettes of social studies teaching as a way to begin a critical conversation about the "what" and "how" of social studies. These snapshots of teaching practice invite us to recognize ourselves in them and then to look both for the positive elements and, even more importantly, for the areas where improvement is possible.

Read the vignette Finding the Facts, but before reading the author's comments, conduct your own analysis of the lesson: What are its positive aspects? What shortcomings do you notice? How might you improve upon the lesson? Repeat this process after you've read the other two vignettes.

In reviewing the vignette Finding the Facts, it is important to acknowledge the lesson's positive attributes. James thought the teacher was both knowledgeable and enthusiastic in her approach to teaching social studies. She systematically exposed students to

important background facts that might serve as a platform from which students could build a greater understanding of Canadian history. For a handful of students, the class discussion enabled them to make personal the information contained in their reading assignment.

The lesson, however, raises several basic questions. What organizing themes or concepts frame students' investigations? There is no evidence that the information presented amounts to anything more than a series of facts. It may be what Walter Parker calls "teaching by mentioning" or the "parade of facts" approach: "the teacher tells students a few facts about a person or event and then moves on to telling a few facts about another person or event" (1989, 40).

What insights or lessons are students asked to draw from the information? The larger picture—the general significance of the jobs performed by pioneers—is neither apparent to nor appreciated by most students.

What level of responsibility or accountability should individual students take for their own learning? The lesson relies heavily on the textbook, with the teacher engaging students in a "search and rescue" attempt to discover the facts contained within it. This methodology tacitly encourages compliance from most students, and does little to increase the number of students who actively participate in discussions or think critically about underlying issues. Although the lesson is presented clearly, and represents a solid effort to introduce new knowledge, students have little opportunity to connect this knowledge to previously learned facts and concepts, nor are they motivated to do so. Finally, the teacher does not develop a segue to subsequent investigations that may invoke fuller and more critical analysis by students.

We are left to conjecture how this lesson might be enlarged beyond the mere acquisition of facts to learning that would be both compelling and challenging for students. This challenge brings us to the second vignette, Trekking Through Town, which moves outside the textbook to the world beyond the classroom.

A number of positive features are apparent in this scenario. Students are actively engaged in the experiences, at least insofar as they all show genuine interest in how each organization they visit functions. Their teacher is committed to providing them with positive experiences that carry them beyond textbooks into the real workings of their community. He is well organized and uses a broad variety of community resources. Students clearly expand their general knowledge of occupations in their community.

The levels of student enthusiasm in this scenario are higher than those described in the first vignette; many of the same questions must, however, be asked. To what extent are students motivated to learn from these experiences? Kieran Egan (1990, 1997) contends that children are typically underwhelmed with the study of everyday experiences, and that greater learning potential exists within the more distant worlds of fantasy and imagination. When social studies concepts are taught in the context of legends and mythology, for example, students are propelled by the power of story to consider important lessons about honour and shame, trust and betrayal, and other fundamental human notions. Egan believes these to be far more relevant and motivating than a trip to the fire hall could ever be. Involving students in direct experiences, as portrayed in this field trip vignette, should not be assumed to be educationally sound simply because students eagerly participate in them.

A related concern is student accountability. In field trip activities, what responsibility do students have for their own learning? Much as James did in the first vignette, these students are participating in a free ride (albeit with legs moving), and feel little obligation to inquire into their community. The field trips might have been enriched if students had identified and completed specific investigations during the trips. After collecting data in the field, students might then have reported their findings to the class. The field "trip" could thereby have been transformed into a field "study" that provided a rich source of fresh concepts and ideas emerging from well-constructed investigations. Such a scenario works best if a teacher involves students in deciding on the most interesting and challenging questions to guide their inquiries.

TREKKING THROUGH TOWN

Mr. Stevens is upbeat. He is continually drumming up enthusiasm among his young students for their community study, tirelessly opening up new avenues for exploring local organizations. Mr. Stevens quickly steps out of the line of children and parent helpers in front of the school and checks off each student's name. After a quick review of the field trip rules, the class walks single file for three blocks, soon reaching the local fire hall where the chief and four firefighters await them.

For the next hour, the class tours the facility. The hosts explain their jobs, telling students about some of the funny and sad things that they encounter in their work. They describe the various pieces of firefighting equipment. Children slide down the fire pole from half-ceiling height, try on rubber boots and coats, and clamber onto the fire truck. When asked by the fire chief whether they have any special questions, silence ensues among the students, broken only when one student asks whether all firefighters are permitted to drive the truck. Another asks whether the chief has ever seen anyone die, and then a third asks what the firefighters do all day and night when there are no emergency calls. At this point, the allotted time is up, and the class heads back to school, arriving just in time for gym class.

In the next social studies period, the class visits the local grocery store and spends time talking with the staff. They tour the back of the store, look at the butchers' work area, examine the throwaway vegetable section, and visit the offices. After a brief conversation with the manager, the students return to class and resume other activities. The community study proceeds in a similar fashion for three weeks, with field trips to two local businesses, the town hall, and a farm. Three parents also volunteer as guest speakers to explain their occupations. The students listen, and the teacher encourages them to ask the guests questions about their work. At the end of the unit, Mr. Stevens presents a summative assignment: "Pick your favourite job or organization and write five things about it."

TACKLING THE BIG ISSUES

It seemed a bit funny. Grade 4 students reading fairy stories in social studies, especially the old version of "The Three Little Pigs." Then Mrs. Arnell—"Ms. A," the students call her—reads them a version of the tale told from the wolf's point of view. In *The True Story of the Three Little Pigs* (Scieszka 1999), the wolf defends his badly tarnished reputation. Students begin to understand how selected events may be interpreted and reported in very different ways, depending on the point of view taken. Students compare the events of the classic version of the tale with the wolf's version and prepare to take on the different roles of the story characters in a simplified mock trial. The trial is going to determine whether the wolf is innocent or guilty of first-degree murder in the death of two pigs.

The wolf (the defendant), who pleads not guilty, works with his legal defence team to review the events reported in the story and to select information that supports his claim of innocence. Crown Counsel and her team of students are given one hour to study the case and develop arguments supporting their position that the wolf is guilty of premeditated murder. The judge and jury study the general background of the case and learn about their responsibilities in the trial proceedings. The next day, the wolf's trial is held. The teacher videotapes the proceedings, and, using jointly generated criteria, helps students assess their own and their peers' presentations. "Interesting," the students think, "a lot of work and even a bit of fun. So what does this have to do with what we are supposed to be studying about Canadian history?"

Ms. A starts the third day's class with a story and drawings showing Captain Cook's first encounters with the "Nootka" peoples of the west coast of Canada in the late eighteenth century. She summarizes the European views of the key events and, for homework, asks students to read Cook's account reprinted in the textbook. The next day she provides students with an entirely different perspective—this time from some of the recently published accounts of Maquinna and the Nuu-chah-nulth peoples who were the inhabitants of Friendly Cove on Vancouver Island. These accounts present an entirely different side of the story that has been passed on through oral tradition. They contain detailed descriptions of humiliation and assaults endured by the coastal peoples at the hands of European explorers. Ms. A. then asks the class to compare the two versions of "The Three Little Pigs" with the two versions of the encounters between Cook and the Nuu-chah-nulth people. She helps students use the proper language to compare the fictional with the historical events, and to refine their rough ideas so they are able to write in their journals about the similarities and differences between them.

Next, the students prepare for a second mock trial. This time, Captain Cook is charged with destroying the way of life of an indigenous people. Students employ the same model they used in the wolf's trial. Each student, first independently, then in a group, researches events related to the first contact in Friendly Cove. They write a summary of these events and with the help of a small group of peers construct arguments either defending or prosecuting Cook. As a culminating activity, they present their arguments in a mock trial.

In this field trip lesson, what insights of importance have students gained? What new knowledge or concepts have these students acquired? Although they may pick up tidbits of information incidentally, it is unclear from the vignette that students entered or exited the field trips with a rich context for framing and extending their study. The experiences appear as serial pop-up activities with only a modest expectation that students will connect or apply this information to some larger question or problem. It is unrealistic to expect that students will make these connections by themselves. Engaging children in direct experiences for the sake of active learning without helping them make the important connections may be interpreted as largely providing entertainment. John Dewey (1938), the twentieth-century advocate of experiential education, exhorted teachers to legitimate active learning by systematically linking it to reflective practice and helping students make meaning out of their experiences by drawing conclusions from them. The main message: direct experiences such as field trips must be linked closely to concepts and theories through reflective thought. But this brings us back to our primary question.

What will make the teaching of social studies a motivating and educationally significant experience for students? It is frequently suggested that schooling should do more to help students learn how to learn and to assess knowledge critically, solve problems, and make sound decisions. The third vignette seems to more directly address this vision of social studies teaching. But, as we review the lesson, we will see that it too provides some cause for concern.

Clearly, students in the third vignette, Tackling the Big Issues, are actively engaged in a series of diverse activities. Each student has individual responsibilities within the learning tasks. Students such as James in the first vignette would have had difficulty evading this kind of assignment. To succeed in the mock trials, for example, each student is required to produce written arguments based on research and analysis, and then present them in a persuasive manner. It was intended that students would develop these skills first in relation to the fairy tale, and later by applying them to historical events related to European and aboriginal contact on the west coast of Canada. The objectives for the lesson extended well beyond the text of a classic piece of children's literature. Building on Egan's idea that story and literature can serve as a vehicle to teach important concepts, students learned about "points of view" by comparing the traditional version of the fairy tale with a modern counterpart. The teacher invited students to think critically—asking them to analyze information, decide what information would support their arguments, create and present arguments, and, ultimately, to make ethical judgments about an important historical figure. All is well thus far.

So what are the problems in this teaching scenario? The concerns with this vignette are found in the manner in which students are cast into an extremely complex historical context with insufficient background information, concepts, and skills for them to analyze the issues competently.

If students are to move beyond a superficial indictment or vindication of Captain Cook, they need a more thorough knowledge of both peoples involved: the Nuu-chah-nulth people—their history, economy, and social patterns, their previous and subsequent experiences with European and American traders, and their changing attitudes towards the white visitors; and, on the other side, the European explorers—their methods of pursuing trade, and the competition that drove their sponsors to expand their boundaries and increase the volume of trade. Without this understanding, students may be unable to judge responsibly whether or not Cook was guilty of destroying a nation of indigenous people.

A related concern stems from the skills and concepts presupposed by the very sophisticated challenges students were given. Expecting each student to successfully develop a cohesive argument is an immense stretch if students are not coached and supported in the requisite "tools." For example, will students recognize when a reason supports a conclusion and when it is largely irrelevant? Can they distinguish unfounded or exaggerated statements from grounded ones? Are students disposed to look at potential counter-arguments to their position or will they quickly reach a conclusion and be closed to all other options? Fundamental, too, is students' appreciation of the ethnocentrism that may colour each group's perceptions of events. Even the question posed—guilty or innocent—may fuel an unproductive "all or nothing"

view of an issue that may better be cast in shades of gray. As exciting and challenging as they might appear, the trials and associated debating exercises are highly sophisticated and complex practices that may result in superficial outcomes unless preceded by deliberate and comprehensive preparation. The required abilities in critical thinking do not come naturally to most students, and many will need the support of a systematic progression of instruction and guided practice to prepare them for such complex challenges. Thus, although there is much that is educationally exciting about this third vignette, there are significant gaps that may undermine student learning.

As our discussion of these three vignettes suggests, effective social studies teaching is a complex and demanding enterprise. There are many choices to make concerning what to teach and a great deal of thought is involved in making these studies educationally rewarding for our students. In reviewing the three vignettes, we see how each offers a piece of the puzzle, yet if used on its own, each presents an incomplete picture. Students must acquire knowledge, yet our teaching must reach beyond transmitting factual information to developing thoughtful understanding. There is a need to involve students in mindful exploration of the world around them. This involves much more than providing active, hands-on experiences; it requires helping students frame, think about, and apply these experiences in meaningful and fruitful ways. As well, there is more to promoting thoughtfulness than posing provocative issues or dilemmas for discussion; we must identify and carefully develop the requisite skills and knowledge that will empower students to competently and responsibly tackle these challenges. Finally, the diverse curricular and pedagogical decisions regarding what and how to teach social studies must be influenced by one additional consideration—students have to be engaged in and by their social studies before they can be expected to learn what this subject has to offer.

REFERENCES

Bognar, C., W. Cassidy, and P. Clarke. 1997. *Social studies in British Columbia: Results of the 1996 provincial learning assessment.* Victoria, BC: Evaluation and Accountability Branch, Ministry of Education, Skills and Training, Province of British Columbia.

Case, R. 1993. *Summary of the 1992 social studies needs assessment.* Victoria, BC: Queen's Printer.

Dewey, J. 1938. *Experience and education.* New York: Free Press.

Egan, K. 1990. *Teaching as story telling*. London, ON: Althouse Press.

———. 1997. *The educated mind: How cognitive tools shape our understanding*. Chicago: University of Chicago Press.

Goodlad, J. 1984/2004. *A place called school*. 20th anniv. ed. New York: McGraw-Hill.

Parker, W. 1989. How to help students learn history and geography. *Educational Leadership* 47 (3): 39–43.

Scieszka, J. 1999. *The true story of the three little pigs*. New York: Viking.

2

Creating Meaningful Goals for Elementary Social Studies

Roland Case and Mary Abbott

SOCIAL STUDIES IS... A POEM

What is social studies?
What a question to ask.
How will I answer?
What a difficult task.

Should the focus be religious?
Early settlers felt it was the key
The Revolutionary War
Brought a new philosophy.

Is social studies history
With a focus on the past?
Or sociology
Where the subject seems so vast!

Is social studies geography?
Where we look at population.
Or is it anthropology?
Where we look at culture's creation.

Is social studies political science?
And a view of government.
Or is it economics?
And a view of money spent.

When I am learning social studies
Should I start with me?
This is called the spiral curricula
And it could hold the key.

Should my lessons be directed
By the teacher or me?
Or can I learn about the subjects
By my own discovery?

While writing this poem
It seems I do digress.
Overall, I think the definition of social studies
Should include human development and progress.

—Donna Robinson

An Enduring Dilemma

Although social studies has been a part of the school curriculum for almost a century, there remains little agreement on what constitutes a worthwhile social studies program. As the preceding poem suggests, there are likely as many answers to the question "What is social studies?" as there are social studies educators. Although lack of consensus is not necessarily undesirable—standardization, *per se*, is not a precondition for sound social studies teaching—the diversity of conceptions has been characterized as "an incredible heap of miscellany" comprised of:

> some odd pieces of the past held together by habit, a few bits of several social sciences (themselves in need of major rethinking), the remnants of a dozen ill-digested fads, an assortment of responses to demands of state legislators and special interest groups, and other odds and ends assigned to social studies because they do not seem to fit anywhere else. (Brady 1989, 80)

The problem is captured in the cartoon "What Should be Included in the Social Studies Curriculum?", which shows bewildered educators peering at many jigsaw puzzle pieces. Each piece represents a different dimension of social studies (for example, citizenship education, generalizations, global education, skills, social action, history). The onlookers are unable to figure out how all the pieces fit together. Significantly, the caption reads: "It might help if we had a picture of what this is supposed to look like."

WHAT SHOULD BE INCLUDED IN THE SOCIAL STUDIES CURRICULUM?

Cartoon by John Anfin. Courtesy of the artist.

This lack of a clear picture is evident in the disconnected, irrelevant learning that many teachers report when asked what they remember of their own elementary social studies classes. Isolated facts, endless colouring of maps, and tedious research reports figure strongly in their recollections. When we asked a group of preservice teachers to informally survey intermediate level students to determine their attitudes towards social studies, the majority of students cited social studies as their least favourite subject. The very title of a popular professional book, *If This Is Social Studies, Why Isn't It Boring?* (Steffay and Hood 1994) is a further indictment of the subject. Clearly, social studies has the potential to be an exciting, dynamic, and thought-provoking subject, but all too often it fails to achieve this potential. So how do we decide what we should be doing and where would we begin to look?

Our goal here is to suggest how teachers might develop clearer pictures of what meaningful social studies looks like. The solution is not to be found in a definition of social studies, but in the answer to a fundamental question: "What am I really supposed to be teaching in social studies?" It is not imperative that everyone identifies exactly the same answer. Rather, it is important that individual teachers come to a coherent and defensible purpose that drives their social studies teaching. Developing this "picture" is a long-term aim that may take years to realize fully. But the alternative of not bothering to figure it out is much less satisfying—it results in what Brady referred to as "a chaotic state" and "an incredible heap of miscellany."

Finding Purpose in Curriculum Documents

Faced with the dilemma of what to teach, a teacher might reasonably turn to the prescribed curriculum for direction. Surely all we need to do is look at the provincial documents to learn what the government expects us to teach in social studies. As we will see, it is not as simple as that, but it is important to know what we will find in these documents and to understand their role in developing a purposeful social studies program.

TABLE 2.1 TYPICAL OUTCOMES AND ACTIVITIES		
ONTARIO GRADE 4 (ONTARIO MINISTRY OF EDUCATION 2004)	**ALBERTA GRADE 4 (ALBERTA LEARNING 2006)**	**BRITISH COLUMBIA GRADE 5 (BC MINISTRY OF EDUCATION 2006)**
Knowledge outcome: describe aspects of daily life for men, women, and children in medieval societies (e.g., food, housing, clothing, health, religion, recreation, festivals, crafts, justice, roles) (27)	**Knowledge outcome:** analyze how Albertans interact with their environment by exploring and reflecting upon ... How are natural resources used by Albertans (i.e., agriculture, oil and natural gas, forests, coal)? (14)	**Knowledge outcome:** describe the location of natural resources within BC and Canada (93)
Skill outcome: use graphic organizers to summarize information (e.g., ... timeline showing dates of innovations and events, T-chart showing comparison of peasants' and lords' lifestyles) (28)	**Skill outcome:** use graphic organizers, such as webbing or Venn diagrams, to make meaning of information (22)	**Skill outcome:** gather a body of information from a variety of primary and secondary sources (86)
Typical activity: Students might gather relevant information from the textbook about medieval societies and complete a three-column chart comparing aspects of daily life for men, women, and children.	**Typical activity:** Students might research an assigned resource using a government website. Groups could create a web diagram showing the uses that Albertans make of an assigned resource.	**Typical activity:** Students might research the distribution of resources in a particular province or territory using atlases, CD-ROMs, or online maps. Groups could present their research through models or maps that use grids (for example, longitude and latitude) and scales to show location.

SPECIFIC CURRICULUM OUTCOMES

In provincial curriculum guidelines, the most specific and, one would think, most practical place to look is the lists of specific learning outcomes for a particular grade level—also called specific expectations or objectives. Let's see if these outcomes provide a clear sense of direction and purpose. In Table 2.1 are listed typical outcomes from three social studies curricula and sample activities that a teacher might use to address these outcomes.[1]

In each of these examples, undertaking the suggested activity would satisfy the identified knowledge outcome and address (at least partly) the skill outcomes. The teacher could then confidently proceed to the next knowledge expectation in the curriculum and begin to address it.

The Ontario teacher might move from daily life in medieval times to castles and castle life (sports, entertainment, and justice). Students might draw pictures of a castle showing people undertaking typical activities. From here, the teacher could move to the next curricular outcome, which involves tracing the effects of various events including the Crusades, the opening of the Silk Road, and the Black Death.

The Alberta teacher might turn from uses of natural resources to an outcome dealing with competing demands on the land (for example, recreational use, food production, resource extraction). Students might brainstorm potential uses for a particular plot of land in their community or region.

The British Columbia teacher might move from the distribution of resources to explore the difference between renewable and non-renewable resources. Students might do this by sorting various resources into the two categories.

In each case, the teacher would continue in a similar vein until all outcomes had been covered. But it is worth asking what has been achieved. What is the reason for wanting students to learn about daily life a thousand years ago or to web different products developed from a natural resource? The effect of attempting to "cover" each outcome is to drag students through the curriculum for no apparent reason other than that the ministry curriculum guide states that topic X and skill Y must be taught. The problem is compounded when we realize that a given grade level may list many dozens of outcomes. For example, the 2004 Ontario grade 4 social studies curriculum lists 45 specific expectations, the 2006 Alberta grade 4 curriculum lists 102 specific outcomes, and the 2006 BC curriculum for grade 5 prescribes 24 learning outcomes.[2]

"Covering" the specific outcomes in the curriculum doesn't lead to engaging, meaningful learning for at least four reasons.

- **Outcomes don't dictate teaching method**. Curriculum that is specified in terms of outcomes or expectations describes what students should know or be able to do as a result of completing the lesson, but it doesn't indicate how teachers might involve students in learning the topic in the first place. For example, asking students to describe life in medieval times may be a way of assessing what they have learned, but we might teach them this information by reading a novel that transports students back to that time period. The tendency to teach the topic by asking students to perform the task mentioned in the outcome fuels this pattern of "covering the curriculum" that students find boring.

- **Outcomes aren't organized in teachable clusters**. Specific outcomes need not be taught in the order in which they are listed, nor for that matter need they be taught individually. The pattern when "covering" the curriculum is to proceed from one outcome to the next, often in a drawn-out manner. This is what Brady (1989, 80) is referring to as an "incredible heap of miscellany." This need not be the case. For example, all eighteen outcomes related to the study of medieval times in the grade 4 Ontario curriculum (plus numerous language arts outcomes) could be addressed through one large project—namely, inviting students to research, write, and perform a play about medieval life.

- **Outcomes don't specify priority**. Not all outcomes are of equal importance nor will they have equal value for students in a given class. Consequently, each outcome does not warrant the same amount of teaching time. In fact, a few outcomes may have great priority and deserve extended treatment, whereas others should be touched upon very quickly. The tendency when "covering" the curriculum is to teach a topic for as long as it takes to complete the selected activity—even if this means less important outcomes receive more attention than do vitally important ones.

- **Outcomes don't indicate purpose**. As previously mentioned, outcome statements don't indicate why we want students to achieve these results. If a teacher doesn't know why, it is almost certain that students won't know either. A likely result when "covering" the curriculum is to do things because the curriculum says so or because it's in the textbook.

TYPES OF SOCIAL STUDIES GOALS

Although curriculum documents and writers categorize them differently,[3] it may be helpful to organize social studies around four general goals—content knowledge and understanding, and three kinds of competency:

- **Content knowledge and understanding.** This goal specifies the breadth and depth of understanding students should possess about their world. It includes knowledge of specific facts (for example, key figures in local community history, the capital of Canada, major current events), generalizations or theories (for example, people have many shared needs, Canada is a land of immigrants), and concepts (for example, community, democracy, fairness). However, the emphasis is increasingly towards understanding of the implications and importance of knowledge and not mere recall of information.
- **Critical, creative, and collaborative thinking.** This goal refers to students' ability and inclination to thoughtfully access ideas and beliefs, imaginatively create ideas and products, and learn from and build on the ideas of others.
- **Communicative competence including various literacies.** This goal specifies a range of abilities related to students'

capacity to function or be literate in text, oral, visual, and digital worlds. It includes accessing and interpreting information from a variety of sources (for example, textbooks, magazines, internet, social media, artifacts, images, community resources), and representing ideas in text, oral, and visual forms using digital and traditional technologies.

- **Personal and social responsibility.** This goal refers to competence in handling individual and societal situations (for example, regulating one's behaviour, dealing with siblings and fellow students, combatting school- and community-based problems, or acting on national and international concerns). It involves developing students' abilities to analyze problems in their personal lives and in society, to plan appropriate courses of action individually and in co-operation with others, to put their plans into action, and to evaluate the efficacy of their efforts. It also includes nurturing individual values (for example, self-esteem, integrity, personal identity) and social values (for example, equality, respect for persons, justice, national pride, international solidarity) that are characteristic of healthy individuals, communities, and nations.

Think back to your own experiences as a student in elementary social studies. Make a list of your clearest memories of these experiences—both positive and negative. Review these experiences in light of the four factors listed above: teaching method, meaningful organization, clear priorities, and a sense of purpose. To what extent can the nature of your experiences be attributed to choices your teachers made in light of these four considerations? What implications might this have for your own choices as a teacher of elementary social studies?

GOING BEYOND SPECIFIC OUTCOMES

Ken Osborne suggests that the danger of a preoccupation with specific outcomes is that "teachers come to see themselves, or be seen by others, not as teachers of history [or social studies] but as achievers of outcomes, and history becomes little more than a sequence of outcomes to be checked off in a teacher's day-book" (2004, 4). The antidote to this problem is a return to the question "What is our purpose?" If we know why we are teaching something, we have a better idea of its priority relative to other outcomes and we can better decide how to structure learning effectively to achieve this end.

As the highlighted text suggests, educational writers use different terms to identify the important

ideas that guide teachers' interpretation of curriculum outcomes. It does not matter whether one's reason for teaching a specific outcome is characterized as a "big idea," "linchpin," "essential understanding," or "enduring understanding." What does matter is that we know why we are teaching the outcome.

Let's return to the example of the grade 4 Alberta curriculum and consider possible reasons for studying how Albertans use their natural resources.

- **Economic purpose**: to decide which of Alberta's natural resources are the most promising to develop. If Alberta intended to reduce its dependence on oil and gas, which would be the best resources to develop?
- **Geographical purpose**: to investigate why some resources are more plentiful in some regions than in others.
- **Environmental purpose**: to explore how Albertans could better conserve and sustain their resources. Which resource uses are the most wasteful? Should we continue to use coal to generate electricity?
- **Personal purpose**: to appreciate the importance of these resources in the students' own lives. How do students and their families benefit from Alberta's natural wealth?
- **Historical purpose**: to learn about the directions

that Alberta's resource use are taking by studying past and present patterns. Can we learn anything about our present challenges by studying how resources were used in the past?

Each of these purposes offers plausible reasons for teaching the identified outcome. Some may be more interesting or relevant to students, and may be more important in the bigger scheme. Developing a coherent purpose that excites and challenges students requires thoughtful consideration of what learning will contribute to their ability to interact in and contribute to the world. Perhaps any one of these reasons would work. Does it simply depend on the direction we personally want to take our students?

Asking "why" helps us uncover important aspects of content and to situate learning experiences in a more relevant context. But how will we know which learning experience is the best one or even the one intended by the government? The answers to these questions require us to look at various elements embedded in curriculum documents that typically provide the bigger picture.

The Bigger Curricular Picture

Teachers are expected to work within the guidelines provided by the provincial curriculum. This is the framework within which instructional decisions are made. It is teachers' responsibility to connect specific outcomes in meaningful ways and develop them in a context that furthers an overall vision for social studies. Identifying these connections and planning towards this purpose breathes life into the curriculum.

Three features of the curriculum are central in formulating this broader vision for social studies. These are the general goals that social studies promote, the strands around which subject matter is organized to promote the desired goals, and the ultimate rationale for the subject. We consider each of these elements and their role in giving purpose to social studies. As we will see, they leave much for the teacher to fill in.

GENERAL GOALS

The goals of a course or a unit are the general educational outcomes that are to be promoted by addressing the specific outcomes. Although the precise wording differs from jurisdiction to jurisdiction (for example, they are called "Overall Expectations" in Ontario and "General Outcomes" in Alberta), their common function

is to provide a more general description of what we are trying to achieve. Perhaps these goals will help in giving purpose to our teaching.

Goals are typically categorized into types. The most widely used categories of goals are knowledge, skills, and attitudes. Despite its popularity, this categorization is confusing. Supposed "skills"—such as conducting research—require knowledge (of the strengths and key features of various information sources) and attitudes (attention to detail, curiosity). It is increasingly common to organize goals according to (1) what students know and understand and (2) what students are competent to do. We explain more about these goals in the adjacent highlighted text.

One obvious purpose in categorizing the kind of goal we are trying to achieve is that it orients us in a particular direction. For example, it is helpful to realize whether our primary goal is to promote understanding of the subject matter or foster individual responsibility or promote digital literacy.

The Ontario grade 4 curriculum identifies three "overall expectations" that students should achieve in the course of their study of medieval times:

- **Knowledge:** "identify and describe major features of daily life and social organization in medieval European societies from about 500 to 1500 C.E. (Common Era)" (27).
- **Print and digital literacy:** "use a variety of resources and tools to investigate the major events and influences of the era and determine how they shaped medieval society" (27).
- **Application of knowledge:** "relate significant elements of medieval societies to comparable aspects of contemporary Canadian communities" (27).

As is typical of many curricula, these goals summarize in general terms what is stated in the specific outcomes. Unfortunately, they don't seem to suggest why we would teach these outcomes. What is the point of having students learn about medieval European societies and compare elements in these societies with contemporary elements in Canadian communities? We won't find the kind of clarity of purpose that we need from these goals.

The Alberta curriculum offers the following "General Outcome" for the cluster of specific outcomes we have discussed previously:

Students will demonstrate an understanding and appreciation of how elements of physical geography, climate, geology, and paleontology are integral to the landscapes and environment of Alberta. (2006, 13)

This broad outcome appears to include both content and attitudinal goals and suggests a geographical or environmental orientation, but it is not clear why we would want to further these goals. Are we to nurture environmental literacy or perhaps to cultivate understanding of the work of geographers and geologists? It seems that the stated goal helps to some extent by eliminating some options, but we are still left with choices to make. These examples are instructive: general curriculum goals may sometimes suggest directions for our teaching, but they don't eliminate all the possibilities and often provide little help in understanding why we might want students to achieve this goal.

CURRICULUM STRANDS

Strands are another element commonly featured in social studies curriculum documents. The word "strand" refers to the parts that are bound or woven together to form the whole. There are two kinds of strands: "underlying themes," which are main threads or concepts that run throughout the curriculum, and "organizing themes," which are the categories used to structure or cluster segments of the curriculum (units within a single course or different courses within a kindergarten to grade 12 program). Both kinds of strands serve a similar purpose: they provide ways to identify the focus and organize the delivery of the curriculum.

UNDERLYING THEMES

The underlying themes highlight the continuing emphasis or the backbone of the curriculum. For example, Alberta (2006, 6–7) identifies six strands as the threads running throughout the entire K–12 curriculum:

- time, continuity, and change—essentially history;
- the land (places and people)—essentially physical and human geography;
- power, authority, and decision-making—essentially politics and law;
- economics and resources—essentially economics;
- global connections—essentially global education;
- culture and community—essentially anthropology and sociology.

The curriculum specifically links two of these

strands—essentially geography and economics—to the outcomes that we have used as our example. These strands are described as follows:

- **The Land: Places and People.** Exploring the unique and dynamic relationship that humans have with the land, places, and environments affects decisions that students make and their understanding of perspectives, issues, citizenship, and identity. Students will examine the impacts of physical geography on the social, political, environmental, and economic organization of societies. The examination also affects students' understanding of perspectives and issues as they consider how connections to the land influence their sense of place (7).
- **Economics and Resources.** Exploring multiple perspectives on the use, distribution and management of resources and wealth contributes to students' understanding of the effects that economics and resources have on the quality of life around the world. Students will explore the basic economic systems, trade, and the effects of economic interdependence on individuals, communities, nations, and the natural environment. Students will also critically consider the social and environmental implications of resource use and technological change (7).

The many ideas raised by these two strands suggest that several of the previously identified purposes—economic, geographical, environmental, and personal—may apply. It seems that here too the teacher must choose among the possibilities.

ORGANIZING THEMES

Organizing themes are the topics that subdivide a given grade level or distinguish one course focus from another. For example, in the Ontario curriculum, each social studies course (grades 1 to 6) is divided into two strands: "Heritage and Citizenship," which is very loosely a historical theme, and "Canada and World Connections," which is loosely a geographical theme. The subject "social studies" disappears in grade 7 and beyond and is then organized in separate history and geography courses (and in later grades, into courses in economics, civics, and law). The elementary curriculum in British Columbia (2006) is organized around five strands at each grade level:

- skills and processes of social studies
- identity, society, and culture

- governance
- economy and technology
- human and physical environment

Across grades the most common organizing theme for elementary social studies is the expanding horizons approach. In the early grades, the focus is on what is near and familiar to students and progresses to the distant and increasingly unfamiliar. Although there are variations, the organizing themes of the British Columbia, Alberta, and, to a lesser extent, Ontario curricula are the individual, family, school, community, province, nation, and the past.

The diagram in Figure 2.1 illustrates the structure of the grade 4 curriculum for Alberta.

PROGRAM RATIONALE

While curriculum strands suggest how the outcomes are to be divided (in a discipline-based or a social dimensions arrangement), they don't tell us why we are teaching them. The rationale identifies the ultimate reasons for a program. In other words, a rationale for a social studies program explains the point of pursuing the goals discussed above. In this respect, the rationale is the "bottom line" of a program. In the face of uncertainty or conflicting directions, the rationale provides a basis for deciding which direction to pursue.

The tendency among some teachers is to regard discussion of the rationale for a subject as a rather abstract and irrelevant exercise. This attitude is unfortunate. Getting clear about our rationale—the reason for doing something—gives us a sense of purpose. The danger when we are unclear about the ultimate reason for doing what we do is that we will teach a topic merely for the sake of covering it. Thus, the rationale for a subject—whether it is clearly spelled out in the curriculum or one we develop and refine individually—should serve a practical function: it should give us some sense of direction when interpreting and implementing the curriculum. This direction is especially important since, as we have tried to illustrate, curricula leave teachers considerable latitude in deciding the specifics of what will be taught and how.

Consider the following official rationales for social studies:

- **Ontario:** prepare students "to function as informed citizens in a culturally diverse and interdependent world and to participate and compete in a global economy.... [and] to develop attitudes that will

motivate them to use their knowledge and skills in a responsible manner" (2).

- **Alberta:** enable students "to become engaged, active, informed, and responsible citizens" with an emphasis on "recognition and respect for individual and collective identity" in a diverse, pluralistic, inclusive, and democratic society and awareness of "their capacity to effect change in their communities, society and world" (1).
- **British Columbia:** "develop thoughtful, responsible, and active citizens who are able to acquire the requisite information to consider multiple perspectives and to make reasoned judgments" (11).

All of these rationales refer to preparing citizens, but there is vagueness and variation in what this means. On first glance, the qualities of an ideal citizenship are so general and open-ended—"informed" and able to "function" in a "diverse" world—that almost any kind of citizen might be implied. On closer investigation, the tone of the visions suggests some differences. The Ontario curriculum stresses an economically viable citizenry, whereas Alberta has a more socially active vision of the ideal citizen. The British Columbia rationale emphasizes informed decision-making as a quality of citizenship. Our challenge, then, is to use these rationales to inform and give purpose to our teaching of the specific outcomes listed in these respective curricula. A more extensive discussion of the visions of citizenship embedded in social studies curricula is the focus of chapter 3, "Defining the Purposes of Citizenship Education."

For the time being, it will be useful to consider briefly how a rationale might shape our teaching. What, for example, are the implications of the Ontario rationale for the grade 4 curriculum? How does teaching about medieval life foster the development of an ideal citizen? Several possibilities come to mind:

- **Understanding of diversity.** The study of medieval life might be used to foster understanding of diversity as students learn that individuals within societies haven't always had the same rights, opportunities, values, and beliefs.
- **Understanding interdependence.** The study of medieval life might be used to foster understanding of interdependence as students learn how various aspects or sectors (for example, religion, innovations, architecture, social structures) of medieval life were dependent upon and influenced each other.
- **Respect for rights and peaceful problem solving.** The study of medieval life, especially the violence and

abuses that were common, might be used to foster respect for others and encourage responsible behaviour.

- **Building teamwork**. The study of medieval life in and of itself may not be especially important to developing the ideal citizen, but it might provide an opportunity (for example, by mounting a play and getting an audience to attend) to nurture students' ability to work co-operatively in pursuit of a common goal.

The specific expectation for the grade 4 curriculum states: "describe aspects of daily life for men, women, and children in medieval societies (e.g., food, housing, clothing, health, religion, recreation, festivals, crafts, justice, roles)" (Ontario 2004, 27). The teaching activity offered when we first introduced this outcome was to ask students to gather information from the textbook about life for men, women, and children in medieval societies. We can see how adopting any of the suggested rationales listed above would give meaning and relevance to the activity. Students are no longer collecting information for its own sake, but using this as an opportunity to understand interdependence or develop competence in working together. Having a purpose is not simply motivational for students, it influences what they learn from the activity. As Van Sledright notes, "How students view the purpose of engaging in topical or disciplinary study appears deeply connected to what they eventually learn and understand" (cited in Osborne 2004, 37).

Comparable examples could be developed for other curricula, but the conclusions would be the same. The stated rationales in curriculum documents indicate the kinds of purposes that we should set for our teaching, but even these leave open possibilities we must choose among.

This does not mean that we are free to do whatever we wish—we must work within the parameters set out by the curriculum even if the form and emphasis of that understanding may vary among us. As professionals, we have a responsibility to develop a program that is educationally sound and ethically defensible. In reaching decisions about the substance and shape of our social studies teaching—in refining the vision for our program— several factors are particularly relevant:

- the needs and expressed wishes of our students;
- the expectations embedded in the provincial curriculum in its stated outcomes, goals, strands, and rationale;
- the nature of social studies as a subject and the range of purposes that social studies is expected to serve;

- the expressed wishes of the local community;
- the priorities and needs of society generally;
- our own priorities and strengths as educators.

The Task Ahead

The word curriculum is derived from the word *curricle* which means "the path to follow"—hence, the notion of a course of study. Teachers must know where they are going if they are to lead students through the curriculum in a meaningful and productive way. One might think by covering each of the outcomes that a more complete picture would emerge—just as joining the dots by tracing lines between each point reveals a hidden image. It is not obvious that there is a single clear picture embedded in prescribed curriculum documents—joining the dots (covering the outcomes) may not reveal any image— it may simply mean a string of activities. As a British Columbia Ministry of Education document noted:

> Curriculum is no longer "ground to be covered." Instead, curriculum evolves from the teacher's mediation between the goals of the program and the curriculum and the individual learning styles, interests, and abilities of students. (1990, 25)

An earlier British Columbia curriculum guide explained that "A curriculum is an organized statement of *intended learning outcomes that serves as a framework for decisions about the instructional process* [emphasis added]" (1988, 4). In other words, curricula are guidelines to assist teachers in developing a program of study for their own students.

It is incumbent on us as social studies educators to explore and assess the nature and implications of each of the elements of a curriculum—rationale, strands, goals, and specific outcomes (or expectations)—when developing our social studies programs. To some extent, choices will have been dictated by the provincially prescribed curriculum, but surprisingly, most curricula require considerable teacher discretion in deciding what specifically to include and emphasize, and how to organize these items for instructional purposes.

Engaging in purposeful social studies is not an easy task—it will no doubt evolve over years of teaching and reflection. However, we can begin by thinking about our vision for social studies. If we have only the vaguest idea of what social studies is supposed to look like, how will our students learn from us?

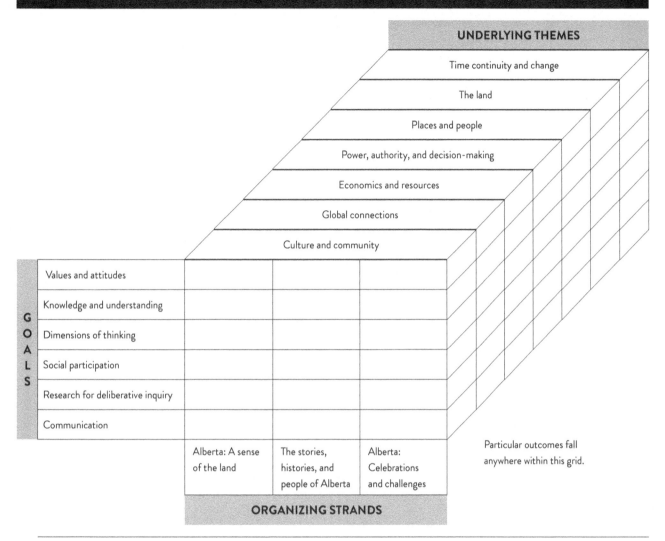

Identify one or more specific outcomes prescribed in social studies curriculum for a particular grade. Make a list of different activities you might undertake to help students meet this outcome. Review the rationale offered in the curriculum guide and formulate a particular purpose that would give meaning to the specific outcome(s) you identified and shape the activities you might ultimately select to meet the outcome. Justify your choice of rationale and teaching activity.

ENDNOTES

1   As of the Fall 2012 these were the current versions, but some jurisdictions were in the process of revising their social studies curricula.

2   Because of the problem of "content overload," curriculum revisions underway in some jurisdictions are expected to reduce the number of learning outcomes for each grade level.

3   Ontario organizes its goals into four categories: (1) knowledge and understanding; (2) thinking, which includes research, analysis, and decision-making; (3) communication; and (4) application, which is the use of knowledge and skills to make connections. Alberta has three categories of goals: (1) values and attitudes; (2) knowledge and understanding; and (3) skills and processes, which are subdivided into thinking, social participation, inquiry, and communication. British Columbia has no formal set of categories for its goals. Instead the curriculum guide simply describes a diffuse range of types of outcomes including developing understanding, making connections, applying knowledge, practising active citizenship, and demonstrating respect (2006, 11).

REFERENCES

Alberta Learning. 2006. *Social studies—Kindergarten to grade 12*. Edmonton, AB: Author. Available online at www.education .alberta.ca/teachers/program/socialstudies.aspx.

Brady, M. 1989. *What's worth teaching? Selecting, organizing and integrating knowledge*. Albany, NY: State University of New York Press.

British Columbia Ministry of Education. 1988. *Social studies curriculum guide: Grades 8–11*. Victoria, BC: Author.

———. 1990. *The intermediate program: Learning in British Columbia*. Victoria, BC: Author.

———. 2006. *Social studies K to 7: Integrated resource package 2006*. Victoria, BC: Author. Available online at www.bced.gov .bc.ca/irp/pdfs/social_studies/2006ssk7.pdf.

Chiodo, J. 1990. Social studies poems. *Social Education* 54 (7): 466–468.

Duplass, J.A. 2004. *Teaching elementary social studies: What every teacher should know*. New York: Houghton Mifflin.

Erickson, L.H. 1998. *Concept-based curriculum and instruction: Teaching beyond the facts*. Thousand Oaks, CA: Corwin Press.

Ontario Ministry of Education. 2004. *The Ontario curriculum— Social studies grades 1 to 6; History and geography grades 7 and 8* (revised). Toronto: Author. Available online at www.edu .gov.on.ca/eng/curriculum/elementary/sstudies18curr.pdf.

Osborne, K. 2004. Canadian history in the schools. Unpublished report by Historica Foundation, Toronto, January.

Steffay, S. and W.J. Hood. 1994. *If this is social studies, why isn't it boring?* York, ME: Stenhouse Publishers.

Wasserman, S. 1990. *Serious players in the primary classroom*. New York: Teachers College Press.

Wiggins, G. and J. McTighe. 2005. *Understanding by design* (second edition). Alexandria, VA: Association of Supervision and Curriculum Development.

3

Defining the Purposes of Citizenship Education

Penney Clark and Roland Case

Citizenship has been recognized as the rationale or defining aim of social studies since its inception as a school subject. In 1916, the report that marked the formal introduction of social studies in the United States argued that the "conscious and constant purpose" of social studies was "the cultivation of good citizenship" (cited in Dougan 1988, 14–15). Since then citizenship has been called "the primary, overriding purpose" and the "distinctive justification" of social studies.[1] As Fitzgerald aptly describes it, again and again social studies reformers have come "reeling back to the old lamppost of citizenship training" (1979, 187). In Canada, George Tomkins claims that "the goal of 'citizenship' probably comes closer than any other to identifying the purpose that Canadians have usually believed that the social studies should serve" (1985, 15). Echoing Benjamin Barber's sentiments, Larry Booi writes that "public education is the vital vehicle for developing citizens of a democratic society and that social studies teachers have the main role to play in this regard" (2001, 22).

Unfortunately, general acceptance of citizenship education as the *raison d'être* for social studies does not provide much guidance or direction since there is little agreement as to what constitutes the ideal citizen. Citizenship is such an amorphous concept that it may be used to legitimize virtually anything in social studies (Longstreet 1985). Apparent consensus about the centrality of citizenship education is almost meaningless because of widely disparate conceptions of citizenship (Marker and Mehlinger 1992; Sears 1996), which range from nationalistic loyalty to international solidarity (Cogan and Derricott 2000).

In this chapter, we outline four interrelated rationales underlying citizenship education; each at varying times in the history of social studies has served as the defining purpose of the subject. Before looking at each of these, it is useful to explain why as social studies teachers we should care about which purpose (or mix of purposes), if any, undergirds our teaching.

A Direction for Social Studies

For many of us, decisions about what to teach in social studies will likely be informed, consciously or not, by our image of the type of person and world we hope to promote. If our model citizen is someone who is well informed about social matters, we will devote much of our time to helping students acquire a breadth of knowledge. If our focus is the ability to make ethically sound decisions about complex issues, then we will likely engage students in investigating and discussing social issues. Perhaps our ideal citizen is someone who is committed to acting on his or her beliefs. In this case, students might undertake community enhancement projects or explore ways of living and acting in personally responsible ways. Each of these choices should, and likely will, be influenced by an implicit view of what our subject is all about.

For some of us, our conception of the "good" citizen may be so completely established that further discussion will make no difference. For others, however, exploring options may help us become more focussed and resolute in our orientation or perhaps cause us to modify our outlook in light of an appreciation of alternative purposes that might be served. If we take seriously our role as educators charged with making complex judgments about our students' well-being, then we must articulate with some clarity our ultimate educational aims. As Ken Osborne writes in *Teaching for Democratic Citizenship*:

> Good teachers possess a clear vision of education and of what it will do for their students. They are not simply technicians who take prescribed curriculum, or the textbook, and work their students through it. They incorporate the curriculum into their philosophy of education and use what it has to offer in ways that make educational sense. This involves thinking carefully about goals and about how to achieve them, and such thinking inevitably takes a teacher beyond the confines of the classroom. Educational goals do not exist in a vacuum. They emerge from thinking about what one wants for students and for the society in which they live. (1991, 119)

During the nearly one-hundred-year history of social studies in North America, the four ideals listed below have traditionally been offered as "competing" rationales for citizenship education.[2] Two of the rationales identify specific *social purposes*—that is, their focus is the type of society we hope to promote through social studies—and the other two rationales serve *individual purposes*—these focus on the type of individuals that we want social studies to foster.

- **Social initiation**. This rationale posits that the primary purpose of social studies is to initiate students into society by transmitting the knowledge, abilities, and values that students will require if they are to fit into and be productive members of society.
- **Social reform**. This rationale holds that the primary purpose of social studies is to empower students with the understandings, abilities, and values necessary to improve or transform their society.
- **Personal development**. According to this rationale, the primary purpose of social studies is to help students develop fully as individuals and as social beings. Its direct purpose is neither to reform society nor to maintain the status quo, but to develop each student's talents and character.

- **Intellectual development**. This rationale suggests that the primary purpose of social studies is to develop students' capacity for understanding the complex world they face by introducing them to the bodies of knowledge and forms of inquiry represented in history and the other social sciences.

Each of these rationales comprise variations. For example, the particulars of a social initiation rationale will vary depending on whether we are more liberal or conservative; similarly, social reformers may be radical or moderate in their outlook on social improvement. There is, as well, inevitable blurring of the lines between these camps—for example, at what point does a concern for social justice move from an accepted principle of mainstream Canadian society towards a commitment to social reform? Even pedagogical approaches overlap considerably. For example, although social initiation is typically associated with textbook-based programs, and intellectual development with engaging students in analysis of primary documents and social science research, the reverse is not inconceivable. The point of categorizing different rationales is not to pigeonhole each of us in one camp or another, but to invite reflection about the options facing us when deciding upon our purpose—*our ultimate reason*—for teaching social studies.

The choices we are forced to make each day of our teaching lives should reflect these priorities. Although the differences are more matters of emphasis than of mutual exclusivity, in important respects the different purposes require choices among competing objectives. As illustrated by the examples in the "four visions" of the building of the Canadian Pacific Railway in Table 3.1 and the study of families in Table 3.2, the underlying rationale will significantly affect the nature and outcomes of the study.

It is likely—even desirable—that many of us will endorse aspects of all four rationales. We might, for example, think that promoting a sense of responsibility for others and a recognition of the need to pull one's own weight are part of a core set of values that all citizens ought to abide by. To this extent we have some affinity for the social initiation camp. Perhaps we are concerned that many students are overly accepting of mainstream attitudes that contribute to environmental destruction, exploitation, inequality, and other social ills. In this case, we are espousing elements of a social reform perspective. We must also decide how best to prepare students for these civic responsibilities. If our inclination is to emphasize students' feelings, needs, values, issues, and problems, we are in effect

TABLE 3.1 FOUR "VISIONS" OF A CURRICULAR TOPIC: BUILDING THE CANADIAN PACIFIC RAILWAY

UNDERLYING GOALS

Social initiation: to promote knowledge of and pride in important events in Canadian history	**Social reform:** to encourage scepticism about the official versions of history and a concern for past injustices in Canada	**Personal development:** to nurture students' ability to work with each other and to plan and carry out self-directed studies	**Intellectual development:** to introduce students to the methods used by social scientists to inquire into the world

SAMPLE ACTIVITIES

• learn about the "glorious" saga of the CPR's construction and the impressive engineering feats that occurred • learn about famous people who were instrumental in building the railroad, including John A. Macdonald, Donald Smith, William Van Horne, and Sanford Fleming • explore the historical significance of the railroad—opening the West to European immigration, defence against American Manifest Destiny, fulfilling the Confederation promise • explore the railroad as a symbol of Canadian nationhood—the iron ribbon that binds Canada and the Last Spike at Craigellachie, BC—the linchpin joining East and West	• learn about the alternative story of the railroad's construction, including the exploitation of immigrant workers and the corruption and greed that resulted in the "Pacific Scandal" • learn about the personal sacrifices of the Asian workers who actually constructed the railroad • explore the hidden cost of its development, including the dislocation and abuse of First Nations and the demise of the buffalo • explore the myth of nationhood—for example, the symbolic Last Spike was stolen the first night	• allow students to select any aspect of the topic that interests them personally and decide on a way to represent their learning • explore potential career choices—engineers, developers, politicians—by considering the contribution each made to the railway • use co-operative activities, such as having students work together to create a mural depicting some aspect of the railway, and role-play to develop their ability to work with others	• learn about historical inquiry by developing an account of an event using primary sources • learn about geographical inquiry by plotting the demographic effects of the railway on local terrain or by planning a route using contour maps • learn about archaeological inquiry by developing an account of camp life based on artifacts recovered from a simulated "dig"

TABLE 3.2 FOUR "VISIONS" OF A CURRICULAR TOPIC: STUDYING FAMILIES

UNDERLYING THEMES

• **Social initiation:** promote students' knowledge of the role of the family and a sense of responsibility towards their family	• **Social reform:** encourage sensitivity towards and support of family structures and predicaments that may not be universally accepted by students	• **Personal development:** nurture students' pride in their families	• **Intellectual development:** teach students how to gather and represent information used by social scientists

SAMPLE ACTIVITIES

• learn about the important needs that families meet in society • learn about different family roles and the ways that family members work to support one another • learn about the responsibilities that each child has to contribute towards the harmonious operation of a family • learn about important celebrations that acknowledge parents' contributions (Father's Day, Mother's Day)	• explore and promote acceptance of less traditional family structures (including families with same-sex parents) and unfamiliar family practices from other cultures • learn about families who are less fortunate and what might be done to assist these families • carry out a project to help a family in need • learn how to recognize and respond when family members are acting improperly	• each child learns about his or her own family background • each child develops a treasure box representing the most powerful, positive family memories • each child plans a personal commemoration or personal act of kindness for a family member	• learn to interview family members and identify important information and ideas obtained • learn various ways of recording and presenting information and ideas (family tree, timelines, graphs, webbing) • learn how to formulate powerful questions to ask of a guest who is coming to talk about families

adopting a personal development view of citizenship. This is certainly a widely held rationale for social studies, but we may nevertheless be concerned that helping students become "personally and socially fulfilled" may not do enough to prepare them to thoughtfully address the issues that they will encounter. The often quoted expression by George Santayana, "Those who do not remember the past are doomed to repeat it," suggests that students who have not studied much history will have little insight into or context for making sense of contemporary questions. Perhaps, then, preparation for civic life should focus on the knowledge and the principles of inquiry that drive history and the other social science disciplines. If this is the case, we have moved towards an intellectual development focus.

Think of a social studies unit you have taught or have seen taught. Using the "four visions" chart as a guide, identify the dominant rationale or rationales underlying this unit. Select a rationale not significantly represented in the unit and think of activities that would reflect this new rationale.

In formulating our own more specific set of purposes for social studies education, it is useful to view the four traditional camps as positions on two intersecting continuums (as shown in Figure 3.1):

- **Social acceptance/social change spectrum**. Social initiation and social reform represent a range of positions on a social acceptance/social change spectrum. At one extreme, the point of citizenship education is to promote complete conformity with mainstream social norms and practices; at the other extreme, it is to promote total transformation of the social fabric. Seen in this light, the differences between the social initiation and social reform camps are matters of degree about the extent and depth that citizenship education should encourage social conformity/social transformation.
- **Subject-centred/student-centred spectrum**. Personal development and intellectual development represent a range of positions on a subject-centred/student-centred spectrum. At one extreme is a view that the best form of citizenship preparation is achieved by nurturing the whole child by focussing exclusively on his or her interests, concerns, problems, values, and so on; at the other extreme, the best form of citizenship preparation is thought to be achieved by disciplining the mind exclusively through exposure to the bodies of knowledge and forms of reasoning found in the social sciences.

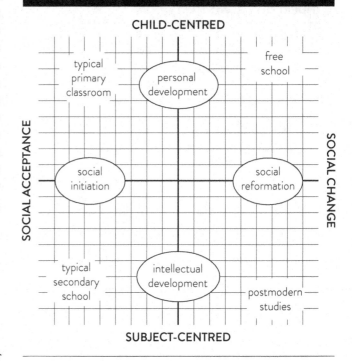

FIGURE 3.1 CITIZENSHIP EDUCATION MATRIX

Let us look at each of the traditional camps of citizenship education and consider how the differences between the camps can be explained in terms of where they fall within the matrix created by these two continuums.

Social studies rationales tend to be defined exclusively in terms of one of the continuums, either "social acceptance/change" or "child/subject-centred." Labelling a view as "social initiation" simply means that the dominant but by no means exclusive purpose is social acceptance. The closer the rationale is, for example, to the left of the social acceptance end of the continuum, the greater the emphasis placed on promoting the status quo. As a rationale moves towards the "social change" pole, the emphasis on the status quo diminishes until, at some point, the social reform purpose begins to dominate.

Plotting rationales within a matrix allows us to position camps in light of both sets of poles. For example, the "free school" movement in the 1960s was a radical child-centred approach to education with a strong social change mandate. Consequently, it belongs in the upper right-hand corner of the matrix. The typical secondary school program with a liberal arts emphasis is strongly subject-centred with a clear social acceptance mandate. Hence it belongs in the lower-left quadrant. Many primary classrooms would be located in the upper-left quadrant because of their child-centred, social acceptance mandate. Postmodern studies with their emphasis on making problematic the position from which scholarship is written would fall in the lower-right corner because of its critical discipline-based focus. A view of schooling in the very centre of the matrix would weight all four purposes equally: encouraging students to accept some aspects of society but to challenge others, and nurturing students' individual development in certain domains while seeking intellectual development through the disciplines.

The Social Acceptance/Social Change Spectrum

As indicated above, two of the traditional visions of citizenship education—social initiation and social reform—can be distinguished by the extent to which conformity with mainstream values, social practices, and world view are encouraged.

Citizenship Education as Social Initiation

The most common and long-standing view of the purpose of social studies, and, for that matter, of public schooling in general has been to promote a core body of beliefs and to instill the essential values and skills that are thought necessary to function in and contribute to society (Barr, Barth, and Shermis 1977, 59). The socializing role of schooling that prevailed in the 1800s was evident in the teaching of patriotism and character training, the primary components of social education at that time. Aspects of it were also evident in Canadian social studies curricula in the 1930s and 1940s, in which teachers were urged to use fables and stories about heroes (and occasionally heroines) as a means of inculcating values such as patriotism, loyalty, and courage. The "back to basics" movement of the 1970s reinvigorated, in a very conservative voice, the call to provide all students with core knowledge and values. This tradition continues with the recent emphasis on learning the essential facts of our culture and history. J.L. Granatstein's (1998) call to teach Canada's "common cultural capital" and E.D. Hirsch's (1988) "cultural literacy" and Charles Quigley's (1991) "civic liberty" in the United States are well-known examples of this vision. Headlines in Canadian newspapers on July 1 of each year reporting on the Dominion Institute's Canada Day History Quiz

attest to continuing public interest in promoting knowledge of the basic facts of Canadian political and social history. Social initiators are likely to espouse the kinds of values (such as respect, responsibility, honesty, perseverance, optimism) advocated by the character education movement (Glaze, Hogarth, and McLean 2003) and the workplace skills of personal management, teamwork, and communication outlined in the *Employability Skills Profile* published by the Conference Board of Canada.

The social initiation rationale appears to be widely shared by social studies teachers. Jim Leming believes that in the United States, social studies teachers generally espouse a conservative version of social initiation involving "the transmission of mainstream interpretations of history and American values" (1992, 294). Linda McNeil (1986) found in an ethnographic study of teachers in six schools that a major goal was helping students maintain positive attitudes towards American institutions. In order to achieve this goal, teachers avoided content that would expose students to the injustices and inadequacies of economic and political institutions. In a survey of almost 1,800 elementary and secondary social studies teachers in British Columbia, approximately 70 per cent supported social initiation as a dominant purpose for social studies (Case 1993, 3). This compared with approximately 57 per cent who supported a social reformist role, and 38 per cent who supported intellectual development. (Respondents were not asked to comment on a personal development rationale.)

Social initiation does not necessarily require indoctrinating students into a narrow set of beliefs and values. Although nineteenth- and early twentieth-century versions of social initiation in Canada had a decidedly pro-British assimilationist bent, more recent versions embody a more multicultural, pluralistic aim (Sears 1994). An individual's perception of the prevailing, mainstream image of a good citizen may be broad-minded, including values such as an abiding respect for the rights of others and, in particular, tolerance of individual and cultural differences and freedoms. As Ken Osborne suggests, "While avoiding nationalistic chest-beating, history curricula are designed to instill in students a sense of Canadian identity, which all provinces describe as based upon respect for diversity, pluralism, and democracy" (2004, 6). Nor is social initiation inconsistent with critical thinking; but there are parameters within which this questioning is to occur—students would not be taught or encouraged to question the received interpretations of history and the foundations of the dominant world view. For example, advocates of a social initiation rationale would be less inclined to invite students to question seriously issues such as whether Confederation is something to celebrate, whether Canada is a token democracy, and under what conditions students should engage in civil disobedience. Social initiation is compatible with an active participatory citizenship; however, it would be more likely to emphasize community service projects rather than boycotts of consumer products, and voting in elections rather than political lobbying (see, for example, Alter 1997; Rappoport and Kletzien 1997).

Citizenship Education as Social Reform

As its name implies, social studies as social reform focusses on encouraging a better society. It posits that there is much to be improved about society and that the role of social studies is to help students acquire the understandings, abilities, and values that will launch them on this path. Although both social initiation and social reform approaches would teach students about the history and workings of our nation and the world, their dominant purposes pull in opposing directions. In the case of social initiation, the overriding point is to get students to endorse the implied world view, whereas social reformers believe the emphasis should be to prepare students to critique the existing society. And unlike the social initiation approach, where the emphasis is on getting students to participate in and contribute to the established ways of operating, the social reform approach aims to empower students to work towards a "different" society. The reform position need not imply a radical anarchistic view of social change, but by definition social reform is more controversial than the social initiation position. Jim Leming (1992) and others believe it is for this reason that social reform is espoused more often by university professors than by classroom teachers.

Social studies' closest turn towards a social reform orientation occurred in the 1970s. Jerome Bruner, earlier a proponent of an intellectual development rationale, announced in a 1971 article entitled "The Process of Education Revisited" a "moratorium" or at least a "de-emphasis" on teaching the structure of history and instead argued for teaching history in the context of the problems facing American society (21). He identified social problems such as poverty, racism, the unpopular war in Vietnam, and the extent to which schools had become "instruments of the evil forces in our society" (20) as desired foci for social studies instruction.

Osborne points out that Canada, too, had a "crisis of values" at this time, with the October Crisis of 1970, new societal concerns such as sexism, the stirring of discontent among Native peoples, and a breakdown in federal/provincial relations (1984, 95). Others point to Black studies, women's studies, and Third World or development studies, which have been regularly offered in Ontario as examples of a social reform vision of social studies (van Manen and Parsons 1985, 6). More recently, some environmental education programs have raised critical consideration of local problems such as land use and conservation, as well as larger issues such as overpopulation, pollution, and resource depletion. The recent Alberta curriculum has elements of social reform in that it encourages debates around unresolved issues in Canadian identity such as the nature of federalism, the meaning of democracy, and differing conceptions of social justice (Osborne 2004, 7).

An important thread of the social reform camp is teaching students to be what Walter Werner and Ken Nixon call "critically minded"—to be inclined as a general orientation to ask hard questions about much of what we encounter (1990, 2). Students need, for example, to be taught that public media do not simply convey information but, as Neil Postman suggests, they "conceptualize" reality: "They will classify the world for us, sequence it, frame it, enlarge it, reduce it, and argue a case for what it is like" (1979, 39). The very fact that public media pay attention to or ignore an event determines what we come to see as important or worth knowing. So too with what gets taught in schools. We shape students' perceptions of what is important in school and in life by celebrating the individual efforts of famous figures (for example, Van Horne built the CPR, Cheops built the Great Pyramid) and not the collective toil of ordinary, often exploited people, or by focussing on the military outcomes of battles and not on their environmental outcomes. A social reformer would want students to be critical (in an intellectually healthy way) of the very sources and selection of information they encounter—including their teacher and their textbooks. In contrast, a social initiator, even one close to the reform camp, would want students to be more generally accepting of these sources.

Within the last thirty years, a more radical version of social reform espoused by critical theorists has appeared in the social studies literature. This version presumes that knowledge is never impartial but always represents a value position because it is constructed by people with particular values and interests (Smits 1997;

Stanley 1981). Representing any knowledge as a given or as objectively true obscures its social, economic, political, and historical contexts. Social science knowledge shapes our society in conformity with some values and in opposition to others since the dominant culture within society has a major influence on the development and maintenance of social institutions. This radical form of social reform calls for "root criticism" of all knowledge in the social sciences, including critical study of gender, race, nationalistic, or social class domination of social structures and knowledge (Nelson 1985, 370). Canadian proponents of this conception include van Manen, who espouses the "emancipatory" suggestion that "a socially conscious person" ought to engage in "social criticism of all forms of hegemony including the authority of the knowledge and value orientations taught in school" (1980, 114).

A second key element in many versions of social reform is the importance attached to social action. Since the overarching goal is to improve society, students should be assisted in acquiring the abilities and the inclinations to act on their beliefs. Fred Newmann's book *Education for Citizen Action* has been influential in urging that students develop "environmental competence" (1975, 157) and engage in social action as the natural outcome of considering public issues. There has been a somewhat spotty and ambiguous inclusion of "social action" in Canadian social studies curricula. For example, the new Alberta curriculum identifies "social participation" as one of four core skills. Most of the examples refer to developing leadership skills in school and community groups, but the curriculum document does indicate that this goal "could include social action" (2005–2007, 9). Similarly, the current social studies curriculum in British Columbia (2006, 1997) mandates action projects outside the classroom for students at several grades. However, it is ambiguous as to the rationale. It is consistent with a social initiation rationale to engage students in non-controversial forms of social participation such as cleaning up the litter around the school grounds and raising money for a local charity. A reform purpose for social action would involve students in projects that do more than perpetuate the way things are done by filling in the gaps in existing social services (Wade 2000). For example, elementary students have been involved in social reform by writing letters to the newspaper about the way baboons were caged at a Calgary zoo (Dueck, Horvath, and Zelinski 1977) and McDonald's use of styrofoam packaging (Roth 1991).

The Child-centred/Subject-centred Spectrum

Unlike the two purposes of citizenship education already discussed, which have an implied stance towards the status quo—either that the existing state of affairs is basically sound or that it is not and should be changed—the next two camps that we discuss posit no such assumption. Perpetuating or altering the social order are not their preoccupation. Rather, their concern is where to focus in identifying and developing the desired knowledge, abilities, and values. Are they found with the individual by looking to and working with the range of personal needs and everyday predicaments of students, or do they reside in the subject area, in this case in the storehouse of intellectual insight offered through the social science disciplines? The tension between these two poles was expressed by the principal of a prestigious school in India that we visited. His school and many other élite schools in India have a strong intellectual development focus. This principal implicitly acknowledged the social development emphasis of a certain rival school when he commented with a hint of criticism, "Oh yes, you can tell students from that school, they are always so well-adjusted."

Citizenship Education as Personal Development

The focus of personal development is on nurturing students who are fulfilled—personally and socially. It is believed that the "good" society will follow from creating well-adjusted individuals. Important elements of this tradition are traced to John Dewey's progressivist philosophy. Osborne suggests that "Canadian progressivism spoke in terms of the growth and development of students, of meeting students' needs, of teaching the whole child, and much less of social reform or reconstruction" (1996, 42). Instead of an imposed body of knowledge or predetermined direction for social studies education, the desired understandings, abilities, and attitudes are very much those that are required to cope with and make sense of students' own lives and experiences. As Shermis explains, in this tradition "a problem is not a problem unless an individual senses it as such" (1982, 49).

The personal development rationale has had a long history. It can be seen in the 1916 report of the National Education Association Committee on Social Studies in which it was suggested that instruction be organized "not on the basis of the formal social sciences, but on the basis of concrete problems of vital importance to society and of *immediate interest to the pupil* [emphasis added]" (cited in Jenness 1990, 77). This progressive-inspired tradition came into prominence in Canada in the 1930s, a decade during which every province initiated major curricular reform. Revised provincial curricula exemplified new "child-centred" approaches, which implied correlation of subject matter to the needs and interests of the child. The emphasis was on the "whole" child who would "grow physically, emotionally and spiritually, as well as mentally" (Newland 1941, 12). Curricula were activity-oriented, with a focus on group investigation of problems or issues of interest to students; the activities were intended to promote co-operation, communication, and decision-making. Social studies formed the basis of these group investigations, called "enterprises" at the elementary level in many provinces (Alberta Department of Education 1936, 288). "The social studies classroom instead of being a place where children 'learn' history, geography, and civics, is to be a real laboratory, where co-operation, initiative, originality and responsibility are developed" (Alberta Department of Education 1935, 36). At the secondary level, this approach found expression in programs referred to in different provinces as core curriculum, life adjustment curriculum, or an integration of social studies with language arts and the humanities.

In the 1960s, the values clarification movement was an important addition to the personal development orientation. Values clarification is a model for teaching values developed by Louis Raths, Merrill Harmin, and Sidney Simon (1966). It encourages students to choose their own system of values. The values clarification model has been described as "extraordinarily influential" in the development of the 1971 Alberta social studies curricula (Milburn 1976, 222).

The personal development rationale remains in evidence in contemporary social studies, especially in the elementary school. Key features of this vision include: (1) a belief that the content of what is learned is not as significant as students finding what they study personally relevant to their lives, (2) an emphasis on supporting students in pursuing their own directions and developing their own interests, (3) an emphasis on exposing students to a wide range of situations and experiences where they can work out their beliefs and develop their own positions on issues, and (4) a priority given to supporting students in feeling confident about themselves and their beliefs over challenging students to think differently or to question their values.

Citizenship Education as Intellectual Development

The definition of social studies that exemplifies the intellectual development rationale is Edgar Wesley's: "the social studies are the social sciences simplified for pedagogical purposes" (1937, 4). The defining feature of this tradition is not simply or even essentially a matter of acquiring a body of knowledge as it is mastery of the norms and methods used by scholars to gain new knowledge. It is believed that the various social science disciplines have generated the richest insights and investigative techniques for understanding our social world. Hence, developing the minds of students as social scientists and historians is thought to provide the best preparation for citizenship in a complex world. Unlike the personal development camp, intellectual development rationales see the disciplines, more than the students, providing the problems worth considering. Initiation into the academic traditions is more important than exposure to problems of immediate and personal concern, and coming to one's own conclusions is not as important as coming up with intellectually defensible conclusions.

This tradition came into its own with the publication of Jerome Bruner's slim book *The Process of Education* in 1960. Bruner referred to the "structure of the disciplines," by which he meant teaching the component parts or basic structures—the concepts, canons of reasoning, and techniques of inquiry—particular to each discipline. He believed that the basic ideas lying at the heart of the disciplines are simple enough for students at any level to grasp. Bruner argued that "intellectual activity anywhere is the same, whether at the frontier of knowledge or in a third-grade classroom" (14). Consequently, rather than simply presenting students with the findings of a discipline, students should take on the role of social scientist and use the inquiry techniques of the disciplines to make discoveries themselves. Before social studies was itself a subject, proponents of history education were stressing the importance of analysis of source documents for the "mental training which may be obtained from their use" (Caldwell, 1899, reported in Osborne 2003, 482). This tradition has been evident in Canada in the texts and other curriculum materials used in the late 1960s and 1970s. It also appeared in texts used for university social studies curriculum and instruction courses, such as *Teaching the Subjects in the Social Studies*, where the authors identify helping school children begin to learn the thinking patterns, or structure, of the social sciences as a major purpose of elementary social studies (Moore and Owen 1966, v). These authors explain that "a better democratic citizen [is one] who can think historically or geographically, who can think as an economist or as a political scientist, whenever these approaches are relevant to the assessment of contemporary situations" (ibid.).

A similar philosophy underlies a 1960s-approach to teaching geography in the elementary school:

> the child learns, at his own level, the structure of geography and the methods used by the professional geographer. He will learn of, through use at his own level, the various subjects which contribute to the subject of geography. He will also learn through practice in the field, and later with pictures, to observe details carefully, to record these details in many ways, to analyze the data, and then to synthesize selected data to answer a problem. (Social Studies Advisory Committee 1962, 139)

While the structure of the disciplines approach has been somewhat discredited,[3] the calls to promote disciplined historical and geographical understandings are as strong as they ever were. In fact, there is considerable pressure, including calls from Canadian academics (Seixas 1994, 1997; Granatstein 1998), to replace social studies with the teaching of history and geography. As Peter Seixas (1997) argues, students should approach historical accounts critically. Yet this is unlikely to happen as long as students are taught only generic critical thinking or information processing approaches. The distinct challenges of thinking within the disciplines—notions in history such as what counts as a historically significant event, the difficulties of developing historical empathy, and the bases for accepting historical claims—require discipline-specific instruction. Without a developed capacity for historical thinking, teaching about the past is little more than the "simple accretion of increasing amounts of information" (Seixas 1994, 105). According to proponents of an intellectual development rationale, since the social science disciplines are the most rigorous and insightful forms of inquiry about our social world, they represent the best tools that social studies educators can offer students in

preparation for citizenship. As Osborne wrote in the context of history, "The important tasks in teaching history are to arouse in students an interest in, and even love for, the past; to give them a sense of connectedness linking the present with both the past and the future; to help them think historically; and to show them the range of human behaviour" (2000, B3).

Having a Sense of Purpose

It is evident from the foregoing discussion that the factors that influence adoption of a particular conception include deep-rooted assumptions about the role of schooling, the perceived nature of challenges facing society and students, and the teacher's personal values and theories of knowledge and learning. Because of these ideological divisions, many have despaired of arriving at a common vision for citizenship education (Marker and Mehlinger 1992, 832). Attempts to reach consensus typically result in statements of purpose that are so vague they provide no helpful direction and are of dubious educational value. For example, a 1982 survey of provincial curricula by the Canadian Council of Ministers of Education concluded that the common focus is on inquiry approaches towards a goal of providing "students with the knowledge, skills, values and thought processes which will enable them to participate effectively and responsibly in the ever-changing environment of their community, their country and their world" (4). This statement could include anything imaginable and can be interpreted to apply to any of the four camps. Not only is consensus on an identifiable set of desired attributes of citizenship not currently present, the prospects of it are remote. It is no wonder that it is frequently observed that "The content of social studies is a smorgasbord of this and that from everywhere; it is as confusing and vague as is the goal of citizenship" (Barr, Barth, and Shermis 1977, 2).

In order to fill this serious gap, each of us must of necessity develop our own guiding purpose for social studies. After reading the above discussion, we may be inclined to actively promote aspects of all four rationales for citizenship education. Perhaps the most appropriate way of framing the challenge is by asking, "In what respects should each of these purposes be promoted?" However, we must be careful that this does not amount to unfocussed borrowing from all four camps. Vague and indiscriminate choices have produced the smorgasbord referred to above. Barr, Barth, and Shermis, later in the same book, characterize social studies in even less

TABLE 3.3 ILLUSTRATIVE GOALS FOR EACH RATIONALE

GOALS	SOCIAL INITIATION	SOCIAL REFORM	PERSONAL DEVELOPMENT	INTELLECTUAL DEVELOPMENT
Content knowledge and understanding	• mainstream view of history and the world • knowledge of core facts about Canada and the world • knowledge of rights and responsibilities	• alternative world views (post-colonial, feminist) • knowledge of "overlooked" facts about Canada and the world • knowledge of human rights	• self-knowledge • knowledge of personal events and background	• principal and core concepts of social sciences • broad general knowledge in each social science area • knowledge of historiography
Critical, creative, and collaborative thinking	• framed social issues—thinking within "givens"—for example, how to better contribute to society, evaluate situations • innovative solutions to enhance the existing system	• probing issues at the foundations of society • imaginative alternatives to challenge the received order • sceptical of what is presented	• personal issue analysis • exploring personal viewpoints • pursue creative endeavours to further personal ambitions	• canons of historical reasoning and evidence • discipline-based academic issues • develop alternative explanations to established theories
Communicative competence	• use of mainstream sources including electronic technology • established conventions for presenting information	• accessing "alternative" sources of information and viewpoints • persuasive presentations • deconstructing popular media	• mainstream sources of information to meet personal information needs • exploring personal forms of expression and representation	• use of academic resources including original sources and field research • research papers and other forms of academic presentations
Personal and social responsibility	• national pride and trust in civic institutions • honesty, loyalty, and respect for others • work ethic and assume responsibility for self • community service, school enhancement projects, and work placement • ability to work with others to solve problems	• global affiliations • abiding social and environmental conscience • direct political and social action (lobbying) • public advocacy and networking	• personal and cultural pride • personal integrity • individual values clarification • self-help and personal interest projects • personal advocacy	• academic self-confidence • intellectual curiosity and pursuit of knowledge • intellectual work ethic • field studies in academic areas • team research projects

flattering terms, referring to complaints that the subject is "social sludge" and "social stew" and amounts to "a confusing hodge podge" (57). One reason for developing a focussed and discriminating sense of purpose is that few of the attributes of citizenship that are truly worthwhile can be nurtured quickly. Those that we are most serious about will require considerable thought and effort to bring about. Students will not, for example, develop mastery of the social science disciplines without considerable exposure to the body of knowledge and

standards of reasoning in these areas. Promoting all of the purposes in a half-hearted way may mean that nothing is done very well. Besides, there is never enough time. We must inevitably establish priorities, even if these priorities change over time and depend upon the particular class we are teaching.

Table 3.3 provides a sampling of the ways in which each of the main goals in social studies might be developed, depending on the rationale. This table suggests that the range of social studies goals will be present in any given vision, but that the particular emphasis of each will vary.

In addition to our conscious choices as teachers, the influences of the hidden curriculum subtly but pervasively impose a tacit vision of citizenship on us. For example, reliance on a single "authoritative" text is likely to suppress key attributes of social reform and intellectual development, as will an emphasis on recall of received "accepted" facts over student-initiated interpretations of events. One way or another, consciously or unconsciously, we will likely advance a particular rationale. For all of these reasons, we should be cautious about assuming that we can do it all, or that it does not much matter which vision or collection of attributes we judge to be most defensible. It should be stressed that the choice of a dominant purpose should not be a whimsical personal preference. Rather, it requires thoughtful and professional judgment based on a number of factors including the needs, best interests, and rights of our students, their parents, and of society, more broadly.

The vague generalities common in most social studies curriculum frameworks create considerable latitude for teachers to interpret and implement their own clear sense of purpose. Many teaching activities and materials—such as use of textbooks and primary documents, analysis of issues, field trips—are common to all four camps. These standard teaching approaches may be employed in different ways depending on the ultimate purpose for teaching social studies—for example, by varying the topics debated, the amount of deference to the authority of the textbook, and the importance attached to students' wishes. This possibility of massaging teaching objectives, activities, and resources to align with a particular purpose offers the most compelling reason for each of us to think clearly about the sort of citizen that ought to guide our social studies teaching. Every day in countless, often unconscious ways we shape students' development as members of society. If we are unclear about the direction, we will likely perpetuate the bland smorgasbord that has typified mission statements in social studies. If this is the case, we can hardly complain about a passive, unreflective, and apathetic citizenry, since we may have nurtured this "vision" by default—by failing to infuse our teaching with a coherent direction. Each of us needs a clear and reasonable rationale, even if it differs from the teacher's rationale that students encountered the year before and will encounter the year after. In fact, a diversity of well-conceived rationales may be healthy. Doing things well even if the goals differ is preferable to consistently doing

things in a tepid and diluted manner. Far fewer students will be inspired or assisted by a social studies program that lacks clear focus and strong direction. To paraphrase a familiar proverb, "Where there is no vision, programs perish."

Refer back to the "Citizenship Education Matrix" on page 22. Locate the most defensible position for you on this grid by thinking of the students you currently teach or anticipate teaching, and the problems facing them and their society. Which mix of rationales would best meet these needs? Justify your position by thinking of why you would not want to be farther along each of the continua that form this grid.

ENDNOTES

1   These comments are by Barr, Barth, and Shermis (1977) and Jenness (1990).

2   The conceptual framework for social studies developed by Robert Barr, James Barth, and Samuel Shermis (1977, 1978) has had the most impact and the greatest longevity. Their typology, which places citizenship as the ultimate goal of social studies, consists of three traditions: citizenship transmission, social studies as social science, and social studies taught as reflective inquiry. Our four-rationale framework differs from the three traditions of the Barr et al. model in three ways. Our "social initiation" is a narrower notion than their "citizenship transmission." They include any form of transmission of a world view—one which may be a mainstream view or a rather esoteric view held by a minority. For our part, we limit "social initiation" to mainstream world views and any vision of society that is different from the mainstream view as "social reform." Following Jean Fair (1977) and Brubaker, Simon, and Williams (1977), we believe that "reflective inquiry" neglects an important tradition in social studies—the child-centred, personal fulfillment vision. We offer "personal development" to reflect this strand. Finally, following Suzanne Helburn (1977), we collapse the Barr et al. account of "reflective inquiry" with "social science" into what we call "intellectual development." Other conceptual frameworks include the five-camp model (Brubaker, Simon, and Williams 1977), seven program types (van Manen and Parsons 1985), and "elitist and activists" conceptions (Sears 1996).

3   The structure of the disciplines approach has been criticized on numerous counts (Fenton 1991; Massialas 1992; Dow 1992). Criticisms include charges that it relies overly on knowledge objectives and inquiry procedures from the social science disciplines, while ignoring the needs and interests of

students and societal problems; that it uses materials that are too sophisticated for the students for whom they are intended; that it fails to involve typical teachers in material development; that it ignores the hidden curriculum of gender, social class, ethnic, and religious issues; that the logistical complexity of many of the projects is problematic; and that it fails to bridge the cultural gap between theory and the real world of teaching with its large classes, multiple preparations, and often resistant students.

REFERENCES

Alberta Department of Education. 1935. *Programme of studies for the elementary school.* Edmonton, AB: Author.

———. 1936. *Programme of studies for the elementary school.* Edmonton, AB: Author.

Alberta Learning. 2005–2007. *Social studies—Kindergarten to grade 12.* Edmonton, AB: Author. Available online at www.education.alberta.ca/teachers/program/socialstudies.aspx.

Alter, G. 1997. The emergence of a diverse, caring community. *Social Studies and the Young Learner* 10 (1): 6–9.

Barr, R., J.L. Barth, and S.S. Shermis. 1977. *Defining the social studies.* Arlington, VA: National Council for the Social Studies.

———. 1978. *The nature of the social studies.* Palm Springs, CA: ETC Publications.

Booi, L. 2001. Citizens or subjects? *AlbertaViews* March/April: 28–33.

British Columbia Ministry of Education. 2006. *Social studies K to 7 integrated resource package.* Victoria, BC: Author.

British Columbia Ministry of Education, Skills and Training. 1997. *Social studies 8 to 10 integrated resource package.* Victoria, BC: Author.

Brubaker, D.L., L.H. Simon, and J.W. Williams. 1977. A conceptual framework for social studies curriculum and instruction. *Social Education* 41: 201–205.

Bruner, J. 1960. *The process of education.* Cambridge, MA: Harvard University Press.

———. 1971. The process of education revisited. *Phi Delta Kappan* 53: 18–21.

Case, R. 1993. *Summary of the 1992 social studies needs assessment.* Victoria, BC: Queen's Printer.

Cogan, J. and R. Derricott, eds. 2000. *Citizenship for the twenty-first century.* London: Kogan-Page.

Council of Ministers of Education, Canada. 1982. *Social studies: A survey of provincial curricula at the elementary and secondary levels.* Toronto: Author.

Dougan, A.M. 1988. The search for a definition of the social studies: A historical overview. *The International Journal of Social Education* 3 (3): 13–36.

Dow, P. 1992. Past as prologue: The legacy of Sputnik. *Social Studies* 83: 164–171.

Dueck, K., F. Horvath, and V. Zelinski. 1977. Bev Prifit's class takes on the Calgary zoo. *One World* 17: 7–8.

Fair, J. 1977. Comments of Jean Fair. In *Defining the social studies*, R. Barr, J.L. Barth, and S.S. Shermis, 106–109. Arlington, VA: National Council for the Social Studies.

Fenton, E. 1991. Reflections on the "new social studies." *Social Studies* 82: 84–90.

Fitzgerald, F. 1979. *America revised: History schoolbooks in the twentieth century.* Toronto: Little Brown.

Glaze, A.E., B. Hogarth, and B. McLean, eds. 2003. Can schools create citizens?: An exploration of character and citizenship education in Canadian, US, and UK schools. Special issue, *Orbit* 33 (2).

Granatstein, J.L. 1998. *Who killed Canadian history?* Toronto: Harper Collins.

Helburn, S.W. 1977. Comments of Suzanne W. Helburn. In *Defining the social studies*, R. Barr, J.L. Barth, and S.S. Shermis, 110–113. Arlington, VA: National Council for the Social Studies.

Hirsch, E.D. 1988. *Cultural literacy: What every American needs to know.* New York: Vintage.

Jenness, D. 1990. *Making sense of social studies.* Toronto: Collier Macmillan.

Leming, J.S. 1992. Ideological perspectives within the social studies profession: An empirical examination of the "two cultures" thesis. *Theory and Research in Social Education* 20 (3): 293–312.

Longstreet, W.S. 1985. Citizenship: The phantom core of social studies curriculum. *Theory and Research in Social Education* 13 (2): 21–29.

Marker, G. and H. Mehlinger. 1992. Social studies. In *Handbook of research on curriculum*, ed. P.W. Jackson, 830–851. Toronto: Maxwell Macmillan.

Massialas, B.G. 1992. The "new social studies": Retrospect and prospect. *Social Studies* 83: 120–124.

McNeil, L. 1986. *Contradictions of control: School structure and school knowledge.* New York: Routledge and Kegan Paul.

Milburn, G. 1976. The social studies curriculum in Canada: A survey of the published literature in the last decade. *Journal of Educational Thought* 10: 212–224.

Moore, E. and E.E. Owen. 1966. *Teaching the subjects in the social studies: A handbook for teachers.* Toronto: Macmillan.

Nelson, J.R. 1980. The uncomfortable relationship between moral education and citizenship instruction. In *Moral development and politics*, ed. R. Wilson and G. Schochet, 256–285. New York: Praeger.

———. 1985. New criticism and social education. *Social Education* 49: 368–371.

Newland, H.C. 1941. Report of the supervisor of schools. In *Thirty-sixth annual report of the Department of Education of the Province of Alberta*. Edmonton, AB: A. Schnitka, King's Printer.

Newmann, F.M. 1975. *Education for citizen action: Challenge for secondary curriculum*. Berkeley, CA: McCutchan.

Osborne, K. 1984. A consummation devoutly to be wished: Social studies and general curriculum theory. In *Curriculum Canada V: School subject research and curriculum/instruction theory*. Proceedings of the Fifth Invitational Conference of Curriculum Research of the CSSE, ed. D.A. Roberts and J.O. Fritz. Vancouver, BC: Centre for the Study of Curriculum and Instruction, University of British Columbia.

————. 1991. *Teaching for democratic citizenship*. Toronto: Our Schools/Our Selves Education Foundation.

————. 1996. Education is the best national insurance: Citizenship education in Canadian schools—past and present. *Canadian and International Education* 25 (2): 31–58.

————. 2000. Who killed Granatstein's sense of history? Misguided criticisms. *National Post*, May 27.

————. 2003. Fred Morrow Fling and the source-method of teaching history. *Theory and Research in Social Education* 31 (4): 466–501.

————. 2004. *Canadian history in the schools*. A report prepared for Historica Foundation, Toronto. Available online at www.histori.ca.

Postman, N. 1979. *Teaching as a conserving activity*. New York: Delta Books.

Quigley, C.N. 1991. *Civitas: A framework for civic education*. Calabasas, CA: Center for Civic Education.

Rappoport, A.L. and S.B. Kletzien. 1997. Kids around town: Civic education through democratic action. *Social Studies and the Young Learner* 10 (1): 14–16.

Raths, L.E., M. Harmin, and S.B. Simon. 1966. *Values and teaching: Working with values in the classroom*. Columbus, OH: Charles E. Merrill.

Roth, A. 1991. Battle of the clamshell. *Report on Business Magazine*, April: 40–43, 45–47.

Sears, A. 1994. Social studies as citizenship education in English Canada: A review of research. *Theory and Research in Social Education* 22 (1): 6–43.

————. 1996. "Something different to everyone": Conceptions of citizenship and citizenship education. *Canadian and International Education* 25 (2): 1–15.

Seixas, P. 1994. A discipline adrift in an "integrated" curriculum: The problem of history in British Columbia schools. *Canadian Journal of Education* 19 (1): 99–107.

————. 1997. The place of history within social studies. In *Trends and issues in Canadian social studies*, ed. I. Wright and A. Sears, 116–129. Vancouver: Pacific Educational Press.

Shermis, S.S. 1982. A response to our critics: Reflective inquiry is not the same as social science. *Theory and Research in Social Education* 10 (1): 45–50.

Smits, H. 1997. Citizenship education in postmodern times: Posing some questions for reflection. *Canadian Social Studies* 31 (3): 126–130.

Social Studies Advisory Committee, Faculty of Education, University of British Columbia. 1962. *History and geography teaching materials*. Vancouver, BC: University of British Columbia.

Stanley, W.B. 1981. The radical reconstructionist rationale for social education. *Theory and Research in Social Education* 8: 55–79.

Tomkins, G. 1985. The social studies in Canada. In *A Canadian social studies*, rev. ed., ed. J. Parsons, G. Milburn, and M. van Manen, 12–30. Edmonton, AB: University of Alberta.

van Manen, M. 1980. A concept of social critique. *The History and Social Science Teacher* 15: 110–114.

van Manen, M. and J. Parsons. 1985. What are the social studies? In *A Canadian social studies*, rev. ed., ed. J. Parsons, G. Milburn, and M. van Manen, 2–11. Edmonton, AB: University of Alberta.

Wade, R.C. 2000. Beyond charity: Service learning for social justice. *Social Studies and the Young Learner* 12 (4): 6–9.

Werner, W. and K. Nixon. 1990. *The media and public issues: A guide for teaching critical mindedness*. London, ON: Althouse Press.

Wesley, E.B. 1937. *Teaching social studies in high schools*. Boston: D.C. Heath.

PART 2 Learning and Thinking Within and Outside the Disciplines

4

Teaching Elementary Students to Think Historically

Amy von Heyking

Contrary to the prevailing opinion, history is not the story of the past. It is not a purely factual record of events that happened long ago. Rather, it is best seen as a form of inquiry that helps us construct an understanding of our individual and collective lives in time. It is an interpretive discipline, requiring students to determine the validity and credibility of evidence in order to analyze, construct, and reconstruct narratives about past people, events, and ideas. In other words, it is a form of inquiry that requires historical thinking. The Alberta social studies curriculum (2005–2007, 9) describes historical thinking as "a process whereby students are challenged to rethink assumptions about the past and re-imagine both the present and the future." This approach is a significant departure from past practices. Traditionally, the history taught in many elementary schools has consisted of a single narrative—for example, the heroic contributions of settlers, or the wondrous achievements of ancient civilizations.

Understanding the interpretive nature of history is essential if students are to value the construction of valid alternative stories about the past and acknowledge the controversial nature of those constructions. For example, How different is the settlement of the West when seen through aboriginal eyes? Ancient Egypt is a "great" civilization from an architectural point of view, but what about from a human rights perspective? Creating this opening helps children explore their own and their families' connection to the past, empowers them to imagine possible futures and consider significant themes and questions in history, encourages them to be critical

readers of historical narratives, and acknowledges the diversity of questions and topics of interest to historians beyond past politics and basic needs. History of this kind is powerful and exciting. It requires that children move beyond memorizing isolated facts or accepting a given story, and instead engages them in creating stories about the past. How can elementary school children do this?

Children's Historical Understanding

Early studies of children's cognitive development seemed to indicate that history was largely meaningless to students until the age of fourteen. Using Piaget's stages of cognitive development, researchers concluded that students under the age of sixteen could not be expected to cope with abstract concepts or tasks such as hypothesizing beyond what is readily apparent in source material or synthesizing ideas drawn from different sources. Clearly, if this assessment were valid, history as investigation, analysis, and interpretation would be beyond the ability of elementary school children.

Researchers now have largely rejected universal cognitive development theories. Instead, they define learning as a reordering of prior knowledge according to "scripts" that vary depending on the subject area (Levstik 1993). In other words, learners use their existing mental structures when confronted with something new. Accordingly, teachers should acknowledge that elementary children do indeed bring considerable prior beliefs to the learning of history. Seixas (1996) reminds us that from a very young age children encounter traces of the past in the natural and human landscape (weather-worn trees, deserted houses), in the relics of the past (old coins, antiques), in the language they use ("when I was little," "in Gramma's day"), and in the cultural institutions of which they are a part (school, church). Moreover, children experience many accounts of the past on television and film, in books, in family stories, and in commemorations. British researcher Hilary Cooper argues:

> The past is a dimension of children's social and physical environment and they interact with it from birth. They hear and use the vocabulary of time and change: old, new, yesterday, tomorrow, last year, before you were born, when mummy was little, a long time ago, once upon a time. They ask questions about the sequence and causes of events: When did we move here? Why? What happened in the story next? Children encounter different interpretations of past times in nursery rhymes and fairy stories, family anecdotes, theme parks, films, and pantomime. They encounter historical sources: old photographs, a baby book, an ornament, a statue, a church, maybe a closed-down factory or a derelict cinema being replaced by new roads and flats ... before children start school there are many contexts in which they are implicitly aware of the past. (1995, 1–2)

Research on children's prior understanding of time and history suggests that students have some conception of history as the study of significant events in the past and, as early as grade 2, may have some understanding of particular historical events (Levstik and Pappas 1987). Children's historical understandings are shaped by their environment and experiences, but also by the television shows and films they watch and the stories they read. Consequently, all elementary teachers would be well advised to provide opportunities within their history units for students to share prior beliefs.

Many studies indicate that elementary school children can develop sophisticated historical thinking within an appropriate context of active engagement with source material, exposure to alternative accounts, and teaching that scaffolds their emerging understanding and skills (Barton 1997b; Foster and Yeager 1999; Levstik and Smith 1996; VanSledright 2002b). It is helpful, therefore, to examine the specific historical thinking concepts that define this domain, review current research in order to determine the extent and nature of children's work with

these elements, and suggest ways in which teachers can nurture children's understanding of history.

Select a historical event that might be familiar to elementary school children. Identify two or three children who are willing to discuss this event with you. Individually, explore their understanding by asking the following questions:

- Who was involved?
- What were the main events?
- Where did it take place?
- When did it occur?
- Why is it an important event?
- How did it come about?

Compare the children's responses and identify areas of understanding and misunderstanding. Look beyond what may be simple factual errors for evidence of more foundational perceptions of the event in particular, and of history in general.

Historical Thinking

Although there are different explanations of historical thinking, in Canada, Peter Seixas (2006) and the Historical Thinking Project offer a coherent framework and a useful entry point for deepening students' historical thinking. This project identifies six concepts:

- historical significance;
- evidence and interpretation;
- continuity and change;
- cause and consequence;
- historical perspective taking; and
- the ethical dimension.

These concepts are interrelated. If students are investigating whether life is better now or in "the good old days," they would address concepts of change and continuity over time, of historical perspective, and would likely consider the validity of the evidence they collected. A role-playing exercise in which students explore the meeting of Jacques Cartier and Chief Donnacona would require the consideration of varying historical perspectives and the use of valid historical sources to create a plausible account. It may also challenge students to consider the significance of this historic meeting. In other words, the six concepts are not typically addressed in isolation in separate learning activities. Without these concepts, students lack the tools needed to make sense of historical accounts and to construct their own interpretations.

HISTORICAL SIGNIFICANCE

History is not a chronicle of everything that happened in the past, but only a filtered representation of a very small part of what has occurred. Consequently historians must make decisions about what is significant and students need to be able to distinguish between what is historically trivial and what is important.

In some cases, historical significance is determined by the long-term impact of an event, idea, or person. For example, we might study the use of cedar by First Nations peoples because it had a great influence on their lives at the time, or we might learn about the battle on the Plains of Abraham because of its lingering effects on Canada's cultural and political landscape. But historical significance is also determined by our current interests and values. The priorities of the present shape the questions we ask about the past and the nature of the evidence we use. For example, comparing social studies textbooks from fifty years ago with modern ones, we would notice a greater focus on women and children in the latter. This is because earlier writers of these texts were preoccupied with political or economic concerns, for example, Why do we have this form of government? How did these particular patterns of trade develop? The everyday lives of people—particularly women, children, people of the working class, and people of ethnic minorities—were not thought of then as particularly significant from a historical point of view, whereas it is now thought important to encourage students to investigate the history of their local communities and of everyday life in the past.

Research suggests that even children as young as seven can distinguish between "history" and "the past" (Levstik and Pappas 1987). By the time they reach grade 6, students are able to explain and support their definitions with examples, suggesting that historical events are often rooted in conflict and result in social change. But teachers must be deliberate in their discussions with children about historical significance. Researchers stress the important opportunities available to teachers for engaging students in discussions about why some events, people, or ideas are included in school history curricula and texts while others are omitted. Historical events that are significant to students or are contentious because they occurred within the living memory of parents and grandparents provide particularly rich opportunities to consider what makes certain episodes and people of the past important. CBC Television's *The Greatest Canadian* contest in 2004 sparked lively discussion and debate over just this question. The choice of Tommy Douglas, widely championed as the creator of Canada's public health care system, is a powerful illustration for children of the extent to which history embodies the viewpoint of the present.

Young children can address the element of historical significance by considering for whom their school or other places in the community are named. Why are these people important? Have students learned about other individuals in their community for whom something should be named? They could consider what will be significant in their own lives by creating time capsules to illustrate life in the beginning of the twenty-first century. Students should explain why they have included certain artifacts and omitted others. They might compare the choices they have made with those of students in a more senior grade or with those their own parents might make. Students could engage in different kinds of writing exercises about historical figures in order to consider what information might be included and/or omitted in an obituary, a commemorative plaque, or a newspaper story. Such exercises prepare children for later studies that further illustrate that historical significance depends largely on the purpose of the account (for example, to create a positive impression, to focus on a particular theme, to tell all sides of the story) and that this in turn depends on one's point of view.

EVIDENCE AND INTERPRETATION

Another important element of historical thinking involves understanding the basis for claiming to know about the past. How do we determine what happened at a given time? For example, What was Champlain's role in the conflict between the Huron and the Iroquois? What evidence do we have? How reliable is this evidence? How can we explain historical accounts that offer different, even contradictory, interpretations of past events? We should not leave children with the impression that there is one true story of the past, or that history is a report from the past. Nor should they think that historians make things up. Children need to understand that history is the way we make sense of the past based on many different kinds of evidence.

Children in elementary school can begin to explore the range of evidence that historians use: written primary sources such as letters and diaries; oral sources such as interviews; and physical remains such as artifacts. Given the emphasis in elementary school curricula on aboriginal culture and history, there are many opportunities for teachers to help children understand how we can come to know about events and people, even in our distant past.

Researchers suggest that children can begin to appreciate how historians might use the same information about the past but differ in their conclusions about what that information means. Children certainly have difficulty determining the credibility of evidence, weighing different kinds of evidence, and understanding how historians use evidence to weave different narratives when they are studying topics or events that are unfamiliar or abstract. But children can collect and interpret historical evidence and write their own narratives if they are investigating historical topics that are familiar to them, such as the history of their own families or communities. Children can examine photographs, analyze physical artifacts, and interview relatives in order to create accounts of their own past. They can compare and contrast these with those of their parents or siblings. They can consider who might be a more credible source of information about their family's history: a sibling, parent, or grandparent?

When studying the history of their school or community, children can draw inferences from a school backpack or an antique trunk full of objects. Who do you think this belongs to? What do you think this person is like? What does he or she like to do for fun? These activities require children to make tentative assumptions based on the evidence they have and generate questions to guide further inquiry. Peter Knight (1993, 95) reminds us that even very young children can improve their historical reasoning by responding to three questions when presented with any traditional primary source: "What do you know for certain about it? What can you guess? What would you like to know?"

Students might be invited to reach conclusions about life in an earlier period by interpreting images depicting past scenes. For example, in one resource (Case and Misfeldt 2002), students study various illustrations, including the one of political life in ancient Egypt included here, looking for clues and drawing conclusions to answer the 5W questions (who, what, where, when, and why). Their conclusions must be well supported by clues and provide a detailed portrayal of life (for example, Is the man sitting to the left of the stage an accountant? A scribe? A tax collector? What clues can we find? Is the figure sitting on the throne kind or nasty? Poor or wealthy? What clues can we find?). Students are invited to reserve judgment and consult other sources if the clues are insufficient for them to reach a clear conclusion.

Multiple interpretations, provided they are supported by plausible evidence, are accepted provisionally, subject to the discovery of additional sources of evidence that might support a more conclusive interpretation.

Many studies indicate that upper elementary children are capable of sophisticated reasoning when appropriately supported through analysis of historical evidence and accounts (Barton 1997b; Foster and Yeager 1999; Levstik and Smith 1996; VanSledright 2002a, 2002b, 2002c; VanSledright and Kelly 1998). But researchers concede that several challenges remain. For example, although twelve-year-olds in one study were able to critique sources by detecting bias and identifying gaps in the evidence, they naively insisted that finding a kind of "middle ground" among their sources would yield a definitive account (Foster and Yeager 1999). They had difficulty assessing the validity of sources and using that assessment to weigh differing viewpoints. Other students, without sufficient content background or contextual information, assessed the validity of a source solely by the amount of information provided (VanSledright and Kelly 1998). Students' use of this criterion is not surprising given that this is often how multiple sources are used in elementary classrooms. Clearly, teachers need to help children analyze accounts and assess the quality of evidence upon which they are based.

Barton (1997b) was impressed with the ability of grade 4 and 5 students to identify historical sources, evaluate evidence, and reconcile contradictory accounts of a famous battle during the American Revolution. His study, however, revealed that when asked to construct their own accounts of the battle, students ignored the evidence they had spent so much time and effort analyzing. Instead, they largely invented their own stories. These students did not see the need to ground their historical narratives in the available evidence. This suggests that elementary teachers should exercise caution when using fictional narratives in their history teaching. Since students at this age are most familiar with narrative as a fictional (invented) form, they need explicit instruction as well as opportunities to examine the evidence on which such narratives are constructed. They should, for example, use source material to determine which episodes in a story or novel are likely to be true and which invented by the author. They need to compare and contrast historical fiction with non-fiction. They also need to engage in historical inquiries of immediate relevance to them that require using evidence to create original narratives.

ANCIENT EGYPT

Illustration by Danna deGroot. Courtesy of The Critical Thinking Consortium.

CONTINUITY AND CHANGE

Understanding change over time is central to historical thinking. So, too, is the need to recognize the constants that continue through time. Obviously, age is an important factor in gaining this understanding: an older person simply has had more direct experience with historical change and continuity—in technology, social values, customs—and therefore has a better sense of what has and has not changed. But researchers suggest that age is not the only factor. Life experience can help even young children appreciate the nature of change. A young person who has lived through a war or a refugee experience, who immigrates to a new country, or who has had to move because a parent lost a job, may better understand historical change than one who has always lived in a stable environment. But beyond experience, there are concepts that children must understand.

First, children must have a grasp of time-related concepts such as "past" and "present," "yesterday," and "long ago." Primary children's understanding of time concepts is generally vague. They can read clock time; recite days, months, and seasons in order; and use terms like "tonight" or "tomorrow" to describe a point in time. Units of time that require an understanding of decades and centuries must wait for the upper elementary grades. But researchers stress the importance of helping even very young children with time categories such as "past" and "present" or "then" and "now." Children should begin by examining objects and photographs from their

own childhoods and learning about the lives of elders in their community (Seefeldt 1993). They can also examine archival and current photographs of familiar scenes—schools or local streetscapes—and categorize them as past and present (H. Cooper 1995). Illustrated picture books provide opportunities to identify elements of the story or illustration that provide clues as to its setting in time (for example, When did this story take place? How do you know? Are there clues in the illustrations?).

Sequence is another key concept in understanding temporal change. Researchers working with very young children stress the importance of developing students' understanding of a sequence of events by using familiar contexts (C. Cooper 2003). Early primary children can begin by sequencing photographs that show the activities and routines of their school day and gradually learn to sequence months and special events in the year for a classroom "memory line" or a personal timeline. Students can examine photographs of the school and its playground dating from ten years previously to compare and contrast their school "then" and "now."

Studies indicate that when faced with pictures and photographs from various eras, even young children can place them in the correct chronological sequence (Barton and Levstik 1996). Using clues from the material culture portrayed in the photographs, they could identify the sequence even if they lacked the appropriate time vocabulary to label the pictures. Upper elementary children are more likely to identify historical eras and include references to political history; they also rely less on evidence of technological change when sequencing pictures, but draw on their background knowledge of school history as well as information gleaned from the media, family history, and popular fiction and non-fiction.

Sequencing activities do not by themselves aid students' understanding of change and continuity. It is important to structure opportunities for young children to observe and record changes in themselves, their school, and their community, perhaps by following seasonal changes of a tree in the schoolyard, keeping records of children's own growth, or tracking a neighbourhood construction project. According to Seefeldt (1993, 147), these activities help children understand that "(1) change is continuous and always present; (2) change affects people in different ways; and (3) change can be recorded and become a record of the past." While it is a useful starting point, we should not limit young children to exploring personal dimensions of change. With appropriate support, they can begin to think about changes over time in their families, schools, and communities.

Researcher Keith Barton (2002, 178) believes that upper elementary students are adept at observing changes in material culture, technology, and social life, and are able to categorize events according to broad historical periods, especially if they explore when those things happened: "which came earlier or later (sequencing), what other things were going on at the same time (grouping), and how far apart they are from each other or the present (measuring)." In other words, students need to see connections if they are to make sense of the broad sweep of time.

Children, however, are prone to constructing simplified narratives that distort history. They seemed to assume, for example, that historical change follows a uniform and linear pattern: immigrants came to North America, they lived in small cabins, they built cities. They are confused by evidence of "pioneer" life well after the establishment of cities in some parts of the country. Students tend to believe that once a "problem" has been solved, it is no longer an issue. For example, Barton reports that children believed that once women's suffrage was achieved, women were equal and no longer faced discrimination. Children should be exposed to a wide range of lifestyles and experiences in any given historical period:

> Whether studying ancient Egypt, colonial America, or the 1960s, for example, students should constantly be comparing the experience of men and women, urban and rural residents, and upper, middle, and lower socio-economic classes. Moreover, students should learn about the relationships among these groups, so that they see historical societies as consisting of many connected groups rather than as idealized stereotypes of explorers, settlers, and so on. (Barton 1996, 74)

Related to their tendency towards simplification, many studies suggest that elementary students believe that history is the story of constant progress, that life— whether in terms of political participation, technological advantages, or amount of leisure time—has always improved over time. In fact, when American children were asked to identify the most important events in their country's history, they rejected any idea or event that challenged the dominant message that the nation has continuously progressed towards greater liberty and freedom for all. This assumption is not surprising since textbooks typically convey an underlying positive message of physical, intellectual, and social advancement. Challenging these dominant messages by provoking students with examples that encourage alternative readings might create the cognitive dissonance necessary for a more balanced understanding.

When studying a particular era in history, it may be helpful to ask students to consider in what ways life has improved and in which ways life has worsened since the period being examined. If children are interviewing parents or elders about their childhoods, they could be directed to ask these adults whether life had improved or declined and in what ways. The purpose of such considerations is not to produce cynics or sunny optimists, but rather to encourage a more complex understanding of continuity and change.

CAUSE AND CONSEQUENCE

Research suggests that elementary children hold simplistic notions of the reasons for historical change. While human agency is always an essential consideration for historians when they consider how and why certain events occurred, children tend to see history as a record of the accomplishments of a few important people: Sir John A. Macdonald was responsible for the confederation of the British North American colonies, or the five women involved in the "Famous Five" case convinced Canadians of the need for women's equality. This is hardly surprising given the traditional "great people" interpretations of history presented in many elementary textbooks. Good quality biographies, however, may help children better understand the context in which historical figures lived and the constraints they faced (Fertig 2008).

Children also often misunderstand the scale or numbers of people involved in historic events. For example, Barton (1996, 66–67) found that after studying the American Revolutionary War, grade 5 students "did not understand that there were many thousands of soldiers, engaged in many different conflicts throughout the colonies; they thought there were simply two bodies of troops who kept meeting each other in battle."

Elementary children have difficulty appreciating the social, economic, and political factors that lead to change; they do not understand the role of social and political institutions (Barton 1997a). Children would view the deportation of the Acadians between 1755 and 1763, for example, as the action of a bullying British governor in Acadia rather than the tragic consequence

FIGURE 4.1   GRAPHIC WEB

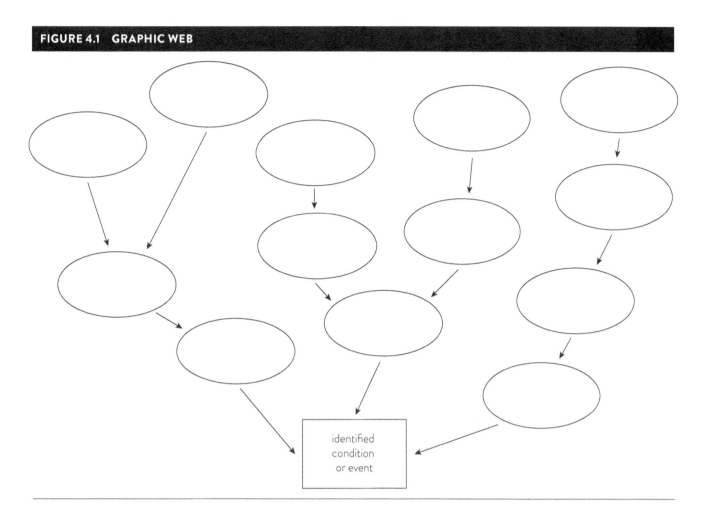

of a global conflict between two empires. Lengthy or detailed study of political, military, and economic history is inappropriate for elementary children. Yet the biographical approach to history should also be approached with caution. Because children appreciate so readily that history is about real people, history teaching at the elementary level may encourage an inflated sense of personal efficacy if students do not understand the institutional constraints on individual action. Teachers can help children analyze the complex questions of historical agency by distinguishing between direct and indirect influences on events.

A graphic web such as the one in Figure 4.1 is useful when students are analyzing the chain of factors or influences that contributed to a particular historical event. For instance, in considering why nineteenth-century immigrants moved to Canada, students might identify economic hardships, political conditions in their home country, the promise of free land, and so on. They would then investigate how these influences came to be (for example, economic hardships might be traced to unfair land practices). For young students, the

activity may be more appropriately done using a simple wall-sized web while the class considers the reasons a particular historical figure acted as he or she did. Older students might complete the chart individually and then discuss their findings collectively.

HISTORICAL PERSPECTIVE AND THE ETHICAL DIMENSION

According to historian Gerda Lerner (1997, 201), meaningful historical study "demands imagination and empathy, so that we can fathom worlds unlike our own, contexts far from those we know, ways of thinking and feeling that are alien to us. We must enter past worlds with curiosity and respect." This imaginative leap into times and places long ago is extremely challenging for children. How can they appreciate and understand the experience of fur traders in the nineteenth century, or settlers struggling to establish homesteads in the Canadian West in the early twentieth century? And yet one of the most important contributions of the study of history to the development of citizenship is that it forces us to confront and make sense of an enormous range of human behaviours and beliefs. It provokes insights into the thoughts and experiences of people in the past. Because people generally acted on diverse or even conflicting beliefs, we must examine multiple perspectives when we investigate historical events, people, ideas, or issues.

Hilary Cooper (1995, 3) explains how exploring historical perspective develops children's moral awareness, because it encourages children "to ask questions, to discuss and to speculate about the reasons for people's behaviour, attitudes and values in other times and other places." Research, however, consistently demonstrates that elementary children initially bring a "presentist" perspective to their understanding of the past: they judge the people of the past according to present standards; they see the people of the past as deficient in some way (Barton 1996; Lee and Ashby 2001; VanSledright 2002c). When examining a photograph of students in a classroom one hundred years earlier, elementary school children commented on the dinginess of the room, the children's uncomfortable clothing, and the lack of books, even though textbooks were clearly visible in the photograph (von Heyking 2011). When asked to comment on the difference between the classroom in the photograph and their own, all the students commented that their own was much better. Elementary school children typically see people in the past as not just intellectually, but also morally, inferior. This makes it difficult for them to consider ethical questions about Europeans' attitudes towards and treatment of Canada's aboriginal people within the context of the time. It interferes with their ability to consider the intelligibility of Governor Lawrence's deportation of the Acadians even as they acknowledge the injustice of the act. In other words, children's natural inclination to see historical issues through contemporary perspectives and morality makes understanding and articulating diverse historical perspectives very challenging for them.

Sometimes teachers inadvertently reinforce presentist attitudes by asking children to imagine themselves in a historical era. Instructions for a writing exercise, for example, may say: "Pretend you are a fur trader for the Hudson's Bay Company. Write a letter to your family in England." Many children will literally imagine themselves in this situation like time travellers struck by the discomfort and difficulties of the environment, particularly if they have little historical information or evidence that might provide more authentic insights into the perspectives of the men of that time and place.

Rephrasing the instructions to more accurately represent what students should do would help them avoid the error of presentism: "From the perspective of a fur trader, write a letter to your family in England." Sometimes well-timed questions or interventions can help students acknowledge the presentist assumptions they are making. For example, teachers might ask: "Would the settlers then have felt the same way you do about their household work? Why or why not?"

Many teaching strategies—including using imaginative play stimulated by stories about previous times—can help very young children begin to understand historical perspectives. Although play is largely driven by fantasy rather than any connection to historical evidence, H. Cooper (1995, 21) believes that setting play in a historical context helps children find out about and try to understand and reconstruct past times. Activities such as role plays, simulations, and field trips to historic sites—if supported with appropriate structure, guidelines, and constructive intervention by the teacher—can help elementary children understand the perspectives of people of earlier times.

For older children, historical fiction can provide insights into the thoughts, values, and perspectives of people in the past. Because of its emotional power, children often have difficulty reading historical fiction critically, but it is important to ask students to consider whether the imagined historical perspectives of a novel's characters are credible. For example, students reading Scholastic's *Dear Canada* diaries or the *I Am Canada* journals should consider how the authors of these fictional accounts have created main characters who seem like "real" historical figures, but who also appeal to modern readers. Is it realistic that girls in these historical eras would keep diaries? That the diaries would survive until the present day? In what ways are the journals crafted to appeal to boys today? Thinking about the choices authors make in writing historical fiction helps children appreciate that their own perspective is one that is grounded in a particular time and place.

The most effective way for children to begin to recognize, understand, and appreciate historical perspectives is to hear and read the voices of historical figures. Barton argues that one of the most important reasons to use primary sources in history teaching is to provide us with direct evidence of the thoughts and experiences of people long ago. Reading excerpts from diaries, letters, or speeches can help children consider questions such as: "Just what were these people trying to say? What did they think about the choices they were making, and what reasons did they give for their actions? How did they feel about their lives and circumstances, their triumphs and tragedies? What hopes and dreams did they entertain, and what were their everyday feelings and opinions?" (2005, 753).

In order to help elementary school children understand diverse historical perspectives, teachers should make connections to stories with multiple perspectives, as well as the students' own experiences with events in their past that might have been interpreted differently by different people. For example, students have little difficulty understanding the story of the three little pigs from the wolf's perspective. Likewise, they appreciate that certain events that took place in the school playground may be interpreted differently by different students or their supervisors. Like detectives, historians need to listen to all the "witnesses'" perspectives in order to answer questions about the past. This will prepare them to consider why some Nova Scotians supported Confederation in 1867 and others did not, or why the Métis and the Canadian government saw the events in Red River in 1869 and 1870 very differently.

The paradox of historical perspective, and its value in developing historical understanding, is that it involves confronting difference at the same time that we recognize a common humanity that transcends time. It allows us to recognize something familiar, while at the same time acknowledging that times have changed in profound ways. It prevents us from making unreasonable moral judgments, but encourages us to learn something from the past that will help us consider the ethical dimension of our actions today. This is essential when we are faced with commemorating past events or people, and when we confront our responsibility for facing the legacies of historical injustices. Encouraging historical perspective cultivates humility and prudence in our attempts to understand the past and the present.

Conclusion

It is possible for primary and upper elementary students to think historically, to understand the interpretative nature of history, and to engage in the creation of stories about the past. They need to see the relevance of their historical inquiries and to participate to the extent possible in hands-on activities that explore how people lived in the past. It is helpful to encourage children to share their thoughts at the beginning of historical inquiries, develop their own questions about the past, and examine evidence in order to reach their own conclusions. History teaching that focusses on developing children's understanding of the six historical thinking concepts introduced in this chapter will ultimately help create citizens who are critical thinkers and who look to the future with imagination, empathy, and hope.

The author's fundamental point is that it is not enough to teach elementary students about the past; we should also help them think critically about any historical account. Select a topic from the curriculum that involves some historical thinking (whether about personal memories or earlier civilizations). Identify at least two of the historical thinking concepts (for example, significance, evidence, perspective) and identify various activities that would help students think about this topic in a historically more meaningful way.

REFERENCES

Alberta Learning. 2005–2007. *Program of studies: social studies—Kindergarten to grade 12.* Edmonton: Author.

Barton, K.C. 1996. Narrative simplifications in elementary students' historical thinking. In *Advances in research on teaching.* Vol. 6. *Teaching and learning in history,* ed. J. Brophy, 51–84. Greenwich, CN: JAI Press.

———. 1997a. "Bossed around by the Queen": Elementary students' understanding of individuals and institutions in history. *Journal of Curriculum and Supervision* 12 (4): 290–315. Accessed from the Proquest database. Available online at www.library.ualberta.ca/getit.

———. 1997b. "I just kinda know": Elementary students' ideas about historical evidence. *Theory and Research in Social Education* 25 (4): 407–430.

———. 2002. "Oh, that's a tricky piece!": Children, mediated action, and the tools of historical time. *The Elementary School Journal* 103 (2): 161–183.

———. 2005. Primary sources in history: Breaking through the myths. *Phi Delta Kappan* 86 (10): 745–753.

Barton, K.C. and L.S. Levstik. 1996. "Back when God was around and everything": Elementary children's understanding of historical time. *American Educational Research Journal* 33 (2): 419–454.

Case, R. and C. Misfeldt. 2002. *Legacies of ancient Egypt.* Richmond, BC: The Critical Thinking Consortium.

Cooper, C. 2003. History: finding out about the past and the language of time. In *Teaching across the early years 3–7,* ed. H. Cooper and C. Sixsmith, 153–167. London: Routledge Falmer.

Cooper, H. 1995. *History in the early years.* London: Routledge.

Fertig, G. 2008. Using biography to help young learners understand the causes of historical change and continuity. *Social Studies* 99 (1): 147–154.

Foster S.J. and E.A. Yeager. 1999. "You've got to put together the pieces": English 12-year-olds encounter and learn from historical evidence. *Journal of Curriculum and Supervision* 14 (4): 286–317.

Knight, P. 1993. *Primary geography, primary history.* London: David Fulton.

Lee, P. and R. Ashby. 2001. Empathy, perspective taking, and rational understanding. In *Historical empathy and perspective taking in the social studies*, ed. O.L. Davis, Jr., E.A. Yeager, S.J. Foster, 21–50. Lanham, MD: Rowman & Littlefield Publishers.

Lerner, G. 1997. *Why history matters.* New York: Oxford University Press.

Levstik, L.S. 1993. Building a sense of history in a first-grade classroom. In *Advances in research on teaching. Vol. 4. Research in elementary social studies*, ed. J. Brophy, 1–31. Greenwich, CN: JAI Press.

Levstik, L.S. and C.C. Pappas. 1987. Exploring the development of historical understanding. *Journal of Research and Development in Education* 21: 1–15.

Levstik, L.S. and D.B. Smith. 1996. "I've never done this before": Building a community of historical inquiry in a third-grade classroom. In *Advances in research on teaching.* Vol. 6. *Teaching and learning in history*, ed. J. Brophy, 85–114. Greenwich, CN: JAI Press.

Seefeldt, C. 1993. History for young children. *Theory and Research in Social Education* 21 (2): 143–155.

Seixas, P. 1996. Conceptualizing the growth of historical understanding. In *The handbook of education and human development*, ed. D.R. Olson and N. Torrance, 765–783. Cambridge, MA: Blackwell Publishers.

———. 2006. Benchmarks for historical thinking: A framework for assessment in Canada. Unpublished paper. Vancouver: Centre for the Study of Historical Consciousness, University of British Columbia. Accessed online at www.historical thinking.ca.

VanSledright, B. 2002a. Confronting history's interpretative paradox while teaching fifth graders to investigate the past. *American Educational Research Journal* 39 (4): 1089–1115.

———. 2002b. Fifth graders investigating history in the classroom: Results from a researcher-practitioner design experiment. *The Elementary School Journal* 103 (2): 131–160.

———. 2002c. *In search of America's past: Learning to read history in elementary school.* New York: Teachers College Press.

VanSledright, B. and J. Brophy. 1992. Storytelling, imagination, and fanciful elaboration in children's historical reconstructions. *American Educational Research Journal* 29 (4): 837–859.

VanSledright, B. and C. Kelly. 1998. Reading American history: The influence of multiple sources on six fifth graders. *The Elementary School Journal* 98 (3): 239–265.

von Heyking, A.J. 2011. Historical thinking in elementary education: A review of research. In *New possibilities for the past: Shaping history education in Canada*, ed. P. Clark, 175–194. Vancouver: University of British Columbia Press.

SUPPLEMENTARY READING

Ashby, R. and P. Lee. 1987. Children's concepts of empathy and understanding in history. In *The history curriculum for teachers*, ed. C. Portal, 62–88. London: Falmer.

Barca, I. 2005. "Till new facts are discovered": Students' ideas about objectivity in history. In *International review of history education.* Vol. 4. *Understanding history: Recent research in history education*, ed. R. Ashby, P. Gordon, and P. Lee, 68–82. New York: Routledge Falmer.

Barton, K. 2001a. Primary children's understanding of the role of historical evidence: Comparisons between the United States and Northern Ireland. *International Journal of Historical Learning, Teaching, and Research* 1 (2): 21–30.

———. 2001b. A sociocultural perspective on children's understanding of historical change: Comparative findings from Northern Ireland and the United States. *American Educational Research Journal* 38 (4): 881–913.

Barton, K. and L. Levstik. 1998. "It wasn't a good part of history": National identity and students' explanations of historical significance. *Teachers College Record* 99 (3): 478–513.

Barton, K. and A. McCully. 2005. History, identity, and the school curriculum in Northern Ireland: An empirical study of secondary students' ideas and perspectives. *Journal of Curriculum Studies* 37 (1): 85–116.

Boix-Mansilla, V. 2000. Historical understanding: beyond the past and into the present. In *Knowing, teaching, and learning history: National and international perspectives*, ed. P. Stearns, P. Seixas, and S. Wineburg, 390–418. New York: New York University Press.

Boix-Mansilla, V. 2005. Between reproducing and organizing the past: students' beliefs about the standards and acceptability of historical knowledge. In *International review of history education.* Vol. 4. *Understanding history: Recent research in history education*, ed. R. Ashby, P. Gordon, and P. Lee, 98–115. New York: Routledge Falmer.

Booth, M. 1983. Skills, concepts, and attitudes: the development of adolescent children's historical thinking. *History and Theory* 22 (4): 101–17.

Foster, S. and E. Yeager. 1998. The role of empathy in the development of historical understanding. *International Journal of Social Education* 13 (1): 1–7.

Hunt, M. 2000. Teaching historical significance. In *Issues in history teaching*, ed. J. Arthur and R. Phillips, 39–53. London: Routledge.

Lee, P. 2004a. Understanding history. In *Theorizing historical consciousness*, ed. P. Seixas, 129–164. Toronto: University of Toronto Press.

———. 2004b. "Walking backwards into tomorrow": Historical consciousness and understanding history. *International Journal of Historical Learning, Teaching, and Research* 4 (1). Accessed at www.centres.exeter.ac.uk/historyresource/journalstart.htm.

Lee, P. and R. Ashby. 2000. Progression in historical understanding among students ages 7–14. In *Knowing, teaching, and learning history: National and international perspectives*, ed. P. Stearns, P. Seixas, and S. Wineburg, 199–222. New York: New York University Press.

Peck, C. and P. Seixas. 2008. Benchmarks of historical thinking: First steps. *Canadian Journal of Education* 31 (4): 1015–1038.

Phillips, R. 2002. Historical significance—the forgotten "key element"? *Teaching History* 106: 14–19.

Portal, C. 1987. Empathy as an objective for history teaching. In *The history curriculum for teachers*, ed. C. Portal, 89–99. London: The Falmer Press.

Seixas, P. 1994. Students' understanding of historical significance. *Theory and Research in Social Education* 22 (3): 281–304.

———. 1997. Mapping the terrain of historical significance. *Social Education* 61 (1): 22–77.

———. 2006. What is historical consciousness? In *To the past: History education, public memory, and citizenship in Canada*, ed. R. Sandwell, 11–22. Toronto: University of Toronto Press.

VanSledright, B. 2004. What does it mean to think historically . . . and how do you teach it? *Social Education* 68 (3): 230–233.

Yeager, E.A., S.J. Foster, S.D. Maley, T. Anderson, and J.W. Morris III. 1998. Why people in the past acted as they did: An exploratory study in historical empathy. *International Journal of Social Education* 13 (1): 8–24.

5 Teaching Elementary Students to Think Geographically

Andrew Young

This past year my daughter Zoë "graduated" from elementary school. Aside from a class trip, there was no school celebration to commemorate this significant milestone in her young life. To show Zoë how proud of her we were and to honour an important transition in her life, my wife and I decided that I would take her to a sunny location at the end of the summer just before she started high school. This would allow Zoë and me time together to reflect on her elementary school experiences and talk about her goals and dreams while enjoying luxurious sunshine on a sandy beach.

After much anticipation and patiently counting down the days until our departure, my daughter and I finally found our way to a small slice of paradise. Seen through the eyes of a biased father, I can state with some certainty that Zoë is an adventurous thirteen-year-old girl with a keen interest in understanding both people and culture. Every night after dinner we walked on the beach talking about the people we saw, the food we ate, the music we listened to, and the place we were immersed in. One night, a few days into our adventure, we made it our goal to talk with other people who were staying at the same hotel as we were so that we could learn a little bit more about the world. Yes, even on vacation a teacher never stops teaching.

Sitting at the swimming pool, we struck up conversations with the people around us. Being from a different country holds a certain cachet for travellers, and I was fascinated to watch my daughter absorb the information about people's lives and their homes. Soon Zoë sought out the companionship of people closer to her own age. I looked over to the hot tub and saw my daughter surrounded by a group of young girls all chatting away. Not long after, Zoë made her way back over to me with a slightly bewildered look on her face, shaking her head, mumbling, "Oh my goodness."

Not wanting to pry but nonetheless curious to know what had caused this reaction, I simply asked, "How did that go?" Her reply went something like this: "First they asked me where I was from, not what my name is. So I told them that I was from Canada and they were all interested and stuff." She sat there with a bemused look about her, so I prodded a bit, "Well isn't it nice that they are interested in where you're from? So what happened?" Soon enough she explained the source of her frustration:

They finally asked me what my name was and when I told them they said you mean like zee-oh-ee-why? And I said no, there's no "y" at the end, it's spelled zed-oh-ee. Then they were like what's zed? And I said it's the last letter in the alphabet. Then they said cool, you have an extra letter in your alphabet? I said no, it's the last letter. And they said you mean after zee, right? I didn't even tell them about the dots [the umlaut] because that would've just confused them more.

Remember how I said earlier that a teacher never stops teaching, even on vacation? There are some moments that come along in life that appear to be so perfect to serve as lessons that they somehow look manufactured or scripted. This was one of those moments, and the geography teacher in me couldn't resist. I said, "You know, Zoë, that's a really good example of geography in action." Her eyes rolled back into her head and she groaned loudly, followed quickly by "Dad, that's not geography." After a prolonged comedic tit-for-tat of "is not"/"is too," I stopped laughing and said, "Seriously, Zoë, the miscommunication you girls just had is a perfect example of cultural geography, where you speak the same language but culturally there's a huge difference." What came out of my daughter's mouth next would send any geography teacher into fits of apoplexy, "Dad, I know you teach geography, but to me geography is just colouring and drawing maps." And there it was, the culmination of seven years of elementary geography . . . colouring maps.

Geography Is More Than Just Maps

Now don't get me wrong, I love maps. When I was a kid my family would take road trips and I would plop myself down in the back seat contented to look at the world whizzing by through the window and follow along with the map on my lap. Perhaps in this lay the kernels for my passion for geography. Even though maps are crucial to the understanding of geography, they are part of the subject, not the subject itself. In his book, *Why Geography Matters*, Michigan State University geography professor Harm de Blij states:

> It is often said that a picture is worth a thousand words. If that is true then a map is worth a million, and maybe even more. Even at just a glance, a map can reveal what no amount of description can. Maps are the language of geography, often the most direct and effective way to convey grand ideas or complex theories. (2005, 23)

I like the metaphor of map as language; there is so much information encoded in maps and the information contained within them is universally accessible. Maps do speak; they tell the stories of the land and provide the reader spatial information that allows us to make sense of what we see. In this metaphor, then, a map can be seen as a tool of the geographer, a way to convey complex spatial information in a graphic format. However, it is important to note while maps are synonymous with geography, the study of geography is more than just maps.

So what is geography? Natoli and Gritzner (1988) define it as the study of the spaces where events occur.

De Blij (2005) explains that historians look at the world temporally while geographers look at the world spatially. So the concept of space is crucial to understanding what geography is all about. If I were to present this idea to my daughter, her initial reaction would probably be to say that geography and astronomy sound like they are the same. By space, then, I mean the physical distribution of objects in the Earth system.

I like to think of geography as a frame of mind or a way to look at information. Peter Jackson (2006, 199) argues that geography is not just factual but is also conceptual in nature; it is a subject that "enables a unique way of seeing the world, of understanding complex problems and thinking about inter-connections at a variety of scales." Thinking like a geographer, then, is thinking spatially in a systems manner. This involves looking for patterns, relationships, and connections in order to comprehend large, complex, self-regulating systems. Since this is the case, geography is inherently cross-curricular. Biology, chemistry, physics, Earth science, English, music, history, languages, food studies, economics, civics, and leadership are all subjects in geography. What distinguishes geography from these subjects? Daniel Edelson argues that geography:

> focuses not just on specific systems, but also on the interactions among systems. Where disciplines like biology, Earth science, and political science each focus on physical, biological, and social systems respectively, geography has always looked at interactions among them across space. (2008, 2)

Seen in this light, geography is an overarching holistic subject that provides a skill set that is fundamentally important for our students. We should, therefore, establish how to use it effectively in our schools so that it is more than what my daughter experienced, "just drawing and colouring maps."

What is important to note is that teaching geography beyond mere subject matter includes the skills and processes associated with geographic thinking, along with making sense of how you can use these skills in the social studies classroom for content organization, acquisition, and reinforcement. Consider the following:

> Geography as a perspective is clearly within the reflective inquiry tradition of the social studies. Although the questions that ask who, what, where, why, and so what provide general guidelines for developing a geographic perspective,

each person's perspective will be slightly different from every other's. As a result, teaching geography as a perspective links closely with developing the questioning abilities of students and makes use of such teaching techniques as inquiry teaching, values clarification, and individual assignments and reports that require the student to analyze, verify, and evaluate information . . . Although a teacher can compartmentalize the teaching of geography as topic or as a social science in a unit and feel confident that the students accomplished some worthwhile short-term learning objectives, this is not the case with teaching geography as perspective. Working on developing a perspective is a long-term repetitive task. Essentially learning to look at the world like a geographer involves solving problems, receiving feedback, improving the solution, and working on more problems. (Libbee and Stoltman 1988, 39)

Therefore, you could say that geography is a frame or a lens through which you can organize and teach social studies content. This way of approaching the subject provides a useful framework to help students make sense of the world.

Teaching Social Studies with a Geographic Lens

One of the most promising ways to view geography not as content *within social studies* but as an organizer for social studies, is the five theme approach.[1] In 1984, the National Council for Geographic Education and the Association of American Geographers introduced the five themes of geography in *Guidelines for geographic education: Elementary and secondary schools*. The five themes have been widely adopted in provincial curricula across Canada and are a simple way to introduce geographic skills and content throughout all grade levels. The five themes of geography are a framework to help geographers understand the complex interrelationships that exist amongst all spaces and all places. No one theme can be understood without the others; they are connected to each other, as are all the components of our world. Using the five themes of geography as an organizational tool for social studies curricula allows students to interpret discrete data and make connections among the data in order to comprehend complex information through the lens of geography.

THE FIVE THEMES

Location helps to describe the positions and distribution of people and places on the earth's surface. A location can be *Absolute* (the exact location of something in grid coordinates, latitude and longitude, or street addresses) or it can be *Relative* (where something can be found in relation to something or somewhere else, usually expressed in time, direction, and/or distance). This is the most common entry point to geography in most social studies classes, where we ask students, "Where are things located?"

Place addresses the question "What is it like to be there?" This theme considers the characteristics that make one place different from all other places on earth. The characteristics are *Physical* (the makeup of the natural environment—geological, hydrological, atmospheric, and biological processes) or *Human* (constructs and ideas of human beings—land use, language, religion, architecture, and political systems).

It is important to note that the themes of Location and Place, taken together, provide a basis for observation and interpretation in geography. They help to answer the questions "Where is it?" and "What is it like to be there?" They also help to answer the question "Why is it there?" Consider this example: Why is the city of Vancouver located where it is? Think about its location and place. It can be found at the mouth of the Fraser River. Now consider where the mouth of the Fraser River is in the context of southwestern British Columbia, and what physical and human features are present. This allows you to start to paint a picture about why Vancouver is located where it is.

Human–Environment Interaction looks at how the physical and human characteristics of a place are related. The relationships between humans and their environment can be looked at in three ways:

1. Humans depend on the environment.
2. Humans modify the environment.
3. Humans adapt to the environment.

We meet our basic needs from the environment and in doing so we modify it (we build dams for electricity, which gives us heat and light; we cultivate and irrigate land to produce food). We change our lifestyle in order to live in particular climates (consider living in Nunavut) that affect how we live, which, in turn, affects our culture.

Movement helps a geographer understand how and why places are connected with one another. Consider the following scenario: You can sit at home watching a Vancouver-based television station broadcasting a sitcom made in Los Angeles that has actors from New Delhi, London, and Nashville. You can drive a Japanese-made car, listening to songs that you purchased online through a music site for a band in New Zealand on an MP3 player made in China that is transmitted through a German-made stereo system. Then you can go to the grocery store to purchase bananas produced in Ecuador by a company based in Spain. All of these scenarios are practical everyday examples of movement.

Relationships between people in different places are shaped by the constant movement of materials and physical systems (such as wind and ocean currents). Obvious evidence of global interactions are transportation and communication links. These include roads, railways, shipping routes, air routes, telephone lines, satellite communications, and the internet. Not-so-obvious examples of global interactions include weather systems, wind, erosion, urbanization, fashion, and changing attitudes. In essence, movement can also be seen as change; our world is constantly moving and changing and we, as geographers, need to understand those changes and why they happen.

Region is defined as an area that has unifying characteristics, which make it either distinct or similar to other areas. Regions can be:

1. Political (country, province, state, county, city).
2. Socio-economic (North American Free Trade Zone, European Common Market, Association of Southeast Asian Nations).
3. Physical (Western Cordillera, Prairies, Canadian Shield).
4. Climatic (Maritime, Continental).
5. Linguistic (Francophone, Anglophone, Inuktitut).

Joel Garreau (1981) used the concept of a region in order to reconceptualize North America in his book *The nine nations of North America*. The underlying premise of the book is that the conventional borders of North America are artificial constructs. Garreau argues that the modern political borders of Canada and the United States should be replaced with cultural and economic regions such as the Pacific Northwest coast of Ecotopia (southwest Alaska, along with coastal British Columbia, Washington, Oregon, and northern California) or the Central Plain States and Prairie Provinces of the Bread

Basket. Garreau's book provides a sophisticated example of how geographers use region to make sense of a complex world.

Although the five themes of geography were introduced in 1984, they still provide an excellent means to introduce complex contemporary material in a structured approach that supports students in thinking in a geographic manner.

EXAMPLE: TEACHING ABOUT FOOD USING THE FIVE THEMES

One of the things my daughter liked on our trip last summer was the food we ate. For the first time in her life she tried funnel cakes and voraciously finished a plate of cake and ice cream. We talked at length about the food we were eating and made every effort to try something new and different each day. Ordering *machaca con huevos* became an opportunity to talk about the climate of northern Mexico and the need to dry meat. Eating grilled fish tacos on the beach allowed Zoë to listen to surfers talk and observe their intimate knowledge of local ocean conditions. Remember how I said earlier that a teacher never stops teaching, even on vacation? Food became a point of discovery and a way for Zoë and me to talk about the different ways that people live.

Food as a subject of study can be embedded within almost any topic in social studies. Food is a basic need for humans (we make and eat food on a daily basis), and often a source of conflict. Food connects humans to each other and to the environment where it is grown. In many ways, food defines culture and establishes a way of life that connects individuals to each other and to societies. It is important to note that there are many other components of culture that make it complex; therefore, a simplistic correlation between food and culture misses out on the intricate and nuanced elements that make culture. However, since food is part of the consciousness of society and is relevant in the social studies curriculum, why not make a study of this topic meaningful and relevant to young social studies students? This can be done using the five themes of geography.

One way to introduce a unit on food is to invite students to examine the contents of their kitchen cupboard at home (Pike and Selby 1988). Ask students to identify the origins of ten food items in their home pantry, cupboard, refrigerator, or deep freeze. Using their lists, direct students to create an individual or collective "Where in the world is my food from" map. This map addresses the first theme of geography: location. On the map direct students to draw pictures of the foods they identified on the countries that they came from and show transportation routes or connections between the country of origin and country of consumption. This portion of the activity covers the geographic theme of movement. Encourage students to research the origins of any processed food on their map and to identify where the components of the food originated. Alternatively, ask students to research why one or more of their food items grows where it was exported from and not where they live. This portion of the activity involves students in looking at the geographic themes of place and region. The human-environment interaction theme is addressed by researching how a food item is grown and why it is an important nutritional or economic source for the people that grow it. After this, you could ask the students what their favourite food on their lists or map is, and have them develop a critical inquiry into their food focussed on the question "What makes food popular?" Depending on the age of the group you are working with, you could have them try to identify the forces that determine what people eat or don't eat and what makes food popular or not. You could then have the students predict what the favourite food is for the entire class. Here the students can use the background knowledge they've already acquired, determine the validity of their information, form a judgement, test their theory, and then evaluate their thinking.

Taking your class on a field study to a local grocery store provides further opportunities for integrating the five themes of geography. The National Geographic Society has a series of lessons on their education website, one of which, called Geographic Groceries, involves an exploration of a grocery store (education.nationalgeographic.com/education/activity/geographic-groceries). In this lesson, students examine the regions (or sections) of a grocery store in order to make sense of how food is arranged using geographic organizational and analytical skills. Students create a floor plan of the grocery store and map out the food items that they observe as they walk through the aisles. Students are encouraged to identify patterns and ask questions about why food is located in the manner that the store has chosen. All five themes of geography can be seen in this activity: identifying location of food items; explaining what each section contains and describing its physical attributes (refrigerators, freezers, heat lamps, boxes, or carts); classifying food product sections; examining how food sections are related, where food is from, and how food is organized to move people throughout a store; and evaluating how people live based on what food they consume and how they obtain it.

This field trip can be extended by asking students to compare and contrast various grocery stores, especially if local and national grocery stores operate within the community. Choosing a national grocery chain for a visit is valuable because it is ubiquitous in North American society and is reflective of the cultural values of the broader Western world. A regional grocery store may reflect a different set of values towards food and a local supermarket or grocery store may say even more about a difference between cultural worldviews. Taking the students to a farmers' market or to a farm or fish dock may allow students to meet local producers and see the process of food production from its origin to table. These options allow students to extend their study of food and begin to look at the world like a geographer. These lessons move geography away from understanding discrete content and shift it towards a perspective on the world. Through this approach you are helping students think geographically and moving the subject away from what my daughter so succinctly described as "just colouring and drawing maps."

SAMPLE RESOURCES ON FOOD AND THE FIVE THEMES

A simple online search for lessons on food and the five themes of geography will produce reams of pages. One of the best sources of resources and ideas are the educational arms of geographical associations. For example:

The Canadian Council for Geographic Education has many online lessons in a searchable database, including lessons on food: www.ccge.org/resources/learning_centre/lesson_plans.asp. The Canadian Atlas Online also has many online lessons in a searchable database, including lessons on food: www.canadiangeographic.ca/atlas/learningtools.aspx.

The Geographical Association in the United Kingdom has a wonderful online course series on the geography of food: www.geography.org.uk/cpdevents/onlinecpd/geographyoffood.

National Geographic in the United States has archived the educational "Xpeditions" website, which includes many food activities in the "Lesson Plans" section, such as:

- Addressing world hunger: education.national geographic.com/archive/xpeditions/lessons/18/g68/tghunger.html;
- Spice geography: education.nationalgeographic.com/archive/xpeditions/lessons/16/g68/ingredient.html;

- Sushi bar: You, me, sushi: education.national geographic.com/archive/xpeditions/lessons/16/g68/sushi.html;
- Spices in your favorite foods: education.national geographic.com/archive/xpeditions/lessons/16/g35/favfoods.html

Concluding Thoughts

What concerned me most about my daughter's summation of geography was not that it came from her, but that it was a theme that I have heard repeated many times. Clearly there are dynamic classrooms where geography is more than just colouring maps, yet over and over I have seen this engaging and important subject relegated to a small portion of the social studies curriculum. A report from the National Geographic Society (2005) suggests one source of the problem may be the lack of geographic background of most social studies teachers. For teachers who are unsure of what to do in geography beyond asking students to fill in maps and learn place names, utilizing the five themes of geography provides an accessible alternative.

The five themes of geography are easy to understand and can be adapted to any social studies unit. Imagine you have a grade 4 unit on aboriginal cultures of Canada and the impact of first contact with European explorers and settlers. Describing and comparing the characteristics of two or more pre-contact aboriginal cultures can lead the students to an understanding of how a location can impact the ways in which people live. This provides students with an opportunity to examine culture through a geographic lens. Examining where societies existed and developed looks at the theme of location. Identifying the physical characteristics of where cultures developed looks at the theme of place. Investigating how cultures relied upon and were affected by their environment looks at the theme of human-environment interactions. Analyzing the impact of one culture on another and then evaluating the transfer in technology between them looks at the theme of movement. Identifying similarities between cultures examines the theme of regions.

Using the five themes you can have the students examine the economic and trade structure of different civilizations and assess the impact of their interactions. The five themes of geography are a tool to:

- identify and clarify a problem, an issue, or an inquiry;
- gather and organize a body of information from primary and secondary print and non-print sources, including electronic sources;
- interpret and evaluate a variety of primary and secondary sources; and
- assess a variety of positions on controversial issues.

These are the "bread and butter" of social studies skills, and using these five themes is a great way to engage students with geography.

ENDNOTE

1   Another way to position geography as an organizer for social studies is a critical inquiry approach. Bahbahani and Huynh (2008) identify six portals to geographic thinking: geographical importance; evidence and interpretation; patterns and trends; interactions and associations; sense of place; and geographical value judgements. Using these portals as a form of inquiry, teachers can provide "a means for turning the factual content of geography into the subject of analysis for students" (7). These portals provide an excellent opportunity to examine social studies content through the lens of geography where students can begin to think like a geographer. There is much to like about the portals, and although focussed towards a middle and senior school audience, these portals could be carefully adapted to meet the needs of an elementary classroom.

REFERENCES

Bahbahani, K. and N.T. Huynh. 2008. *Teaching about geographical thinking*, ed. R. Case and B. Sharpe. Vancouver: The Critical Thinking Consortium.

Blij, H.J. de. 2005. *Why geography matters: Three challenges facing America*. New York: Oxford University Press.

Canadian Council for Geographic Education. 2001. *Canadian national standards for geography: A standards-based guide to K–12 geography*. Ottawa: Royal Canadian Geographical Society.

Edelson, D.C. 2008. *Repositioning geography education: From neglect to necessity*. Washington, D.C.: National Geographic Society.

Garreau, J. 1981. *The nine nations of North America*. Boston: Houghton Mifflin.

Jackson, P. 2006. Thinking geographically. *Geography* 91 (3): 199–204.

Libbee, M. and S. Stoltman. 1988. Geography within the social studies curriculum. In *Strengthening geography in the social studies*, ed. S.J. Natoli, 22–41. Washington D.C.: National Council for the Social Studies.

National Council for Geographic Education and Association of American Geographers. 1984. *Guidelines for geographic education: Elementary and secondary schools.* Washington, D.C.: Author.

National Geographic Society. 2005. *Marketing solutions that drive results.* Washington, D.C.: Author.

Natoli, S.J. and C.F. Gritzner. 1988. Modern geography. In *Strengthening geography in the social studies*, ed. S.J. Natoli, 1–9. Washington D.C.: National Council for the Social Studies.

Pike, G. and D. Selby. 1988. *Global teacher, global learner.* Toronto: Hodder and Stoughton.

6

Teaching Elementary Students the Tools to Think Critically

Roland Case and LeRoi Daniels

Neither the hand nor the mind alone would amount
to much without aids and tools to perfect them.
—Francis Bacon, *Novum Organum* (1620)

The idea of critical thinking is not new. For decades—no, for centuries—it has been recognized as an important goal in education. Curriculum documents and learning resources in all subjects and at every level recommend that students be taught to think critically. Despite this expectation, the extent of critical thinking and the way it is taught are disheartening. Many studies document how little class time is devoted to thinking but instead focusses on the transmission of information and the rote application of "skills."

It is a depressing irony that critical thinking is so valued but so inadequately taught. Or, as Walter Parker (1991, 234) puts it, teaching thinking remains "more wish than practice."[1] There are numerous reasons for this. One enduring dilemma is to get students to think for themselves while simultaneously teaching them subject matter. This tension is captured in the so-called division between the teaching of "content" and the teaching of "process." Confusion about how to integrate these goals has led to opposing camps, with some theorists urging a focus on content, and others emphasizing skills. This division is educationally bankrupt. It is based on a false dichotomy: thinking without content is vacuous, and content acquired without thought is inert.

The problem of students learning information through transmission without thinking about it is that they frequently adopt ideas without understanding them. For example, a large proportion of university students who have passed examinations in physics are unable to provide credible explanations for simple real-world problems. In one study (Mackenzie 1988), undergraduates studying physics could not predict which of two balls, one heavier than the other, would hit the floor first. In explaining this anomaly of knowing facts without understanding, teacher-author Richard Feynman concludes: "After a lot of investigation, I finally figured out that the students had memorized everything, but that they didn't know what anything meant" (cited in Mackenzie 1988, 61).

Even educators who try to engage their students in thinking critically about content are often hampered by vagueness about what that means. Without a clear understanding of critical thinking, teachers are likely to adopt a superficial approach, have significant gaps in treatment, or proceed ineffectually, if not counterproductively.

Take a moment to think of someone you know who is an excellent critical thinker. List several qualities that make this person such a good thinker.

Profile of Exemplary Critical Thinkers

A useful strategy to unpack confusing notions of any sort is to consider examples of what it looks like when it is present and what it looks like when it is absent.

TABLE 6.1 ATTRIBUTES OF EXEMPLARY CRITICAL THINKERS

 HABITS OF MIND	 THINKING STRATEGIES	 BACKGROUND KNOWLEDGE	 CRITICAL THINKING VOCABULARY	 CRITERIA FOR JUDGMENT
• open to new ideas • persist when thinking through a problem • empathetic; appreciate other points of view • courageous in their convictions; not afraid to take a stand • question ideas; do not accept everything at face value • do not jump to conclusions • flexible and willing to change tactics • do not take themselves too seriously • can live with ambiguity; do not require black-or-white answers • welcome challenges	• restate a problem in clear language or graphics • restate in their own words to confirm understanding • ask questions to probe for more information • examine issues from different perspectives • look for connections between what is already known and what is new • test ideas using a "reality check" • focus on one thing at a time; break complex challenges into manageable bits • consider the assumptions behind a position • look for possible counter-arguments or negative consequences	• have extensive general knowledge and/or experience • are well read • are knowledgeable about the topic	• recognize common informal fallacies (for example, "straw person," "slippery slope," overgeneralizing)	• recognize arguments that are well supported • value clarity and specificity

Table 6.1 represents what critical thinking looks like when it is present. The list of traits typically exhibited by exemplary critical thinkers has been compiled from the responses of workshop participants over time. The list has been divided into five columns to reveal the nature of the attributes of a good critical thinker.

HABITS OF MIND

Column 1 in Table 6.1 contains more attributes than any other. What is the common feature of this set of qualities? They are attitudes. This suggests, perhaps surprisingly, that an individual's attitudes—or, to use the term that we prefer, habits of mind—are key to good critical thinking. For example, people who are closed to new ideas are seriously impaired in their ability to arrive at fair solutions to issues.

Recognizing the role of attitudes in critical thinking challenges the perception that critical thinking is a skill or set of skills. This perception is unfortunate because no amount of "skill" will ever overcome the limitations of closed-minded thinking or prejudice. People who deny the Holocaust are a case in point. Such individuals may be clever, have extensive knowledge of the events, and be able to marshal persuasive arguments. They may possess many other qualities on our list of attributes. However, these individuals are fundamentally mistaken in their belief that the Holocaust did not happen because their prejudices prevent them from impartially considering the evidence.

Open-mindedness is only one habit of mind possessed by critical thinkers. Another crucial habit of mind is an inclination to deliberate—to think before leaping to conclusions or acting on those conclusions.

Successful critical thinking is significantly (but not exclusively) a matter of attitude.

THINKING STRATEGIES

The qualities listed in column 2 of Table 6.1 most closely match what are often called "skills," which we call thinking strategies. Good critical thinkers use a variety of strategies to work their way through challenges. These strategies may be elaborate, such as a decision-making model that begins with identifying the issue, then considering the consequences, researching each option, and so on. Simpler strategies for specific tasks might involve restating a problem in our own words to better understand it, asking others to help clarify it, or representing the problem graphically. There are literally thousands of thinking strategies: procedures, models, graphic organizers, helpful hints, and so on.

Because critical thinking typically has been labelled a skill, such attributes have received considerable attention by teachers. This strong association of critical thinking with skills has often meant that the other attributes of good thinking have been overlooked.

BACKGROUND KNOWLEDGE

Column 3 of Table 6.1 reveals that critical thinking requires background knowledge as well as strategies and habits of mind. Many of us are incapable of thinking very critically about certain difficult topics, for example, nuclear physics or baroque art—not because we lack appropriate habits of mind or thinking strategies, but because we are not knowledgeable about these subjects. Likewise, students cannot think critically about a topic they know little about. If we treat critical thinking as a set of general skills that can be applied independently of subject matter, the importance of background knowledge to good critical thinking is overlooked.

Consider attempting to teach students how to analyze. If analysis is considered a general skill, then students should learn to analyze any object or event, without reference to knowledge of the topic. However, without adequate background knowledge, students must guess or speculate blindly. If they are guessing wildly, they are not thinking critically and we are teaching them to do the very opposite of what we intended. We cannot effectively teach students to analyze a poem for its metre, rhyme, and symbolism in the same way as they would analyze a historical document for its authenticity. Although both forms of analysis may share a few strategies (such as isolating each discrete part and reading between the lines), successful completion of the task is largely determined by having relevant background knowledge. Students won't be able to analyze a historical document for authenticity if they know little of the events and period described in the document.

The "generic skills" approach to teaching critical thinking is not only ineffective but potentially counterproductive; it may encourage or reinforce student habits in making hasty or uninformed judgments. Our list of attributes of good critical thinkers suggests that analysis requires suitable habits of mind, such as an inclination to attend to detail and refraining from jumping to a conclusion; appropriate thinking strategies, such as isolating each discrete part and listing the features of each; and relevant background knowledge.

ANOTHER KIND OF BACKGROUND KNOWLEDGE: CONCEPTS

Good critical thinkers not only require knowledge about the field of investigation but also knowledge about the concept of investigation itself. Although knowledge of concepts or vocabulary related to critical thinking is not usually considered a key attribute of critical thinkers, it is reflected in column 4 of Table 6.1, "avoidance of fallacies."

Teachers of young students or students who are non-native speakers have long recognized the importance of understanding concepts. For example, students cannot understand a passage in a story without understanding the meanings of key vocabulary. Similarly, they cannot understand a science or social studies concept if they do not understand the meanings of the words being used to describe it. What has not been so widely appreciated is the need to teach the vocabulary of thinking. Students cannot analyze a poem if they do not understand the concept "analyze," nor can they make a "judgment" without understanding what a judgment is. Similarly, students cannot converse deeply about their thinking if they do not have the words to identify or recognize key concepts. Students cannot provide sound justifications for their opinions if they cannot distinguish the concept of evidence from conclusion.

The distinction between the related concepts "what I like" versus "what is worthwhile" is key to students' ability to think critically. For example, if asked to determine whether a hamburger or salad is the better dietary choice, many students, especially younger ones, will select the option they like to eat best. They merely report their preference without thinking about the relative merits of each. Critical reflection can only occur if students can distinguish between considering what is worthwhile, such as what would be a good dietary choice (nutritious, environmentally sound, easy to prepare, tasty, widely available, inexpensive)—and what is merely liked. Without a sound knowledge of critical thinking vocabulary, we are left in a conceptual haze.

The final attribute of exemplary critical thinkers is shown in column 5 of Table 6.1 "recognize arguments that are well supported and value clarity and specificity." Criteria are the basis by which critical thinkers make a judgment. While a poor critical thinker may rush to conclusions, a critical thinker looks for well-supported arguments. Thinking critically requires assessment of the reasonableness of the alternatives. And assessments inevitably are done on the basis of criteria. For example, in judging whether or not a movie is good, we typically have reasons. The movie may have made us laugh—in which case, a criterion for a good movie is humour. But we may have more elaborate criteria: a poignant message, breathtaking visual effects, and/or engaging actors. Additional criteria for our assessment are implicit in these reasons, such as the relevance of the message to our own lives, the quality of the cinematography and the editing, and believability of the acting. Not only are criteria an important aspect of critical thinking, but they define critical thinking. To think critically is essentially to make a judgment based on appropriate criteria.

Notice that students may judge movies on quite narrow and inappropriate criteria, such as the amount of adventure and violence. Our job in helping students think more critically about movies includes encouraging them to use a wider, more adequate set of criteria. Paying attention to relevant "criteria for judgment" is an important and often overlooked aspect of teaching critical thinking.

The close relationship between the term "critical" thinking and "criteria" is worth noting. Matthew Lipman (1988) suggests that the word "critical" should be seen as a synonym for "criterial"—to think critically is to think using criteria. To put it another way, criteria are what give judgments rigour. When thinking critically about a movie, we are not asserting a personal preference ("it's good because I like it") or reaching a conclusion based on dubious considerations ("it's good because it contains lots of bloodshed"). Rather, we are offering a reasoned assessment of the merits of the movie, a judgment based on an ample set of relevant criteria. An important objective in teaching critical thinking is to help students identify and appreciate relevant criteria for making diverse judgments across the curriculum.

The "Tools" in a Nutshell

To summarize, we believe the basic building blocks of critical thinking are not generic skills or mental operations. We do not learn to analyze, interpret, predict, and so on and then simply apply these "processes" to any given situation. Exemplary critical thinkers have five types of attributes that are all important for thinking critically: habits of mind, thinking strategies, critical thinking vocabulary, background knowledge, and criteria for judgment. We suggest that promoting critical thinking among students is largely a matter of helping them to increase their mastery of these intellectual tools. The ability to think critically develops over time as individuals acquire more of the tools of good thinking.

The metaphor of intellectual tools is preferable to the notion of mental operations because students can only learn to analyze or predict in specific contexts. Just as a geologist might use a hammer differently than a carpenter, mastery of the tool in one field does not transfer to mastery of the tool in another. Students will only become better at predicting weather, earthquakes or story endings if they acquire the relevant background information; understand the concept of prediction; develop thinking strategies to extrapolate information; and develop the habit of mind of being attentive to detail. Notice that there is no "process" of predicting that is discrete from "content": we cannot predict weather thoughtfully without knowledge of meteorology, and predicting weather thoughtfully does not mean we can automatically predict the stock market.

Our categories of attributes of a good critical thinker are supported by the diverse literature on thinking. There are schools of thought regarding critical thinking that focus separately on each of the five categories we identify. In the critical thinking as background knowledge school of thought, we find advocates such as John McPeck (1981), E.D. Hirsch (1988), and Daniel Willingham (2007) arguing that sound thinking is best served by promoting student mastery of subject matter. David Perkins and his associates (1993) believe the central ingredients of good thinking are thinking dispositions—what we call habits of mind. Harvey Siegel (1988) also suggests that these are the most important features of a critical thinker, while Stephen Norris and Robert Ennis (1989) list dispositions as one of two essential ingredients of critical thinking.

Matthew Lipman (1988) and Richard Paul (1988) are among the prominent advocates for the central importance of criteria for judgment (also called intellectual

FIGURE 6.1 PROMOTING CRITICAL THINKING

HABITS OF MIND   THINKING STRATEGIES   BACKGROUND KNOWLEDGE   CRITICAL THINKING VOCABULARY   CRITERIA FOR JUDGMENT

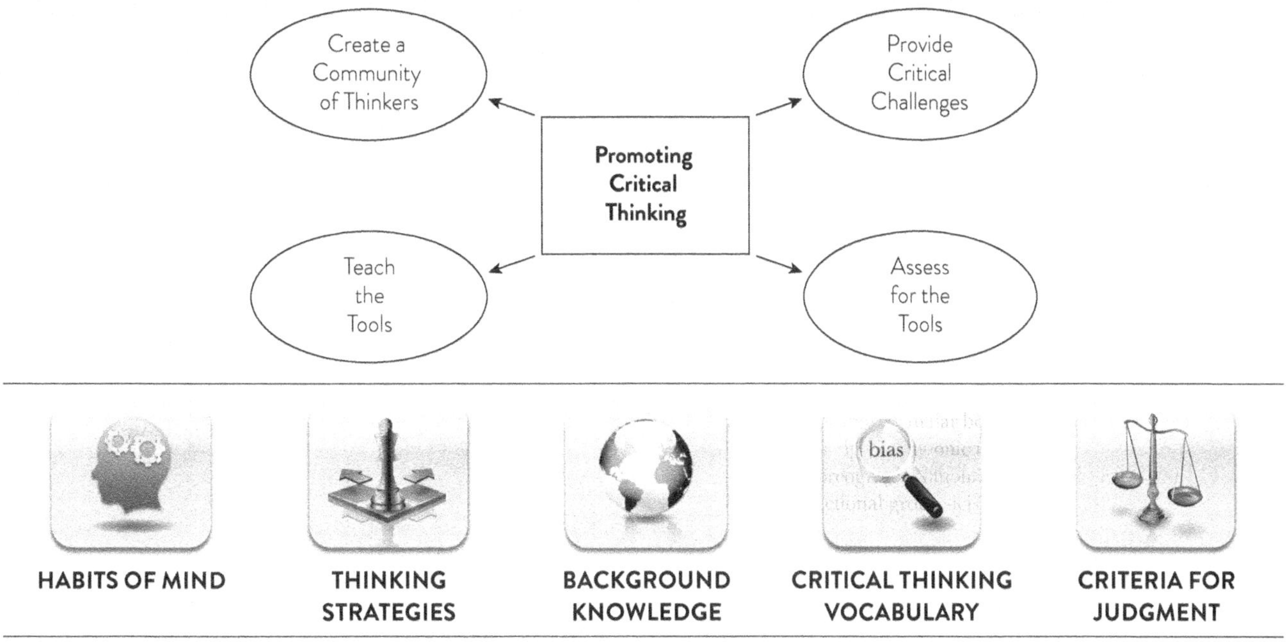

© The Critical Thinking Consortium

standards). The "informal logic" school of thinking stresses two categories from among our tools: those criteria for judgment that are reflected in the formal and informal rules of logic and what we refer to as critical thinking vocabulary—concepts such as argument, validity, credibility, truth, soundness, induction, deduction, and various informal fallacies. Much of the literature on promoting critical thinking skills focusses on teaching strategies for carrying out various operations (e.g., Glaser 1984), which is parallel to our category of intellectual tools or thinking strategies.

Collectively, the different schools of thought on critical thinking theory support all five of our intellectual tool categories. This is grounds for considering our conception to be the most complete synthesis of critical thinking attributes to date.

Applying the Tools

Nurturing critical thinking is a long-term goal. Students develop an ability to think critically gradually as they expand and enrich their intellectual tools. This requires incremental, collective effort; no one teacher can do it quickly or on her own. We must take the long view. The work of promoting critical thinking is a kindergarten to university challenge, but each of us is responsible for doing our part in promoting it.

Note that critical thinking is a matter of degree; an individual's sophistication and ability as a thinker is related to his or her range and mastery of the tools. All of us, including young children, think critically to some extent in some circumstances. All of us possess and use some of the tools for thought. It is equally true that all of us can improve our ability to think critically.

Based on scholarly research and professional work with thousands of teachers, we are convinced that developing the tools for thought requires teacher effort in four areas of practice. These four prongs are represented graphically in Figure 6.1, and explained briefly below.

TEACH THE TOOLS

Students require instruction in how to use the tools to enable them to develop as critical thinkers. Students should be introduced to the range of tools required for the tasks they are asked to do. The ability to think critically develops over a lifetime by acquiring and refining the vast repertoire of intellectual tools that an expert draws on to respond to problems.

Attention should be paid to explicitly teaching all five kinds of tools:

- **Background knowledge:** relevant information about a topic that is required for thoughtful reflection.

- **Criteria for judgment:** the appropriate criteria or grounds for deciding the most sensible or defensible response to a challenge.
- **Critical thinking vocabulary:** the concepts and distinctions that facilitate thinking critically, concepts that are foundational to thinking critically—for example, the difference between conclusion and premise or cause and effect.
- **Thinking strategies:** the repertoire of procedures, heuristics, organizing devices, and models that are useful when thinking through a critical challenge.
- **Habits of mind:** the values and attitudes of a careful and conscientious thinker.

CREATE A CRITICAL COMMUNITY

Critical thinking cannot be learned independently of the broader forces operating within the classroom and the school. Consequently, it is essential to foster communities in our classrooms in which teachers and students interact in mutually supportive ways to nurture critical thinking. The point of a critical community is to create a climate that embodies and reinforces the tools of intellectual thought. This is especially important for acquiring the habits of mind for thinking critically, as these are only likely to develop if they are modelled and continuously supported.

Building a community of thinkers is also important to counter the view of thinking as a solitary enterprise. Although we want students to be independent-minded and to make up their own minds, we should not expect them to do so entirely on their own. There is a key difference between thinking for oneself and thinking by oneself. Good critical thinkers regularly engage in dialogue with others to broaden their knowledge, test their ideas, and understand alternative perspectives. Learning to contribute to and make use of other people's wisdom can only be learned through participation in a community of thinkers. Further discussion of this aspect of teaching critical thinking is found in chapter 10, "Supporting a Community of Critical Inquiry."

PROVIDE CRITICAL CHALLENGES

The intellectual tools are best learned within the context of curriculum-based problems. Students need abundant opportunities to use the tools to work through meaningful challenges. If curriculum content is presented outside the context of a problem, that is, if there is only one plausible option or a correct answer is obvious, then it does not call for critical thinking—it is not a critical challenge. Further discussion of this area of teaching critical thinking is found in chapter 7, "Getting Beyond Inert Facts in Elementary Social Studies."

ASSESS THE TOOLS

It is not sufficient merely to teach the intellectual tools. Because assessment influences what is learned, we must also assess the tools. Teachers signal to students what is and is not important by assigning marks to some assignments and not to others and by "weighting" aspects of assignments with different values. If student mastery of the tools is not assessed, not only are students (and teachers) left in the dark about their growth, but they are implicitly encouraged to believe that critical thinking is unimportant.

THE TOOLS IN ACTION

The value of conceiving critical thinking as the competent use of intellectual tools is best illustrated with examples of them in action. Our first example, Table 6.2, is adapted from work by our colleague Jerrold Coombs. It describes a hypothetical student's deliberations about a proposal to compromise the development and conservation of a mature, old-growth forest. The tools are identified at each step of her deliberations to illustrate how our model reflects the diverse elements of sound thinking.

An important function of the tools approach is to help teachers identify what students need to be taught in order to undertake a given task in a critically thoughtful manner. To illustrate the instructional value of our model, we examine two case studies in which students are taught the tools they need to ask thoughtful questions.

In the case study "Developing Powerful Questions," Tami systematically aids her primary students to construct questions thoughtfully by teaching four tools. Tami does not do the thinking for them; rather, she helps students develop the skills to complete the task thoughtfully for themselves. Not only is students' ability to pose powerful questions enhanced by the teaching of these tools, but so is their understanding of the subject matter—the significance of Remembrance Day.

In a second case study, "Developing Test Questions," Karen, a junior high school teacher, helps students think critically about questions for an end-of-unit test in social studies. The required background knowledge in this scenario is knowledge of the Civil War period in seventeenth-century England. Karen offers a thinking strategy to complement brainstorming to help students generate questions: she suggests that students focus their thinking on the features of good test questions. The criteria she sets is that students ask nontrivial questions. This requires students to think about what is important about the historical period, and what contributed to their understanding of the subject matter. Including student-generated questions on the class test requires students to think deeply about the historical period because these questions cannot be answered by the mere recall of information. Karen insists that she would have been bombarded with complaints if she had put the very questions her students did on an exam: "How do you expect us to know this? You never told us the answers to this!" Instead, students not only took the assignment seriously (in some cases reading the textbook for the first time), but they were more motivated to study for the test because the questions were posed by their peers.

This last point—the motivational value of critical thinking—is important. Although not all students welcome opportunities to think critically, more often than not students prefer to think about matters than to regurgitate facts. This is especially true when the topics students are asked to think about are meaningful.

TABLE 6.2   THINKING CRITICALLY ABOUT LOGGING OLD-GROWTH FORESTS[2]

Outlined in the left-hand column is a hypothetical response by a young woman to the question: Should the government's plan to permit logging in some areas of a forest and designate other areas as a wilderness park be endorsed or rejected? The intellectual tools in her critically thoughtful response are indicated in the right-hand column.

SCENARIO	CRITICAL THINKING TOOL
A young woman reads a number of arguments for and against the government's plan that have appeared in the local newspaper, as follows:	
Anti-development side Environmentalists claim that the government has sold out to the forestry industry and unions. Some claim that we cannot afford to lose any more old-growth forest. They point out that forests are needed to prevent the buildup of carbon dioxide that causes global warming, that the forests are home to many species that are endangered by reductions to their habitat, and that old-growth forests enrich the aesthetic quality of life. Some feel so strongly about the need to preserve old-growth forests that they have publicly announced that they have "spiked" (driven long nails into) many trees in the area and plan to recruit volunteers to spike many more.	**Background knowledge:** knowledge of the arguments made by the proponents of the anti-development side
Pro-development side Supporters of the government plan argue that the forestry industry needs to log at least part of the area and other old-growth forests if it is to continue to provide jobs for people, supply lumber to build houses, and contribute to government revenues. They claim that the land set aside for the park and for limited logging will be more than enough to maintain the aesthetic beauty of the area and to preserve the species that depend on it. They also argue that, since the logged areas will be replanted, there will not, in the long run, be any reduction in forested land.	**Background knowledge:** knowledge of the arguments made by the proponents of the pro-development side
Several of the student's friends have joined demonstrations protesting against the government's decision to permit logging. The student checks her impulse to rush out and join her friends because she wants to be sure that she is doing it for the right reasons, not simply to avoid disappointing her friends.	**Habits of mind:** open-mindedness and independent-mindedness
The student considers the possible consequences of stopping to deliberate the best thing to do rather than making a decision right away. She decides there is sufficient time for more careful deliberation before acting.	**Criteria for judgment:** practicality and desirability of deliberation
She attempts to understand all the reasons for supporting the government's decision and the reasons for protesting and trying to change that decision.	**Criteria for judgment:** adequacy of evidence
She considers whether she should believe the claims of the government, the forestry industry, and environmentalists about the likely consequences of the government's policy.	**Habits of mind:** an inquiring or "critical" attitude

TABLE 6.2 THINKING CRITICALLY ABOUT LOGGING OLD-GROWTH FORESTS[2] (CONT.)

SCENARIO	CRITICAL THINKING TOOL
She considers whether all of these groups have access to experts in economics and ecology, and also if and what they stand to gain by misrepresenting the facts.	**Criteria for judgment:** reliability of authorities
She considers how adequate the newspaper accounts of reasons for and against the government's decision are likely to be.	**Criteria for judgment:** the accuracy and unbiased nature of information sources
She is also aware that the emotionally charged language and other persuasion techniques used in the newspaper reports could influence her to adopt views without good reasons. She makes a point of watching for and dismissing any fallacies.	**Critical thinking vocabulary:** can recognize informal fallacies
She considers whether she has any assumptions or preconceptions that would influence her from making an unbiased assessment of this issue.	**Habits of mind:** fair-mindedness
She decides her attachment to environmentalism and lack of contact with persons whose livelihood depends on logging may lead her to undervalue economic reasons for permitting logging.	**Habits of mind:** open-mindedness
Consequently, she decides to talk to forestry workers to get a more sympathetic understanding of their point of view.	**Criteria for judgment:** broadness of inquiry **Thinking strategy:** seeks counsel from a variety of parties in a dispute
She is aware that there may be other options open to her besides simply accepting the government's decision or joining protest marches. She tries to think of other plausible courses of action that would produce desirable consequences.	**Thinking strategy:** looks for multiple, perhaps novel, options
Because she is aware that others may already have thought of alternative courses of action, she seeks out knowledgeable people to discuss what they think ought to be done and why.	**Thinking strategy:** confers with recognized experts
In the course of the discussions, she asks for clarification of the terms other people use and gives examples of what she means by various terms she uses to make sure she is communicating her thoughts clearly.	**Thinking strategy:** check for clarity and shared meanings of terms by asking for and providing examples
Having identified the likely consequences of each plausible course of action, she considers whether any of the options involves treating others unjustly or otherwise acting immorally.	**Criteria for judgment:** fairness and morality
She decides to rule out the option of joining the tree-spiking expeditions, because she has good reason to believe that this course of action could cause serious injury to persons working in the lumber industry and could subject her to criminal prosecution.	**Criteria for judgment:** acceptability of judgment even if the person were one of those adversely affected by the action
Accordingly she tries to imagine what it would be like to be a lumber mill worker facing the choice of not working or risking serious injury. She decides it would be morally wrong to subject them to such risk if there are other options available for adequately preserving forests.	**Thinking strategy:** test the fairness of moral judgments by sensitively imagining oneself in the situation of others
Having ruled out those options that she has good reason to regard as immoral, she considers which of the remaining courses of action would produce the best consequences overall—which would most fully realize the things she values without producing unacceptable negative consequences.	**Habits of mind:** commitment to decide on rational grounds
Having made a tentative decision about which course of action is best, she decides to discuss it with others (including those who might have reached a different decision), explaining her reasoning and inviting counter-arguments.	**Thinking strategy:** talk through one's thinking on an issue, inviting others to poke holes in the reasoning
She wants to be sure she hasn't overlooked any important considerations or failed to appreciate the significance of any of the likely consequences for other things she values.	**Habits of mind:** intellectual work ethic
Lacking any good reasons for changing her decision, she proceeds to act on it.	**Habits of mind:** commitment to act on the basis of reasoned judgment

DEVELOPING POWERFUL QUESTIONS[3]

Tami McDiarmid's kindergarten to grade 3 class was to learn about the significance of Remembrance Day. Tami invited a guest who was to speak about his World War II experiences, and prior to the event asked her students to think of questions they might ask him. Tami sought to support her students in thinking critically about questions they might ask by focussing their attention on four tools: background knowledge, critical thinking vocabulary, criteria for judgment, and a thinking strategy.

Tami developed relevant background knowledge during the three weeks preceding the guest's visit by reading and discussing various children's stories relating to the war. Without the knowledge acquired from these stories, many students would be incapable of asking a thoughtful question.

A few days prior to the visit, Tami reintroduced key vocabulary to remind her students about two kinds of questions: "weak" questions and "powerful" ones. Armed with this distinction, the class discussed what powerful questions "look like or sound like." To use our terminology, they discussed the criteria for judging whether a question is powerful. Tami recorded on chart paper the following student-generated criteria:

Powerful questions ...

- give you lots of information;
- are specific to the person or situation;
- are open-ended; can't be answered by yes or no;
- may be unexpected; and
- are usually not easy to answer.

Next, Tami made use of a thinking strategy—brainstorming, which her students were already familiar with—and asked them to generate as many ideas of questions for the guest as they could. Brainstorming is a useful strategy to help with the generation of ideas. While brainstorming, individuals are discouraged from making judgments about the proffered ideas; the point is simply to come up with as many ideas as possible. The critical thinking began in earnest when students, working in pairs, began to assess the brainstormed questions using the agreed-upon criteria. Students discussed whether their proposed questions were likely to elicit lots of information, were obvious or predictable, and so on. Some "weak" questions were rejected; others were modified to make them more powerful. Here is a sample of the questions students asked the World War II veteran:

- Where did you live during the war?
- Were there any women in World War II? If so, what were their jobs?
- What started the fighting?
- Why was Canada involved?
- What was your safe place?
- Why did you fight in the war?
- Do you remember some of your friends from the war?
- Which countries did you fight over?

ASSESSING THE TOOLS IN ACTION

The tools approach is also useful because of the parallel between instruction and assessment. Assessment is a major obstacle for many teachers in their efforts to promote critical thinking. If there is no single correct answer to look for in student responses, knowing what to assess is often difficult. As our case studies illustrate, students might pose a multitude of effective questions. Does this mean that virtually any student response is acceptable? If not, on what basis should we assess their responses?

The topic of assessing critical thinking is discussed more extensively in chapter 26, "Embedding Authentic Assessment Practices in Elementary Classrooms," but the use of the tools to assess the case studies is detailed here to help illustrate the benefits of the approach. The key consideration is not whether we agree or disagree with the conclusions students reach but rather to assess the quality of the thinking that supports their answers. In assessing critical thinking, we should look for evidence that students' answers embody the relevant tools competently. An appropriate approach is to assess those tools that students were expressly expected, and taught, to employ in a task. Let's look at how this happens in practice.

ASSESSING THINKING ABOUT POWERFUL QUESTIONS

In learning to pose powerful questions to the war veteran, Tami's primary students were expressly taught four tools, which could potentially be the criteria for assessing students' thinking. Notice our use of criteria in two contexts: we talk about assessment criteria and criteria for judgment. Assessment criteria are the grounds for assessing students' work and, in the area of critical thinking, we recommend using all five tools as sources of assessment criteria. The tool we refer to as criteria for judgment is one of five criteria used to assess critical thinking.

To assess students' use of the intellectual tool "criteria for judgment," we could assess how well the questions they posed met the agreed-on criteria. We could

DEVELOPING TEST QUESTIONS[4]

Karen Barnett, a junior high humanities teacher, borrowed an idea from a fellow teacher, Bob Friend. Instead of exam questions focussed on their study of seventeenth-century England, she had her students create an end-of-unit test consisting of six questions and an answer key. Students were informed that their class test would be drawn exclusively from the question pool developed by the class.

To support her students in completing this task, Karen provided them with three tools: background knowledge, criteria for judgment, and a thinking strategy. The required background knowledge—knowledge of the focus of the questions—was acquired by reading the relevant chapter in their textbook and by undertaking a variety of related assignments. When framing their six questions, students were instructed to consider four criteria.

Questions:

- must be clear so that fellow students understand what is required;
- should address a non-trivial aspect of the chapter contents;
- can be answered within a half page (or twenty minutes); and
- require more than mere recall of information.

Karen further supported her students' efforts by offering a thinking strategy—the use of "question frames"—to help generate questions that went beyond mere recall of information.

More specifically, students were invited to frame questions using prompts such as the following:

- Compare ... with ...
- What conclusions can be drawn from ...
- Decide whether ... was correct when ...
- Predict what would have happen if ...
- What was the effect of ...
- Decide which choice you would make if ...

A list of the best student-generated questions was distributed to the class well before the test. The following questions were submitted by students:

1. Compare the ideas of Thomas Hobbes and John Locke on government.
2. Do you think Cromwell was correct in chopping off the king's head, and what advantage did government gain over royalty because of this?
3. What were the effects of the civil war on the monarchy and the peasantry?
4. If you were the king, how would you handle the pressures of government and the people?
5. Compare the power of the government in the early 1600s to the power it has today.
6. What do you think would have happened if the people hadn't rebelled against the king?

do this either by judging the questions ourselves or by asking students to explain how their question satisfies each criterion.

To assess background knowledge, we could examine student questions for factual errors. To assess the thinking strategy of brainstorming, the teacher could circulate among the groups, observing whether students readily volunteered questions and accepted all suggestions without criticism. Since the purpose of brainstorming is to generate lots of questions, the quantity of questions can also be used to assess effective use of this tool.

Students' understanding of the conceptual distinction between weak and powerful questions could be assessed by providing sample questions and asking students to identify which are weak and which powerful.

ASSESSING DEVELOPING TEST QUESTIONS

In the second case study, students were provided with three tools to support their thinking about test questions: criteria for effective test questions, the "question frame" strategy for generating questions, and background knowledge on the historical period. The student-generated questions could be assessed on all three grounds: how well they satisfied the stipulated criteria, the variety of question frames, and the knowledge of the period implied by the questions asked. (A more appropriate way to assess students' background knowledge would be the answer key that accompanies each student's questions, which is not included here.)

Since the focus of this case study is on posing test questions, we made no mention of the tools needed to help students think critically about their answer key (or their answers on the test). It would be instructive to briefly consider what these tools might be. The tools assessed will depend on the teacher's priorities for the assignment, the perceived needs of the students, and the demands of the curriculum, so our suggestions are just that.

A useful place to begin thinking about how to assess the tools students use to answer questions thoughtfully is to imagine a weak response. Consider the following question: "What do you think would have happened if the people hadn't rebelled against the king?," and the following flawed answer: "If the people hadn't rebelled they would have quickly forgotten their troubles and gone back to watching television."

What relevant tools are absent from this answer? For one, there is the historical error of the existence of television in the seventeenth century; the background knowledge is incomplete. Then there is the bald assertion that the citizenry would quickly forget their problems, which is vague, somewhat implausible, and not supported with any evidence. These deficits suggest gaps in understanding the criteria for a thoughtful response. To address these gaps in criteria for judgment, we might explore the importance of a detailed, specific answer, its plausibility, and how it is supported by evidence (or reasons). These three criteria for judgment might raise the need to teach critical thinking vocabulary, since all students might not know the difference between plausible and actual outcomes. We might also try to nurture an empathetic habit of mind. If students were inclined to put themselves, metaphorically speaking, into the heads and hearts of those living in the seventeenth century, their answers to the questions might be more detailed and plausible. A thinking strategy that might help students construct a thoughtful answer is to suggest a "template" for their answers, such as a three-point outline:

1. Briefly summarize the position taken;
2. Elaborate on what is meant or implied by the position; and
3. Offer several pieces of evidence to justify the position.

We might also supply hypothetical student answers, including ideal answers to help elaborate and refine our list of tools. For example, our exemplary answers might include alternative positions and evaluations of the relative merits of each. If we thought these were reasonable and appropriate expectations, we might introduce additional tools, such as teaching the concepts of "argument" and "counter-argument" and revise the suggested three-point outline to add a new step:

4. Anticipate possible objections to the position and provide a counter-argument for each.

There are many possibilities for tools to teach and, in turn, to assess the questions and answers students generate. The point is that students' answers will likely be much better if they have been taught to use a variety of intellectual tools.[5]

Consider an assignment you intend to assign that involves critical thinking. What tools might you teach and assess to help your students complete the assignment more thoughtfully?

In any critical thinking task it is inevitable that background knowledge and criteria for judgment are needed. Tools of the other three types—critical thinking vocabulary, thinking strategies, and habits of mind—are often, but not always, applicable. You might want to anticipate student responses (both exemplary and poor) in order to develop a list of tools to teach and assess. Two criteria to use to judge what tools to include and what to leave out are whether they are realistic and appropriate.

ENDNOTES

1   The widely cited study of one thousand American classrooms by John Goodlad (2004) concluded that from the early grades, students are conditioned to reproduce what they are taught, not to use and evaluate information. Fred Newmann's (1991, 324) research on sixteen schools observed that most instruction "follows a pattern of teachers transmitting information to students who are expected to reproduce it." Sandra McKee (1988) found in her study of high school teachers that 4 per cent of classroom time was devoted to reasoning and an average of only 1.6 student-posed questions per class.

2   Developed by Jerrold Coombs, first published in Bailin, Case, Coombs, and Daniels (1999). Used with permission of the author.

3   This example is based on a lesson described in McDiarmid, Manzo, and Musselle (2007, 115–119).

4   Based on personal communication with Karen Barnett.

5   To learn more about teaching the tools, view the two detailed lesson plans, "Sample Primary Lesson: Passing Along Kindness" and "Sample Upper Elementary Lesson: Arctic Survival" available for downloading at Pacific Educational Press's web page for *The Anthology of Social Studies*: www.pacificedpress.ca/?p=2687.

REFERENCES

Bailin, S., R. Case, J. Coombs, and L. Daniels. 1999. Conceptualizing critical thinking. *Journal of Curriculum Studies* 31 (3): 285–302.

Glaser, R. 1984. Education and thinking: The role of knowledge. *American Psychologist* 39 (2): 93–104.

Goodlad, J. 2004. *A place called school: Twentieth anniversary edition*. Whitby, ON: McGraw-Hill.

Hirsch, E.D. 1988. *Cultural literacy: What every American needs to know*. New York: Vintage Books.

Lipman, M. 1988. Critical thinking: What can it be? *Educational Leadership* 45: 38–43.

Mackenzie, J. 1988. Authority. *Journal of Philosophy of Education* 22 (1): 57–65.

McDiarmid, T., R. Manzo, and T. Musselle. 2007. *Critical challenges for primary students*. Rev. ed. Vancouver, BC: The Critical Thinking Consortium.

McKee, S.J. 1988. Impediments to implementing critical thinking. *Social Education* 52 (6): 444–446.

McPeck, J. 1981. *Critical thinking and education*. New York: St. Martins.

Newmann, F.M. 1991. Promoting higher order thinking in social studies: Overview of a study of 16 high school departments. *Theory and Research in Social Education* 19 (4): 324–340.

Norris, S.P. and R.H. Ennis. 1989. *Evaluating critical thinking*. Pacific Grove, CA: Midwest Publications.

Parker, W. 1991. Achieving thinking and decision making objectives in social studies. In *Handbook of research on social studies teaching and learning*, ed. J. Shaver, 345–356. Toronto: Collier Macmillan.

Paul, R.W. 1988. *What, then, is critical thinking?* Rohnert Park, CA: Center for Critical Thinking and Moral Critique.

———. 1993. The critical connection: Higher order thinking that unifies curriculum, instruction, and learning. In *Critical thinking: How to prepare students for a rapidly changing world*, R. Paul, 273–289. Santa Rosa, CA: Foundation for Critical Thinking.

Perkins, D.N., E. Jay, and S. Tishman. 1993. Beyond abilities: A dispositional theory of thinking. *Merrill–Palmer Quarterly* 39 (1): 1–21.

Siegel, H. 1988. *Educating reason: Rationality, critical thinking, and education*. New York: Routledge.

Willingham, D.T. 2007. Critical thinking: Why is it so hard to teach? *American Educator*, Summer: 8–19.

SUPPLEMENTARY RESOURCES

The Critical Thinking Consortium offers a vast array of print and digital resources through its website to support the approach to critical thinking described in this chapter (www.tc2.ca). These include:

- *Tools for Thought*: an online collection of lesson plans designed to introduce students to specific intellectual tools to improve their ability to think through a wide array of tasks.
- *Critical Challenges*: a searchable online collection of lesson plans in various subject areas, but especially in social studies, that provide critical thinking tasks and support for specific tools in the course of teaching the subject matter.
- *Critical Challenges Across the Curriculum*: a collection of print publications that provide individual lessons and units that embed critical thinking into the teaching of various curriculum topics.

7

Getting Beyond Inert Facts in Elementary Social Studies

Roland Case

It cannot be too strongly impressed, that Education consists not in travelling over so much intellectual ground, or the committing to memory of so many books, but in the development and cultivation of all our mental, moral, and physical powers. The learned Erasmus has long since said: "At the first it is no great matter how much, but how well you learn it." (Ryerson 1847, 56–57)

Each year reports from groups such as the Historica Dominion Institute decry students' ignorance of historical facts and petition educators to teach more Canadian history.[1] Similar reports are made about Canadians' geographic illiteracy based on students' inability to recall basic information (Royal Canadian Geographic Society 2005). Should we be alarmed about these consistently poor results? Does this necessitate spending more time on content knowledge in history and geography?

Perhaps the root of the problem is not that we don't teach enough history and geography but—as suggested by the quotation above—the ways in which these topics are taught, which may contribute to the forgetting of these facts. Ironically, if we stress covering more facts, we may fuel a worse problem than lack of recall of details. Consider the following interview between Sam, a ten-year-old student, and Pauline, a student teacher at the University of Calgary:

Pauline: Out of the things you do in school, what would you say is the subject that you like least?

Sam: Probably language arts and social studies because they're boring. I don't like writing that

much, so I don't like language arts too much, and social studies you've got to listen and learn words and stuff.

Pauline: So in social studies you're sitting there, listening to the teacher talk, are you?

Sam: Yeah, but it's still boring. We listen to her talk and we have to read these things. Last year we did about the war, Alberta, its history and stuff like that. And we had to read stuff and the teacher had to read stuff too. Just have to memorize these vocabulary and stuff and write them down.

Pauline: So if someone said, "What do you do in social studies?" what do you think you'd tell them?

Sam: Listening, memorizing, and writing. (Carswell 1990, 15)

As this young student's comments suggest, there is an important difference between "remembering" historical or geographic information—factual recall—and "understanding" these events. As historian George Wrong noted in 1924, "Education is what is left when we have forgotten most of the facts we have learned" (cited in Osborne 2000, 36).

Understanding the key ideas is more complicated and more important than simple recall of dates, place names, and terminology. Education is concerned with the development and cultivation of mental, moral, and physical powers. As Erasmus said, "It is no great matter how much, but how well you learn it" (Ryerson 1847,

56–57). Unfortunately, many public reports calling for the teaching of more "content" fail to grasp this.

In this chapter, I explore how to teach social studies content to foster understanding rather than mere recall of information. The chapter's title reference to "inert" facts comes from Alfred North Whitehead's famous book, *The Aims of Education*, in which he suggests that "the central problem of all education" is preventing knowledge from becoming inert (1929/67, 5). By inert, Whitehead means "ideas that are merely received into the mind without being utilized, or tested, or thrown into fresh combination." Harvard educational psychologist David Perkins defines inert knowledge as "knowledge that learners retrieve to answer the quiz question, but that does not contribute to their endeavours and insights in real complex situations" (1993, 90). Calling attention to the need to see our task as engendering understanding, not transmitting information, has been a persistent theme in social studies. In *How We Think*, John Dewey wrote that "the aim often seems to be—especially in such a subject as geography—to make the pupil what has been called a 'cyclopedia of useless information'" (cited in Hare 1994, 72). In 1960, Shirley Engle warned of a "ground-covering fetish" by which he meant the practice of "learning and holding in memory, enforced by drill, large amounts of more or less isolated descriptive material" (302). Howard Gardner concurs: "Coverage is the enemy of understanding" (cited in Antonelli 2004, 42).

Walter Parker (1989, 41) urges that learning be seen as the "progressive construction of understandings" rather than "the warehousing of facts" and teaching be not the "telling of fact" but rather the leading of a construction project. The teacher acts as a contractor, not building the house but contracting the job out to students to do the labour that will build the house.

This chapter provides strategies to teach factual information in ways that promote understanding. By factual information, I mean beliefs about the way the world is and why it is this way. These include what in social studies are typically called "facts" and "generalizations." "Confederation occurred in 1867" and "John A. Macdonald was Canada's first prime minister" are examples of facts. "Early European exploration of North America was motivated by the desire for economic and political gain" and "Natural resources have dominated Canada's economic and social development" are examples of generalizations.[2] Ways to teach concepts to promote conceptual understanding are discussed in the next chapter.

Teaching for Understanding

Let's clarify what it means to understand information. Three characteristics of understanding are especially important:

- **Understanding implies comprehension of information**. At the least, understanding implies that students can thoughtfully rephrase an answer in their own words. Richard Lederer has compiled an amusing "history" of the world gathered from students who poorly understood what they were taught:

    > Eventually the Romans conquered the Greeks. History calls people Romans because they never stayed in one place very long. At Roman banquets, the guest wore garlics in their hair. Julius Caesar extinguished himself on the battlefields of Gaul. The Ides of March murdered him because they thought he was going to be made king. Nero was a cruel tyranny who would torture his poor subjects by playing the fiddle to them. (Lederer 2006, 12)

- **Understanding implies appreciation of context**. Remembering that Confederation occurred in 1867 is not the same as understanding this fact. Understanding Confederation requires knowing the significance of this event and how it fits into the larger historical picture. Imagine asking students: "Which is the more important event in Canada's development as a nation—Confederation or the first basketball game?" If students really understand Confederation, they won't choose the first basketball game. Imagine also asking: "Is Canadian self-rule related to Confederation?" If students cannot see a connection, there is cause to doubt that they understood Confederation, since they seem to have little appreciation of the constellation of ideas surrounding it. Amassing facts adds little to understanding; it is interrelationships between the facts that are important.

- **Understanding implies some grasp of the evidence**. A final aspect of understanding is the need to appreciate, to some extent, the kind of evidence required to decide whether one should accept or reject a proposed fact. Imagine students are told that certain statements in their textbook are thought to be false, say, that Confederation was not in 1867 or that early European exploration of North America was not motivated by the desire for economic gain. If students had no idea about what evidence might support or refute these claims, we might wonder how well they understood what these facts signify.

If we want to promote understanding, our task is to help students comprehend, connect, and seek justification for the information they receive. The following sections provide suggestions to engage students and foster understanding based on two general themes:

- inviting students to think critically about the content, and
- framing effective critical challenges.

Thinking Critically about the Content

In 1847 Egerton Ryerson wrote in his *Report on a System of Public Education for Upper Canada*:

> If the mind of the child when learning, remains merely passive, merely receiving knowledge as a vessel receives water which is poured into it, little good can be expected to accrue. It is as if food were introduced into the stomach which there is no room to digest or assimilate, and which will therefore be rejected from the system, or like a useless and oppressive load upon its energies. (58)

Ryerson's conclusion that students must, in some fashion, "digest" the ideas they encounter, put them into use and assimilate or own them, is not achieved by answering comprehension questions after reading a text and/or taking notes while listening to the teacher. As Alfie Kohn (2004, 189) reports, "Lecturing was defined by writer George Leonard as the 'best way to get information from teacher's notebook to student's notebook without touching the student's mind.'" Students only digest content when they think deeply about the material—that is, when they make reasoned judgments about it (or with it). As Parker (1988, 70) notes, "Thinking is how people learn." This does not mean that it is inappropriate to transmit information—we must transmit information to our students. The point is that passing on information, including "covering" the pioneers and "doing" human migration, is not the heart of our task but merely a means to an end. Our ultimate objective is to support students' ability and inclination to think rigorously about these ideas.

The need for students to think continually about content is crucial. It is not sufficient to "front-end load" content and at a point near the end of a unit or term invite students to reflect on the ideas. As Ryerson's metaphor suggests, information that has been passively acquired is not digested in a way that makes it available for future use. It ceases to be—in fact never was—food for thought. We must find ongoing ways to involve students in thinking as they learn, so that they will, in fact, learn.

The most powerful way I know to help students digest what they are learning is to invite them to think critically about it using an approach I helped develop with The Critical Thinking Consortium.[3]

WHEN TO INVITE CRITICAL THINKING

The obvious place to begin to engage students in thinking critically is with the questions and tasks we present them. What does a question that invites critical thinking look like? And how does it differ from other good questions we might ask? Asking students to "think" about things may, on its own, fall short. To illustrate, consider the questions in Table 7.1.

Although all three types of questions are appropriate and valuable, only one type invites students to think critically: those in column 3.

- **Factual questions**. The questions in column 1 ask students to recall or locate a correct answer from a source. Typically, these questions have a single correct answer. The answer already exists and the student's job is to locate it—in students' notes, their textbooks, the library, or in their memory. For this reason, I sometimes refer to these as "Where's Waldo?" questions. Although finding the correct answer can be difficult, it is not a "critical thinking" challenge. Students are not required to think through a problem. These questions are useful for bringing ideas to students' attention. However if we ask only these questions, we cannot presume that students have digested the information. They have likely just regurgitated it.
- **Preference questions**. The questions in column 2 invite students to share their feelings—what they like and dislike. There are no wrong answers to these questions; they are matters of taste. Some students like living in large cities, others prefer smaller communities; some students welcome adventure, other students do not. This type of question invites students to offer their "opinions" or personal preferences on matters. All answers are valid. Like factual questions, preference questions are valuable—they have a place in any teacher's repertoire.

TABLE 7.1: THREE TYPES OF QUESTIONS

TOPIC	QUESTIONS OF FACTS	QUESTIONS OF PREFERENCE OR LIKING	QUESTIONS REQUIRING REASONED JUDGMENT
Communities	Where is Medicine Hat?	Would you prefer to live in Toronto or Medicine Hat?	Would moving to Toronto or Medicine Hat better meet your family's needs?
Community roles	How do police officers contribute to our community?	If you could be anyone you wished, would you want to be a police officer?	Which contribution made by police officers is the most important to our community?
Inuit	What did the Inuit traditionally use to make tools?	Which Arctic animal would you like to have as a pet?	Which animal—the seal or the caribou—contributed more to traditional Inuit life?
Explorers	What three First Nations peoples did Simon Fraser encounter on his descent down the river?	How would you have felt if you were with Simon Fraser on his journey?	Was Simon Fraser a rogue or a hero?

- **Reasoned judgment questions**. Factual and preference questions do not invite students' "critical" reflection. Only the questions in column 3 invite students to think critically because they require students to make a judgment. When students think critically, they do not merely report what they know or like, they offer a judgment or an assessment among possible options. They must determine which is the more reasonable or justifiable choice. Although there may be several or even many reasonable answers to the questions in column 3, some answers are unreasonable. For example, plausible arguments can be made for having a hamster or a frog as a class pet, but a lion is not a good idea.

The significant feature of a reasoned judgment is that it requires some basis other than our own preferences and whims for selecting one option over another. A reasoned judgment is based on criteria. For example, in deciding whether Toronto or Medicine Hat better meets a family's needs, it is useful to consider criteria such as: health factors, availability of suitable employment, quality of life, safety, and ease of travel.

The close relationship between the term "critical" and "criteria" is instructive. Mathew Lipman (1992) suggests that "critical" thinking is "criterial" thinking—thinking using criteria. It can be defined as follows: "To think critically is to assess the reasonableness of various options in light of appropriate criteria."

In our examples of critical questions, students need to use criteria to form a reasoned judgment. For example, in judging whether Simon Fraser was a hero or a rogue, students might use criteria such as his contribution to society, hardship endured, personal attributes, and respect for others. Students might also use narrow and dubious criteria such as looks, fame, and wealth. A central part of our job in helping students think critically is to assist them to use appropriate criteria when coming to conclusions.

EFFECTIVE CRITICAL CHALLENGES

To develop effective questions and tasks that invite students to think critically, it is beneficial to think critically ourselves about the questions and tasks we choose. That involves using criteria. We need to consider what criteria we use to judge whether a question or task is an effective critical thinking activity or not.

We believe effective critical challenges meet four criteria. They:

- invite reasoned judgment among plausible alternatives;
- are perceived by students to be meaningful;
- advance understanding of the curriculum; and
- are focussed.

These criteria are explained in Table 7.2. In the right-hand side of the table, they are applied to a question we might ask about the illustration "The 'Suburb of Happy Homes'" (Wilson, in Evenden 1995, 20), which shows life in Burnaby, British Columbia, in 1942. We could, of course, ask any number of questions including information or factual questions (e.g., "How many people do you see in this picture?") and preference questions (e.g., "Would you like to live in this house?"). Instead, let us focus on a question to invite reasoned judgment: "What is the season and the period of day (morning, afternoon, evening, or night) of the scene depicted in this illustration?" Older elementary students may be asked a more specific and challenging question: "What is the month, day of the week, and time of day (within an hour) of the scene depicted in the drawing?" Let's explore the merits of this question for inviting critical thinking by considering four criteria for an effective critical challenge.

Applying the criteria for an effective critical challenge is an important step in developing critical challenges. When developing critical challenges, it is important to check the questions and tasks you have created to ensure that they meet these four criteria for effectiveness:

- include criteria for judgment;
- are meaningful to students;
- are based on curriculum; and
- are focussed.

THE "SUBURB OF HAPPY HOMES"

Illustration by Fraser Wilson.

TABLE 7.2: THE BURNABY PICTURE ACTIVITY

CRITERIA FOR EFFECTIVE CRITICAL CHALLENGES	CRITERIA IN ACTION: WHAT IS THE SEASON AND TIME OF DAY?
Clearly invites reasoned judgment among plausible alternatives: poses questions or tasks that invite students to judge the reasonableness of plausible options or alternative conclusions. Criteria give judgments rigour, so the appropriate criteria should be implicit in the question. For example, when deciding which solution is the most reasonable, students might consider feasibility, effectiveness, and fairness.	Students must choose among the seasons and times of the day. Whether this choice is "reasoned" judgment or mere expression of preference depends on whether criteria are used as the basis for judgment. How will students judge whether summer or winter is a more reasonable suggestion for the time of year? The implicit criterion for judgment is consistency with the available evidence. Students will judge which conclusion (spring or winter) is most consistent with the evidence in the picture (for example, the clothing worn, height of the vegetation), and with their general knowledge about the world (for example, the look of plants at different times of the year).
Are perceived as meaningful by students: challenges that students view as irrelevant and unimportant are unlikely to be taken seriously. Over time, students are likely to regard critical thinking as boring or trivial.	The challenge to decipher the time period of the scene is likely to be more engaging than determining the number of people in the picture and or deciding whether they would like to live in the house. If students had just studied the seasons, they might be especially intrigued by the invitation to apply their knowledge to solve the puzzle. Generally speaking, it is engaging to be asked a question that invites exploration, discovery, or reflection.
Advance students' understanding of curriculum content: Critical thinking should not be an add-on, nor should it interrupt the pursuit of other curricular goals. Rather, challenges should involve students in thinking critically about what we want them to learn.	By thinking critically about the seasons and time of day in this picture, students will learn about family life in a suburban community more than sixty years ago. This might be one of the outcomes in the curriculum. Alternatively, if the curricular outcome deals with the differences between past and present communities, then a more appropriate critical question to pose might be whether the quality of life was better for people living at the time of the drawing or in contemporary times.
Are focussed enough to require limited background knowledge: If students are without crucial background knowledge, they will not be able to complete the critical challenge and its value will be lost.	The proposed challenge is relatively focussed compared to related questions such as, "What is the month, day of the week, and hour of the day of the scene depicted?" The greater the number of choices (twelve months as opposed to four seasons; four time periods as opposed to twenty-four hours) the more sophisticated the knowledge required. The addition of the question about the day of the week adds further complexity, including requiring knowledge of the customs in Burnaby in 1942. Would a family toil in their garden on a Sunday? Would the children go to school? Compare the background knowledge required to determine the time of day for the scene with that required to answer the following: What is the approximate annual income of this family? This latter question requires considerably more background knowledge about the living conditions of wartime Canada.

None of the following questions are effective invitations to think critically. For each question, decide which of the four criteria discussed in Table 7.2 are lacking. The answers are provided in endnote 5.[4]

1. Which African animal is the fastest?
2. What is your favourite part of the school playground?
3. Name three things that you noticed about this website.
4. After reading this passage, identify the reasons why ozone is being depleted.

Strategies for Creating Effective Challenges

Initially, at least, it is deceptively difficult to generate effective critical challenges. Many experienced teachers have commented that it is much like the early days of planning lessons. Our very first lesson took many of us days to plan. Our second lesson plan was a little quicker and our tenth was many times faster. A similar pattern occurs when developing critical challenges: initially it takes time and persistence, but eventually it becomes second nature. Here are some strategies to help you develop effective critical challenges that satisfy each of the four criteria.

INVITING REASONED JUDGMENT

Over the years we have noted that effective critical challenges take several forms, and we have identified at least six ways of inviting students to make reasoned judgments. Each of these is discussed in Table 7.3. It may help you to think of these different forms when creating your own critical challenges. Start with the curriculum matter you wish to teach, and use these six types of challenges like a menu of options to help stimulate ideas about ways to frame your questions and tasks.

MEANINGFUL QUESTIONS

Terrell Bell offers the following advice: "There are three things to remember about education. The first one is motivation. The second one is motivation. The third one is motivation" (source unknown). In addition to ensuring that our questions or tasks invite critical thinking, it is important that they motivate students to learn.

One of the most compelling reasons for using critical challenges as a method of teaching subject matter is that it is inherently appealing to be asked to think about one's beliefs instead of simply finding answers others have produced. The feature "The Power of Critical Challenges" is typical of many testimonials I have received about the motivational effect of inviting students to think critically.

The following kinds of qualities in a critical challenge increase appeal to students:

- real-life consequences (for example, sending a letter to an actual official instead of drafting a letter to a fictional person);
- connections to present-day, topical issues;
- personalized to students' lives;
- tied to compelling themes (for example, justice, mystery);
- sensational details or images;
- fun or engaging activities (for example, simulations); and
- activities that open with an engaging hook (for example, an anecdote, role play, or a powerful example).

Another way to promote student engagement is to decrease aspects of a task that students might find boring. Here are a few suggestions:

1. Strip away trivial or extraneous details. For example, study two or three major explorers or regions in depth, not all of them.
2. Minimize "drudgery" tasks:
   - provide manageable chunks of information. (e.g., avoid assigning long reading passages); and
   - limit the products that students are required to produce without sacrificing core understanding. For example, instead of asking students to write an extended paragraph, ask them to summarize their arguments in note form on a chart.
3. Minimize student frustration:
   - keep the task focussed. For example, if the main purpose of an activity is to develop students' ability to analyze a current issue, supply them with a few relevant background pieces rather than expecting everyone to find their own sources; and
   - ensure that students have the tools they will need to successfully address the task.

UNDERSTANDING THE CURRICULUM

To foster student understanding of the content of the curriculum, the content must be made problematic in some way so students think critically about it rather

TABLE 7.3 SIX WAYS TO INVITE REASONED JUDGMENT

TYPE OF CRITICAL CHALLENGE	EXAMPLES OF PRIMARY-LEVEL CRITICAL CHALLENGES	EXAMPLES OF UPPER-ELEMENTARY CRITICAL CHALLENGES
1. Critique the piece. Invite students to assess the merits and/or shortcomings of various social studies: a. people (e.g., historical figures, literary characters, contemporary leaders) b. actions (e.g., proposed solutions to a problem, historical events) c. products (e.g., passages in a textbook, posters, essays, media reports) d. performances (e.g., speeches, presentations, role plays)	• Are these questions for our guest speaker "powerful"? (Possible criteria: give lots of information, are not too easy, mean something to the person) • Has this author explained what actually happened? • Is the wolf in *The True Story of the Three Little Pigs* good or bad? • Is the person in this picture contributing a lot, some, or a little to the community?	• Is Simon Fraser a hero or a rogue? (Possible criteria: contribution to others, hardship endured, character traits, respect for others) • Does this passage of text accurately describe the quality of life of a slave in ancient Rome? • Is this poster an effective presentation for the intended audience? (Possible criteria: catchy, convincing, clear, and concise) • Did the event of Confederation have a positive or negative effect on aboriginal peoples? • On a scale from great to horrible, assess what it would be like to live in ancient China (or some other time and place) considering the quality of the environment, comforts, and fun things to do.
2. Judge the better or best. Invite students to judge which of two or more options is better or best, given agreed-upon criteria.	• Which one of the communities we are studying would better meet the needs of your family? (Possible criteria: safe, healthy, fun, jobs) • Which of these three ideas is the best way for you to make a contribution to the environment? (Possible criteria: safe, possible for you to do, would help) • What is the best thing about being in school (or in a family or club)? • Which celebration is the most impressive? (Possible criteria: applies today, means a lot, lasted the longest in history) • What is the biggest difference between our present community and past community (or another community)? • Which of the two characters in the story is a better friend? (Possible criteria: helps people, does not say mean things, forgives mistakes)	• Who was the greater explorer, Vancouver or Cook? • Which is the more effective Arctic transportation: dogsled or snowmobile? • Which of these five items is the most impressive legacy of ancient Egypt? • Which threat to safe freshwater supply is the greatest concern and why? Identify and analyze possible solutions to the threat and decide which one has the most realistic chance of success. • You have been asked by a museum curator to select the painting from this list which best exemplifies the Group of Seven. Which painting do you choose? • What is the best course of action for this empty land on the edge of town: build a recreation building or leave the land undeveloped? • Would life for a young person in our community be better sixty years ago or right now?
3. Rework the piece. Invite students to transform a product or performance in light of new information, or a differing perspective or focus (e.g., from the point of view of a logger or an environmentalist, a king or a peasant, or someone else).	• Rewrite this story from the point of view of another person or character. (Possible criteria: must include same details, be believable, show a difference) • After reading the traditional version of the *Three Little Pigs* (told from the pigs' points of view) and *The True Story of the Three Little Pigs* (told from the wolf's point of view), write a fair-minded account of what happened at the third pig's house.	• Rewrite a historical letter written by a non-aboriginal person about the practice of potlatches from the traditional perspective of First Nations peoples. • Rewrite a picture book to show changes in society over time. • Predict what might have happened if this historical event had turned out differently. • Redraw the picture showing the pioneer family scene as it would appear in the present time (or in a different season of the year).

TABLE 7.3   SIX WAYS TO INVITE REASONED JUDGMENT (CONT.)

TYPE OF CRITICAL CHALLENGE	EXAMPLES OF PRIMARY-LEVEL CRITICAL CHALLENGES	EXAMPLES OF UPPER-ELEMENTARY CRITICAL CHALLENGES
4. Decode the puzzle. Invite students to use clues to solve a mystery or to explain a confusing or enigmatic situation.	• *Tell the story.* Based on our simulated dig (dinosaur remains, pioneer community), tell the story of what occurred here. (Possible criteria: uses all the evidence, is believable, clearly tells the story) • *What am I?* Identify the purpose and function of a mystery object or person. (Possible criteria: fits all the evidence, makes sense) • *Solve the mystery.* Using clues in the images, explain who, what, where, when, and why. (Possible criteria: based on information in the picture, uses lots of clues) • Put these images into the correct order.	• What is the cartoonist really saying in this drawing? • Using the clues in these images, identify the four communities. • Find out as much as you can about the region using the mapping technique you have been assigned (e.g., scale, colour, contours).
5. Design to specs. Ask students to develop a product that meets a given set of conditions or specifications that provide the criteria for judging the quality of the design.	• Design a rich habitat that meets the needs of a class pet animal for exercise, shelter, food, and privacy. • Using the materials provided, build a structure to achieve the specified results. • Design a plan for a web page that meets class-developed requirements. • Design a symbol that shows three of our community's qualities. (Possible criteria: fits the qualities, has sufficient detail) • Prepare a package of three helpful items for a homeless person. (Possible criteria: easy to carry, meets needs, shows we care) • Take a photograph that captures a community quality (e.g., peaceful, safe, active). (Possible criteria: fits the caption, has sufficient detail) • Create a family shield that represents your family heritage and tells something about your identity. • Write a poem about the key features in a community that represent its land and people.	• The premier has asked for concise notes on the day's front-page news. Your notes must be less than one-half page in length, focus on the important issues, and clearly summarize the main points. • Create a travelogue or itinerary to be used by a family planning their vacation to our province. • Prepare a persuasive letter (or an oral statement) directed to a specific group that expresses your views on the preservation of national parks. • Create a poster-sized advertisement to discourage fellow students from smoking, effectively employing the techniques of persuasion without distorting the evidence. • Generate three "powerful" questions to ask a classroom visitor. (Possible criteria: informative, relevant to the person, requires some thought in order to answer) • Create a plan to address a community or national concern. (Possible criteria: effective, efficient, sustainable, culturally responsible) • Write a story that is true to the time period, involves all the characters in a meaningful way, and captures the mood of the scene.
6. Perform to specs. Invite students to perform a task or undertake a course of action that meets a given set of conditions. Perform to specs is very similar to design to specs with one important difference: perform to specs involves acting in real time.	• Personally make a lasting contribution to a family member, a community member, or the school. • *Charades.* Portray a mystery community member using clues which don't include words, and are informative. • Perform an act of kindness to another member of the class. (Possible criteria: makes the other person happy, you feel good about it, is simple to do)	• Mount a school-wide media campaign on an issue of concern to students. • Undertake an action that makes a lasting contribution to someone else's life. • Create a tableau that accurately and clearly expresses the feelings and tensions present during the assigned historical event. • Provide feedback to a fellow student in a manner that is constructive, respectful, clear, and honest. • Dramatize a role that is true to the time period, involves all the characters in a meaningful way, and captures the mood of the scene.

than regurgitate it. Thus, a key requirement of any critical challenge is that it addresses the curriculum we want students to understand. The examples in Table 7.4 illustrate how curricular understanding is promoted through critical challenges.

Developing critical challenges that help students "uncover" the curriculum takes practice, but critical challenges need not be large-scale undertakings. Although in-depth challenges are valuable, there are many opportunities to pose "mini" challenges that take ten minutes or so to complete (for example, which of the three differences between an Inuit and a southern community would have the biggest impact on daily life?). Even when critical challenges are extensive, the time spent can be justified provided many curriculum outcomes are addressed.

Many teachers despair at finding the time to address all of the subject matter that needs to be taught (Onosko 1989). In a study of 1,800 social studies educators in British Columbia, one teacher wrote, "I don't have enough time to cover even 10 per cent of the textbook and other resources" (Case 1993, 6). More recently, Osborne (2004, 25–26) noted that the pressure of high-stakes testing forces teachers to "cover" their courses even when they know that they need to spend more time on certain topics if students are to properly understand them.

The perceived need to cover large quantities of material may arise to some extent from a belief that our crucial task as elementary social studies teachers is to transmit information about the world. However, as we've seen in this chapter, promoting understanding is our

TABLE 7.4 LINKS TO CURRICULAR UNDERSTANDING

CRITICAL CHALLENGE	CURRICULAR UNDERSTANDING
Decode the Burnaby picture	Learn about the customs and lifestyle within a suburban community in the 1940s.
Ask powerful questions of a World War II veteran who has come as a class visitor	Learn what the war meant to people who were involved in it and why society continues to commemorate this event.
If you were required to move either to Medicine Hat or Kingston, which community would best meet your family members' needs?	Learn how different communities meet people's needs in different ways.

crucial task. This means that we need not "get through" the textbook or "cover" every explorer or region in order to meet our responsibilities to the curriculum.

Years ago, Hilda Taba offered useful advice about balancing the quantity of information with the quality of understanding. She believed that "coverage" of topics was impossible—there was always too much to cover. Instead teachers should sample rather than survey the content. Thus, the important question for Taba was not "how many facts, but which facts we want students to think about" (Fraenkel 1992, 174). John Dewey talked of "generative knowledge"—knowledge that had rich ramifications in the lives of learners (Perkins 1993, 90). The most generative knowledge is found in powerful conceptual and factual insights that apply across many circumstances. For example, is it important that students study all the major early Canadian explorers or is it sufficient that they consider one or two explorers and come to appreciate the extent to which personal, economic, and cultural motives drove early exploration? Is it imperative that students study all the major technological inventions and their effects or is it sufficient that students come away with a few broad understandings, grounded in specific instances, of the way technology has transformed (for better and worse) Canadian society? These broader insights, which span cultures and time periods, are the sorts of generative understandings that are worth emphasizing.

It is sometimes thought that devoting considerable amounts of time to in-depth studies results in students acquiring very narrow understandings. This possible shortcoming can be avoided by sampling the content. Just like a geologist explores an area by surveying the surface and then probes carefully selected sites, a teacher may sample the curriculum and probe deeply at carefully selected topics. Students may get highly condensed overviews of a period or culture via mini-lectures, films, or fact sheets to set the context for more focussed case studies of particular issues.

To illustrate how critical thinking challenges can address multiple curricular outcomes, the feature "Bundling Curriculum Outcomes" outlines the outcomes in the grade 2 Alberta curriculum that are addressed by the critical task of deciding who the school should be named after, if it was to be renamed.

MANAGING BACKGROUND KNOWLEDGE

Students need background knowledge to deal competently with critical challenges. Without it, the value of posing challenges will be lost; students are less likely to develop their ability to think critically if they are fumbling in the dark. It is important to anticipate and manage the information required by a challenge. This is done either by narrowing the challenge's scope or by finding effective ways for students to acquire the information they need.

LIMIT THE INFORMATION NEEDED

One way to limit the amount of background knowledge required is to narrow the challenge or, as my colleague Selma Wassermann would say, "make it compact." Answering the question "Who is the greatest hero in our community's history" is a task that could fill a book. A more focussed challenge is preferable, possibly, "Of the three people we have studied, who is the greatest hero?" Similarly, completing the task "Assess the legacy of the Industrial Revolution" could fill volumes. A more focussed challenge might ask, "Based on the following two reports and your own knowledge, is the steam engine the most significant invention of the Industrial Revolution?" or, perhaps, "In the first fifty years of the Industrial Revolution, which invention most altered industry and commerce?"

PROVIDE INFORMATION EFFICIENTLY

Acquiring background knowledge is obviously necessary, but teaching it can get in the way of critical thinking. It is useful to remember that "background knowledge" is the focussed information needed to address the task at hand; this is not the same as "general information," which might be described as the fuller range of facts about a topic acquired for general interest or potential value. We often tell students more than they need to know and thereby reduce the amount of time available for them to think about what they really need to know. The following list includes several strategies to teach background knowledge:

- **Don't front-end load**. Students can acquire necessary information as they work through the challenge and even after they have begun to answer the challenge (for example, after students offer their considered response invite them to undertake further study to confirm whether they are right or not).
- **Deliver it economically**. One way to communicate background knowledge is to use picture books in critical challenges. In this way, students acquire the information they need simply by listening to or reading a story. Other mechanisms for the efficient communication of information include the following:
  - provide point-form notes;
  - deliver short mini-lectures on key ideas;

  - distribute teacher- or student-prepared briefing sheets; and,
  - use visuals.
- **Use students as information sources**. It is often productive to tap into the collective wisdom of the class through class and group sharing. For example, in analyzing the Burnaby picture, each student might work with a partner and then share their tentative conclusions with the entire class so that everyone has the benefit of each other's insights. Another strategy is to divide topics among groups of students who pursue specific areas in some depth and then share their findings with the rest of the class, thereby broadening the scope of everyone's understanding.
- **Think carefully about student research**. Despite its popularity, independent library research is typically neither efficient nor reliable as a means of acquiring background knowledge: many students waste considerable time looking for material that does not give them the information they need. Library research projects may be best directed to teaching students how to conduct research and not used as a means for acquiring background knowledge.
- **Frame the acquisition of background knowledge as a critical challenge**. Find ways to chunk a body of knowledge into smaller bits and then frame a challenge for each segment. For example, if students are to consider whether life was better now than it was sixty or more years ago, the Burnaby picture challenge could be used to teach them about life in the 1940s. In addition, students might be asked to think critically about questions they would ask of people who were alive at the time. The following critical challenges can be used to invite students to think critically as they acquire background information:
  - Select the five most important facts or events from the chapter;
  - Decode the contents of the picture (answer the 5Ws, who, what, where, when, and why);
  - Rank the causes or benefits in order of importance;
  - Rate the effect of a particular event or policy from the perspective of various groups;
  - Which of the provided sources offers the least reliable information?; and
  - Think of a powerful question and a thoughtful answer on an assigned topic.

Conclusion

Learning is not a matter of acquiring information, but of developing understanding of the ideas behind the facts. Superficial coverage of facts for their own sake is of marginal value and much of it is forgotten almost as soon as it is taught. Our primary task is not to present students with prepackaged information for mental storage but to help them internalize, question, and utilize relevant information. Engaging students in thinking critically about, and with, the content of the curriculum is most effectively accomplished through meaningful, focussed challenges.

Create several critical challenge questions or tasks based on a curriculum resource you already use. Endeavour to meet all of the following criteria when framing each critical challenge:

- Does it invite students to make a reasoned judgment?
- Is it likely to be perceived as meaningful by students?
- Does it promote understanding of curriculum content?
- Is it focussed to limit the amount of background knowledge?

ENDNOTES

1   See the list of annual reports on the Historica Dominion Institute website at www.historica-dominion.ca/content/polls. More generally, surveys throughout the twentieth century show repeatedly that students remember very little of the history learned in schools (Osborne 2004, 35–36).

2   The word "concept" is used ambiguously in social studies by some to refer to generalizations and by others to refer to the ideas or meanings captured by words such as "justice," "table," "sustainable," and "community." We use "concept" exclusively in this latter sense.

3   For further information about The Critical Thinking Consortium, which has worked with many thousands of social studies teachers and published numerous resources, visit their website at www.tc2.ca.

4   The missing criteria in these four questions are: 1. Criteria for judgment; 2. Criteria for judgment, curriculum-driven; 3. Criteria for judgment, focus, meaningful to students; 4. Criteria for judgment, meaningful to students.

5   This example was developed by The Critical Thinking Consortium for Alberta Education as part of its online guide to support implementation of the provincial social studies curriculum. Many other critical challenges can be found on the LearnAlberta website: www.learnalberta.ca.

REFERENCES

Antonelli, F. 2004. *From applied to applause.* Toronto: Ontario Secondary School Teachers' Federation, November.

Carswell, R. 1990. Social studies through students' eyes. *One World* 27 (2): 14–16.

Case, R. 1993. *Summary of the 1992 social studies needs assessment.* Victoria, BC: Queen's Printer.

Engle, S.H. 1960. Decision making: The heart of social studies instruction. *Social Education* 34 (8): 301–306.

Evenden, L.J., ed. 1995. *The suburb of happy homes—Burnaby: Centennial themes.* Burnaby, BC: Community Economic Development Centre and the Centre for Canadian Studies, Simon Fraser University.

Fraenkel, J.R. 1992. Hilda Taba's contributions to social education. *Social Education* 56 (3): 172–178.

Hare, W. 1994. Content and criticism: The aims of schooling. In *Papers of the annual conference of the Philosophy of Education Society of Great Britain,* ed. J. Tooley, 72–89. Oxford: New College, University of Oxford.

Kohn, A. 2004. Challenging students—and how to have more of them. *Phi Delta Kappan* 86 (3), November: 184–194.

Lederer, R. 2006. *Anguished English. An anthology of accidental assaults upon our language* (revised, expanded and updated). Layton UT: Wyrick & Company. E-book online at books.google.ca/books?id=y2-YPs29zVwC.

Lipman, M. 1992. Criteria and judgment in critical thinking. *Inquiry* 9 (2), May: 3–4.

Onosko, J. 1989. Comparing teachers' thinking about promoting students' thinking. *Theory and Research in Social Education* 17 (3): 174–195.

Osborne, K. 2000. Who killed Granatstein's sense of history? Misguided criticisms. *National Post,* May 27.

———. 2004. Canadian history in the schools: A report prepared for Historica Foundation, Toronto.

Parker, W. 1988. Thinking to learn concepts. *Social Studies* 79 (2): 70–73.

———. 1989. How to help students learn history and geography. *Educational Leadership* 47 (3): 39–43.

Perkins, D. 1993. The connected curriculum. *Educational Leadership* 51 (2): 90–91.

Royal Canadian Geographical Society. 2005. *The perceived importance of geography, comprehension of geography, and geographic literacy in Canada.* Prepared for the RCGS by Kendric, Smith, and Partners, Inc., May 2005. Available online at www.ccge.org/default.asp

Ryerson, E. 1847. *Report on a system of public education for Upper Canada.* Montreal: Lovell and Gibson.

Whitehead, A.N. 1929/1967. *The aims of education and other essays.* New York: Free Press.

8 Promoting Conceptual Understanding in Elementary Classrooms

John Myers and Roland Case

A few years ago, my niece (Roland's) came home with the results of an end-of-unit quiz on thirty of the most difficult concepts in social studies. The concepts included capitalism, communism, totalitarianism, liberalism, and dozens of other complex political notions. She received 96% on the quiz—the highest mark in the class. Seeking to celebrate her success and engage her in political conversation, I asked what "capitalism" meant. She immediately recited in a rather hypnotic tone a dictionary-perfect definition. I responded, "Yes, but what does it actually mean?" and my niece said she wasn't exactly sure. So I agreed that it was a difficult concept to explain and asked if she knew whether or not Canada was a capitalist country. My niece responded, "How should I know?" She was the top student in the class and she didn't really understand anything of these concepts.

Concepts are the neglected content dimension in social studies. While generally speaking we may be in danger of having an obsession with teaching factual information, we are guilty of devoting very little attention to teaching concepts. Even when concepts are taught, we often do little more than provide a definition and an example. This is unfortunate because concepts are powerful tools for making sense of our world, and memorizing definitions doesn't go very far in helping students understand their meaning. The result, to use Hilda Taba's phrase, is "the rattle of empty wagons," where students learn to parrot the labels for concepts without grasping their meaning (Parker 1988). This chapter makes a case for the importance of teaching concepts, explains what this involves, and offers teaching and assessment strategies for conceptual understanding.

The Role of Concepts

A concept is "a mental construct or category represented by a word or phrase" (Wiggins and McTighe 2005, 340). Although concepts are abstractions—meaning they are ideas—examples representing concepts do exist. For example, the concept "mountain" is a mental construct, but individual mountains do exist. Concept groupings help us organize our experiences—we can distinguish mountains from hills, and both of these from plains and valleys. Our ability to make sense of the world would be greatly impaired if we did not use concepts as organizing constructs. For example, there may be as many as 7.5 million distinguishable colours, but we can manage this diversity by grouping them into a dozen or so basic categories (Bruner 1973). In short, concepts provide the intellectual categories or lenses through which we recognize and classify the world.

A simple way to illustrate this point is to draw attention to the drawing on the following page. When asked what they see, people will typically answer "a rabbit," "a duck," "a puppet," or some other creature. These answers arise only because we possess the concepts "rabbit," "duck," and "puppet." If we were not familiar with these concepts, we would not recognize them in

DUCK OR RABBIT?

Courtesy Roland Case.

the drawing. Hence, the difference when looking at the drawing between seeing undefined markings and seeing representations of objects is the possession of relevant concepts. Even animals recognize and classify objects as "food" or "non-edible" and distinguish fellow animals as "prey," "mate," "predator," or "other." Concepts actually shape what we see or, as a Chinese proverb puts it, "We see what is behind our eyes." If our students do not understand, for example, the concepts "justice" and "rights," they will not see injustice in a situation where a person's rights are being violated. Similarly, Roland's niece couldn't recognize Canada as a capitalist country because she did not truly understand the concept of "capitalism."

The metaphor of concepts as intellectual lenses is especially apt in that some individuals' glasses or eyesight are not well focussed—they see the world in a blurred, sometimes incorrect form. Our task, then, is not solely to introduce students to new concepts in social studies, but also to continually refine their conceptual understandings so that they learn to see the world in increasingly discriminating ways. In fact, the major focus of the primary social studies curriculum is on helping students grasp concepts that are central to understanding social life (such as teaching students to distinguish "needs" from "wants," to recognize when

a group of people is a "community" and when it is not, and to understand the difference between a "right" and a "responsibility"). Because concepts organize or categorize our world, they often make most sense when paired with what they are not; we typically distinguish "need" from "want," "renewable" from "non-renewable," "capitalism" from "communism," and so on.

In addition to helping us classify and find meaning in our world, conceptual understandings are the essential building blocks for knowledge. Concepts are the basis upon which facts, theories, principles, and generalizations are constructed. Roland's niece might eventually learn that Canada is a capitalist country, but this fact still won't mean anything to her until she understands the concept of "capitalism." Studies going back almost a century in the area of history-learning show that emphasizing the facts at the expense of teaching the concepts impairs understanding and even retention of these facts (Wineburg 2001).

Challenges in Teaching Concepts

Despite their importance in helping us make sense of our world, concepts are not, generally speaking, taught effectively (Seiger-Ehrenberg 2001). Common impediments to effective conceptual teaching include:

- uncertainty over the very large number of concepts to teach, and which of those are most important to reinforce with students;
- lack of clarity about the precise distinctions between the various concepts we hope to teach (for example, How is "bias" different from "point of view"?);
- conflation of concepts with other constructs such as facts and generalizations, and assuming that concepts can be taught the same way we teach facts;
- teaching concepts in a superficial manner by providing a definition and possibly an example or two.

Much of the rest of this chapter is devoted to suggestions on how to address these challenges.

One of the obvious difficulties is the sheer number of concepts we use in social studies. Every sentence contains concepts. Because of this, it is important to be selective. There is no point in teaching a concept merely because it is found in the curriculum or textbook. Students may already have a good grasp of the idea. For instance, most primary students will have some understanding of "family" before they begin to work with it in social studies. Most students will have lived in a family of one type or another for much of their lives. Rather, they need experiences such as looking at pictures, reading stories, and talking with other children, which will help them see that some families are different from the ones they are familiar with (for example, they may have only one parent living in the home), but they are nevertheless families. Our efforts should be directed towards extending understanding and correcting misperceptions of familiar concepts.

As well, we should introduce students to unfamiliar concepts that have significant generative potential. By "generative," we mean concepts that represent significant ideas and can be linked with other important concepts. Consider the following pairs of concepts: "plateau" and "renewable resource" or "fashion" and "culture." The first concept in each pair identifies a rather narrow notion that does not have nearly the same breadth of use as does the second concept in each pairing. Clearly, we must prioritize our teaching towards developing those concepts that will have the biggest payoff in shaping and refining students' ability to make sense of their world.

Key Features of a Concept

It is helpful, when learning to teach concepts in ways that promote student understanding, to recognize four key features of any concept (Bennett and Rolheiser 2001).

- **Concepts have a label or a name.** Young children understand many sophisticated concepts long before they learn the conventional terms or labels for them. For example, long before they learn the word "discrimination," many children will understand that some individuals are picked on unfairly simply because they happen to be different. Similarly, many young students can draw conclusions from a given fact without knowing that this is called an "inference" (for example, the fact that the person waves his hand in a particular way suggests that he wants me to come towards him). As teachers, our role includes connecting students' existing conceptual understanding with the traditional words used to label these concepts. While it is helpful to know and use these labels, it is more important that students understand the meaning behind the vocabulary than for them to be able to use the words themselves.
- **Concepts are explained when examples are identified.** According to Gagné (1985, 95), concept learning refers to "putting things into a class" and being able to recognize members of that class. The American

philosopher William James said: "A word is a summary of what to look for" (cited in Parker and Perez 1987, 164). Thus, recognizing the examples that fall within the concept and those that do not is at the core of understanding the concept. For instance, it would be difficult to claim that students understand the concept of "responsible citizenship" if they cannot identify picking up litter as responsible and throwing a candy wrapper on the sidewalk as irresponsible.

- **Many concepts are matters of degree.** Although some concepts are black or white—either a body of land is an island or it is not—many others are matters of degree. For example, at what point does a river become a stream? If democracies take away rights of citizens during times of war or other disasters, at what point does a country cease to be a democracy and become a dictatorship instead?
- **Concepts are delineated by shared attributes.** The criteria that determine which examples belong within a conceptual category can be called attributes (also referred to as features, characteristics, or traits). For example, having three sides is an attribute of the concept "triangle"; an attribute of the concept "rule" is that it regulates actions. Some attributes are absolutely necessary for inclusion. These are essential attributes (for example, we cannot refer to an object as a triangle if it doesn't have three sides; the right to vote is an essential attribute of a democratic society). Some attributes may not be shared by all examples of a concept (for example, being able to vote for political parties, while a feature of most democratic societies, is not essential, since democracies such as ancient Athens operated without a party system as do some municipal governments today).

Helping students recognize non-essential attributes deepens their understanding of a concept. Non-essential attributes include "typical" features that are often associated with the concept and may be helpful in understanding it but are not necessarily present in all cases. For example, "mountains are (often) very high" and "mountains may have snow" are typical but non-essential attributes. Typical attributes of "rules" are that they often involve punishment or negative consequences if broken, and that they often prohibit or prevent action but may also protect or permit action. Another typical attribute of rules is that they are often written down. It may be the case that teaching students about typical features is as important as teaching them about essential features. But students must understand that a typical attribute

TABLE 8.1	KEY ATTRIBUTES OF SELECTED SOCIAL STUDIES CONCEPTS
CONCEPT	**ATTRIBUTES**
bias	• an unfair preference or prejudice that colours observations or conclusions • a predisposition to praise or blame without sufficient evidence • comes in many forms: ethnocentrism, sexism, racism
change	• all things change over time • growth is change • change is necessary for survival • change may be negative or positive • change may be gradual or dramatic
co-operation	• co-operation does not always mean doing what you are told or that you have to "give in" • involves listening to each other in decision-making • means working together for a common goal • not all "group work" is "co-operative" work
culture	• human response to the surrounding environment • changes over time • includes many different aspects of a society (for example, language, religion, customs, laws, art, music) • is more than costumes, clothing, and food • shapes our beliefs and values in powerful ways
needs	• refers to things that are basic for survival or a minimal level of functioning; are not simply wanted • different types of needs exist, both psychological and physical • some needs are common to everyone and some vary from person to person
perspective	• orients what we see and how we see things • can be physical (standing on top of or at the bottom of a hill) or mental (viewed from a teacher's, parent's, or student's perspective) • can't be avoided: everything must be viewed from some perspective • may be narrow or broad, empathetic or closed, biased or fair-minded • some perspectives are more defensible than others • we can and should be self-conscious about the perspectives we take on a given issue

need not always be present for the concept to apply (for example, heroes are often famous, but someone may not be famous yet may still be a hero).

The task of identifying attributes can be challenging, especially in the case of abstract concepts. (Many social studies concepts are concrete in that they represent physical objects such as lake, mountain, ocean, valley, map, and globe; other concepts are abstract such as large, prime minister, power, time, culture, and discrimination.)

Clarity about the attributes is key when teaching for conceptual understanding. Table 8.1 suggests key attributes for a sampling of elementary social studies concepts. Once the key essential and non-essential attributes of a concept have been identified, it is important to select from this list those items about which students are most in need of instruction. It is generally unwise to attempt to teach all attributes of a concept at any one time. Instead, begin by teaching the particular attributes that students most need to understand.

Promoting Conceptual Understanding

Learning a concept involves more than simple transmission of a label or a definition. It is centrally connected with recognizing the range of application or scope of the concept. For this reason, learning to recognize whether something is or is not an example of the concept lies at the heart of conceptual understanding.

In teaching concepts that refer to concrete objects such as "chair" or "tree," young students need to see numerous examples of the range of chairs and trees that exist. This is also the case with concepts that refer to non-physical notions such as "co-operation" or "needs." For these, students require examples that highlight the particular attributes you plan to teach. For example, in teaching that "needs can be both psychological and physical," we would include examples of psychological needs such as hope and emotional security along with examples of physical needs such as food and clean water.

Equally important in coming to understand a concept is knowing the limits or boundaries beyond which the

TABLE 8.2 THE CONCEPT "PENCIL"

ATTRIBUTES	ESSENTIAL ATTRIBUTE	NON-ESSENTIAL ATTRIBUTE	EXAMPLES AND NON-EXAMPLES
contains lead	✓		if it did not contain lead, but ink, it would be a pen
needs to be sharpened		✓	mechanical pencils do not need to be sharpened
made of wood		✓	mechanical pencils can be made of metal or plastic
used for writing or drawing	✓		if it wasn't, it would be a stick or pointer
has an eraser		✓	erasers are a typical but not essential attribute

concept does not apply. For this reason, non-examples are very useful in teaching. Non-examples are not simply any non-instance of the concept. Rather, they are closely related non-examples—instances that are frequently confused with the concept or are very similar but different in important respects (for example, a much-wanted toy or a special privilege are non-examples of a "need").

In Table 8.2, we see examples and non-examples that might be offered to help students recognize the various attributes (essential and non-essential) of the concept "pencil." For example, students might be asked whether or not a pencil has to be made of wood and, if it is not, why not (it could be a mechanical pencil made of plastic or metal).

Strategies for Teaching Concepts

There are three general approaches offering different orientations to the use of examples and non-examples in fostering conceptual understanding: concept recognition, concept attainment, and concept formation.

Test how well you have understood some of the ideas related to the teaching of concepts. Table 8.3 contains a list of features that may or may not be necessary attributes of a mountain. For each feature, identify whether it is essential, typical, or not an attribute of a mountain. In each case, provide an example or a non-example to illustrate this feature. A sample answer for the first feature is provided.

CONCEPT RECOGNITION

Concept recognition is the most straightforward of these approaches. It begins with the selection of the concept(s) to teach, identification of a few key attributes, and creation of a list of relevant examples/non-examples for students to consider. Students are introduced to the concept and explicitly or implicitly to the attributes that

define the concept. Students then sort the examples and non-examples according to the identified attributes and discuss the reasons for their choices. The teacher checks for understanding and then involves students in applying the concept in some meaningful context.

In the following example, adapted from Abbott, Case, and Nicol (2003, 83), the objective is to help students understand short-term and lasting differences. In particular, three attributes were identified:

- some differences don't last very long and others continue for a very long time.
- short-term and lasting differences can result from objects and from actions.
- short-term and lasting differences can be positive or negative.

The concepts are introduced by reading a story about a girl who tried to make a lasting difference in the lives of others. The teacher also discusses the different effects particular actions can have, such as doing someone's homework for them rather than helping the person learn how to do their own homework. Students are then given sets of cards with situations or actions similar to those reproduced in Figure 8.1 and asked to work with a partner to sort them into two labelled piles: "short-term differences" and "lasting differences." Finally, in applying the concept, students are asked to think of and carry out an action that would make a lasting difference in someone's life.

CONCEPT ATTAINMENT

The idea of concept attainment originates with cognitive psychologist Jerome Bruner (Bruner, Goodnow, and Austin 1967). It is a structured inquiry approach in which students are given examples and non-examples, but the particular concept is not indicated to them. In this approach, teachers select the concept they want students to attain, decide in advance on the attributes they want

TABLE 8.3   THE CONCEPT "MOUNTAIN"

FEATURES	ESSENTIAL ATTRIBUTE	TYPICAL ATTRIBUTE	NON-ESSENTIAL ATTRIBUTE	EXAMPLES AND NON-EXAMPLES
has snow on top		✓		a mountain need not have snow
is found with other mountains				
is taller than a hill				
has trees on it				
rises above its surroundings				

students to "discover," and then create or control a set of approximately ten paired examples/non-examples that will help students decipher these attributes. The examples/non-examples might be recorded as single words, phrases, actions, or images, and they may be introduced all at once to students or introduced one pair at a time as an unfolding mystery. The students' task is to ascertain which attributes explain why the examples fall into one category and the non-examples in another.

The scenario described in "Teaching About Natural Resources" illustrates a grade 3 teacher's efforts to use a concept attainment approach to teach about "natural resources." The teacher begins by introducing the task and a set of ten appropriately paired examples and non-examples. She presents the clearest contrasting pairs first and asks students to think about the difference between them. Gradually she presents pairs representing increasingly subtle distinctions. Meanwhile, students are generating and testing their hypotheses about the attributes that distinguish the examples from the non-examples. Students who catch onto the idea are able to identify the concept and are invited to suggest their own examples, while other students continue to try to formulate the concept. A "no call-out" rule allows everyone to stay involved. At an appropriate stage, the teacher offers test examples for students to classify. These serve as initial checks for understanding. To conclude, the teacher shares the conventional label or phrase for the concept and helps the class reach consensus on the concept and its defining attributes. Students discuss the changes in their thinking during the analysis of the paired examples.

The successful use of concept attainment as an unfolding mystery that students are to decipher depends on the choice and sequencing of the paired examples. The initial set of paired examples shared with the class ought to suggest several hypotheses. As they work through the set, more clearly discriminated pairs should help students eliminate various hypotheses.

CONCEPT FORMATION

The concept formation approach evolved out of the work of social studies educator Hilda Taba (1967). In this instructional method, students begin by examining data that may be generated by the teacher or by students. Students are encouraged to explore ways of classifying or sorting the data and attach descriptive labels to their groupings. Working individually, or better yet, in teams, students might use a mind map.[1] Students are helped to form their own understanding of a concept by linking the examples to the labels and by explaining their reasoning. Finally, students apply their understanding of the concept or concepts by predicting consequences, explaining unfamiliar phenomena, or hypothesizing and testing their hypotheses.

Consider the use of concept formation after a field trip in the local community. The teacher might engage

FIGURE 8.1   RECOGNIZING SHORT-TERM AND LASTING DIFFERENCES

Sort the following cards into short-term or lasting differences.

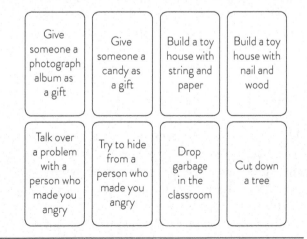

Give someone a photograph album as a gift	Give someone a candy as a gift
Build a toy house with string and paper	Build a toy house with nail and wood
Talk over a problem with a person who made you angry	Try to hide from a person who made you angry
Drop garbage in the classroom	Cut down a tree

TEACHING ABOUT NATURAL RESOURCES

Serena Pierre has decided to use a concept attainment approach to teach her grade 3 class about natural resources. She identifies two attributes that are key to understanding the concept:

- natural resources are products that are considered valuable in their relatively unmodified (natural) form;
- natural resources are extracted from the earth or purified; they are not made or created by humans (for example, mining, oil extraction, fishing, and forestry are generally considered natural-resource industries, while farming is not).

Later, she might introduce a more complex attribute, the idea that natural resources can be classified into renewable and non-renewable resources.

For each attribute, she thinks of approximately three or four pairs of examples and non-examples. She makes a simple drawing and caption for each one on flash cards.

When it is time for social studies, she begins: "We are going to play a guessing game about some of the things we use in our world. I am placing pairs of things on the board under the headings YES and NO." Ms. Pierre puts a card with the word "trees" under the YES column and another card with the word "paper" under the NO column. Then she takes a second pair of cards. She puts "bears" under the YES column and "steak" under the NO column. Next she puts "wind" under the YES column and "plastic" under the NO column. She then asks the class to consider the three examples under the YES column and discuss how they are alike. "What do they have in common?"

"No call-outs, please. If you have an idea, I want you to hang onto it and see whether your idea works with the next few sets of pairs." She proceeds to put "sunlight," "clay," and "crude oil" under the YES

column and "electricity," "bread," and "gasoline" in the NO column.

Now there are six cards under each column. She asks, "What idea links all the items in the YES column? If you know, can you think of a new pair of items to go in the YES and the NO columns?"

Several students raise their hand. At the teacher's request, Maria offers "water" for the YES column and "ginger ale" for the NO column.

"That's correct," replies Ms. Pierre.

"I have another pair," says Gorinder, "'wild berries' for the YES and 'wheat' for the NO column."

Other students nod their heads in agreement. Most raise their hands when asked whether they think they know the idea that links the items in the YES column. At this point, Ms. Pierre selects a card and holds it up. She asks: "Which column does 'plastic bag' go under?"

"NO."

"What about 'sand'?"

"YES."

"Where would 'cars' belong?"

"NO."

"How about 'gold'?"

"YES."

Ms. Pierre concludes by asking what the YES items have in common and offers the label "natural resources" to describe things that we use and that occur in nature. These two features are essential attributes of the concept. She invites students to describe their thinking during the analysis of the data as a way of reconfirming the critical attributes. The teacher and students discuss the purpose of distinguishing natural from human resources, and begin their study of Canada's natural wealth.

---

students in discussing what they saw and heard. After listing the items on the chalkboard, the teacher invites students to look for ways of grouping the items (for example, "What things belong together?"). Students might arrange items by identifying common properties (such as clustering houses, apartments, and townhouses into one category, and grocery stores, clothes stores, and hardware stores into another). The teacher might prompt students with questions such as:

- How are these categories different from or similar to …?
- What does this tell us about …?
- Why do you think this would happen …?

Each group would be asked to explain its rationale for the classification system. Drawing attention to the

different ways in which students classify is an important purpose of the activity. At some point the teacher should ask students to assign labels or names to grouped items (for example, "living places," "shopping places," "office places," "fun places").

In another class on communities, the teacher might provide students with sets of photographs of various types of communities (such as urban, suburban, and rural). Working in groups, students could sort the photographs into categories and distinguish among the categories. Students could then explore the differences and similarities, and perhaps also the advantages and disadvantages, of living in urban, suburban, or rural communities.

Concept formation provides students with an opportunity to explore ideas by making connections and seeing relationships between items. This method can help students develop and refine their ability to recall

TABLE 8.4   A CONTINUUM OF LEARNING EXPERIENCES FROM REAL TO ABSTRACT

	REAL EVENTS AND ACTUAL OBJECTS	PHYSICAL REPRESENTATIONS AND ROLE PLAYS	VISUAL REPRESENTATIONS	VERBAL REPRESENTATIONS
Sources	On-location sites and actions; genuine artifacts	Toys or replicas; simulations	Photographs, drawings, and picture books	Stories and words
Samples of teaching the concepts "hill" and "co-operation"	• during a field trip, climb a hill • take part in classroom activities where students are allowed to work together and where they must work alone	• make a papier mâché model containing hills, mountains, and valleys • role-play situations where students are co-operative and where they are not	• examine photographs of hills and mountains • look at pictures depicting people both co-operating with each other and not co-operating	• read a story involving someone who lives atop a hill • read stories and discuss situations where students are co-operative and where they are not

and discriminate among key ideas, to see commonalities and identify relationships, to formulate concepts and generalizations, to explain how they have organized data, and to present evidence to support the way in which they have organized the data.

CHOOSING AMONG THE APPROACHES

A decision about which of the three approaches to use depends partly on the nature of the concept to be taught. Concept recognition and concept attainment are best used with concepts that have clearly defined attributes. Most concrete concepts such as "island" have one clear set of attributes that define examples (that is, either it is completely surrounded by water or it is not). Many concepts in social studies are of this type (for example, democracy, primary source, secondary industry, hypothesis, fact, assimilation), as are most concrete concepts found in geography and economics. Other concepts are "relational"—best defined when compared to other concepts (for example, an aluminum can might be considered as waste when thrown out as garbage but would not be if it were recycled). Examples of this class of concept include "strong," "deep," "opposite," and "pollution." Relational concepts can also be taught using concept recognition or concept attainment when the pairs represent examples at opposing ends of a continuum (such as comparing the size of a needle to that of an elephant). If a concept has an "or" in its definition, it likely has two or more sets of alternative attributes (for example, a citizen can be either a native-born or a naturalized member of a state). Such concepts as "symbolism," "equality," "justice," "controversial," and many abstract concepts in history are of this kind. Concept formation may work best with such concepts. Table 8.4 contains examples of concept teaching using a continuum of real to abstract sources and activities.

OTHER STRATEGIES

Although the use of example/non-example pairs is the most powerful means to help students understand concepts, other strategies are potentially useful complementary strategies. These strategies include the following.

• **Provide an opportunity to "experience" the concept**. Whether it is concrete or abstract, it is important for students to "experience" a concept. The need for tangible first-hand experience is especially acute with primary students (Seefeldt 2005, 197). With concrete concepts, these experiences may be provided by using actual physical objects or pictures, rather than merely referring to examples. In the case of abstract concepts, it is often more difficult, but even more necessary, to provide students with opportunities to "experience" key attributes of the concept. In teaching about "co-operation," for example, we might involve students in simulated situations where they work at odds with each other's goals, side by side in parallel, and in interdependent ways. It may be useful to examine Table 8.4, which represents a continuum from real to abstract. Where feasible, start as far as possible to the left of the chart in providing students with opportunities to experience a concept.

• **Provide or generate a definition**. Although on their own definitions do not capture all the attributes of a concept, providing or having students create a definition (especially if they have explored examples and non-examples) contributes to their conceptual understanding.

TABLE 8.5 OTHER STRATEGIES

TEACHING IDEAS	"RULES"
Experiential introduction	• Play a "rotten rules" game. Without any introduction, throw an inflated balloon into the class. Students will automatically react by batting the balloon back and forth. As students do this, assign points on the blackboard and draw students' attention to this by verbalizing the process: I am giving Suzy one point for hitting the balloon the highest. I am giving Joshua a point for hitting it quietly. Points can be given for highest, lowest, sex, colour of hair, or type of clothing of the hitter, and so on. Be inconsistent in scoring; take off a point for the same action or characteristic for which a student earlier received a point. Students will react with frustration and will try to figure out the basis for assigning points. End the game when the frustration level gets high. Discuss the following questions: • When the game began, what did you think you had to do? • Did you ever figure out the rules for the game? • How did you feel when you realized you didn't know what was going on? • Did anyone enjoy playing this game? Why or why not? • What were the rules? • How could we improve this game if we played it again? • How many would like to play the game again under the new conditions? • Are there times in real life when rules are needed or when rules that exist seem unfair?
Definition	• a principle or regulation governing conduct
Etymology	• "regula," meaning a straight stick, pattern
Derivative words	• to rule—to control, guide, direct, or govern • a ruler (straight edge)—a device for guiding the drawing of lines • unruly—uncontrolled • a (court) ruling—a decision as to what is to be done in a particular case
Synonyms or antonyms	• laws and regulations

- **Explore the etymology of the word that represents the concept.** Etymology explores the linguistic origins of a word and its formation and development through time. Sometimes a word's origins provide a clue identifying an essential attribute of the concept. For example, the origin of the concept word "rule" is the Latin word that refers to a straight stick.
- **Compare derivative words.** Derivative words are words that come from the same stem as the concept under investigation. It is interesting, for example, to compare the notion of a ruler (that is, a straight edge) with the concept of a rule. A ruler is a physical device for guiding the making of lines, whereas a rule is a verbal device for guiding our actions.
- **Examine synonyms and antonyms.** Often synonyms and antonyms are helpful because students may be more familiar with these other words and their understanding of the concept under investigation can be reinforced.

Table 8.5 summarizes the strategies mentioned above and their specific applications to the teaching of the concept of "rules." All five strategies would rarely be used at any one time.

Assessing Conceptual Understanding

Numerous strategies can be used to assess how well students have understood a concept.

- **Recognize instances of the concept.** Provide students with original examples and non-examples and ask whether they are instances of the concept. Are the following examples of rules?
  - No one is allowed to use my radio without my permission.
  - Every sentence must end with a period, a question mark, or an exclamation point.
  - Many people vote in federal elections.
  - I don't like it when people run in the school hallway.
- **Generate examples.** Ask students to provide their own original examples of the concept:
  - Give two examples of a family rule or a school rule.
  - List two problems that you sometimes encounter at school.
- **Explain specific attributes.** Ask students to address questions about specific attributes:

- Do all rules forbid action and are all rules written down?
- Give an example of a rule that prohibits and a rule that enables.

- **Distinguish similar concepts**. Ask students to distinguish non-examples from examples:
  - Explain in your own words the difference between a request and a rule. Give examples of each.
  - Explain in your own words the difference between a problem and a question. Give an example of each.

- **Apply the concept**. Ask students to apply the concept in an assignment:
  - Create a set of class rules to guide how we should treat each other in class.
  - What problems did the character in the story we have just read face? Which of these was the most difficult?

Identify an abstract concept that is not discussed in this chapter but that is central to social studies at a particular grade level. Identify at least three important attributes and develop a set of between six and eight paired examples/non-examples that you might use in a concept recognition or concept attainment lesson to teach these attributes.

Conclusion

The focus of this chapter is on teaching concepts in ways that foster understanding. We have argued that conceptual knowledge is not a matter of transmitting bits of vocabulary to students. Rote acquisition of definitions is not worthwhile—students can't use the concepts and they will have difficulty making sense of any factual information that relies on these concepts. In promoting conceptual understanding, we have emphasized the importance of identifying key attributes for selected concepts and teaching these largely through the use of examples and non-examples. Providing opportunities to "experience" concepts is also valuable, especially for younger students. Our goal should be to teach important concepts using strategies powerful enough to make them meaningful, memorable, and usable.

ENDNOTE

1   Mind maps and other visual tools such as Venn diagrams can be used to help students explore concepts and for teachers to assess student understanding. For ideas and resources on using visual tools such as mind maps, concept maps, and other graphic organizers, see Bennett and Rolheiser (2001) and McEwan and Myers (2002).

REFERENCES

Abbott, M., R. Case, and J. Nicol. 2003. *I can make a difference.* Richmond, BC: The Critical Thinking Consortium.

Bennett, B. and C. Rolheiser. 2001. *Beyond Monet: The artful science of instructional integration.* Toronto: Bookstation.

Bruner, J.S. 1973. *Going beyond the information given.* New York: Norton.

Bruner, J., J.J. Goodnow, and G.A. Austin. 1967. *A study of thinking.* New York: Science Editions.

Gagné, R.M. 1985. *The conditions of learning and theory of instruction,* 4th ed. New York: Holt, Rinehart & Winston.

McEwan, S. and J. Myers. 2002. Graphic organizers: Visual tools for learning. *Orbit* 32 (4). Available online at www.oise.utoronto.ca/orbit.

Parker, W. 1988. Thinking to learn concepts. *Social Studies* 79 (2), 70–73.

Parker, W. and S.A. Perez. 1987. Beyond the rattle of empty wagons. *Social Education* 51 (3), 164–166.

Seefeldt, C. 2005. *Social studies for the preschool/primary child,* 7th ed. Columbus, OH: Pearson.

Seiger-Ehrenberg, S. 2001. Concept development. In *Developing minds: A resource book for teaching thinking,* 3rd ed., ed. A.L. Costa, 437–441. Alexandria, VA: Association for Supervision and Curriculum Development.

Taba, H. 1967. *Teacher's handbook for elementary social studies.* Palo Alto, CA: Addison-Wesley.

Wiggins, G. and J. McTighe. 2005. *Understanding by design,* expanded 2nd ed. Alexandria, VA: Association for Supervision and Curriculum Development.

Wineburg, S. 2001. *Historical thinking and other unnatural acts: Charting the future of teaching the past.* Philadelphia: Temple University Press.

PART 3

Engaging in Individual and Collective Inquiry

9 Infusing a Spirit of Inquiry in Elementary Social Studies

Garfield Gini-Newman and Laura Gini-Newman

From Piaget to the present, educational research suggests that students learn best when actively engaged: arithmetic is mastered through the use of manipulatives, science through experimentation, and physical education through participation in athletics. So how do we engage students in the study of far-off lands or long-ago events? The answer, we believe, lies in critical inquiry. Teachers can engage students in learning about social studies by involving them in shaping questions that guide their study, giving them ownership over the directions of these investigations, and requiring them to analyze critically rather than merely retrieve information. In these ways, we shift classrooms from places where teachers "cover" the curriculum to places where students "uncover" the curriculum.

This uncovering of the curriculum occurs only when students investigate questions that have a clear, worthwhile purpose and present problems or challenges that they perceive as meaningful. We use the term "critical" inquiry to mean inquiry that is not essentially the retrieval of information but rather a process of reaching conclusions, making decisions, and solving problems. Of course, some students may enjoy gathering information, but all students' depth of learning and sense of engagement are greatly enhanced when tasks require them to think critically at each step of the way. The typical research-project scenario described in the featured text "Researching a Topic" illustrates this point.

If we expect students to become critical thinkers and problem solvers, then we must challenge them to solve problems and embark on personally relevant journeys

of inquiry. This outcome is unlikely if students are fed mounds of information with little opportunity to pose their own questions or to thoughtfully re-examine their emerging conclusions. Even well-planned, interesting, and colourful lessons can fail to involve students in thinking meaningfully about the ideas. Active involvement requires that students digest and make personal sense of the ideas, not simply listen and recite or read and record.

Optimal Conditions for Engaged Inquiry

For deep learning to occur, teachers must pay attention to students' engagement and the factors that contribute to or undermine a desire to learn. Extending the work of Mihaly Csikszentmihalyi (1990) to an educational context, Shernoff (2002) suggests that student engagement combines three facets of flow experiences: concentration on a specific problem or challenge, interest in the topic, and enjoyment of the activity. When we manage to create a state of flow for students while they are learning, they experience a sense of personal discovery and higher performance. Building a desire to learn is an important reason for encouraging critical inquiry (McGaugh 2003).

Linking social studies to issues meaningful to students is crucial if we expect to engage them (McMahon and Portelli 2004; Armstrong and McMahon 2002). Where there is no engagement, students do not pay attention and consequently are

FIGURE 9.1   MAXIMIZING STUDENT ENGAGEMENT

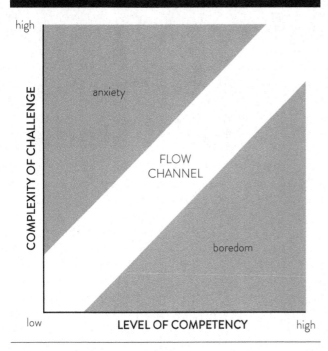

Students in grade 2 are asked to select any topic they wish, provided it deals with animals, and to prepare a short presentation supported by a display board summarizing their research. Samantha chooses cats. On the day of the presentation, she relays to her classmates the information she has found. Soon her classmates begin to ask questions. "Do you have a cat?" asks one student. "No," replies Samantha. "Do you want to have a cat?" asks another classmate. "No," replies Samantha. "Do you like cats?" asks another. "No!" Samantha exclaims, becoming somewhat frustrated by the questions. "Why is there a dog on your display?" comes a final question. "Let's move on to the next presentation," the teacher interjects.

What went wrong with this task? The absence of purposeful inquiry made Samantha select a topic and prepare a report without needing to think critically about the choices she was making or the significance of the information she was gathering. Had she been supported in asking a more purposeful question and processing the information critically, she might have selected a topic of genuine interest to her that would have led her to think more deeply about her findings. Samantha could have been asked, for example, to consider what kind of pet would make the best addition to her family. She then could have generated criteria for a suitable choice, including personal preference, cost to purchase and maintain, amount of care needed, habitat requirements, and diet. Using these criteria, she might then have researched several animals before making her choice. What's more, she would need to reach a conclusion and explain her thinking. Clearly, in this scenario Samantha would have been more involved, cognitively and emotionally, in her inquiry.

The Dynamics of Critical Inquiry

Critical inquiry is an attempt to infuse a spirit of exploration throughout the curriculum. At its heart is a provocative question or challenge that arises out of the interplay of asking, investigating, reflecting, creating, and sharing. With these multiple entry points, teachers are better able to tailor instruction to meet the varied needs of their learners. For example, students may respond to a challenge first by reflecting on what they know, sharing initial thoughts and ideas with peers, and then carrying out an investigation. Others may choose to investigate, share their preliminary findings, reflect on what they know and do not know, and then return to further investigation. Similarly, once students have completed their investigation, opportunities to share and reflect are integral parts of any creative process. Figure 9.2 outlines the dynamic nature of critical inquiry.

unlikely to learn. Engagement is more likely when our curriculum is built around meaningful questions (including ones formulated by students themselves), stimulating challenges, and relevant projects. In a classroom of critical inquiry, unsolved problems, intriguing mysteries, and purposeful questions are used to excite students to learn.

While recognizing the need to challenge students, teachers also need to scaffold learning for student success. Csikszentmihalyi (1990) offers three conditions for optimizing flow: a challenge that is clear and allows for goal-directed learning; student confidence that their skills are adequate to cope with the challenge; and frequent and timely feedback on how students are performing throughout their learning. Failure to provide the necessary scaffolding and to adequately challenge students can have equally detrimental effects on students' learning, either by creating anxiety in students who find the work too demanding or boring those who find it too easy. Ideally, we want to provide all students with moderate to high challenges in a safe environment that provides the necessary scaffolds to learning. Figure 9.1 illustrates the positive impact on engagement when the complexity of challenges presented to students is increased along with an increase in student competency with the intellectual tools.

FIGURE 9.2   DYNAMIC ELEMENTS OF CRITICAL INQUIRY

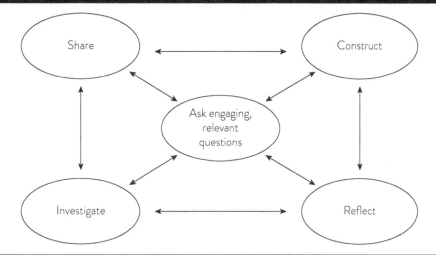

Ask: Inquiry begins with meaningful questions that are connected to the world around us, build on prior knowledge, and excite curiosity.

Construct: The invitation to build on existing ideas and knowledge to construct new conclusions and understandings is a key step in inquiry. This may lead to a product or other representation of learning or may result in the coalescence of ideas leading to the generation of additional thoughts, theories, and lines of inquiry.

Reflect: Reflection on the path taken and the conclusions formed is an integral part of the dynamics of inquiry as it assists in the consolidation of learning. Reflection may lead to revisions in the investigation, affirm conclusions, or open new lines of inquiry.

Investigate: Investigation puts curiosity into action. As they gather information, students are likely to refine or redirect their questions, clarify ideas, and begin to make connections.

Share: Sharing with others the product of their journey of inquiry allows students to refine their ideas and reflect on how they arrived at this point.

Asking Questions

As suggested by the scenario described in the featured text "Researching a Topic," students are too often detached from their research projects, a situation which usually guarantees that learning will be limited and of little lasting value. Framing effective inquiry questions is an important first step in any research.

Building on prior knowledge and asking questions of broad significance are vital to the success of social studies curricula. Students are more likely to become engaged if they are working from a question of more universal than particular importance. Also, the open-ended nature of the questions asked is crucial to the success of an inquiry-based classroom. Questions that send students to textbooks and other sources seeking the "correct answer" or which encourage them merely to prepare lists for their response do little to develop critical thinking or create genuine interest in social studies. Consider, for example, this question: "What are some of the advantages and opportunities of living in a small town?" The question requires students to locate information and prepare a list. When revised to read "Considering the interests and needs of each member

of your assigned immigrant family, would moving to a small town be a good idea for them?", this is a more thought-provoking question and addresses the reality that some destinations may be more suitable for individuals and families than others.

INQUIRY QUESTIONS AS UNIT ORGANIZERS

A powerful and engaging method of curriculum development is to build the entire year around provocative questions that challenge students to explore and apply their learning. When a course has a central inquiry question at its heart, it assists students in looking for the "big ideas" or the "enduring understandings," to use the term of Grant Wiggins and Jay McTighe (2005). Overarching questions reduce the likelihood of students bogging down in the details of history and geography. A provocative inquiry question provides them with a central reference point to reflect on as the year unfolds. Such central questions serve as excellent summative assessment questions. For example, a central question such as "Is Canada a country we can be proud of?" provides a focus for learning about the history of the country. Around this central question, more specific

SAMPLE "BIG" INQUIRY QUESTIONS IN ELEMENTARY SOCIAL STUDIES

Family and Community Traditions

- What information would most help a newcomer understand the different family traditions—past and present—in our community and across Canada?

Rules and Responsibilities

- What are the three most important rules you must follow each day, at home, at school, and in your community? How might your day change if there were no rules and no one had any responsibilities?
- What are the biggest differences between the rules and responsibilities in your life and those that your parents, grandparents, or teachers had to follow?

Early Societies

- In some areas such as Egypt, China, and India, early civilizations developed along river valleys. In other areas such as Mexico, Chile, and Japan, they did not. How important was the role of geography in shaping early civilizations?
- How should we measure the greatness of past civilizations? Which of the early civilizations did the best job at meeting the needs of the people who lived in it?
- When people of the future study us they will learn that tall office buildings and huge stadiums were built in most cities. When we study the early societies we see that pyramids, great walls, cathedrals and castles were often the most important structures. What can we learn about a society by the buildings they built?

New France

- For whom did the change in regime matter the most following the transition from French to British rule in Quebec?

critical inquiry ones addressing particular aspects of the curriculum might be framed:

- Does Canada offer a welcoming home to newcomers from around the world?
- Have Canada's aboriginal people been treated with dignity and respect?
- Is Canada a model of responsible environmental stewardship?
- Is Canada a model of international co-operation and leadership?
- Have scientific and technology developments in Canada improved the lives of all Canadians?

EFFECTIVE QUESTIONS FOR CRITICAL INQUIRY

Not all questions are created equal. As illustrated in Table 9.1, care must be taken to distinguish between questions of factual recall, questions of preference, and questions of critical inquiry. While each has value when used correctly, inappropriate use can become a barrier in meeting the intended learning objectives. If critical thinking is considered an integral part of a social studies program, then questions of critical inquiry are vital to the program's success.

Factual recall questions that have a single correct answer or a limited range of responses are useful as checks for understanding. When the purpose is to assess students' comprehension of key facts and processes, narrowly focussed questions are useful; but if the purpose of posing a question is to prompt student thinking, then open-ended questions of critical inquiry are necessary. Critical inquiry questions require thoughtful consideration of evidence gathered against a set of criteria. Although answers will often vary, a question such as "What is your favourite flavour of ice cream?" is not an inquiry question but rather one of preference. A question such as this does not build on human curiosity; it does not require investigation, the convergence of new learning with prior understandings, or the application of criteria. (For more about framing questions that invite critical thinking, see chapter 7, "Getting Beyond Inert Facts in Elementary Social Studies.")

SUPPORTING STUDENTS IN ASKING QUESTIONS

Equally important to the quality of questions posed by teachers is the students' own ability to ask powerful questions. In genuine critical inquiry, provocative questions, which form the basis of the inquiry, should come from students as well as the teacher. Yet all too often, students are unaccustomed to or ill equipped for asking critical questions. Beginning in the primary grades, students are presented with research projects that often follow a similar process: students select a research topic, reflect on what they already know about the topic, consider what more they would like to know about it, and, following their research, summarize what they have learned. The intent of this type of exercise is commendable, though it often has a glaring flaw: rarely are students taught how to frame meaningful critical inquiry questions. As a result, their questions are

| TABLE 9.1 | THREE TYPES OF QUESTIONS |

FACTUAL RETRIEVAL	PERSONAL PREFERENCE	CRITICAL INQUIRY
Ask students to locate information.	Ask students to express a personal opinion or preference.	Ask students to reach a conclusion or solve a problem.
• Answers are often "right there." • Answers have a single correct answer. • Useful in assessing comprehension of key facts.	• Answers are not grounded in careful reasoning, but invite an emotional or "gut" response. • There are no wrong answers; it depends entirely on how each person feels towards the topic.	• Answers require thoughtful consideration of evidence in light of a set of relevant factors or criteria. • Typically open-ended and there are often several reasonable answers.

typically limited to factual retrieval. Consequently, there is often little purpose to their research and no expectation that students will draw conclusions, merely that they will gather information.

If students are to become effective critical thinkers, they must learn to ask as well as respond to powerful questions. Throughout the school year, teachers should encourage students to ask critical inquiry questions on important issues, including events in the news and issues related to their school and community. Explicit teaching of the three types of questions, accompanied by opportunities to practise answering them, are vital if students are to move from questions of factual recall to critical inquiry questions. Teachers may wish to consider beginning a unit with factual recall questions and invite students to work in small groups to tweak the questions into critical inquiry questions. For example, students might move from considering "What three challenges did aboriginal peoples encounter during this period?" (factual retrieval) to "What was the most significant challenge that aboriginal peoples encountered during this period?" (critical inquiry). Students could also review questions from a chapter in their textbook and group the questions into the three types, then suggest rewording of several of the factual recall questions so that they become questions of critical inquiry. Activities such as these support students in learning to frame effective questions while deepening their understanding of the subject matter and developing their capacity for critical thinking.

Throughout the process, teachers should encourage students to sustain their focus on critical inquiry by continuous self-monitoring and reflection on the quality and relevance of their questions. This helps to create self-directed, self-motivated students because their research empowers their thinking, leading to the creation of new knowledge rather than merely inviting regurgitation and organization of a body of information culled from other sources.

Assemble a list of five research questions or topics (either think of ones you have completed, look in a teacher resource, or ask students to suggest examples). Critique their effectiveness in light of the criteria discussed in this chapter (are open-ended, have broad significance, require thoughtful consideration). Keeping the same general topics, reframe each of these research projects into a more engaging critical inquiry.

Reflecting on Ideas and Strategies

Metacognition is a vital part of learning. Throughout an inquiry, students should be encouraged to take time to reflect on how the new information they uncover either challenges or affirms their beliefs, and to consider the validity of their conclusions in light of the evidence. Also important is self-reflection about the choices students make in conducting their research. Careful reflection occurs as students consider the nature of the questions they pose, assess the sources they are using, generate the criteria for guiding their decision-making or judgments, weigh the evidence gathered in light of these criteria, consider the process by which they arrived at their conclusions and the validity of their conclusions, and finally, consider how purpose and audience will inform the presentation of their conclusions.

Earlier we saw how provocative questions can be an effective means to frame a unit of study. These same questions can be used at the beginning of a unit to prompt student reflection on their prior knowledge and beliefs. Posing questions as an anticipation guide (see Figure 9.3 for an example) can be useful for raising important questions and garnering a sense of students' prior knowledge and attitudes before delving into a unit of study. Anticipation guides are generally used as a literacy strategy to prepare students to read a piece of text. Adapted, they become an excellent framework for a unit and a diagnostic activity. After responding to the anticipation guide questions, the teacher might debrief with students and explain that these are the essential questions for the unit. In fact, the questions can became focus questions for individual lessons and serve as the basis for an end-of-unit assessment.

Investigating Topics

Being engaged by provocative questions primes the pump for learning, but providing support to meet students' varying needs is vital if all students are to experience success. Before setting students free to conduct research, teachers need to lay some foundations, such as graphic organizers, which can help students structure and make sense of the information they uncover in their investigations.

A teacher presentation road map can be a useful tool to help students learn from short lectures. Essentially, the road map "chunks" the teacher's presentation into meaningful pieces much like the outlines that are often put on the board before a talk begins. When using a road map, encourage students to record three or four key points in each box. Remembering that students can only pay attention for 10 to 15 minutes before needing to process what they have taken in, teachers should employ a think/pair/share strategy after addressing a couple of points on their presentation road map. This allows students to review what they have heard, share and support one another, and consolidate their learning by explaining their notes to their peers.

Another strategy to support students is collaborative note-taking (see Figure 9.4). Collaborative note-taking encourages students to make point-form notes from a reading or during a presentation and then exchange notes with a peer. Each student reviews a fellow student's notes, adds information that was missed, and asks reflective questions. Afterwards, students

---

FIGURE 9.3   ANTICIPATION GUIDE

CIRCLE THE ANSWER THAT BEST DESCRIBES YOUR OPINION.

1. Considering the causes of the War of 1812, it is difficult to assign blame to one country.

| Strongly agree | Agree | Don't know | Disagree | Strongly disagree |

My explanation:

2. There were several heroic figures in the War of 1812.

| Strongly agree | Agree | Don't know | Disagree | Strongly disagree |

My explanation:

3. The outcome of the war was determined by several key battles.

| Strongly agree | Agree | Don't know | Disagree | Strongly disagree |

My explanation:

4. Considering the causes and outcome of the War of 1812, Canada was the winner of the war.

| Strongly agree | Agree | Don't know | Disagree | Strongly disagree |

My explanation:

FIGURE 9.4 COLLABORATIVE NOTE-TAKING

Reflective questions:

My point-form notes on key facts, terms, ideas, and concepts:

-

-

Reflective questions:

-

-

-

Reflective questions:

-

-

-

Fellow students' additional notes:

-

-

-

-

-

-

-

-

-

Connections with other topics or the contemporary world:

FIGURE 9.5 COMPARING THE ROLE OF WOMEN IN ANCIENT EGYPT AND CONTEMPORARY CANADA

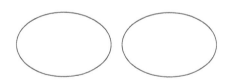 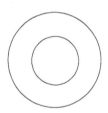 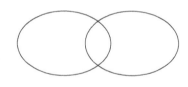

This graphic suggests that the role women played in the two societies was completely different and that there was no overlap or continuity.

This graphic suggests that the role of women expanded from ancient times (centre) so that by the present day in Canada, women were continuing to fulfill all the roles they had in ancient Egypt and had added several more roles.

This graphic suggests that while there were some roles they played in both societies, there were also roles unique to each society.

jointly discuss and make notes on how the noted information connects with their world or with the central question(s) of the unit.

Students most often encounter Euler diagrams in mathematics classes. But consider their power when they are used to invite students to draw conclusions about the relationships among people, places, and things. For example, students might be asked to determine which of the Euler diagrams in Figure 9.5 best represents the relationship between the role of women in ancient Egypt and in contemporary Canadian society. In responding to this question, students would search a variety of sources, including textbooks and websites, in order to locate words, phrases, or visuals that they can place within each circle to support their conclusion. It would be helpful for students to explain their conclusions in small groups and to adjust their findings based on the discussion.

Students need to search broadly for evidence and to consider multiple perspectives. To do this, they should consult a variety of sources to gather as many views as possible. They should be encouraged to gather information from various textual and non-textual sources (books and magazines, electronic sources, field visits to museums and other sites, visuals, interviews). They need to be taught how to read various text forms including a wide range of primary source material. Teachers should explicitly teach students how to read and decode visual text forms such as cartoons, artworks, and maps. (See other chapters in this volume for strategies on promoting these forms of information literacy.)

Sharing of Ideas

The opportunity to seek assistance, receive feedback, and hear responses from peers, parents, and teachers is a vital part of critical inquiry. As the previous examples suggest, graphic representations of ideas and conclusions are excellent vehicles that enable students to share their thoughts and conclusions prior to completing a summative task. Similarly, various forms of in-class debate and discussion, such as the "Academic Controversy" strategy described in the featured text, provide a forum for the exchange of ideas that, when combined with reflection, extend student learning and challenge students' thinking. Infusing opportunities to share through inquiry provides students with feedback that will enrich their understanding of the curriculum.

Think back to a research project you were asked to undertake in social studies. Using ideas discussed in the five elements of critical inquiry (ask, construct, reflect, investigate, and share) suggest revisions to your original research project that would make it more personally engaging and educationally worthwhile.

Constructing New Understanding

The model of critical inquiry we propose is grounded in a constructivist learning theory that assumes learners are not blank slates onto which information is etched through didactic forms of instruction. Rather, we believe that learners construct new knowledge through the continuous integration of past experiences with new information and interactions with their environment. It is important that this view of constructivist learning not be confused with constructivist pedagogy that

ACADEMIC CONTROVERSY

Academic controversy is a strategy created by David and Roger Johnson (described in Bennett and Rolheiser 2008) that establishes small co-operative groups of four to six students to explore both sides of a designated issue. Each group is divided into A and B teams. The controversy is then identified in the positive (for example, "Canada should work with the United States to provide direct and indirect military aid to eradicate terrorism"). The A students prepare the "pro" side and the B students prepare the "con." Once students have prepared their opening arguments, each team shares its ideas with the opposing students. To encourage students to present ideas concisely, each team is allowed no more than ninety seconds. While each team presents its points, the opposing team practises active listening and takes notes. There should be no interruptions. Once both sides have presented their views, the A and B teams each gather to plan a rebuttal. In planning their rebuttal, they should consider the flaws in the opposing team's arguments. Each team has approximately sixty to ninety seconds to present its response. Once both sides have presented their rebuttal, the teams switch sides and repeat the process. The final step in the academic controversy is to hold a round robin. During the round robin, students explain where they stand on the issue individually.

posits that teachers should never directly tell students anything. Constructivist learning theory suggests that all new knowledge is constructed from previous knowledge regardless of how it was acquired.

Although the term "construct new knowledge" has come to be a commonly used phrase, it is a term too often left ill-defined. What does it mean to construct new knowledge and how has the advent of the digital revolution contributed to the advancement of constructivist learning? Constructivism is grounded in the belief that learning is a dynamic process; it is perhaps best understood when we separate information from knowledge and knowledge from wisdom. In 1934, T.S. Eliot first alluded to what would become known as the Data-Information-Knowledge-Wisdom (DIKW) hierarchy in his poem "Choruses from the Rock." Eliot wrote:

Where is the Life we have lost in living?
Where is the wisdom we have lost in knowledge?
Where is the knowledge we have lost in information?
(excerpted from T.S. Eliot, *The Rock*, 1934)

Traditional approaches to learning see knowledge as something that is acquired rather than constructed, leading to classrooms where teachers utilize textbooks, lectures, and even films to transmit information to the learners as if they are vessels to be filled. Transmissive classrooms are, by their nature, hierarchical in their structure. Students are expected to acquire knowledge from perceived experts, be they the authors of the textbook, the filmmaker, or the teacher. Sam Wineburg points out that school textbooks rarely use hedges, instead presenting information as if handed down from some omnipotent source, not to be questioned. Similarly, films shown in class are most commonly used as a vehicle to transmit content, which is then invariably gathered through the ubiquitous worksheet. Once the information has been transferred, various forms of assessment are used to see if the student has "retained" the intended information.

In a classroom of critical inquiry, learners construct new knowledge in a dynamic and iterative process, using information and interactions with others to continually deepen their understanding of important curriculum concepts that ultimately help them to better understand themselves and the world around them. In this classroom, textbooks and films become but a few of many resources to be explored and scrutinized; the information gleaned from them can be woven into our understanding of the world past and present. Teachers, rather than being transmitters of information, become important members of a community of thinkers, coaching students to actively engage with the information uncovered through the rigorous application of filters to determine the credibility of sources, the careful analysis of the information, and the innovative interpretation of facts and ideas to construct new solutions or reach new conclusions on complex issues.

The digital age is creating exciting opportunities for classrooms to become much less hierarchical and much more of a network of inquirers through which the construction of knowledge is not the mere drawing of conclusions by students but rather a complex interplay of prior learning, new learning, networked exploration involving thinking, re-thinking, and re-conceptualizing understandings as new ideas emerge. Learning becomes an active process of critical reflection, creative exploration, and collaborative meaning-making.

The comparative study of various communities in a transmissive classroom might simply ask young students to locate various sources of information about similarities and differences between people, places, or things (for example, in one community people make houses out of wood and in another they make houses out of ice), and

invite young students to reflect on the significance of the differences they notice. Students might simply record or draw the features being compared (for example, types of houses, modes of travel, health conditions). In a constructive classroom, students would be asked to use this information to draw their own conclusions, offer an assessment of the amount of difference between the compared features, and explain their thinking. After comparing individual features, students might offer an overall assessment of the degree of difference and then share their summary conclusions with the class. Or, based on their assessment of the differences, students might reach a conclusion about the relative suitability of each location as a home for a particular family or group of people.

Assessing for Thinking

Opportunities for students to create new knowledge through the fusion of prior knowledge and current learning are largely dependent on the nature of the tasks assigned by teachers. Tasks that are narrowly focussed on recall of pre-determined information preclude critical inquiry and present fewer opportunities for students to take ownership over their learning. Conversely, assessment tasks that invite students to engage in critical inquiry tend to encourage students to apply their learning in meaningful and relevant ways.

In effective classrooms, assessment drives instruction. Knowing what students are to achieve and how they will demonstrate it should be the basis on which daily instruction is planned. Differentiated assessment ensures that students with varying learning styles, interests, and aptitudes are given opportunities to demonstrate their learning. The key to differentiated assessment is establishing clear targets and not confusing methods with targets. For example, assessment targets might include student understanding of the "big ideas and concepts" being studied and the abilities to conduct research, think critically, and communicate their findings and conclusions effectively, considering purpose and audience. If these were the assessment targets (or objectives), then a variety of methods might be used to assess student learning. Students could write a report, prepare a visual essay, create a bulletin board display with relevant images and captions, or deliver an oral presentation. Encouraging students to select the best method to demonstrate their learning is yet another way to shift the focus of learning from teacher- to student-directed learning.

Assessment tasks can further student learning and

THE GREAT SAND CASTLE/SNOW SCULPTURE COMPETITION[1]

The Challenge

Throughout the ages, people have created lasting landmarks. From the Great Pyramids of Egypt to the Great Wall of China, from the soaring cathedrals of medieval Europe to the grace and perfection of the Parthenon, architecture tells us much about the people who created the buildings.

The Great Sand Castle/Snow Sculpture Competition invites you to build an accurate scale model of an ancient site at a local beach or in the snow. To prepare for the challenge, you will need to find books with pictures and information about the site and the society that constructed the architecture. You will need to look carefully at the pictures and take research notes. Once you are familiar with the structure, its purpose, and the sponsoring society, you should prepare a detailed plan including a sketch, required tools, and any extra materials needed to construct the model out of sand or snow. You are also to prepare an informative viewers' guide in the form of a brochure that provides details of the original structure and explains why this structure best represents the early civilization from which it came. Information you might include in the brochure includes:

- Who built it?
- What was its purpose?
- Where was it built?
- When was it built?
- How was it built?
- Why is it an important site?

In meeting this challenge, you will work in groups of three to complete the steps outlined below.

Each Student's Responsibilities

- Prepare a bibliography of between four and seven sources.
- Prepare two to three pages of research notes and gather four or five visuals related to the society and the structure.
- Prepare a sketch of the structure.
- Write a 250–300-word summary explaining the purpose of the structure, its method of construction, and how the structure was reflective of various aspects of the society that built it, including:
  - the influence of religion on the social and/or political structure of the society;
  - social divisions within the society; and
  - the relationship between those in positions of authority and the general population.
- Actively participate in the construction of the scale model.
- Be able to explain to observers the structure, its purpose, and its relationship to the civilization that built it.

Each Group's Responsibilities

- Establish deadlines for each of the steps relative to the date established by the teacher for the building of the structure.
- Assign responsibility to individuals for preparing the final sketch and gathering the tools and materials needed (one student) and preparing a viewer's guide (two students). Then produce a group agreement that clearly lists the agreed due dates and individual responsibilities.
- Collaboratively scan sources to select a suitable structure.
- Prepare a detailed plan for the construction of the scale model drawing using sketches and notes of group members.
- Gather necessary tools and resources in preparation for the construction of the model.
- Construct the scale model in sand or snow.

not simply measure it; when clear targets are provided from the outset and when students receive frequent feedback, they have opportunities to improve their work through revision, editing, and polishing. Throughout these tasks, students need appropriate scaffolding to ensure success and to encourage them to reflect on what they are learning (Earl 2003). At some time this may require allowing students to "fail forward." Learning from their mistakes can often provide powerful and lasting learning. But to have the confidence to fail forward, students need to know that their teacher is available to support them as needed and that failed attempts will not affect their final grade negatively. This requires that teachers embrace the concept of "assessment as learning" and provide feedback and guidance

without grading students on the process of learning. Of course, at some point, students will need to demonstrate their learning through some kind of performance, and teachers do need to grade students on performances.

The authentic assessment task described in the featured text "The Great Sand Castle/Snow Sculpture Competition," which is built around critical inquiry, challenges students to create and explain a replica of an ancient landmark.

Concluding Comments

Organizing the social studies curriculum around critical inquiry ensures a focus on key curricular ideas and concepts while allowing students to explore topics and issues of personal interest and relevance. In addition to engaging students, critical inquiry contributes to their cognitive development by challenging them to make decisions, solve problems, and draw connections. The abilities to conduct focussed research and to analyze critically are crucial life skills.

There is no question that the most efficient means to "cover" an over-built curriculum is to teach from a teacher-focussed, lectured-based approach. Teaching students the skills they need to be successful takes time. Putting the proper scaffolding in place to assist them in meeting the expectations of the curriculum requires time spent on teaching critical thinking skills. And so the age-old debate rages on. Should teachers take the time to teach effectively or make sure they cover the entire curriculum? On closer inspection, however, it is evident that this debate exists only when curriculum is viewed through the eyes of the teacher. When viewed through the eyes of the learner, can there really be any debate? Should we quickly cover curriculum knowing that little of what is taught is retained beyond the final exam, or should we develop students' ability to learn independently and to think critically about the world around them, thus preparing them for the challenges they will face for a lifetime? Perhaps we need to consider the success of our classes based on what students retain in the years to come rather than on ephemeral results of tests.

ENDNOTE

1   Details of the Great Sand Castle/Snow Sculpture Competition can be found in Newman (2001).

REFERENCES

Armstrong, D. and B. McMahon. 2002. Engaged pedagogy: Valuing the strengths of students on the margins. *Journal of Thought*, Spring.

Bennett, B. and C. Rolheiser. 2008. *Beyond Monet: The artful science of instructional integration*. Toronto: Bookation.

Csikszentmihalyi, M. 1990. *Flow: The Psychology of Optimal Experience*. New York: Harper and Row.

Earl, L. 2003. *Assessment as learning: Using classroom assessment to maximize student learning*. Los Angeles: Corwin Press.

McGaugh, J.L. 2003. *Memory and emotion*. London: Weidenfield and Nicolson.

McMahon, B. and J. Portelli. 2004. Engagement for what? Beyond popular discourses of student engagement. *Leadership and Policy in Schools* 3 (1): 59–76.

Newman, G. 2001. *Echoes from the past: Teacher's resource*. Toronto: McGraw-Hill Ryerson.

Shernoff, D.J. 2002. "Flow states and student engagement in the classroom." Wisconsin Center for Education Research, University of Wisconsin. Statement to the California State Assembly Education Committee.

Wiggins, G. and J. McTighe. 2005. *Understanding by design* (2nd ed.). Alexandria, VA: Association for Supervision and Curriculum Development.

Wineburg, Samuel S. 1991. "On the reading of historical texts: Notes on the breach between school and academy" in *American Educational Research Journal*, 28 (3): 551.

10

Supporting a Community of Critical Inquiry

Roland Case and Philip Balcaen

Critical thinking does not develop in a vacuum. Rather, we should actively develop, supplement, and test our ideas in conjunction with others. Lasting gains cannot be expected from isolated efforts, and ongoing practices and structures that reinforce thoughtful reflection must be established. As Barbara Rogoff suggests, this requires more than "piecemeal incorporation of innovative techniques into an otherwise inconsistent fabric" of traditional teaching and learning (1994, 214). This chapter discusses what is involved in supporting a community of critical thinkers in schools and classrooms.

Creating a Community Atmosphere in the Classroom

Over the past two decades it has become popular to talk about the classroom in terms of a community. This is an especially attractive metaphor to us because a community atmosphere is conducive to critical thinking. Various writers identify four aspects that define a community (Lipman 1991; Newmann 1990). A community is a group of people who:

- are committed to a common goal;
- work together to pursue the goal (i.e., they communicate and co-operate);
- agree on the general "rules and procedures" to follow; and,
- each take personal responsibility for their role in achieving the goal.

Of course, there are many kinds of classroom communities: caring communities, learning communities, and communities of inquiry. The underlying commonality is the commitment to creating a community atmosphere within the classroom. These kinds of classroom communities differ subtly in their common goal and some general procedures. For example, a "caring" community gives priority to emotional support and nurturing feelings of trust. A community of "inquiry" emphasizes the shared pursuit of knowledge through individual exploration of content. The differences are small, as the conditions that support a community of inquiry overlap extensively with those that support a caring community: students cannot learn in conditions of distrust, lack of co-operation, and disrespect.

Our conception of a community of critical thinkers has more in common with these other kinds of classroom communities than it has differences. For example, a "critical" community presupposes a deep and abiding concern for each other's feelings and ideas, and in this respect it is also a caring community.

Distinguishing "Traditional" and "Community" Classrooms

What is a community classroom? Rogoff (1994) distinguishes a classroom community from teacher-run and student-run classrooms, which she argues are opposite ends of a spectrum, whereas classrooms as communities are in a different category altogether. Studies suggest that traditional teacher-directed classes do not

TABLE 10.1 TEACHER- AND STUDENT-RUN CLASSROOMS

	TEACHER-RUN CLASSROOM	STUDENT-RUN CLASSROOM
Decision-making	teacher initiates and dictates; students react and comply	students initiate and decide for themselves; teacher responds and permits
Principles of teaching and learning	teacher transmits knowledge and practices; students absorb and adopt	students construct their own understandings and ways of doing things; teacher encourages but does not "interfere" in student learning
Teaching practices	teacher-directed instruction (for example, show and tell, repetition, drill and correction)	student-directed learning (for example, self-discovery, unaided exploration, hit and miss)
Dominant values	compliance and replication	permissiveness and individual expression

create an atmosphere conducive to student thoughtfulness (e.g., Newmann 1991, 330). Goodlad's study of more than a thousand schools in the United States found that in many schools the rhetoric of promoting creativity, individual flexibility, and independent thinking was strikingly different from the reality of practice: "From the beginning, students experience school and classroom environments that condition them in precisely opposite behaviours—seeking 'right' answers, conforming, and reproducing the known." (2004, 291).

Many educators think that the alternative to a teacher-run classroom is a student-run classroom. Rogoff argues that neither teacher-run nor student-run classrooms support thinking as well as a classroom community. This comment is potentially confusing because a classroom community is often referred to as a student-centred classroom. To clarify, we will distinguish teacher- and student-run classrooms, and then contrast these with community classrooms. The key differences between teacher- and student-run classrooms are summarized in Table 10.1.

Rogoff suggests that on the spectrum of teacher- and student-run classrooms, any decrease in teacher control directly increases student control. In the area of decision-making in the extreme teacher-run class, the teacher makes all the rules, determines what is studied, sets the schedule for the class, and so on. The student's role is passive: merely to comply with the teacher's dictates. The dominant values of the teacher-run classroom are control and student replication. The nineteenth-century American educator William Torrey Harris put it this way: "The first requisite of the school is order: each pupil must be taught to conform his behaviour to a general standard, just like the running of the trains" (cited in Barell 1991, 29).

Conversely, in a student-run classroom, in order not to inhibit students' creativity and initiative, teachers

assume a laissez-faire or hands-off approach. In the most extreme version of a student-run classroom, individual students are left to decide for themselves what to study, when, and how. While teaching and learning in a teacher-run classroom is largely through direct instruction in the accepted beliefs and ways of proceeding, there is no direct instruction in the student-run classroom, no telling, no "right or wrong" answer, and no correct way of doing anything (Richardson 2003). The teacher's role is largely to encourage students as they individually make their own sense of the material. The dominant values of a student-run classroom are a permissive atmosphere and the free expression of ideas and actions. Student-run classrooms have never operated extensively, although there was a "free" schools movement in the 1960s and 1970s.

Clearly, a completely teacher-run class and a completely student-run class are extremes. Rogoff points out that a middle ground between these poles—the classroom that is partly teacher-run and partly student-run—could be interpreted as a classroom in which the teacher initiates, directs, and controls some of the time and the students control at other times. When it is the teacher's turn to control, students are expected to comply, and conversely when it is the students' turn to control, the teacher stands back and permits. When the topic demands a right way or a correct answer, the teacher transmits the knowledge and students receive it; when no correct answer is expected, students freely discover and conclude for themselves.

THE CLASSROOM AS COMMUNITY

Rogoff invites us to see the classroom as community as an alternative to any position on the teacher/student-run continuum. A classroom community is not a matter of deciding whether the teacher or the student is "in charge." Rather it requires collaborative participation

TABLE 10.2 CLASSROOM AS COMMUNITY	
Decision-making	teacher and students negotiate mutually acceptable decisions within established parameters
Principles of teaching and learning	teacher orients, mentors, and monitors while students engage rigorously with the subject matter in concert with others
Teaching practices	teacher teaches the "tools" to enable students to reach thoughtful responses to structured but open-ended tasks
Dominant values	norm-guided participation and collaboration

and decision-making—a community effort—involving differentiated roles and responsibilities. The principles of a classroom as community are summarized in Table 10.2.

To illustrate what a classroom community might look like in practice, we will examine two case studies, first Roland's and later Philip's attempts to create communities within their university-level courses. As you read about Roland's attempt to create a community of thinkers in his methods course, try to identify the features of a classroom community.

Decision-making in a community is not an either/or proposition, but rather a shared responsibility. Notice that Roland and the students negotiated the course contents. Similarly, the regular implementation of ideas emerging from the weekly circles signalled to the students that their voices were being heard. According to some researchers, students' sense of influencing their learning, as opposed to relying exclusively on a teacher to direct them, is a significant factor in encouraging students to think for themselves (Barell 1991, 71; Resnick 1989, 9). In a classroom as community, teaching and learning are collaborative—the teacher does not tell students what to think, and, conversely, students are not free to think whatever they happen to feel like. The teacher's role is to frame the tasks, actively mentor students, and support students in developing the tools they need in order to reach thoughtful conclusions.

For their part, students must work within the negotiated structures and shared norms as they engage seriously with the subject matter. Norm-guided participation and collaboration among all community members are the dominant values.

This picture of a classroom as a community may sound idealistic. How can such an environment be nurtured in a classroom? There are two aspects of teaching practice to be considered: scrutinizing our existing practices to ensure they match our goals, and introducing specific strategies to support a community of critical thinkers.

Examining Existing Practices

The need to look closely at our current practice arises because we may be missing out on opportunities to support critical thinking, or worse, we may be undermining thinking. A particularly important dimension of classroom climate is what is loosely called the "hidden curriculum," the largely unintentional, mixed messages our students get in our classrooms. These messages often have greater effect on student learning than our deliberate efforts. Studies of various educational programs designed to promote respect for others confirm this effect (Daniels and Case 1992). For the most part, specific programs and activities intended to increase respect for others had marginal impact. What affected students was the climate within the classroom: whether or not teachers provided a safe forum for student dialogue, solicited and valued student opinions, and otherwise acted in ways that modelled respect for the feelings and ideas of others.

Even a commonplace activity such as "teacher talk" may have an unintended message for students. For example, studies of the factors that influence students' willingness to contribute to class discussions suggest that teachers commonly monopolize the talk. Not only does this reduce opportunities for students to contribute, it creates the impression that student opinions don't really matter (Hess 2004, 152). One study found that 80 per cent of students would talk less in class if they felt their opinions weren't valued.

Consider the effects of the hidden curriculum in the context of the traditional classroom debate. The objective for each team in this activity is to prove that the other side is without merit by refuting, belittling, or ignoring opposing arguments. There is a tacit prohibition against changing one's mind partway through the debate. Increasingly, teachers are replacing this adversarial format with more open-ended discussions in which students are encouraged to see the merits of all sides and to recast binary options as polar positions

ROLAND'S ATTEMPT TO CREATE A COMMUNITY OF THINKERS

After years of talking about the factors that promote student thoughtfulness in the classroom, I decided to "walk the talk" and try to develop a community of thinkers in my pre-service social studies course. Typically, my routine is to begin the first class with a talk about my expectations for the course, and a detailed handout outlining the topics, required readings, and the assignments—including their length, format, and due date. With the goal of creating a critical community, I instead invited students to help design the course contents.

We began by sharing our most memorable (both positive and negative) experiences as students in elementary and secondary social studies, first in small groups and then as a class. Students then examined two documents—the provincial curriculum and a recent Ministry of Education report on the state of social studies teaching. Students were to identify key elements of effective social studies teaching and the key challenges for prospective teachers. Finally, I offered my own critique of the "good, the bad, and the ugly" of social studies.

Working in groups, students identified what they would need to master if they were to teach the curriculum successfully, based on their personal experiences, the published documents, and my observations. In other words, they collaborated to define a common goal. They also made general suggestions about the activities, readings, assignments, and resources that would help them to achieve the goal. They had agreed upon a common procedure.

We compiled a list of these objectives and strategies and I returned the following week with a proposed outline of our course of study. I warned that some of their suggestions might not be feasible given my limitations, the constraints we faced, and university policy (for example, I had to assign grades). I indicated that I might add a few topics of my own that past experience had taught me were valuable for beginning teachers, but I would provide a rationale for these additions.

Only minimal additional preparations were necessary to carry out the collective plan, since the topics and activities students identified were remarkably similar to those that I usually include. The common goals were partly directed by me, because my course had always been focussed on trying to address the very questions I put to them. I also provided the documents and commentary that oriented their thinking.

I implemented various other strategies to create a critical community. Three of these were especially significant:

- **Avoiding "what should I do?" questions.** During the second class, we discussed and affirmed that my proposed course outline captured the spirit and many of the specifics of the students' recommendations. I then suggested that there were two kinds of questions that students could ask of teachers: "Tell me what to do and say" and "Help me advance my thinking and actions." I announced that for the first three weeks of class students were allowed to ask either kind of question, but that after that date, I would respond only to "Help me advance my thinking" questions. I offered examples of the first kind of question that students might pose if they wanted more information about the first assignment for the course (for example, How long does it have to be? Must it be typed? Should we offer our own opinion? What kind of answer are you looking for? Do we have to cite our sources?).

  We then practised reframing questions so they assisted students in furthering their own thinking rather than dictated what they should do. Initially, several students offered more specific restatements of the "tell me what to do" kind of question (for example, Can it be less than five pages? Is it okay if I don't type it?). The class grew silent as they realized they were hard pressed to frame these questions differently. I offered an example: "I see the first assignment is worth 10 per cent of the final grade, has two parts, and is largely a personal reflection. I write concisely and think I can do a competent job in three pages. Does this seem reasonable to you?"

  We practised reframing other questions and the first attempts were of limited success. My typical response to these partial successes was, "What do you think?" and then, "Why do you think that?" This promoted student thinking so they could eventually frame the second kind of question. More often than not, students actually worked out their own thoughtful answer during the process.

- **Group discussion to build community.** Every three-hour class, we arranged our chairs in a circle and spent thirty minutes discussing emergent concerns, news and updates, and listening to students present on an assigned mini-topic. My role was to moderate the conversation and listen. Wherever possible, I took action the following week based on students' ideas. In this way, I signalled to students that their opinions mattered.

- **Self- and peer assessment.** Students were expected to self- and peer assess major assignments using carefully developed rubrics, which the class had reviewed and modified if necessary. Initially, students did not often use the descriptors as the basis for their assessments; either they had not internalized these criteria or they ignored them. This was especially problematic when students were invited to assign marks. This aspect improved with practice and the addition of a rubric that evaluated students' ability to self- and peer assess. The result was a significant shift away from the teacher as the sole arbiter of standards to a shared responsibility with students.

(continued on next page)

The result of these efforts was the most satisfying teaching experience of my career. Students acquired a much deeper understanding and competence than I had previously seen. They reported working harder in this course, and found it very satisfying (this is not the same as enjoying the course, as many students agonized over tasks that pushed the boundaries of their teaching). Most felt that they had not simply acquired ideas and strategies, but that the course had changed them as teachers.

I tried to replicate these conditions in the next course I taught, with much less satisfying results. Although many of these students reported a similar experience, one-third of the students did not. I was so dissatisfied with this group's performance that I felt compelled to withhold their grades until they had redone the major assignment. I suspect the disappointing results with this group were because of things I did differently or because of their modest level of commitment to the course. They likely lacked a defining element of community—a commitment to a common goal. Instead of caring about advancing their professional learning, they seemed more interested in completing the course. This epilogue does not undermine the power of creating a community of thinkers—in the first course and for the majority of students in the second, the results were superior—but it does remind us that there are no quick fixes or universal remedies in education.

along a continuum. In this way, less dogmatic attitudes are encouraged and the value of provisionally held positions is recognized.

Nurturing a classroom community of thinkers is an orientation that must pervade all of our actions. Not only must we be proactive in introducing elements that will support thinking, we must also be vigilant in identifying and altering existing habits that undermine it.

Consider a recent class situation where you were a student or a teacher. Make a list of all the teaching and learning actions that in some way supported thinking and a parallel list of the actions that did not. Consider why each action had the effect that it had. Identify ways you might strengthen the supportive actions and improve, or avoid, the non-supportive actions.

Strategies for Building Community

Each of us can build and sustain communities of thinkers in our classrooms by working on five fronts:

- setting appropriate classroom expectations;
- implementing appropriate classroom routines and activities;
- personally modelling the attributes of a good critical thinker;
- teaching the tools students need to participate in a reflective community; and
- shaping the communicative interactions within the class to encourage thinking.

Before exploring specific strategies in each of these areas, we offer an account of Philip's efforts at creating a virtual community of learners.

Classroom Expectations

The expectations we set for students influence the tone of the classroom. One significant factor in Roland's attempt to create a community was his expectation of the kind of questions students asked. Typically, at the outset of each year we establish behavioural expectations (for example, students are expected to be punctual, keep the classroom clean, and treat each other respectfully). It is also worth considering the following kinds of classroom expectations to support thinking:

- Students are expected to make up their own minds, not simply take someone else's word.
- Students and teacher are expected as a matter of course to support their observations, conclusions, and behaviour.
- Students and teacher are expected to consider other perspectives on an issue and alternative approaches to a problem before reaching a firm conclusion.
- All persons are to be treated respectfully by everyone, even if their ideas seem wrong or silly.
- It is expected that students will disagree with one another; however, differences of opinions must never be personal attacks.
- It is not acceptable merely to criticize and complain—the pros of a position should always be examined as should possible solutions to problems.
- The insincere use of critical techniques to show off or to be contrary is not tolerated (this does not mean that there is no place for well-intentioned devil's advocacy).

Classroom Routines and Activities

A community of thinkers is supported by daily routines

PHILIP'S ATTEMPT TO SUPPORT A VIRTUAL COMMUNITY OF THINKERS

For several years I have been using online technologies with pre- and in-service teachers to support the teaching of thinking. Initially I relied on these technologies as convenient tools to communicate with students between class periods. I began with e-mail exchanges to monitor concerns and address student questions. Later, I used a dialogue forum to post information about the course and provide a means for students to discuss practical matters. Both approaches had some benefit; for one, all of us arrived to the face-to-face sessions better informed about our views and questions.

Recently I have begun creating more authentic virtual learning communities that do more than act as peripheral support. I now use Knowledge Forum (KF) software (discussed in Scardamalia and Bereiter 1991) to support "knowledge building." My students actively collaborate to develop the content of the discussions—the topics and resources to consider as well as how we will operate and be assessed. The software provides the architecture for participants to structure the discussion and collectively construct understanding. It has played a significant role in nurturing communities of thinkers in my classes.

Below I describe how I have tried to support these virtual communities by acting on the five aspects of building community:

- **Setting appropriate expectations.** At the outset, my students and I agree on general expectations including:
  - participants take the topic being discussed seriously;
  - participants attend to others responses; and
  - participants contribute to the building of a positive virtual community.

    In one group, participants identified a negative tone in peer discussion and as a consequence developed a code of etiquette for deliberation. This specified that we would always acknowledge contributions made before offering contrary points of view, and that the discussion would focus on ideas and avoid personal criticisms.
- **Implementing appropriate routines.** The most fundamental routine involves making frequent contributions to the forum: students and I regularly post messages (usually one per week) intended to "advance understanding of the topic" and regularly respond to several messages (usually two per week). We routinely provide structural clues to help everyone keep up

with the discussions. These include the following:
- creating informative and engaging titles for each post (for example, Kohn trashes standardized testing);
- mentioning the question we are addressing (for example, Do cell phones have a constructive role to play in the classroom?);
- identifying "keywords" in our messages (for example, inference, bias, conclusion, opinion) to help others search and organize the database;
- quoting other participants' messages (for example, X says "…," but I think …, because …); and
- embedding external sources including internet links, graphics, and video clips.
- **Personal modelling of critical thinking attributes.** I try as best I can to model sound thinking and respectful discussion. To encourage student use of software features, I identify the kind of contribution I am making to the discussion with "scaffolding" labels ("An Alternative Point of View," "My Conclusion," or "Flaws in the Argument"), which help participants identify the thinking concepts involved.
- **Tools for a reflective community.** Success is unlikely if a majority of participants lack the skills to contribute to a virtual community. I have found it imperative to teach participants both how to use the software effectively to build community and the thinking tools needed to contribute.
- **Shaping communicative interactions.** The structure and pace of online communication within a virtual community provide rich opportunities to ask probing questions and offer thoughtful responses. KF software is particularly effective at helping participants move beyond offering opinions to weighing multiple options and seeking informed consensus. These virtual interactions lead to more thoughtful face-to-face discussions in the classroom.

While the results have generally been pleasing, not every group has been entirely successful in building a virtual critical community. One explanation for the less successful cases is participant unwillingness to use the technology. Another is the vulnerability felt by some participants over posting their thoughts. This sense of vulnerability requires careful attention during face-to-face encounters, supported with actions, to assure participants they will be treated with thoughtful consideration.

and activities that habituate students to habits of mind conducive to a thinking community. The weekly discussion in Roland's class was an ongoing mechanism for students to air their concerns and influence the direction of the course. The following is a list of some routines that support a critical community:

- Using critical thinking vocabulary as a matter of course in classroom discussion (for example, "What can you infer from this picture about the individual's mood?", "What assumptions are you making?").
- Consistently assigning tasks, including those that are for marks that contain a non-trivial commitment to thinking critically.

- Involving students in scrutinizing accounts, textbooks, news articles and reports, and other "reputable" sources of information for bias, stereotyping, overgeneralization, and inaccuracy.
- Regularly soliciting student ideas and suggestions and (when appropriate) using them to set assignments, establish rules, and establish criteria for assessment.
- Praising thoughtfully supported, insightful, or empathetic responses (even if flawed).
- Regularly inviting students to explore and defend positions from particular points of view, especially from others' perspectives.
- Regularly involving students in identifying and defending criteria used to evaluate their classroom behaviour and work, and applying these criteria to self- and peer assessment.
- Providing students with adequate time to reflect on their learning and to think about their answers before being asked to respond.

Teacher Modelling

Albert Schweitzer is reported to have noted, "Example is not the main thing in influencing others, it's the only thing" (reported in Norman 1989, 27). If we want our students to be good critical thinkers we must model these attributes ourselves:

- Don't be dogmatic and don't always have an answer. Live with ambiguity—be satisfied with tentative conclusions until a full review of complex issues can be carried out.
- Sincerely attempt to base all comments and decisions on careful and fair-minded consideration of all sides.
- Be willing (if asked) to provide "good" reasons for your decisions and actions (this does not mean that the lesson must be interrupted every time a student asks for a justification).
- Be careful to avoid making gross generalizations and stereotypical comments about individuals and groups, and seek to expose stereotypes in books, pictures, films, and other learning resources.
- Be willing to change your mind or alter your plans when good reasons are presented.
- Regularly acknowledge the existence of different positions on an issue (for example, look at events from different cultural, gender, and class perspectives).
- Don't be cynical—instead, adopt a realistic but questioning attitude towards the world.

Tools for Community Participation

Just as students need instruction about how to function effectively as citizens in society, so too do they need to be taught how to be effective contributors to a community of thinkers. Initially, many students may not be willing or able to contribute to and benefit from collaborative reflection. Tools they may need to be taught include: how to listen well, how to accept criticism, how to monitor what they say, and how to have confidence in their ability to contribute. Students need many intellectual tools to participate effectively in a community of thinkers. Here are some of these tools:[1]

- **Background knowledge**
  - individuals may see things in significantly different ways;
  - how individuals can be expected to react in various situations.
- **Criteria for judgment**
  - relevance of comments to the discussion;
  - clarity of comments to the community.
- **Critical thinking vocabulary**
  - unanimous, consensus, minority positions, perspective.
- **Thinking strategies**
  - group-management: taking turns, assigning co-operative roles, active listening, keeping a speaker's list;
  - critiquing in a non-threatening manner: putting a comment in the form of a question, preceding a comment with a caveat, preceding a comment with positive remarks;
  - presenting information in group settings: limiting comments to a few points, speaking from notes, connecting remarks to others' comments.
- **Habits of mind**
  - independent-minded—willingness to make up one's own mind;
  - sensitivity to others—attention to the feelings of others;
  - self-monitoring—attention to how one's actions are affecting the group.

Communicative Interactions

The "talk" that goes on within a classroom has a powerful influence on atmosphere. Classroom communication can be divided into three categories:
- teacher interactions with individual students;
- communication among students; and
- whole class discussions.

INTERACTIONS WITH INDIVIDUAL STUDENTS

A community of thinkers is affected by teacher interactions with individual students. On one hand, responding to individual students' questions helps them learn; on the other hand, students may be discouraged from thinking for themselves if they know that the teacher will provide the answers. Although there are many occasions when student questions should be answered directly, it is worth considering ways of encouraging students to answer their own questions. The scenario of Roland's university methods course presented earlier illustrates how students may find it very difficult to answer their own questions. To encourage them, try the following:

- Turn the question back on the student or onto others in the class (for example, "What do you think? What is your best guess to the answer? How would you respond?").
- Prompt students with clues or present an example or new situation that might help them come to a response (for example, "Have you considered…?").
- Suggest tentative answers, including flawed answers (for example, "Well I'm wondering if it could be…? I'm not sure, some people might think…").

INTERACTIONS AMONG STUDENTS

There is much that could be said about helping students to communicate respectfully and thoughtfully with each other. Peer feedback is one important occasion for inter-student communication involving critical thinking. When asked to offer peer feedback, students are thinking critically about another's work—they are offering assessments based on identifiable criteria. The following suggestions may guide students during feedback sessions:

- Emphasize peer feedback as an invitation to see the positives as well as the negatives.
- Begin by critiquing the work of those not in the class, or have the class critique something you have done (for example, an essay you wrote as a student, a class presentation you made). When it is time for peer critique, start with group assignments so the responsibility is shared among several students.
- In the early days of peer critique, do not allow negative comments but only positive remarks. When students voluntarily ask each other to identify what is missing or could be improved with their work, this is a good indication they're ready for more rigorous critique.

- Set a few simple guidelines for peer critique and model them. For example, insist that each student start with two (or more) positive comments before offering a (single) concern, and that negative comments be phrased in the form of a query (for example, "I'm unclear why you did it this way. Could you explain what you had in mind?").
- Ensure that the early instances of peer feedback are low-risk, easy to perform, and have an obvious benefit.

WHOLE CLASS DISCUSSIONS

Diane Hess (2004, 152) has identified four impediments to successful classroom discussions:

- a tendency for teachers to talk too much;
- "discussion" questions that don't invite discussion;
- lack of focus and depth in student contributions; and
- unequal participation by students (some students monopolize discussions and others are marginalized).

The obvious solution to teacher dominance of class discussions is to remind ourselves constantly that most of the talk should come from our students. It may also help to avoid signalling to students our own opinions on the issue under discussion. Raising questions or offering statements that invite disagreement will avoid an abrupt end to discussion.

Another significant determinant of student participation in whole class discussion is the nature of the questions asked. Questions of factual or personal preference provide little opportunity for students to engage in genuine debate. With factual questions, there is relatively little to discuss other than to assert an answer. Disagreements surrounding factual questions typically hinge on factual details (for example, Did they or did they not have cars?).

Preference questions are difficult to debate since they are largely matters of personal inclination (for example, You would like living without electricity and I would not). The most productive kinds of questions for classroom discussions are critical challenges. These questions do not have a pre-specified right answer. Students must instead render their own judgments based on relevant factors (for example, Considering social, physical, and mental health, was the quality of life for the average young person better now or a hundred years ago?). Such questions leave lots of room for debate, especially if students are well prepared for the discussion.

The following strategies support reluctant discussants (Wilen 2004, 53):

- Base discussion on a common experience or text students have shared.
- Invite students to think about the topic beforehand and write down a few questions.
- Provide students an opportunity to review information or gather their thoughts prior to the discussion.
- Divide students into pairs to develop questions and prepare and rehearse a few points they might offer.

Teacher questioning during discussion can support critical thinking. A discussion can be initiated by asking one student to state and support a position and, if necessary, to clarify the position or the supporting reasons. Other students may be invited to offer their positions and supporting reasons, and then to respond to those in disagreement. The teacher might also draw attention to unrecognized information or add provocative clues to stimulate further discussion. In asking these questions, teachers help students articulate their beliefs, extend their thinking, and engage with others. The following list of questions illustrates non-intimidating ways to frame these prompts:

INVITE A JUDGMENT OR REASON:

- What is your conclusion and what causes you to think this?
- Can you tell me what you think about the issue and a reason why?

SEEK GREATER CLARITY (ONLY IF JUDGMENT OR REASON IS UNCLEAR):

- That's interesting; can you give me an example?
- Can you help me understanding what you're saying? Is your point "this" or "this"?

SOLICIT OTHER STUDENTS' JUDGMENTS AND REASONS:

- Does anyone have a different opinion? Why or why not?
- Who has the same opinion, but for different reasons?

INVITE STUDENTS TO RESPOND TO EACH OTHER'S COMMENTS:

- What might you say to those who don't agree with your position?
- Does everyone agree that . . . is a convincing reason?

ADD NEW INFORMATION OR PROVIDE CLUES TO PUSH STUDENTS' THINKING

- No one has mentioned . . . Would this make a difference to your thinking?
- Do you think it is important that . . .

List strategies for supporting a critical community for each of the five fronts below, and select one or two strategies from the list that you can effectively implement in your teaching:

- Setting appropriate classroom expectations.
- Implementing appropriate classroom routines and activities.
- Personally modelling the attributes of a good critical thinker.
- Developing the tools for student participation in a reflective community.
- Shaping the communicative interactions within the class to encourage reflection.

Conclusion

We have argued in this chapter the importance of the atmosphere of a classroom to student thinking. Building on the metaphor of the classroom as community, we have distinguished classrooms in which students are partners in the decision-making process from teacher- or student-run classrooms. The core features of a classroom community include: a commitment to a shared purpose, agreed-on procedures, and joint responsibility. Using examples from our own university teaching, we have illustrated various ways in which teachers might nurture a community of thinkers in their own classrooms.

ENDNOTE

1   The tools referred to in this list are explained in chapter 6, "Teaching Elementary Students the Tools to Think Critically" by Roland Case and LeRoi Daniels.

REFERENCES

Barell, J. 1991. *Teaching for thoughtfulness: Classroom strategies to enhance intellectual development.* New York: Longman.

Daniels, L. and R. Case. 1992. *Charter literacy and the administration of justice in Canada.* Ottawa: Department of Justice, June.

Goodlad, J. 2004. *A place called school: Twentieth anniversary edition.* Whitby, ON: McGraw-Hill.

Hess, D.E. 2004. Discussion in social studies: Is it worth the trouble? *Social Education* 68 (2): 151–155.

Lipman, M. 1991. *Thinking in education.* Cambridge: Cambridge University Press.

MacKinnon, A. and C. Scarff-Seatter. 1997. Constructivism: Contradictions and confusions in teacher education. In *Constructivist teacher education: Building new understandings,* ed. V. Richardson, 38–56. London: Falmer.

Newmann, F.W. 1990. Higher order thinking in teaching social studies: A rationale for the assessment of classroom thoughtfulness. *Journal of Curriculum Studies* 22 (1): 41–56.

———. 1991. Promoting higher order thinking in social studies: Overview of a study of 16 high school departments. *Theory and Research in Social Education* 19 (4): 324–340.

Norman, P. 1989. *The self-directed learning contract: A guide for learners and teachers.* Burnaby, BC: Faculty of Education, Simon Fraser University.

Resnick, L.B., ed. 1989. *Knowing, learning and instruction: Essays in honor of Robert Glaser.* Hillsdale, NJ: Lawrence Erlbaum.

Richardson, V. 2003. Constructivist pedagogy. *Teachers College Record* 105 (9): 1623–1640.

Rogoff, B. 1994. Developing understanding of the idea of communities of learners. *Mind, Culture, and Activity* 1 (4): 209–229.

Scardamalia, M. and C. Bereiter. 1991. Higher levels of agency for children in knowledge building: A challenge for the design of new knowledge media. *The Journal of the Learning Sciences* 1: 37–68.

Wilen, W.W. 2004. Encouraging reticent students' participation in classroom discussions. *Social Education* 68 (1): 51–56.

11

Escaping the Typical Research Report Trap with Elementary Students

Penney Clark

onsider this scenario: We assign a research report on a topic—a famous person, perhaps, or ancient Greece, or pioneers. Students surf the net or the library shelves and stop at the first three sources they find. They copy or download a paragraph from the first source, one from the second source, and so on, until their report meets the required word count. Come presentation time, students troop one by one to the front of the class to read their reports in low, monotonous voices. It seems that they understand little of the content since they can't answer questions based on the information they've just presented. And judging from the largely irrelevant questions from other students, the rest of the class didn't understand the presentation or simply weren't listening.

What can we do to avoid this disappointing, yet all-too-common, scenario? Perhaps the place to begin our escape from this largely fruitless, time-consuming trap is to clarify why we engage students in conducting research and preparing reports in the first place. Is it primarily so students can learn about famous people, ancient Greece, or pioneers? No, because while acquiring information may be one of our objectives, there are faster, more efficient ways to achieve this end. Surely the more important purpose is to develop students' abilities to inquire independently, to synthesize their findings in meaningful ways, and to clearly communicate those findings to others. As the above scenario suggests, many so-called research projects may do little to help students develop these abilities.

In this chapter, I present a seven-step model for teaching students at primary and upper-elementary levels how to carry out and present research. The key

to success is to devote as much, or more, attention to the process of conducting research as to the final product, a report of some kind. Teacher and teacher-librarian guidance along the way is crucial. We should not send students unaided to the library, assignment in hand, and expect them to present a well-written, original, and thoroughly researched report on the due date. The complex task of conducting and reporting on research can be interesting, profoundly satisfying, and educationally useful if we implement strategies that teach students how to successfully complete the various tasks involved in a research project:

1. select and focus a topic;
2. develop guiding questions;
3. identify relevant information sources;
4. extract information from sources;
5. record and organize information;
6. synthesize and present information;
7. assess student research.

Select and Focus a Topic

Any successful research project begins with thoughtful selection of a topic and the narrowing of that topic to manageable proportions.

SELECT A TOPIC

Three interrelated considerations are relevant when choosing a topic:

- **Mandated curriculum**. Student research provides an opportunity to develop a richer understanding of curriculum content than can be achieved by using a textbook or other single resource, because it can involve a variety of resources and perspectives. But since research is time consuming, topics should be selected carefully for their relevance to the curriculum.
- **Availability of resources.** The choice of topic depends to some extent on the suitable resources available. Teacher-librarians can be a great help in locating resources with diverse perspectives and rich detail. They will often place materials on reserve so they are available to students when needed. If school resources are limited, teacher-librarians can also assist by borrowing outside resources on a short-term basis.
- **Student interest.** Research projects provide opportunities for students to explore individual interests. They can have powerful motivational value if students care about the topic. The teacher can stimulate interest in topics by raising provocative questions. Allowing students a say in selecting topics is another way to increase interest. This can be as simple as providing students with a list of curriculum-related topics from which they can choose.

FOCUS THE TOPIC

Research projects are unmanageable if the scope is too grand or vague. Since students often have trouble zeroing in on a topic, they may need assistance in articulating the scope of their research. Before directing students to choose their own topic, model with the entire class the focussing strategy illustrated by the following example.

Begin with a broad general theme, such as "European Exploration and Trade in North America" and, as a class, brainstorm a list of categories within this theme. The list might include:

- famous explorers
- causes and consequences of exploration
- inhabitants of the northern part of North America at the time of the fur trade
- the fur trade

Then select one of these categories and generate more specific topics that fall within its scope. For instance, narrower topics under the heading "Fur Trade"

might include:

- fur forts
- fur trade routes
- methods of trapping fur-bearing animals
- daily life on the trap lines
- role of women in the fur trade
- beaver hats and fur fashions
- aboriginal peoples and the fur trade
- the Hudson's Bay Company

These narrower topics then become the focus for individual or group research projects. After modelling this procedure with the entire class on a topic unconnected to the theme(s) of the actual research project, invite students, individually or in small groups, to undertake a similar process when selecting their own topics. Students may want to consult with friends and family and scan the textbook or other resources for help in generating a list of categories and topics. Before allowing students to proceed with their research, check that their topic choices are not too broad.

Develop Guiding Questions

Inviting students to frame questions to answer through their research is often helpful in providing even greater focus and purpose. When generating guiding questions that will have meaning for the students, start with what they already know about their topic and then move to what is unknown.

START WITH WHAT STUDENTS KNOW

Students are often pleased to discover that they already know quite a bit about a topic. Helping them record this information at the outset encourages them to connect it with the information they acquire during their research. One caution: some of the information that students already "know" may be incorrect. But it can be recorded anyway. Then, as they gather new information, students can check the accuracy of their original claims.

As demonstrated in Figure 11.1, "What We Already Know about Fur Forts," webbing is a way to generate and record what is already known. Ask students to think of everything they can that links to the keywords or ideas contained in their topic. Webbing encourages the free flow of ideas since students make any links that come to mind, rather than fitting information into predetermined slots.

FIGURE 11.1   WHAT WE ALREADY KNOW ABOUT FUR FORTS

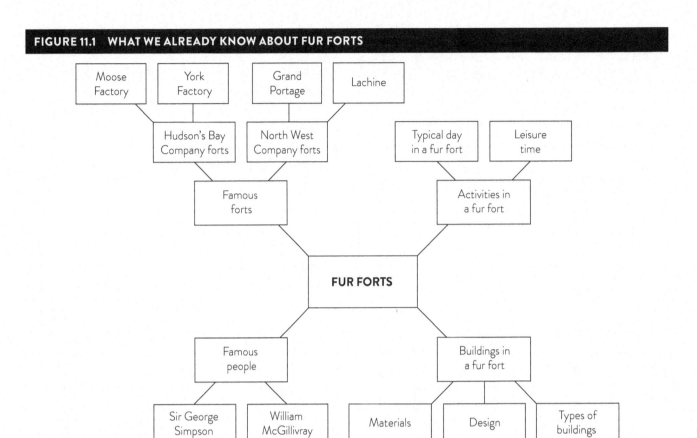

MOVE TO THE UNKNOWN

Once students have reviewed what they already know about the topic, they can turn their attention to what more they would like to know. If students are interested in a topic, there will be many questions. Listing and then organizing these can help students target the most important and interesting aspects of the topic.

One strategy is to list student questions about a topic on chart paper, and then cut up the paper so that each question is on a separate piece. Either as a whole class or in smaller groups, students can sort the questions into categories and develop a single, more general question for each one. As Table 11.1 shows, the topic of fur forts might elicit specific questions that could be grouped under three general questions.

A variation of this approach for use with primary students is to ask every student to write (or have scribed) on an index card a question about the chosen topic. Arrange students in a circle and invite them to individually place their card on the floor in the centre. If others think they have a question that could be grouped with one already presented, they place their card in line just below the first card and explain why it belongs there.

When all questions have been clustered in this manner, students choose a general question from those in each group, or formulate a new question that subsumes the specific questions on the index cards.

Armed with a few general questions (that summarize the many specific ones they have), students can use information sources more effectively. With a clear focus for reading, students have less difficulty separating relevant from less relevant information. Otherwise, they will often assume that if the author considered it important enough to mention, it must be important enough to include in their notes. With questions in mind, students can scan for answers rather than reading every word and constantly wondering how to decide what to record.

Identify Relevant Information Sources

A third step in conducting research is to help students learn how to identify possible sources of information and then select the most relevant and reliable sources. Identifying information sources is an area where the teacher-librarian can be of particular assistance, both in making appropriate resources available and in helping students locate the most useful ones.

TABLE 11.1 STUDENT QUESTIONS ABOUT FUR FORTS

BRAINSTORMED QUESTIONS	GENERAL QUESTIONS
• Were there schools in the forts? • What did people do if they didn't take part in the fur trade? • How did people obtain food? • How did people preserve and prepare food? • Was life hard or easy for people living in the forts?	What was it like to live in a fur fort?
• Where were the forts built? • What factors were considered in choosing a location? • What materials were used to build the forts? • Why were these materials chosen?	How and where were fur forts built?
• Why were fur forts needed? • When did fur forts stop being used? • Are there any fur forts still standing?	What was the role of the fur forts in the fur trade and why were they eventually no longer needed?

IDENTIFY POSSIBLE SOURCES

The possibilities for information sources are infinite. It may be useful, before students begin their research, to brainstorm specific options as a group. If this is not feasible because individual projects are too varied, encourage students to brainstorm individual lists. Information sources can include print, people, places, audiovisual materials, computer databases, and the internet.

- **Print texts.** These include reference books, magazines, almanacs, non-fiction trade books, literature, and newspaper clipping files, which can all be found in school and public libraries. Printed information can also be found in the kinds of materials that are not meant to be long lasting. Many such items are not found in libraries because they are frequently updated and therefore not saved, for example, pamphlets and bulletins published by advocacy groups such as environmental organizations, government departments, and agencies such as tourist bureaus and travel agencies. (See chapter 16, "Bringing Community Resources into Elementary Social Studies," for use of these kinds of print resources.)

- **People and places.** Parents, businesses, professional and lobby groups, and community organizations such as local historical societies and ethnic group associations can all be sources of guest speakers or interviewees. Places might include historic sites, museums, parks, zoos, and various kinds of resource centres. These can be particularly useful information sources for less capable readers. (See chapter 16, "Bringing Community Resources into Elementary Social Studies," for suggestions on interviewing people, hosting guest speakers, and conducting field trips.)

- **Visual and audiovisual sources.** These include photographs, drawings, graphs, slides, posters, DVDs, and CD-ROMs. (See chapter 15, "Exploring Visual Resources with Elementary Students," for use of visual and audiovisual materials as information sources.)

- **Electronic and web-based information sources.** Electronic databases and the internet have become increasingly useful for conducting research. It is crucial, however, that students learn how to use search engines and other tools to manage these sources and assess their credibility. (See chapter 14, "Integrating Computer Technologies into Elementary Social Studies," for a discussion of locating and selecting appropriate electronic and web-based information sources.)

SELECT RELEVANT AND RELIABLE SOURCES

Once students have generated a list of possible information sources, encourage them to think about which sources seem the most promising. With young students, it might be best to simplify by presenting them with a pair of resources and asking them to explain which would be the better source for a given research purpose (for example, "If we want to know what 'voyageur' means, should we consult a newspaper or a dictionary?" and "If we want to know what voyageurs do, should we consult an electronic encyclopedia or a dictionary?").

Older students require more complex challenges. Figure 11.2 presents the chart that teacher-librarian Elizabeth Smith and teacher Rachelle Beaulieu used to help grade 4 students at Shaughnessy Elementary

School in Vancouver evaluate the suitability of various information sources on early Canadian explorers. In groups, students researched their assigned explorer using the nine sources listed on Figure 11.2. While doing this, they assessed the quality of the content in light of student-generated criteria. They were asked to offer reasons for each rating. After totalling the scores and rank-ordering the sources, each group reported its findings to the rest of the class.

Select a topic in the social studies curriculum and locate three relevant print, electronic, or web-based information sources suitable for students at this grade level. Plan an activity with student-ready materials to teach students how to judge which of these sources is the most appropriate for the assigned topic.

Extract Information from Sources

The next step in conducting research is to extract the desired information from the source. To do so effectively and efficiently, students need to use such tools as tables of contents, indices, keywords, and site menus competently. It should not be assumed that all students are adept at using these information retrieval tools, especially with electronic resources.

This is yet another step in which the teacher-librarian can be of assistance. Some teachers and teacher-librarians team-teach research skills. Preparation work is cut in half when the teacher and teacher-librarian each prepare a lesson on a specific skill (for example, using a table of contents or an index, or navigating a website) and teach that lesson to half the class and then to the other half.

Record and Organize Information

The next step—learning to record and organize information in a form that will be helpful in completing a report—requires specific teaching. Four strategies for helping students record and organize information are described below: partner talk, guiding question folders, note-taking columns, and data charts.

PARTNER TALK

Partner talk is a strategy for organizing information that relies heavily on extended discussion prior to any written recording. Before beginning to write their reports, individual students explain to a partner what they already know or have found out. This approach can be used whether students in each pair have different topics or the same one.

Here is one way to organize a partner talk, developed by Ann McIntyre, who was a teacher-librarian in Edmonton public schools:

- Students work in pairs The partners take turns telling each other what they already know about the topic and explaining what they found out about each of the guiding questions. The partners also ask each other questions.
- Individually, partners find a source and read relevant sections.
- Partners return and relate the new information they found.
- Partners question each other for clarification of ideas and to find out what additional information is required.
- Partners turn to the resources used previously, or to new ones, to answer these additional questions.
- Partners share answers. Repeat previous steps until all needed information has been gathered. (McIntyre recommends that students do not take notes prior to this point in the process.)
- Students prepare their reports.

GUIDING QUESTION FOLDERS

Students can use a folder to store the results of their research. They begin by writing each of their general questions at the top of a separate sheet of paper. They create an additional final sheet with the title "Bibliography." All sheets are kept in the folder. As students conduct research, they record information on the appropriate sheet, always remembering to record the source on the bibliography page, indicating the title, author, date and place of publication, and the publisher's name. When students write their first draft, the required information is already organized

The following list is an adaptation of this procedure for a group report with primary students:

- Brainstorm with students what they already know about the topic. List these "facts" on strips of cardboard and place them in a pocket chart for easy reference.
- List the questions students have about the topic. Choose three or four key ones.

FIGURE 11.2   EVALUATING RESOURCES ON CANADIAN EXPLORERS

3 = Effective   2 = Acceptable   1 = Ineffective

	Detailed (depth of info)	Up to date (currency)	Information from "around the world"	Includes the "whys" of history (causes)	Includes the "consequences" of history	Cites references	TOTAL	RANK
Canadian Encyclopedia Online	3 2 1	3 2 1	3 2 1	3 2 1	3 2 1	3 2 1		
World Book Print edition	3 2 1	3 2 1	3 2 1	3 2 1	3 2 1	3 2 1		
Wikipedia	3 2 1	3 2 1	3 2 1	3 2 1	3 2 1	3 2 1		
Ebsco Magazine Search tool	3 2 1	3 2 1	3 2 1	3 2 1	3 2 1	3 2 1		
Internet	3 2 1	3 2 1	3 2 1	3 2 1	3 2 1	3 2 1		
Non-fiction trade books	3 2 1	3 2 1	3 2 1	3 2 1	3 2 1	3 2 1		
Historical fiction	3 2 1	3 2 1	3 2 1	3 2 1	3 2 1	3 2 1		
Historical documentaries	3 2 1	3 2 1	3 2 1	3 2 1	3 2 1	3 2 1		
Historical docudramas	3 2 1	3 2 1	3 2 1	3 2 1	3 2 1	3 2 1		
Historical films (fictional)	3 2 1	3 2 1	3 2 1	3 2 1	3 2 1	3 2 1		
Textbook	3 2 1	3 2 1	3 2 1	3 2 1	3 2 1	3 2 1		

- Write each key question at the top of a sheet of chart paper. Ask students to print the questions at the tops of their own sheets of paper. Add a sheet called "Book List," where the books used as information sources are recorded.

- Read aloud all or parts of the books chosen as information sources. Encourage students to draw information from the pictures as well as from the words. Students are to raise their hands any time one of their questions is answered. Record answers in note form on the appropriate piece of chart paper. Students can print the answer on their papers as well.

As they listen, they can also check the validity of the information they already knew. They may find some of their information is incorrect. If a "fact" is incorrect, discard the card on which it is written. If correct, tape the card to the appropriate sheet of chart paper.

- Generate and print on chart paper statements based on the information gathered. The information from each page will form one paragraph of the report.
- Choose a title for the report.
- Invite students to copy the report for themselves and illustrate it.

FIGURE 11.3 ASSESSING STUDENTS' NOTES[1]

	WELL-DEVELOPED 5	COMPETENT 3	UNDERDEVELOPED 1
Relevant ideas in left-hand column	Almost all relevant ideas and no irrelevant ideas are highlighted or listed.	Many relevant ideas and several irrelevant ideas are highlighted or listed.	Very few relevant ideas and many irrelevant ideas are highlighted or listed.
Clear and understandable notes	Almost all the relevant ideas and no irrelevant ideas are highlighted or listed.	Approximately half of the notes are expressed clearly and with enough detail to be understandable.	Very few of the notes would make sense to someone reading them.
Brief and in point form	All of the notes are written in very brief phrases.	Approximately half of the notes could be shortened without any loss of meaning.	Almost all of the notes are too long.
In student's own words	Everywhere appropriate, notes are in the student's own words.	Approximately half of the notes are copied exactly from the text.	Almost all of the notes are copied exactly from the text.

NOTE-TAKING COLUMNS

Columns for note-taking are made by taking sheets of paper and drawing a line down the middle of each one. Write each guiding question on a separate sheet, as in the guiding question folder strategy. Students use the left-hand column to jot down information from the reference source. An alternative way to use the left-hand column is for students to paste a photocopy or printout of every text they are referencing. If necessary, they may use the back, or make their own form. Then they underline or highlight sentences directly in the photocopied or printed text. Stress that they are to focus only on information that pertains to the research question. In the right-hand column, students restate the information in their own words. This increases the likelihood that they will understand what the notes mean. Emphasize that their notes should be clear and understandable (so they can remember the important information) and expressed in point form (so that the notes are not too long). Student note-taking can be assessed using the rubric reproduced in Figure 11.3. Afterwards, students can cut the notes in the right-hand column into strips and use them to create an outline for their report. To reduce the likelihood of plagiarism, compare the ideas (underlined or recorded) in the left-hand column of the sheets with the student's final report in order to ascertain how closely these sources match the final product.

DATA CHARTS

Data charts are an effective format for recording information for three reasons: the limited space requires students to record information in point form; the framework encourages use of several information sources; and the listing of only a few questions or topics focusses students on the major issues. Until everyone is comfortable with the format, it is advisable to use data charts as a class rather than having students use them individually. Group practice runs should focus on topics unrelated to the topics students will explore for their individual projects.

The steps involved in class use of data charts are illustrated in Figure 11.4, "Data Chart: Peru," and are further explained here:

- Provide a blank data chart using a SMART Board or whatever technology is available in your classroom, and individual charts for each student. Ask students to record information on their individual sheets as the information is recorded on the SMART Board.
- Identify and record a title for the research topic.
- Generate numerous questions. Invite students to discuss which of these questions are the most important or interesting. List four or five major questions in the first column.
- In the second column, record what students already know in response to each question.
- Provide students with the titles of two or three brief resources that they will use as information sources. So that students do not become bogged down in any one source, choose brief ones. Pictures or poems are useful not only because they are brief but also because they illustrate the variety of possible information sources. Record the titles at the top of the remaining columns.

FIGURE 11.4 DATA CHART: PERU

OUR GENERAL QUESTIONS	WHAT WE ALREADY KNOW	SOURCE:	SOURCE:	SOURCE:
1. What are the most interesting physical features of the country?				
Summary statement:				
2. What are major cultural aspects of the country?				
Summary statement:				
3. What are important industries? Is this a poor country?				
Summary statement:				
4. Are there environmental/ sustainability issues? If so, how are they being dealt with?				
Summary statement:				
5. How would you describe the roles of women in this society??				
Summary statement:				

- Read or show the first resource to students. Invite students to share information from this source that answers any of the questions in column one. Decide as a class on the best and briefest response to each question. Record each response in point form.
- Repeat this procedure with all other sources.
- Working together as a class, develop a summary response statement for each question.

Synthesize and Present Information

The most common methods of synthesizing and presenting research information are written reports and oral presentations.

STRATEGIES FOR WRITTEN REPORTS

- **Explain to a colleague.** Ask students to explain their topics to other students, using their notes as a guide, prior to drafting a written report. This provides an opportunity to practise expanding their notes into sentences and to sequence their information logically. In addition, questions asked by other students may indicate information gaps that need to be addressed. (This approach is similar to partner talk except that students work from notes. Partner talk is oral until the final step.)
- **Draft without notes.** It can be useful to have students write the first draft of the report without reference to their notes. This encourages them to think carefully about what they are writing and helps them to make the report their own. They can return to their notes for their second draft.
- **Selective efforts.** Polished written reports require several drafts, each of which must be edited. It may not be necessary, however, to take every report through to final polished product. One option, from among the reports assigned over the given year, is to allow each student to choose which one will receive the extra effort. These are the ones that will receive a professional-looking laminated cover and be displayed publicly.
- **Writing from a point of view.** Students can represent what they have learned from their research from a particular point of view. It is more interesting for students to write—and for the teacher to read—a letter from a settler on the Prairies to relatives in

the Ukraine than a straightforward description of life on a prairie homestead. Similarly, a child's day-to-day journal of a hypothetical visit to contemporary China may be more engaging than a summary of historic sites, industries, and cultures.

- This type of writing is often referred to as RAFT writing—Role, Audience, Format, Topic. Students write in role (for example: from the point of view of a world leader, journalist, pioneer, inventor, or famous person in history) to a particular audience (for example: to newspaper readers, a relative, prospective employers, or television viewers) using a particular format (for example: newspaper editorial, poem, letter, journal entry, telephone conversation, or rap song) on a certain topic.

Offer students opportunities to display their reports in prominent locations. The teacher-librarian can help in this regard since the school library is an appropriate place for public displays of student work.

Elementary students should be expected to include a bibliography in a formal written research report, but they will need help. Upper-elementary students can be expected to write a simple reference list using an example as a model:

Braid, Kate. 2001. *Emily Carr: Rebel Artist.*
Lantzville, BC: XYZ Publishing.

Primary students can be provided with a simple format such as the following and they can simply fill in the blanks.

SOURCES

Author   _____

Title   _____

Publisher   _____

Place   _____

Date   _____

STRATEGIES FOR ORAL REPORTS

- **Using visual aids.** Visual aids help make presentations more interesting to an audience. Students who are not aural learners may have difficulty listening for any length of time to an oral presentation. Visuals also provide memory cues to guide the oral delivery. Visual aids help presenters feel more at ease; they will know that the eyes of the audience will be directed elsewhere for at least part of the presentation. In addition, pointing to a picture or map gives presenters something to do with their hands, thus reducing nervousness.

- **Synthesizing another student's report.** To encourage students to listen carefully when others are presenting their reports, it is useful to ask students to take notes. One approach is to ask each student to use his or her notes to write a summary of another student's report. The example in the highlighted text, "Summary of Emily's Talk," was done by a student in a grade 3 class, where students made oral presentations on a topic of their choice.

There is no rule that says a student must deliver his or her oral report in front of the entire class. There are alternatives to the whole class presentation:

- **Rotating presentations.** Locate speakers at different spots around the room and arrange for small groups of students to rotate from one speaker to the next. It is not essential that every student hears every other student's presentation. This approach has several advantages over the whole class/one-speaker-at-a-time method. First, it is far less intimidating for a student speaker to make a presentation to a small group than to the entire class. Second, the speaker has the opportunity to repeat the speech several times, gaining confidence and improving delivery with each presentation. Third, members of the audience may be more attentive in this format because they are not forced to sit in one place for long periods. Also, they have more opportunity to ask questions because there are fewer questioners.

- **Co-operative group presentations.** In this approach, a group of students works together to make the presentation, each focussing on a particular aspect of the topic. One student might serve as a moderator, introducing the topic and panellists, calling on questioners, and keeping things running smoothly. This approach is helpful to the speakers. They can assist one another with difficult questions and the burden of response does not fall on a single individual. In addition, students have an opportunity to develop group participation skills such as co-operating with and listening to others and taking responsibility for contributing to discussions. Students, however, should not simply be thrust into a co-operative project without being helped to develop the tools needed for effective co-operation. These include the willingness and ability to listen carefully to others in the group, await one's turn to speak, and share materials. (See chapter 12, "Learning Co-operatively in Elementary Classrooms," for skill-building strategies.)

ALTERNATIVE REPORTING FORMATS

There are many alternatives to formal oral and written reports. "Alternative reporting ideas" lists a number of suggestions, any of which can be approached in various ways. For instance, a timeline may consist entirely of words, it may be illustrated, or it may be presented "live." Pat Shields (1996) suggests that in a "living timeline" format, students prepare role plays using costumes and props to suggest historical figures, either real or fictional, whom they have researched. The role plays are presented in chronological order so viewers can see how perspectives changed over time.

The depth of understanding of the subject need not be diminished when students use an unusual format. In fact, the level of understanding must often be greater in order to make the writing ring true. For instance, it would be more challenging for students to write entries in the diary of the gold miner Billy Barker during his exploits in the Cariboo area of British Columbia than a straightforward account of the Cariboo gold rush. To write entries in Barker's journal, students must know about key events and also understand how Barker might have viewed them. Instead of writing a straightforward description of the building of the CPR, they could describe the events from the perspectives of various stakeholders by means of "interviews" with individuals such as the general manager William Van Horne, the financier Sir Donald Smith, an Irish or a Chinese navvy, Chief Crowfoot, or Agnes Macdonald (the wife of John A. Macdonald, who travelled through part of the Fraser Canyon sitting on the "cowcatcher" of the locomotive pulling the train). In trying to view events through the eyes of different participants, students will develop a richer understanding of circumstances, individual motivations, limitations, and causes and effects.

Similarly, writing and illustrating a picture book intended for young students is more challenging than it may seem. The information has to be distilled down to the essentials and presented in clear, simple language, yet still hold the interest of its intended readers. (Since illustrations are a key element of this project, more and less artistically capable students could be teamed or students could access the internet for visuals in the public domain.)

SUMMARY OF EMILY'S TALK
by Laura Brown

If you want to know anything about anaesthetics just ask Emily.

Anaesthetics are drugs that make it possible for operations and other medical treatment to be carried out painlessly. Anaesthetics are made from laughing gas. Horace Well invented anaesthetics.

A long time ago even the most minor operation was quite painful because back then they didn't have anaesthetics.

The main anaesthesias are local and general. A general anaesthetic is when you get a needle put through your vein.

A local anaesthetic is when they don't put you to sleep such as when the dentist puts a needle through your gum when you have a filling.

The other anaesthetic is when some ointment is swabbed on with a Q-tip or a cotton ball to numb the feeling in a certain area. The method called inhalation is when the doctor gives you gas through a mask.

This example of a summary was written by a grade 3 student at Caulfeild Elementary in West Vancouver, BC.

Alternative reporting ideas

- advertisement
- annotated bibliography
- audiotape
- banquet
- bulletin board display
- cartoon
- chart
- collage
- collection
- computer program
- crossword puzzle
- debate
- demonstration
- digital scrapbook
- diorama
- DVD
- field trip (student planned)
- game
- illustrated timeline
- itinerary for imaginary trip
- journal or diary
- learning centre
- letter
- map
- mobile
- model
- mural
- newspaper
- panel discussion
- photo documentary
- photo essay
- picture book
- play
- poem
- position paper
- poster
- PowerPoint presentation
- resumé
- review
- role play
- simulated interview
- skit
- slides
- song
- story
- TV or radio quiz show

Assess Student Research

It is misleading to place assessment at the end of this model, since assessment should not be viewed as the last step in a research project, but rather as an ongoing part of the entire process. Three strategies for effective assessment of student research projects are to:

- generate and share assessment criteria prior to completion of any assignment;
- assess research procedures in addition to products; and
- include self- and peer assessment.

SET CRITERIA BEFOREHAND

Set out, or better yet, negotiate the assessment criteria at the very outset or at an early stage of the research project. This way, there are fewer surprises. Assessment is less menacing for students if they know how their work will be assessed and if they have had some say in establishing the basis for assessment. Encourage students to use the criteria to assess their own work before presenting it for teacher assessment. For example, the criteria listed below could be discussed with students when preparing an oral presentation or a written report.

Criteria for assessing an oral or written report

Content:
- is accurate;
- covers major points;
- is sufficiently detailed; and
- is interesting.

Organization:
- begins with an effective introduction;
- is arranged in logical sequence; and
- has an effective closure.

Presentation (oral):
- is easily heard;
- is delivered while looking at audience; and
- is delivered with an expressive speaking voice.

Presentation (written):
- is clearly written;
- uses correct spelling and punctuation; and
- uses descriptive language.

Visual aids:
- effectively illustrate key points;
- are clear; and
- are visually appealing.

ASSESS PROCEDURE AND PRODUCT

All aspects of the research process can and should be assessed, starting with students' ability to focus their topics and frame guiding questions through the effective use of data charts, to the quality of the final written, oral, and visual products. Assessing along the way makes the task less onerous for the teacher and provides students with ongoing feedback, which reduces the likelihood that mistakes made early in the process will scuttle the entire project. A form such as "Research Project Feedback," illustrated in Figure 11.5, could be used for ongoing teacher notes on each student's progress through the research project.

INCLUDE SELF- AND PEER ASSESSMENT

Self-assessment and peer assessment should be part of every research project because they provide students with additional, more immediate feedback than a teacher alone can provide. Students must learn how to provide constructive feedback to others; this in itself is a valuable learning experience. Students need to think about and learn ways to make comments in a positive and sensitive manner (for instance: precede any concerns with several positive features; put forth concerns in the form of a query or issue to think about).

Figure 11.6 is an example of a joint assessment sheet that can be used by students and teachers to assess a poster presentation.

Parting Comment

Throughout this chapter, I have pointed to the value of making maximum use of teacher-librarians. They can be helpful in many ways, including identifying appropriate resources in the school resource centre, obtaining other materials from outside sources, designing activities that require resource centre support, instructing students in skills needed to work through the research process, and providing a public venue for displaying finished reports.

The most dramatic example I have heard about co-operative planning and teaching between a classroom teacher and a teacher-librarian involved a grade 2 class that was researching dragons. Under the guidance of their teacher and the teacher-librarian, students examined portrayals of dragons in literature, determined the characteristics of dragons, and then formulated three questions they would ask a dragon if they happened to meet one. As students were discussing possible questions,

FIGURE 11.5 RESEARCH PROJECT FEEDBACK

TOPIC:	NAME:

SKILLS	COMMENTS
Topic: • is worth pursuing; • is narrow enough to be manageable.	
Guiding questions: • are relevant to topic; • adequately summarize specific questions.	
Information sources: • are relevant to topic; • provide reliable information.	
Extracting information: • uses appropriate locator aids (for example: index, table of contents, guide words, computerized directory to library resources).	
Recording and organizing information: • notes are brief; • notes are well organized; • notes cover important points related to topic; • notes are drawn from several sources; • notes are expressed in student's own words.	
Presenting information: • written drafts have been carefully edited and corrected; • presentations are appropriate for audience and topic; • visuals are thoughtfully designed and constructed; • written and oral reports are thoughtfully sequenced; • reporting (in any form) clearly and accurately presents the collected information.	

a dragon (the grade 6 teacher) burst into the classroom and attempted to kidnap their teacher. Of course, she was eventually saved by St. George (the custodian). But, true to form, the librarian played a key role in keeping the dragon from being ripped apart by students until St. George could arrive. This life-saving gesture was necessary because St. George had been momentarily delayed by a custodial emergency, and these grade 2 students were determined to protect their beloved teacher. The now subdued dragon turned out to be meek and mild, and only too happy to be interviewed—and, of course, forever grateful for the services of the teacher-librarian.

Research projects are more time-consuming than simply supplying students with information. How should you decide when a topic is best addressed through student research? Examine the topics for a specific grade in the social studies curriculum. Decide which and how many of these topics over the course of the school year might best be addressed in a research project. Would you structure each research assignment in a similar manner? If not, how might you alter them to best achieve the information-gathering and reporting outcomes in the curriculum?

FIGURE 11.6   SELF- AND TEACHER-ASSESSMENT OF A POSTER

	TEACHER RATING				SELF RATING			
	Definitely	Mostly	Partly	Not at all	Definitely	Mostly	Partly	Not at all
Important content/ message								
Clear content/ message								
Well laid-out/ designed								
Visually appealing								

ACKNOWLEDGMENT

I wish to thank Marg Franklin, a retired elementary school principal and University of British Columbia sessional instructor in elementary social studies, for her helpful suggestions on an earlier revision of this chapter.

ENDNOTE

1   This chart is adapted from J. Nicol and R. Case, eds. 2002, *The resourcefulness of the Inuit.* Vancouver, BC: The Critical Thinking Consortium, p. 116.

REFERENCES

Harrison, J., N. Smith, and I. Wright, eds. 2004. *Selected critical challenges in social studies—Intermediate/middle school.* Vancouver, BC: The Critical Thinking Consortium.

Nicol, J. and R. Case, eds. 2002. *The resourcefulness of the Inuit.* Vancouver, BC: The Critical Thinking Consortium.

Shields, P. 1996. Experiencing and learning through simulations and projects. *Canadian Social Studies* 30 (3): 142–143.

SUPPLEMENTARY READINGS

Barron, B., D. Schwartz, N. Vye, A. Moore, A. Petrosino, L. Zech, J. Bransford, and the Cognition and Technology Group at Vanderbilt. 1998. Doing with understanding: Lessons from research on problem- and project-based learning. *The Journal of the Learning Sciences*, 7 (3–4), 271–311.

Britt, M. and C. Aglinskas. (2002). Improving students' ability to identify and use source information. *Cognition and Instruction*, 20 (4), 485–522.

Hass, M.E. 2008. Conducting interviews to learn about World War II. *Social Education*, 72 (5): 264–267.

Hubbard, J. 2010. Using social studies themes to investigate modern Egypt. *Social Education*, 74 (4): 226–231.

Rowell, C.G., M.G. Hickey, K. Gecsei, and S. Klein. 2007. A school-wide effort for learning history via a time capsule. *Social Education*, 71 (5): 261–270.

Selwyn, D. 2011. Encouraging student research. *Social Education*, 75 (5): 277–280.

Selwyn, D. 2010. *Following the threads: Bringing inquiry research into the classroom.* New York: Peter Lang Publishing.

Sweda, C. 2009. Our school as living history. *Middle School Learning*, 34 (1): 8–9.

Trenkle, A. 2009. Researching our school's history. *Middle School Learning*, 34 (1): 2–7.

VanSledright, B.A. 1995. How do multiple text resources influence learning to read American history in fifth grade? NRRC Ongoing Research. *NRRC News: A Newsletter of the National Reading Research Center*, 4–5.

VanSledright, B.A. and L. Frankes. 2000. Concept- and strategic-knowledge development in historical study: A comparative exploration in two fourth-grade classrooms. *Cognition and Instruction*, 18 (2), 239–283.

Woodward, A., D.L. Elliott, and K.C Nagel. 1986. Beyond textbooks in elementary social studies. *Social Education*, 50 (1), 50–53.

WEB RESOURCES

1.   **Canadian Letters and Images Project:**
www.canadianletters.ca
The Canadian Letters and Images Project is an online archive of the Canadian war experience, from World Wars I and II, as told through the letters and images of Canadians themselves.

2. **Digital History: Using New Technologies to Enhance Teaching and Research:** www.digitalhistory.uh.edu
This site contains an extensive array of digitized documents organized according to eras in American history; topics such as beauty and fashion, children, courtship, architecture, and political cartoons; virtual exhibitions; and voices (e.g., Asian-American immigrants, children, women).

3. **The EvidenceWeb: Library and Archives Canada:**
www.collectionscanada.gc.ca/education/sources
The EvidenceWeb is part of Library and Archives Canada's Learning Centre and provides teachers with original documents, art, and video and audio clips. Each original document includes detailed descriptions, zoom-in capacity, and links to other websites. The EvidenceWeb can be searched by theme, site, format, and place, or sources can be browsed by theme (Aboriginal Peoples, The Arts, Disasters and Phenomena, Exploration and Settlement, Landmarks and Landscape, Notable People and Accomplishments, Politics and Government, Sports and Leisure, and War and Military). EvidenceWeb Educational Resources include various guides to improve students' research skills, their ability to analyze a variety of different primary sources—including oral histories, photographs, maps, political cartoons, and diaries—as well as three seven-lesson units of study: The Confederation Chronicles; Hidden in the Documents: Discovering Loyalist Stories; and Canada and the Cold War: The Gouzenko Affair.

4. **Great Unsolved Mysteries in Canadian History:**
canadianmysteries.ca
This prize-winning site presents visual and print primary source documents related to a number of Canadian historical mysteries such as: "Who Discovered Klondike Gold?", "Death over a Painted Lake: The Tom Thomson Tragedy," and "Heaven and Hell on Earth: The Massacre of the 'Black' Donnelleys." Students don't need to "solve" the mysteries in order to access this treasure trove of documents.

5. **McCord Museum, Keys to History:**
www.mccord-museum.qc.ca/en/keys
This digital online collection contains 137,000 artifacts organized in categories: Paintings, Photos and Drawings, Costume and Textiles, Ethnology and Archaeology, Decorative Arts, Notman Photographic Archives, and Textual Archives.

6. **Multicultural Canada:** www.multiculturalcanada.ca
This website includes collections of newspapers, oral histories, photographs, books, newsletters, legal documents, meeting minutes, and other materials highlighting the presence and contributions of numerous cultural and ethnic communities in Canada. It also includes resources for finding information on cultural or ethnic groups not listed on this site, including Encyclopedia of Canada's Peoples, BC Multicultural Photographs, Miscellaneous Collections, and Related Sites.

7. **Picture History: The Primary Source for History Online:**
www.picturehistory.com
The focus of this site is American history. It is organized according to topics such as Arts and Entertainment, Places and Social Conditions and Trends, and War and Military, or by decade, photographers, or anniversary.

8. **The History Education Network:** www.thenhier.ca
See also www.thenhier.ca/en/content/primary-sources-and-teaching-links for an extensive list of annotated websites organized according to Canadian history topics.
See also chapter 15, "Exploring Visual Resources with Elementary Students" for a further list of websites.

12 Learning Co-operatively in Elementary Classrooms

Tom Morton

In the 1980s, co-operative learning marched—sometimes with considerable fanfare—to the centre stage of accepted educational practice. Researchers and practitioners alike applauded its power to improve academic achievement, especially among students who had traditionally not done well in school, and its potential to enhance interpersonal relations, especially among ethnic groups and between physically challenged and able-bodied students.

Many teachers have embraced co-operative learning. Many others, however, have run up against the common barriers to implementing new practice, and abandoned the approach in favour of more traditional group work or whole-class instruction. Speaking of the United States, Seymour Sarason (1995, 84) bluntly suggests that what passes frequently for co-operative learning is a charade or a misnomer for traditional group work. Although research on the current situation in Canada is sparse, the reality of co-operative learning, especially in secondary schools, may be less like a mainstage performance than a fringe festival play—creative, exciting, but marginal. This situation arises partly from a failure to appreciate that co-operation is not merely a teaching technique, but a commitment to a set of core values.

Morton Deutsch (1949) coined the term "co-operative learning" more than sixty years ago, but the idea of group learning has been around much longer. At the beginning of the twentieth century, John Dewey recommended that students work together on problems relevant to their lives. He also wrote about the barriers to effective group work. For example, Dewey described his attempt to buy work tables for his elementary school; he could not find anything other than individual desks. Finally, a salesperson identified the problem: "I am afraid we have not what you want. You want something at which the children may work. These are all for listening!" (1907, 48). Similar practical and philosophical barriers impede effective implementation of co-operative learning today.

This chapter clarifies key elements of effective co-operative learning in elementary classrooms and suggests ways to implement co-operative approaches in social studies. I begin by offering three reasons why co-operative learning should play an important role in our subject and then explore three challenges to its implementation. I then introduce two of the best-known approaches to co-operative learning—the Learning Together model, developed by brothers David and Roger Johnson with help from their sister Edythe Holubec, and the Structural Approach, first developed by Spencer Kagan and recently revised with help from his wife, Laurie, his son, Miguel, and other associates. I explore the principles behind each approach, offer sample lessons, and distinguish these models from each other and from traditional group work and direct instruction.

Why Adopt Co-operative Learning in Social Studies?

Co-operative learning is an approach to teaching in which students work together in small groups that are carefully designed to be cohesive and mutually supportive. At the same time, group members are individually accountable for their own learning and for contributing to the group's learning. This approach to learning can contribute to the goals of social studies in at least three ways:

- **Academic achievement.** Considerable research suggests that properly implemented co-operative learning promotes academic achievement. In social studies, this achievement involves the acquisition of a body of knowledge in the social science disciplines and the ability to investigate and communicate these ideas. Two notable reviews, a meta-analysis of 475 research studies (Johnson and Johnson 1989) and a similar review with stricter selection criteria of 60 studies (Slavin 1989), concluded that co-operative learning produces significant gains in achievement when compared to control conditions.

- **Constructivist learning.** Considerable cognitive research suggests that learners must "construct" knowledge if it is to be internalized. Co-operative learning facilitates the construction of ideas, perhaps because explaining ideas to others is one of the more effective ways of making personal sense of them. This concept was expressed by the Roman philosopher Seneca when he said, "Qui docet, discit": whoever teaches, learns (also translated: when you teach, you learn twice).

- **Citizenship values and attitudes.** Co-operative learning promotes values. Well-planned co-operative lessons offer students opportunities to express themselves and reflect on their civic competence—the abilities and values of citizenship (Myers 2003a, 2003b). Since its early years, co-operative learning has been closely linked with promoting mutual respect and liking regardless of differences. It does this by encouraging students to appreciate their own background and those of others, and by fostering commitment to a set of foundational values that includes respect for civic responsibilities, freedom of expression, fairness, and equality.

Challenges to Co-operative Learning

During the rise in popularity of co-operative learning in the 1980s, the prominent researcher Robert Slavin warned educators that it was being "oversold and undertrained." At the time, teachers were encouraged to implement an approach to teaching that may have been at odds with their philosophy and/or not adequately understood. If co-operative learning is to be more than the charade Sarasan describes, teachers must recognize and commit to overcoming the challenges that come with its implementation. Three of these challenges are described below: the need for teacher commitment and study, aligning classroom practices and values, and building student skills and habits.

TEACHER COMMITMENT AND STUDY

One of the conditions for co-operative learning is recognition of the commitment and study required to implement it competently. Co-operative learning is not a technique for varying the usual classroom fare. An occasional group task or a lesson or two in co-operation in the midst of business as usual will not create a learning community and will not improve interpersonal relations. As David and Roger Johnson (1992, 45) note: "Simply placing students in groups and telling them to work together does not in and of itself result in co-operative efforts—or positive effects on students."

Implementing co-operative learning creates problems and raises questions: What do I do about students who resist being in the same group? What about the quiet students? What about the group that doesn't get down to work, finishes early, or talks too loudly? Most of us will need help in resolving these problems and, over time, forging a learning community from what may be very diverse and reluctant learners. Help may come from a co-operative support group of teachers—much like the groups we expect students to be part of, through independent study, or through outside help from a school board consultant or support teacher. (Contact information for co-operative learning groups is listed at the end of this chapter.)

ALIGN CLASSROOM PRACTICES AND VALUES

The basic values of co-operative learning, such as collaboration, equality, and inclusion, may conflict with teaching philosophies, curriculum content, and classroom organization. Aligning the classroom with the practices and values of co-operative learning requires effort. One source of conflict is the importance given to social or interpersonal goals in co-operative learning. Most co-operative models teach interpersonal skills and encourage reflection. In many classrooms, however, learning means academic learning only and social goals may be downplayed or actively suppressed by factors such as seating in rows to minimize student interaction.

Co-operative learning may also conflict with deeply held beliefs about individualism and competition. In a

FIGURE 12.1   PARTICIPATION PIE

Divide the pie to illustrate how much each member of your group participated in the task. Write down each member's name in their pie section. Give your reasons for the way you divided the pie and suggest things you might do to improve co-operation in the group.

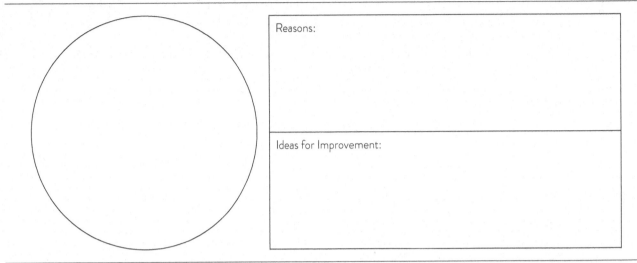

Reasons:

Ideas for Improvement:

co-operative classroom, common watchwords are "two heads are better than one" and "you have a right to ask any group member for help and a duty to help anyone who asks." Students sit facing each other, they know the names of their classmates, and they may ask to study together before a test or have a partner for a project. Teachers who believe strongly in individual learning and competition may be uncomfortable with this kind of classroom.

Even if students are not separated from each other in the classroom, they are often pitted against each other. We send enduring messages that peers are potential barriers to success whenever we grade by the curve, display only the best papers on the wall, sort children into winners and losers in spelling bees, and encourage students during a teacher-led discussion to compete to get the answer quickly. In his book *No Contest: The Case Against Competition*, Alfie Kohn (1992) summarizes the research on the effects of these sorts of classroom practices. His findings suggest that competition is associated with less generosity, less inclination to trust, less willingness to see other viewpoints, and poorer communication.

Co-operative learning will never be more than a fringe methodology or a charade unless the practices and values in our classrooms embody it. Almost everything we do or say in class can influence co-operation (Sapon-Shevin and Schniedewind 1992).

BUILD STUDENT SKILLS AND HABITS OF CO-OPERATION

Not all, or even most, students enter our classes with well-developed interpersonal skills. For co-operative learning to be effective, we need to teach students interpersonal skills and attitudes as well as how to reflect. Problems such as a conflict or reluctant participation should be discussed and resolved with student participation. One motto of the Johnsons' has been, "Turn problems back to the group to solve." They insist that co-operative groups put their academic tasks to one side to address personal problems. By teaching social skills and establishing the habit of reflection on group dynamics, students can recognize that they have the power to make co-operation work.

Two Approaches to Co-operative Learning

By one account (Myers 1991), there are more than twenty co-operative learning models. In this section I explore two popular models: The Johnsons' Learning Together model and the Kagans' Structural Approach. My purpose is to show the key ingredients involved in co-operative learning, identify the ways in which it differs from traditional group work, and give some useful ideas for implementing both models.

ELEMENTS OF THE LEARNING TOGETHER MODEL

The Johnsons' model offers one of the best-known explanations of the principles of co-operative pedagogy (Johnson, Johnson, and Holubec 1998). Their model describes five elements essential for effective co-operation:

- **Establish positive interdependence.** Group work will be co-operative only if there is positive interdependence: group members must believe that their success depends on the success of others or, as the Johnsons say, "We sink or swim together." Positive interdependence can be seen as both an element of lesson design and a spirit of mutual helpfulness. Teachers might create positive interdependence by asking small groups to come up with a single product or to share a limited number of resources such as one instruction sheet, glue stick, or pair of scissors. Planning for positive interdependence is especially important in the early months of the school year, when students may not yet have the skills or motivation to co-operate.
- **Require individual accountability.** Individual accountability can be seen both as an element of lesson planning and the attitude that everyone contributes and is valued for that contribution. When students know that they are accountable for their own learning and for helping the group learn, both group productivity and individual achievement are enhanced. However, resentment is likely if some members are not pulling their weight; in such instances, the harder-working group members may lessen their effort to avoid being "suckers." To encourage individual accountability, we might require each student to explain the contents of the group's product or assign each student a specific section of a shared product.
- **Encourage face-to-face interaction.** Co-operative learning requires face-to-face interaction where the conversation helps students advance their thinking. This element is often referred to as "purposeful talk" and it emphasizes the role of talk in thinking. To achieve a high level of academic achievement, students must meet in groups to discuss and refine their thinking. To achieve a feeling of caring and commitment, students must encourage and help each other. Sitting together, but working independently and occasionally copying each other's notes, is not interaction.

PLANNING A LEARNING TOGETHER LESSON

Specify lesson objectives
- academic content
- social skills

Decide operational details
- group size
- assignment to groups
- room arrangement
- materials
- student roles

Introduce lesson
- explain the academic task
- structure positive interdependence
- create individual accountability
- explain expected use of social skills
- set criteria for success

Monitor students
- look for evidence of the expected social skills (by student or teacher observation)
- provide opportunities for processing

Evaluate
- academic achievement
- group functioning

- **Teach interpersonal or social skills.** Social skills refer to behaviours that enable a group to work together, such as sharing, listening, and encouraging. Students do not necessarily know how to behave co-operatively and we may have to teach "good classroom manners." For example, students should move quickly and quietly to groups, use a person's name, talk in quiet voices, stay with the group, avoid wandering around, and sit facing each other. In the primary grades or in classes with many impetuous students, it may be several months before we can introduce more advanced social skills such as encouraging participation or active listening. The timing and particulars may differ, but the need to teach rather than assume social skills is crucial.
- **Allow for processing.** Research suggests that academic achievement is greater when co-operative groups reflect on their interaction. Students require time and appropriate strategies to analyze their group's functioning and their individual mastery of social skills. It is advisable to regularly devote

between five and fifteen minutes of group time for students to write or talk about group interactions. The Participation Pie described in Figure 12.1 is one tool for facilitating group reflection.

Planning an effective Learning Together lesson may take considerable time to master. A suggested sequence of steps is outlined in the feature "Planning a Learning Together Lesson."

Apart from the five elements described in Planning a Learning Together Lesson, there are a number of operational details to attend to. Group composition requires prior planning and warrants special consideration. Group size should be small, from two to five students, and groups should be mixed according to academic level, ethnicity, gender, and socio-economic status. Compatibility is another ingredient to consider. Considerable research and teacher experience suggest that heterogeneous groups enhance class cohesiveness, interpersonal relations, and academic achievement for all students.

However, when unaccustomed to co-operative learning, students typically want to choose their own group members, mainly friends who are similar to themselves. Consequently, there may be tension when teachers choose groups. To lessen this tension, spend some time explaining the reasons for mixed groups, such as:

- Social studies class is where we learn how to be good citizens and part of that is learning to work with others who are different from us but share this classroom and this planet.
- We often work better with those who are not our friends; there is less social talk about sports, movies, and the like.
- Each student will probably work with everyone in the class at some point during the year.
- You don't have to like your teammates; you only have to work with them.
- When we play sports, go to church/temple/synagogue, join a trade union, or are born into a family, we are in a team, so why not in the classroom?
- Especially for a highly diverse class: There are lots of different people in this classroom and in our neighbourhoods; in this country we say this is a good thing, and that we should respect each other and learn to work together.
- Especially for older students: Learning to work with others is key for career success; when hired for a job, we do not choose our fellow employees and we certainly do not choose our customers. Business research suggests that people who get fired from their first jobs do so because they can't get along with their boss and their co-workers.

Some students may still disagree with you, but they will know that you have a clear plan and purpose for your groupings.

Although most experienced practitioners argue strongly in favour of teacher-selected teams, during the early part of the year when we are unfamiliar with our students—or at any other time of the year for a break in routine—random choice is recommended. There are several creative ways to do this: distributing playing cards with the common cards sitting together, counting off the names of famous figures, a foreign language, or lining up according to birth date without talking—a challenge—and then grouping students next to each other. As a class develops into a learning community, one that is inclusive in habit and attitude, students may be able to choose their own heterogeneous groups.

MAKE-OVER LESSON BASED ON LEARNING TOGETHER MODEL

The significance of the Johnsons' Learning Together model can be seen by contrasting its five elements and key decisions with traditional group work. In a lesson described in *Critical Challenges for Primary Students* (McDiarmid, Manzo, and Musselle 2007), students are asked to develop criteria for powerful questions in preparation for a visit by a classroom guest. The criteria include "questions that will give you answers with a lot of information" and "questions that require some thought." Students use the criteria to assess questions they might ask the guest and each student selects one question. How would a Learning Together approach to this lesson differ from traditional group work?

- **Preparation.** In traditional group work, students might select their own groups. Most students would choose their friends, resulting in more homogeneous groups. Group size might vary from two to twenty. Few of the social goals of co-operation would be realized in these groups, and in some groups the academic goals would probably not be achieved either. In contrast, the Learning Together teacher would carefully select groups to include a high achiever, a low achiever and one or two middle-level achievers for a group of three or four. Gender, ethnicity, and

FIGURE 12.2   PAIR REFLECTIONS

NAME:

NAME OF PARTNER:

	Never	Once in a while	About half of the time	Most of the time	Always
I made certain my partner and I both understood the material we were studying.	0	1	2	3	4
I listened to the contributions of my partner.	0	1	2	3	4
I felt that my partner listened to me.	0	1	2	3	4
We stayed on task.	0	1	2	3	4

Write down two adjectives that describe how you feel about your work together:

1.

2.

general compatibility would also be considered. In the primary grades, most co-operative work is done in pairs. (It is hard to get left out of a pair!) Students would be comfortable with a number of routines such as seating arrangement—what the Johnsons call "eye to eye and knee to knee"—and a quiet signal to indicate the time to stop group work and pay attention to the teacher. Often, the success of a lesson depends on these and other details.

- **Positive interdependence.** The Learning Together teacher would explain the academic task and set the interdependence and individual accountability criteria. For the first step of this critical thinking lesson, groups could have goal sharing (namely, the common task of establishing criteria for a powerful question). There could also be resource sharing if each group was given a single poster on which to write the criteria for powerful questions, and role interdependence if there were different but complementary roles, such as:
  - **Checker:** confirms that everyone in the group agrees with each decision and can explain the reasons for it.
  - **Recorder:** writes down the questions and reads them back to the group to confirm wording.
  - **Encourager:** invites more quiet members to share their ideas and encourages the group if it gets bogged down.

- **Gatekeeper:** ensures a balanced discussion by politely asking students who are dominating to give others a turn.
- **Individual accountability.** This could be established by asking each student to be ready to explain why their criteria are key to powerful questions. The teacher might randomly ask students to respond. If the student's answer is reasonable, the teacher compliments the whole group for the work, not just the individual student, as is typical in traditional group work. If the answer is unreasonable, the group needs to go back to work and the teacher returns to the same student to ask the question again.

Students might also be held individually responsible by taking turns to offer a criterion. Assigning roles gives special responsibilities to each student. In traditional group work, in contrast, there is little positive interdependence or individual accountability. All students use their own notebooks and groups are instructed to create criteria and share their answers. Students who are co-operative by nature might do this and produce a common list, but there would be no clear impetus to do so and little motivation to refine the list. Without individual accountability, some students would say and do little and merely copy the work of others.

For the next step in the lesson, in which each student writes one powerful question to ask the guest, a

Learning Together approach would also expect student teams to have a common goal (for example, each student is to have a powerful question written down to ask the guest) and individual accountability (for example, individual students are able to explain how their question meets the criteria).

- **Social Skills.** Social skills are often omitted entirely in traditional group work, or superficially addressed by general admonitions such as "I want you to listen." In the Learning Together model, the teacher discusses why listening is a good idea and teaches specific strategies. For example, the teacher might ask: "What kinds of things would you be likely to say if you were listening carefully to someone?" or "What would you look like as you were listening carefully?" The teacher might record responses on a poster or ask three or four students to role-play positive and negative examples. Understanding the importance of social skills and being able to use them well are major learning objectives in the Johnsons' model of co-operative learning.

- **Processing.** At some point, co-operative groups will be asked to reflect on how well they worked together in order to improve social skills, resolve group problems, and celebrate successes. This reflection might be done in various ways: students could keep a journal; the teacher could make observations and report them to the class; the group could discuss what they did well and identify areas for improvement; or, individuals may complete a reflection form such as Pair Reflections described in Figure 12.2. In contrast, student reflection in typical group work is solely about the content of the lesson.

Select a lesson you have planned. Using the remake of the "powerful questions" lesson into a co-operative lesson as a guide, modify your lesson's activities to embody the Johnsons' five elements of effective co-operative learning.

THE STRUCTURAL APPROACH

Another popular co-operative learning model, the Structural Approach, includes similar elements to the Johnsons' but with a few key differences. The Johnsons' approach focusses on the elements of co-operative learning so that teachers can develop lessons embodying these principles. The Kagans and their associates have instead provided planned lesson structures that have co-operative elements built into them. At first glance, their repertoire of co-operative structures or lesson formats may appear to be a "cookbook," but each structure has a solid co-operative foundation and is suitable for different teaching situations.

The Kagans define structures as content-free ways to organize social interaction within the classroom. The structures are the "how" of instruction while the lesson content is the "what." The more than 150 structures in the Kagan model may seem daunting. However, there is no need to use all or even most of the structures. In fact, the Kagans advocate teaching students one structure a month. The large repertoire provides flexibility in choosing co-operative learning formats for a specific topic or learning objective.

Structures can be simple and brief, such as Think-Pair-Share, which can take mere minutes. In this structure, the teacher poses a problem or a question and students individually think, write, or draw an answer. Then, one person shares their ideas with a partner and the partner listens and offers feedback. The two students then switch roles. Finally, the teacher asks students to share their ideas with the entire class.

Structures can also be quite involved, such as Co-op Co-op, which is a ten-step structure for group research projects involving considerable student autonomy. In Co-op Co-op, students form groups with others who share an interest in a topic. Each student researches an aspect of that topic, then they pool their knowledge to prepare a class presentation. Co-op Co-op may take a full semester to complete. Other Kagan structures suitable for elementary grades are described in the feature "Co-operative Structures Appropriate for Elementary Students."

From grade 4 up, almost any structure can be used. The simplest structures are best for the younger grades and any class that is new to co-operative learning. For example, groups of two can use RallyRobin or Timed-Pair-Share, while students ready for a bigger group of three or four can use Placemat. More complex structures like Numbered Heads Together and Academic Controversy are appropriate for older students.

Each Kagan structure incorporates the same positive interaction and individual accountability as in the Johnsons' model, but the Kagans suggest two alternative principles: "equal participation" (the use of strategies such as taking turns that promote broad involvement of all students) and "simultaneous interaction" (as many students as possible contributing at the same time). The acronym for the Kagans' principles is PIES:

CO-OPERATIVE STRUCTURES APPROPRIATE FOR ELEMENTARY STUDENTS

- **Numbered Heads Together.** Students number off in teams. The teacher asks a question with complex or multiple answers and the teams discuss possible responses. The teacher calls a number and the student with that number in each group explains his or her group's answer.
- **Corners.** The teacher poses a question, statement, or issue and offers four or so possible responses, assigning each to a corner of the room. Students move to the corner that best represents their choice and pair up to explain to each other the reasons for their choice. The teacher then calls on students to explain their choices. If students have learned to paraphrase, the teacher asks students to paraphrase the reasoning of students from other corners.
- **RoundRobin and RoundTable.** The teacher poses a question that has multiple answers. In RoundRobin, students take turns giving an answer or idea orally. In RoundTable, students write down or construct answers in turn or simultaneously on a single sheet of paper. Example topics in social studies include: listing jobs in the community, cities, details from a picture, or recollections from a field trip or video.
- **RallyRobin, RallyTable, or RallyRead.** These structures use the same steps as RoundTable and RoundRobin but are done in pairs. RallyRobin is organized turn-taking. Primary students could take turns saying the letters of the alphabet or counting numbers. Students could also take turns drawing part of a forest or impressions of a story. In RallyRead, students take turns reading sentences or paragraphs to each other.
- **Timed-Pair-Share.** This is a very versatile approach that is a more carefully structured form of Think-Pair-Share, where students turn to a partner and talk about something. With younger students it helps to structure the think time and the share time or one person may do all the talking. In Timed-Pair-Share, one student shares his or her thoughts for a measured time—twenty seconds to two minutes—while the other listens. The students then switch roles. Almost any thought-provoking question a teacher could ask of a whole class could become Timed-Think-Pair-Share. For example, after looking at a picture or listening to a story, you could ask, "What does this tell us about . . . ?"
- **Review.** Students could write down everything they remember and then share, or they could do an oral review, answering the question, "What have we learned from reading this story or newspaper article?" Other possibilities include:

- A question asking for a reason why something happened.
- A question asking for a prediction.
- A question asking students to reflect on how they think, for example, "What steps do we need to follow when we interview someone about their work?" or "What should we be thinking about when we try to help someone?"
- Kindergarten and grade 1 students could draw, midway through a story, a prediction of what happens next, or express their feelings by drawing a sad, happy, angry, or scared face.

- **Placemat.** This begins with a similar approach to RoundTable. Teams of two to four students are given a large sheet of paper with a square or circle in the middle and the rest of the space divided into sections according to the number of students in the group. Students are given a question and write or draw their answer in one of the sections. The steps include:
  - Assign students a topic or question that requires reflection; perhaps what they know about a city, Canada, the government, or some controversial issue.
  - Each student writes down or draws their response in his or her own space, leaving the centre blank.
  - Students take turns sharing their thoughts with the group or rotate the paper to view each other's responses. Optionally, they may place a star beside the most important idea each of the other students has written.
  - As a group, students combine their ideas to write their best answer or a consensus answer in the central section of the placemat.
- **Team Web.** Each team is given a large sheet of paper and each student a different colour pen. Students are asked to construct a web about a topic. Optionally, the teacher may provide all or some of the sub-topics and ask students to provide a detailed explanation and identify connecting links. The key to this exercise is the coloured pens: each student must contribute to the web and write in a different colour, thus making individual accountability easy to monitor.
- **Carousel Sharing.** One person from each team stays at the team's workplace to be a spokesperson for their topic. The other team members rotate from spokesperson to spokesperson learning as much as they can about a topic, which they must understand in order to complete a task. After the carousel, each rotating group of students provides feedback to their own spokesperson about what they learned from the other teams' spokespeople.

positive interdependence, individual accountability, equal participation, and simultaneous interaction. Equal participation would be reflected, for example, in the timed aspect of Timed-Pair-Share or the turn-taking step in RoundRobin and RoundTable. Simultaneity is reflected in the importance given to pairs in most of the structures.

There is also a different emphasis on social skills in the Kagans' approach. In an article contrasting the two approaches, Kagan (2001) agrees with the value of social skills but argues that there is no need to take extra time to teach them and process their use when they are embedded into the lesson structure. For example, a social skill such as active listening is integral in Corners and encouraging participation is important in RoundTable.

MAKE-OVER LESSON USING THE STRUCTURAL APPROACH

To better understand the structural approach and its four principles, let us consider an example of their application to direct, whole-class instruction. In the critical thinking lesson "What Is Canada Like?" (Harrison, Smith, and Wright 2004), students learn about what makes a powerful metaphor. They then view the video *Kids' View of Canada* to identify the metaphors that are offered to describe Canada. They then analyze these metaphors and create their own metaphor according to agreed-upon criteria. Finally, they create a group poster using an image to illustrate their metaphor.

The following description of lesson activities assumes the teacher has used the Learning Together model to form groups and arrange seating. In addition, it assumes that the class is familiar with the structures. Students begin in a team of four, then separate into pairs before reassembling in groups of four again. Note that for the purpose of illustrating the variety of applicable structures, the description below uses more structures than most teachers would want in a single lesson.

The lesson could begin by asking students to describe themselves metaphorically by choosing one of the words in a pair and writing their response to: "How would you describe yourself? more cat or dog?... solid or liquid?... Monday or Saturday?... eagle or dolphin?... radish or strawberry?" After each of these questions, students use the RoundRobin structure to share their responses.

Next, students are asked to consider the meaning of these and other social studies metaphors, such as

describing the United States as a cultural "melting pot" and Canada as a multicultural "mosaic." This could be done in pairs with a Timed-Think-Pair-Share, followed by whole-class instruction on the definition of a metaphor.

The teacher continues in the mode of whole-class instruction to explain the features that make a metaphor powerful: broad application (an accurate comparison, usually on many points), original, revealing (gives insights), and surprising (intriguing or lively). Students are asked to use these criteria to judge which is the more powerful metaphor: "television is a fountain of information" or "television is bubble gum for the mind."

Returning to Think-Pair-Share, students now suggest metaphors to represent common aspects of their lives, such as playing, eating, school, or family. They list these metaphors and ask which are powerful and why.

So far, the steps illustrate one aspect of the Kagan approach: a mix of short co-operative activities with teacher-directed instruction. The Kagans believe that a teacher will seldom give a fully co-operative lesson, but almost every lesson should have some co-operative activity.

The next activity, watching the National Film Board video *Kids' View of Canada*, uses the Pairs View structure, described in the feature "Co-operative Structures Appropriate for Elementary Students." This structure contrasts clearly with direct instruction (Morton 1996), or what John Myers calls "full frontal instruction." A typical form of direct instruction using a video might appropriately be labelled the "Whole Class View-Question-Answer" approach. It has three parts:

- The teacher shows the video.
- Students individually complete worksheets or answer questions during or after the showing.
- When the assignments are completed, the teacher calls on students one by one for their answers to the questions.

In this approach, during the showing of the video there is little interaction among students or between students and teacher. If a section of the video is confusing or complex, students get little or no help until the end. The question-and-answer session is intended to help all students learn, but in many classes it may be competitive if students are vying for the teacher's attention with cries of "Me! Me!" Student interaction is competitive when strong students triumph, while those who are not quick with the answer or not aggressive enough to win the teacher's attention lose. In contrast, the Pairs View approach is rich in both student-student and student-teacher interaction.

Once the video has been viewed, the next step is for students to analyze interesting metaphors from the video and add at least one metaphor of their own creation using the criteria for a powerful metaphor. This could be done co-operatively using Numbered Heads Together.

Following this, students choose the most powerful metaphor and create a group poster indicating the points of application between Canada and the powerful metaphor. This too could be done with Numbered Heads Together or perhaps a modification of the Team Web, in which each student uses a different colour of felt pen to draw the poster.

Finally, each group shares its poster. A Carousel Sharing structure might be appropriate so that students can listen to each group's explanation of the power of its metaphor.

Although I have suggested possible co-operative structures, these last few activities would be inconsistent with the Kagans' approach because they lead to giving a group grade. The Kagans oppose group grades because of concerns about fairness and because they believe group grades fuel negative reactions against co-operative learning from high-achieving students. The Johnsons, while recognizing the risks, nevertheless believe that group grades may sometimes be acceptable if teams

are well prepared and individual accountability is well planned. The Kagans would recommend that the Structural Approach be used for the introduction, the input of information, and guided practice aspects of the lesson, after which students would demonstrate their learning with an individual project or test. According to the Kagans, co-operative learning is a method of teaching, not an approach to the evaluation of learning.

With the Kagans' approach, the final few steps of analysis and a group poster could be preparatory work followed by individual team members writing a paragraph or illustrating one of the metaphors that the group has analyzed. Individual students might also be given a new metaphor, perhaps from a political cartoon about Canada, and asked to decide whether it is a powerful metaphor and to explain why.

Avoiding Common Mistakes When Introducing Co-operative Learning

In his article "Four Fatal Flaws: Avoiding the Common Mistakes of Novice Users of Co-operative Learning," Paul Vermette of Niagara University outlines four particular mistakes to watch out for when introducing co-operative learning (1994). The first fatal flaw he identifies is allowing students to choose the participants in their groups. He argues, as I do, that teachers should build the teams.

The second fatal flaw is to launch students into a major group project before completing smaller activities to build teams and establish social skills and habits of co-operation.

The third common fatal flaw is assigning group projects to be done out of class, rather than having the groups do the work in the class. "To help monitor the effectiveness of co-operative learning, the teacher *needs to see it!*" writes Vermette (1994, 258–259). (The italics are his, but could have been mine.) He lists many advantages of doing co-operative work in class. For example, teachers can offer suggestions and praise to students, boost the efforts of reluctant learners or shy students, and help groups reflect on their behaviour. When teachers give students group projects to complete outside class, none of this happens. Moreover, unequal participation is almost inevitable.

The fourth fatal flaw is found with group grades: "Nothing offends an industrious student more than having someone else (Paul or Paula Parasite?) do nothing and share an A!" (Vermette 1994, 259). If group grades are to be assigned, it is imperative that all students get what, and only what, they deserve.

Co-operative learning is a valuable approach to teaching and learning, worthy of attention and thoughtful implementation by elementary school teachers. Although it does demand a commitment on our part, an alignment of our values with the approach, and a willingness to address the social side of learning, there is help from research, practical guides, and experienced teachers, some of which are listed in the references.

Select a lesson you have planned. Using the remake of a traditional lesson into a co-operative lesson as a guide, modify the activities and structure of your lesson to embody the Kagans' four principles of effective co-operative learning.

REFERENCES

Deutsch, M. 1949. A theory of cooperation and competition. *Human Relations* 2: 129–152.

Dewey, J. 1907. *The school and society.* Chicago: University of Chicago Press.

Harrison, J., N. Smith, and I. Wright. 2004. *Selected critical challenges in social studies—Intermediate/middle school.* Vancouver: The Critical Thinking Consortium.

Johnson, D. and R. Johnson. 1989. *Cooperation and competition: Theory and research.* Edina, MN: Interaction Book Co.

———. 1992. Approaches to implementing cooperative learning in the social studies classroom. In *Cooperative learning in the social studies classroom,* ed. R. Stahl and R. VanSickle, 45–51. Washington, DC: National Council for the Social Studies.

Johnson, D., R. Johnson, and E. Holubec. 1998. *Cooperation in the classroom,* 7th ed. Edina, MN: Interaction Book Co.

Kagan, S. 2001. Kagan structures and learning together—what is the difference? *KaganOnLine Magazine.* Available online at www.KaganOnline.com.

Kohn, A. 1992. *No contest: The case against competition.* Boston: Houghton Mifflin.

McDiarmid, T., R. Manzo, and T. Musselle. 2007. *Critical challenges for primary students.* Rev. ed. Vancouver: The Critical Thinking Consortium.

Morton, T. 1996. *Cooperative learning and social studies: Towards excellence and equity.* San Juan Capistrano, CA: Kagan.

Myers, J. 1991. Cooperative learning in history and social sciences: An idea whose time has come. *Canadian Social Studies* 26 (2): 60–64.

———. 2003a. Assessing citizenship and character using co-operative learning. *Orbit* 33 (2): 47–49.

———. 2003b. Co-operative learning: Steps toward an anti-racist education. *Orbit* 33 (3): 29–32.

Sapon-Shevin, M. and N. Schniedewind. 1992. If cooperative learning's the answer, what are the questions? *Journal of Education* 174 (2): 11–37.

Sarason, S. 1995. Some reactions to what we have learned. *Phi Delta Kappan* 7 (1): 84.

Slavin, R.E. 1989. *Cooperative learning: Theory, research, and practice.* Englewood Cliffs, NJ: Prentice-Hall.

Vermette, Paul. 1994. Four fatal flaws: avoiding the common mistakes of novice users of cooperative learning. *The High School Journal,* February/March: 255–260.

HELPFUL WEBSITES

BC Cooperative Learning Association is the professional specialist association of the BC Teachers' Federation: psas.bctf.ca/BCCLA.

Cooperative Learning Center at the University of Minnesota: www.co-operation.org.

Great Lakes Association for Cooperation in Education (GLACIE) is based in Toronto: www.glacie.ca.

International Association for the Study of Cooperation in Education is a group of teachers and researchers from around the world who produce a magazine called *Co-operative Learning*: www.iasce.net.

Kagan Publishing and Professional Development: www.Kagan Online.com.

Saskatoon Public School Division offers a substantial collection of online resources for interactive learning strategies, including online tutorials, assessment tools, templates, and sample lessons that support co-operative learning: olc.spsd.sk.ca/DE/PD/instr/strats/coop.

13

Conducting Social Action in Elementary Social Studies

Penney Clark

It is generally agreed that the preparation of citizens is the *raison d'être* of social studies. However, establishing that citizenship education is the ultimate purpose of social studies doesn't tell us very much. The crucial question is: What are the qualities of a good citizen? Is it sufficient that students are capable of informed debate on social issues? Or does effective citizenship also require developing the will and the ability to "act" to address local, national, and global problems?

Prominent Canadian (Osborne 1982) and American educators (Newmann 1975, Goodlad 2004) have long argued that students should be taught not only to discuss social issues but also to act on them. This attention to social action is apparent in recent provincial curricula. For example, the Alberta curriculum states that the role of social studies is to help students "become active and responsible citizens, engaged in the democratic process and aware of their capacity to effect change in their communities, society and world" (Alberta Education 2005, 1). Starting with grade 3, the "Social Participation" outcomes in this curriculum include expectations that students will contribute to the well-being of their school or the broader community (Alberta Education 2005). Similarly, the British Columbia social studies curriculum expects elementary students to "develop the skills and attitudes necessary to become thoughtful, active participants in their communities and as global citizens" (British Columbia Ministry of Education 2006, 11). In grade 6 they are asked to "individually or in groups implement a plan of action to address a problem or issue" (98). The curriculum suggests that this might involve a fundraising or letter-writing campaign, a clothing drive, writing an editorial for a school or community newspaper, or circulating a petition. In the Atlantic provinces, students in grade 3 are expected to develop "a class action plan to promote positive interactions among people. . . . The plan might involve helping out at a retirement home (ageism), working at a food bank (poverty), or creating an awareness campaign (racism)" (Department of Education, Prince Edward Island 2012, 68).

Of course, it is not enough simply to ask students to undertake a project. If they are to succeed in this endeavour and truly learn about active citizenship, they need to be taught how to plan and implement social action projects responsibly. This chapter focusses on developing these abilities by discussing various examples of social action undertaken by elementary students and by presenting a framework to guide teachers in selecting and conducting social action projects.[1]

Types of Social Action

A useful starting point is to identify the different types of social action that students might undertake. One classification views social action projects along a continuum extending from, at one end, "direct action" (directly addressing a problem oneself) to, at the other end, "indirect action" (influencing, or using as intermediaries, those who hold power and who are in a position to effect change). Elementary students are most likely to engage in direct and indirect action at the local level and indirect action at provincial, national, and global levels.

LOCAL ACTION PROJECTS

Examples of **direct** local action might include tending a school garden, cleaning up the school grounds or a local park, contributing nonperishable food items to a food bank, visiting the elderly at a senior citizens' home, caring for animals at a local wildlife shelter, or conducting a winter clothing drive. Viscount Alexander School in Cornwall, Ontario, for example, collects socks and slippers at the beginning of the winter season. They are hung in the hallways throughout the school for a time before they are donated to a local organization for distribution. Students might also raise money for playground equipment or other school improvements. Fundraising strategies include baked goods, used toy or book sales, read-athons, or earning money in their own homes or neighbourhoods and contributing it to the cause.

Elementary students in two North Vancouver schools engaged in **indirect** local action as a result of problems they examined in their social studies program.[2] They sought to bring about action by lobbying officials in political and government positions who had the authority and influence to take action if they could be convinced to do so. The grade 4 and grade 5 French immersion classes at Ross Road Elementary made a presentation to North Vancouver District officials advocating the suspension of a proposed residential development in a wilderness area. Prior to the presentation, students toured the district hall and discussed forest management with the mayor and with a forest industry representative. They also performed a play involving a developer who wanted to cut down trees in a small town.

Kindergarten and grade 4 students from Maplewood Community School in the same school district engaged in indirect social action against the planned development of land owned by the Vancouver Port Corporation. These students sent letters to the port corporation, the North Vancouver District mayor, the federal transport minister, the prime minister, the provincial premier, and environment critics for the opposition parties. One grade 4 student wrote in his letter, "Without the mud flats no one will see the animals again. The only time you will see birds is when they pass by. How would you like it if animals took away your buildings? I do not think you would like that."

NATIONAL AND GLOBAL ACTION PROJECTS

Students can fundraise for national causes. An example of **indirect** action on a national level is the Terry Fox

FRAMEWORK FOR SOCIAL ACTION PROJECTS

There are many things to consider when guiding students through a social action project. Below is a framework identifying six tasks. Depending on the project, not all will be required and with younger students especially it will be necessary to address the relevant steps in a more simplified manner:

Laying the groundwork

1. **Preplan for the project**
   - What should a teacher consider before starting the project? Select a focus.
   - Secure advice and approval from key parties.
2. **Introduce the idea to students**
   - How might the teacher introduce the project to students? Consider how to connect this project to students' interests and to topics in the curriculum.

Guiding students through the project

3. **Clarify the problem**
   - What is the problem? Students gather information and articulate a clear statement of the problem.
4. **Agree on a sound solution**
   - What are the different ways in which the problem could be addressed? Which is the most promising approach? Students assess the relative merits of alternative approaches and decide on the best option.
5. **Plan an effective course of action**
   - How will the problem be addressed? Students consider specific challenges, resources, and strategies and develop an action plan.
6. **Implement and evaluate the action**
   - Students implement the plan. They debrief the experience and determine how well it worked.

National School Run Day, in which more than half the schools in Canada participate. The expectation is that students will engage in fundraising for cancer research prior to participation in the event, which might be a run, a walk, a skate-athon, hockey game, bake sale, or other activity. (See www.terryfox.org/SchoolRun.)

An example of **indirect** global action is fundraising to support relief organizations such as UNICEF (United Nations International Children's Emergency Fund). "Project Love" is an example. This project is sponsored by CODE (Canadian Organization for Development through Education), an organization that supports literacy in the developing world. Students assemble Project Love kits containing basic school supplies—a pencil, eraser, notebook, and ruler—packed in a reusable plastic bag, and send them to developing countries such as Belize, Guyana, Ethiopia, and Tanzania. Students raise funds to help cover the cost of the supplies and shipping (www.codecan.org/project-love). Other examples are provided by the Youth: Take Action project described under Web Resources at the end of this chapter (www .freethechildren.com/getinvolved/youth/campaigns).

When students engage in **indirect** action, particularly at national and global levels, there is no direct contact with the people affected, they have no control over how the funds they raise or the items they send are administered, nor can they observe specific results of their actions, unless, perhaps, they are able to convince a relief worker to send them a video. However, they still experience a sense of having made a difference.

Planning a Social Action Project

The rest of this chapter examines the specific considerations involved in each of the six tasks outlined in the highlighted text, "Framework for Social Action Projects."

TASK 1: PREPLAN FOR THE PROJECT

Select a suitable focus and secure the advice and approval of key participants.

SELECT A SUITABLE PROJECT FOCUS

Five questions are useful to consider when selecting and shaping the focus for a project:

- Is it relevant for my students?
- Is it appropriate for my school and community?
- Does it grow out of and support the curriculum?
- Are there adequate resources?
- Is it worth the effort?

STUDENT RELEVANCE

There is little point in attempting a project if students do not support it. Rahima Wade (1995) found, when working with a grade 4 class in a suburban American school over the course of a school year, that unless students saw a meaningful or enjoyable connection between a social action project and their own lives, they had little interest in further involvement. For example, Wade tried to interest students in fundraising to purchase a goat for a poor family in Haiti. Although

most students voted in favour of participating in the project, only three students came to an out-of-school meeting to plan a course of action. Wade abandoned the project, concluding that it was too far removed from the students' own interests and life experiences.

Barbara Lewis describes how her upper elementary students from a low-income area became excited about school because of a social action project. As she says, "it was not an imaginary situation or a case study in a textbook—it existed in their neighborhood" (1991, 47). She describes how engagement in social action made the curriculum relevant for these students:

> Children anxiously await answers to letters, and track legislation. No one knows for sure what will happen next. When the Jackson children sat in the Utah Legislature watching the votes for their hazardous waste fund flash on the wall, they exhibited as much enthusiasm as if they had been counting points on the scoreboard at a basketball game. (49)

We should not presume that students will always be enthusiastic about the same projects that would interest adults (Wade 1995). For example, in the context of creating a class Bill of Rights, students in a grade 4 class decided to write letters to their principal requesting permission to chew gum and wear hats in class. Most adults would not consider these issues of great importance, but the grade 4 students felt differently and decided to act on their concerns. Students' sense of empowerment can result only when they take ownership of, and feel enthusiasm about, a project. Of course, all students need not participate in a particular project. Nor should those who do not wish to become involved prevent others from having the opportunity to do so. To the extent possible, we should allow for alternative routes for students who are not committed to the selected project or who want to pursue an alternative course of action.

APPROPRIATENESS FOR THE COMMUNITY

It would be inappropriate for a teacher to encourage students to engage in a project that violates the values of the community. The uproar caused by such an action may negate students' feelings of efficacy and make them unwilling to engage in future projects. When assessing a project's suitability in light of the cultural, religious, political, and economic characteristics of the school and community, we might ask ourselves the following questions:

- Does it respect the belief systems and cultural values of students and parents, as well as local histories and sensitivities?
- Would it lead to unproductive conflict or stress? A project that is appropriate in one school may create unproductive controversy in another. Although controversy will be part of any project related to sensitive issues, it may be wise to modify a project's focus if there is potential for unproductive conflict.

CURRICULUM MATCH

Social action projects have the potential to promote many curricular outcomes, including the skills needed to organize information, write proposals and reports, deliver public presentations, co-operate with others to achieve a shared goal, listen thoughtfully to the ideas and opinions of others, construct a compelling argument, and interact effectively with adults. Teacher Syma Solovitch-Haynes (1996) details her grade 2 students' success in achieving many such curricular goals. These students in Central Harlem set out to rename a street Mary McLeod Bethune Place after they noticed there were no streets in their area named after African-American women. In the course of working to achieve this goal, students learned how to research needed information, access the legislative process, organize and get signatures on a petition, and prepare and present a compelling argument in public forums.

Content knowledge is also promoted through social action projects. For instance, academic peer-tutoring projects in reading and math have been shown to positively affect achievement scores for both tutors and their pupils (Hedin 1987). Lewis (1991) describes the academic benefits as her elementary students sought to eliminate hazardous waste sites in Utah. Not only did students hone their speaking and writing skills as they learned to communicate effectively by means of telephone calls, letters, and proposals, they also learned the process of passing a bill, and used mathematics to compile survey data and calculate the anticipated profits from their fundraising efforts.

ADEQUATE RESOURCES

Facilities, materials, time, knowledge, and abilities are needed to complete a project successfully. The following questions are worth considering:

- Do students have the background experience, prior knowledge, and developmental maturity for grappling with the concepts, complexities, and implications of this action? Can they be expected to acquire what they are missing or can "outside experts"—parents and community members—make up for any shortfalls in expertise?
- Can parents be counted on to provide assistance and materials that may be needed? If outside activities are involved, will adequate supervision and transportation be available?
- Is the project doable within the available time? Would holidays interrupt the project? How will it fit with the time demands of other school events? Success often depends on having sufficient time.

WORTHWHILE

Social action projects may require students and teachers to spend considerable in-class and out-of-school time on the project. Thus, it is important that the benefits warrant the effort. In addition to achieving curriculum outcomes, an important measure of the success of a social action project is its impact on student empowerment. Involvement in social action projects contributes to student assertiveness and self-esteem (Kohn 1990). Students who work in projects where they see that they have made a difference feel valued and involved (Yaeger and Patterson 1996). Wade (1995) believes that student ownership of a project is central to developing a sense of empowerment. Students must see a connection between the activity and their own interests. Other critical factors are the teacher's willingness to relinquish some control over decision-making, and the teacher's actions that foster empowerment, such as providing choices and including time in the school day for student-initiated projects.

"You know, I didn't think something I did could really matter. Now I know that I can make a difference" (reported in Reindl 1993, 44). This was the message given by many students in grade 4 and grade 5 classes to their teacher following an extensive local action project. These students conducted food drives to help the needy in their community, persevering despite heckling from older students because the project was important to them. They also "adopted" a battered women's shelter and raised funds to purchase a swing set for children staying at the shelter. In the teacher's words:

MONKEY BUSINESS

Bev Priftis took her grade 7 students to the Calgary Zoo in order to observe the nature and behaviour of baboons and other animals as part of a study of the unique characteristics of humans.[3] The purpose of the unit, which was called "Man: A Course of Study," was to promote student inquiry into the question, "What is human about human beings?"

As a result of their field trip experience, many students became concerned with the contradiction between what they had learned in class about social organization and territoriality, and the practice of caging baboons and other animals. The students decided to write letters of protest to the Zoological Society, the mayor of Calgary, the Queen, and the editors of two daily papers.

The newspapers printed stories on the students' actions. One paper, in particular, emphasized the conflict between the attitudes of the Zoological Society and those of the students. The teacher was portrayed as incompetent, the students uncontrolled, and the zookeeper inflexible. The head of the Zoological Society wrote a three-page letter charging that the students' criticisms were childish and irresponsible and that they had not been properly prepared for their field trip.

The response to her students' actions could have had negative repercussions on the career of this teacher. It was only her second year of teaching and permanent certificates were not granted until the end of two years' teaching experience. Fortunately, Ms. Priftis had laid the groundwork. She had become acquainted with the resources for the unit she was teaching by means of a professional workshop. This program was clearly consistent with the provincial curriculum and the supervisor of social studies had promised to purchase the material in order to pilot the program in the Calgary school system. Parents had been given an opportunity to become familiar with the program through informational meetings. Many were pleased at the enthusiasm it generated in their children, particularly those children who had not previously been interested in social studies. This teacher also received a great deal of support from colleagues, including her principal and the professor who had originally introduced her to the program.

The teacher made use of the controversy that surrounded her students' social action to advance student learning. For instance, students compared the story as it appeared in the newspaper with the notes the teacher kept when the newspaper reporter interviewed her for the article. They examined the story for contradictions and evaluated it for bias and personal motives.

Largely because of the groundwork that was done, this story has a happy ending. The Zoological Society and the community as a whole eventually endorsed the "Ban the Bars" movement. The baboons were removed from the zoo because it was not a suitable environment for them. The program continued to be taught in Calgary schools. Bev Priftis was recognized for her expertise in social studies pedagogy and became a social studies consultant with the Calgary Board of Education.

I found myself trusting them more and more as the year went on and seeing that they could handle it, that it wasn't going to be devastating for them because they were having the opportunity to do something about it. With children you just can't let them feel hopeless. I think they can deal with almost anything as long as they know it doesn't have to be that way. (44)

These students saw situations that disturbed them and, with the encouragement of their teacher, did something about them. As a result of their actions, they developed a sense that they could indeed change the world around them for the better. The teacher, too, felt a sense of empowerment: "If I never do anything else with kids for the rest of my life, I will feel that, in letting these kids do this, I made a contribution" (46).

If students feel they lack the abilities and resources to effect change, they are unlikely to wish to participate. For this reason, particularly for young children, it may be worthwhile to focus their social action on the classroom or school environments. These are places where they should feel comfortable and where they can actually see the changes that their actions have wrought. Such a project might involve forming a "Green Team" to promote recycling, operating a "buddy" system for new students, sponsoring a bicycle safety program, forming a team of crosswalk guards, or tutoring other students.

SECURE SUPPORT FROM KEY PARTIES

It is always a good idea to secure community and administrative support for any proposed project. Social action projects are more public and may be more controversial than other school activities and some people may consider it inappropriate for students to be involved in social action projects during the school day. More often than not, potential criticisms can be avoided by keeping parents and the school administration informed about the project.

Clearing the project beforehand with the school administration by pointing out the congruence of project objectives with the curriculum will help if there are any negative parental or public reactions (Kreisberg 1993).

Informing parents of the proposed activities by letter allows them to air concerns and helps to garner their support. This is preferable to explaining after the fact if some controversy emerges. It can also be helpful to have parents and others participate in planning discussions or as panel members when different perspectives on the issues are presented.

In the example described in the highlighted text, "Monkey Business," a grade 7 teacher and her class were criticized in the press for questioning the ethics of keeping animals in cages. Support for their actions came by pointing to the congruence between project objectives and curriculum objectives, and by securing approval ahead of time for the project from the school administration, curriculum specialists, and parents.

The author recommends five factors to consider when selecting a social action project:

- relevance for students
- appropriateness for the school and community
- curriculum match
- available resources
- whether it is worthwhile

Identify four or five possible projects for students to undertake at your grade level and use these criteria to assess each option. Identify and justify your selection of the one or two most promising options.

TASK 2: INTRODUCE THE IDEA TO STUDENTS

Many social action projects arise from students' interests and concerns. For example, in teacher Solovitch-Haynes' case, on the way to school one morning, her grade 2 students noticed the absence of street signs honouring female African-Americans and wanted to do something about it.

Other projects arise from curriculum units already taking place in the classroom. For example, while learning about community services, primary students might decide that there is a need for a swimming pool in their own community and then embark on a plan to see what they can do to help bring this about. Upper elementary students studying transportation networks might decide that sections of the Trans-Canada Highway require upgrading and begin lobbying efforts to that end. Even historical units can lead to social action projects. For instance, upper elementary students who are learning about Canada's aboriginal peoples in the past may wish to investigate current land claims issues and make their opinions known.

If a project does not naturally arise from student concerns or from the curriculum, it is important to stimulate student interest. Possibilities include inviting a guest speaker who has personal experience with the issue, using a newspaper article, news clip, or documentary film, or organizing a field trip to the site of the controversy. In the highlighted text, "Leaving a Legacy," teacher Steve Oldenberger directed his grade 6/7 students' attention to the pollution of the Fraser River by means of several field trips.

TASK 3: CLARIFY THE PROBLEM

An important part of learning to participate in social action is developing the ability to clearly identify the problem to be solved. Two useful strategies are to involve students in researching the problem and then in exploring its complexities.

GATHER INFORMATION

Students need to collect information about a problem just as they would with any other research project, and they may need assistance with this research. This can involve helping students to frame clear questions, determine their information needs, and develop strategies for gathering the necessary information. See chapter 11, "Escaping the Typical Report Trap with Elementary Students," for specific teaching suggestions.

RECOGNIZE COMPLEXITY

Successful projects depend on students recognizing the complexity of the problem under investigation, and appreciating the various perspectives that are held, as well as multiple contributing causes. The difficulties that emerge when this is not done are illustrated by an incident involving a grade 1 girl who came home from school and accused her logger father of being a murderer because his tree-cutting was eventually going to kill everyone. The little girl had been read a story at school about British Columbia's Carmanah Valley and environmentalists' efforts to save the old-growth trees there. Officials in the IWA-Canada (International Woodworkers of America) local were concerned about what they saw as an unbalanced treatment of logging

LEAVING A LEGACY

Steve Oldenberger's grade 6/7 classroom in Queen Elizabeth Elementary is just a stone's throw from the Fraser River, which winds through the community of New Westminster, British Columbia. Steve asked his students to see what they could discover about the river. They began by taking class field trips there in order to observe seasonal water levels, turbidity, and temperature as well as water quality, what was floating on it, and what was on the riverbanks. They recorded information by taking photographs and writing their observations in logbooks. In different spots, they also collected samples of river water and tested it with lab equipment borrowed from the Marine Science Centre at the Vancouver Aquarium. With the Science Centre's help, they dredged samples of the muddy bottom of streams that feed the Fraser. They used nets to gather insects from the water surface. They carried out systematic samplings of the invertebrate population that inhabited the tributaries leading to the river, and carefully examined the health of minnows in the local streams. They enlisted the help of marine life experts, environmentalists, and others to make sense of their data.

The students' findings were disturbing. There was litter on the riverbanks. Wood debris from upriver was stifling wetland growth. Pollutants such as oil and agricultural runoff were threatening the more delicate inhabitants of the river. Large fish were rare and bird habitat was decreasing.

The students decided that they wanted to do something about the problems they had discovered. They considered a variety of alternative solutions, such as:

- writing articles for publication in the local newspaper;
- raising money for a particular campaign, such as building bird nesting boxes;
- producing a video about the river that could be shown at the school and perhaps other schools in the district; and
- creating a website to publicize the problems.

In the end, the students voted to launch a River Day in May for the entire school and the community. Students organized guest speakers, study stations, observation sites, publicity booths, and food tables. They prepared posters, brochures, and displays of their photographs, log entries, and drawings. They organized a shoreline cleanup to involve their visitors in a hands-on restoration activity.

The first River Day was an enormous success. The entire school and many neighbours participated. Reporters and photographers from the local media also attended, as well as a representative from city hall. River Day has been held now for several years. Six students presented at the 2002 International Children's Conference on the Environment held in Victoria, BC. The result of this ongoing social action project has been a great deal of effort directed at cleanup of the Fraser River environs. The students in Mr. Oldenberger's grade 6/7 classes have encouraged community members and students from nearby schools to become involved. "And instead of tin cans and broken bottles, the riverbanks near Queen Elizabeth School are sprouting wildflowers and native grasses."[4]

---

and took the issue up with the local school board (Rees and Fraser 1992). This child should have been reminded that she used wood, in various ways, every day of her life. She needed to understand that loggers do not simply "murder" trees, but chop them down in order to meet very real human needs. Even at six years old, a child can begin to appreciate the complexity of environmental issues, and that solutions to them are more often a matter of balance than of taking an either-or position. Teachers have a responsibility to see that students are well informed about opposing views.

In another situation, after observing volunteer students at community food programs for three years, one researcher concluded that understanding of the underlying problems was not promoted through these experiences (Willison 1994). When asked why they thought people went to the programs to obtain meals, students responded that clients were "hungry, homeless, excessive users of drugs and alcohol, unemployed, sick, uneducated, and do not want to work. On some occasions, students responded that the clients 'did not have any self-respect'" (89). These exclusively negative stereotypes were reinforced by a teacher who made comments such as, "See how much sugar these people take, they need sugar because of drug addictions" (88). Willison points out that these stereotypical notions were true for only a portion of the food program clients. Many were actually employed, but their income was insufficient to meet their needs. Student preparation for this project should have included examination of the underlying conditions of poverty, and of the history of local food provision programs.

Advocates for total banishment of child labour in Third World countries have been cautioned by UNICEF about the complexity of the issues involved. Child factory workers in developing countries are often the sole support of their families. If all child labour were banned, the families might starve and these children might be forced to turn to more oppressive sources of income, such as prostitution. Instead, many aid workers advocate working

FIGURE 13.1   CONSEQUENCES FOR STAKEHOLDERS

STAKEHOLDER GROUP:

Identify the anticipated consequences for each proposed solution and indicate whether they will be negative (–), positive (+), or mixed (?) for an assigned stakeholder group or for various stakeholders.

OPTIONS	ANTICIPATED CONSEQUENCES
	+ – ?
	+ – ?
	+ – ?

to improve children's working conditions and providing health care and educational programs, rather than outright banning of child labour (Vincent 1996). A UNICEF report recommends that governments focus on increasing educational opportunities, enforcing labour laws, and addressing social problems such as caste and ethnic divisions that exacerbate the problem (Stackhouse 1996). Clearly social action is complex, and unintended consequences must be considered carefully.

TASK 4: AGREE ON A SOUND SOLUTION

The next stage after defining a problem is to agree on a solution. While it is impossible for students to anticipate all the consequences of their proposed action, they should carefully examine possibilities and likely courses of action under various circumstances. Careful consideration of a social action project was evident when a grade 8 class considered "adopting" a child in Africa (Ashford 1995). After considering this plan, class members realized that the project was not as desirable as it had initially seemed. It was a long-term project that could not be continued when students left grade 8, and there was no guarantee that the incoming grade 8 class would be willing to carry on with the commitment.

Students need to be well informed about the potential impact of various action options. Students in Toronto were highly successful in their efforts to have fast-food giant McDonald's change from its Styrofoam clamshell packaging to paper (Roth 1991). However, scientific experts, as well as environmentalists, have since argued that McDonald's has caused more harm than good by this move. For example, James Guillet (1990), professor of chemistry at the University of Toronto, states that his own twenty-five years of research, as well as other scientific studies, simply did not support students' claim that when the foam disintegrates, it produces a chemical that has been associated with a breakdown of the Earth's ozone layer. As well, the volume of trees needed to provide the new paper packaging and the magnitude of pollution produced through paper production may be more harmful to the environment than the plastics were. Guillet concludes with the following caution:

> Environmental problems are extraordinarily complex. There is no magic solution to pollution. What we must do to minimize environmental damage is to make informed and intelligent choices. Media-supported campaigns such as this make great television, but they also exploit the natural altruism of young children and do little to inform the public. Children's crusades should have no place in the formulation of public policy. (1990, D7)

Grade 5 students in Surrey, BC, sent letters to the *Vancouver Sun* (June 25, 1996) expressing concern about

FIGURE 13.2 ACTION PLAN

ACTIONS TO BE TAKEN	RESOURCES REQUIRED	WHO WILL BE RESPONSIBLE?

the exploitation of Indonesian factory workers who make Nike products. These students were justifiably angry at Nike for paying their workers wages of $2.20 a day, while at the same time paying basketball superstar Michael Jordan $20 million a year to represent the company. Many of the students called for a boycott of Nike products. These students thought it worthwhile to take the time to write letters in order to publicly air their concerns. They may well have chosen the best action under the circumstances. However, they would have confidence in their decision only if they had carefully investigated the situation before reaching their conclusion. For instance, did they consider the possibility that driving up wages in Indonesia might result in Nike moving its factories to another country where labour costs are lower? Did they anticipate that other large corporations considering options for locating their factories might also avoid Indonesia? What alternatives to a boycott of Nike did they consider? Perhaps it would be more desirable to encourage all companies or countries in the region to establish minimum-wage laws. Perhaps, as more large corporations build factories in Indonesia, they will compete for the labour that is available and wages will rise. Canadian businessman Subhash Khanna, who imports clothing from South

Asia, argues, "If you don't do business with Third World countries you will increase their poverty and have more kids dying of hunger" (cited in Vincent 1996, 50). It is important that students consider potential consequences before reaching a decision.

Figure 13.1, "Consequences for Stakeholders," is intended to help students explore the implications of each proposed solution for one or more groups who may be affected by the actions.

TASK 5: PLAN AN EFFECTIVE COURSE OF ACTION

After deciding on a solution, the next task is to develop a plan to put the solution into effect. The purpose of an action plan is to guide students in implementing the project. The quality of the plan depends largely on the thoroughness of students' deliberations. Use of a simple task analysis chart such as Figure 13.2, "Action Plan," can support students in identifying the many steps to be taken, the resources required to complete each step, and the people responsible.

While planning a course of action, invite students to reflect on the soundness of their proposals by considering the following criteria:

- **Clear.** Are the goals and tasks of the plan clear to us?
- **Effective.** Are the proposed strategies likely to lead to the desired solution? What might some other effects of these strategies be (i.e., unintended consequences)?
- **Respectful.** Does the proposed strategy respect the feelings of all sides? Have we judged how the strategies will affect people? Does it respect the rights and legitimate interests of those who might be affected?
- **Realistic.** Is the plan doable given our time and available resources? How much class time is realistically available to devote to the project? How much outside help will be necessary?
- **Comprehensive.** What did we have to leave out of the plan? Does it contain and sequence the important tasks necessary for successful implementation?

TASK 6: IMPLEMENT AND EVALUATE THE ACTION

By this stage, students should have a good sense of their project and what needs to be done next. Now the teacher's task is to help students bring the project to a successful conclusion. Wade (1995) found that students responded enthusiastically to projects where they were closely supervised and assisted by their teacher or other adult. Students did not carry through on projects where they were left to their own devices. For instance, a group of students planned to write letters to American soldiers in Saudi Arabia after one student suggested the plan, but no one followed through. However, most students were enthusiastic about and participated in a project initiated, organized, and supervised by Wade in which students made puppets to send to India to teach villagers to make a simple solution for curing diarrhea, a common killer of children.

As students work through their project, and after its completion, encourage them to assess their decisions and actions in light of their own opinions, the opinions of other students, the responses of those who were affected by the social action project, and both short- and long-term consequences. Figure 13.3, "Reflecting on Our Project," suggests questions to ask students as they debrief their experiences.

There is a risk that students will feel that, in spite of all their efforts, they were ultimately unsuccessful in achieving their goals. Lewis (1991) gives a description of the discouragement one boy might feel early on in his project:

Successful phone calling is a simple place to begin. Students often fail at this initial step. For example, Joe may get access to use the school phones (which might require a notarized letter from his parent). He dials the main number for the Department of Transportation seeking information on the placement of a street light near the school. It takes four transfers before he reaches the correct party who can help him. Ms. So-and-So says she will mail some information to Joe and asks for the school address.

Joe panics. Although he can instantly recall all the states in the NFL, he doesn't know the school address. He asks Ms. So-and-So to wait, then runs into the secretary's office to find out the address. Seven people are lined up at the secretary's desk. By the time Joe gets the address and returns to the phone, Ms. So-and-So has hung up. Joe can't remember how to get through to her again and gives up. His first attempt to become involved in citizenship, and he stubs his toe and loses interest. (48)

Two ways to reduce the likelihood of perceived failure are to prepare students to carry out the steps necessary to complete the project and to encourage students to define "success" very broadly. Suggestions for developing the necessary competencies have been discussed throughout this chapter. In terms of students' definition of success, this need not mean that the intended change is achieved. It can simply mean that students develop a sense of efficacy by actively participating in the process to effect change, even if, ultimately, that change does not occur. If students feel proud that they acted on their convictions, they are likely to want to engage in more projects. Students should also be reminded that even though no immediate positive consequences stemmed from their social action, desirable changes could yet occur over the long term. (Chapter 23, "Teaching for Hope," looks at the importance of nurturing student hopefulness and the factors that affect this goal.)

Conclusion

There is no doubt that engaging in social action involves uncertainties. It can place both teachers and students in situations where they are unfamiliar with the circumstances and unsure how to proceed. Social action can be much more visible, and also more controversial, than

FIGURE 13.3 REFLECTING ON OUR PROJECT

Identify two ways in which you think this social action project was successful.

List three factors that helped and three factors that hindered the success of the project.

HELPING FACTORS	HINDERING FACTORS
•	•
•	•
•	•

What might you and your fellow students have done differently to make the project more successful?

Identify the most important thing you have learned from this project about planning and conducting social action.

---

other social studies activities and can invite criticism from outside sources. Nevertheless, there are significant benefits. Prominent among these is a sense of empowerment, possession of which increases the likelihood that students will become active citizens in their adult lives. In the final analysis, it is difficult to conceive of social studies as citizenship education without the possibility of social action. The "cost" of a social studies program that is all talk and no action is the preparation of citizens who are unqualified and unwilling to work to improve their community, their nation, or their world.

The author stresses the need to prepare students with the knowledge and abilities required to complete the social action project they have embarked upon. Identify a suitable project for students at your grade level and plan mini-lessons on how you would teach two or three of the most important social action competencies required by this task.

ACKNOWLEDGMENT

The author is grateful to Marg Franklin, retired elementary school principal and sessional instructor in elementary social studies curriculum and instruction at the University of British Columbia, for her helpful comments on the manuscript of this chapter.

ENDNOTES

1   This chapter draws on the framework and ideas in *Active Citizenship: Student Action Projects* (Case et al. 2004), a teaching resource designed to develop students' abilities to think through each step of a social action project.

2   These examples were described in "Students wake up to environmental concerns," by Michael Becker in the *North Shore News*.

3   This example of social action is based on an article by Dueck, Horvath, and Zelinski (1977).

4   This example of social action was adapted from "Leaving a legacy" in Case et al. (2004, 83–84). Thanks to Steve Oldenberger and his students at Queen Elizabeth School, New Westminster, BC, and the Vancouver Aquarium.

See Vancouver Aquarium: Act and Make a Real Difference (www.vanaqua.org/act) for other social action projects involving the well-being of our marine life.

REFERENCES

Alberta Education. 2005. *Social studies—Kindergarten to grade 12.* Edmonton, AB: Author. Available online at www.education .alberta.ca/media/456082/sockto3.pdf. Note that the preamble is identical for K–12.

Ashford, M-W. 1995. Youth actions for the planet. In *Thinking globally about social studies education*, ed. R. Fowler and I. Wright, 75–90. Vancouver: Research and Development in Global Studies, University of British Columbia.

British Columbia Ministry of Education. 2006. *Social studies K to 7: Integrated resource package 2006.* Victoria, BC: Author. Available online at www.bced.gov.bc.ca/irp/irp/pdfs/ social_studies/2006ssk7.pdf.

Case, R., C. Falk, N. Smith, and W. Werner. 2004. *Active citizenship: Student action projects.* Vancouver, BC: The Critical Thinking Consortium.

Department of Education, Prince Edward Island. 2012. *Atlantic Canada Social Studies Curriculum, Prince Edward Island, Grade 3.* Summerside, PEI: Author. Available online at www .gov.pe.ca/photos/original/eecd_SocialSGr3.pdf.

Dueck, K., F. Horvath, and V. Zelinski. 1977. Bev Priftis' class takes on the Calgary zoo. *One World* 17 (4): 7–8.

Goodlad, J. 2004. *A place called school: Twentieth anniversary edition.* Whitby, ON: McGraw-Hill.

Guillet, J. 1990. Kids' crusades bad idea. Letter to the editor, *Globe and Mail*, December 1.

Hedin, D. 1987. Students as teachers: A tool for improving school climate and productivity. *Social Policy* 17: 42–47.

Kohn, A. 1990. *The brighter side of human nature: Altruism and empathy in everyday life.* New York: Basic Books.

Kreisberg, S. 1993. Educating for democracy and community: Toward the transformation of power in our schools. In *Promising practices in teaching social responsibility*, ed. S. Berman and P. La Farge, 218–235. Albany, NY: State University of New York Press.

Lewis, B.A. 1991. Today's kids care about social action. *Educational Leadership* 49 (1): 47–49.

Newmann, F. 1975. *Education for citizen action.* Berkeley, CA: McCutcheon.

Osborne, K. 1982. *The teaching of politics: Some suggestions for teachers.* Toronto: Canada Studies Foundation.

Rees, A. and K. Fraser. 1992. Book turns 6-year-old against her father. *The Province*, February 20.

Reindl, S. 1993. Bringing global awareness into elementary school classrooms. In *Promising practices in teaching social responsibility*, ed. S. Berman, and P. La Farge, 27–49. Albany, NY: State University of New York Press.

Roth, A. 1991. Battle of the clamshell. *Report on Business Magazine*, April.

Solovitch-Haynes, S. 1996. Street-smart second-graders navigate the political process. *Social Studies and the Young Learner* 8 (4): 4–5.

Stackhouse, J. 1996. Hazardous child labour increasing. *Globe and Mail*, December 12.

Vancouver Sun. 1996. Air Jordan comes in for a crash landing with Surrey students. Letters to the Editor, June 25.

Vincent, I. 1996. The most powerful 13-year-old in the world. *Saturday Night*, November.

Wade, R.C. 1995. Encouraging student initiative in a fourth-grade classroom. *Elementary School Journal* 95 (1): 339–354.

Willison, S. 1994. When students volunteer to feed the hungry: Some considerations for educators. *Social Education* 85 (2): 88–90.

Yaeger, E.A. and M.J. Patterson. 1996. Teacher-directed social action in a middle school classroom. *Social Studies and the Young Learner* 8 (4): 29–31.

SUPPLEMENTARY READINGS

Alter, G. 1995. Transforming elementary social studies: The emergence of curriculum focused on diverse, caring communities. *Theory and Research in Social Education* 23 (4): 355–374.

Association for Supervision and Curriculum Development. 1990. *Educational Leadership* 48. This issue is devoted to the theme of social responsibility.

Baydock, E., P. Francis, K. Osborne, and B. Semotok. 1984. *Politics is simply a public affair.* Toronto: Canada Studies Foundation.

Berman, S. 1990. Educating for social responsibility. *Educational Leadership* 48 (2): 75–80.

Berman, S. and P. La Farge, eds. 1993. *Promising practices in teaching social responsibility.* Albany, NY: State University of New York Press.

Botting, D., K. Botting, K. Osborne, J. Seymour, and R. Swyston. 1986. *Politics and you.* Scarborough, ON: Nelson.

Chamberlin, C. 1985. Knowledge + commitment = action. In *A Canadian social studies*, rev. ed., ed. J. Parsons, G. Milburn, and M. Van Manen, 231–248. Edmonton, AB: Faculty of Education, University of Alberta.

Clarke, P. 1999. Smoking salmon for social justice. *Teacher: Newsmagazine of the BC Teachers' Federation* 11 (5).

Conrad, D. 1991. School-community participation for social studies. In *Handbook of research on social studies teaching and learning*, ed. J.P. Shaver, 540–548. New York: MacMillan.

Conrad, D. and D. Hedin. 1991. School-based community service: What we know from research and theory. *Phi Delta Kappan* 72 (10): 743–749.

Engle, S. and A. Ochoa. 1988. *Education for democratic citizenship.* New York: Teachers College Press.

Foran, A. 2004. Social studies and service-learning: The Aleph of democratic citizenship? *Canadian Social Studies* 38 (3). Available online at www.educ.ualberta.ca/css/Css_38_3/ARforan_aleph_democratic_citizenship.htm.

Hartmann, T. 2000. Peace cranes. *Teacher: Newsmagazine of the BC Teachers' Federation* 12 (7).

Kielburger, M. and C. Kielburger. 2002. *Take action! A guide to active citizenship.* Toronto: Gage Learning.

Lyman, K. 1995. "AIDS—You can die from it." Teaching young children about a difficult subject. *Rethinking Schools* 10 (2): 14–15.

Nickell, P. 1997. Big lessons for little learners. *The Social Studies Professional: Newsletter of the National Council for the Social Studies* 127: 3–4.

Saye, J.W. and T.A Brush. 1999. Student engagement with social issues in a multimedia-supported learning environment. Teaching and Research in Social Education 27 (4), 472–504.

Shaheen, J.C. 1989. Participatory citizenship in the elementary grades. *Social Education* 53 (6): 361–363.

Van Scotter, R. 1994. What young people think about school and society. *Educational Leadership* 52 (3): 72–78.

Wade, R.C. 1994. Community service-learning: Commitment through active citizenship. *Social Studies and the Young Learner* 6 (3): 1–4.

———. 1996. Prosocial studies. *Social Studies and the Young Learner* 8 (4): 18–20.

Wade, R.C. and D.W. Saxe. 1996. Community service-learning in the social studies: Historical roots, empirical evidence, critical issues. *Theory and Research in Social Education* 24 (4): 331–359.

Werner, W. 1999. Selecting "hot" topics for classrooms. *Canadian Social Studies* 33 (4): 110–113.

WEB RESOURCES

- HSBC Fraser River Sturgeon Education Program: hsbc.frasersturgeon.com

  This online resource includes a set of six lessons about the white sturgeon in the Fraser River of British Columbia. Lesson 6 in the Elementary Module introduces students to the concept of sturgeon stewardship and assists them to generate practical ideas for ways to protect the imperiled sturgeon by improving its environment.

- ImagineAction: www.imagine-action.ca

  Working with the Canadian Teachers' Federation, The Critical Thinking Consortium (TC²) has developed short video and booklet versions of the framework for social actions described in this chapter. The resources are targeted for French and English students at three grade ranges: K–4, 5–8, and 9–12. The videos offer inspirational examples of social action undertaken by youth in the targeted grades. The booklets provide a thumbnail summary of the steps in preparing students to thoughtfully plan and implement a social action project.

- Project Love: www.codecan.org/project-love

  This website contains background information about the project and includes a teacher's guide, as well as videos and photos of Canadian students preparing Project Love school supply kits and students in developing countries using them. The site also provides information about other Project Love opportunities such as the "Adopt a Library" program.

- Youth: Take Action: www.freethechildren.com/getinvolved/youth/campaigns

  Created by Free the Children—an international organization educating youth about global awareness—this website contains projects that students can become involved in as a class that will benefit parts of the world that require additional assistance. These include building a school, providing water, and giving alternative income, all to teach children to be global citizens.

- Terry Fox School Run: www.terryfox.org/SchoolRun

  This comprehensive website explains how to organize a school event to raise funds for cancer research.

PART 4 Accessing Learning Resources

14 Integrating Computer Technologies into Elementary Social Studies

Susan Gibson

The Partnership for 21st Century Skills (www.p21.org) calls for schooling that prepares digitally literate citizens who are proficient in the skills of critical thinking, problem solving, communication, collaboration, creativity, and innovation. In both social studies curriculum (Alberta Education 2005) and in classroom practice, there has been a shift to a constructivist view of children as active and engaged inquirers (Albion and Maddux 2007; Bolick, McGlinn, and Siko 2005; Doolittle and Hicks 2003; Zhao 2007). As a result, teaching social studies in today's technology-driven world demands the use of the latest digital tools to both support and enhance students' development of these important twenty-first century skills. This chapter explores how the diversity of technologies now available is changing the way students and teachers are accessing and using information, interacting with others, and building knowledge together.

Educational Uses and Benefits

Based on over a decade of educational research we know that a technology-rich environment can help to develop and deepen children's subject-specific knowledge (Angeli 2004; Bai and Ertmer 2008; Beaudin and Hadden 2005; Belland 2009; Brown and Warschauer 2006; Brush and Saye 2009; Dexter, Doering, and Riedel 2006; Magliaro and Ezeife 2007). Recent years have also seen a shift in the capabilities of the technology that provide even greater support in designing these types of learning experiences for students.

The original version of the internet, known as Web 1.0, was valuable for the access to vast amounts of information that it afforded, but it focussed mainly on acquisition of information, was highly structured and content driven, and mostly provided read-only capability. Now with the evolution to Web 2.0, there has been a change to more of a "culture of sharing" through the "read-write" web, which allows for both presentation and participation.

> The latest evolution of the Internet, the so-called Web 2.0, has blurred the line between producers and consumers of content and has shifted attention from access of information toward access to people. New kinds of online resources—such as social networking sites, blogs, wikis, and virtual communities—have allowed people with common interests to meet, share ideas, and collaborate in innovative ways. Indeed, the Web 2.0 is creating a new kind of participatory medium that is ideal for supporting multiple modes of learning . . . technology has begun to change the game in education by leveraging the potential of social learning. (Brown and Adler 2008, 16–17)

Rosen and Nelson (2008, 220) argue that Web 2.0 students are "a new generation of learners who are comfortable with and enthusiastic about using collaborative technologies to participate in the world wide web as creators rather than consumers. These students gravitate towards group activity, seeking interaction with thriving online communities of generative individuals."

WEB-BASED HISTORICAL ARTIFACTS

Students can access the collections of a number of virtual museums where they are provided with opportunities to analyze primary documents and engage in the processes that historians use (Levstik and Barton 2011). One site, assembled by the Canadian Broadcasting Corporation (www.cbc.ca/archives), contains clips from radio and television stories about people, conflict and war, disasters and tragedies, arts and entertainment, politics and economy, life and society, science and technology, and sports. This site has a teacher section that includes educational materials and activity ideas for using the resources provided on the website. Other web-based news services can also be used to help students develop critical awareness of current events. (See, for example, www.canada.com and www.thecanadianpress.com.)

The UK National Archives website (www.nationalarchives.gov. uk/education) is an excellent example of a web-based museum collection that presents a number of issues for students to investigate using primary documents. For example, there is a section on the evacuation of British children to Canada during World War II. Through this site (www.nationalarchives.gov.uk/education/homefront/evacuation/britain), students can engage in a problem-solving activity that requires them to examine primary source evidence, including official Canadian and British government documents and records, to investigate the issue of child evacuation during wartime. The Children of World War II site (www.bbc.co.uk/schools/primaryhistory/world_war2) addresses a similar issue. Here students use photos, posters, letters, documents, radio clips, and sounds to inquire into topics including a wartime home, rationing, and being an evacuee.

The McCord Museum (www.mccord-museum.qc.ca/en/keys) offers a free online "history laboratory" in which images and objects from 1840–1945 are given a central role. This laboratory draws upon the Keys to History resource, a vast database of images and artifacts, developed in collaboration with other Canadian museums. This fully bilingual world wide web resource provides tools that allow students to access information, organize and synthesize facts, and share knowledge. They are invited to analyze primary documents and engage in the process that

historians or museologists use. Thematic tours (through video, images, and text) provide insights into major events in Canadian history and aspects of daily life that shaped the Canadian experience. This site includes quizzes and role-playing games such as placing objects in their proper context; recreating period dress; discovering the identity of unusual objects; locating the odd man out in period settings; finding the link between two historical figures; and Mind Your Manners! (a game that explores the Victorian period and the Roaring Twenties). Although these resources and tools were developed for the general public and for secondary schools, they would also be of interest to upper elementary students.

Another tool at the McCord Museum site is My McCord space, which allows users to create their own visual presentation based on images from the collections, adding comments, personal images, and hyperlinks. Using this tool, students carry out their inquiry and can integrate resources from elsewhere.

Other web-based Canadian museum collections that social studies teachers should find useful are the Canadian Museum of Civilization (www.civilization.ca), the Virtual Museum of New France (www.civilization.ca/virtual-museum-of-new-france), the British Columbia Archives (www.bcarchives.gov.bc.ca/exhibits/timemach/index.htm), and the Glenbow Museum (www.glenbow.org/mavericks/).

Online databases, such as ones developed by Statistics Canada (www.statcan.gc.ca/edu/index-eng.htm), are also helpful resources for supporting research in social studies. The benefit of using an online database is that it tends to be kept relatively up to date. The Statistics Canada site has a section that is designed primarily for teachers. It contains examples and grade-appropriate exercises on how to read, use, and create a variety of tools to organize data. This site also offers activities that engage students in using historical census data. In one of these activities, "Jean Talon does a count" (www.statcan.gc.ca/kits-trousses/cyb-adc2001/edu04_0035d-eng.htm), students are provided with access to the census data from 1665 and 1666 and are challenged to use this data to take on the role of Jean Talon as he tries to convince the King of France to take a greater interest in New France.

Web 2.0 collaborative technologies "allow students' work to be read and commented on by a larger participant audience than afforded in traditional constructivist education" (221). Accordingly, Web 2.0 is leading to a shift in schooling that is referred to as "Education 2.0."

> Education 2.0 emphasizes social constructivist pedagogy ... [which] signals the addition of a new dimension, a 21st century digital dimension rooted in collaborative technologies that enable groups to move past their usual ways of working together, and, as a result, to a) build a collective wisdom that transcends that of the individual, in which the wisdom of the whole is greater than the sum of the parts, and b) transform the constructivist classroom into an Education 2.0 classroom (i.e., into an interactive, participatory, adapting, living organism of learning and generating content). (Rosen and Nelson 2008, 222)

SCAVENGER HUNTS AND TREASURE HUNTS

Scavenger hunt and treasure hunt websites are good places to introduce strategies for effective online searching to students by getting them used to accessing information, navigating around different types of websites, and "reading" a variety of media to locate specific information. Scavenger hunts and treasure hunts provide topic-related searching challenges for students using pre-selected websites.

One such site, the Ancient Olympic Cyberhunt (www2 .lhric.org/pocantico/olympics/ancienthunt.htm), presents a series of questions about the first Olympics and then provides links to specific websites where students search for appropriate responses. This is also a good way to begin a resource list for further research for a unit of study on ancient Greece or the beginnings of the Olympic Games. Another site, the Cyberhunt Kids' Library (www.teacher.scholastic.com/prod-ucts/instructor/cyberhunt_kids.htm), offers similar activities on the Aztecs (www.scholastic.com/teachers/lesson-plan/cyberhunt-amazing-aztecs), ancient China (www.scholastic.com/teachers/lesson-plan/cyberhunt-ancient-china), the Vikings (www.scholastic.com/teachers/lesson-plan/cyberhunt-here-come-vikings), and the voyages of Christopher Columbus (www.scholastic.com/teachers/article/web-hunt-christopher-columbus). Other similar sites, such as Adventures of Cyber Bee (www.cyberbee.com/primary/Letter/investigation_sites.html), engage students with primary source documents as they try to answer questions posed.

VIRTUAL FIELD TRIPS

Virtual field trips can be used to support student inquiry and knowledge construction as they allow students to travel through time and space to places that would otherwise be out of reach. Often these tours provide images and text describing the particular site being toured. For example, on the topic of ancient civilizations, students can access interactive sites such as www.villa-rustica.de/tour/toure.html, which features a tour of an ancient Roman villa. In another example, students can virtually traverse the Great Wall of China at www.thebeijingguide.com/great_wall_of_china/index.html. Such websites give children important contextual information to help them personalize their study of a country from afar. The VirtualTourist website (www.virtualtourist.com/) allows children to take virtual trips through any country in the world simply by highlighting their choice on a world map. History can be brought to life as well through virtual field trips. For example, the study of the history of Canada's peoples can be enhanced through the Underground Railroad site (www.nationalgeographic.com/features/99/railroad/), which follows the footsteps of Harriet Tubman, who led hundreds of runaway slaves to freedom in Canada.

they perform at a much higher level than when they complete an assignment only to turn it in to the teacher; students are motivated to show what they know because of the necessity of getting their audience to understand them. (Levstik and Barton 2011, 19)

Gutnick, Robb, Takeuci, and Kotler (2011) conducted a meta-analysis of seven recent studies on children and their use of digital media and found that young children today are spending more time with digital media than ever before, especially from age eight, and they prefer to use portable mobile media the most (i.e., cell phones, music players, hand-held video games, and so on). The prevalence of digital media in children's lives is a reality that educators would be wise to embrace as they look for ways to make it work for them in the classroom.

The research literature on learning tells us that engagement in active, co-operative, constructive, intentional, and authentic learning experiences with technology has been found to make their learning experiences much more meaningful for students (Belland 2009). Students are motivated to learn more deeply when they are able to contribute what they know to the web and share their ideas with others (Richardson 2006).

When students communicate for a real audience,

While developing literate citizens who can locate, evaluate, and ethically use information, think critically and creatively, problem solve, and make informed decisions have long been critical outcomes for social studies teachers, the term "literacy" itself has also changed in the digital age (Ribble and Bailey 2007; Warlick 2009). Leu, Kinzer, Coiro, and Cammack (2004, 1572) explain that digital literacy includes not just the traditional literacies of reading, writing, and arithmetic, but also "the skills, strategies and dispositions necessary to successfully use and adapt to the rapidly changing information and communication technologies and contexts that continuously emerge in our world and influence all areas of our personal and professional lives." Jones-Kavalier and Flannigan (2006, 9) add that digital literacy incorporates "the ability to read and interpret media (text, sound, images), to reproduce data and images through digital manipulation, and to evaluate and apply new knowledge gained from digital environments." Addressing these digital literacies in the way we teach social studies is imperative.

MS. YOUNG'S INTERNET RESEARCH PROJECT

Ms. Young has a grade 4 class this year. In social studies, her class is currently studying geography and its effect on the quality of life. The focus inquiry question is: "How do certain geographical elements affect climate and industry in the various regions of Canada?" Students are working in groups of five to investigate the six physical regions of Canada (the Atlantic, the Great Lakes/St. Lawrence Lowlands, the Canadian Shield, the North, the Cordillera, and the Plains). Each group has chosen a different region. Their challenge is to prepare a multimedia production designed to "sell" their area as the best place to live in Canada to an audience of their peers. The class begins by brainstorming a list of topics to investigate, including climate, weather, natural resources, industries, occupations, population, cities, landscape, and environmental concerns and conservation. Students begin data retrieval by accessing information from a number of sources to support each of the topics. The internet is the primary research resource. Ms. Young has created a class wiki using the Wikispaces tool (www.wikispaces.com), where students are to post text, photos, and videos about the region they are studying. A wiki is a website that is effective for collaboration because it allows for editing by anyone who has been granted access. Students are also encouraged to e-mail contacts (i.e., relatives, friends, ePals (www.epals.com)) in the various regions to collect more information. Using the Glogster tool (www.glogster.com), they can also prepare a poster advertising their region.

MR. MACDONALD'S GRADE 6 ONLINE INQUIRY PROJECT

Mr. Macdonald has created an interactive online scrapbook for his grade 6 social studies class that asks "Should the Oilers build a new downtown arena?" To design this current events scrapbook, he used Zoho Notebook (www.notebook.zoho.com), which is an online application that allows users to add pages as well as audio, video, text, and web links. He feels that exploring an issue such as this provides opportunities for students to investigate the intricacies of local government, see how the relationship between lobby groups and government can change, and develop a better understanding of how civic government functions. By engaging students in decision-making on a civic issue, he also hopes that they will better understand how to become active citizens and to think critically about issues that affect their lives. Having the majority of the materials for students to use in their investigations available in an online format such as an online scrapbook makes the resources easily accessible for students and allows for easy updating of sites.

The online scrapbook represents the views of three main groups involved in this issue: the Katz Group run by Darryl Katz, the owner of the Oilers hockey team in Edmonton, who are lobbying for a new arena; Edmonton Northlands, a non-profit organization that currently leases Rexall Place to the Oilers; and the Edmonton city council and the people of Edmonton. The diverse opinions on the issue provide a good opportunity for students to examine differing viewpoints and to experience decision-making for themselves

Mr. Macdonald begins the investigation of this issue by discussing the relevance of the new arena to the City of Edmonton. The students then brainstorm a list of questions they would like answered in order to feel more informed about the issue. Next Mr. Macdonald divides the class into three groups, one representing each interest group. Group members work together to research the various perspectives on the issue, using the resources provided in the scrapbook (see www.notebook.zoho.com/nb/public/isaacam/book/261622000000005661). When the three interest groups have assembled sufficient information, a class debate is held and then the class is encouraged to come to a consensus on the issue based on the evidence presented.

Students could also use the Zoho Notebook tool to create their own scrapbook on a current issue. Another example of a similar user-friendly application is Mixbook (www.mixbook.com).

Constructing Knowledge through Technology

In addition to developing digital literacies, students need experiences that lead to deeper understanding of social studies content. Such experiences include opportunities for honing critical and creative thinking skills, for collaborative knowledge building around authentic problems, and for learning through inquiry.

In social studies there are numerous avenues for incorporating inquiry-based learning that examines authentic problems supported by technology. One such avenue is through the study of controversial issues. Controversial issues can be defined as "those topics that are publicly sensitive and upon which there is no consensus of values or beliefs. They include topics on which reasonable people may sincerely disagree" (Alberta Education 2005, 6). Providing opportunities for students to engage with controversial issues assists "in preparing students to participate responsibly in a democratic and pluralistic society. Such study provides opportunities to develop the ability to think clearly, to reason logically, to openmindedly and respectfully examine different points of view and to make sound judgments" (6).

Learning to consult a variety of sources in any investigation to ensure the accuracy of the information presented and to examine a range of viewpoints is equally important. The study of current events offers a key opportunity for locating topics or issues for study and for finding diverse perspectives on them.

> Ongoing reference to current affairs adds relevance, interest and immediacy to social studies issues. Investigating current affairs from multiple perspectives motivates students to engage in meaningful dialogue on relevant historical and contemporary issues, helping them to make informed and reasoned decisions on local, provincial, national and global issues. (Alberta Education 2005, 6)

Using current events in social studies creates an opportunity for students to become more engaged and interested in their learning. This interest leads to questioning, which is of utmost importance for successful learning. "An issues-focused approach that incorporates multiple perspectives and current affairs helps students apply problem-solving and decision making skills to real-life and controversial issues" (Alberta Education 2005, 6). Investigating current relevant controversial issues can also help students to understand the importance of getting involved in their community and effectively making their opinions heard.

Developing Communication and Collaboration Skills through Telecollaboration

Today's children are growing up in a world where technology is pervasive, and that makes the world a much smaller place. Social studies teachers need to take advantage of the opportunities that the latest technologies provide for children to make global connections in their learning. It's no longer enough to simply read second-hand information about other countries in a textbook when opportunities exist to acquire that information through digital technologies. Through access to technology, students' ability to communicate, collaborate, and learn with others beyond the classroom walls is powerfully enhanced.

The telecollaborative inquiry project is a great way to engage students in open-ended inquiry and collaboration with others. Effective inquiry projects engage students with a problem to solve related to the curricular topic, as well as requiring that students consult a variety of sources and examine a number of different ways of looking at the problem. Students as inquirers are encouraged to critically examine and evaluate evidence and find a way to resolve the problem in consultation with other learners. Collaborative inquiry projects can take on many forms, including working with outside experts, exchanging information with other learners, shared problem solving, or participating in social action projects. Digital technologies such as blogs, wikis, websites, and so forth can be used in a variety of ways, from a simple exchange of e-mail between children in different locations, to developing a new website on a class topic. A more ambitious project might collect original data from all over the world to produce new knowledge and original insight into the nature of our world.

Blogging is one readily available tool that can be used to collaboratively engage students. Students can blog individually, contribute to a class blog, or be part of a collaborative blog where they work with students from other classrooms (Poling 2006). Blogs offer many benefits to teachers and their students, including teaching students twenty-first century skills (Richardson 2006). Blogs can provide authentic opportunities to practise reading and writing skills (McPherson 2006) and to advance literacy through storytelling and dialogue (Huffaker 2004). The relationship between blogs and reading, writing, and thinking skills is echoed by Davis, who has written in her own blog about a blogging project with her students:

WEBQUESTS

A WebQuest is a teacher-designed website that engages students in a task or inquiry to solve a problem using web-based resources. Most of the resources used for the inquiry are other websites that have been vetted and linked directly to the WebQuest site. Through WebQuest, students can actively explore issues from a number of different viewpoints, find answers, and reach moral and ethical decisions about real contemporary world problems. A WebQuest can help to develop critical and creative thinking, problem-solving, and decision-making skills. WebQuests can easily be tailored for diverse needs in the classroom.

A WebQuest is typically divided into five sections. The first part lays out the task or problem to be investigated. Students are then assigned roles or provided with differing perspectives on the issue or problem being investigated. Working either independently or in groups, they explore the issue or problem in a manner that is meaningful to them, with guidance from the teacher. Students access the information provided, analyze it, synthesize and evaluate it, then transform it in some way to demonstrate their understanding of the view they are adopting. They then share their findings with the whole class. The teacher acts as a facilitator, checking to see that students understand the role they are to take and that they stay on task.

Here are some samples of WebQuests with a Canadian focus. The Travel Canada WebQuest (olc.spsd.sk.ca/de/webquests/travelcanada) challenges students to collect information about Canada in preparation for writing an article for *Canadian Geographic* magazine. Parks Canada has a WebQuest on climate change (www.pc.gc.ca/apprendre-learn/prof/sub/quete-quest/index_e.asp) that invites students to design a campaign to advertise the effects of climate change on northern Manitoba. Quest Garden (www.questgarden.com) not only hosts a large number of teacher-designed WebQuests for all grades and subject areas, but also features an online authoring tool whereby teachers can create their own WebQuests. A similar database of WebQuests can be found at Bernie Dodge's and Tom March's official site, www.webquest.org. However, much of the content at the latter two sites is American.

Weblogs have proven to be an excellent way to focus on writing and thinking. Student writing improved. Student motivation soared! Students experienced a learning community that went beyond the school walls. We want to continue the learning journey (2004, Aug. 4).

Richardson (2006) adds that blogging encourages students to do more than just write because blogs provide opportunities for students to express their ideas and thoughts and to reflect on their own and other people's writing. Blogs also allow students to save and share their work over time. Students can learn to select the posts that best represent their writing. In this way, blogs can become a type of digital portfolio (Huffaker 2004; Richardson 2006).

As well, blogs offer expanded opportunities for interaction beyond the classroom environment and traditional school schedule constraints (Chan and Ridgway 2006). Students who use blogs can easily be encouraged to collaborate with their peers around the world, providing them with opportunities to practise working with other people from diverse settings. The presence of this large, potentially worldwide audience can be a strong motivator for students (Huffaker 2004; Richardson 2006). An online community can form in which ideas are shared and participants challenge and build on each other's ideas by offering different perspectives and sharing links (Huffaker 2004; Richardson 2006; Siemens 2002). Opportunities for scaffolding arise as new ideas and perspectives are added (Ferdig and Trammell 2004). In this way, blogs can be places for sharing meanings and understanding as part of a collaborative construction of knowledge:

> Knowledge is acquired and shaped as a social process resulting in spiraling: I say something, you comment on it, I evaluate it, comment and present a new perspective, you take it to the next level and the process repeats until a concept has been thoroughly explored. (Siemens 2002, Implications Section, ¶7)

In this way, blogs offer a democratic space where everyone can participate and everyone has a responsibility for ownership of a shared classroom space (Huffaker 2004; Richardson 2006).

Select a topic from the curriculum or from a student textbook. Using digital resources mentioned in this chapter or located elsewhere, develop an activity in which students use technological tools not to gather information but to solve problems or organize and synthesize ideas and to share and collaborate with other learners. Plan how you will help students undertake this knowledge construction and collaboration task using technology.

MISS PETERSON'S GRADE 3 TELECOLLABORATION PROJECT

Miss Peterson designed this telecollaborative project to encourage her grade 3 children to gain an understanding and appreciation of diverse traditions, celebrations, and stories from around the world. Through the study of geographic, social, cultural, and linguistic aspects of various communities, her students get a chance to develop an understanding of how people live in other places, and they learn to appreciate the role that global diversity has in their lives. At the same time, the students also learn about Canada's involvement with these particular communities, ultimately expanding their concept of global citizenship. By immersing students in an in-depth investigation of four diverse contemporary communities, in this case, India, Tunisia, Ukraine, and Peru, this inquiry allows students to learn about how a variety of factors impact quality of life.

First using ePals Global Community (www.epals.com), Miss Peterson looks for partner schools in each of the countries being studied that might be interested in collaborating on this project. Classes in the partner schools are responsible for composing and posting a blog entry about their specific cultural traditions onto a central blog that Miss Peterson has created using WordPress (www.wordpress.com). All of the students use this blog to communicate with the other locations, to share information about their own traditions, and to ask questions in order to learn more about others' traditions. As this blog exchange continues to develop, the local class is divided into four smaller groups, each of which communicates with classes in one country so that they become knowledge experts about that country. At the conclusion of the project, Miss Peterson sets up a culture fair in the classroom where the students share the diverse traditions they have learned about.

MS. MUNRO'S GRADE 2 INUIT RESEARCH PROJECT

Ms. Munro is beginning a unit on Canadian communities with her grade 2 class. She wants her students to understand how geography, weather, culture and traditions, language, industry and resources, community, and people shape and change Canada's communities. She has created a class webpage using Weebly (www.weebly.com) to provide a place for her students to blog about what they are learning about the Inuit. Students are engaged in research about the Inuit using a number of websites provided by Ms. Munro, including the following:

- www.kativik.qc.ca/inuktitut-computer-games
- www.collectionscanada.gc.ca/settlement/kids/021013-2071.5-e.html
- www.slideshare.net/martinmurga/the-inuit-the-people
- www.youtube.com/watch?v=8IqOegVCNKI
- www.gamesmuseum.uwaterloo.ca/VirtualExhibits/Inuit/english
- www.learnalberta.ca/content/ssognc/inuitLifestyle
- www.google.com/earth
- www.nunavuttourism.com
- www.comeexplorecanada.com/nunavut

The students in Ms. Munro's class are encouraged to ask questions on the blog about what it is like to live in an Inuit community. The blog is also a place for students to communicate their thoughts and questions about what they are learning about the Inuit. In this way, students can communicate their learning to others in the class and to the teacher. As a part of the research on the Inuit, Ms. Munro arranges a videoconference session using Skype (www.skype.com) with a class of children in the Arctic. Students are encouraged to ask and answer questions as a part of this videoconference session.

CONNECTED LEARNING PROJECTS

The International Education and Research Network (iEarn) website (www.iearn-canada.org/) provides opportunities for students to engage in telecollaborative projects. One such project is the My Hero Project (www.myhero.com/go/home.asp), which involves students in learning about everyday heroes and encourages them to see themselves as change agents. Another project, Children's Rights (media.iearn.org/projects/childrens-rights), has students explore the Convention of the Rights of the Child. The Local History Project (media.iearn.org/projects/localhistory) engages children in the global community in exploring and sharing local heritage. A fourth project, Holiday Card Exchange (media.iearn.org/projects/holidays), has children design and share greeting cards with classrooms around the world. Teachers can also make contracts with other teachers through iEarn to promote telecollaborative exchanges that support their own teaching plans.

Other examples of telecollaborative projects to support social studies learning outcomes are:

- Square of Life: www.ciese.org/curriculum/squareproj/
- Global Grocery List Project: www.landmark-project.com/ggl
- Voices of Youth: www.unicef.org/voy
- The Day I Was Born: www.dayiwasborn.net
- Electronic Emissary: emissary.wm.edu
- The Tooth Tally Project: www.toothtally.com
- The Global Schoolhouse: www.globalschoolnet.org

Conclusion

The main focus of this chapter is how to prepare digitally literate students through the use of digital technologies in social studies. I believe that the most effective uses of digital technologies are those that foster meaningful learning by engaging learners in authentic, inquiry-oriented learning experiences that recognize the active and collaborative role of the learner in constructing meaning about the world. A number of internet-based tools provide support for students throughout their inquiry. These tools—including blogs, ePals, videoconferencing, virtual museums, and field trips—have the potential, if used in meaningful ways, to develop students' ability to think critically and creatively, solve problems, make sound decisions, and collaborate with one another.

REFERENCES

Alberta Education. 2005. *Social studies kindergarten to Grade 12 Program of Studies*. Edmonton, AB: Author.

Albion, P. and C. Maddux. 2007. Networked knowledge: Challenges for teacher education. *Journal of Technology and Teacher Education* 15 (3): 303–311.

Angeli, C. 2004. The effects of case-based learning on early childhood preservice teachers' beliefs about the pedagogical use of ICT. *Journal of Educational Media* 29: 139–151.

Bai, H. and P. Ertmer. 2008. Teacher educators' beliefs and technology uses as predictors of preservice teachers' beliefs and technology attitudes. *Journal of Technology and Teacher Education* 16 (1): 93–113.

Beaudin, L. and C. Hadden. 2005. Technology and pedagogy: Building techno-pedagogical skills in preservice teachers. *Innovate* 2 (2). Accessed at www.innovateonline.info/index.php?view=article&id=36.

Belland, B. 2009. Using the theory of habitus to move beyond the study of barriers to technology integration. *Computers & Education* 52: 353–364.

Bolick, C., M. McGlinn, and K. Siko. 2005. Twenty years of technology: A retrospective view of social education's technology themed issues. *Social Education* 69 (3): 155–161.

Brown, D. and M. Warschauer. 2006. From the university to the elementary classroom: Students' experiences in learning to integrate technology in instruction. *Journal of Technology and Teacher Education* 14 (3): 599–621.

Brown, J.S. and R.P. Adler. 2008. Minds on fire: Open education, the long tail, and learning 2.0. *Educause Review* 43 (1): 16.

Brush, T. and J.W. Saye. 2009. Strategies for preparing preservice social studies teachers to integrate technology effectively: Models and practices. *Contemporary Issues in Technology and Teacher Education* 9 (1): 46–59.

Chan, K. and J. Ridgway. 2006. *Students' perceptions of using blogs as a tool for reflection and communication*. Accessed at www.dur.ac.uk/resources/smart.centre/Publications/ALT-C EdinburghCHAN.doc.

Davis, A. 2004. *Welcome to the write weblog!* The Write Weblog, August 4. Accessed at itc.blogs.com/thewrite weblog/2004/08/index.html.

Dexter, S., A. Doering, and E. Riedel. 2006. Content area specific technology integration: A model for educating teachers. *Journal of Technology and Teacher Education* 14 (2), 325–345.

Doolittle, P. and D. Hicks. 2003. Constructivism as a theoretical foundation for the use of technology in socials studies. *Theory and Research in Social Education* 31 (1): 72–104.

Ferdig, R. and K. Trammell. 2004. Content delivery in the "Blogosphere." *T.H.E. Journal* 31 (7): 12–16.

Gutnick, A, M. Robb, L. Takeuci, and J. Kotler. 2011. *Always connected: The new digital media habits of young children*. New York, NY: Sesame Workshop and the Joan Ganz Society Cooney Center. Accessed at www.ictliteracy.info/rf.pdf/jgcc_alwaysconnected.pdf.

Huffaker, D. 2004. The educated blogger: Using weblogs to promote literacy in the classroom. *First Monday* 9 (6). Accessed at www.firstmonday.org/issues/issue9_6/huffaker/index.html.

Jones-Kavalier, B. and S. Flannigan. 2006. Connecting the digital dots: Literacy of the 21st century. *Educause Quarterly* 2: 8–10.

Leu, D.J., Jr., C.K. Kinzer, J. Coiro, and D. Cammack. 2004. Toward a theory of new literacies emerging from the Internet and other information and communication technologies. In *Theoretical Models and Processes of Reading*, 5th ed., ed. R.B. Ruddell and N. Unrau, 1568–1611. Newark, DE: International Reading Association.

Levstik, L. and K. Barton. 2011. *Doing history: Investigating with children in elementary and middle schools*, 4th ed. New York: Routledge.

MacGregor, S. and Y. Lou. 2006. *Web-based learning: How task scaffolding and website design support knowledge acquisition*. Accessed at www.maryborougheducationcentre.vic.edu.au/successforboys/resources/pdf/ict/ict_resource22.pdf.

Magliaro, J. and A. Ezeife. 2007. Preservice teachers' preparedness to integrate computer technology into the curriculum. *Canadian Journal of Learning and Technology* 33 (3): 95.

McPherson, K. 2006. School library blogging. *Teacher Librarian* 33 (5): 67. Accessed at proquest.umi.com/pqdweb?did=10714 40891&Fmt=7&clientId=12301&RQT=309&VName=PQD.

Poling, C. 2006. Blog on. *Output—Education Computing Organization of Ontario*, 26 (4): 8. Accessed at proquest.umi.com/pqdweb?did=1138836521&Fmt=7&clientId=12301&RQT=309&VName=PQD.

Ribble, M. and G. Bailey. 2007. *Digital citizenship in schools.* Washington, DC: International Society for Technology in Education.

Richardson, W. 2006. *Blogs, wikis, podcasts, and other powerful web tools for classrooms.* Thousand Oaks, CA: Corwin Press.

Rosen, D. and C. Nelson. 2008. Web 2.0: A new generation of learners and education. *Computers in the Schools* 25 (3): 211–225.

Siemens, G. 2002. *The art of blogging—part 1: Overview, definitions, uses, and implications.* Accessed at www.elearnspace.org/Articles/blogging_part_1.htm.

Warlick, D. 2009. *Redefining literacy 2.0.* Columbus, OH: Linworth Books.

Zhao, Y. 2007. Social studies teachers' perspectives of technology integration. *Journal of Technology and Teacher Education* 15 (3): 311–334.

SUPPLEMENTARY RESOURCES

Beheshti, J., A. Large, K. Kee, and C. Cole. 2006. Designing virtual environments in an educational context. *Canadian Association for Information Science/L'Association canadienne des sciences de l'information Conference.* Accessed at www.cais-acsi.ca/proceedings/2006/beheshti_2006.pdf.

Borun, M., D. Schaller, M. Chambers, and S. Allison-Bunnell. 2010. Implications of learning style, age group and gender for developing online learning activities. *Visitor Studies Today* 13 (2): 145–159.

Britt, M., C. Perfetti, J. Van Dyke, and G. Gabrys. 2000. The sourcer's apprentice: A tool for document-supported instruction. In *Knowing, teaching, and learning history: National and international perspectives*, ed. P. Stearns, P. Seixas, and S. Wineburg, 437–470. New York, NY: New York University Press.

Bruno-Jofre, R. and K. Steiner. 2007. Fostering educative experiences in virtual high school history. *Encounters on Education* 8, 69–82.

Brush, T. and J. Saye. 2000. Implementation and evaluation of a student-centered learning unit: A case study. *Educational Technology Research and Development* 48 (3): 79–100.

———. 2001. The use of embedded scaffolds with hypermedia. *Journal of Educational Multimedia and Hypermedia* 10 (4): 333–356.

Kee, K. 2008a. Re-presenting Canadian history on-line: 'The cyberterrorism crisis' web site as a test case of history and citizenship education on the web. In *The Emperor's New Computer: ICT, Teachers and Teaching*, ed. T. Di Petta, 29–44. Rotterdam: Sense Publishers.

———. 2008b. Computerized history games: Narrative options. *Simulation and Gaming* 20 (10).

Lee, J. and W.C. Clarke. 2003. High school social studies students' uses of online historical documents related to the Cuban missile crisis. *Journal of Online Learning* 2 (1).

Lévesque, S. 2008a. The impact of digital technologies and the need for technological pedagogical content knowledge: Lessons from the virtual historian. In *The Emperor's New Computer: ICT, Teachers and Teaching*, ed. T. Di Petta, 17–28. Rotterdam: Sense Publishers.

———. 2008b. "Terrorism plus Canada in the 1960's equals hell frozen over": Learning about the October Crisis with computer technology in the Canadian classroom. *Canadian Journal of Learning and Technology*, 34 (2). Accessed at www.cjlt.ca/index.php/cjlt/index.

Lipscomb, G. 2002. Eighth graders' impressions of the Civil War: Using technology in the history classroom. *Education of Communication and Information* 2 (1): 51–67.

Milson, A. 2002. The internet and inquiry learning: Integrating medium and method in a sixth grade social studies classroom. *Theory and Research in Social Education* 30 (3): 330–353.

Sandwell, R. 2005. The great unsolved mysteries of Canadian history: Using a web-based archive to teach history. *Canadian Social Studies* 39 (2). Accessed at www.quasar.ualberta.ca/css.

Sandwell, Ruth. 2004. "Who killed William Robinson?": Exploring a nineteenth century murder online. *Social Education* 68 (3): 210–213.

Swan, K. and D. Locascio. 2008. Evaluating alignment of technology and primary source use within a history classroom. *Contemporary Issues in Technology and Teacher Education* 8 (2): 175–180.

15

Exploring Visual Resources with Elementary Students

Penney Clark

The statement "a picture is worth a thousand words" is a truism. Photographs, paintings, films, and other visual resources can convey immense detail at a glance—detail that would take pages of print to describe. They can depict nuances of colour, texture, and facial expression that are difficult to convey in words. They may also be artifacts that provide rich historical insights. Certain photographs are so powerful that they come to represent an era, such as the poignant image of John Kennedy, Jr. saluting his father's coffin, Pierre Elliott Trudeau pirouetting behind the Queen, or the sole Chinese student in front of sixteen tanks in Tiananmen Square. Much of Canada's early history (and that of other countries, too, for that matter) was recorded for posterity by painters, before photography came into common use. For example, Paul Kane produced more than a hundred oil paintings of aboriginal people based on sketches done in his travels from the Great Lakes to Vancouver Island between 1845 and 1848. We are indebted to Frances Anne Hopkins, whose husband was the secretary to George Simpson, governor of the Hudson's Bay Company, for her detailed paintings of the voyageurs on several canoe journeys that she took with them between 1858 and 1870.

Given their importance, visual resources should be a key part of a social studies program. If students are to make effective use of visual resources, they first need to see them as an important part of the variety of information sources available to them. Yet, visuals are often overlooked. For instance, pictures in textbooks are ignored while students scour the print segments for information. Students need to learn to examine pictures from a critical perspective. They are not only a rich source of information and insights, but deliberate constructions, rather than mere reflections, of reality; and as constructions, they represent their creators' purposes and perspectives. Coupled with this is the need to examine visuals actively to uncover the meanings that lie under their surface images. In order to make them yield all that they have to offer, students must spend time studying them and learn to ask compelling questions about them.

This chapter discusses the thoughtful classroom use of photographs and paintings, as well as visual resources with an audio component, such as DVDs.

Paintings and Photographs

The most abundant and accessible visual resources are photographs and paintings. Most authorized textbooks are full of them. Other sources include:

- travel brochures
- calendars
- newspapers
- magazines
- government publications
- discarded textbooks
- store advertising displays
- digital museum exhibitions
- digital archives
- art books
- family albums
- public relations material
- art galleries

In this section I look at concerns about interpreting paintings and photographs at face value and offer a few strategies for "interrogating" these visual resources.

PAINTINGS

Paintings (and other art forms) can give students a powerful sense of how the world was viewed in the time and place in which they were produced. However, students need to be aware that paintings are not necessarily intended to represent events as they actually happened. For instance, a famous painting depicting the death of French commander the Marquis de Montcalm, at the Siege of Quebec, shows him dying on the battlefield. In fact, he died the next morning in Quebec. An equally famous painting of the death of General Wolfe, the British commander, depicts people who weren't actually present, and some who were there are not shown.

Students should discuss why artists do not always represent events as they actually happened. One of the reasons for altering the details is to represent the artist's social and political purposes. Students can see the influence of national perspective on the depiction of events by comparing paintings by different artists on a particular incident. For example, American artist John Trumbull's painting of the death of the American commander Richard Montgomery during the 1775–76 American invasion of Quebec shows Montgomery as the centre of attention. The painting by British artist Johan Frederick Clemens shows a chaotic battle scene with many more things happening at once. It is interesting to note that neither painting is authentic in that Montgomery died on the battlefield on December 31, but his frozen body was not found until the next day.[1]

Students can use historical paintings to construct a written account of life in a particular place at a particular time in the past. For instance, Peter Rindisbacher, a Swiss settler who lived at Red River from 1821 to 1826, created numerous drawings and paintings depicting the activities of aboriginal people in the area. (*Life at Red River: 1830–1860*, a text in the Ginn "Studies in Canadian History" series, contains reproductions of several Rindisbacher paintings.) Students could examine these paintings and then write a few paragraphs describing what they see. They might also compare the information extracted from the drawings and paintings to information extracted from written sources and attempt to account for any differences.

PHOTOGRAPHS

"While photographs may not lie, liars may photograph" (Lewis Hine, quoted in Everett-Green 1996, E1). Students (and many others) tend to take photographs at face value, while they are ready to accept that drawings and paintings represent the perspectives of their creators (Gabella 1994). It is difficult to repudiate the visual evidence of a photograph because it is a record of a particular moment in time. Students may not stop to consider that even photographs are not always what they seem and that the person behind the camera will likely have constructed the picture to suit particular purposes. Photographic evidence may be unreliable in four ways:

- Photographers or subjects may stage photographs in order to deliver a particular message.
- Photographs may depict an atypical situation or event, one that is not representative of the people or circumstances shown.
- Photographs may be deliberately altered.
- Photographs may exclude important aspects of a situation.

STAGED PHOTOGRAPHS

Photographers may arrange subjects or objects in a photo in order to deliver a particular message. For example, a famous photo by Alfred Eisenstaedt shows a sailor and a nurse kissing in the middle of a crowd on VJ Day (official end of the fighting between the Allies and Japan in World War II). The photographer had two people pose for the shot. He did not happen upon a spontaneous eruption of joy, as most people who see the photograph imagine. Such photos are clever and capture the imagination, but they are not "real," in that they would not have happened without the photographer's intervention.

Photographs can be "created" in much less dramatic ways than the VJ Day example. It was common practice for nineteenth-century photographers, intent on preserving traditional images of Native people for posterity, to stage their photographs. For instance, Edward S. Curtis, who photographed Native peoples from Alaska to the American Southwest, used wigs and costumes, as well as other props, so his subjects would appear as he imagined First Nations people would have looked before being affected by European culture.

In other cases, it is not so much that the photos have been deliberately staged, but rather that the reality they

GRAFLEX CAMERA PHOTOGRAPH

THE SHAME OF THE CITY—CAN WE GIVE OUR CHILDREN NO BETTER PLAYING SPACE?

"The shame of the city: Can we give our children no better playing space?"—Winnipeg, 1912
Library and Archives Canada (C-030947).

are intended to convey has been slightly altered to suit the momentous occasion of the photograph itself. For instance, the photograph above shows children dressed in ragged and dirty clothing, yet with freshly scrubbed faces. Someone has prepared the children for this photograph. Students have to be aware of such anomalies so that they do not take such photographs at face value (no pun intended). It is interesting to speculate about the photographer's motives and the effect on the audience of seeing poorly dressed children with fresh faces.

A photograph may also, in some sense, be staged by its subjects. Joy Kogawa, in *Obasan*, a novel about a Japanese family that was transported first to an internment camp and then to an Alberta beet field, says of a photograph of another Japanese family taken at the time: "'Grinning and happy' and all smiles standing around a pile of beets? That is one telling. It's not how it was" (1981, 197). The photo did not reflect the reality of the lives of the subjects of the photo. The camera can create its own reality.

Students need to learn to look beyond distortions created by photographers or subjects to examine other evidence that photographs may offer. J. Robert Davison (1981–82) describes a photograph labelled "Indians, Fraser River," taken around 1868 by photographer Frederick Dally. The photograph, which appears on page 163, shows a group of Native people "praying." However, the photographer contradicts the evidence of the photograph by writing underneath, "Indians shamming to be at prayer for the sake of photography." Above the photo is written, "At the priests [sic] request all the Indians kneel down and assume an attitude of devotion. Amen." Even without the help of the caption, close examination of the photograph reveals that it is a sham:

The two priests have set a fine, holy example, but their spiritual and physical distance from the group is palpable; they are easily picked out standing (here kneeling) apart—curiously not aloof, for in this case it is the Native group that is aloof. They have gone along with the play, but there is little conviction. Some emulate the priests, but only tentatively, as if they were unsure of what exactly constitutes an "attitude of devotion." A few others seem to have

"Indians shamming to be at prayer for the sake of photography. Fraser River."—Frederick Dally British Columbia Archives (E-04419).

thought it barely worth the effort. They have pulled their dignity and their pride around them like their blankets, refusing the pious assault on their spirit. (Davison 1981–82, 2)

Much can be ascertained from such a photograph and its captions. It can be used to demonstrate to students that critical examination of a visual resource can reveal messages that are not evident at first glance. Students could discuss why it might be in the best interests of the priests to have such a photograph taken and how it might be used. Also, it would be interesting to consider why the photographer, in writing his captions, refused to go along with the sham. Students could examine other photographs and their captions to determine how a caption can alter the message conveyed by a photograph.

UNREPRESENTATIVE IMAGES

A second way photographs lead viewers to draw unwarranted conclusions occurs when they are highly unrepresentative of the reality of the person or the situation. The famous photograph showing candidate Robert Stanfield fumbling a football kickoff during a national election campaign is an example of this. The photograph, which was widely reprinted, left the impression that Stanfield was an incompetent bungler. Other evidence does not support this impression. Students could be shown such a photograph and asked to locate additional evidence that supports or refutes the impression conveyed by the picture. They could then be asked to draw a conclusion about the person or event based on the wider array of evidence, which they now have at hand. They should also consider the power of such impressions, where connections can be made that are not warranted. In this case, competence in football is not related to competence in politics or, for that matter, governing, but these connections were made.

Daniel Francis points out that early photography technology was instrumental in developing an image of nineteenth-century aboriginal people that was less than accurate. Francis says:

A mask-like quality was particularly pronounced in early photographs, because exposure times were prolonged and subjects had to keep themselves and their expressions immobile for up to half a minute. Since photographs were often the only glimpse most non-natives got of native people, this simple technological imperative may have contributed

to the stereotype of the grim, stoical, cigar-store Indian. (1996, 2)

Here, the camera has created rather than captured unrepresentative images. The result is the same—a misleading impression is created.

To help students appreciate that photographs may lead viewers to draw unwarranted conclusions, students could role-play particular historical events while another student takes photographs at dramatic moments. Invite students to examine the photographs and discuss what they convey about the event and what is misleading. Students might also speculate about the conclusions historians using family photo albums as evidence might draw about contemporary family life. Using their own family albums as an example, students may conclude that a historian would judge the family to be avid travellers and partygoers, without realizing that these were the types of events that family members recorded by means of photographs. Such albums often do not record the more typical routines of daily life.

ALTERED PHOTOGRAPHS

With the advent of digital technology, photographs are "as malleable as clay" (Grady 1997, A23). People can be moved from one location to another, objects can be placed in the photograph, unwanted people can be removed, and so on. However, these sorts of alterations did not suddenly appear with the advent of the computer. They have occurred since photography was invented. Stephen Jay Gould describes his unearthing of "conscious skulduggery" (1981, 171) in the work of psychologist H.H. Goddard. Goddard maintained that the "feeble-minded" could be recognized by their facial characteristics and "proved" this point by means of photographs of poor families. Seventy years after publication of the photographs, examination by experts revealed that facial features had been altered to make the people appear mentally disabled. Communist regimes have rather routinely altered historical evidence, including photographs, to suit current political thinking. For instance, in *The Book of Laughter and Forgetting*, Milan Kundera (1980) describes a scene on the balcony of a palace in Prague in 1948, where Communist leader Klement Gottwald was addressing hundreds of thousands of Czechoslovakian people. Photographs of the group on the balcony were reproduced widely in posters and textbooks. However, after Vladimir Clementis, who was on the balcony and in the photographs, was executed for treason in 1952, his image was removed from the

DECONSTRUCTING THE LAST SPIKE

"Hon. Donald A. Smith driving the last spike to complete the Canadian Pacific Railway"—November 7, 1885, Alexander Ross, Ross, Best & Co., Winnipeg. Alexander Ross/Library and Archives Canada (C-003693).

"Staged by construction party that missed the official ceremony."—November 7, 1885, Alexander Ross, Ross, Best & Co., Winnipeg. Library and Archives Canada (C-014115).

photographs—which, once doctored, showed a bare palace wall where he had stood.

More commonly, a photograph intended for publication will be cropped before printing in order to suit layout requirements, sometimes radically altering its meaning in the process. Students can apply two L-shaped frames to photographs from magazines and newspapers in various ways in order to see for themselves how the meaning can be altered by the practice of cropping.

SELECTIVE FOCUS

Photographs can also exclude; that is, they may only represent "part" of a story. An example of this is the famous photo, which has appeared in many textbooks, of Donald Smith and other dignitaries at the Last Spike ceremony to mark the completion of the Canadian Pacific Railway at Craigellachie, British Columbia. It is important in such a case to ask who is included and who excluded. Another, less famous photo shows the labourers who had built the railway holding their own Last Spike ceremony while they waited for the train that would take them back east. A comparison of these two

photographs, which appear on page 165, can be used to show that the historical record is selective. However, it is not only the first photo that excludes. Encourage students to note who is missing from the photograph of the labourers as well. Even though there was a large contingent of Chinese workers on the railway, they are not represented in the second picture. This, too, tells students something about historical perspectives. Many textbooks dwell on the activities and achievements of prominent Caucasian men, while ignoring those of working-class people, people of other races, and women.

The feature "Questions to Ask about These Pictures" could be used with the two Last Spike photographs. Similar questions aimed at helping students consider who is excluded, as well as who is included in the photos, could be posed about many historical pictures. For instance, there is a photo showing the Fathers of Confederation at the Charlottetown Conference. Since historians (Cuthbert Brandt 1992) have acknowledged that the social aspects of the Conference were key to its success, it seems fair to ask why the politicians' wives, who organized these social events, do not appear in official photographs.

Students can also take their own photographs as a way of helping them understand that photographs offer selective views of the world. Primary students can be assigned a word that describes a quality of their community (for example, co-operation, safety, peace). Then they can take a photograph within the school grounds or in the neighbouring community that captures that particular quality. It might also be interesting to ask students to take pictures that capture the opposite attributes (for example, isolation, danger, discord). Photographs and captions can then be separately taped to the board and class members guess which caption belongs with each picture and explain why they think it fits. The students who take each photograph are expected to provide an adequate explanation as to why it is an appropriate photograph for their caption. Finally, students may create a neighbourhood montage with magazine photographs representing the original captions.[2]

STRATEGIES FOR INTERROGATING PHOTOGRAPHS AND PAINTINGS

John Ruskin, the famous art and social thinker, noted that the evidence found in photographs "is of great use if you know how to cross examine them." His point is that images are sources of many different kinds of information depending on the questions we ask of them and on

INTERROGATING A PAINTING: AN EXAMPLE FOR UPPER ELEMENTARY STUDENTS

"Canoe Manned by Voyageurs Passing a Waterfall"—1869, Frances Anne Hopkins.
Library and Archives Canada (C-002771).

General Content
- Describe the people you see in this painting. Note the clothing and various types of headgear.
- What are the people doing?
- What objects do you see? Describe them.

Geographic data
- What is in the foreground of the painting? The background?
- Where do you think these people are?

Historical data
- What can you learn about the voyageurs from this painting?
- What questions would you like to ask the artist about the lives of the voyageurs?

Sociological data
- Who are the woman and man in the centre of the canoe? What clues suggest this?
- Why do you think they are not paddling? Is this explanation supported by anything in the painting?

Emotional context
- How do you think the voyageurs felt about having the well-dressed man and woman in the canoe with them? How might their presence affect the behaviour of the voyageurs?
- What aspects of this painting convey a sense of tranquility?

Aesthetic qualities
- How is light used in this painting? What is the purpose of this use?
- What are some of the ways the artist has made the painting artistically pleasing?

Photographer's or artist's perspective and purpose
- Why do you think the artist chose to paint a journey by voyageurs?
- Why might the artist have chosen to convey the voyageurs amid such a tranquil scene?
- Do you think the artist has a positive feeling for voyageurs?

INTERROGATING A PHOTOGRAPH: AN EXAMPLE FOR PRIMARY STUDENTS

"Sharing a moment"—Penney Clark.

General Content

- What do you see here?
- What or who do you see in this picture? What do you see in the background?
- What do you think the people are doing?

Geographic data

- What natural objects do you see? What is the land like?
- What do you think the weather was like on the day the photo was taken? What clues help you to answer this question?
- Where do you think the man and the child are?

Sociological data

- What can you tell about the people by the way they are dressed?
- Do you think the man and the child are related? How do you think they might be related? Why do you think this?

Emotional context

- What words could be used to describe how these people are feeling? Are they in a hurry? Relaxed? Comfortable? Anxious?

Aesthetic qualities

- What are some things that the photographer has done to make this photo one that you enjoy looking at?

Photographer's or artist's perspective and purpose

- Who do you think might have taken the photograph? Why do you think it was taken?
- Do you think the people in the photo knew it was being taken? Why or why not? If not, why would the photographer choose to take the photo when the people did not know it was being taken?

COMPARING VISUAL IMAGES

Using multiple carefully selected images on a common theme may be more effective than solitary images because students can rely on clues from the various images to aid in their analysis. The following images depict two immigrant groups involved in occupational activities—Chinese Canadian men working on the railway in 1883 in British Columbia and Ukrainian Canadian women clearing land in the 1930s in Alberta.

Housing built for Chinese labourers working on the Canadian Pacific Railway. Courtesy of Royal BC Museum, BC Archives (I-30869).

Ukrainian Canadian women clearing land in the 1930s in Alberta. Library and Archives Canada/Canadian National Railway Company (C-019134).

Sample lines of inquiry

- Explain an image: The most widely used line of inquiry is undoubtedly the approach popularly attributed to news reporters to explain the action in an image by asking the 5W questions (Who? What? Where? When? and Why?). This inquiry may not advance beyond the obvious if students are not encouraged to look deeper and probe for specificity. For example, it is obvious that one of the pictures involves women chopping down trees. However, there is more to be gleaned from this image. For example, when asking "Who?," can students find clues about the ages of the women—whether young girls are working along with adult females? When thinking about "When?," can students locate clues suggesting the approximate time of day (shadows), season (foliage), or even the century (clothing, technology)? In exploring the picture of the railway camp, can students identify clues that answer "Why?" the men are there and what kind of settlement is represented?

- Explore daily life: A highly useful line of inquiry for social studies purposes is to examine several images for clues about the lifestyle, practices, and conditions of historical and contemporary people and places. See Figure ZZ for an activity sheet that supports students in making accurate and relevant observations and drawing plausible and imaginative inferences about various aspects of daily life. For example,

what technology did the people have available to them? If the women in one of the images were chopping down the trees, what roles might the men have played?

- Unpack the sensorial experience: Another line of inquiry invites students to explore an image from the sensory perspective of someone in the time and place. What smells, touches, tastes, and sounds would the people in the image encounter? For example, How might their hands feel after chopping and sawing trees for days on end? What might be some of the odours coming from the log houses in the work camp?

- Investigate inner thoughts. We can invite students to enter inside the perspective of a contemporary or historical person or group by looking for clues about their values, fears, and beliefs. For example, can we tell anything about Ukrainian women's values from their clothing and the work they carried out?

These lines of inquiry are only some of the avenues that may be pursued. And it should be obvious that different questions can be used in tandem. For example, explaining the action depicted in a photograph is an accessible way to get students into an image. Students might then unpack the subjects' sensory experiences and eventually explore their inner thoughts. Ensuring that students have the tools they need to probe images for different kinds of information is perhaps the most important factor in tapping into the potential answers that images can provide.

☐ shelter/housing	☐ diet/health	☐ clothing
☐ transportation	☐ art/entertainment	☐ religion/spirituality
☐ tools/technology	☐ government	☐ community life
☐ freedoms	☐ economic activity	☐ _____

OBSERVATIONS	INFLUENCES

Criteria for an informative profile

- **Accurate and relevant observations:** offers many observations that accurately describe the details in the image that are relevant to the specified theme(s);
- **Plausible and imaginative inferences:** offers varied inferences that go beyond the very obvious conclusions and are supported by details from the image or based on other known facts about the topic.

our ability to probe their contents. We can use images more effectively in elementary classrooms by encouraging various lines of inquiry and teaching students how to "read" visual sources to extract the information they contain. The lines of inquiry that students might pursue include the following:

- general content (e.g., objects and people in the picture);
- geographic data (e.g., climate, landscape);
- historical data (e.g., type of clothing, hairstyles, furniture);
- sociological data (e.g., social class, relationships);
- emotional context (e.g., feelings of people depicted);
- aesthetic qualities (e.g., general appeal, use of colour, light, texture); and
- the photographer's or artist's perspective and purpose (e.g., intended audience, messages conveyed).

Questions that fit within one category may not necessarily be asked all at once. It may be helpful to follow a sequence emerging from students' responses. The features "Interrogating a Painting" and "Interrogating a Photograph" offer two examples of using questions to interrogate visuals. The first example, intended for upper elementary students, uses the painting "Canoe Manned by Voyageurs Passing a Waterfall" by Frances Anne Hopkins. The second example is intended for primary students and uses a contemporary photograph of a grandfather and his grandchild.

Select three or four pictures pertaining to a particular topic in the curriculum (for example, a specific community, historical event, or time period). Develop a lesson where you teach students to read the pictures and notice the similar and contrasting information contained in them.

Audiovisuals

Audiovisual resources have many positive features that make them useful in teaching social studies:

- Students with different learning styles may benefit from their use because they deliver information through both auditory and visual means.
- They provide alternative ways to gather information for less capable readers.
- In some cases, they can be more useful for data gathering than field trips because they focus on the most important aspects of the experience and eliminate extraneous details.
- They can convey a great deal of information in a relatively brief span of class time.
- Through such methods as animation, slow motion, time-lapse photography, and microphotography, they allow students to view scenes they would otherwise not have an opportunity to observe. Processes that can be difficult to visualize when described in print can be seen in action.

- Motion can also add to student interest.
- They can be more motivating than many other resources.
- They are usually less intimidating than textbooks.

Historian Graeme Decarie has warned us to "beware of technologies standing under streetlights, calling, 'Hi, sailor'" (1988, 98). He was referring to the production and indiscriminate classroom use of poor-quality (both technically and in terms of meeting curriculum objectives) audiovisual aids of various kinds. He urged teachers to choose audiovisual resources carefully and use them selectively. With the advent of computer technology, there are many more audiovisual materials available now than there were a decade ago. Therefore, it is more important than ever that they be chosen carefully and used selectively.

The type of audiovisual technology chosen will depend on its accessibility and the purpose for which it is being used. Specific audiovisual resources should be selected for classroom use based on criteria such as interest, accuracy and currency of content, conceptual level, whether content fits intended purposes, quality of photography and sound, and the way in which information is organized for presentation.

HELPING STUDENTS BECOME CRITICAL VIEWERS

As with other visual resources, it is important to help students see that audiovisual resources have been created by human developers with particular perspectives and for particular purposes. Like other visual resources, they must be actively investigated in an effort to reveal the messages that lie underneath the surface. Below are sample questions (adapted from Cates 1990) for deconstructing an audiovisual resource:

- **Dialogue.** Notice consistent use of words that have positive or negative connotations. What is the effect of using the word "cheap" instead of "inexpensive," or "conceited" in place of "high self-esteem," or "forthright" instead of "domineering"?
- **Actors.** Is there any relationship between the type of character played and the physical appearance of the actor? For instance, do homely actors play "bad guys," while attractive people play the "upstanding characters"? Are people of a particular race overrepresented among the evil characters?

- **Character development.** Are characters stereotypical (for example, are Native people presented as uniformly good or uniformly bad, or are attractive blonde women presented as unintelligent)?
- **Colour and lighting.** Is the depiction light and airy, dark and brooding, or some variation of this? Are some scenes lighter and brighter than others? What is the content of these scenes? What about the darker scenes? Are any scenes in black and white? Why do you think this is the case?
- **Music.** Can you find examples where the choice of music or its volume influences the way you view particular characters or events?
- **Camera angle and choice of shot.** Is the action ever shown from the viewpoint of a character? If so, in what cases and for what purposes?
- **Selection and arrangement of scenes.** Does the film alternate among different viewpoints, places, or people? Are different viewpoints given equal time and emphasis?
- **Overall impression.** What is the developer of this resource attempting to convey through use of some of the devices presented here?

Use of audiovisual resources need not be limited to those developed specifically for classrooms. Popular films, for example, can be used to help students learn to analyze a medium to which they receive constant exposure in their daily lives. This is important to do for the following reasons: many people are predominantly visual learners; films present details graphically that may not necessarily be communicated through writing; their dramatic telling can amplify and illuminate themes and ideas from history; they are an important art form in their own right because of their pervasiveness in our culture; and they are a gauge of the tastes and ideologies prevalent in North American culture (Johnson and Vargus 1994).

IDEAS FOR USING AUDIOVISUAL RESOURCES

This section discusses previewing, viewing, and follow-up activities for use with audiovisual resources. It is, generally speaking, not sufficient merely to turn on the DVD player and let students sit back and watch the show. The following activities are helpful in turning what may simply be an entertaining interlude into an educational experience.

FIGURE 15.1   DATA KNOWLEDGE CHART

REGION OF CANADA:

	PRIOR KNOWLEDGE	ADDITIONAL KNOWLEDGE
Topography		
Climate		
Vegetation		
Natural resources		
Industries		
Major cities		
Transportation and communication		
Wilderness preserves		

PREVIEWING ACTIVITIES

Previewing activities should arouse interest, build background knowledge, clarify purposes for viewing, and reveal what students already know about a topic. In order to arouse interest and build background knowledge, teachers might briefly describe the topics to be explored in the audiovisual resource and ask students to bring pertinent newspaper and magazine pictures and articles to class. These materials could form part of a bulletin board display that would evolve throughout the unit of study. In order to clarify purposes for viewing, students can be given key questions that identify main ideas, establish relationships among different aspects of a topic, or help students examine the material for accuracy, authenticity, or bias. These questions need not be numerous; one general question may be sufficient. The important point is that students have the questions prior to, rather than following, the viewing to provide a focus or purpose for their viewing. Students can be assigned different questions and therefore have different purposes. Then they pool their information following the viewing. A previewing activity might also consist of a discussion

of students' prior knowledge of the topics dealt with in the audiovisual resource. They could record what they already know in a retrieval chart (such as Figure 15.1, which is intended for use with an audiovisual resource on an assigned Canadian region). After viewing, students can refer back to their charts to add to and confirm the accuracy of the information they recorded prior to viewing.

Previewing activities signal to students that the viewing is to be an educational rather than a recreational experience. Because students are so accustomed to viewing DVDs for entertainment, they develop a mindset that such materials are for pleasure use only. Unless reminded by means of previewing activities, students may not view DVDs with the same intensity that they might read a textbook or other "serious" information source.

VIEWING ACTIVITIES

The purpose of viewing activities is to give students a focus while encountering the resource. It is preferable that students not take detailed notes during the viewing

FIGURE 15.2 VIEWING GUIDE

SURVEY. Listen to your teacher read you a brief summary of the DVD. List five topics you think will be addressed in this DVD.

1.

2.

3.

4.

5.

QUESTION. Create a question about an important aspect for each of the above topics. Write your questions below.

1.

2.

3.

4.

5.

VIEW AND RECORD. View the DVD to find the answers to your questions. Record your answers below. All of your questions may not be answered in the DVD. You may want to check other sources for those answers.

1.

2.

3.

4.

5.

REVIEW. Review your answers above. Use this information to write a summary of the DVD.

because there is a danger that the recording task will occupy their attention to such an extent that they will miss important points. Audiovisuals can be stopped frequently in order to check on student comprehension and to discuss and clarify points made. The entire audiovisual need not be viewed if only a portion is appropriate to curricular intents. If the entire audiovisual is pertinent, one viewing can be insufficient to allow students to cope well with the information. It may be best to view it in its entirety once and then show selected portions a second time, or as many times as necessary.

FOLLOW-UP ACTIVITIES

Following the viewing, students might record and then compare their responses to questions asked during the previewing phase. If there are discrepancies, pertinent sections of the audiovisual can be viewed again to determine why. If students have recorded hypotheses prior to viewing, they might confirm their accuracy. Other follow-up activities might relate the material in the audiovisual to the ongoing unit of instruction in which they are engaged. For example, students might use an audiovisual resource as one of a set of information sources to prepare for a talk or a report that they will prepare.

The example in Figure 15.2 (adapted from Clark 1991) of an approach to previewing, viewing, and follow-up activities uses the well-known SQ3R (Survey, Question, Read, Record, Review) strategy for dealing with print material. Its purpose is to provide students with a structured format that gives them purposes for viewing, ways to record information, and ways to summarize the information once recorded. Students can then proceed to more sophisticated strategies involving probing underneath the surface discourse for the author's purpose, and so on. They may also wish to view the resource a second time.

Conclusion

Visual resources should be a key part of a social studies program. They add interest and variety. Their use teaches students that the print medium is not the only means by which information can be acquired. However, visual resources, like other learning resources, represent the perspectives of their creators. Visual resources are particularly seductive sources of misleading information because of the powerful effect they can have on the viewer. Therefore, students need systematic strategies for interrogating these sources of information and they should view these resources with the same healthy scepticism with which we would want them to view any other resource.

Select a visual resource that has been recommended for use in a particular grade level. Identify specific outcomes in the curriculum that might be addressed using this resource. Design an activity and student support material to achieve these outcomes using the selected resource.

ACKNOWLEDGMENT

The author is grateful to Marg Franklin, retired elementary school principal and sessional instructor in elementary social studies curriculum and pedagogy at the University of British Columbia, for her helpful comments in the preparation of this chapter.

ENDNOTES

1 Trumbull's painting of the death of Montgomery can be found at en.wikipedia.org/wiki/Invasion_of_Canada_(1775); Clemens's painting can be found at explorer.monticello.org/?s1=0|s4=4_42.

2 The Critical Thinking Consortium and The History Education Network THEN/HiER have co-published a set of lesson plans, *Investigating images* (Abbott, Woytuck, and Nicol 2009), which explores nine kinds of questions (or lines of inquiry) and identifies tools to help students mine historical and contemporary images.

3 Reprinted from *Investigating images* (Abbott, Woytuck, and Nicol 2009) with permission of the Critical Thinking Consortium.

REFERENCES

Abbott, M., W. Woytuck, and J. Nicol. 2009. *Investigating images.* Vancouver, BC: The Critical Thinking Consortium.

Cates, W.M. 1990. Helping students learn to think critically: Detecting and analyzing bias in films. *Social Studies* 81: 15–18.

Clark, P. 1991. *Government in Canada: Citizenship in action.* Montreal: National Film Board of Canada.

Cuthbert Brandt, G. 1992. National unity and the politics of political history. *Journal of the Canadian Historical Association* 3: 2–11.

Davison, J.R. 1981–82. Turning a blind eye: The historian's use of photographs. *BC Studies* 52: 16–35.

Decarie, G. 1988. Audio-visual aids: Historians in Blunderland. *Canadian Social Studies* 23 (2): 95–98.

Everett-Green, R. 1996. Photography's white lies. *Globe and Mail*, November 9.

Francis, D. 1996. *Copying people, 1860–1940.* Saskatoon, SK: Fifth House.

Gabella, M.S. 1994. Beyond the looking glass: Bringing students into the conversation of historical inquiry. *Theory and Research in Social Education* 22 (3): 340–363.

Gould, S.J. 1981. *The mismeasure of man.* New York: Norton.

Grady, M. 1997. Photography as "monster." *Vancouver Sun.* May 17.

Johnson, J. and C. Vargus. 1994. The smell of celluloid in the classroom: Five great movies that teach. *Social Education* 58 (2): 109–113.

Kogawa, J. 1981. *Obasan.* Boston: David R. Godine.

Kundera, M. 1980. *The book of laughter and forgetting.* New York: Knopf.

Scott, D., C. Falk, and J. Kierstead. 2002. *Legacies of ancient Egypt.* Richmond, BC: The Critical Thinking Consortium.

Wilson, K. 1970. *Life at Red River: 1830–1860.* Toronto: Ginn.

SUPPLEMENTARY READINGS

Allen, R. 1994. Posters as historical documents: A resource for the teaching of twentieth-century history. *Social Studies* 85 (2): 52–61.

Allen, R.F. and L.E.S. Molina. 1993. Snapshot geography: Using travel photographs to learn geography in upper elementary schools. *Canadian Social Studies* 27: 62–66.

Braun, J.A. and D. Corbin. 1991. Helping students use videos to make cross-cultural comparisons. *Social Studies and the Young Learner* 4 (2): 28–29.

Burke, P. 2001. *Eyewitnessing: Uses of images as historical evidence.* Ithaca, NY: Cornell University Press.

Challenger, M. 2007. The 'stolen voices' project for the United Nations international day of peace, Imperial War Museum, London. *Intercultural Education* 18 (5): 501–504.

Clark, P. and D. Bryant. 2006. Historical empathy and Canada: A people's history. *Canadian Journal of Education,* 29 (4): 1039–1064. Accessed at http:www.csse.ca/CJE/General.htm.

Considine, D.M. 1989. The video boom's impact on social studies: Implications, applications, and resources. *Social Studies* 80 (6): 229–234.

Cromer, M. and P. Clark. 2007. Getting graphic with the past: Graphic novels and the teaching of history. *Theory and Research in Social Education* 35 (4): 574–591.

Downey, M.T. 1980. Pictures as teaching aids: Using the pictures in history textbooks. *Social Education* 44 (2): 92–99.

Epstein, T. and J. Shiller. 2005. Perspective matters: Social identity and the teaching and learning of national history. *Social Education* 69 (4): 201–204.

Felton, R.G. and R.F. Allen. 1990. Using visual materials as historical sources: A model for studying state and local history. *Social Studies* 81 (2): 84–87.

Foster, S., J. Hoge, and R. Rosch. 1999. Thinking aloud about history: Children's and adolescents' responses to historical photographs. *Theory and Research in Social Education* 27 (2): 179–214.

Fournier, J. and S. Wineburg. 1997. Picturing the past: Gender differences in the depiction of historical figures. *American Journal of Education* 105 (2): 160–185.

Harnett, Penelope. 1993. Identifying progression in children's understanding: The use of visual materials to assess primary school children's learning in history. *Cambridge Journal of Education* 23 (2): 137–154.

Hennigar-Shuh, J. 1988. Learn to look. *History and Social Science Teacher* 23 (3): 141–146.

Hou, C. and C. Hou. 1997. *Great Canadian political cartoons, 1829 to 1914.* Vancouver BC: Moody's Lookout Press.

———. 2002. *Great Canadian political cartoons, 1915 to 1945.* Vancouver, BC: Moody's Lookout Press.

———. 2011. *Great Canadian political cartoons, 1946–1982.* Vancouver, BC: Moody's Lookout Press.

Jackson, D. 1995. A note on photo CDs: A valuable resource for the classroom. *Canadian Social Studies* 30 (1): 28–29.

McCormick, T.M. and J. Hubbard. 2011. Every picture tells a story: A study of teaching methods using historical photographs with elementary students. *The Journal of Social Studies Research* 35 (91): 80–94.

Morris, S. 1989. *A teacher's guide to using portraits.* London: English Heritage Education Service.

Nelson, M. 1997. An alternative medium of social education—The "horrors of war" picture cards. *Social Studies* 88 (3): 100–107.

Osborne, K. 1990. Using Canada's visual history in the classroom. In *Canada's visual history,* 4–19. Ottawa and Montreal: National Museum of Civilization and National Film Board of Canada.

Pazienza, J. and G. Clarke. 1997. Integrating text and image: Teaching art and history. In *Trends and issues in Canadian social studies,* ed. I. Wright and A. Sears, 175–294. Vancouver, BC: Pacific Educational Press.

Poyntz, S. 2008. Images of the past: Using film to teach history. In *The anthology of social studies: Issues and strategies for secondary teachers,* ed. R. Case and P. Clark, 336–347. Vancouver, BC: Pacific Educational Press.

Sandwell, R. 2005. The Great unsolved mysteries of Canadian history: Using a web-based archives to teach history. *Canadian Social Studies* 39 (2). Accessed at http://www.quasar.ualberta.ca/css/Css/_39_2_ARSandwell_mysteries.htm.

Segall, A. 1997. "De-transparent-izing" media texts in the social studies classroom: Media education as historical/social inquiry. In *Trends and issues in Canadian social studies,* ed. I. Wright and A. Sears, 328–349. Vancouver, BC: Pacific Educational Press.

Seixas, P. 1987. Lewis Hine: From "social" to "interpretive" photographer. *American Quarterly* 39 (3): 381–409.

———. 1994. Confronting the moral frames of popular film: Young people respond to historical revisionism. *American Journal of Education* 102 (3): 261–285.

———. 2007. Popular film and young people's understanding of the history of native American-white relations. In *Celluloid blackboard: Teaching history with film,* ed. A.S. Marcus, 99–120. Greenwich CT: Information Age Publishing.

Shand, K. 2009. The interplay of graph and text in the acquisition of historical constructs. *Theory and Research in Social Education* 37 (3): 300–324.

Stevens, R.J. and J.A. Fogel. 2009. Comparing FSA photographs by Ben Shahn: A lesson in media literacy. *Middle Level Learning* 35, M2–M9.

Sunal, C.S. and B.A. Hatcher. 1986. How to do it: Studying history through art. *Social Education* 50 (4): 1–8.

Werner, W. 2000. Reading authorship into texts. *Theory and Research in Social Education* 28 (2): 193–219.

———. 2002. Reading visual texts. *Theory and Research in Social Education* 30 (3): 401–428.

———. 2004. Towards visual literacy. In *Challenges and Prospects for Canadian Social Studies*, ed. I. Wright and A. Sears, 202–215. Vancouver, BC: Pacific Educational Press.

Wineburg, S. 1991. Historical problem solving: A study of the cognitive processes used in the evaluation of documentary and pictorial evidence. *Journal of Educational Psychology* 83 (1): 73–87.

OTHER RESOURCES

INTERNET RESOURCES

Archives Canada: www.archivescanada.ca/english/index.html

British Columbia Archives, "Amazing Time Machine": www.bcarchives.gov.bc.ca/exhibits/timemach/index.htm

Canada Science and Technology Museum, "Picturing the Past": www.images.technomuses.ca

Canadian Heritage Gallery: www.canadianheritage.org

Canadian Historical Portraits: www.bac-lac.gc.ca/eng/portrait-portal/Pages/portrait-portal.aspx

Canadian Museum of Civilization: www.civilization.ca

Canadian War Museum: www.warmuseum.ca

CBC Digital Archives: www.archives.cbc.ca

Critical Thinking Consortium, "Investigating Images" and "Investigating Sources Online": www.tc2.ca/cmsms/index.php?page=investigating-sources-online

Critical Thinking Consortium, "Picture Sets": sourcedocs.tc2.ca/picture-sets/about-picture-sets.html

Framing Canada: A Photographic Memory: http:www.collectionscanada.gc.ca/framingcanada/index-e.html

The History Education Network: www.thenhier.ca. See also www.thenhier.ca/en/content/primary-sources-and-teaching-links for an extensive list of annotated websites organized according to Canadian history topics.

Images Canada: www.imagescanada.ca

Library and Archives Canada: www.collectionscanada.gc.ca

Library and Archives Canada, "Detecting the Truth: Fakes, Forgeries and Trickery": www.collectionscanada.gc.ca/forgery

McCord Museum, "Keys to History": www.mccord-museum.qc.ca/en/keys

Royal Ontario Museum: www.rom.on.ca

A Scattering of Seeds: www.whitepinepictures.com/seeds

United States Holocaust Memorial Museum: www.ushmm.org

Virtual Museum: www.museevirtuel-virtualmuseum.ca

WebMuseum, Paris (also known as LeWebLouvre): www.ibiblio.org/wm

FILMS

Canadian Broadcasting Corporation. *Canada: A People's History*, vols. 1–4. 2000. Toronto: Author. Uses visual documentary sources and enactments to depict the history of Canada from prehistory to 1990.

National Film Board of Canada. 1972. *Paul Kane goes west*. Montreal: Author. Features Paul Kane paintings depicting Canada's early history. All NFB films listed below, except as noted, can be accessed at www.nfb-onf.gc.ca/eng/collection.

———. 1980. *A visit from Captain Cook*. Montreal: Author. Illustrates how European artists projected their own ethnocentric perspectives on what they observed and recorded.

———. 1997. *Canada's visual history*. Montreal: National Museum of Civilization and National Film Board of Canada. This rich source of visual information deals with Canada's social and economic history, including visuals from pre-European contact to the recent past and suggestions for further reading.

———. *Postcards from Canada*. 2000. Montreal: Author. Includes stunning postcard-like images from coast to coast.

———. *Transit series*. 2000. Montreal: Author. These documentaries examine Canada's geography using these five themes: Air: Climate; Water: Reserves and Networks; Land: Territory and Resources; Fire: Energy; and Life: People, Fauna and Flora.

———. *Images of a forgotten war: Films of the Canadian expeditionary force in the Great War*. n.d. Accessed at www3.nfb.ca/ww1.

———. *On all fronts: World War II and the NFB*. 2008. Accessed at www3.nfb.ca/ww2.

National Film Board (NFB) contact information:
www.nfb.ca/store
National Film Board of Canada
P.O. Box 6100, Station Centre-Ville
Montreal, Quebec H3C 3H5

16

Bringing Community Resources into Elementary Social Studies

Penney Clark

Garnet McDiarmid (1970) tells the story of a teacher who wrote that he did not teach science in his elementary school because the school had neither textbooks nor laboratory equipment. McDiarmid points out that the school was located in an area of uranium mines, moraines and other post-glacial deposits, running water, ponds, and abundant flora and fauna—all of which could have been exploited as fascinating sources for scientific investigation.

A similar point might be made about the availability of outside resources for social studies. Every school has many historic and geographically interesting sites to explore nearby or further afield. Every teacher has access to local people who are willing to be interviewed or come to school to share their expertise. Many organizations will send text-based and visual materials or realia free-of-charge (McKoy 2010). Students in urban areas can step outside their school to investigate traffic patterns, community development, museums, recreational facilities, and commercial sites. Students in rural locations can visit metropolitan areas, regional or local industries, historic sites, and transportation routes. The value and accessibility of the community as a learning resource in social studies is richly illustrated by the examples described in the featured text, "Globe-trotting Teddies." Unfortunately, many of us overlook the educational potential of what is outside our classroom walls.

Learning to make effective educational use of the community requires that these encounters become more than "isolated experiences," unrelated to curriculum learning outcomes. As one writer warns, field trips may involve little more than "wandering in a long line (rather like a snake that has just shed its skin and is doubtful about its boundaries) through museum corridors with half-minute halts to gape at an exhibit or collect stragglers" (quoted in Oliver 1970, 22). The lost educational potential of field experiences is reflected in an episode of the television show *The Wonder Years* in which the junior high school protagonist Kevin Arnold and his classmates visit a museum. In the episode, teacher and students have very different agendas. The teacher, of course, views the trip as an opportunity to expose students to the richness of the past. For Kevin and his friends, the exhibits become a mere backdrop to more important personal concerns—who likes whom, who is going to which party on the weekend, and so on.

If students lack clear curricular purposes and the educational context in which to place them, embarking on a community experience can become a mere diversion from classroom routine—a welcome relief perhaps, but ultimately not an experience that furthers the goals of social studies. In this chapter, I explore the value of and strategies for effectively bringing the outside into the curriculum in the context of three types of community resources: field experiences, local experts, and materials developed by non-educational agencies.

Field Experiences

Involving students directly in the community through field experiences can foster rich understandings not available from textbook study. When conducted in the

GLOBE-TROTTING TEDDIES

Wendy Newport and Jenny Murdie, two primary teachers at Irwin Park Elementary School in West Vancouver, found an interesting way to help their grade 2 students learn about the wider world. Early in the year, each student brings a teddy bear to school. Each teddy is given an identification card, travel journal, instructions, and a tote bag. The first entry in the journal describes the student's/owner's interests and geographical location. Each teddy is then given to someone who will be travelling to other parts of the province, country, or world. This individual might be a family member, friend, parent's work colleague, or acquaintance. The traveller is asked to pass the teddy on to someone else, but only after that person agrees to one condition: an entry must be made in the travel journal and a postcard mailed to the student.

Each year the class receives several hundred postcards, as the teddies are passed from one person to another. One year, postcards arrived from more than fifty countries. When a postcard arrives, its contents are read to the class and discussed, and its origin is located on a world map. Whoever has the teddy on April 30 is asked to mail it back to the school. By the end of the school year, at least 80 per cent of the teddies, with their travel journals and often souvenirs, make their way back to their owners. What a wonderful way for young children to begin to learn about the world! They read first-person accounts of places and events, living vicariously through their teddies.

The "Flat Stanley" project is a variation on this strategy. More than one thousand schools around the world have sent paper dolls to classes in other countries. Flat Stanley's daily experiences are recorded in a journal, which is sent along when he is returned by mail. The idea originated with a book called *Flat Stanley* by Jeff Brown (1964). The story is about a boy who is squashed flat by a bulletin board. He makes the best of his situation by embarking on adventures such as mailing himself to a friend in California. Flat Stanley has posed with US President George W. Bush, and spent a day at the White House after receiving security clearance. He has also been on an episode of the television drama *The West Wing*.

In a similar vein, Karlo Cabrera's grade 4 class at Fenside Public School in North Toronto mailed "Flat Mark" to Paul Martin shortly after he became prime minister. Martin welcomed the idea and invited Flat Mark to the swearing-in ceremony at Rideau Hall. Martin told the students that "Flat Mark got into some trouble, and there are stories I don't think I should tell you, but he did a terrific job.... He was extremely helpful when the transition team was devising policy." Flat Mark was returned to the students accompanied by a binder of photographs and captions and a journal describing his experiences. In exchange, students sent three books describing their "hopes and dreams and wishes for Canada," including wishes that there would be no more SARS, and that people would be kinder to animals, stop robbing banks, and cease waging war (Taber 2003; Galloway 2004; Globe-trotting teddies 1998).

context of an ongoing unit or theme, a field trip becomes much more than a pleasant break from daily routines. For example, art galleries and museums can enliven the study of ancient civilizations or pioneer times. Field experiences, particularly those involving overnight stays, are ideal for outdoor studies and environmental investigations.

During a unit on pioneer life, a combined grade 3/4 class in Alberta visited a typical pioneer home, a wealthier pioneer home, a historical costume collection, and the first schoolhouse built in their school district more than one hundred years earlier. In the typical pioneer home, the students chopped wood, carded wool, and made butter, ice cream, scones, and candles. In the home of the wealthier family, they did needlework, baked cookies, and acted as guests in the drawing room. When viewing the historical costume collection, students imagined what it would be like to wear corsets and stiff collars. During the morning spent in the schoolhouse, they enacted a typical 1881 school day with a teacher "in role." Through these simulated experiences, students gained a feeling for life during pioneer times

in their community. This is evident from three students' unedited journals following the field experience in the schoolhouse (McKay 1990, 153–154):

> **Penney:** Today at the 1881 School I learned how things were back in the 18S mostly. Such as reading, games, aned a spelleing B. the teacher called us lassies and ladies. I also learned that there wre severeal additions to the school because the amount of children was growing alot the games were called Anti-I-over, marbles jacks, count the rabbits and fox and geese. I also learned that the old school was once a House and the people that lived in it loved walpaper and I learned that the school house was down by saskatchewan river and it flooded so they tied it down by a hool on the back of it so it wouldn't float away. I also learned that the first legestlatetive building was in the gym of Macy avenue school.

Adam: I lrnd that 1881 school is srikt with the kids. The kids play anty anty I over and the boys playd kech and rabits

Timothy: it was scarry when adam was talking to Jason and the teacher turned around and smacked the stick on the desk and said put your hands on the desk and I thought she was going to smack adams nuckles but she didn't. then she turned to me and said stand up and put your hands on your desk and then I thought she was going to smack me on the bum but she didn't.

I also was intereted and thought that was neet was the little kinds of porjectors, one you would put a candel in it and that would be the light and you would put a little sort of film and it would show up on the wall.

Timothy's relief that both he and Adam were spared the teacher's wrath is palpable. Because they actually were pioneer children for a time, all three students gained a more powerful understanding than they might have attained through reading about or viewing such a scene. The students also acquired historical information on topics such as children's games of the time, the first legislative building in the province, audiovisual techniques used by nineteenth-century teachers, and disciplinary methods. This information enabled students to build their impressions of what life was like during the period—impressions that would expand as they engaged in follow-up activities upon their return from the trip. (See White 2010.)

A field trip can provide accurate information and direct experience that also enrich contemporary social studies topics. Students might investigate topics such as:

- roles of community members
- community services
- community rules and laws
- cultural makeup of the community
- local government
- transportation networks
- industry and commerce
- architecture
- zoning
- recreation

Field experiences must be carefully planned. Activities that take place prior to and following the field experience may be of equal importance to those activities that take place during it. Prior activities set the context for the experience and help students participate with inquiring attitudes. Follow-up activities allow students to clarify impressions, share ideas, and apply what they have learned. The featured text, "Field Trip Checklist," contains a checklist of logistical and educational factors to consider when organizing a field trip. I will elaborate on three sets of considerations:

- choosing to go on a field trip;
- choosing the site; and
- developing preparatory, on-site, and follow-up activities.

CHOOSING TO GO ON A FIELD TRIP

Two factors should govern the decision to include a field experience in a social studies program: feasibility and educational efficacy. Feasibility refers to the reasonableness of undertaking the proposed activity given the typical constraints—transportation logistics, insufficient adult supervisors, expensive admission fees, safety considerations, and parental resistance due to lack of understanding of the connection between the experience and curriculum objectives. Many of these difficulties can be overcome with careful planning.

A second consideration is educational efficacy—whether the benefits outweigh the risks and drawbacks. Will the gain in learning justify the valuable class time and effort involved? Could the same learning outcomes be attained as richly and efficiently by staying in the classroom? A field experience should be chosen only if important benefits are realized that could not be achieved in the classroom. Clear communication is helpful in assuring parents, students, and school (and school board) administration that a field experience is the best way to meet specific curriculum goals.

CHOOSING THE SITE

The key criterion in choosing a field-trip site is that it advances curricular objectives by extending and enriching areas of investigation that are being (or will be) pursued in the classroom. Field experiences should be seen as one more data source to be accessed in a unit.

We need not limit our choices of field site to destination settings such as museums, local historical sites,

FIELD TRIP CHECKLIST

Early preparation

☐ Review school and district policies regarding field trips.

☐ Obtain information about the field trip, including talking to other teachers who have organized similar outings.

☐ Clarify educational objectives. Make them as concrete as possible.

☐ Obtain permissions from principal and on-site authorities.

☐ Book trip and arrange transportation.

☐ Make students aware of objectives and solicit student input.

☐ Visit site. Could take along a student committee.

☐ Arrange for helpers.

☐ Inform parents of the purpose of the trip, departure and arrival times, eating arrangements, costs, supervision arrangements, and any special clothing or equipment requirements.

☐ Obtain permission from parents or guardians.

Just prior to trip

☐ Provide checklist for students:

- money;
- equipment;
- clothing; and
- food.

☐ Collect money, if required.

☐ Prepare students logistically:

- discuss safety issues;
- could role-play expected behaviour;
- review rules of conduct; and
- establish work groups and buddy system.

☐ Brief adult helpers:

- discuss purposes of trip;
- discuss duties; and
- discuss safety issues.

☐ Prepare students educationally:

- review objectives;
- share students' prior knowledge about the place; and
- assign and review individual and group tasks.

On the trip

☐ Use the travel time to the site as part of the experience (for example, have students take note of types of buildings, industries, and transportation observed en route).

☐ Once on site, point out boundaries and key spots (for example, washrooms, meeting area, lost and found space).

☐ Elicit student questions and discussion.

☐ Remind students about gathering and recording data:

- go over charts to be filled in or questions to be answered;
- assign one or more students to take photographs as a record of the trip;
- create field sketches; and
- interview people on-site.

☐ Plan for return trip (for example, take a different route back to the school to capitalize on the commuting and what can be observed while travelling).

Follow-up

☐ Organize, synthesize, and present collected data.

☐ Formally thank hosts and helpers.

☐ Evaluate trip.

---

or other typical attractions. A field experience might be as simple as a walk through the neighbourhood to record the range of home types, a trip to the shopping mall to observe product marketing, or a visit to the local public library to access information, if these will help attain curriculum objectives. One of the most successful field experiences I am aware of took place at a construction site of new government offices, which was around the corner from the school. Several grade 2 students had observed the beginning of construction on the way to school one morning and reported this event to the class. The teacher, eager to capitalize on this serendipitous lesson on community change, took students to the site almost every day during construction. Students observed construction plans, materials, and methods, and interviewed construction workers. After the building opened, and government workers had moved in, students interviewed them to find out how well their new offices met their needs. What made this experience so successful was the uniting of keen student interest with the achievement of social studies objectives. (See Schuler 2002 for a delightful account of her grade 2 class's rewarding exploration of their community.)

In considering alternatives, a site should not be rejected out-of-hand merely because most students may have been there before. I remember my surprise when I learned that a little boy in my grade 4 class in a suburb of Vancouver had never visited Stanley Park. In the nine years of his life, his family had never climbed into a car or onto a bus and travelled there to spend the day at the zoo or aquarium, or simply exploring the seaside. We cannot assume that all students will have had these seemingly common experiences. As well, a family excursion can and should be quite a different experience than a structured field trip. During a field experience, students observe with particular purposes in mind, which guide their information gathering. Also, field trips offer opportunities for in-depth activities. For instance, it is always

FIGURE 16.1 SAMPLE FIELD TRIP PERMISSION FORM

In conjunction with their local history study, our class will be visiting McAdam Heritage Home. Volunteers at the home will involve students in activities in which people living in the home would have been engaged in the late 1800s.

Date of trip _____ Destination _____

Duration _____ Transportation _____

Time leaving school _____ Time of return _____ Cost to student _____

Items to bring _____

_____

Teacher's name _____ Phone _____

PLEASE RETURN THIS SECTION

I give my permission for _____ to participate in the trip to the McAdam Heritage Home on October 3, 2015.

Signature _____ (parent/guardian)

Phone number: Home _____ Work _____

Email address _____

Emergency contact _____

---

enjoyable to visit an aquarium, but it is a much richer experience when students are invited behind the scenes to observe feeding routines or attendants caring for a sick animal.

Table 16.1, "Range of Field Sites," outlines various possibilities available in many communities, and suggests questions or tasks to focus these experiences. There has been no attempt to assign sites according to grade level. Many sites visited in the primary years for one purpose may well be revisited in later grades for other purposes.

PREPARATORY ACTIVITIES WITH STUDENTS

Prior activities set the context for the experience, and help students participate with an inquiring attitude. First and foremost, students need to be aware of field-trip objectives. For instance, the reason for a trip to a local branch of the public library might be to discover the special services offered to particular community groups (for example, children, seniors, visually impaired)

and how these services are delivered. A second objective might be to explore how these services or their delivery might better meet people's needs. Such a trip could be part of a larger unit on community services. Do not assume that students will automatically make the connections between their experiences on the trip and other learning activities. The objectives to be addressed should be discussed explicitly.

Provide students with site-related pamphlets, posters, websites, kits of sample items, or video programs that preview the field experience. Students can use these materials to generate questions to guide their observations at the site. You can also give key questions to the students.

Prior to the trip, a permission form providing basic facts about the trip, such as the one shown in Figure 16.1, should be sent home. Considerable preparation is required if interviews or surveys are to be conducted at the site. The featured text, "Advice on Conducting Interviews and Surveys," offers suggestions for carrying out interviews and surveys.

ADVICE ON CONDUCTING INTERVIEWS AND SURVEYS

Preparation

- Decide what information is needed to meet the research objectives.
- Consider whether a survey or an interview is the better format to obtain the required information. Use surveys when a minimal amount of common information is needed from a fairly large number of people. An interview works best when smaller numbers are involved and the answers may be lengthy or need to be clarified.
- Research background information before the interview or survey. The more information you have, the more pertinent your questions are likely to be.
- Decide on the type of questions to ask: questions where people can indicate YES/NO or AGREE/DISAGREE, or the type where people explain their answers. Generally with interviews it is preferable to avoid questions that could be answered with a simple "yes" or "no" because these may not be particularly enlightening. Long answers on surveys involve more work from the respondents and may be more difficult to interpret and categorize.
- Generate a list of possible questions and select those questions that most clearly and directly address the desired information. Ask as few questions as possible.
- Decide on the "sample" (the group who will answer the questions). Check with possible respondents beforehand to ensure that they are comfortable sharing information on the research topic.
- Discuss as a class the guidelines for effective interviewing.
- Provide an opportunity for students to practise interviews with peers, parents, or other familiar individuals.

Survey guidelines

- Decide whether respondents will be asked questions or if they will fill out the form on their own. Response rates are lower when respondents fill out their own forms because some will not do so.
- Decide whether responses will be anonymous. This will depend on the type of questions and respondents' wishes.
- Provide information on the survey in an accompanying letter. The information should include why the survey is being conducted, who is conducting it, and how the person can find out the results of the survey.

Interview guidelines

- Clearly state who you are, your purpose, how the information will be used, and how long the interview is expected to take.
- Visit with the interviewee for a few minutes before and after the interview. This will help you to see the interviewee as a person and to make the interviewee feel comfortable.
- Allow the interviewee time to think about the question before responding.
- Clarify ambiguous responses. Restate the question using other words. Or say, "Is this what you meant?" and restate the intended meaning of the response.
- Ask new questions that grow out of the interviewee's comments. By sticking to the prepared questions, valuable opportunities to delve deeper and explore ideas may be missed.
- Use a tape recorder (with the interviewee's permission) or notes to record the interview. Use the interviewee's exact words in the notes. Choice of words may be an important indicator of feelings.
- Summarize the main points for the interviewee at the end of the interview. Don't offer comments that could be interpreted by the interviewee as critical of his or her responses.
- Thank the interviewee at the end of the interview.

Follow-up

- Send a thank-you note to all interviewees.
- Summarize impressions in writing as soon as possible after the interview. Tabulate survey results by adding up the totals of similar answers and clustering common themes contained in open-ended answers.
- Prepare an oral and/or written report of the results.
- Send a copy of the report to all those who wish to have it.

TABLE 16.1 RANGE OF FIELD SITES

FIELD SITES	FOCUS QUESTIONS OR TASKS
School • physical layout • roles of various staff members	• What types of rooms are in our school (for example, classrooms, offices, gym)? How is each one used? • What types of occupations are there in our school? • What tasks do people do? How are these tasks important? • How could the physical layout be altered to better meet the needs of the people who use the school?
Local neighbourhood • modes of transportation • safety measures (for example, crosswalks, sidewalks, signs, fire hydrants)	• How do people get to work and to school? • What do people in the neighbourhood think of the transportation services? • How could they be improved to better meet people's needs? • What safety features are in our neighbourhood? • What is the function of each? • Are other safety features needed? • How could we go about getting them?
Public services • fire station • police station • public library • public health unit	• What places in our community provide services? • Which services does the government provide? • Which services are special to our community and which are provided in most communities? • Are other services needed in our community? • How could we go about getting them?
Retail businesses • grocery store • bakery • shopping mall	• Which places sell goods? • Are there enough goods and services available in our community? • Do all communities need goods and services from other communities?
Manufacturing or commercial sites • assembly line • newspaper plant • warehouse • advertising agency	• What is the product(s) here? • Where does the facility fit in terms of the product's production, distribution, marketing, or sale? • What happens at this site? • What happened to the product before it arrived at this site? What happens next? • Is it safe working here? Why or why not?
Community celebrations • multicultural festivals • Remembrance Day ceremonies • heritage days	• What things do people in our community choose to celebrate? • What is the history of this event? • Why are these celebrations important to people in this community?
Historical sites • restored homes, forts, and villages • graveyards and monuments • museums (local and provincial)	• What can we learn about the past at this site? • Is it important to maintain sites like this one? Why or why not? • What might life have been like when people lived and worked here?
Resource development sites • mines • lumber mills • farms • refineries	• What resource is being developed? Give a step-by-step description of the process used to develop this resource. • What are the environmental effects of development of this resource? • What environmental protection measures are used here? Are these measures sufficient? • Where does the product(s) go? • How are transportation systems used to transport the product from this site?
Environmental preservation sites • fish hatchery • water-treatment plant • landfill facility	• What happens at this facility? • How does it contribute to environmental preservation? • Does this site create any pollution?

TABLE 16.1   RANGE OF FIELD SITES (CONT.)

FIELD SITES	FOCUS QUESTIONS OR TASKS
Government operations • all-candidates meeting • provincial legislature in session • city council in session • ratepayer meeting on a local issue • mock trial in a courtroom	**All-candidates meeting:** Choose two election issues. • What is each candidate's stance on these issues? • Which issues seem to be of most concern to the audience? • Who are the strongest candidates? Why? **Simulated city council meeting:** • What strategies did you use to try to win others over to your point of view? How successful were you? • Did you change your position in any way based on what others said? **Actual city council meeting:** Describe the decision-making process used by the city council. • Were points in favour of each argument taken into consideration? • Did some opinions seem to carry more weight than others? • What recommendations would you offer to city councils about the process of making decisions?
Transportation and communication venues • railway station, bus depot • port facilities • television station • post office • airport	• How are things organized so that employees work together to keep things running smoothly? Draw a flow chart. • Describe what it would be like to work at a job at one of these sites. • What are some examples of the technology used at this facility?

ON-SITE ACTIVITIES

An ideal field experience is structured and purposeful. Students observe and record their observations in an organized manner. Here are some approaches to recording information at the site:

- **Tally sheets.** Students may find tally sheets useful if they are looking for specific information that can be counted. The following example shows how students might calculate on a tally sheet how much traffic goes over the school crosswalk during a specific period of time. Students could also use a tally sheet to solicit opinions for a survey.

TRAFFIC OVER A CROSSWALK	
TIME PERIODS	**NUMBER OF PEOPLE**
8:00–8:15	|||
8:15–8:30	||||
8:30–8:45	
8:45–9:00	╫╫ ╫╫
…	

- **Maps.** A simple street map of the community can be used to record the location of community features such as housing types (for example, apartments, single-family dwellings, duplexes).

- **Note-taking sheets.** Encourage students to record responses during the field experience on sheets with teacher- or student-made questions. The questions should direct students to the features of the site that relate to the intended understanding, especially those that students may not notice otherwise.
- **Digital photographs/recordings.** One or more students could record important aspects of the trip using a digital camera or camcorder. These visual records assist in making detailed observations following the trip and in preparing multimedia presentations, bulletin boards, class booklets, or websites.
- **Sketches.** Drawings are a useful way to record information because students can focus on particular details rather than record everything as a camera would.
- **Journals.** Students could record impressions in a journal, perhaps writing in the role of someone working at a site or living in a particular historic time.
- **Interviews.** It may be appropriate for students to conduct interviews at the site. Primary students could use a chart, such as the one in Figure 16.2, to record interview information obtained from members of the school or the local community.

Think of a particular site that would enhance the study of a topic in the social studies curriculum. Develop an activity sheet based on one of the ideas discussed above that would structure students' experiences while at this site. Focus the activity so that the field experience provides students with insights that they could not achieve from a classroom-based study.

FIGURE 16.2 SAMPLE INTERVIEW FORM

Hello,

Our names are _____

Thank you for agreeing to answer our questions.

Q. What is your role or job in our community?	A.
Q. Where do you work?	A.

We have been studying how people in our community help meet each other's needs.

Q. In your role, do you help people LEARN? If yes, how?	A.
Q. In your role, do you help people be SAFE? If yes, how?	A.
Q. In your role, do you help people be HEALTHY? If yes, how?	A.
Q. In your role, do you help people have FUN? If yes, how?	A.
Q. In your role, do you help people BELONG? If yes, how?	A.
Q. In your role, do you help people GET AROUND? If yes, how?	A.
Q.	A.

Thank you for answering our questions.

FIGURE 16.3   NOTE OF APPRECIATION

To: _____

Role: _____

Place: _____

We appreciate many things that you do to help our community meet its needs:

1. _____

2. _____

3. _____

But we REALLY appreciate how you help the community meet its need to

_____

when you _____

Thank you very, very much.

Signed _____

FOLLOW-UP ACTIVITIES

After a field experience three kinds of activities are helpful:

- Students organize and interpret the data they have gathered.
- Students share their findings with others.
- Students review and assess the experience itself, including its preparatory and follow-up activities.

In preparation for interpreting data, students should review their notes, diagrams, photographs, drawings, or other records and then select and organize this information. (The pre-visit questions or the recording charts provide an organized format for the data.) Students should then interpret and draw conclusions from the information. This might include asking questions such as the following:

- Is there a particular point of view from which this information was presented?
- Is there another side to this story?
- What conclusions can I draw from this information? Does other evidence support these conclusions?
- Was I able to answer all my questions or do I need to consult other sources?
- What other questions arise now that my original questions have been answered?

Encourage students to develop effective and interesting ways of presenting their findings. Presentation formats include individual or group bulletin board displays, models, photo albums, stories, reports, letters, poems, digital recordings, journals, articles in the school newspaper, a play to be put on for other classes, and so on. Choices are as varied as for any other kind of research. (See chapter 11, "Escaping the Typical Report Trap," in this volume for other ideas.)

Finally, it may be useful to invite students, orally or in writing, to review and assess the field experience itself. Students could address the following questions:

- What were our purposes in engaging in this community experience?
- Did we achieve our purposes?
- Are there things we could have done differently in order to achieve our purposes?
- Was the trip the best way to obtain the needed information?
- Was the trip interesting? Why or why not?
- What were some of the pleasant and unpleasant surprises we encountered? How could we reduce the possibility of encountering the unpleasant surprises in another field experience?

Students could write letters reviewing the experience and send them as thank-you notes to coordinators at the site. Figure 16.3, "Note of Appreciation," provides a structure for primary students to communicate their findings and to acknowledge community members' contributions.

Local Experts

Local resource people provide students with unique learning opportunities to initiate relationships with adults they may not normally meet. Students enjoy asking their own questions, receiving first-hand responses to those questions, and drawing their own conclusions.

Bringing in a resource person can be used to dispel stereotypes. For example, in the unit on pioneer life discussed earlier in this chapter, a local senior who had lived in the community as a child spoke to the class. For one child, a predominant impression from the experience was how healthy the senior was. The guest had announced to the class that the reason she had come a day early was because she was going skiing the next day. Clearly, the child's conception of "elderly" was broadened considerably when he realized that a seventy-six-year-old woman could be so physically healthy and active

(McKay 1990). A similar result occurred when a grade 6 class invited local seniors to the school for a senior citizens' tea (Sears and Bidlake 1991). The students served refreshments, provided entertainment, and interviewed their guests. Not only did students learn about local historical events, they developed empathy for seniors and interest in their life decisions and experiences.

SOURCES OF EXPERTS

If given the opportunity, many people are willing to come to the classroom and share their expertise with students:

- **Parents or guardians.** It is easy to forget this rich source that is so close at hand. Every classroom will have parents or guardians who have travelled widely. Many may have come to Canada as immigrants. They will also have a variety of occupations and interests. It can be useful to send a form home at the beginning of the year outlining topics that the class will be exploring, and asking for parents or guardians who have some related expertise to share it.

- **Industry and commerce representatives.** Chambers of commerce, public relations departments of large firms, business lobby groups, owners of small businesses, and professional people such as doctors and lawyers are often prepared to come to schools or to arrange for interviews.
- **Interest and service groups.** Representatives from community organizations such as local historical societies, environmental lobby groups, veterans' organizations, and ethnic group associations are often prepared to meet with students. Museums sometimes provide resource people, as well as kits of materials they will send to classrooms.
- **Government officials.** Politicians are often willing to visit schools to present their perspectives on pertinent issues and to answer student questions. Local law courts, police departments, embassies, and consulates are other possibilities.
- **Individuals with unique backgrounds.** Some people have unique life experiences to share. Such people might include Holocaust survivors, refugees from war-torn countries, and workers for humanitarian organizations in developing countries. The possibilities are limitless.

PREPARATION

Hosting a resource person is likely to be a profitable experience only if both students and guest are adequately prepared. In her article "Beyond Guest Speakers," Diana Hess (2004) discusses the futility of having guests who lecture the class for thirty minutes and answer a few vague or irrelevant student questions. A guest expert's visit is far more likely to be a meaningful experience if there is genuine interaction between the resource person and students. This may mean that the guest does not simply speak to the class but shares artifacts, documents, or websites for students to examine and discuss. The featured text, "Checklist for Guest Experts," suggests planning ideas to ensure a meaningful experience.

FOLLOW-UP ACTIVITIES

Follow-up activities should provide students with opportunities to compare ideas provided by the expert and previously acquired information, interpret the lessons learned, draw conclusions, and develop further questions. The visit should be acknowledged with a written thank-you letter. Students might also send copies of pictures, stories, or other projects to the visitor.

GOVERNMENT-RELATED RESOURCES

The Parliament of Canada website has two very helpful compilations of annually updated resources and programs about parliamentary democracy and citizenship education.

- "Background Resources for Educators" lists resources produced by parliamentary groups, organized under three headings:
  - Parliament
  - Senate
  - House of Commons

  This web page can be found online at www.parl.gc.ca/About/Parliament/Education/Resources/index-e.asp.

- "Related Resources" lists contact information and educational resources available from numerous federal and provincial departments and educational organizations organized under six headings:
  - Information about Parliament
  - Parliamentary history
  - Multimedia
  - Professional development
  - Youth programs and contests
  - Provincial and territorial assemblies

  View this web page at www.parl.gc.ca/About/Parliament/Education/Resources/related/index.asp.

Community-Developed Materials

In addition to the community resources already discussed—field experiences and resource people—community organizations offer an amazing variety of materials for teachers and students:

- **Consulates.** A vast array of materials is available from some countries (for example, Japan, Switzerland).
- **Federal agencies.** Many national government agencies (for example, Canadian International Development Agency, Library and Archives Canada, National Film Board of Canada, Elections Canada, Citizenship and Immigration Canada) are rich sources of print, electronic, and video resources.
- **Provincial and local services.** Materials are available from fire and law-enforcement services, municipal and provincial bodies, and many local agencies. Museums often have kits of materials that schools can borrow.
- **Political parties.** The websites of major political parties contain information about the party, its organization, and its position on key issues.

- **Resource industries.** Industry associations often have teacher-developed materials (for example, provincial mining or forestry associations).
- **Environment and development organizations.** Non-governmental groups (for example, Greenpeace, Western Canada Wilderness Committee) can provide materials.

Community-developed resources may be particularly useful in providing information that presents an alternative, more current perspective than that found in textbooks. Because these materials may not have been originally intended for use in classrooms, the information and views contained in them must be scrutinized carefully. The following questions may help teachers critically examine these materials:

- What are the aims of the organization? Are these acceptable in a public education system?
- How are these aims reflected in the materials available to teachers and students?
- Does the organization have any formal ties to education or the production of educational materials?
- How suitable are the materials for classroom use and what levels might they be appropriate for? Can they be adapted for use?
- Which curricular objectives can these materials be used to help attain?
- If the organization provides human resources for classroom or professional purposes, how can these resources be used to enhance social studies?

Select a topic in the social studies curriculum and brainstorm the range of field experiences, resource people, and community-developed resources that might be used to supplement or even replace the traditional educational resources used to address this topic.

Conclusion

A rich social studies program requires access to a wide array of resources, including those in the community. Community resources offer important experiences and insights that can deepen student understanding of social studies. Careful preparation is the key to making the most of such resources. Preparation includes carefully choosing a field-trip site or resource person, making students aware of the purposes for using the resource, and helping students develop questions to guide their discovery. Most importantly, unlike the teacher cited at the opening of this chapter, let us not ignore the exciting possibilities all around us. The rewards are immense.

ACKNOWLEDGMENTS

Thanks to Marg Franklin, retired elementary school principal and University of British Columbia sessional instructor in elementary social studies, for her helpful comments on this chapter. I would like to thank Marjorie Redbourn, a student in a Simon Fraser University social studies methods class, for reminding me of the episode of *The Wonder Years* and its applicability to field experiences.

REFERENCES

Brown, J. 1964. *Flat Stanley.* New York: HarperCollins.

Galloway, G. 2004. The adventures of Flat Mark and Paul Martin. *Globe and Mail*, January 21.

Globe-trotting teddies provide geography lesson for students. 1998. *Vancouver Sun.* May 5.

Hess, D. 2004. Beyond guest speakers. *Social Education* 68 (5): 347–348.

McDiarmid, G.L. 1970. The value of on-site learning. *Orbit* 1 (3): 4–7.

McKay, R. 1990. Children's construction of meaning in a thematic unit. Unpublished doctoral dissertation, University of Alberta, Edmonton.

McKoy, K. 2010. Realia: It's not just about field trips anymore. *Social Education* 74 (2): 73.

Oliver, H. 1970. Philadelphia's Parkway Program. *Orbit* 1 (3): 22–23.

Schuler, D. 2002. Studying the community. *Social Education* 66 (5): 320–324.

Sears, A. and G. Bidlake. 1991. The senior citizens' tea: A connecting point for oral history in the elementary school. *Social Studies* 82 (4): 133–135.

Taber, J. 2003. Flat Mark has the next prime minister's ear. *Globe and Mail.* December 10.

White, W.E. 2010. Historic sites and your students. *Social Education*, 74 (2): 73.

SUPPLEMENTARY READINGS

Anderson, D. and Z. Zhang. 2003. Teacher perceptions of field-trip planning and implementation. *Visitor Studies Today!* 6 (3): 6–11.

Anderson, D. and H. Shimizu. 2007. Recollections of Expo 70: Visitors' experiences and the retention of vivid long-term memories. *Curator: The Museum Journal* 50 (4): 435–454.

Anderson, D. and V. Gosselin. 2008. Private and public memories of Expo 67: A case study of recollections of Montreal's World's Fair, 40 years after the event. *Museum and Society* 6 (1): 1–21.

Anderson, D., B. Piscitelli, K. Weier, M. Everett, and C. Tayler. 2002. Children's museum experiences: Identifying powerful mediators of learning. *Curator: The Museum Journal* 45 (3): 213–231.

Baird, O. 2008. I want the people to observe and to learn! The St. Petersburg "Kunstkamera" in the eighteenth century. *History of Education* 37 (4): 531–547.

Butler, P. and R. Loomis. 1993. Evaluation for an historic house museum: The Moody Mansion as a case study. *Visitor Studies* 5 (1): 154–164.

Camhi, J. 2008. Pathways for communicating about objects on guided tours. *Curator: The Museum Journal* 51 (3): 275–294.

Carson, C. 2008. The end of history museums: What's plan B? *The Public Historian* 30 (4): 9–27.

Dockett, S., S. Main, and L. Kelly. 2011. Consulting young children: Experiences from a museum. *Visitor Studies* 14 (1): 13–33.

Downey, S. 2000. Findings and implications from an evaluation of school programs at the United States Holocaust Memorial Museum. *Visitor Studies Today!* 3 (2): 13–16.

Giese, R., J. Davis-Dorsey, and J. Gutierrez. 1992. School/museum collaboration in curriculum design and delivery. *Visitor Behaviour* 7 (1): 4–6.

Graft, C. 1990. Incorporating evaluation into the interpretive planning process at Colonial Williamsburg. *Visitor Studies* 2 (1): 133–139.

———. 2001. Improving interaction between live interpreters and children. *Visitor Studies Today!* 4 (3): 1–5.

Gruenewald, D., A. Elam, and N. Koppelman. 2007. "Our place in history": Inspiring place-based social history in schools and communities. *Journal of Museum Education* 32 (3): 231–240.

Higgs, P. and S. McNeal. 2006. Examining a culture from museum artifacts. *Social Studies and the Young Learner* 18 (4): 27–30.

Holtschlag, M. 2000. The big history lesson. *Visitor Studies Today!* 3 (3): 15–17.

Leach, D. 2011. Children's recollections of a historical house visit: Recall of experiences and use of cognitive tools. *Visitor Studies* 14 (1): 34–47.

Lévesque, S. 2006. Integrating museum education and school history: Illustrations from the RCR Museum and the London Museum of Archeology. *International Journal of Historical Learning, Teaching, and Research* 6 (1). Accessed at centres.exeter.ac.uk/historyresource/journalstart.htm.

Lohman, J. 2007. Bringing history to life. *Education Journal* (105): 16.

Risinger, C. 2005. Take your students on virtual field trips: Exploring museums of the arts and humanities on the internet. *Social Education* 69 (4): 193–194.

Seixas, P. and P. Clark. 2011. Obsolete icons and the teaching of history. In *New possibilities for the past: Shaping history education in Canada*, ed. P. Clark, 282–301. Vancouver: University of British Columbia Press.

Stewart, A. 2008. Whose place, whose history? Outdoor environmental education pedagogy as "reading" the landscape. *Journal of Adventure Education and Outdoor Learning* 8 (2): 79–98.

Wunder, S. 2002. Learning to teach for historical understanding: Preservice teachers at a hands-on museum. *The Social Studies* 93 (4): 159–163.

17 Responding to Literature in Elementary Social Studies

Roberta McKay

The idea of incorporating fictional and non-fictional literature into a social studies program is not a new one. Young people enjoy stories and poems that relate to social studies and many teachers have long known that literature can be used to teach content directly. In this chapter, I address a different role for literature, arguing that literature has an essential place in social studies because of its aesthetic qualities—qualities that educate the heart and complement a subject area that cannot be mere facts, but includes human feelings and emotions.

I begin by considering what literature is and the importance of an aesthetic experience in social studies. I then discuss specifically how literature as an aesthetic experience contributes to the major knowledge, skill, and attitude dimensions of social studies. I discuss general considerations in choosing literature for aesthetic purposes in social studies and sources of annual lists of high-quality literature. As well, I identify characteristics and criteria for selecting particularly relevant categories of literature, including contemporary realistic fiction, historical fiction and biography, and folk tales. In the final section, I suggest an approach to encouraging students' aesthetic responses to literature. The chapter concludes with lists of references on dealing with various kinds of literature.

The Power of Literature

Charlotte Huck and Barbara Kiefer, noted experts in children's literature, define literature as "the imaginative shaping of life and thought into the forms and structures of language" (Huck and Kiefer 2004, 3). In literature for children, language works with pictures to evoke what Huck and Kiefer describe as an inner experience of art, an aesthetic experience, which enables the reader to perceive patterns, relationships, and feelings. The subject matter of literature is the human condition and the experience of literature is the coming together of text and reader. While literature for children and young people exhibits similar qualities to adult literature, it is important that literature for children appropriately reflects their emotions and experiences.

The power of literature rests in its ability to engage simultaneously with the feelings and thoughts of the reader or listener. Young people need to be introduced to literature as a source of wonder, delight, joy, and sorrow—as a window on the human condition. Literature engages us at an affective and aesthetic level, connecting us with our own experiences and the experiences of others. Literature helps us to shape and understand our human experience on affective and cognitive dimensions simultaneously. Literature connects us to the human community through time and space—it provides a doorway to other worlds. Imagination and curiosity are fuelled by literature. As young people enter other possible worlds, they encounter new perspectives on people, events, places, times, and ideas. The realms of possibility are widened and deepened on every dimension as children engage with literature. "Literature enables us to live many lives, good and bad, and to begin to see the universality of human experience" (Huck and Kiefer 2004, 9).

The Role of Literature in Social Studies

Textbooks are written primarily to transmit information. Although literature can enhance social studies knowledge and attitudes, its primary purpose is to engage us aesthetically. We must not violate this purpose by utilizing literature as a textbook to "teach" social studies (McKay 1995). Literature should be used in social studies for literature's sake—to provoke an aesthetic response, to stir a feeling of affinity with the human condition, to capture our hearts and imaginations as well as our minds, and to connect us to ourselves and others. These qualities of literature can make a lasting contribution to the social studies program. In light of their different purposes, literature requires different teaching and learning responses than those needed to teach from a textbook. While literature often includes considerable information about the world both past and present, it should not be used as a textbook, or, as Huck and Kiefer assert, "literature should never be distorted to fulfill the purposes of a lesson" (2004, 552).

Louise Rosenblatt (1991) distinguishes a reading continuum which streched from the "efferent" stance—reading for information—to the "aesthetic" stance—reading for the aesthetic experience. Rosenblatt asserts that all readings are a mix of efferent and aesthetic stances. For example, we may read the story *Sadako and the Thousand Paper Cranes* (Coerr 1977), which deals with the aftermath of war, and experience the poignancy in the death of Sadako while acquiring some information about World War II. Because readings have this mix of efferent and aesthetic stances, it is essential to be clear on the purpose for which we are having students read. Because children's literature is written predominantly from an aesthetic stance, young readers should first experience the piece, then recapture and reflect upon it, followed perhaps by further aesthetic responses (for example, talking, drawing, singing, writing, or engaging in dramatic forms such as tableaux, mime, reader's theatre, or role plays). Rosenblatt suggests that secondarily to the aesthetic responses, the text may be discussed for informational purposes, but, she states, "first, if it is indeed to be 'literature' for these students, it must be experienced" (1991, 447). For example, when studying Canadian history, a novel about prairie settlement is valuable primarily as a way of experiencing what it would have been like to live at that time. Factual information contained in the literature may be recalled at a later time as a starting place for further research or to enrich prior information.

There is one exception to my belief that the role of literature in social studies should first be to evoke aesthetic response. Non-fiction is a category of literature for children that is slightly different: while non-fiction books are not textbooks, they are also not fiction. These books characteristically have aesthetic value as a result of being finely written and illustrated and thereby evoke reader satisfaction and delight. But such non-fiction books also fulfill a specific teaching function in that their primary purpose is to provide information, usually on a single topic. These non-fiction books often provide depth and a richness of detail about a topic that is unlikely in a textbook. These books are written with a predominantly efferent stance and while they may also have some aesthetic value as noted above, they certainly may be utilized primarily for information gathering purposes. The pairing of non-fiction and fiction books in dealing with a social studies topic or theme is a powerful way to introduce children to the value of using a variety of sources.

Literature and Social Studies Objectives

Incorporating literature into the social studies as aesthetic experiences enriches the curriculum both directly and indirectly. Immersing young people in literature enhances the knowledge, skill, and attitude dimensions of social studies in the following ways.

- **Personalizes and contextualizes people, events, and situations.** Knowledge outcomes are enhanced as people, events, and situations are personalized and contextualized. Factual information and concepts are developed through the familiar format of story. Literature enables young people to relate facts, concepts, and generalizations to their own lives, thereby facilitating individual construction of meaning. Literature offers entry into many possible worlds and provides vicarious experience that enables young people to gain insight into people, places, events, situations, and times far removed from their immediate experience. Their world view is expanded. Literature often acts as a springboard for research as inquiries generated from a story motivate a quest for further information.
- **Develops language.** In addition to engaging children at a profoundly aesthetic level, literature simultaneously develops language on several crucial

dimensions. Oral language is enhanced by listening to stories and poetry and engaging in conversation about them. Literature provides experience with abstract language patterns and structures that are similar to those encountered in school. A sense of story is developed and there is exposure to a vast vocabulary. Reading fluency is increased by reading many and varied books, and the content, structure, vocabulary, and conventions in young people's writing reflects the amount and type of reading to which they are exposed. Reading as an enjoyable and thoughtful experience is promoted and young people become acquainted with additional authors and memorable characters, plots, and moods. They also get further exposure to language structures and vocabulary present in literature. Because of a definite link between language and thought, literature plays a role in developing thinking abilities.

- **Develops multiple skills.** Many skills outcomes of social studies can be realized through literature. Creative thinking and problem solving are stimulated in a variety of contexts. Reading is an individual meaning-making activity, providing opportunity to draw conclusions, speculate and imagine, and make self-initiated discoveries. Comparing, contrasting, analyzing, synthesizing, and evaluating are all required when listening to and reading stories and poetry. Communication and participation skills are meaningfully used as young people respond to literature individually and collectively through talking, writing, drawing, and dramatizing.

- **Nurtures empathy, sensitivity, and other social values.** It is perhaps in the area of the value and attitude outcomes that literature makes its most profound and powerful contribution to the social studies. Literature evokes feeling, stimulates emotion, and helps shape our human experience. Values and attitudes are personalized in literature and are treated as living forces that motivate human behaviour and are embedded in complex situations. Conflict, change, and ethical dilemmas are presented as part of what it means to be human. Through aesthetic engagement with literature, young people can come to understand their own lives more fully by seeing that they share areas of conflict in their lives with other human beings who, for better or for worse, have responded to these conflicts in their lives. Empathy and the ability to view life from different perspectives are promoted. Through literature, young people identify and analyze the values and attitudes of characters in literature and often relate these to their own experiences, past, present, or future. This can develop positive attitudes towards themselves and others in their immediate as well as the global environment.

- **Addresses delicate topics sensitively.** Literature can be a vehicle for considering many sensitive social issues. Authors currently writing for young people deal with a wide range of contemporary topics including sibling and peer relationships, divorce, death, adoption, sex roles, and discrimination. Reading or listening to stories and poetry that concern the feelings and responses of other young people in similar situations can be very beneficial to young people in the classroom who are facing these situations in real life. Literature can provide models of alternative behaviours that are removed from an individual and personal context. Folk tales and fairy tales also provide a rich array of value-laden dilemmas and conflicts to stimulate reflection and discussion.

- **Builds community.** Literature can also contribute to a sense of classroom community and other citizenship goals by focussing on the qualities required for living with others (Orr 1995). Literature often celebrates uniqueness, considers friendship and acceptance, and deals with concepts related to sharing and caring for others. These aspects of human relationships can be catalysts for young people to reflect individually and collectively on their own classroom community. For instance, literature that reflects themes of caring for and about others may encourage young people to examine their own behaviour towards one another in the classroom. Providing opportunities for listening to, reflecting upon, and responding to literature may help young people develop a sense of what a classroom community could be.

- **Celebrates diversity.** Literature can form the heart of multicultural education by celebrating and building upon the diversity in young people's backgrounds and experiences. Rosenblatt has argued that aesthetic responses evoked by literature, such as heightened sensitivity to the needs and problems of others and greater imaginative capacity, are "part of the indispensable equipment of the citizen in a democracy" (cited in Pradl 1991). It is currently popular to promote multicultural education through literature, and many professional resources are available (Ramirez and Ramirez 1994; Zarrillo 1994; Bieger 1996; Finazzo 1997; Harris 1997; and Cai 2002).

TABLE 17.1   INCORPORATING LITERATURE INTO MULTICULTURAL EDUCATION

BANKS' LEVEL OF INTEGRATION OF ETHNIC/CULTURAL CONTENT IN THE CURRICULUM	USE OF LITERATURE	NATURE OF COMMITMENT TO DIVERSITY AND SOCIAL JUSTICE
Contributions Cultural concepts and content are "separate" from the curriculum and are introduced as a result of special ethnic/cultural holidays, heroes, customs, or contributions.	• In February, reading literature about Chinese New Year.	• Eurocentric perspective is used as the basis for selection of elements to be studied. • May reinforce stereotypes and mistaken beliefs. • A focus on visible aspects of a culture may lead to superficial understanding. • Diverse views of events and issues are presented.
Additive Cultural concepts and content from a Eurocentric perspective are "added" to social studies curriculum.	• During a Canadian history unit, reading about European immigration.	
Transformative Cultural concepts and content "alter" the structure of the curriculum as perspectives of various ethnic/cultural groups are included.	• During a Canadian history unit, reading literature (including historical fiction and biography) about immigration that incorporates perspectives of diverse cultural groups (for example, Native, Ukrainian, Chinese, German).	• Diverse cultures are recognized and presented in the curriculum.
Decision-making and social action Cultural concepts and content "alter" the structure of curriculum by including diverse perspectives and related social issues.	• During a Canadian history unit, reading literature about immigration that identifies and deals with social issues (for example, discrimination). • Social issues are discussed in relation to students' own school or community, leading to social actions.	• Diverse views and social issues are recognized and explored through solving problems, decision-making, and social action.

The four-level model proposed by James Banks (1989) is helpful when integrating ethnic and cultural content into the curriculum because it reduces the likelihood of superficial treatment of multicultural concepts. Banks' model for integrating ethnic and cultural content into the curriculum is hierarchical, based on the degree to which multicultural issues are central to the curriculum, the extent to which changes occur in the traditional curriculum, and the extent of teacher and student commitment to diversity and social justice. His model provides a theoretical framework for incorporating literature into multicultural education. Making use of literature at the transformative and decision-making/social action levels can assist young people to understand and value cultures and experiences different from their own.

Choosing Literature

Choosing literature for social studies is both challenging and rewarding. Our opportunities to find high-quality material for young people are better now than ever before, but our need to select wisely is also heightened. I offer three general considerations when choosing

literature for our students: literary value, curriculum fit, and student suitability. I introduce other criteria, particular to various literary genres, when I discuss specific categories of literature.

LITERARY VALUE

Because of my emphasis on literature as an aesthetic experience, the first criterion for choosing literature in social studies is literary or aesthetic qualities. These qualities in fiction are traditionally judged by the elements of plot, setting, theme, characterization, style, point of view, and format. According to Huck and Kiefer, high-quality fiction for children includes "a well-constructed and well-paced plot, a significant theme, an authentic setting, a credible point of view, convincing characterization, appropriate style and an attractive format" (2004, 24). They provide an excellent expanded explanation of these elements, useful guidelines for evaluating literature for children (14), and specific guidelines for evaluating the literary merit of poetry (368). Young people evaluate literature by their responses to it and as teachers we need to value their interpretations and judgments while also acquainting them with the qualities in a story or a poem that make it acclaimed for its literary and aesthetic merit. Professional organizations in the United States such as the International Reading Association (IRA) and the National Council for the Social Studies (NCSS) publish annual annotated bibliographies of exemplary children's books. In addition to these annual listings, the journals *Social Education*, *Social Studies and the Young Learner*, *Language Arts*, and *The Reading Teacher* often publish excellent practical articles for teachers on ways to incorporate literature into social studies. (See the resource list at the end of this chapter.[1])

CURRICULUM FIT

A second criterion to consider when choosing literature for social studies is "curriculum fit"—the suitability of a work to the specific content and issues in the social studies curriculum. Selecting appropriate books is a serious responsibility because the best books can enhance social studies understandings while poor selections may reinforce misconceptions and stereotypes. Sullivan (1996) offers four criteria to guide literature selection to enhance global understanding:

- shows our common humanity;
- provides sound geographic, social, historical, political, economic, and/or religious information;
- shows that other people have different but valid approaches to our common human concerns and needs; and
- increases understanding, empathy, and the ability to learn from other peoples and cultures.

As previously discussed, stories and poetry may present only one perspective on an event, issue, or topic and several selections may be chosen to represent varying points of view.

STUDENT SUITABILITY

While suitability to the age and reading level of the students is a third consideration, student interest is often the more important criterion. Many stories and poems that young people express interest in, enjoy, and understand may be too difficult for individual reading, but can be read out loud by the teacher. Quality picture books that may appear to be suitable for a younger audience can stimulate discussion and writing, and art and drama projects with older students.

Locate one or two pieces of children's literature that have been used or recommended for students in a grade level of your choice. Assess how well this resource(s) meets each of the three criteria mentioned by the author. Would you "Highly recommend," "Recommend," or "Not recommend" this book(s)? Explain the reasons for your rating.

Categories of Literature

Four categories of literature for children are particularly powerful in promoting the aesthetic dimension in social studies. These are contemporary realistic fiction, historical fiction and biography, folk literature, and poetry. The nature and criteria for selecting suitable titles of each for use in the classroom are explored separately.

CONTEMPORARY REALISTIC FICTION

Contemporary realistic fiction can make a powerful contribution to a social studies program because of the nature of the story and the topics explored. Contemporary realistic fiction is imaginative writing that accurately reflects life as it could be lived today, including its opportunities, challenges, and values (Huck and Kiefer 2004). Through contemporary realistic fiction, young people may experience the social issues of our times in relation to growing up, coping with the problems of the human condition, and living in a diverse world. Through such literature, young people experience models, both good and bad, that may assist them in making sense of their own life experiences and, ultimately, of the human condition. Contemporary realistic fiction has changed dramatically in recent decades in its depiction of life. Studies of young people's preferences consistently show it to be the most popular category of story (Huck and Kiefer 2004). This category of book is often controversial and is closely scrutinized for bias and stereotyping because its realistic content addresses issues such as family and peer relationships and changes, developing sexuality, physical and mental disabilities, aging and death, and ethnic and racial diversity.

Multicultural literature is one type of contemporary realistic fiction and deserves particular attention in social studies. There continues to be debate surrounding the definition of the term multicultural literature (Cai and Bishop 1994). Bainbridge and Pantaleo (1999, 114) suggest that "literature can be considered multicultural today when it contains a central character, plot, theme, setting, or style that is culturally or socially diverse in nature." Contemporary multicultural literature provides young people with opportunities to enhance their self-concepts and to understand and develop pride in their own cultural heritage. It also provides opportunities for students to experience cultures other than their own in ways that foster respect, appreciation, and sensitivity.

Multicultural literature should meet the previously discussed general criteria for literary and aesthetic value, as well as specific criteria for both text and illustrations. Cultural accuracy is a major criterion in selection. Since no single book can portray the full range of experience in a culture, it is important to provide a collection that portrays members of a culture in a wide spectrum of occupations, educational backgrounds, living conditions, and lifestyles. Young people need to understand that within any culture there is diversity. Illustrations should reveal differences in individual appearances while portraying distinctive characteristics of a group or race. Stereotyping of appearance, artifacts, and occupations in the text and illustrations should be avoided. Huck and Kiefer (2004, 23) offer a set of guidelines for evaluating multicultural literature and suggest that the term "literature of diversity" might provide an alternative to the term multicultural literature that would help us broaden our understanding of the term culture. Authors of contemporary realistic fiction are increasingly sensitive to such stereotyping and the number of books that positively and fairly depict our diverse population is increasing. Historical realistic fiction and traditional literature such as folk tales present cultures and ethnic groups from views and values of times past and are considered biased and stereotypical when evaluated by criteria for selection of contemporary multicultural fiction. However, these forms should not be eliminated from classrooms when they may actually be historically authentic or true to a traditional genre. Issues related to historical fiction and folk tales are discussed separately in this chapter.

HISTORICAL FICTION AND BIOGRAPHY

Historical fiction and biography are categories of literature for children that are in particular demand in social studies. Although neither of these are as popular with young readers as contemporary realistic fiction is, there are many outstanding books available that not only enhance social studies but also expand young people's experiences with a category of literature that they may not choose on their own. Historical fiction and biography draw upon both fact and imagination. Historical fiction encompasses "all realistic stories that are set in the past" (Huck and Kiefer 2004, 484) and depends on the author's ability to present the facts of the past accurately while also being able to speculate imaginatively on what it was like to live during that time. Biography is a life story that reads like fiction but centres on facts and events that can be documented. Huck and Kiefer suggest that the best biographies "combine accurate information and fine writing in a context that children enjoy—the story that really happened" (588). Both historical fiction and biography embed the facts that young people encounter in social studies textbooks within the context of human emotions. As discussed previously, this elicits an aesthetic response that enables the content to be experienced on a more personal dimension.

Historical fiction helps young people develop a sense of what history is and a feeling of continuity as they realize through story that their lives and times are linked individually and collectively to past lives and times. This linking of past to present helps young people see themselves as part of a continuum of human experience and to understand that the current way of life is a result of the past, and will have an impact on our way of life in the future. Historical fiction offers vicarious experience of past conflicts, accomplishments, tragedies, and high points along the journey of what it means to be human. Comparisons with the present are inevitably created, and conflicting points of view on issues are presented. Through the aesthetic experience of historical fiction, young people learn that while change is inevitable there are certain aspects of being human that remain constant through time. Our interconnectedness as a human community is reinforced.

In selecting historical fiction, the first consideration, as discussed previously, is aesthetic quality—that it engages us in story. There are several other considerations and issues in the selection and use of historical fiction. While the factual details should be accurate and authentic, they should be background to the story, blended with the fiction. At the same time, contradictions and distortions of the actual record of history must be avoided. In addition to accurate and authentic portrayal of the facts, the story must also reflect the values and spirit of the times as accurately as possible. Huck and Kiefer (2004, 485) state, "historical fiction can't be made to conform to today's more enlightened point of view concerning women or minorities or knowledge of medicine." Teachers have a rich opportunity to help students examine the values and attitudes of today in light of those reflected in historical fiction. The language of the times also reflects values and attitudes. While authenticity of language is important in historical fiction, some vocabulary used in previous times is offensive by today's standards. Derogatory and demeaning labels for particular people and cultural groups are examples of language that may have been used in the past but is unacceptable today. The use of these labels in historical fiction is helpful in understanding characters and events of the past provided they accurately and authentically reflect the values and attitudes of the times. Young people should be taught to respond to these labels in the context of the past and make links to the present, while appreciating the hurt and damage that derogatory and demeaning labels inflict. In this way, another essential feature of good historical fiction is realized—insight into the problems of today, as well as those of the past, is stimulated.

A final consideration when including historical fiction in social studies relates to recognizing that there are many and varied points of view on the issues and events of the past as well as the present. The use of different pieces of historical fiction on a particular topic or event can assist young people in recognizing that there is never only one point of view on any historical event. Events such as the Riel Rebellion need to be understood from the perspectives of the Métis and other Native peoples, as well as from the perspectives of the Canadian government and European settlers. The perspectives of women have often been ignored in Canadian history, as well as the perspectives of Native peoples, Asian Canadians, and other cultural groups. As discussed previously in this chapter in relation to Banks' hierarchical model, in order for literature to make a meaningful contribution to social studies, it must be incorporated at the transformative and social action levels. In terms of historical fiction, this may require using multiple pieces of literature on any historical event in order to present the event from the points of view of the various peoples and cultures involved.

FOLK LITERATURE

Folk literature, also termed traditional literature, is another category of literature that can have a profound impact on social studies because it is "literature derived from the human imagination to explain the human condition" (Huck and Kiefer 2004, 237). Folk tales, fables, myths, epics, and legends are included in this category of literature, which many consider the foundation of the understandings about the human condition

that are reflected in modern literature. Folk literature derives from oral tradition as human beings sought to explain themselves and their world—in short, it is oral history. Bruno Bettelheim (1976), noted child psychologist, suggests in his book *The Uses of Enchantment: The Meaning and Importance of Fairy Tales* that there is more to be learned from this literature about our inner problems and possible solutions to our predicaments than from any other type of story that a child can comprehend. Folk literature can provide insights into inherent cultural values and beliefs, as well as into human motivations and inner feelings. It can have a profound impact in social studies because it engages young people with universal patterns of experience.

Folk literature is popular with young people because the engaging stories demand full use of the imagination. They tend to be short, fast-moving, concrete, and deal with the imponderables of life such as truth, beauty, good, evil, and justice. They often include inspirational concepts such as courage, nobility of character, accomplishment, tenderness, and optimism. Folk literature is a compelling resource because it deals with universal issues and problems of daily life that have embedded within them ethical and moral dimensions.

Every culture has folk literature that can provide insights into the beliefs, values, jokes, lifestyles, and histories of that culture. In this way, folk literature can help young people understand other cultures. Because similar types of stories can be traced from country to country and continent to continent, a cross-cultural study of folk literature can help young people see universal patterns that show the similarities in our experiences of being human. Cinderella-type stories are a good example of folk literature that appears in many versions across many cultures. Huck and Kiefer (2004) list a number of cross-cultural folk tale versions as well as cross-cultural motifs, for example, the motif of magical powers that appears in folk literature from many cultures.

Folk literature has been criticized for being violent, sexist, and even ageist (sorcerers and witches are often portrayed as old men and women). But, as previously suggested, experts in the area of literature for young people maintain that folk literature should not be eliminated for being true to its genre. As with historical fiction that is authentic for the historical period, folk literature must be introduced as stories that present cultures, views, and values from times long past.

POETRY

Poetry is a category of literature that can enrich the social studies program because the use of language is particularly vivid, intense, and aesthetically evocative. Contemporary poetry for young people often reflects experiences of hurt, fear, and sadness, as well as experiences of happiness, satisfaction, and expectation. In social studies, poetry can be introduced in conjunction with prose. Huck and Kiefer (2004, 394–396) provide one listing of thematically arranged poetry/prose connections that include themes such as family, death/loss, sibling rivalry, relationships, courage, and holocaust/war. Poetry in social studies must be presented as an aesthetic experience. Poetry that is too difficult, sentimental, or abstract is to be avoided, as are required memorization and detailed analysis (391). Social studies teachers can deepen learning and foster delight in poetry by selecting contemporary poems that reflect familiar experiences and humour and that employ poetic forms such as narrative verse, limericks, and rhymes.

Responding to Literature from an Aesthetic Stance

Throughout this chapter, I have stressed that literature should be incorporated into a social studies program to evoke an aesthetic response—to stir a feeling of affinity with the human condition, to capture our hearts and imaginations as well as our minds, and to connect us to ourselves and others. In this section, I outline an approach to responding aesthetically to literature. In language arts, engaging young people with literature in this way is called a reader-response perspective. In reader-response, the major focus is on reading the literature for its own sake. This stance encourages engagement, personal involvement, and connection with the literature, and the use of personal response to build further interpretive response (Tompkins and McGee 1993). Although not widely held by social studies educators, this stance towards literature has received increased recognition and attention within social studies (Lamme 1994, Kornfeld 1994, Koeller 1996, Mathis 2001).

We can support students' aesthetic response to literature in social studies by creating three kinds of opportunities:

- experiencing the literature aesthetically;
- responding personally; and
- revisiting the piece in ways that enable personal response to be connected to broader concepts, issues, and values.

EXPERIENCING THE LITERATURE AESTHETICALLY

Whether young people personally read the stories, poems, and novels, or listen to them, literature related to social studies topics and issues should first be encountered whole, not in parts or in fragments reproduced in textbooks. That is, literature should be engaged in aesthetically—its flow and complexity should not be interrupted by predetermined questions, probes, and activities. In this way, young people can experience and respond to literature for the sheer joy and pleasure it evokes.

SAMPLE AESTHETIC RESPONSE (K–3)
THE NEW LAND: A FIRST YEAR ON THE PRAIRIE

This beautiful Canadian piece of historical fiction, written by Marilynn Reynolds and illustrated by Stephen McCallum (1997), details a family's journey by boat, train, and wagon to their new home on the prairies and describes their first year there. The story begins in the springtime as the family leaves the old country. It takes us along with them through their long voyage, and we accompany them as they locate their homestead's iron stake, find water, build a house, and survive their first winter. As spring comes to the prairies, the family plants apple trees "that would bloom every spring, just like the trees they had left behind."

Purpose
- To experience what it might have been like for one family who moved to the western prairies from the old country.

Experiencing the story
- Prior to reading the book, read the title to students and show them the cover of the book (an illustration of the family on their ox-drawn wagon). Ask them what they think this story might be about and how the title and picture makes them think this.
- Ask if any of them has ever moved to another country or province and how they felt. Alternatively, you could ask students to speculate on how they might feel if they did move. Encourage students to listen to the story and imagine what it would have been like for the children in the story.
- Read the book through once without interrupting the flow of the text, even to show the pictures. Read the book a second time and show students the stunning pictures that complement the text on each page, giving them ample time to enjoy and comment on the details.

Responding personally
- Personal response to the book will have begun in the form of questions and comments students have as they listen to the story and look at the illustrations. Questions that facilitate personal response may include:
  - Did the story remind you of anything that has happened to you or that has happened in another story that you know?
  - What was the most significant or important part of the story for you and why?
- What feelings did you have as you listened to the story? Why?
- Alternatively, students could be asked to write in their journals in response to one of these questions or more generally on what they liked about or learned from the story.

Revisiting the story
- Invite students to recreate the sequence of the story in a series of tableaux representing:
  - the voyage by sea
  - the ox-cart journey across the prairie
  - finding the iron stake on their homestead
  - finding water
  - building a house
  - surviving the winter
  - the arrival of spring

  Divide students into seven groups and assign each group the task of creating a "frozen picture" or tableau of one of the scenes. Students may use facial expressions, placement of body, gestures, and stances to convey the scene. Give students enough time to discuss the aspect of the story their tableau will represent and how they will achieve this, and to prepare their expression, placement, and stance. When they are ready each group "freezes" in their picture (that is, no talking, no movement) and the rest of the groups observe. The teacher may ask the observing students to comment on what the scene shows and how this is conveyed.
- Have students choose from the following revisiting possibilities:
  - Write an "I" poem from the viewpoint of the father, mother, the boy (John), or the little girl (Annie). For example:

    I am Annie, a little girl.
    I am scared to leave my friends.
    I am only six years old.
    I was sick for fourteen days on the boat.
    I loved the train ride to the prairie.
  - Draw a picture that interprets the story or some aspect of it.
  - Create a collage of words and/or pictures that represents the experiences of the pioneer family in the story.
  - Construct a "soddie" like the first home of the family.
  - Read another book, informational story, or poem about pioneer family life.

SAMPLE AESTHETIC RESPONSE (GRADES 4–8)
GHOST TRAIN

This award-winning Canadian piece of historical fiction, written by Paul Yee and illustrated by Harvey Chan, won the Governor General's Literary Award in 1996 and the Amelia Frances Howard-Gibbon Illustrator's Award in 1997. Through the story of the love between a daughter and her father, readers get a glimpse of the building of the Canadian railway from the perspective of the Chinese labourers, many of whom lost their lives during the construction of the railway through the mountains of British Columbia. The author and illustrator, both Chinese Canadians, provide an insider perspective on Chinese-Canadian history and culture. In the story, Choon-yi comes to Canada to join her father, who has been working on building the railroad. When she arrives, she learns that her father has been killed in a railway accident. Choon-yi, a gifted artist, attempts to paint a train as a memorial to her father. The night before she is to return to China, her father appears before her in a dream and Choon-yi then begins a fantastical journey through which she glimpses the hardships of the Chinese railroad workers. The faces of the many dead workers become part of Choon-yi's painting, which her father instructs her to take home to China and burn so that the souls of the men may "sail on the four winds" and find their way home. This is a complex story and the teacher will need to preview the book and be alert for issues that might be sensitive in his or her particular classroom.

Purpose
- To experience what the building of the Canadian railway might have been like from the perspective of one Chinese labourer and his daughter.

Experiencing the story
- Prior to reading the book, read the title to students and show them the front and back covers of the book (on the front, an illustration of a Chinese girl on a railroad track holding a stick of burning incense and on the back, an illustration of a train engine and two figures, the same girl and a man). Ask them what they think this story might be about and what in the title and pictures make them think this.
- Ask if any students have a parent who has ever gone to a different city, province, or country to work while the rest of the family stayed home. Some students may wish to share how they felt and what this experience was like for them and their family. Ask the students to listen to the story of Choon-yi, the young girl in the story, and her father who decided to leave his home in China and come to Canada to work on the building of the railway and imagine how this decision changed their lives.
- Read the book through once without interrupting the flow of the text. Read the book a second time and give the students ample time to look at, savour, and comment upon the stunning illustrations that complement the text.

Responding personally
- Personal response to the book will have begun in the form of questions and comments students have as they listen to the story and look at the illustrations. Questions that facilitate personal response may include:
  - Did the story remind you of anything that has happened to you or that has happened in another story that you know?
  - What was the most significant or important part of the story for you and why?
  - What feelings did you have as you listened to the story? Why?
- Alternatively, students could be asked to write in their journals in response to one of these questions or more generally on what they liked or learned from the story. Students who wish to could be given the opportunity to share some of what they wrote with class members or a smaller group.

Revisiting the story
Following are a number of revisiting possibilities from which to choose. Tableaux and readers' theatre are powerful whole-class strategies that are very motivating to many students in this age group.
- Have students recreate the sequence of the story in a series of tableaux such as the following, or others that they may choose:
  - the father's decision to leave China for work in Canada building the railroad
  - Choon-yi arriving in Canada and learning of her father's death
  - Choon-yi painting the train
  - the ghost train journey
  - the painting arriving home in China

Divide the students into the same number of groups as there are scenes. Each group must create a "frozen picture" or tableau of one of the scenes. Students may use facial expressions, placement of body, gestures, and stances to convey the scenes. Give the students enough time to discuss the aspect of the story their tableau will represent and how they will achieve this, and to prepare their expressions, placements, and stances. When they are ready each group "freezes" in their picture (that is, no talking, no movement) and the rest of the groups observe. The teacher may ask the observing students to comment on what the scene shows and how this is conveyed. A "thoughts in the head" strategy may also be used. While students are in their tableau, the teacher touches a character in the scene on the shoulder.

At this time, the student, in the role of the character, says the thoughts that are going through his or her mind. The student may remain silent if he or she does not wish to speak. For example, in the scene where Choon-yi's father leaves China, one of the characters might be Choon-yi. During the "thoughts in the head" strategy, the student who is Choon-yi might say, "Oh, how I will miss my father. I am scared that he is going so far away. What will happen to him? What will happen to our family?"

- Assist the students to prepare a readers' theatre script from part or all of the story. In the readers' theatre format, the emphasis is on oral reading of the script, not memorization of it. The script is based on the story and can be a combination of wording from the actual story as well as rewritten portions of the original text. In a readers' theatre script for *Ghost Train*, there would be two main characters who speak (Choon-yi and her father) and a narrator. More dialogue could be scripted, for example, for the mother and railroad official, as well as dialogue created for some of the Chinese railroad workers on the ghost train. In the readers' theatre, students practise and then read their parts. Voice, gesture, and facial expressions are used to communicate the story as it is read.

- Suggest that students draw scenes, characters, or interpretations from the story. The style of the illustrator could be examined for technique.

- Have students retell the story or a portion of the story by writing a personal journal, with various entries, from the point of view of Choon-yi or her father.

- Suggest that students find a "factual" account of the building of the Canadian railway. For example, they could consult the *Canadian Encyclopedia* (www.thecanadianencyclopedia.com) and compare information on the Chinese workers in a factual account with that presented in *Ghost Train*. Students may also wish to examine the photograph of the Last Spike, which celebrated the completion of the railway, and discuss who is in the photograph and who is absent.

- Suggest that students read another piece of historical fiction, an informational book, or a poem about the building of the Canadian railway.

RESPONDING PERSONALLY

Responding to literature aesthetically means acknowledging and valuing the personal connections, meanings, and questions young people construct as they read and listen to stories and poems. Students will respond differently to the same piece of literature depending on age, life experience, and literary and reading experience. Answering other people's questions, taking someone else's perspective, and aiming for someone else's purposes do not facilitate aesthetic response. Our role as teachers is to enable young people to express their responses and then to revisit the literature with a range of activities that deepen and enrich personal meanings by connecting them to understandings about other people and the world. Tompkins and McGee (1993, 137) suggest that aesthetic reading is stimulated by questions that focus on personal meaning:

- What did the story or poem remind you of?
- What images came to mind as you read?
- What were your feelings as you read?
- What do you think?

Questions such as these provide opportunities to express personal responses in conversations and in expressive writing such as journal writing. Although sharing personal responses should never be forced, individual meaning is enriched by hearing the range and diversity of responses evoked by a piece of literature. Where young people feel that their personal responses are valued by the teacher and classmates, most of them, over time, will want to share personal meanings and connections.

REVISITING THE PIECE

After young people express their personal responses to literature, it is important to "revisit" the piece. Revisiting experiences are defined by their relevance to students' interests and questions. This means allowing for student choices in how to engage with the piece. Revisiting experiences are characterized by active learning and open-endedness and by their ability to reflect the "inner experience of art" evoked by the piece. While the possibilities for this type of experience are almost endless, they include art and media, writing and reading, collecting and constructing, drama and talk, and singing and movement.[2]

The featured texts "Sample Aesthetic Response (K–3)" and "Sample Aesthetic Response (Grades 4–8)" illustrate the three phases of an aesthetic response for primary and intermediate level literature.

Conclusion

Social studies is about the human condition in all its complexity, and literature enables young people to access that complexity. Literature should not be used as a social studies textbook. "In social studies classes, literature is a work of art enabling the study of character issues and relationships between persons sharing contexts or ideas" (Koeller 1996, 102). The role of literature in social studies is to evoke the aesthetic response—to illuminate, inspire, inform perspective, and educate the heart as well as the mind. Promoting the aesthetic experience through the use of literature in social studies is necessary for the full development of humane and responsible citizens.

The aesthetic value of children's literature depends in part on its ability to bring students inside the lives of others and to reflect on this experience. Select a piece of children's literature that you already know and describe a few activities that you might plan for students that would help them powerfully engage in this experience.

ENDNOTES

1   Although these listings and articles originate in the United States, many of the titles and ideas are applicable to Canadian social studies. Teacher librarians, public librarians, and school district and professional associations can provide local and provincial listings of available literature for use in social studies. The Canadian Children's Book Centre publishes an annual listing of the best Canadian books published for children, and the Toronto Public Library's list "One Hundred Best Canadian Books for Children" is available online. Bainbridge and Pantaleo (1999), in their text on using literature in the Canadian elementary classroom, highlight Canadian authors, illustrators, and award-winning Canadian books, many of which have a place in the social studies program.

2   Huck and Kiefer (2004), Hoyt (1992), and Tompkins and McGee (1993) provide outstanding descriptions of a wide range of specific revisiting experiences to engage young people. Lamme (1994), Kornfeld (1994), and Koeller (1996) provide examples of personal response and revisiting experiences related to various social studies topics.

REFERENCES

Bainbridge, J. and S. Pantaleo. 1999. *Learning with literature in the Canadian elementary classroom.* Edmonton, AB: University of Alberta Press and Duval House Publishing.

Banks, J.A. 1989. Integrating the curriculum with ethnic content: Approaches and guidelines. In *Multicultural education: Issues and perspectives,* ed. J.A. Banks and C.A.M. Banks, 189–207. Boston: Allyn and Bacon.

Bettelheim, B. 1976. *The uses of enchantment: The meaning and importance of fairy tales.* New York: Knopf.

Bieger, E.M. 1996. Promoting multicultural education through a literature-based approach. *Reading Teacher* 49 (4): 308–311.

Cai, M. 2002. *Multicultural literature for children and young adults: Reflections on critical issues.* Westport, CT: Greenwood Press.

Cai, M. and R. Bishop. 1994. Multicultural literature for children: Towards a clarification of the concept. In *The need for story: Cultural diversity in classroom and community,* ed. A. Haas Dyson and C. Genishi, 57–71. Urbana, IL: National Council of Teachers of English.

Canadian Children's Book Centre. 2012. *Best Books for Kids & Teens.* Accessed at www.bookcentre.ca/publications.

Coerr, E. 1977. *Sadako and the Thousand Paper Cranes.* New York: G.P. Putnam's Sons.

Finazzo, D. 1997. *All for the children: Multicultural essentials of literature.* Albany, NY: Delmar Publishing (ITP).

Harris, V., ed. 1997. *Using multiethnic literature in the K–8 classroom.* Norwood, MA: Christopher Gordon Publishers.

Hoyt, L. 1992. Many ways of knowing: Using drama, oral interactions, and the visual arts to enhance reading comprehension. *Reading Teacher* 45 (8): 580–584.

Huck, C. and B. Kiefer, with S. Hepler and J. Hickman. 2004. *Children's literature in the elementary school,* 8th ed. New York: McGraw-Hill.

Koeller, S. 1996. Multicultural understanding through literature. *Social Education* 60 (2): 99–103.

Kornfeld, J. 1994. Using fiction to teach history: Multicultural and global perspectives of World War ll. *Social Education* 58 (5): 281–286.

Lamme, L.L. 1994. Stories from our past: Making history come alive for children. *Social Education* 58 (3): 159–164.

Mathis, J. 2001. Respond to stories with stories: Teachers discuss multicultural literature. *Social Studies* 92 (4): 155–160.

McKay, R. 1995. Using literature in social studies: A caution. *Canadian Social Studies* 29 (3): 95–96.

National Council for the Social Studies (NCSS). 2012. *Notable Social Studies Trade Books for Young People.* Accessed at www.socialstudies.org/notable.

Orr, J. 1995. Classroom as community. Unpublished doctoral dissertation, University of Alberta, Edmonton.

Pradl, G.M. 1991. Reading literature in a democracy: The challenge of Louise Rosenblatt. In *The experience of reading: Louise Rosenblatt and reader-response theory,* ed. J. Clifford, 23–46. Portsmouth, NH: Boynton/Cook.

Ramirez, G. and J.L. Ramirez. 1994. *Multiethnic children's literature*. Albany, NY: Delmar.

Reynolds, M. and S. McCallum, illus. 1997. *The new land: A first year on the prairie*. Victoria, BC: Orca.

Rosenblatt, L. 1991. Literature—S.O.S.! *Language Arts* 68 (6): 444–448.

Sullivan, J. 1996. Real people, common themes: Using trade books to counter stereotypes. *Social Education* 60 (7): 399–401.

Tompkins, G. and L. McGee. 1993. *Teaching reading with literature*. New York: Macmillan.

Yee, P. and H. Chan, illus. 1996. *Ghost train*. Toronto, ON: Groundwood Books.

Zarrillo, J. 1994. *Multicultural literature, multicultural teaching*. Orlando, FL: Harcourt Brace Jovanovich.

SUPPLEMENTAL READINGS

LITERATURE IN SOCIAL STUDIES (GENERAL)

Alter, G., ed. 1995. Varieties of literature and elementary social studies. Special issue, *Social Studies and the Young Learner* 8 (2).

Billig, E. 1977. Children's literature as a springboard to content areas. *Reading Teacher* 30 (8): 855–859.

Combs, M. and J.D. Beach. 1994. Stories and storytelling: Personalizing the social studies. *Reading Teacher* 47 (6): 464–471.

Cromer, M. and P. Clark. 2007. Getting graphic with the past: Graphic novels and the teaching of history. *Theory and Research in Social Education* 35 (4): 574–591.

Cullinan, B.E., M.C. Scala, and V.A. Schroder. 1995. *Three voices: An invitation to poetry across the curriculum*. York, ME: Stenhouse.

den Heyer, K. and A. Fidyk. 2007. Configuring historical facts through historical fiction: Agency, art-in-fact, and imagination as stepping stones between then and now. *Educational Theory* 57 (2): 141–157.

Edwards, G. and J. Saltman. 2010. *Picturing Canada: A history of Canadian children's illustrated books and publishing*. Toronto: University of Toronto Press.

Eeds, M. and D. Wells. 1991. Talking, thinking, and cooperative learning: Lessons learned from listening to children talk about books. *Social Education* 55 (2): 134–137.

Farris, P.J. and D.J. Fuhler. 1994. Developing social studies concepts through picture books. *Reading Teacher* 47 (5): 380–386.

Fredericks, A.D. 1991. *Social studies through children's literature: An integrated approach*. Englewood, CO: Teacher Ideas Press.

———. 2000. *More social studies through children's literature: An integrated approach*. Englewood, CO: Libraries Unlimited.

Friedman, A.A. and C.A. Cataldo. 2002. Characters at crossroads: Reflective decision makers in contemporary Newbery books. *Reading Teacher* 56 (2): 102–112.

Gramlich, K. and J. Bainbridge. 2001. Listening to children learning: Discovering Canada through picture storybooks. *Teacher-Librarian Today* 7 (2): 32–38.

Hartman, K.J. and C. Giorgis. 2001. Exploring maps through children's literature. *Social Studies and the Young Learner* 13 (3): 14–16.

Hennings, D.G. 1982. Reading picture storybooks in the social studies. *Reading Teacher* 36 (3): 284–289.

Hoodless, P. 2004. Spotting the adult agendas: Investigating children's historical awareness using stories written for children in the past. *International Journal of Historical Learning, Teaching, and Research* 4 (2). Accessed at www.centres.exeter.ac.uk/historyresource/journalstart.htm.

Krey, D.M. 1998. *Children's literature in social studies: Teaching to the standards*. Washington, DC: National Council for the Social Studies.

Kurkjian, C., N. Livingston, and Y. Siu-Runyan. 2003/4. Building text sets from the Notable Books for a Global Society Lists. *Reading Teacher* 57 (4): 390–398.

Long, T.W. and M.K. Gove. 2003/4. How engagement strategies and literature circles promote critical response in a fourth-grade, urban classroom. *Reading Teacher* 57 (4): 350–361.

Macken, C.T. 2003. What in the world do second graders know about geography? Using picture books to teach geography. *The Social Studies* 94 (2): 63–68.

McGowan, M.J. and J.H. Powell. 1996. An annotated bibliography of resources for literature-based instruction. *Social Education* 60 (4): 231–232.

McGowan, T., guest ed. 1996. Telling the story of citizenship. Theme issue. *Social Education* 60 (4).

National Council for the Social Studies. 1998. Children's literature and social studies. Theme issue. *Social Education* 62 (4).

Needham, R.L. and C. Sage. 1991. Intermediate children and notable social studies picture books. *Social Studies and the Young Learner* 4 (2): 11–12.

Pantaleo, S. 2000. Canadian picture books in social studies instruction. *Canadian Social Studies*, 34 (3): 48–52.

Rosen, H. 1986. The importance of story. *Language Arts* 63 (3): 226–237.

Roser, N.L. and S. Keehn. 2002. Fostering thought, talk, and inquiry: Linking literature and social studies. *Reading Teacher* 55 (5): 416–426.

Sandmann, A.L. and J.F. Ahern. 2002. *Linking literature with life: The NCSS standards and children's literature for the middle grades.* Silver Spring, MD: National Council for the Social Studies.

Waters, S.D. 1999. Children's literature: A valuable resource for the social studies classroom. *Canadian Social Studies* 33 (3): 80–83.

Woll, C.B. 1991. Support resources for whole language lovers. *Social Studies and the Young Learner* 4 (2): 26–27.

Zarnowski, M. and A.F. Gallagher, eds. 1993. *Children's literature and social studies: Selecting and using notable books in the classroom.* Washington, DC: National Council for the Social Studies.

CONTEMPORARY REALISTIC FICTION (GENERAL)

Banaszak, R.A. and M.K. Banaszak. 1997. Trade books for reducing violence. *Social Education* 61 (5): 270–271.

Barnes, B.R. 1991. Using children's literature in the early anthropology curriculum. *Social Education* 55 (1): 17–18.

Gallagher, A.F. 1991. Peace (and war) in children's literature. *Social Studies and the Young Learner* 4 (2): 22–23.

Hoffbauer, D. and M. Prenn. 1996. A place to call one's own: Choosing books about homelessness. *Social Education* 60 (3): 167–169.

Houser, N.O. 1999. Critical literature for the social studies: Challenges and opportunities for the elementary classroom. *Social Education* 63 (4): 212–215.

McCall, A.L. and M.P. Ford. 1998. Why not do something? Literature as a catalyst for social action. *Childhood Education* 74 (3): 130–136.

McGowan, T., M. McGowan, and R. Lombard. 1994a. Children's literature: Empowering young citizens for social action. *Social Studies and the Young Learner* 7 (1): 30–33.

———. 1994b. Children's literature: Social education as the curriculum integrator: The case of the environment. *Social Studies and the Young Learner* 6 (3): 20–22.

Owens, W.T. and L.S. Nowell. 2001. More than just pictures: Using picture story books to broaden young learners' social consciousness. *Social Studies* 92 (1): 33–40.

Rule, A. and J. Atkinson. 1994. Choosing picture books about ecology. *Reading Teacher* 47 (7): 586–91.

Reed, C.A. 1992. Children's literature and antiracist education: A language-planning project. *Alberta Teachers' Association Multicultural Education Journal* 10 (2): 12–19.

Social Education. 2004. Notable children's trade books in the field of social studies. May/June. 1–15.

Yenika-Agbaw, V. 1997. Taking children's literature seriously: Reading for pleasure and social change. *Language Arts* 74 (6): 446–453.

CONTEMPORARY REALISTIC FICTION (MULTICULTURAL)

Au, K.H. 1993. *Literacy instruction in multicultural settings.* Orlando, FL: Harcourt Brace Jovanovich.

Bainbridge, J., S. Pantaleo, and M. Ellis. 1999. Multicultural picture books: Perspectives from Canada. *Social Studies* 90 (4): 183–189.

Bieger, E.M. 1996. Promoting multicultural education through a literature-based approach. *Reading Teacher* 49 (4): 308–311.

Finazzo, D. 1997. *All for the children: Multicultural essentials of literature.* Albany, NY: Delmar.

Galda, L. 1992. Exploring cultural diversity. *Reading Teacher* 45 (6): 452–460.

Gillespie, C., J. Powell, N. Clements, and R. Swearingen. 1994. A look at the Newbery Medal books from a multicultural perspective. *Reading Teacher* 48 (1): 40–50.

Hillard, L.L. 1995. Defining the "multi-" in "multicultural" through children's literature. *Reading Teacher* 48 (8): 728–729.

Koeller, S. 1996. Multicultural understanding through literature. *Social Education* 60 (2): 99–103.

Madigan, D. 1993. The politics of multicultural literature for children and adolescents: Combining perspectives and conversations. *Language Arts* 70 (3): 168–176.

Mathis, J.B. 1999. Multicultural literature: Mirror and window on experience. *Social Studies and the Young Learner* 11 (3): 27–30.

Mikkelsen, N. 1984. A place to go to: International fiction for children. *Canadian Children's Literature* 35/36: 64–68.

Pang, V.O., C. Colvin, M. Tran, and R.H. Barba. 1992. Beyond chopsticks and dragons: Selecting Asian-American literature for children. *Reading Teacher* 46 (3): 216–224.

Ramirez, G. and J.L. Ramirez. 1994. *Multiethnic children's literature.* Albany, NY: Delmar.

Rasiniski, T.V. and N.V. Padak. 1990. Multicultural learning through children's literature. *Language Arts* 67 (6): 576–580.

Stewig, J.W. 1992. Using children's books as a bridge to other cultures. *Social Studies* 83 (1): 36–40.

Taylor, S.V. 2000. Multicultural is who we are: Literature as a reflection of ourselves. *Teaching Exceptional Children* 32 (3): 24–30.

Yokota, J. 1993. Issues in selecting multicultural children's literature. *Language Arts* 70 (3): 156–167.

Yokota, J. and the Committee to Revise the Multicultural Booklist. 2001. *Kaleidoscope: A multicultural booklist for grades K–3*,
3rd ed. Urbana, IL: National Council of Teachers of English.

Zarrillo, J. 1994. *Multicultural literature, multicultural teaching*.
Orlando, FL: Harcourt Brace Jovanovich.

HISTORICAL FICTION

Caldwell, J.J. 1988. Historical fiction as a modern tool. *Canadian
Journal of English Language Arts* 11 (1): 24–32.

Collins, F.M. and J. Graham, eds. 2001. *Historical fiction for children: Capturing the past*. London: David Fulton Publishers.

Danielson, K.E. 1989. Helping history come alive with literature.
Social Studies 80 (2): 65–68.

Drew, M.A. 1991. Merging history and literature in teaching
about genocide. *Social Education* 55 (2): 128–129.

———. 1995. Incorporating literature into a study of the Holocaust: Some advice, some cautions. *Social Education* 59 (6):
354–356.

Erlandson, B. and J. Bainbridge. 2000. Living history through
Canadian time-slip fantasy. *Language and Literacy: A Canadian E-journal*. Accessed at www.langandlit.ualberta.ca/
archives/vol32papers/timeslip.htm.

Fisher, S.R. 2011. *Boys and girls in no man's land: English-Cana-
dian children and the First World War*. Toronto: University of
Toronto Press.

Freeman, E.B. and L. Levstik. 1988. Recreating the past: Historical fiction in the social studies curriculum. *Elementary School
Journal* 88 (4): 330–337.

Galda, L. 1993. Stories of our past: Books for the social studies.
Reading Teacher 46 (4): 330–338.

Handley, L.M. 1991. Sarah, plain and tall: A model for thematic
inquiry. *Social Studies and the Young Learner* 4 (2): 24–25.

Harms, J.M. and L.L. Lettow. 1993. Bridging time and space:
Picture books with historical settings. *Social Education* 57
(7): 363–367.

———. 1994. Criteria for selecting picture books with historical
settings. *Social Education* 58 (3): 152–154.

Johnson, N.M. and M.J. Ebert. 1992. Time travel is possible:
Historical fiction and biography—Passport to the past.
Reading Teacher: 45 (7): 488–495.

Kazemek, F.E. 1994. Two handfuls of bone and ash: Teaching our
children about Hiroshima. *Phi Delta Kappan* 75 (7): 531–534.

Kornfeld, J. 1994. Using fiction to teach history: Multicultural
and global perspectives of World War II. *Social Education*
58 (5): 281–286.

Lamme, L.L. 1994. Stories from our past: Making history come
alive for children. *Social Education* 58 (3): 159–164.

Levstik, L.S. and K.C. Barton. 2001. *Doing history: Investigating
with children in the elementary and middle schools*. Mahwah,
NJ: Erlbaum.

Tunnell, M.O. and R. Ammon. 1996. The story of ourselves:
Fostering multiple historical perspectives. *Social Education*
60 (4): 212–215.

Von Heyking, A. 2008. *Teaching with Dear Canada*, vol. 4.
Markham: Scholastic.

FOLK LITERATURE

Hickey, M.G. 1995. Focus on folk tales. *Social Studies and the
Young Learner* 8 (2): 13–14.

Spagnoli, C. 1995. These tricks belong in your classroom: Telling
Asian trickster tales. *Social Studies and the Young Learner* 8
(2): 15–17.

Taub, D.K. 1984. The endearing, enduring folktale. *Instructor* 94
(4): 61–70.

Wason-Ellam, L. 1988. Making literacy connections: Trickster
tales in Canadian literature. *Canadian Journal of English
Language Arts* 11 (1): 47–54.

Young, T.A., J. Bruchac, K. Livingston, and C. Kurkjian. 2004.
Folk literature: Preserving the storytellers' magic. *Reading
Teacher* 57 (8): 782–792.

18

Reading for Comprehension in Social Studies

Paul Neufeld

Historical Neglect

The importance of teaching reading comprehension strategies in social studies should be obvious. Since social studies is a text-laden subject, being able to read and comprehend texts effectively is crucial for success. Despite research confirming that students can effectively be taught strategies for improving their reading comprehension (National Reading Panel 2000), such instruction is not as common as it should be (Durkin 1978/79, Ness 2011, Pressley 2002a).

Before World War I, little thought was directed towards teaching students how to better comprehend what they were reading. Typically, reading instruction consisted of oral reading practice, the hallmarks of which were accurate and fluent recognition and pronunciation of words. In the decade after the war, the emphasis shifted from improving oral reading towards gaining meaning from text. For the next forty years, reading comprehension instruction consisted largely of students answering teacher-presented questions about specific selections (Pearson and Dole 1987). After observing more than ten thousand minutes of instruction in her landmark study of reading and social studies instruction, Dolores Durkin concluded that giving, completing, and checking assignments consumed a large part of the teaching periods and that no actual instruction in how to comprehend was taking place (1978/79, 481). Despite the importance of reading in social studies and other subjects, and a growing body of research suggesting the efficacy of teaching students how to comprehend, more than two decades after Durkin's famous study,

researchers continue to document the limited extent to which such instruction actually occurs (Pressley 2002b).

In this chapter, I present the basic principles and introductory tools required to teach reading comprehension in social studies. In the process, I hope to communicate why reading comprehension instruction should not be viewed as the exclusive domain of English/language arts but instead has an important place in social studies. I begin by defining reading comprehension and outlining the role of intentional thinking in reading comprehension. The bulk of the chapter focusses on specific reading comprehension strategies and offers a framework for developing students' self-regulated use of a repertoire of such strategies.

Reading Comprehension as Thinking

Comprehension can be defined as the act of constructing a reasonable understanding of a text (Neufeld 2005). Three principles underlie this deceptively simple definition: 1) comprehending a text requires active, intentional thinking through which a reader constructs meaning (Alexander and Jetton 2000); 2) varying interpretations of texts are to be expected because of differences in people's background knowledge and experiences; and 3) not all interpretations of a given text can be considered valid (Pressley 2002b). Clearly, comprehension is a function of both what the reader brings to the text (for example, his or her background knowledge of the topic) and the ideas conveyed through the words themselves. Thus, two students reading the same historical account may reach differing impressions about some aspects of the text. If both readers have comprehended the text, however, the essential understanding they construct from it should be similar (Pressley 2002b).

Comprehending a written text is a multifaceted undertaking, requiring both automatic and intentional thinking. Readers must engage in thinking at the word level (for example, decoding of words, accessing one's memory of word meanings) and at what has been called the above-word level. Thinking at the above-word level consists of the purposeful use of procedural or "how-to" strategies when attempting to comprehend a text (Alexander and Judy 1988). Although my focus in this chapter is solely on developing above-word-level strategies, other challenges to reading comprehension must not be overlooked. These include the reader's general knowledge of the world and specific knowledge of the particular topic; knowledge of relevant vocabulary; the ability to activate such knowledge; and competence in word-level processes such as decoding and fluency (that is, the ability to read at an appropriate rate and with expression). Difficulties in any of these areas may render above-word-level strategies unavailable to the reader. Consequently, comprehension-strategy instruction should complement, not replace, various long-standing practices such as providing vocabulary instruction and building students' background knowledge prior to having them read. Indeed, students' prior knowledge of both the topic and related vocabulary are strong predictors of successful reading comprehension (Stahl, Jacobson, Davis, and Davis 2006). Importantly, then, teachers should teach content knowledge and vocabulary related to the topics they want students to read about.

A substantial body of research supports the value of teaching students to use question asking and answering to support their efforts to comprehend what they read (Rosenshine, Meister, and Chapman 1996, Wilson and Smetana 2011). Question asking and answering can be viewed as the foundation for all the other strategies. In other words, the process of asking and then answering questions of oneself and of the text drives the other strategies. What differs from one strategy to the next is the type of questions one asks. Developing the ability to ask and answer questions of oneself and the text before, during, and after reading is an essential part of becoming a strategic reader. The ultimate goal is for question asking and answering to become a habit—a natural and pervasive part of a student's reading routine.

Without instruction, many students will not spontaneously generate and use effective comprehension strategies. Such students benefit from explicit instruction in a few well-researched strategies, and ongoing guidance in learning to select, activate, and use the strategies without direct prompting from others (Pressley 1998). The strategies described below can be applied regardless of the kind and length of the text—whether one is reading whole books, research articles, chapters within books, or passages within chapters.

Reading Comprehension Strategies

Researchers have identified many individual reading comprehension strategies that are both teachable and useful. These strategies can be clustered into two groups: pre-reading strategies, and during- and after-reading strategies (Schuder 1993).

PRE-READING STRATEGIES

As the name suggests, these strategies help students comprehend texts by involving them in thinking about the text before they actually start to read it. Four of these strategies are discussed below.

- **Clarify a purpose for reading.** A simple but important first step is to encourage students to think consciously about why they are about to read a particular text. Some common reasons for reading social studies texts are to prepare for a class discussion, study for a test, or gather important information for completing a task such as writing a paper. Questions for students to ask include:
  - Why am I reading this text?
  - How should my purpose affect the way I read the text?
- **Overview the text.** Overviewing involves quickly surveying the text before reading it. The intent is to develop an overall sense of the text, determine its relevance to one's purpose for reading, and identify sections that are particularly relevant to that purpose. Implementing this strategy involves considering the title and major headings, reading the introduction and conclusion, and examining text support features such as tables and graphs, with the purpose of answering questions such as:
  - What does this text appear to be about?
  - What major topics are covered in the text?
  - What text structure(s) does the author use to present the information? (for example, enumeration, time order, compare and contrast, cause and effect, problem/solution).

TABLE 18.1   COMMON TEXT STRUCTURES

TEXT STRUCTURE	EXPLANATION	VISUAL REPRESENTATION
Enumeration	Lists items or ideas that follow in order (for example, stages in the passage of legislation, instructions for building an igloo).	
Time order	Lists a sequence of events in time (for example, the daily schedule of a pioneer, major events in the history of a civilization).	
Compare and contrast	Highlights similarities and differences between two or more things or events (for example, comparing life in nineteenth and twenty-first century Canada, differences between capitalism and communism).	
Cause and effect	Shows how events (causes) lead to other events (effects) (for example, causes of poverty, escalation of violence in a dispute).	
Problem/solution	Shows the development of a problem and one or more solutions (for example, dealing with pollution or traffic congestion).	
Description	Presents the main features of a person, event, object, or scene (for example, conditions for new immigrants, daily life in a community).	

- **Activate prior knowledge.** Having developed a general sense of the content and organization during the overviewing process, readers can invoke knowledge they already possess that may be relevant to the text. Prior knowledge provides a mental connection linking ideas in the text with the reader's existing knowledge of the topic and the world. This practice has been shown to improve both recall and comprehension (Anderson and Pearson 1984). At this point, typical questions for students to ask and answer include:
  - What do I already know or think I know about this topic?
  - How does what I already know about this topic relate to this particular text?
- **Make predictions about the text.** Students can learn to make predictions about a text by drawing on answers produced using the overview strategy and by drawing on prior knowledge of the topic (Pressley 2002b). For instance, after scanning an

article on the history of the Olympics, a student might forecast that the text will provide information about sports such as wrestling that were popular in ancient Greece. Such predictions can then be used as hypotheses to test as the student is reading. A typical prediction for students to make and check on is:

- I think this text is going to be about …

Before reading any further, review the questions to ask and answer when overviewing a text. Apply this strategy to the rest of the chapter and then read the chapter to test how well you were able to develop an overall sense of the text and to identify particularly relevant sections.

DURING- AND AFTER-READING STRATEGIES

According to Pressley and Wharton-McDonald (1997), in addition to using strategies prior to reading, students should learn to use strategies while reading a given

TABLE 18.2	USEFUL WORD CLUES				
	ENUMERATION	**TIME ORDER**	**COMPARE AND CONTRAST**	**CAUSE AND EFFECT**	**PROBLEM/ SOLUTION**
Keywords	to begin with	on (date)	however	because	
	first	not long after	but	since	
	secondly	now	as well as	therefore	
	next	as	on the other hand	consequently	
	then	before	not only ... but also	as a result	
	finally	after	either ... or	this led to	
	most important	when	while	so that	
	also	following	although	nevertheless	
	in fact		unless	accordingly	
	for instance		similarly	if ... then	
	for example		yet	thus	

text and after they finish reading it. Strategies applied during these phases are intended to help students: 1) understand and remember what they have read; and 2) monitor their comprehension and remedy misunderstandings when breakdowns in comprehension occur. As was the case with pre-reading strategies, readers' ability and inclination to ask and answer questions of the text, and of themselves, drives the use of any particular strategy. Three types of strategies are addressed.

- **Analyze text structure.** The term "text structure" refers to the organizational logic of a text. It identifies the form in which information is organized for presentation. Most texts are written using relatively few organizational structures—enumeration, time order, compare and contrast, cause and effect, problem/solution, and description (see Table 18.1, "Common Text Structures"). As shown in Table 18.2, adapted from categories proposed by Vacca and Vacca (1999), each of these text structures, with the exception of description, is typically associated with a set of keywords that readers can use to identify the particular structure or structures.

  Helping students identify organizational structure facilitates their comprehension (Taylor and Beach 1984). For instance, recognizing that a particular text compares and contrasts the leadership styles of former prime ministers provides a framework for understanding the information presented. Not surprisingly, once students learn to identify organizational structures, they can apply this strategy when overviewing texts before reading them. Key questions for students to ask are:
  - Do I see any keywords associated with specific text structures?

- What text structures are used to present the information? (for example, enumeration, time order, compare and contrast, cause and effect, problem/solution).

- **Summarize the text.** Another strategy is to teach students to summarize coherently and briefly what they have read. Creating well-developed summaries is difficult. To support this task, students are advised to ask and answer questions such as "What organizational structure(s) does the author use to present the information?", "What is the gist of the text?", and "What are the author's main points?" Three common types of summaries are:
  - *Oral summaries.* Duke and Pearson (2002) recommend the use of oral summaries for "on-the-fly" comprehension checking that involves pausing momentarily after reading a section and checking comprehension by constructing a brief oral summary of what has just been read.
  - *Visual summaries.* Visual summaries include visual organizers such as semantic webs and Venn diagrams, strategies that are not typically regarded as summarizing tools. Vacca and Vacca (1999) point out that visual organizers provide graphic representations of both important information and the structure of knowledge contained in the text. Visual organizers also depict how these ideas relate to one another. Keep in mind that constructing appropriate visual organizers requires that readers be able to identify the organizational structure of a text. For instance, as suggested in Table 18.1, a Venn diagram or matrix can be used to summarize and compare and contrast text structure, but neither can be used to summarize a cause and effect or problem/

solution organizational structure. There are many commercially produced instructional packages about visual organizers. However, such products may not be necessary and may in fact get in the way of students' learning to use visual summaries effectively on their own. The power of visual organizers is realized only when students learn to construct them to accurately represent the particular texts they are reading—something mass-produced visual organizers can seldom accomplish. Furthermore, students find it liberating to create their own tools.

- *Written summaries.* Teaching students to write summaries in complete or partial sentences is another useful strategy. A common approach, as suggested below, is to teach students rules to apply when constructing written summaries (McNeil and Donant 1982):

  1. Delete unnecessary material (for example, delete interesting details that are not germane to the topic at hand).
  2. Delete redundant material (for example, delete repetitious statements made in the text).
  3. Select a word to replace a list of items (for example, replace "beans, flour, sugar, and dried fish" with "food").
  4. Select a word to replace the individual parts of an action (for example, replace a long description of explorers crossing a mountain pass with "the explorers crossed the mountain pass").
  5. Select a topic sentence (that is, one that captures the main idea or gist of a paragraph or passage).
  6. Create a topic sentence if one is not available.

- **Monitor comprehension.** As with previous comprehension strategies, the ability to ask and answer questions is essential for clarifying, comprehending, and correcting misunderstandings. Baker (1985) points out that many readers, particularly younger ones or poor ones, are unable to monitor their understanding while reading. Examples from the seemingly endless number and type of questions that students could ask to assist in monitoring are:
  - Is what I just read clear to me? Do I "get it"?
  - Can I answer who, what, when, where, why questions about the text?
  - What about the text is still fuzzy or unclear?

- **Use fix-up strategies.** Following the identification of a breakdown in comprehension, students must know how to clarify the failure and apply "fix-up" strategies to remedy the situation. Two questions to help remediate a breakdown in comprehension are:
  - Given my purpose for reading, how important is it that I clearly understand this portion of the text?
  - What strategies could I use to help me better understand what I'm reading?
    - Re-read part or all of the text.
    - Look ahead in the text.
    - Relate the information in the text to what I already know about the topic.
    - Examine other resources on this topic (for example, books, web pages, videos).
    - Consult someone who might resolve my confusion (for example, student, teacher, parent).

Review each of the text structures outlined in Table 18.1 and decide which one (or ones) are evident in this chapter.

Instruction in the Strategies

Thus far I have discussed strategies that will help students become better at comprehending what they read. Next I focus on how to teach these strategies. Two phases for teaching reading comprehension strategies are described below: explicit instruction in individual strategies (Roehler and Duffy 1984) and teaching for self-regulated strategy use (Collins-Block and Pressley 2002). The move from explicit instruction to teaching for self-regulated strategy use is not entirely sequential. Instead, there is considerable movement back and forth between the two phases. Students are more likely to master independent self-regulated use of a given strategy if it is taught and learned in a meaningful context that directly applies to the course material they are expected to read (Gambrell, Kapinus, and Wilson 1987). This is accomplished by using actual content materials during both phases of the process.

EXPLICIT INSTRUCTION OF INDIVIDUAL STRATEGIES

This initial phase of instruction focusses on helping students become competent users of the specific comprehension strategies discussed above. I recommend a

FIGURE 18.1 DOCUMENTING THE DETAILS

One way to introduce students to the 5W questions is to use a chart in which the reader provides evidence from the text to support a response to each question.

	MY RESPONSE	EVIDENCE FROM THE TEXT
WHO are the main actors in the text?		
WHAT have they been doing?		
WHERE did the actions take place?		
WHEN did the actions take place?		
WHY have they done these actions?		
Questions I have:		

four-step framework in which the teacher explicitly teaches the strategy to be learned, rather than simply presenting it and hoping that students "catch on."

- **Introduction.** A first step is to introduce the strategy by explaining what it is and why it is useful. This can be done by offering a simple description and/ or definition of the strategy (Baumann and Schmitt 1986). Next, ask students what, if anything, they already know about the strategy, provide a rationale for learning the strategy, and offer evidence of how it can improve their reading comprehension.
- **Modelling.** An effective way to teach students how to use a strategy is to show how it works (Dansereau 1987). Generally speaking, reading and learning processes are covert thinking activities that students seldom get to view in others. As students look on, teachers are advised to demonstrate while thinking aloud and explaining their thought processes while using the strategy.
- **Guided practice.** Guided practice involves providing students with numerous opportunities to use a strategy in an environment where support and feedback are readily available. In this step, the teacher and students share responsibility for implementing a comprehension strategy. For example, after modelling several examples of identifying organizational structure(s), highlight several relevant words in a

new passage and ask students to identify the text structure. Gradually release to students the responsibility for executing the strategy through a progression, starting with the whole class then proceeding towards small-group and individual guided practice. The transition from teacher-directed to student-directed execution with extensive practice in a supportive environment is essential for developing independent use of a strategy (Pearson and Dole 1987). Perhaps the biggest and most crippling deficiency in prevailing approaches to teaching reading comprehension strategies is the failure to provide numerous opportunities for supported practice.

- **Independent practice.** In the final stage, independent practice, students assume full responsibility for using the strategy (Baumann and Ballard 1987). Teacher monitoring and feedback are important, however, to ensure correct use of the strategy and to build student confidence. To reduce the likelihood of a pattern of failure, it is wise after the first few instances of independent practice to discuss students' responses along with their methods of reasoning (Pearson and Dole 1987).

The featured text, "Teaching a Comprehension Strategy in Action," provides an example of explicit instruction in a reading comprehension strategy using this framework.

TEACHING A COMPREHENSION STRATEGY IN ACTION

The scene is Mr. Carling's Canadian history class. Mr. Carling has a well-deserved reputation as an excellent teacher who works tirelessly to instill a passion for history and learning. In addition to having a strong focus on content, his classes are directed towards helping students become more effective learners. It is late September and Mr. Carling is eager to start helping his students learn how to better comprehend the history texts they will be reading through the year. He has chosen to begin by teaching them to overview a text before reading it.

Introduction

Sitting on the table at the front of the class, Mr. Carling addresses the students: "Okay, today I'm going to introduce a strategy, a thinking tool if you like, that will help you become a better reader of your social studies textbooks, and other information books, for that matter. With time and practice, this tool will, if you choose to use it, help you better comprehend what you read in this course and in other courses. The strategy is called overviewing.

"Does anyone have an idea what I mean by overviewing?" A few students raise their hands and take a stab at answering the question. Mr. Carling points to Kevin who says, "This is just a guess but I'm thinking it might be when you skim over what you're supposed to read before you actually read it." Marcy jumps in and adds, "Yeah, I think it means looking over the chapter and trying to figure out what it's about before you actually read it." Nodding in agreement, Mr. Carling says, "You're certainly on the right track." He then adds clarity to the informal definitions provided by the students. "Overviewing," he says, "involves reading through the title, introduction, major headings, and conclusion of a chapter or book prior to reading it in an effort to get a rough idea of what the text is about. Often people will also have a look at things like pictures and graphs as they overview a chapter.

"Now, I hope you're thinking to yourself, 'Why would I want or need to do that? Why wouldn't I just start reading?' Well, the answer to those excellent questions is that because doing so will help you better understand and remember the information in the chapter. In a minute, I'm going to show you how and why this is the case."

Modelling

Mr. Carling jumps down from his perch on the table and says, "Okay, now I'm going to show you how this strategy works. I'm going to demonstrate it for you. As I'm doing this, I want you to pay very close attention to what I am saying. I'm going to share the way I'm thinking with you so that you can think in the same way when it's your turn to do an overview." He then asks students to take out their textbooks and open to page 84, the chapter on the War of 1812. Once the students are settled, he models overviewing for them.

"The title of the chapter is 'The War of 1812.' All right, I'm thinking things are looking pretty straightforward then. It seems obvious that I'm going to be learning about the War of 1812 when I read this chapter, now doesn't it?" Next, Mr. Carling reads the introduction to the chapter, pausing to reflect on what he has read after he finishes. "Hmm, that refreshes my memory a bit, I'm remembering now hearing somewhere that the War of 1812 was between Canadians and Americans. I'm now going to read through the headings and see if I can get a big picture of where the author is going with this chapter. I want to identify the major topics."

He then flips through the chapter pausing to read each of the major headings aloud and then to "think out loud" about how they relate to one another and what he knows or thinks he knows already. In addition, he looks over various illustrations and text boxes that provide interesting tidbits about the war. After reading aloud the first few lines of one text box, he pauses and says, as if to himself, "That's kind of interesting. I didn't know Laura Secord was a real person. Okay, but I need to be careful here; as interesting as that blurb is I don't think it's crucial at the moment. Remember, I'm trying to get a broad sense of what the chapter is about." When Mr. Carling reaches the end of the chapter he reads the chapter summary and then says, "All right, I think I've got a pretty good idea of what this chapter is about. Based on my overview, I'm quite sure, pretty much certain in fact, that I'm going to be learning about the War of 1812, which was a war between Canada and the States, and it looks to me as if we won."

Once he has completed his overview, he discusses the processes he went through. He asks the students if they agree with his assessment and asks them to provide him with reasons for their positions. For instance, when Isabella jumps in and says, "Yes, I totally agree with you," he asks her to explain why she agrees. Isabella says, "Oh that's easy, because the title is 'The War of 1812.'"

After they've spent some time discussing the content of the overview, Mr. Carling says, "Now I want you to think about the thinking I did and the questions I asked and answered as I conducted my overview of the chapter. Can you help me generate a list of things I did?" With guidance from Mr. Carling, the students generate the following to-do list and list of questions to ask and answer for conducting an overview, which he writes on the chalkboard:

Overviewing to-do list:
- Read the title.
- Read the introduction.
- Read the major headings.
- Look at the pictures and other extras (be careful not to get sidetracked).
- Read the conclusion.

Questions to ask and answer when overviewing:
- What does the chapter appear to be about?
- What are some of the major topics?
- Do I know anything about this already?
- How can I use this to help me get ready to read?
- After reading: Was I right?

Finally, after going over a few key vocabulary terms and engaging in an informal discussion with the students centred around what they think they know about the War of 1812, Mr. Carling assigns the chapter for students to read.

Guided practice

After a day working through a series of activities associated with the introductory chapter on the War of 1812, Mr. Carling revisits the overviewing strategy with students. He begins by reminding them about the strategy and his modelling of it. Through discussion, he elicits from the students the goal of the strategy and the major steps involved. Then he tells them that today they will have an opportunity to implement the strategy of overviewing as a class as they prepare for another reading on the War of 1812. After handing out the reading, Mr. Carling asks if anyone can suggest how they might start. Anton answers, "Yeah, we could read the title and talk to ourselves about it like you did the other day." Mr. Carling laughs and says, "Okay, so what would you say to yourself, Anton?" Anton replies, "I'd read the title, 'The War in Upper Canada,' and then I'd say to myself, 'It looks like this is going to be about the part of the war that took place in Upper Canada, wherever that is." Mr. Carling says, "Anton has got us off to a good start. Can someone suggest what we might do next?" Carlos suggests they should be able to get an even better idea about the chapter by reading the introduction. After reading the introduction aloud and eliciting student thoughts on what it tells them about the chapter, Mr. Carling and the students read the headings and the conclusion, working through the overviewing process together as they go. An important aspect of the guidance provided by Mr. Carling is his continual requests of students to provide the reasoning behind their statements. He wants to be sure that students are not simply randomly guessing about the content, but offering informed guesses based on the text and their background knowledge. When they have completed their overview, students read the text.

The process described above occurs repeatedly over the next few weeks. Each time Mr. Carling assigns a new chapter, he and the students overview it before reading it. As the class grows more proficient at this strategy he withdraws from the process, allowing students to take increasing responsibility for its implementation. Moreover, there is a corresponding shift in grouping structures used for the practice sessions, from whole class modelling and practice to small group and ultimately individual practice.

Independent practice

As students develop fluency with overviewing, Mr. Carling provides opportunities to practise this strategy independently as they seek to learn from texts they are reading for assignment purposes. He has already introduced them to making predictions about what they are about to read, and students are adding this technique to their repertoire of reading comprehension strategies.

TEACH FOR SELF-REGULATED USE

The goal of teaching reading comprehension is to foster student mastery of a growing repertoire of individual strategies in a self-regulated fashion. The challenge in becoming an independent strategic reader is not simply a matter of acquiring knowledge of various strategies, but also of knowing exactly when, given the specific purpose and text, to employ particular strategies (Malone and Mastropieri 1992, 278). When assisting students in learning when and where to use each strategy, it is helpful to review why such strategies are useful and to provide multiple opportunities to practise them using actual course content (Gersten and Carnine 1986).

Teaching for self-regulated use should begin as soon as students understand what the particular strategy is and how it works. In practice, then, the two phases are more nearly parallel than sequential, with the teacher providing instruction in when and where to use different strategies as the opportunity arises. For instance, a teacher might model a previously taught strategy while introducing students to text structures. Nonetheless, as students acquire larger repertoires of strategies, there is a natural progression from explicit instruction of individual strategies towards instruction on the coordinated and self-regulated use of multiple strategies.

If students are to become competent strategic readers, they require many opportunities to discuss the texts they read (Pressley et al. 1992). While discussing the content of the texts is important, such discussions should also extend to the *process* students engaged in while trying to comprehend the text. These discussions should take place in small groups where the students discuss both their *understandings of the text* and the *strategies they used* to construct those understandings. In the beginning, students will need considerable teacher input, but as they become more capable, the teacher should gradually withdraw his or her support. Teacher support should focus on prompting students to be active readers by asking them to think about the kinds of strategies they should use (Pressley 2002b). For instance, following reading, a teacher might ask students what kinds of strategies would help them retain the important information from the text and why they would use these strategies. After students implement such strategies, the teacher might ask them to share the information and critique the strategies they used to help retain it. Without making these discussions teacher-centred, the teacher should participate by sharing the understandings he or she constructs and by modelling the strategies used to construct them.

Conclusion

Achieving success in social studies requires that students be able to comprehend the texts of the discipline. Unfortunately, many students struggle to read such texts and learn from them if they are not provided with instruction in how to do so. Moreover, despite research supporting its effectiveness, instruction in how to comprehend is not a feature of many social studies classes. It is my hope that this discussion will help social studies teachers make comprehension instruction a meaningful component of the instruction they provide.

I offer six principles to keep in mind while planning and providing this instruction:

- Remember, the purpose of comprehension instruction is to help students better comprehend challenging texts. Comprehension strategies are a means to this end, not an end in themselves.
- Teach a few comprehension strategies well rather than teaching many strategies poorly.
- Provide many opportunities for students to practise the strategies they are learning for real purposes.
- Help students learn to adapt comprehension strategies to their needs, individual preferences, and the text at hand, instead of using them in a lockstep fashion.
- Be patient. It may take several years to become an effective teacher of reading comprehension.
- Do not forget to build students' background knowledge and vocabulary of topics prior to having them read.

REFERENCES

Alexander, P.A. and T.L. Jetton. 2000. Learning from text: A multidimensional and developmental perspective. In *Handbook of reading research*, vol. III, ed. M.L. Kamil, P.B. Mosenthal, P.D. Pearson, and R. Barr, 285–310. Mahwah, NJ: Lawrence Erlbaum.

Alexander, P.A. and J.E. Judy. 1988. The interaction of domain-specific and strategic knowledge in academic performance. *Review of Educational Research* 58: 375–404.

Anderson, R.C. and P.D. Pearson. 1984. A schema-theoretic view of basic processes in reading. In *Handbook of reading research*, ed. P.D. Pearson, 255–291. New York: Longman.

Baker, L. 1985. How do we know when we don't understand? Standards for evaluating text comprehension. In *Metacognition, cognition, and human performance*, ed. D.L. Forrest-Pressley, G.E. MacKinnon, and T.G. Waller, 155–206. New York: Academic Press.

Baumann, J.F. and P.Q. Ballard. 1987. A two-step model for promoting independence in comprehension. *Journal of Reading* 30: 608–612.

Baumann, J.F. and M.C. Schmitt. 1986. The what, why, how, and when of comprehension instruction. *The Reading Teacher* 39: 640–646.

Collins-Block, C. and M. Pressley, eds. 2002. *Comprehension instruction: Research-based best practices*. New York: Guilford Press.

Dansereau, D.F. 1987. Transfer from cooperative to individual studying. *Journal of Reading* 30: 614–619.

Duke, N. and P.D. Pearson. 2002. Effective practices for developing reading comprehension. In *What research has to say about reading instruction*, 3rd ed., ed. A. Farstrup and J. Samuels, 205–242. Newark, DE: International Reading Association.

Durkin, D. 1978/79. What classroom observations reveal about reading comprehension. *Reading Research Quarterly* 14: 481–533.

Gambrell, L.B., B.A. Kapinus, and R.M. Wilson. 1987. Using mental imagery and summarization to achieve independence in comprehension. *The Journal of Reading* 30: 638–642.

Gersten, R. and D. Carnine. 1986. Direct instruction in reading comprehension. *Educational Leadership* 43: 70–78.

Malone, L.D. and M.A. Mastropieri. 1992. Reading comprehension instruction: Summarization and self-monitoring training for students with learning disabilities. *Exceptional Children* 58: 270–279.

McNeil, J. and L. Donant. 1982. Summarization strategy for improving reading comprehension. In *New inquiries in reading research and instruction*, ed. J.A. Niles and L.A. Harris, 215–219. Rochester, NY: National Reading Conference.

National Reading Panel. 2000. *Teaching children to read: An evidence-based assessment of the scientific research literature on reading and its implications for reading instruction: Reports of the subgroups.* Washington, DC: National Institute of Child Health and Development.

Ness, M. 2011. Explicit reading comprehension instruction in elementary classrooms: Teacher use of reading comprehension strategies. *Journal of Research in Childhood Education* 25 (1): 98–117.

Neufeld, P. 2005. Comprehension instruction in content area classes. *The Reading Teacher* 59 (4): 302–312.

Pearson, P.D. and J.A. Dole. 1987. Explicit comprehension instruction: A review of research and a new conceptualization of instruction. *Elementary School Journal* 88: 151–165.

Pressley, M. 1998. *Reading instruction that works: The case for balanced teaching.* New York: Guilford Press.

————. 2002a. Comprehension strategies instruction: A turn-of-the-century status report. In *Comprehension instruction: Research-based best practices*, ed. C.C. Block and M. Pressley, 11–27. New York: Guilford Press.

————. 2002b. *Reading instruction that works: The case for balanced teaching* (2nd ed.). New York: Guilford Press.

Pressley, M., P. El-Dinary, I. Gaskins, T. Schuder, J.L. Bergman, J. Almasi, and R. Brown. 1992. Beyond direct explanation: Transactional strategies instruction of reading comprehension strategies. *Elementary School Journal* 92: 513–555.

Pressley, M. and R. Wharton-McDonald. 1997. Skilled comprehension and its development through instruction. *School Psychology Review* 26: 448–466.

Roehler, L.R. and G.G. Duffy. 1984. Direct explanation of comprehension processes. In *Comprehension instruction: Perspectives and suggestions*, ed. G.G. Duffy, L.R. Roehler, and J. Mason, 265–280. New York: Longman.

Rosenshine, B., C. Meister, and S. Chapman. 1996. Teaching students to generate questions: A review of the intervention studies. *Review of Educational Research* 66: 181–221.

Schuder, T. 1993. The genesis of transactional strategies instruction in a reading program for at-risk students. *Elementary School Journal* 94: 183–200.

Scott, D., C. Falk, and J. Kierstead. 2002. *Legacies of ancient Egypt.* Richmond, BC: The Critical Thinking Consortium.

Stahl, S.A., M.G. Jacobson, C.E. Davis, and R.L. Davis. 2006. Prior knowledge and difficult vocabulary in the comprehension of unfamiliar text. In *Reading research at work: Foundations of effective practice*, ed. K.A. Dougherty Stahl and M.C. McKenna, 284–302. New York: Guilford Press.

Taylor, B.M. and R.W. Beach. 1984. The effect of text structure instruction on middle-grade students' comprehension and production of expository text. *Reading Research Quarterly* 19: 134–146.

Vacca, R.T. and J.L. Vacca. 1999. *Content area reading: Literacy and learning across the curriculum*, 6th ed. New York: Longman.

Wilson, N.S. and L. Smetana. 2011. Questioning as thinking: A metacognitive framework to improve comprehension of expository text. *Literacy* 45 (2): 84–90.

19

Using Historical Artifacts with Young Students

Linda Farr Darling

The Importance of Historical Inquiry

Developing historical understanding is a central goal for social studies education, but it presents challenges for elementary teachers who wonder about children's readiness to engage in historical investigation. Many teachers are concerned that young children are disconnected psychologically, lack sufficient background knowledge about the past, and are missing concepts dealing with chronology that are required for any understanding of history.

These challenges are important considerations but they are not insurmountable. Various researchers have shown how engaging students in historical inquiry—turning the study of history into an interpretive practice—can be accessible and exciting even to young students. Children continually strive to make "human sense" of the world (Donaldson 1978), and historical inquiries can bring to life stories about people, places, and times that enhance this sense-making. Although children may feel disconnected from broad historical discussions of political movements, wars, revolutions, and so on, they rarely feel disconnected from discovering what life was like for their teachers, parents, and grandparents when they were children. From constructing personal timelines and learning to divide the past into recognizable eras based on family photographs, young students can build chronological sense using narratives found in their own homes and communities. These stories from the past provide starting places for acquiring and refining the concepts necessary for historical understanding.

Paramount in this enterprise is the teacher's role in engaging students in what might be called "disciplined inquiry" by harnessing and shaping the natural curiosity that bubbles up in the form of children's spontaneous questions. The authors of *Doing History* define disciplined inquiry as "purposeful investigations that take place within a community that establishes the goals, standards and procedures of study" (Levstik and Barton 1997, 13). The rich potential embedded in historical inquiry is lost without a teacher framing and guiding the questions that students ask. Too often, questions encountered in the elementary social studies curriculum remain at very concrete and literal levels. Attention stays on gathering information and detail, sometimes at the expense of analysis or synthesis, and without sufficient regard for the "human sense" behind the facts. Unlike fact-finding questions that tend to shut down inquiry, the focus should be on questions that open up inquiry, go beyond recall, deepen understanding, and expand curiosity. Students can engage in sustained inquiries, even without considerable prior knowledge of history. In fact, as the authors of *Doing History* suggest, the inquiry can become the process through which students construct their understanding of historical themes. However, these authors caution that "authentic, disciplined inquiry is not easy; teachers must guide and support students at every step of the process—stimulating their interest, helping them develop questions, modelling procedures for collecting information and so on" (77). Despite these requirements, the rewards of inquiry are worth the effort.

The Role of Artifacts in Inquiry

Before introducing an extended scenario about a primary classroom inquiry, I want to comment on the value of artifacts as starting points for purposeful historical investigation. Levstik and Barton write that "although young children who are still developing their reading skills will have trouble using some kind of written primary sources—particularly from more remote time periods—analyzing photographs and artifacts allows them to use important historical materials in an authentic way" (77). There are several reasons why study of a single historical artifact presents an imaginative entry into larger investigations of the past. Children are attracted to the details about people's everyday lives; physical objects make these lives seem more real and accessible. The opportunity to handle and use physical artifacts stimulates curiosity about "things that work," and engages children's natural inclinations to be active and involved in their learning. Manipulation of hand drills, old egg beaters, and other implements from various eras is absorbing and fun, and importantly adds to children's first-hand knowledge of tools and technologies.

In my own work with young students, I have found that investigations of historical artifacts introduce the past to students in a way that is rooted in something concrete and easy to grasp, but can easily grow to something more. For example, the examination of a glass inkwell or a slate chalkboard can lead to important historical questions about continuity and change in society as reflected in schoolrooms over the last hundred years. I now want to illustrate this potential by describing the inquiry that evolved when I brought a historic artifact to a grade 3 class.

A Classroom Inquiry

As students are getting settled, I look around and see that inquiry is clearly valued in this classroom. There's a large hand-printed letter to author Robert Munsch asking, among other things, "How do you think up your stories?" and "Who do you tell your stories to before you write them down?" On the windowsill are a dozen bean plants of various heights, each with a graph attached and questions about conditions for healthy growth. It's a pleasant jumble of a room, a mixture of works-in-progress and

Photo by Linda Farr Darling.

remnants of last week's literary performances and yesterday's science experiment. Stretching towards the door is a blue rug and on it twenty children are now gathering after a stretch. They are more or less sitting in a semicircle of barely contained energy.

First I introduce the term "artifact," then "historic artifact," and write both on the board with a brief definition. The artifact I have brought is a curious object, a solid wooden sphere the size of a tennis ball with a turned handle protruding two inches from one side (see photograph). I hold up the sphere for students to see and I invite them to raise their hands to ask me what they are curious about. I explain I won't answer right away because there will be so many kinds of questions, and I will need to think about them. Students begin posing their questions:

"Is it really old?"
"Why does it have a handle?"
"Who gave it to you?"
"Is it a toy?"
"Do you have any more of them?"
"Is it breakable?"
"Is it worth a lot of money?"
"Is there something inside it?"

I stop them after the eighth question and say, "You have asked so many questions that I am getting confused. How can we keep track of them?" Someone volunteers that we could make a list and we are off and running with the first stage of our inquiry lesson. I begin recording the questions on the board, but one student notices that some questions are "like other ones kids already asked." Soon it is obvious to some students that there are different sorts of questions and we should find a way to organize them.

We decide to make three columns. We label them, "Questions about what the artifact is like," "Questions about where it came from," and finally, "Questions about what it is for." Our purpose in creating these categories is to frame the questions and eventually the hypotheses that students will generate about the artifact. More questions are asked and students help me decide where to place them in our categories. Then I ask the class to think of how we might find answers to their questions. "We can ask you!"

"What makes you think I will know the right answers?" I reply.

"It belongs to you, so you know." With this response noted, I ask them to imagine that this historical artifact just appeared on their windowsill. How would we learn about it then? They suggest the following methods:

- look in a book;
- ask a grown-up;
- go to a museum or a place with old stuff.

At this stage I want students to understand that we will start building our knowledge of the artifact so we can discover not only what it is, and how it is used, but also how it fits into a historical context. "What do you know about it before you look in a book or find an expert?" I ask. I encourage children to pass the artifact around so that everyone has a chance to touch it, sniff it, and roll it around in their palm. We talk about careful and respectful treatment of artifacts and establish a few rules for handling—no throwing, no hitting it against something, and no dropping.

Next, students work in groups of four to write down everything they already know about the artifact. Collaborative effort is productive in building understanding. Students learn that by observing carefully and putting their observations together they know quite a lot. The object is round, hard, smooth, heavy but not too heavy to hold, somebody made it because it wouldn't grow like that, it's made out of wood, you're probably supposed to hold it by the handle, it probably won't bounce, it is darker in some places than others, and it probably floats. Direct observation has led to additional knowledge and new questions that we add to our three lists.

I invite students to ask me any of the questions we have generated, but I tell them I can answer only "yes" or "no," and I will not answer the same question twice so they will have to keep track. This means that they will have to rethink the form of some of the questions on the board and listen carefully to make sense of my replies. If they get stuck, I may offer another piece of information. They will hear many clues and then they will be asked to form hypotheses about the identity of the artifact.

Through questioning me, students eliminate possibilities and collect further information: No, it was not carved. Yes, the sphere and handle were both created using a special carpenter's tool (a lathe). Yes, it is older than me and my mother and even my grandmother. No, it is not part of a spinning wheel. No, it has no other parts. No, the artifact is not a toy, nor is it furniture. Yes, it is useful, but no, not for cooking or in the kitchen. Yes, more women than men used it, but men travelling on their own (such as gold miners and cowboys) would have found it helpful. Yes, it was used to fix or mend something. Yes, it fixed something most people needed. Yes, other things, most notably burned-out light bulbs once electricity was in wide use, served the same purpose.

There are a few tentative hypotheses offered: it's something for weaving, a tool for knitting. I assure them they are very close and that they have done wonderful work. It is time to demonstrate the artifact in use. I take out a hand-knitted wool sock with a hole in the heel, a thick blunt needle, and some strong white thread. Even those children who have never seen someone darning know exactly what I am trying to do. They can see that the round ball provides the right curve to support mending a hole in the heel. What a useful tool! They are delighted with their efforts as investigators (even though they were not completely successful) and they are eager to hear the story of my artifact, which I can now share.

The artifact is a late nineteenth-century darning ball that came from the family of a friend in the Maritimes. It is made of eastern white oak (a common hardwood in the forests of Nova Scotia and New Brunswick). The wooden ball and handle were turned on a lathe, probably by an amateur woodworker who gave it to his wife, my friend's great-grandmother. The decorative handle bears a strong resemblance to details on country furniture built in the 1870s and 1880s. I hadn't previously seen one like it and it surprises me that darning balls are not more common in attics, antique stores, or at flea markets. Presumably most nineteenth-century European Canadians wore hand-knitted socks that developed holes in their heels. The darning ball is a household object that was at one time rather commonplace. In later decades, burned-out light bulbs were used for the same purpose. There are countless other examples of functional objects that were once familiar in North American homes: hand-held irons, primitive toasting racks, copper bed warmers, wooden butter paddles, carved butter presses, and metal thimbles. Any of these artifacts can lead to "disciplined inquiry" beginning with questions such as, "What are some household inventions that have changed family life since your great-grandparents' day?" This in turn could be linked to other historical questions such as, "What are some ways in which our society has adapted to changing conditions and demands?" Related ideas and topics include:

- obsolescence
- technological innovation
- consumables
- household inventions
- the Industrial Revolution
- textile mills

This time, the darning ball proves to be a catalyst for a social studies unit on recycling and reusing. Part of the study is an investigation of changing societal values. Once socks were mass-produced in knitting mills, people generally attached much less value to them (see Ulrich 2001, especially chapter 11, "An Unfinished Stocking"). Instead of owning only two or three pairs of socks as people did in the eighteenth and nineteenth centuries, today many people own lots of relatively inexpensive machine-made socks. However, if a favourite aunt or other relative had spent the time to knit a pair of socks, the recipient would likely treasure them.

We read *Ox-Cart Man* (Hall and Cooney 1979), the story of a farm family who make almost everything they use. Students draw elaborate illustrations of the way that members of this family grew food, collected goose down for stuffing quilts, built furniture from trees on the property, and so on. On one page of the book, the mother sits by the fire mending torn clothing. The children search Barbara Cooney's illustration for evidence of a darning ball and conclude it must be in the basket of mending at her feet.

The next day, I bring in a colourful pair of warm, hand-made Peruvian socks. They prompt stories of special socks, shoes, and other favourite pieces of clothing that we save even after we outgrow them. This exchange naturally leads to a rich discussion of what we mean when we say we value something. We read Pablo Neruda's poem about a favourite pair of hand-knit stockings called "Ode to my Socks" (1968). I read each line first in Spanish and then the English translation. The poet thinks the socks are too beautiful for his old, tired feet. He calls the socks twin parrots and later in the ode he refers to them as two woven flames. The students look at their feet. They might throw away socks when they get holes (or perhaps turn them into puppets), but it wasn't always this way.

I recite a short poem that my grandmother had cross-stitched on a sampler because it speaks of an important domestic value common to families even two generations ago:

> Use it up,
> Wear it out,
> Make it do,
> Or do without.

The darning ball has done its job—it has stimulated powerful questions that guide our inquiry.

USING ARTIFACTS TO SUPPORT HISTORICAL INQUIRY

- **Artifact study sheet.** Develop a chart, such as the one illustrated below, to accompany artifact investigation that students conduct either in groups, on their own at home (if interviewing family members), or in other settings, such as on a field trip to a museum. Emphasize that students are to offer reasons or evidence for their answers: What clues can we point to that suggest an answer?

- **Old Main Street treasure hunt.** Most towns and cities have a neighbourhood that is full of antique shops, junk stores, second-hand clothing stores, pawnshops, auction houses, consignment stores, or thrift shops. These can be treasure troves for artifact collectors. Sometimes sources for historical artifacts are scattered throughout a wider geographical area. If it seems workable in your situation, consider a field trip for students and arrange for them to have a small amount of money to purchase an artifact or an old newspaper, catalogue, or calendar. If a field trip is not feasible, consider collecting artifacts in a treasure chest of your own. Among the items I have discovered on my own city's Main Street include: biscuit tins, military uniform buttons, initialled handkerchiefs, roller-skate keys, eight-track cassettes, long-playing records, player piano music rolls, apple corers, meat grinders, embroidery hoops, decorative hair combs, stocking garters, hand-forged nails, and inkwells. Each of these offers an imaginative entry into studying how people lived in the past.

- **"Then and now" charts.** Many important questions about societal change and continuity over time can be raised by inviting students to sort artifacts (or representations of objects) into "then" and "now" categories. Primary students can be introduced to Venn diagrams to represent tools, toys, and implements that have changed over the years between the childhoods of their parents, their grandparents, and their own lives. Students can draw pictures of objects that fit into the circle labelled "then" or the circle labelled "now." Certain items may have stayed the same over time and would be placed in the space where the circles overlap. Varying diagrams might be devoted to different themes (for example, kitchen tools, games and toys, women's clothing).

- **Artifact timelines.** A good activity for building understanding of chronology is for young children to arrange artifacts in chronological sequence. Using investigative methods discussed in class, students find out as much as they can about objects brought from home or found in the teacher's treasure chest. In small groups or as a whole class, students use the information gathered to decide where to place artifacts on a timeline. Beforehand, the teacher might write in significant dates, decades, historical periods, or personal time frames (for example, "My grandma's childhood," "My parents' teen years," or "When I was a baby"). Using clothespins, hang drawings of the objects along a clothesline stretched across a corner of the classroom. Alternatively, arrange the actual objects on a windowsill or counter that has been organized into a timeline.

- **Invent the artifact's story.** Invite older elementary students to write their own stories from the point of view of particular artifacts. Based on the knowledge acquired about an artifact and their own abilities to judge the plausibility of various hypotheses, students write a story which explains the following:

  - Who invented me? Why?
  - Who made me? Where?
  - Who has owned me?
  - Where have I lived? Where have I travelled?
  - What have I been used for? Have I been misused or neglected?
  - Does anyone use me now? Has a newer invention taken my place?

ABOUT THE ARTIFACT	CLUES	CONCLUSIONS
Where did it come from?		
Who made it?		
How old is it?		
Who used it?		
For what purpose?		
Is there a modern counterpart?		

Lessons Learned

Through this inquiry, students were introduced to the kinds of standards and procedures that are integral to historical study (for example, we must have reasons or evidence for our conclusions; we have to think for ourselves, the teacher won't always give us the answers; we can tell a lot by looking for clues; we can pool our individual observations). Students worked together to generate both questions and knowledge claims about the artifact. By working as a community of inquirers, the children entered into the practice of actually doing history. Concepts relevant to understanding the contexts in which the artifact might have been used were introduced naturally and informally as questions arose from the students themselves. The students were given opportunities to make sense of important historical themes (for example, technological obsolescence, shifting values, and change and continuity). Throughout the inquiry, the teacher's role was to stimulate children's thinking, help students focus and organize their inquiry, prompt students to think for themselves, help students learn from each other, and, most importantly, raise for consideration the bigger issues embedded in the particulars of their inquiry. In our inquiry, the important point was not the specific fact that we no longer darn our socks. Instead, the broader point was made that things that once had value in our society may no longer be appreciated. A related theme concerned losses and gains associated with technological advances. Certain technologies have qualitatively changed how we live our lives.

Identify a topic in the curriculum dealing with a past event, period, or person. Think of possible artifacts that might be used as an entry point to raise important themes connected with the historical topic you have identified. List several questions you might ask of students to guide them to the bigger issues raised by the artifact.

Clearly, there are countless humble artifacts that could be enlisted as tools to help young students make sense of history. Items need not be expensive or rare to be useful for historical inquiries. Even objects that were commonplace in your own childhood can present wonderful mysteries to young students. The primary criterion for selection is the potential for an artifact to raise important historical ideas (for example, self-sufficiency, changing values, enduring traditions). The artifact is simply the vehicle for grounding and drawing students into a historical inquiry. Other criteria to

remember when selecting artifacts include the following. Artifacts should:

- have the potential to excite children's imagination and to personalize history;
- not be too fragile for young children to handle;
- not be dangerous or cause damage (for example, stain clothing); and
- be easily displayed in a classroom (not too big or too small).

The feature "Using Artifacts to Support Historical Inquiry" includes suggestions for other activities that support historical inquiry using artifacts as the entry point.

Although it is desirable, especially with younger children, to have physical objects to share with students, this is not always feasible—some objects are too big, impossible to find, or are otherwise unavailable. Photographs of artifacts can be useful substitutes for the "real" thing. Many museums have developed virtual collections of artifacts. For example, the Archives Society of Alberta has produced a virtual train station filled with artifacts from Canadian immigrant experiences (www.archivesalberta.org, click on "Letters from the Trunk"). Similarly, the McCord Museum of Canadian history, in partnership with seven museums, has produced "Keys to History" (www.mccord-museum.qc.ca/en/keys), a searchable database of nearly 110,000 images (dating from 1840–1945), of which 2,000 are fully documented.

The example of a slide presentation described in the feature "Same or Different" illustrates how photographic representations of objects from ancient Roman times stimulated a grade 7 class's historical inquiry into the differences between Roman and contemporary societies.

Assemble several objects (or photographs of objects) that have historical significance. Design a lesson involving the use of these items to help students learn about some aspect of the curriculum.

Conclusion

In this chapter I have tried to show how the use of artifacts, or images of them, can be an exciting and effective approach to developing historical understanding, especially in younger children. Historical objects offer accessible opportunities to involve students in historical investigation. The main challenges to effective use

SAME OR DIFFERENT?

Photo courtesy Susan Duncan.

The lesson was introduced using a photograph (shown above) of a clay model of a sheep's liver. Explained in a manner intended to make the practice seem odd, students were told that in ancient times, fortune tellers or soothsayers would sacrifice an animal, slice open its belly, and pull out its organs, which were then "read" for any clues they offered about the future. This clay model was a teaching tool used in Mesopotamia to train would-be fortune tellers about what to look for when reading animal entrails. Each of the squares outlined on the clay model represented a different prediction. For example, a scar or blemish appearing in one part of the grid might indicate five years of good luck or suggest that the person would have many children. A mark in another area of the liver would signal poor health or great financial misfortune. After hearing this explanation, students were asked to indicate whether ancient soothsaying is very similar to or completely different from what happens today. The most common and predictable reaction was reflected in remarks such as "totally weird" and "strange."

The teacher then asked students to more directly consider contemporary fortune-telling. The teacher and students discussed various modern forms (for example, horoscopes, tea leaves, tarot cards, and palm reading) and the basis for predicting used by each (for example, the position of stars and planets, the configuration of leaves in the cup, the symbols on cards, and the length and intensity of lines on the palm). The teacher then observed that instead of the location of the scars on the liver, modern fortune tellers consult the location of the stars in the sky or the lines on the hand. Students were asked to reconsider how different this is from past practices. For many students, what was once a bizarre practice now seemed much less foreign.

The lens guiding their inquiry was now in place—students would look beyond the obvious differences between present and past practices to uncover more basic commonalities and differences. Students were then shown clusters of pictures of Roman objects on a common theme—pictures about entertainment showed the coliseum, gladiators, and chariot races. The teacher shared the stories behind each of these pictures. In small groups, students identified what they saw as the contemporary parallels for each practice. The parallels for entertainment included football stadiums, kick-boxing, and demolition derbies. Students then considered whether or not the differences between then and now were significant. This routine was repeated several times with other aspects of Roman civilization (for example, water systems, architecture, transportation, politics). In each case, students looked at photographs of artifacts from Roman times and identified parallels in their own society. The fact that statues of famous Romans often had their noses and ears broken off was of particular interest to students. One reason for this defacement originated in the time when Christianity took hold in Rome. In the eyes of some Christians, these statues encouraged idolatry and had to be destroyed. Because there were so many marble statues and they were difficult to remove or destroy completely, a common strategy was to mar the face of the statues by breaking off the noses and ears. Students were amused to realize that we still "deface" property—although now more frequently by graffiti than by knocking off appendages.

The culminating activity invited students to offer an overall assessment of the extent to which life in ancient Rome was similar to or different from contemporary society. As they debated their conclusions and shared their evidence, students understood that they were not simply talking about old relics but were engaged in an inquiry into the roots of Western civilization. As one student remarked, "I know why we study ancient Rome. Everything we do now, well, they did something just like it."

are to select objects that can connect with key themes in the curriculum, to engage students' curiosity through strategic questioning, and to support students in drawing out the bigger lessons from their inquiry into the artifact.

REFERENCES

Donaldson, M. 1978. *Children's minds.* New York: Norton.

Hall, D. and B. Cooney. 1979. *Ox-cart man.* New York: Random House.

Levstik, L. and K. Barton. 1997. *Doing history: Investigating with children in elementary and middle schools.* Mahwah, NJ: Lawrence Erlbaum Associates.

Neruda, P. 1968. Ode to my socks. Reprinted and translated in 1994 in *Rethinking schools: Teaching social justice in classrooms.* Milwaukee, WI: Rethinking Schools, Ltd.

Ulrich, L.T. 2001. *The age of homespun: Objects and stories in the creation of an American myth.* New York: Random House.

PART 5 Investigating Perspectives

20

Nurturing Personal and Social Values in Elementary Classrooms

Roland Case

The teaching of values is one of the most important controversial goals in social studies. Many consider the nurturing of personal and social values to be as important in education as acquiring knowledge. Personal values are those we hold about ourselves, such as self-esteem, integrity, personal responsibility for one's actions, and pride in one's work. Social values are those that we hold about others and society in general, such as national pride, commitment to justice, respect for the law and the environment, co-operation, and empathy. Many people see teaching social studies as an important opportunity to promote the fundamental values that society requires of its citizens. But despite the central role of values education, often referred to as character education[1] (Burrett and Rusnak 1993; Glaze, Hogarth, and McLean 2003), there is considerable debate about it. The dominant objections to the teaching of values in schools have revolved around three issues:

- **Should schools nurture values?** Is school the appropriate place to nurture values or should schools be value-free?
- **Which values should be nurtured?** Which values should be promoted in schools? Who decides, and on what basis?
- **How should values be nurtured?** What methods should teachers use to promote values while respecting the rights of students and parents?

In this chapter, I address these three questions in turn, with particular attention to how values should be nurtured in school. I explore three overlapping approaches to help students develop values and think

more critically about them. But before doing so, I offer a few remarks about the other two questions.

Should We Nurture Values?

In some respects, the question whether teachers should teach values in school is moot. Schools cannot be value-free and teachers cannot avoid promoting values. We praise children for being honest, thoughtful, and punctual; these values are embedded in our schools. Every time we permit or prohibit certain behaviour, we implicitly promote certain values: school rules against fighting or throwing rocks, for example, attest to how we value individual well-being and the protection of property.

Educators inevitably, and often unintentionally, influence student values and attitudes—this is often referred to as the "hidden curriculum." For example, if we mark students' work for neatness or praise them for asking probing questions, we are encouraging them to act in particular ways; if we do not reinforce neatness or an inquiring attitude, we implicitly communicate that these behaviours are not valued. Such is the case with everything we do (and do not do) in school. The only real choice teachers have about promoting values is whether their influence will be hidden and unintentional or explicit and systematic.

Daniel Duke (1978) illustrates how schools may affect students' attitudes in unintended and undesirable ways. He suggests the idea that many students develop a cynical attitude towards our legal system as a result of common school practices that run contrary to espoused civic ideals. Duke concludes that it is difficult

TABLE 20.1   WHAT SCHOOLS "TEACH" ABOUT OUR LEGAL SYSTEM

WE TELL STUDENTS...	YET, OFTEN IN SCHOOLS...
• we live in a society based on democratic principles	• rules are determined by those least subject to their application
• all people are to be treated equally before the law	• many teachers fail to enforce school rules consistently
• the punishment should be reasonable and fit the crime	• the consequences for disobeying school rules frequently lack logical relationships to the offences; for example, a common punishment for skipping classes is suspension from school
• society is committed to safeguarding the rights of individuals against abuse by the state	• students have few options if they disagree with a claim brought against them by school authorities
• no one is above the law	• teachers frequently fail to model the rule-governed behaviour they expect of their students

for students to develop respect for law and principled behaviour if their experiences in school consistently reinforce the opposite. Table 20.1 contrasts law rhetoric with common school practices.

Ultimately, the decision of whether schools should intentionally teach values should be made based on a thoughtful assessment of the pros and cons. Table 20.2 lists reasons for and against the intentional teaching of values in schools. It is interesting to note that the majority of listed objections to teaching values intentionally are not against the idea per se, but rather about which values to promote and how to do so responsibly.

Which Values to Nurture?

There are no simple answers for deciding which values to promote intentionally in schools. However, degree of consensus about a particular value is a promising starting point for deliberation. On one end of the spectrum are general values widely acknowledged as acceptable or even highly desirable. Honesty, pride in one's work, concern for the well-being of others, and respect for others' property are examples of values that likely have broad public support.

A justification for including these values in the curriculum derives from the notion that schools must, to some extent, act on behalf of parents. Promoting certain values can be seen as an extension of the upbringing that reasonable parents wish for their children. As suggested in the 1931 Hadow report: "What a wise and good parent would desire for his [or her] children, a national educational system must desire for all children" (cited in Cassidy, 1994).

The kinds of personal and social values listed below seem indispensable for healthy human existence and are likely broadly supported, though some people may object to these suggestions or want to add others. The list is drawn largely from the values advocated fifty years ago by a social studies curriculum committee, cited by Ralph Tyler in his classic book on curriculum design (1969, 92–93). Promoting these values, at least in general terms, is unlikely to conflict with broadly held parental or community values, although from time to time individual parents and community members may not share them. This "consensus" list can serve as a starting point for determining the values to be nurtured in schools.

PERSONAL VALUES

- acceptance of self; realization of one's own worth
- integrity, honesty, and frankness with self
- sense of hope about the future
- willingness to seek adventure; sense of mission
- desire to make a productive contribution to society
- love of truth, however disconcerting
- respect for work well done
- appreciation of beauty in art and the environment
- pride in family and ethnic background
- personal hygiene and health
- self-discipline and self-direction
- independent-mindedness (the courage of one's convictions)

SOCIAL VALUES

- respect for the dignity and worth of every human being
- commitment to equal opportunity for all
- tolerance and kindness

TABLE 20.2 SHOULD SCHOOLS INTENTIONALLY PROMOTE VALUES?

REASONS FOR	REASONS AGAINST
• Teaching values is part of the school's mandate. Official rationales for public education refer to the need to develop the values of productive citizenship. For example, the Ontario Ministry of Education (2004, 2) identifies the need to "develop attitudes that will motivate them [students] to use their knowledge and skills in a responsible manner." Alberta Education (2005, 2) lists a number of values and attitudes that are necessary for active and responsible citizens, including respecting the dignity and equality of all human beings, social compassion, fairness, justice, valuing lifelong learning, and honouring and valuing the traditions and symbols that are expressions of Canadian identity.	• Values promoted in schools may conflict with those shared by individual parents, local communities, or society.
	• Students may be indoctrinated into accepting values that are essentially those of individual teachers or fail to recognize the right to personal inclinations or freedom of conscience.
	• It is feared that schools will do a poor job of promoting values despite best intentions (for example, schools may unintentionally promote condescending attitudes towards various cultural or racial groups).
	• Values often raise extremely sensitive issues that may profoundly upset students.
• Teaching values is a precondition for many other objectives in the curriculum: knowledge and skills cannot be developed without accompanying value components. For example, students will learn little if they do not have self-esteem, curiosity, and open-mindedness. Students will be unable to work co-operatively unless they have some respect for the feelings of others, are willing to play by the rules, and so on.	• Values may be controversial, so actively promoting them may, in certain circumstances, present a professional risk for the teacher (the teacher may become embroiled in a controversy).
• Many important societal values need attention, and schools have a significant, perhaps unique, opportunity to make a difference. If racism and discrimination are promoted within some families, how will these undesirable—and in some cases illegal—values be countered if not by the educational system?	

- desire for justice for all
- acceptance of social responsibility
- commitment to free thought, expression, and worship
- commitment to peaceful resolution of problems
- respect for privacy
- national pride
- environmental stewardship
- fair-mindedness
- concern for well-being of animals
- respect for the law

At the other end of the spectrum are personal and social values that are profoundly controversial, particularly positions on specific issues such as abortion, same-sex parenting, affirmative action, and capital punishment. In these cases, since society is sharply divided, teachers should assume that there is not a single acceptable position; well-informed, thoughtful people will not share the same values. In such cases, if the issue is to be raised in school (and it may be that in many communities some value questions are too controversial to be raised), the objective should not be to promote a specific position, but rather to encourage students to make up their own minds as much as is possible after thoughtful consideration. This expectation must be tempered when students entertain issues that may have

disastrous consequences if they make a poor decision (say, in the case of considering suicide) or when students are trapped in the spell of external irrational influences (say, in the case of Holocaust deniers). As well, we should be careful not to attempt to push students into deciding on an issue before they are ready to make up their minds.

Generally speaking, teachers' responsibility is to act in a respectful and fair manner, seeking to instill appreciation of the need for sensitivity when dealing with divisive issues and to facilitate students' gathering and assessing information before deciding for themselves. A fair manner may not mean that teachers devote identical attention to all sides. If students are already well aware of one side, it may be necessary to spend more effort helping them to see other sides. However, it should be clear that teachers are not favouring a side because it reflects their own position, but rather to ensure that students see all reasonable viewpoints. Because students may be unduly influenced by their teachers, it is important to consider under what conditions teachers should withhold their personal positions.

Many values are largely matters of personal inclination, such as the dictates of religious conscience, life choices, political affiliations, and personal aspiration. In schools that are committed to cultural and political pluralism, it is inappropriate to espouse or favour the values of one religious or political ideology over others.

Consequently, it would be inappropriate, for example, to teach about the law in an attempt to reduce students' objections to current government practices. As Ken Osborne notes, "a well-informed, democratic and interested citizen need not be supportive of government policies" (1982, 59). Since in these matters there is no agreed-upon "correct" set of values (nor should there be), the teacher's role is to encourage students to explore and clarify these values for themselves. Although teachers should not presume which, if any, conclusions students will reach about these values, there may be considerable merit in providing students with opportunities to examine their own belief systems.

Teachers' concerns about imposing personal beliefs may be alleviated by encouraging students to make up their own minds about controversial values. Communicating to parents your commitment to this approach may help alleviate suspicion and opposition. Some issues divide communities deeply, and taking an open-minded view will not satisfy everyone. Our dilemma is, on the one hand, a responsibility to develop students' ability to engage with and resolve value issues in non-violent, thoughtful ways, and on the other, a responsibility to respect the parents' right, within limits, to raise their children as they see fit. Ultimately, these decisions are matters of professional judgment—of deciding what is most defensible in light of the needs and rights of the individuals and groups whom educators have a responsibility to serve. The more contested or individualistic the value, the more sensitive and vigilant teachers must be about empowering students to make up their own minds thoughtfully, and about parents' rights to be informed about and direct their children's education.

That some values may be inappropriate in schools and others, if addressed at all, must be handled with extreme sensitivity, does not mean that consensus about what values can be taught in schools cannot be reached among reasonable people. There are many personal and social values that are essential components of any social studies curriculum. And there may be many others that, if taught appropriately, also have a legitimate place.

Take a moment to think of five values—social or personal—that you most want to nurture in your classroom. Consider why you think these are so important. What might you do to reinforce and model these values in your teaching?

What Methods Should Be Used to Teach Values?

So much has been written about teaching values that it is difficult to get a handle on this field. I believe it useful to focus on three broad approaches:

- creating classroom and school environments that reinforce desired values;
- facilitating direct "emotive" experiences that evoke desired sensitivities; and
- engaging students in thoughtful deliberation about their values.

Although I discuss these approaches separately, they overlap and reinforce each other.

CREATING REINFORCING ENVIRONMENTS

Values do not develop in a vacuum; they are more likely to be nurtured in the complex interactions of a social environment than by short-lived instructional techniques. The literature attests to the power of the environment of a classroom in supporting or inhibiting the acquisition of attitudes. The atmosphere in a classroom is overwhelmingly cited as a primary factor in developing social attitudes (Leming 1991, Patrick and Hoge 1991). Studies reported by Judith Torney-Purta (1983) indicate curriculum content is less influential in developing students' political attitudes than a classroom climate where students express their opinions freely. Teacher behaviour is especially important in signalling to students what values really count. Teachers who are open-minded are more likely to foster this attribute in their students. Similarly, teachers who demonstrate empathy for others are more likely to nurture empathy in their students. There may be no more effective way of promoting a value than by sincerely and consistently communicating through our actions that it matters. Examples of teacher behaviour, expectations, and activities that reinforce concern for others are suggested below:

STUDENT ACTIVITIES AND EXPECTATIONS

- Principles of behaviour towards fellow students are articulated and enforced.
- Verbal or physical abuse of students by students is unacceptable, as is verbal or physical abuse of teachers by students.

- Good deeds by students are acknowledged.
- Students are frequently engaged in role reversals and are asked to think about how others might feel.
- Students are frequently asked to express why they care or do not care about seemingly remote events or people.
- Students are invited to participate in projects in which they do something positive for others.

TEACHER MODELLING

- Teachers refrain from put-downs and sarcasm, and always treat students (and colleagues) with respect.
- Teachers are willing to admit error, either publicly or privately, and attempt redress.
- Teachers often undertake random acts of kindness.
- Teachers are seen by students to care about their concerns and difficulties.

FACILITATING DIRECT EXPERIENCES

A second approach to nurturing personal and social values is to provide opportunities for students to "feel" the effect of caring for such values. Unlike a reinforcing environment, whose goal is to habituate students gradually to particular frames of mind, direct experiences provide students with opportunities to encounter for themselves, vividly and emphatically, the power and merit of certain ways of being. Often these experiences open students' minds to perspectives they would otherwise miss or downplay. There are at least three types of student experiences that nurture values: direct, vicarious, and simulated.

- **Direct experiences.** Students can encounter value-nurturing situations in real-life contexts through field trips, exchanges, and social-action projects. Social-action projects can be important value-nurturing experiences. As Mary-Wynne Ashford (1995) reports in her article "Youth Actions for the Planet," involvement in environmental and humanitarian projects can counter the global hopelessness prevalent among many students.
- **Vicarious experiences.** To live vicariously is to encounter life through the experiences of another. Film and literature—both fiction and non-fiction—can be especially effective in this regard. Vicarious experiences allow students to live the lives of others and to experience the power of feeling and caring about matters that are otherwise foreign or remote. Susan Inman, a teacher at Windermere Secondary

VALUE-BASED STORIES FOR PRIMARY CHILDREN

Students are introduced to the unfairness of inequitable job sharing through *Piggybook*, a children's book by Anthony Browne (2008). It describes a mother who does all the household chores until she leaves home for a short time and the rest of the family learns to recognize their selfish behaviour. After discussing the unfairness of this situation, students list jobs done at home and develop criteria for assigning responsibility in their own family or in an imaginary family. Students are invited to decide on a new job they will undertake. A week or so after assuming their new tasks, students report on their experiences and receive a note of appreciation for their efforts.

Students explore the idea of doing more than expected through *The Gardener* by Sarah Stewart (2007). In this story, a young girl undertakes to cheer up her sombre uncle. Using events from the story, students learn to distinguish acts of kindness from jobs that people have a responsibility to carry out. Students then discuss and apply criteria for an act of kindness before choosing and implementing an appropriate action for a family or community member. When the kind actions are completed, students discuss their contributions to the happiness of others.

The story *Lily and the Paper Man* by Rebbeca Upjohn (2007) tells how Lily is frightened of the Paper Man that she sees on her way home from school, but as winter sets in, she sees he has little protection from the cold and snow and decides to help. It is the anchor for a lesson on developing empathy for homeless people. Students listen to the story, then compare their own lives to that of the main character. After discussing the difficulties that homeless people experience, students select three helpful items they recommend giving to a shelter.[2]

School in Vancouver, uses the National Film Board documentary, *Where the Spirit Lives*, to enhance student sensitivity to the feelings and concerns of First Nations individuals. Prior to viewing this film about the plight and courage of First Nations students in residential schools, several of her students had shown indifference or callousness to First Nations people. The video puts a profoundly human face to what were otherwise stereotypes.

Children's stories also provide powerful vehicles to invite the young to consider important values. The feature "Value-Based Stories for Primary Children" illustrates a few of the many thousands of stories that can serve this purpose.

THE EPORUVIANS COME TO CALL[3]

The following imaginary scenarios are intended to evoke empathy for the historical treatment of First Nations people. The teacher reads each scene and allows students time to reflect (and write) about their thoughts before proceeding.

Scene 1: You're playing in your backyard when a group of odd-looking men dressed in strange clothes walks in. They look dirty and hungry, and are shouting and gesturing in a strange language. They try hard to communicate with you, but you can't understand them. You can tell, though, that what they are saying is important.

Not knowing what else to do, and because they look hungry, you invite them into your house and give them some cake and tea. Soon you are able to communicate with them using hand signals and gestures. You still don't know what they want, but you begin to understand that they are from a faraway land called Eporue. They really like your town and they want to stay.

- How would you feel? Scared? Flattered? Angry? Friendly? Annoyed? Curious? Excited?
- What would you do? Would you help them out? Ask them to leave?

Scene 2: You welcome the Eporuvians. You want to be helpful, and they seem lost. You let them stay in your house, and you keep feeding them. You show them around the town and introduce them to your friends. You begin to notice, however, that they have a habit of taking your things and they are not considerate. You begin to wonder whether making friends with them was such a good idea after all. You also start to wonder if they will ever leave. After a while, you realize that they want to keep living in your house and taking your things. In fact, they think that they own the place—and the land it's on, too. They stick the Eporuvian flag in the ground, and claim your yard for their leader.

- What would you do? Organize your friends to drive them out? Try to reason with them? Trick them into leaving? Give up and be friends?
- How would you feel? Scared? Angry? Puzzled? Disappointed?

Scene 3: By now, they don't bother talking to you much anymore, except when they want something. They bring their relatives, and lots of other Eporuvians, to live in your town. Eventually, they tell you and your family to leave, and give you a broken-down shack to live in, with no yard, no running water, and lots of other people crowded into it (who have all been forced off their land as well).

You never get your land back. For two hundred years, the story of how the Eporuvians forced you off your land is handed down. You tell your children, who tell their children, and so on, for ten generations.

- How will your descendants feel about the Eporuvians? Would you call them heroes or villains?
- If you were a descendant of the Eporuvians, how would you feel about what happened? Would you feel any responsibility to extend friendship to these people?

A skilled guest speaker can do much to change student attitudes. Certainly many of my own stereotypical attitudes towards ethnic and racial groups were exploded when I first encountered articulate and impassioned individuals from these groups. Pen pals are another alternative for providing students with a window into the lives of others.

- **Simulated and role-play experiences.** Drama, role play, and other simulations allow students to act out the predicaments of others. One of the most famous examples of a simulated experience was described in the award-winning documentary *The Eye of the Storm* (Peters 1970). In an effort to help her grade 3 students appreciate the consequences of racism, Jane Elliott began to discriminate against the blue-eyed children in her class, without announcing she was going to do so, and then the next day discriminated against the brown-eyed children. Students were moved by this encounter with prejudice.

In a follow-up documentary, *A Class Divided* (Peters 1985), filmed fifteen years after the simulation, the students in Elliot's class described the profound influence the experience had in shaping their values.

Imagine the power that even simple simulations may have on your students when reading the feature "The Eporuvians Come to Call." A 1986 Australian Broadcasting Corporation film entitled *Babakiueria* —a phonetic spelling of "barbecue area"—offers a similar reversal of perspective with Aboriginal explorers discovering a group of white inhabitants in a campground.

Experiences such as these—whether brought about vicariously, through simulation, or in first-hand encounters—expose students to the perspectives and lives of others and help to evoke sensitivity to important values. The point is not to manipulate students to take on particular perspectives, but to ensure that students view the world beyond themselves and experience the predicaments and feelings that others do.

PROMOTING THOUGHTFUL DELIBERATION

The third approach to values education is to deliberately encourage students to think about their attitudes. On its own, this approach will rarely be sufficient, and perhaps may not be the best first step. But we are in danger of manipulating and indoctrinating students if we do not also encourage them to reflect on the implications and significance of their values. Eventually, students must thoughtfully make up their own minds about their values. Generally, the deliberative approach to attitude development has two strands:

- **values clarification**: to help students clarify the values they hold and understand the implications of these values to themselves; and
- **values analysis**: a more critical examination of their values, in which students assess the adequacy of the reasoning behind them.

VALUES CLARIFICATION

Louis Raths, Merrill Harmin, and Sidney Simon (1966) are the best-known proponents of the values clarification approach, although many others have espoused it and it is widely evident in current educational practice. Its underlying premise is that individuals experience dissonance as a result of being unclear, confused, or uncommitted to their values. Since values are seen to be intensely personal and emotional, the teacher's role is to help students to clarify and affirm their own values. This approach rests on three features of a sincerely held value:

- **chosen**: individuals have considered the implications of a range of alternative values and chosen theirs without pressure or influence from others;
- **prized**: once chosen, individuals are happy with the choice and willing to publicly affirm the value; and
- **acted on**: individuals act consistently to reaffirm and strengthen their commitment to the value.

In this approach, the teacher's primary responsibility is to encourage students to clarify their values for themselves. Teachers facilitate this by organizing activities that stimulate students to think about their values, and by providing occasions for students to publicly affirm, celebrate, and act on them. This was the approach followed in the feature "Value-Based Stories for Primary Children" on page 231. Students were asked to consider what action, if any, they would adopt in response to unfair allocation of tasks, or people in need. To help students clarify their values, teachers might ask questions that invite students to identify their values, to think about their personal meaning and implications, and to consider the consistency of their words and deeds. Here are some sample questions:

- Is this something you value?
- How did you feel when it happened?
- What are some good things about it?
- Have you thought much about it?
- Where does this idea lead? What are its consequences?
- Do you do anything about it?
- Is what you have just said consistent with … [a previous action or comment]?

Other clarifying activities include: inviting students to rank-order alternatives or locate values on a continuum; posing provocative statements, problems, or issues for student discussion; and providing students time to reflect on issues. One classic values clarification activity is to create a personal coat of arms in which students symbolically represent and share their most cherished values. Students may be invited to publicly affirm and act on these values by displaying and explaining their personal coat of arms with their peers. This activity is described in detail in the feature "A Personal Coat of Arms."

VALUES ANALYSIS

Unlike the values clarification approach where the focus is on personally clarifying personal choices, the focus of values analysis is on critical examination of value assumptions and reasoning. This latter approach is based on students not always seeing the gaps or inadequacies in their thinking, resulting in discriminatory or prejudicial attitudes. The values clarification approach would find these values acceptable as long as students are consistent and willing to act on them. In contrast, values analysis holds that some values may be unreasonable and students should be helped to see the limitations of such positions. This is especially important with social or ethical values: those we hold towards others.

There are similarities between the values analysis and values clarification approaches. Both respect the importance of students making up their own minds after thoughtful consideration. The main difference is that the values analysis approach teaches students

A PERSONAL COAT OF ARMS

Creating a personal coat of arms to symbolically represent the values students hold dear is an activity that fits well with social studies units on knights and chivalry, First Nations peoples, patriotism and nationalism, cultural heritage, personal growth, and self-esteem.

- **Create context.** Introduce the project by drawing attention to historical and contemporary uses of coats of arms and heraldry (for example, First Nations, medieval and contemporary nobility, national flags, university and family crests). Explain that many citizens treat their national flag with great reverence because it is a symbol of their homeland. They may be outraged when people burn or damage the flag. Soldiers carry a flag into battle as a symbol of what they are fighting to protect. Desecrating a flag or other crest shows disrespect or scorn for the cherished values. Ask students to consider for a moment the values they would fight to promote or protect.

- **Identify values.** Depending on time available and student level, the crest may contain as few as one or two panels, but more usually between four and six panels, each representing a different value. An outline of a coat of arms (see example below) may be provided to students, either as a prototype for a poster-size design or the final copy. Typically, the teacher establishes the number of panels and the themes. Some common themes are:
    - most cherished family characteristic or event
    - most cherished ethnic/cultural characteristic or event
    - most cherished national characteristic or event
    - most cherished personal character trait(s)
    - most cherished character trait(s) sought in one's friends
    - most significant personal accomplishment(s) to date
    - personal motto or guiding principle
    - most significant personal aspiration(s)
    - most significant contribution(s) one could make to one's friends or family
    - most significant contribution(s) one could make to the world at large
    - what one would hope to be remembered by—one's epitaph.

    Selection of themes should be guided by the specific goals of the project. For example, if increased cross-cultural awareness is an objective, then cultural and national characteristics or events will be especially relevant.

- **Explore values.** Depending on the theme, students might be assigned one or more of the following tasks to explore thoughtfully what the values mean for them:
    - interview a relative about his or her family or ethnic background;
    - read about individuals who exhibit character traits the students admire;

- brainstorm with peers a list of character traits or life goals, and rank-order their priorities;
- think about what they would do if they had one year to live and were guaranteed success in whatever they attempted;
- discuss their strengths and ambitions with others who know them well.

- **Represent one's values.** Although words may be appropriate in some panels (for example, a personal motto), a coat of arms' impact lies in its symbolic representation. Depending on student level, simple drawings, photographs, or magazine illustrations may suffice. Alternatively, students might be asked to create a shield-sized poster.

    Regardless of size, the effect of this exercise is more powerful if students spend time exploring different types of symbols, including corporate logos (e.g., the Nike "swish" represents the wing of the goddess Victory, and victory in Italian is *nike*) and national flags and crests (e.g., the dramatic rising sun in the Imperial Japanese flag, and the olive branches of peace caressing the globe in the United Nations flag). It is especially valuable to point out the symbolism in designs (a dove symbolizes peace, lions symbolize courage). The significance of particular colours may also be explored (white symbolizes purity, red symbolizes life). Encourage students to create original or adapted representations rather than relying on well-established symbols. Some students may be embarrassed about their inability to draw. This can be mitigated by downplaying the artistic element (by not assigning marks for technical merit) and by allowing pictures, computer graphics, and even "commissioned renderings" by artists in the class.

- **Celebrate values.** Since a primary purpose of the project is to publicly affirm students' values, an opportunity to share and celebrate the coats of arms is important. (Students should not be required to participate if they do not wish to.) There are several ways to do this:
    - Each person explains his or her coat of arms to a small group, the whole class, or in a gallery walk.
    - The class might interpret the symbolism in each coat of arms and guess what it means before having creators explain them.
    - The coats of arms may be displayed in the classroom, hallway, or library.

    However the coats of arms are displayed, it is important that students feel safe about sharing their values and feel pride in their representations and the values they symbolize.

to think critically about their values, especially their ethical values. Ethical values are seen to be far less private a matter with the values analysis approach than is presumed by the values clarification approach.

The Association for Values Education and Research (AVER) at the University of British Columbia was a prominent advocate of the values analysis approach. Its work provides a structure to help teachers and students critically reflect on their values. The AVER approach (1978, 1991) is based on reconstructing three elements of the logic of value reasoning:

- **the value judgment:** a statement about what the person judges to be desirable or undesirable or what ought, or ought not, to be (for example, "School should be illegal");
- **the factual evidence to support the judgment:** a descriptive or factual statement of what actually is, was, or is likely to be, which is seen to be relevant to the judgment taken ("I have to work very hard in school"); and
- **the implied or underlying value principle:** the more general value position that the person has accepted implicitly by virtue of the factual reason offered ("Situations that force people to work very hard ought to be made illegal").

When students offer and defend a position on a value issue (for example, when and under what conditions it is right to tell a white lie, or whether Canada should accept more or fewer immigrants), their reasoning can be reconstructed using these elements into deductive arguments, consisting of a major premise (the implied value principle), a minor premise (the factual evidence), and a conclusion (the value judgment). For example, a student might offer the following judgment on the desirability of increased immigration quotas: "It's stupid for the Canadian government to increase immigration levels." When asked to provide factual evidence to support this conclusion, the student might respond: "The more new immigrants we accept, the fewer jobs for current residents." The implied value principle that the student must accept if the reasoning is valid is that "The Canadian government should not adopt policies that cause unemployment among Canadian residents." This reasoning can be summarized thus:

factual evidence	Increasing immigration quotas causes unemployment among Canadian residents.
implied value principle	The government should not adopt policies that cause unemployment among Canadian residents.
value judgment	Therefore, the government should not increase immigration quotas.

The point of reconstructing value reasoning in this way is to provide teachers with three points from which to help students think critically about their views. Students can be taught to query whether or not: (1) the factual evidence is true; (2) the implied value principle is acceptable; and (3) the value judgment follows from the principle and the evidence, especially when all of the reasons are considered.

The unique contribution of this approach is the challenges that students and teachers can apply to assess the acceptability of the implied value principle. University of British Columbia professor Jerrold Coombs (1980) has identified four ways to challenge our principles, though not all four will apply to every principle:

- **Consistency with other basic values.** An obvious test of the acceptability of an implied principle is whether or not it is consistent with more basic tenets in one's value system. It would not be justifiable to accept a principle that is inconsistent with one's fundamental values. For example, if I believe it wrong to discriminate against people on the basis of race, then I would be inconsistent in accepting the principle that white immigrants be given priority. Similarly, if I believe that the lives of people ought to be placed above money, it would be inconsistent to reject refugees whose lives were in danger merely in order to save tax dollars.
- **Consequences for everyone involved.** A second way to evaluate the acceptability of an implied principle is to assess its consequences for all people likely to be affected, especially those most significantly affected. Students should take on these others' perspectives and ask: "How would I feel if I were in their shoes? Would I judge the principle to be fair from their perspective?" If a student finds it unfair to accept the implied principle from someone else's position, this is a reason for finding the principle unacceptable. Even young children use this test when

ANALYZING VALUES ABOUT CANADA'S IMMIGRATION QUOTAS

1 **Identify and clarify the issue under discussion.** Students need to be precise about the nature of an issue. In this case, is the issue the criteria for selecting new immigrants or the size of annual quotas? Students also need to understand that Canada sets quotas for three classes of immigrants: (1) refugees who are fleeing political oppression or desperate conditions; (2) family immigrants who are applying to be reunited with their relatives; and (3) independent immigrants who have no political or family claims.

2 **Generate possible factual reasons.** Once an issue is clarified, students should consider the reasons, pro and con, for a position. It is important that the reasons be framed as factual or description statements (that is, what actually was, is, or is likely to happen). Students may list pro reasons in one column and con reasons in another, as illustrated below.

Issue: Should Canada increase its immigrant quotas for:
- refugees?
- family class immigrants?
- independent immigrants?

PRO	CON
• many immigrants may be in desperate economic need	• many Canadians may feel invaded by more immigrants
• many immigrants may need protection from war and political persecution	• many immigrants take advantage of the system
• increased immigration adds to the population size of Canada	• immigrants drain money away from other Canadians through increased need for social programs
• increased immigration results in enriched lives and lifestyle for many new immigrants	• increased immigration leads to overcrowding in some areas
• many immigrants bring talents and human resources that benefit Canada	• increased immigration drives down the minimum wage
• immigrants provide a pool of workers to fill low paid jobs that may otherwise go unfilled	• increased immigration discourages integration of ethnic groups into mainstream society
• increased immigration helps to unite separated families	• increased immigration fuels racial/ethnic tensions
• increased immigration adds to Canada's cultural diversity	• increased immigration leads to higher housing prices
	• increased immigration will lead to the European culture becoming a minority in Canada
	• increased immigration will lead to the white race becoming a minority in Canada

3 **Investigate the accuracy of the factual claims offered.** Students should be encouraged to resist accepting their factual reasons at face value. Students often have little evidence for their beliefs and consequently may hold beliefs that are inaccurate or only partly true. For example, the idea that increasing immigration drains money away from current residents is not accurate; one of the government's motives for increased immigration is to increase the consumer base for domestic industries and businesses. As well, Canada saves money if it accepts immigrants who have already been trained in essential services, such as medical doctors or computer analysts. After seeking evidence to support or denounce their suggested reasons, students should, where appropriate, modify or reject their ideas. In the immigration scenario, two claims that may be found to be clearly false are: independent immigrants drain money, and immigration of refugees leads to higher house prices.

4 **Test the acceptability of each implied principle.** With each reason that is thought to be fact, students should be helped to identify the implied value principle. For example, the argument that many Canadians feel invaded by increased immigration has an implied value principle along the lines of: "The government should not adopt policies that cause

Canadian residents to feel a sense of invasion." Students can then apply one or more of the principle tests to each of the implied values they identify. Principles found to be unacceptable should be modified or rejected. Three principle tests are useful in assessing the acceptability of the implied principle of not adopting policies that lead to a sense of invasion:

- *Consequences for everyone involved.* Students should put themselves in the position of someone whose parents cannot immigrate or someone who is in danger of being tortured in their home country if their refugee status is rejected because some Canadian residents feel invaded. Do students think the value principle is fair considering these peoples' predicaments? If not, then the principle should be modified or rejected.
- *Consequences in other relevant situations.* Students should think of a different government policy they support that people might find invasive, such as mandatory seat belts. Are students willing to give up on this policy because many Canadians resent it? If not, then they should not accept the value principle that immigration policies should be scrapped because people feel invaded.

- *Consequences for repeated instances.* Students should consider the consequences if every government policy were to be scrapped because of people feeling invaded. Would governments be able to act at all if this principle was accepted? There are few, if any, policies that do not threaten some group, including limits on gun control, smoke-free areas, and anti-discrimination laws. The consequence of the implied value principle, if accepted, might be that governments could never implement any policy.

5 **Weigh all remaining (valid) reasons.** After identifying unacceptable implied principles and eliminating unwarranted reasons, the next step is to assess the collective weight of the remaining reasons. This involves deciding the importance of the implied value principles underlying each one and the extent to which each position affects these values. For example, students must consider what is more important: a modest decline in economic well-being or the life-and-death protection given to political refugees.

6 **Present and defend a judgment on the issue.** Finally, students should determine their own stand on the issue. This may be a simple for-or-against position, but more often it will be a qualified stance. For example, students might decide that immigration quotas should be increased in some areas and decreased in other areas, or that quotas should be increased across the board, provided immigration fraud is reduced. Students are asked to demonstrate how their position is the stronger alternative and how it accommodates the valid concerns of the opposing perspective.

they ask, "How would you like it if I did that to you?"

- **Consequences in other relevant situations.** A third way to test an implied principle is to consider the consequences in other situations. If using the implied principle in other situations is undesirable, this is a reason for rejecting or modifying it. Consider, for example, the implied principle that it is always wrong to tell a lie. It would be appropriate to imagine situations where telling a lie might be justified. Suppose I were living in Nazi Germany during World War II. Would I consider it wrong to lie to soldiers who asked if there were any Jewish people living in my house? If I think I am justified in lying in this situation then I should modify my implied principle to something like, "It is wrong to lie unless it is to protect someone's life." It would then be useful to imagine situations that were not a matter of saving a life but in which I would still consider lying acceptable. The point of the test is to explore other situations to determine if the consequences of adopting the principle in these situations are acceptable. If not, then the principle needs to be modified or rejected.

- **Consequences for repeated instances.** A final way to test the acceptability of an implied principle is by supposing repeated instances of the act in question. If the consequences of repeated actions are unacceptable, then fairness dictates that it is never acceptable. For example, although it may be okay for one person to walk across the grass in a park or to throw a cigarette butt on the ground, the effect of everyone doing it is ruined grass or horrible litter. The philosopher Marcus Singer (1958, 162) refers to this as the generalization argument: "If the consequences of everyone's acting in a certain way would be undesirable, then no one has the right to act in that way without a reason or justification."

Each test needs to be explained to students, perhaps introduced one at a time. Students need to learn when a test is likely to be relevant, perhaps by having students apply a particular test to a list of supplied principles.[4] The feature "Analyzing Values about Canada's Immigration Quotas" outlines a six-step model for values analysis that illustrates how this approach can help students think more critically about their values.

Concluding Remarks

There is a need to teach students how to think critically about their values. Although there are multiple approaches to values education—classroom environment, direct experiences, and values clarification—ultimately teachers must encourage students to reflect critically on their values, especially on their social or ethical values—those pertaining to how others are to be treated.

I close this chapter on values education with a plea for two virtues: sensitivity and perseverance. Although we should be sensitive to our students in all that we do, there is particular need for caution when dealing with values. Not only are values rife with controversy, they are deeply tied to students' emotions. We have a special responsibility to enter into this domain with the greatest of sensitivity for our students.

The consequences of a failure in this regard were demonstrated to me on a visit to a high school in New York City. I had been invited to observe a lesson where an abbreviated version of the personal coat of arms activity was introduced. The teacher opened by sharing a personal coat of arms he had made. It was sketched in pencil on a regular sheet of paper and not readily visible to students. He explained the four panels on his coat of arms, and assigned students the task of developing their own, representing values relating to the following categories: their culture, favourite foods, favourite activities, and the epitaph they would like on their headstone. Their coats of arms were to be photo-copied so that he could hand them out. Students were given a few minutes to think about and sketch a symbol to represent each value. A male student asked if he could complete the activity at home, but he was told to finish it before the end of class. He then volunteered to come back after school to complete the assignment, where-upon the teacher suggested that if he just got down to work immediately he would be finished in no time. With fifteen minutes remaining in the period, the teacher randomly divided the class into groups of four. Students were to explain their coat of arms to the other three members of their group. I noticed one female student being ignored by the three male students in her group. She sat the entire time with her coat of arms in slightly outstretched arms, waiting to be invited by the others to explain her cherished values.

This values lesson was not handled sensitively. The young woman's self-esteem was damaged that day. The male student who wanted to take his coat of arms home to do a proper job learned that "getting it done" was the main thing. And the personal pride of everyone in the class was diminished by having their values treated in such a slapdash fashion and trivialized by such banal questions.

And now a point about perseverance. In talking about the slow pace of significant educational change, Ralph Tyler likens teachers' efforts to the effect of drip-ping water upon a stone: "In a day or week or a month there is no appreciable change in the stone, but over a period of years definite erosion is noted. Correspond-ingly, by the accumulation of educational experiences profound changes are brought about in the learner" (1969, 83). Nurturing personal and social values requires incremental, collective effort—no one teacher can do it quickly or on her own. Each of us is responsible for doing our small part to promote values that will guide students in thinking and acting as responsible human beings.[5]

Arguably, there is no goal more important than this for social studies educators.

Think about one of your five most important values. Make a list of possible activities or resources that you might use to nurture this value, considering all three approaches described in this chapter: creating reinforcing environments, facilitating direct experiences, and promoting thoughtful deliberation.

ENDNOTES

1   Alfie Kohn (1997) draws attention to the fundamental ambi-guity in the term "character education." Character-building in the broad sense refers to any attempt to help children develop desired traits. In the narrow sense, it refers to promoting work ethic and other socially conservative values through exhortations, extrinsic rewards, and other forms of moral training.

2   Lessons can be found in Abbott, Case, and Nicol (2003) and online in the Critical Challenges collection at www.tc2.ca/cmsms/index.php?page=critical-challenges.

3   The Eporuvian role play was developed by Anne Hill, an elementary teacher in Terrace, British Columbia.

4   Teaching activities for introducing principle-testing are described more fully in the Association for Values Education and Research (AVER) teaching materials (1978, 1991).

5   To learn more about nurturing social responsibility with young students, view the detailed lesson plan, "Sample Primary Lesson: Passing Along Kindness" available for downloading at Pacific Educational Press's web page for *The Anthology of Social Studies*: www.pacificedpress.ca/?p=2687.

REFERENCES

Abbott, M., R. Case, and J. Nicol. 2003. *I can make a difference.* Vancouver, BC: The Critical Thinking Consortium.

Alberta Education. 2005. *Social studies—Kindergarten to grade 12.* Edmonton, AB: Author. Available online at education. alberta.ca/teachers/program/socialstudies/programs.aspx.

Ashford, M.-W. 1995. Youth actions for the planet. In *Thinking globally about social studies education*, ed. R. Fowler and I. Wright, 75–90. Vancouver: Research and Development in Global Studies, University of British Columbia.

Association for Values Education and Research. 1978. *Prejudice.* Toronto: OISE Press.

———. 1991. *Peace: In pursuit of security, prosperity, and social justice.* Toronto: OISE Press.

Browne, A. 2008. *Piggybook.* London: Walker Books.

Burrett, K. and T. Rusnak. 1993. *Integrated character education.* (Fastback #351). Bloomington, IN: Phi Delta Kappa Educational Foundation.

Cassidy, W. 1994. An examination of caring and compassion in social studies education. Unpublished paper, Simon Fraser University, Burnaby, British Columbia, May.

Coombs, J.R. 1980. Validating moral judgments by principle testing. In *Practical dimensions of moral education*, ed. D. Cochrane and M. Manley-Casimir, 30–55. New York: Praeger.

Duke, D.L. 1978. Looking at the school as a rule-governed organization. *Journal of Research and Development in Education* 11 (4): 116–126.

Glaze, A.E., B. Hogarth, and B. McLean, eds. 2003. Can schools create citizens?: An exploration of character and citizenship education in Canadian, US and UK schools (special theme issue). *Orbit* 33 (2).

Kohn, A. 1997. How not to teach values: A critical look at character education. *Phi Delta Kappan* 78 (6). Available online at www.alfiekohn.org/articles.htm#education.

Leming, J.S. 1991. Teacher characteristics and social education. In *Handbook on research on social studies teaching and learning*, ed. J. Shaver, 222–236. New York: Macmillan.

Ontario Ministry of Education. 2004. *The Ontario curriculum—Social studies grades 1–6—History and geography grades 7 and 8* (revised). Toronto: Queen's Printer. Available online at www.edu.gov.on.ca/eng/curriculum/elementary/sstudies.html.

Osborne, K. 1982. Civics, citizenship and politics: Political education in the schools. *Teacher Education* 20, 58–72.

Patrick, J.J. and J.D. Hoge. 1991. Teaching government, civics and law. In *Handbook on research on social studies teaching and learning*, ed. J. Shaver, 427–436. New York: Macmillan.

Peters, W. 1970. *The eye of the storm*. ABC News.

———. 1985. *A class divided*. PBS DVD video.

Raths, L.E., M. Harmin, and S.B. Simon. 1966. *Values and teaching: Working with values in the classroom*. Columbus, OH: Merrill.

Singer, M.G. 1958. Moral rules and principles. In *Essays in moral philosophy*, ed. A.I. Meldon, 160–197. Seattle: University of Washington Press.

Stewart, S. 2007. *The Gardener*. New York: Square Fish (Macmillan).

Torney-Purta, J. 1983. Psychological perspectives on enhancing civic education through the education of teachers. *Journal of Teacher Education* 34: 3–34.

Tyler, R. 1969. *Basic principles of curriculum and instruction*. Chicago: University of Chicago Press.

Upjohn, R. 2007. *Lily and the Paper Man*. Toronto: Second Story Press.

21

Enriched by Teaching Aboriginal Content

Lynn Newbery, Cathy Morgan, and Christine Eide

What We Learned

We are three West Coast educators whose combined teaching experience represents about eighty years in the classroom as elementary and secondary teachers and as faculty associates at Simon Fraser University working with student teachers. We are not aboriginal; however, we arrived at places in our teaching careers where we became passionately committed to seeking out aboriginal content and incorporating it into our curricula. We share some of our stories, called "Beginnings" here.

BEGINNINGS 1: LYNN

I was fortunate. As a young teacher, I learned three valuable lessons: the importance of confronting racism and stereotyping, how to infuse the curriculum with aboriginal content, and that there were rewards to becoming a co-learner with my students. This is how it happened.

In the mid-sixties I moved to a British Columbia coastal community from Toronto, where I had taught social studies and English for four years. A teacher shortage in the community of Alert Bay led to my agreeing to teach half days. The assignment included grade 7 social studies—Canadian history, beginning with the explorers. A few days before school started, I was given a textbook that seemed ancient. I knew my class contained about 60 per cent aboriginal students. I was also aware of problems of racism that existed in this small but vibrant fishing community. As I examined the textbook, I was dismayed to find words like "savage" and "uncivilized" used to describe Native people. My impulse was to hide the book, because I was afraid that I could not protect my Native students if other students chose to use this language to make fun of them. My alternative plan for social studies was to focus the year's work on traditional ways of life on the coast. I was ignorant of First Nations culture or history (I realized how deficient my education, which included a degree in modern history from the University of Toronto, had been), any

sense of what I could or should do, or how to go about it. This was probably a good thing. In my naive state, I saw no barriers.

And so began a year of exciting learning for us. We were all teachers and we were all learners. I plunged into reading each night from books I gathered; the students brought their learning and knowledge from home. Together, we shared a rich experience. The non-Native students joined in the project, working with their Native friends and researching in the library. We ended the year by travelling in a fishing boat to the mouth of a river where the students engaged in a "dig" in an old abandoned village midden. It was a year that changed me as a teacher.

I discovered that it was a positive experience to become a co-learner with my students and explore with them the tasks of seeking resources and organizing and sharing knowledge. I learned about First Nations culture on the coast, which was reviving after a hundred years of repression. I began to learn about the history of First Nations because this community had been subjected to the brutal application of the anti-potlatch laws enacted by the Canadian government. I learned that with my increased knowledge I could infuse provincial curriculum with aboriginal content. Since then I have learned that all subjects can be infused with aboriginal content. I also learned that I didn't need to hide biased textbooks but that I could use them to help students deal with racism and stereotyping.

STARTING POINTS FOR CONFRONTING RACISM

Teach the concepts

- Work on the vocabulary: bias, opinion, viewpoint, prejudice, discrimination, stereotyping, racism. (See chapter 8 in this volume for suggestions on how to introduce these concepts.) Discuss prejudices students have encountered as young people ("you are too young"), as males or females, or as members of ethnic and religious groups.
- Expose older students to the use and inadequacy of the common stereotypical references to Native peoples—"noble savage," "silent hunter," "drunken Indian." For an exposé of Native stereotypes in Canadian culture, read *The Imaginary Indian* by Daniel Francis (1992).

Promote awareness of the problems

- Collect pictures that show people of various ages, gender, and ethnicity. Number each picture and post them around the classroom. Distribute a questionnaire containing questions about people in various contexts, for example, "If you were lost in a strange city, which person would you feel most comfortable approaching for help?" Ask students to respond to each question by selecting one of the numbered pictures. Use students' answers to explore stereotypical assumptions and to discuss the problems of systemic discrimination.
- Pose problems that touch upon discrimination. Ask students, for example, to imagine they live in a lovely three-bedroom house but the family is being transferred for a year and the house must be rented. Who will they rent it to? Create applications from a variety of people (for example, three nurses who work in the local hospital; two East Indian male university students; a First Nations family—the dad works for the hydro company and the mom looks after three young children; a Caucasian bank executive whose wife is a social worker with no children). Distribute the applications to groups of students for review. Each group is to select the applicant to whom they would rent the house. Debrief by having a student from each group explain the reasons for their choice and for their reservations about the other applicants.
- Look at First Nations names used for cars and sports teams (for example, Braves, Pontiac, Chieftains, Cadillac) and the use of the "tomahawk chop" by sports fans.
- Examine your textbook for examples of bias or stereotyping.

Provide powerful role models

- Arrange for older students to watch movies that offer powerful portrayals of aboriginal perspectives. Notable examples include *Whale Rider* (New Zealand), *Rabbit-Proof Fence* (Australia), *Atanarjuat* (Canadian), *Powwow Highway* (American with Canadian actor Gary Farmer), and *Smoke Signals* (produced completely by aboriginal people and featuring two Canadian actors in the lead roles).
- Introduce students to aboriginal role models. Most aboriginal groups have produced excellent poster series featuring actors (Adam Beach, Gary Farmer), writers (Thomas King, Eden Robinson, Tomson Highway), doctors, judges, musicians, lawyers, prominent educators, and politicians who have achieved national prominence. Historical figures to introduce include Tom Longboat, Alwyn Morris, Lady Amelia Douglas, Pauline Johnson, and Joseph Brant.
- Watch the National Aboriginal Achievement Awards each spring on CBC television.

We share the lessons we learned. We learned to handle racism and stereotyping, to infuse the provincial curriculum with aboriginal content, to become co-learners with our students, and to discover and appreciate the richness of local sites for learning, and the magic of traditional stories. We share the ways in which we have changed. Underlying our work is the belief that our students have achieved a fuller understanding of the Canadian story, a broader knowledge and understanding of aboriginal experiences and cultures, and a deeper connection to our land. We direct our stories and learning to non-Native teachers who have not travelled this road in the hope that our experiences will encourage you to discover and share with your students the richness of teaching aboriginal content.

Confront Racism, Bias, and Stereotyping

Students are exposed to bias against aboriginal people in print, music, and film, and in real day-to-day situations. We can help them identify, name, and combat this by introducing them to the concepts of racism, bias, and stereotyping; by building awareness and understanding of these problems; and by providing positive role models. I have outlined some ideas about how to accomplish these goals in the featured text above. Many more ideas can be found in a number of professional resources (see, for example, British Columbia Ministry of Education 1998, 2000; Manitoba Education and Youth 2003; McCue and Associates 2000a, 2000b; Sawyer and Green 1990; Sawyer and Lundeberg 1993; Sawyer and Napoleon 1991).

Become a Co-learner with Students

The Canadian history we learned in high schools and universities often omitted aboriginal peoples. As noted by the Royal Commission on Aboriginal Peoples, "From the Commission's first days, we have been reminded repeatedly of the limited understanding of aboriginal issues among non-aboriginal Canadians and of the obstacles this presents to achieving reconciliation and a new relationship" (1996, volume 5, 92). Yet we live with this story today even if we do not know the story. A Gitxsan elder, Marie Wilson, talked about being surrounded by her ancestors whenever she spoke. The Gitxsan have a saying, "We walk on the breath of our grandfathers." The past is alive around us and even though people may not know the events of history, they live with the attitudes and emotions and consequences engendered by past events.

My appreciation for the experiences of aboriginal peoples in this country has grown as I learned about the Indian Act, the denial of the right to vote for aboriginals in the late nineteenth century, the return of the right to vote in the late 1950s and early 1960s, the fight for aboriginal fishing rights, the denial of language and culture (especially as acted out in residential schools), and the loss of the land. Blaming people for their difficulties is easy to do. Understanding the causes of the difficulties requires learning on our part. Many excellent resources on aboriginal history and culture are available for educators and students wishing to learn more (for example, Campbell et al. 2003; Carlson 1997; Kainai Board of Education et al. 2004, 2005a, 2005b; Manitoba Education and Youth 2003).

I invite all of us to leave behind any need to be "the classroom expert" for our students and, instead, acknowledge that we too are constantly learning about aboriginal peoples. The key is to participate in this shared inquiry with enthusiasm, respect, and commitment. The Nova Scotia teachers' guide for the Mi'kmaq history and culture course expresses this well:

> [T]he nature of instructional leadership provided by non-Native teachers will necessarily be different. They will actively share in the learning process with their students. In their attitudes and behaviours they will demonstrate their interest in the history of the Mi'kmaq people, their respect for Mi'kmaq culture and spirituality, and their commitment to open-minded dialogue between the inheritors of different cultures. (cited in Pohl, 2003)

Identify various outcomes or topics in the social studies curriculum for your grade level that provide opportunities to incorporate aboriginal history, culture, and issues. In each case, briefly describe how this might be done in a way that increases understanding both of the curricular topic and of aboriginal people.

Infuse Aboriginal Content

The goal of building understanding and admiration for the resilience of aboriginal peoples everywhere in Canada will not be advanced simply by creating a designated course or unit. We should look for opportunities to infuse aboriginal points of view and issues throughout the social studies curriculum and beyond. Suggestions for integrating aboriginal discussions into the study of traditional topics in social studies, current events, and other curricular subjects are found in the featured text on page 244.

Access Resources: Materials and People

There are many excellent resources developed by aboriginal educators, writers, artists, and filmmakers. This list identifies some of them.

- The seven-video series *First Nations: The Circle Unbroken* (National Film Board) is an excellent resource covering a range of important topics. It is designed for high school students and contains lesson ideas. Historical footage of aboriginal people in traditional settings can be found on the National Film Board website at www.nfb.ca (go to "Educational Resources" and click on "Documentary Lens").
- Curriculum materials developed by school districts and government agencies. Lists of materials can be obtained by contacting almost any school district or provincial ministry of education.
- The Royal Commission on Aboriginal Peoples is available online at www.ainc-inac.gc.ca/ch/rcap/sg/sgmm_e.html.
- Contact Indian and Northern Affairs Canada to locate teaching resources. There is a separate listing for each province in the blue pages. Or call Info Canada, 1-888-O-Canada (622-6232) or go to www.ainc-inac.gc.ca.
- Contact your local friendship centre. Publications by the Ministry of Indian Affairs and Northern

BEGINNINGS 2: CATHY

I arrived in a small northern community in 1971 to teach primary grades, without much background knowledge about the isolated rural area. As a member of the dominant culture, it never occurred to me while I attended public school in the 1950s and '60s that aboriginal people were not represented in the curriculum (except in stereotypical ways such as "Ii" for Indian and "Ee" for Eskimo on the alphabet chart).

I wanted to know more about the local Gitxsan culture in my area, but it was not a topic discussed by the parents of the children in my classroom. I sought books about the local community to familiarize myself with the stories and history of local First Nations groups. I began to make posters and big books that incorporated First Nations material in pattern books such as Bill Martin's *Brown Bear, Brown Bear, What Do You See?* which I adapted to *Eagle, Eagle, What Do You See?* I began to involve children in writing captions for their own stories rather than read from readers that depicted an urban circus story in which all the faces in the crowd were white.

In those early stages, I tried to adapt materials myself without consulting the Native community. Now I seek resources that have been locally developed or approved by Elders or by First Nations Education Committees. I try to find an aboriginal resource person to bring into the class. I recall a quote about the importance of sharing the community's history with my students: "Without history, a society shares no common memory of where it has been, of what its core values are, or of what decisions of the past account for present circumstances" (National Centre for History in the Schools, cited in Bredekamp and Rosegrant 1995, 116).

I understand that history began here long before Europeans arrived so I take my students to visit the First Nations historic sites in the community. I am learning to build lessons that connect students to these sites and to the traditional stories of their aboriginal ancestors. After visiting a local site, students simulated a midden dig in the classroom to think critically about how the various animal bones may have been used in the diet of the original inhabitants of the site. We learned about the prevalence of rabbit bones and understood why some aboriginal inhabitants were called "People of the Rabbit." Building my knowledge of First Nations history and cultures has taken some work, but I learned that I did not have to invent everything and that many resources were available.

I learned to handle my fear of being "politically incorrect." This concern can be simply illustrated by considering the confusion that arises over nomenclature. What terms should be used? What are the distinctions between "First Nations," "indigenous peoples," "aboriginal," "Native," and "Indian"? When considering a specific group of people should we speak of a house, a clan, a tribe, or a nation? And then there are the proper names of specific groups. Many of those names have changed in the last twenty years as First Nations have reclaimed their traditional names. The language groups can also cause confusion. For example, the Gitxsan (formerly spelled Gitksan) language is part of the Tsimshian language group but the Gitxsan cannot be called Tsimshian since that name applies to the First Nation that lives in another area of the West Coast.

It takes a bit of effort to learn the proper terms. I accepted that I was a learner and that I will make mistakes. As I learned, my knowledge deepened. As my knowledge increased, the danger of being trivial lessened. I learned to seek out the human resources living in nearby communities, to seek out the conferences that offered First Nations presenters and themes, and to have the confidence to ask questions. I am also learning to hear quieter voices, to listen before speaking, and to seek the wisdom of the Elders. My classroom was enriched with new learning, new resources, and new strategies, and my classroom became a better place to be.

Development provide contact information for hundreds of aboriginal cultural centres and friendship centres across Canada (McCue and Associates 2000a, 54–67; 2000b, 60–73). Use the yellow pages in the phone book and check listings under "aboriginal."

- Use the internet to find resources. Some useful sites include:
  - Aboriginal Rights Coalition of BC at arcbc.tripod.com
  - Links to aboriginal resources at www.bloorstreet.com/300block/aborl.htm
  - BC Archives at www.bcarchives.gov.bc.ca/index.htm
  - Aboriginal Resources and Services of the Library and Archives of Canada at www.collectionscanada.ca/Aboriginal/index_e.html
- Visit your public library and your school library. You might be surprised at the collections there.
- Speak to someone at your local community college or university to locate human resources. First Nations courses are increasingly available across the country.
- Tune into the Aboriginal Peoples Television Network (APTN).
- Visit the reserve or friendship centre closest to your school on June 21, National Aboriginal Day.
- Make connections with educators, historians,

INTEGRATING ABORIGINAL CONTENT

Embed into traditional social studies topics

There are many opportunities to infuse aboriginal content into the topics normally addressed in social studies. Below are a few examples:

- **War of 1812.** The War of 1812 provides an opportunity to explore the concept of great leaders by studying the visions, activities, successes, and failures of three prominent aboriginal leaders of the time—Joseph Brant, Tecumseh, and Pontiac.
- **Confederation.** This classic event in Canadian history is often studied from French and English perspectives and from the colonial points of view. It would be interesting to explore Métis and First Nations reactions.
- **Human rights.** International instances of human rights abuse can be supplemented with examples of the Canadian government's treatment of aboriginal peoples (for example, the removal of the right to vote, and to meet to discuss land claims, to hire lawyers, or to raise monies to pursue land claims; and the setting up of residential schools for Native children and banning these children from speaking their own languages).
- **Forts and military.** Elementary students enjoy the study of forts, weapons, and knights. First Nations had forts, weapons, armour, rigorous warrior training, and systems of defence and battle tactics.

Infuse aboriginal concerns into current event discussions

Aboriginal perspectives can enrich the study of current events as suggested by the following examples:

- **Catastrophic diseases.** Germ warfare and smallpox epidemics were not new in the twentieth century. Aboriginal peoples suffered the ravages of disease after contact with Europeans. Smallpox epidemics in British Columbia in 1862 reduced the population of Haida Gwaii from about ten thousand to five hundred in a very short period of time. Germ warfare was first used in North America by General Amherst in 1763 when he distributed smallpox-infected blankets to the Mi'kmaq.
- **Repatriation of cultural treasures.** The plundering of cultural artifacts by the Nazis, the destruction of antiquities by the Taliban, and the looting of museums in Iraq can be connected to the experiences of First Nations peoples whose art and bones linger on in many museums and private collections around the world, or whose totems and masks were destroyed in huge bonfires in British Columbia. Recently the Field Museum in Chicago returned the bones of 150 Haida to Haida Gwaii.
- **Arranged marriages.** First Nations had marriages arranged for controlling property rights and status, and as a method of selecting and training chiefs.

Integrate with other subjects

Aboriginal content can be integrated with other subject areas. The following ideas are drawn from *Shared Learnings* (British Columbia Ministry of Education 1998):

- **Physical education.** Invite elementary students to research and learn a traditional aboriginal game or dance to teach to the class.
- **Science.** Investigate traditional uses of plants by aboriginal peoples, traditional ceremonies for honouring the animals and conservation practices, and stories that teach children how to respect plants and animals. Instead of studying simple machines in the context of pyramid-building in ancient Egypt, focus on West Coast First Nations practices that allowed them to raise huge cedar beams for building their large communal houses.
- **Mathematics.** Graph aboriginal information. For example, bar graphs can be used to illustrate the population of aboriginal peoples in each province and territory.
- **Health.** Discuss with students the ideas of balance and symmetry, and their importance in aboriginal life (that is, for a healthy life, the mind, body, and spirit must be in balance). Explore the implications of these qualities for students' own well-being.

---

traditional teachers, and chiefs on the nearest reserve. These people are valuable resources who can help secure guests for your classroom, suggest learning resources, and answer questions about protocols.

Explore Local Sites

No matter where you live in Canada, you are living on someone's traditional territory. The sites are beneath your feet and local aboriginal people can tell you about them. In many places the rocks themselves explicitly point to stories. Here are some points of interest, to name just a few:

- mysterious stone faces at the end of the Baie Verte Peninsula, Newfoundland;
- hundreds of petroglyphs at Bella Coola, British Columbia;
- petroglyphs outside Peterborough, Ontario;
- Dreamer's Rock, Manitoulin Island, Ontario, where visions were sought;
- Siwash Rock in Vancouver, British Columbia.

Sometimes these sites are in the news because of government decisions with regard to the land. Students can discuss the ethics of turning burial grounds into garbage dumps, paving them over for parking lots, or making golf courses over them (an issue in the Oka Crisis in 1990). Teachers have used government decisions to increase sensitivity in students to First Nations concerns and at the same time to practise critical thinking skills and debating techniques.

Teach Local Aboriginal History

The land where we live had ten thousand years of stories embedded in the rocks prior to the arrival of Europeans and a few hundred years of stories since. Until we appreciate what the land means to aboriginal peoples, we will not be able to comprehend the issues surrounding land claims. We should make an effort to seek out the stories of the land where we live. We can learn the stories that are told on the totem poles and in the traditional and the more recent stories. Even something as simple as learning the local aboriginal place names can enrich our knowledge of where we live. Even where the land is paved over, as it is in our major cities, the stories still exist. Finding them can build a sense of belonging and commitment to the land for all students. Imagine being in Wanuskewin Heritage Park in Saskatoon and thinking about the thousands of years that the nomadic tribes of the plains gathered there. Several pre-contact sites have been identified in this place whose Cree name is loosely translated as "living in harmony." People who are aware of the events and stories of the place they are in find their experiences are enriched by their knowledge.

As teachers, we can help our students experience this rich connection to the land. We can do this by seeking the local history of an area. I have learned to ask the following questions wherever I am:

- Who were the original people who lived here? Do their descendents still make it their home today?
- How can we learn about the culture of the local aboriginal people?
- What are the aboriginal names for places here and what do the names mean?
- What stories and oral histories are part of the local aboriginal people's culture?
- Where can we obtain information regarding the history and the stories of this place?
- Who might be able to share these with us and what is the protocol in using this information with our students?
- How can we have all of our students share in this local knowledge?

- What pictures can I find of this area in local, provincial, and national archives?

Teach Aboriginal Stories

Traditional stories are a fundamental part of aboriginal cultures. As Thomas King wrote, "The truth about stories is that that's all we are" (2003, 2). They are the truth on which cultures are built and land is claimed. The stories contain everything of importance—who the people are, how they came to be, how they obtained their crests and territories, what the events of their histories and everyday lives were, what the lessons are that they want to teach their young. Title to land is invested in the stories that are sung and told. Until we try to appreciate the stories, we will never understand land claims. This point is illustrated by the following incident:

> One of the Gitxsan elders asked government officials at a land claims meeting, "If this is your land where are your stories?" He spoke in English, but then he moved into Gitxsan and told a story. All of a sudden everyone understood... how stories give meaning and value to the places we call home; how they bring us close to the world we live in by taking us into a world of words; how they hold us together and at the same time keep us apart." (Chamberlin 2004, 1)

THE ROAD LESS TRAVELLED

I have learned much from aboriginal teaching stories. One example in our area is the story "The Mountain Goats of Temlaham." In this story, young boys are mistreating a young goat. They pay no attention to the voices of their Elders warning them that the whole community will suffer from their lack of respect to the kid. The kid is rescued by one boy who defies the rest. The mountain goat people then invite the boys' people to a feast up on the mountain. When everyone is there feasting, the mountain shakes and tumbles and the people are killed except for the one exceptional boy who had saved the kid that was being mistreated. The mountain that rumbled and fell is now called Roche des Boules: "mountain of the tumbling rocks"—and every once in a while, even today, we hear the rockfalls. It reminds us of the need to be respectful of nature. The equality of all life—human, animal, and plant—is clear and all life is to be respected and treated well.

Cartoon by Erica Ball. Courtesy of the artist.

There are a number of ways to help students appreciate and understand traditional aboriginal stories:

- Expose students to a large selection of the stories, including many local ones. A Ministry of Indian Affairs and Northern Development (2000) publication lists a wide selection of children's literature about aboriginal peoples. Collections of traditional stories can be found at www.hanksville.org/storytellers/alfa.html.
- Provide models for the class of the various types of stories: creation stories, humorous stories, everyday stories, teaching stories, trickster stories, transformation stories, and stories containing the oral histories.
- Form literature circles in which four to five students can share a story they have read and analyze it as to type, purpose, what it reveals about values and beliefs, and about aboriginal world view.
- Ask students to choose the story they like best as a group and present it to the class using the oral traditions.

Conclusions

The three of us were fortunate that our lives took us into areas where First Nations cultures were strong. Most teachers do not have this opportunity, but our experiences have led us to believe that important benefits are available to all Canadian teachers who make an effort to learn about and include aboriginal content wherever we teach to whomever we teach. However, as the cartoon implies, this is unlikely to happen if we remain on the narrow, mainstream culture road.

Some of us began our journey taking very small steps—a lesson here or there, perhaps a guest speaker, perhaps a craft or art approach. Eventually we graduated to integrated units in social studies and language arts. Others of us plunged in, planning an entire year with an aboriginal emphasis. Regardless of where we began, we have arrived at the same place—committed to incorporating aboriginal content into the mainstream of our teaching. It has been a wonderfully enriching journey. We invite the reader also to choose this less-travelled road and find the richness there.

REFERENCES

Bredekamp, S., and T. Rosegrant, eds. 1995. *Reaching potentials: Transforming early childhood curriculum and assessment*, vol. 2. Washington, DC: National Association for the Education of Young Children.

British Columbia Ministry of Education. 1998. *Shared learnings: Integrating BC aboriginal content K–10*. Victoria: Author.

———. 2000. *BC First Nations studies 12: Integrated resource package 2000*. Victoria: Author. Available online at www.bced.gov.bc.ca/irp/irp_ss.htm.

Campbell, K., C. Menzies, and B. Peacock. 2003. *BC First Nations Studies*. Victoria: British Columbia Ministry of Education.

Carlson C.T., ed. 1997. *You are asked to witness: The Sto:lo in Canada's Pacific coast history*. Chilliwack, BC: The Sto:lo Heritage Trust.

Chamberlin, J.E. 2004. *If this is your land, where are your stories? Finding common ground*. Mississauga, ON: Knopf Canada.

Francis, D. 1992. *The imaginary Indian: The image of the Indian in Canadian culture*. Vancouver: Arsenal Pulp.

Kainai Board of Education et al. 2004. *Aboriginal perspectives (Aboriginal Studies 10)*. Edmonton: Duval House.

———. 2005a. *Aboriginal perspectives (Aboriginal Studies 20)*. Edmonton: Duval House.

———. 2005b. *Aboriginal perspectives (Aboriginal Studies 30)*. Edmonton: Duval House.

King, T. 2003. *The truth about stories*. Toronto: House of Anansi Press.

Manitoba Education and Youth. 2003. *Integrating aboriginal perspectives into curricula*. Winnipeg: Author. Available online at www.edu.gov.mb.ca?ks4/docs/policy/abpersp/index.htm.

McCue, H. and Associates. 2000a. *The learning circle: Classroom activities on First Nations in Canada (ages 8 to 11)*. Ottawa: Ministry of Indian Affairs and Northern Development.

———. 2000b. *The learning circle: Classroom activities on First Nations in Canada (ages 12 to 14)*. Ottawa: Ministry of Indian Affairs and Northern Development.

Ministry of Indian Affairs and Northern Development. 2000. *An aboriginal book list for children*. Ottawa: Author.

Pohl, A. 2003. Handling aboriginal curriculum studies appropriately. Coalition for the Advancement of Aboriginal Studies, Faculty of Education, York University, Toronto. Available online at www.edu.yorku.ca:8080/~caas/AbStudies.html.

Royal Commission on Aboriginal Peoples. 1996. *Final report of the Royal Commission on Aboriginal Peoples*. 5 vols. Ottawa: Queen's Printer. Available online at www.ainc-inac.gc.ca/ch/rcap/sg/sgmm_e.html.

Sawyer, D. and H. Green. 1990. *The NESA activities handbook for Native and multicultural classrooms*, vol. 1. Vancouver: Tillacum Library.

Sawyer, D. and W. Lundeberg. 1993. *The NESA activities handbook for Native and multicultural classrooms*, vol. 3. Vancouver: Tillacum Library.

Sawyer, D. and A. Napoleon. 1991. *The NESA activities handbook for Native and multicultural classrooms*, vol. 2. Vancouver: Tillacum Library.

SUPPLEMENTARY RESOURCES

Aboriginal Perspectives: A Guide to the Teacher's Toolkit is a collection of resources designed to help Ontario educators bring aboriginal perspectives into the classroom. Based on the 2007 Ontario curriculum, the collection includes resources for educators at both the elementary and secondary levels. Available online at www.edu.gov.on.ca/eng/aboriginal/toolkit.html.

The Association of Book Publishers of British Columbia publishes an annual catalogue, *Canadian Aboriginal Books for Schools*, selected and evaluated by teacher-librarians. Appropriate grade levels and curriculum correlations are indicated. Available online at www.books.bc.ca/resources/for-teachers-librarians.

The Toronto District School Board publishes *Aboriginal Voices in the Curriculum: A Guide to Teaching Aboriginal Studies in K–8 Classrooms*. Available online at www.r4r.ca/en/resource/aboriginal-voices-in-the-curriculum.

The *BC First Nations Studies Teacher's Guide* contains a comprehensive bibliography of books, articles, journals, and multimedia resources by and about aboriginal people in Canada, many of which are appropriate for upper elementary students. Available online at www.bced.gov.bc.ca/irp/resdocs/bcfns.htm.

Pearson Canada publishes Turtle Island Voices, a series of Canadian books celebrating aboriginal life, culture, and heritage. Series information is available online at www.pearsoncanadaschool.com/index.cfm?locator=PS16Cj.

Fitzhenry and Whiteside publishes a ten-book series, The Land Is Our Storybook, which highlights the languages and cultures of the Northwest Territories. Titles include: *We Feel Good Out Here* by J.-A. André and M. Willett (2008) and *Proud to Be Inuvialuit: Quviahuktunga Inuvialuugama* by J. Pokiak and M. Willett (2010). Order online at http://fitzhenry.ca/.

Fifth House Publishers' Keepers series is available through Fitzhenry and Whiteside. Titles include *Keepers of the Night: Native Stories and Nocturnal Activities for Children*; *Keepers of Life: Discovering Plants Through Native Stories and Earth Activities for Children*; *Keepers of the Animals: Native Stories and Wildlife Activities for Children*; *Keepers of the Earth: Native Stories and Environmental Activities for Children*; and *The Native Stories from Keepers of Life*. Teacher guides are available for some titles. Order online at www.fitzhenry.ca.

22 Infusing Global and Multicultural Perspectives in Elementary Social Studies

Roland Case, Özlem Sensoy, and Michael Ling

Much has been written about the importance of helping students understand the multicultural, globally connected world in which they live. Responding to this challenge should not, we believe, focus on teaching facts about various cultures and countries. Rather, the goal is better served by helping students view the world—and the events and people within it—in new ways. As Louis Perinbaum (1989, 25) observes, global education is a way of looking at the world more than it is the accumulation of information. The same can be said for multicultural education. In other words, the educational goal is to develop multicultural and global perspectives.

Before explaining what we mean by multicultural and global perspectives, we need to clarify the difference between global education and multicultural education. These terms overlap to a great extent, however multicultural education can be viewed as a subset of global education. The cultural dimensions of our global reality are one aspect—albeit a crucial one—of a wider set of political, economic, and social dimensions. Multiculturalism cannot be separated from its global connections, even in a country like Canada where it is a part of national identity. Events such as the "war on terror," trade relations with China or the United States, and outsourcing of jobs to India all have impact on cultural relations within Canada. The difference between multiculturalism and globalism then is largely a matter of emphasis: the "content" of multicultural education is the national and international contexts of culture and cultural relations, whereas global education attends to a broader set of topics that include global development and trade, human rights, the environment, and culture.

What Is a Global/Multicultural Perspective?

A perspective implies a "point of view"—a vantage point from which observations occur, and an "object" of attention—an event, thing, person, place, or state of affairs. Thus an economic perspective (the point of view) considers the financial costs and benefits of a proposed action (the object). Similarly, an ethical perspective looks at the morality of an action. A global/multicultural perspective refers to a point of view or set of lenses for viewing people, places, and things around the world. Like other perspectives, it consists of two dimensions—the object of focus, the substance, or the **substantive dimension**, and the point of view or **perceptual dimension**.

- The "substance" or **substantive dimension** of a global/multicultural perspective is the world events, states of affairs, places, and things that global and multicultural educators want students to understand. This dimension is concerned with fostering knowledge about the people, beliefs, and customs beyond students' own cultural group and country, and knowledge of events, places, and issues beyond the local and immediate.
- The "point of view" or **perceptual dimension** of a global/multicultural perspective is the habits of mind, values, or attitudes that we want students to possess as they perceive the world and the plurality of cultures within it. This dimension, reflected in descriptors such as narrow or broad, ethnocentric or cosmopolitan, and insular or far-reaching, describes

a mindset or outlook. Nurturing this dimension requires developing the capacity to see the "whole picture" of the local and international world in its complexity and diversity.

Before elaborating on these two dimensions, let us consider why we should care about nurturing global/multicultural perspectives in our students.

Why Adopt a Global/Multicultural Perspective?

The aim of promoting global/multicultural perspectives is to expand and enrich students' views of the world so they are not limited by ethnocentric, stereotypical, or otherwise narrow or distorted points of view. Students need to recognize that their particular perceptions are not universally shared, and they need to adopt multiple and far-reaching perspectives. Many students are likely to view the world predominantly through a narrow cultural lens shaped by their location, interests, and experiences.

Research on freehand maps drawn by students from different nations illustrates the importance of helping students perceive the world in diverse ways. In a classic study, Thomas Saarinen (1973) compared sketch maps of the world created by high school students from four cities: Calgary (Canada), Helsinki (Finland), Makeni (Sierra Leone), and Tucson (United States). These sketches suggest how students' understandings are mediated by their perceptions. As expected, most students depicted their home country and home continent with a high degree of accuracy and detail, often locating them in the centre of the map, reflecting a "we are the centre of the world" outlook. Typically, more distant continents were relegated to the "outer reaches" of the page and reduced to vague blotches far smaller than actual size. These depictions reflect reduced levels of awareness and significance attached to "foreign" regions.

Curiously, some international features such as Hawaii, the British Isles, and the "boot" of Italy were exaggerated or rendered with unusual precision. For varying reasons, these "distant" features had particular significance for the map-makers—perhaps the students had visited the place, had relatives living there, or had read about some event or place associated with it.

Instruction in school may unintentionally reinforce students' distorted world views by focussing on quaint and superficial aspects of specific regions and fostering a "we/they" dualism that further estranges other cultures. For example, many curriculum materials promote a "food–costumes–customs" approach to the study of cultures. However, learning about ethnic dishes and "strange" holiday practices is unlikely to enlighten perspective on the lives and concerns of people in "foreign" cultures (Zachariah 1989). These well-intentioned attempts to interest elementary students in other cultures may make people more "alien" and reinforce stereotypical perceptions (Schuncke 1984, 249).

Other distortions are also commonplace. For example, students may regard Africa and South America as primitive frontiers if their exposure to these continents is focussed on issues like subsistence living, genocide, drug runners, and deforestation. Many students are surprised to learn that there are well-educated, affluent people living in modern African cities as the media-based representations they see are often restricted to jungles and rural villages. Similarly, students may regard people in poverty with condescension if they are not shown instances of initiative and self-sufficiency. For example, until quite recently, treatment of Africa, South America, and the Middle East in Canadian social studies curricula focussed predominantly on ancient (and now fallen) civilizations (Case 1989, 6). As late as 1983, the elementary social studies curriculum of British Columbia referred to the study of "primitive" cultures (British Columbia Ministry of Education 1983, 40).

Ethnocentric and stereotypical perceptions like these will not be resolved simply by teaching more information about the world; more information will not advance students' understanding because much of what we notice, and how we interpret it, depends on the lenses through which we filter it. Approaching a cultural study with a narrow attitude is likely to confirm, not dispel, stereotypes and prejudices. We must attend directly to the perceptual lenses that colour students' thinking.

What Comprises the Substantive Dimension?

The substantive dimension refers to the range of global/multicultural topics—world events, states of affairs, places, and things—that students should learn about. It has been described by many writers: Kniep (1986), Hanvey (1976), and Banks (2004) are among the most widely cited. Kniep and Hanvey identify five topics that form the main objects of global study, the first of which is multiculturalism.

- **Universal and cultural values and practices.** Hanvey uses the term "cross-culture awareness" to refer to knowledge and respect for the diversity of ideas and practices found in human societies around the world. Kniep emphasizes the importance of teaching about both commonality and diversity: teaching about universal human values that transcend group identity (for example, equality, justice, liberty) and about diverse cultural values that define group membership and contribute to differing world views (for example, values related to aesthetics, lifestyle, and the environment).
- **Global interconnections.** Kniep talks of "global systems" and Hanvey speaks of "global dynamics" to describe knowledge of the workings—the key features and mechanisms—of interacting systems operating worldwide (for example, economic, political, ecological, social, and technological systems).
- **Present worldwide concerns and conditions.** Both writers identify the need to know about current and emerging global issues—Hanvey calls it "state of the planet awareness." These persistent, transnational issues span security, economic, environmental, and human rights concerns. They include population growth, migration, poverty, natural resource use, science and technology policy, health, and war.
- **Origins and past patterns of worldwide affairs.** Kniep stresses the importance of "global history"—seeing the historical evolution and roots of human values, global systems, and prevailing problems.
- **Alternative future directions in worldwide affairs.** Hanvey stresses the importance of "knowledge of alternatives"—also called "awareness of human choices." This refers to learning about other ways for the world to operate, rather than how it does now, in areas such as economic growth, foreign aid policy, and consumption patterns.

This list of five topics identifies what these prominent global educators see as the main content focus for global education. In essence, they believe that students need to know that:

- people across the world share some values and differ in others;
- events and forces in the world interconnect in powerful ways;
- the world is facing a number of serious issues with deep historical roots; and
- humankind has the potential and, indeed, the obligation to alter existing ways of "doing business."

Challenges in Teaching the Substantive Dimension

While different cultures are an important object of focus in global/multicultural education, there are common misconceptions that create pitfalls in teaching it. One of these misconceptions is the stereotypical notion of "culture" as a unified, fixed entity. In fact, culture is not a "thing" at all, but rather the name we give to the set of beliefs, values, behaviour, and ways of living expressed by a community of people. Culture results from a group of people collectively adapting to their social and environmental circumstances. As circumstances change, so does culture.

One indication of the malleability of culture is the way that peoples of the world have quickly responded to new technology. The Inuit, for example, were incorrectly thought by many in the 1930s and '40s to live a static existence. The snowmobile, however, was very quickly incorporated into Inuit culture and is now an essential part of Inuit life. We have to look no farther than the introduction of telephones into Western culture during our grandparents' lives, television during our parents' lives, and computers during our own lives, to see how new inventions become such a part of the cultural landscape that one wonders how people ever did without them. Thus, a culture must always be made sense of in the context in which it originated and now exists.

Another misconception is that material technologies (for example, costumes, food, housing) are in and of themselves culture. They are not; they are simply physical objects that reveal much about a group. However, it is equally important to recognize that "artifacts" and cultural expressions such as words and gestures are not arbitrary, but rather express how a culture perceives, relates to, and interacts with the world.

And, finally, there is often a dominant cultural tradition that has greater access to opportunity and power. For example, Christianity is the dominant religious tradition in Canada. This historical fact has resulted in the dominance in "our" nation of Christian practices such as Easter and Christmas, and the institutionalization of these celebrations through state-sanctioned holidays. Although other faith communities are celebrated for the diversity they bring to Canadian culture, their cultural practices are not given institutional recognition. Of course, institutional holidays in Japan, India, Iran, and other countries reflect the traditions of the dominant groups in these nations too.

Find text and pictures describing cultural groups in various textbooks and other teaching resources. How are these cultures depicted? To what extent are superficial or unusual aspects profiled? Is there greater emphasis on differences or similarities between the groups' and students' cultures?

What Comprises the Perceptual Dimension?

A major—possibly the key—challenge in developing a global/multicultural perspective is to transform a perspective that comes from a superficial or ethnocentric point of view to a broad-minded perspective that makes sense of the world from varied and "enlightened" points of view. For example, there is little value in promoting knowledge of alternative future directions if students are going to dismiss these ideas offhand because they don't suit students' immediate and possibly narrow interests.

Ironically, we are often unable to see our own cultural responses but are excessively conscious of those of others. For example, those of us who are able-bodied go about entire days, perhaps even weeks and months, without thinking about our ability to access public space. This blindness is called *privilege*. It causes us to overlook how our environment (e.g., restaurants, schools, parks, and transportation systems) accommodates our bodies as the "norm." Only when we encounter those whose bodies are socially defined as outside this norm do we notice. This blindness is also illustrated in aspects of social life. For example, English-speaking Canadians might say that American and British English speakers have accents but that Canadians do not, while both groups say that Canadian English speakers are the ones with an accent. Generally, we think of other groups as having "cultural practices" while we do not.

Our cultural traditions shape our behaviour, identities, environments, and assumptions. When we are part of a group, our culture is the invisible norm against which other cultures are measured. Put another way, a culture provides an invisible screen through which participants interpret and respond to the world, a so-called world view. Culture orients our views so that we respond to "other views" with curiosity and awe at best, resistance or hostility at worst.

To better appreciate what a broad perspective involves and how to promote it, we characterize this dimension in terms of three habits of mind: open-mindedness, full-mindedness, and fair-mindedness.[1]

OPEN-MINDEDNESS

Open-mindedness refers to a willingness to consider new ideas and alternative ways of looking at people, places, and events. Its opposite is closed-mindedness—an unwillingness to explore other ways of looking at things or the inability to see things as others might. Nurturing open-mindedness involves encouraging two traits:

- **Recognizing differences in points of view.** Students must realize that individuals and groups do not always see the world, or explain events that occur in it, in the same way. Thus it is necessary to develop the ability to see things from differing viewpoints.
- **Entertaining various points of view.** Students need to accept the right of others to hold points of view that differ from their own and be willing and able to consider diverse perspectives.

Open-mindedness is *the* crucial feature of the perceptual dimension. It involves more than understanding that people have different opinions on an issue—for example, some people are in favour of mandatory use of seat belts and others oppose it. It involves what Hanvey (1976, 4–5) refers to as "perspective consciousness"—an awareness that individuals and groups have world views or "cognitive maps" that are not universally shared and are shaped by factors that we are unaware of and unable to control. Young students may need particular help to appreciate that events can be interpreted from multiple perspectives. Adopting multiple points of view also requires looking at issues from different disciplines (for example, seeing the economic, environmental, and political implications of an issue) and also from different personal and cultural perspectives.

In introducing point of view to students, it may be useful to encourage them to view and describe concrete objects from different physical locations (for example, the look of a pencil or a classroom from the front, back, and sides). Stories provide another opportunity for students to take on different characters' perspectives to describe events and feelings. It is also useful to invite students to pay attention to changes in their own perspective of a scenario when new information is added. For example, invite students to imagine how they might feel if they saw another student sitting alone eating lunch in the cafeteria. Then ask them to suppose they move closer and notice that the person eating alone is their younger sibling. How does this new information affect their perception of the scene? Or what if it is they themselves who are eating lunch alone? Each piece of information may create a shift in both feelings and description of the event.

A strategy to encourage students to approach the study of other cultures from the point of view of an insider is to invite students to draw mental maps that depict the most relevant characteristics of the world from designated perspectives. This might be the perspective of someone living in their hometown, and then the perspective of a culture that students have been studying in class (Johnson 1997).

When comparing cultural points of view, it is important to remind students of heterogeneity within groups. Although "Europeans" or "Japanese" groups share some points of view, not all members within the group share points of view on all or even most things. A useful analogy can be drawn from a particular grade of students. Students in the same grade share experiences, such as the same teachers, or the same provincial exams. However, there are many distinct points of view within any grade of students.

Students may be open-minded about some issues and not others depending, in part, on personal investment or familiarity. For example, we are less likely to be open-minded when self-interest or deeply held values are at stake.

Teacher modelling is another important way to encourage student open-mindedness (Torney-Purta 1983, 33). To model open-mindedness, teachers must consistently and sincerely base their classroom comments and decisions on careful consideration of all sides, and show a willingness to change their minds when good reasons are given.

FULL-MINDEDNESS

Full-mindedness refers to the inclination to make up one's mind on the basis of adequate understanding of the whole story. Its opposite is simple-mindedness— a penchant for leaping to conclusions or settling for simplistic or incomplete explanations. Promoting full-mindedness includes helping students develop the following traits, which are expanded on below:

- **Anticipating complexity.** The inclination to look beyond simplistic accounts of complex issues for ramifications and interconnections and to see phenomena as part of a constellation of interrelated factors.

- **Recognizing stereotyping.** The ability to identify and dismiss portrayals of people or cultures that are superficial generalizations of cultures or places as quaint, eccentric, or objects of curiosity.
- **Suspending judgment when warranted.** A willingness to withhold conclusions dealing with complex matters until varying viewpoints, and the evidence for them, have been considered.

Fostering anticipation of complexity in students involves encouraging scepticism of explanations that fail to consider the range of interacting factors and consequences of most global events. This is a call to resist seeing world events as isolated and localized. Although it is inevitable, and often desirable, that global/cultural issues be simplified, it is important to discourage superficial or naive views (e.g., black-and-white accounts and definitive lists of the causes of events). If students are not presented the messy reality of many of our enduring global predicaments, or if they refuse to accept this reality, they will have nothing but crude and simplistic responses to problems. Simplified solutions, however, are unlikely to succeed. For example, world famine cannot be resolved by producing more food; we already produce enough food to feed everyone. Similarly, we cannot eliminate poverty by creating more jobs; many people considered to be below the poverty line are fully employed or not capable of working. If students do not anticipate the ramifications of a course of action in a complex situation, they are less likely to advocate adequate proposals for change.

One of the most important applications of anticipating complexity is the consideration of the context in which a cultural practice is expressed, rather than leaping to conclusions. Historical, political, and social factors influence the expression of "culture." For example, swearing in pop music would have been unheard of early in the music genre's development. However, cuss words are now frequent in mainstream pop radio songs, though many have alternate versions such as "Forget You" by Cee Lo Green and "Brand New Chick" by Anjulie, though Pink did not bother with her massive hit "F**kin' Perfect."

The feature "Believe It Or Not" is an activity designed to help elementary students appreciate the sophisticated wisdom behind seemingly "silly" cultural practices.

Educators can discourage simple-mindedness by stressing the context for cultural practices and also by attending to the interrelated factors leading to events

BELIEVE IT OR NOT

Students are invited to react to the "unusual" practices of an unidentified group (the Inuit). The objective of this activity is to encourage students to respond more respectfully to characteristics or practices that seem "foreign" by helping them see the rashness of their initial impressions.

WHAT DO YOU THINK OF A GROUP THAT ...	
	YOUR INITIAL REACTION
once lived in snow houses in winter	
plays soccer at midnight	
used moss diapers for their babies	
softened animal skin by chewing it	
made sleds out of frozen fish	
made sails out of animal intestines	

After recording their initial reactions, students learn about the reasons for each practice (reasons for two of these practices are suggested below) and are invited to reconsider their initial impressions. In this way, students are helped to appreciate the resourcefulness of the Inuit. Though the lifestyle of this and other cultures may seem unusual at first glance, once students understand why people live a certain way, the practices are seen to be, in fact, thoughtful.

RATIONALE/ADVANTAGES FOR SELECTED INUIT PRACTICES	
BEHAVIOUR	**RATIONALE**
moss diapers	• moss is widely available • moss can be stored in the winter • moss diapers are free, absorbent, and soft • moss diapers are environmentally friendly (moss is biodegradable) • moss can be packaged tightly and is lightweight for travel
sails made of intestines	• intestines are strong (they won't rip easily) • intestines are lightweight (they will not slow down the boat and can be transported easily) • intestines are easy to sew together • intestines are available any time animals are killed • the sails are environmentally efficient (parts of animals that may not be eaten or otherwise be used are used)

and the ramifications of actions. For example, solutions to global population problems should be discussed in the context of a complex set of competing social, environmental, historical, and religious factors, which include parents' reliance on their children to supplement family incomes, deep-rooted cultural values and religious beliefs, and state-mandated rules. Young students can be introduced to the complexity of events by exploring the range of influences that have led to an event (for example, all the people and countries that contributed to the breakfast eaten that morning) or tracing the myriad consequences of a single action (for example, the effects of removing one species from a local habitat). Fostering student appreciation of complexity may require replacing superficial exploration of many topics with fewer but in-depth case studies. In general, teachers who model an appreciation of the complexity of issues are likely to promote this trait in their students (Newmann 1991, 330).

Recognizing stereotypes is the ability to identify inadequacy in accounts of people, cultures, or nations due to a narrow range of characteristics or little or no diversity. Unlike anticipating complexity, which focusses on explaining events with appropriate intricacy, resisting stereotyping involves describing groups of people with sufficient diversity. For example, during the Cold War period, there was a tendency in the West to talk about Eastern Europe as if it were a single entity. Similarly, the crude treatment of African culture in many social studies textbooks fails to do justice to the fundamental differences and richness among African cultures (Beckett and Darling 1988, 2–3). Stereotyping occurs in the classroom when educators, however well-intentioned, focus on quaint or exotic features of a culture. For example, curriculum resources regularly stereotype Egypt as a museum or curiosity piece—the land of pyramids and sphinxes.

A particularly relevant form of stereotyping is the focus on "we/they" dualisms. Casting differences as "our" cultural group against "other" cultures is stereotyping whenever it disguises the shared values that underlie supposedly competing interests. Dualisms among international sectors (for example, north-south, east-west, developed-developing countries) involve stereotyping whenever the interests of all countries in a bloc are reduced to the interests of the bloc and set in opposition to the interests of other blocs. These dualisms ignore cross-boundary similarities and shared interests (for example, Eastern Europeans are likely as concerned about cancer as are North Americans) and polarize positions on issues when divisions are not warranted (for example, ending the nuclear arms race was a goal shared by people on both sides of the Iron Curtain). Of course, we can also go to the opposite extreme by exaggerating the extent to which one group's interests are shared by all nations and peoples.

Recognizing stereotypes is important because unflattering stereotypes of people, cultures, or nations are sometimes deliberately encouraged. For example, hostile images of people from an opposing country are sometimes used to fuel distrust or hatred (Silverstein 1989). Even when motives are benign, the effects of stereotyping can be undesirable. The eugenics movement in Western Canada and in many American states is an example of the disastrous effects of well-intended stereotyping. Eugenics called into question the "fitness" of certain groups of people to have and raise children. Based primarily on unflattering stereotypes, people with mild disabilities, or of Eastern European or Aboriginal origin, were considered "feeble-minded" or loose-moralled. They were evaluated by committees that had the power to sterilize those deemed socially undesirable. Well into the twentieth century, eugenics operated in North America at the same time that claims about the superiority of certain races were popular ideology in Western Europe.

As this example illustrates, condescending attitudes (and actions) towards other cultures may be a function of our stereotypical images of them (Werner, Connors, Aoki, and Dahlie 1977, 33). Building students' resistance to stereotypes decreases their inclination to dehumanize or marginalize groups, and instead helps them see different groups as having the full range of human attributes. In other words, we should try to inoculate students against accepting portrayals of members of other cultural groups "as cardboard characters in a stilted puppet play" (Zachariah 1989, 51). On a positive note, we can develop students' resistance to stereotyping by increasing their appreciation of the similarities and shared interests among cultures, and by combatting tendencies to paint issues in black-and-white terms.

The strategies outlined above for promoting an appreciation of complexity are also appropriate for encouraging appreciation of global/cultural diversity. Broad generalizations about people and nations should be discouraged; instead, examples of differences within cultural and national groups should be given. Although more extensive study of fewer cultures or nations may be preferred to relatively superficial study of many, we must guard against the stereotypical impressions that result when studying a heterogeneous entity such as Africa or First Nations through one nation, say Nigeria or the Haida Nation. As a general rule, we should avoid presenting the dominant aspects of a country or people.

Being open-minded also entails a tendency to suspend judgments when an investigation is not thorough or the evidence inconclusive. As the Scottish philosopher David Hume observed, a wise person proportions his or her belief to the evidence. Teachers can encourage full-mindedness in their students by being comfortable with uncertainty—that is, not always having the answer and being satisfied with tentative conclusions when firm conclusions are not warranted.

FAIR-MINDEDNESS

Fair-mindedness is the tendency to give a fair hearing to alternative points of view—to judge matters on the basis of their own merits and not simply in terms of our own interests and preferences. Its opposites are bias and self-absorption. Promoting fair-mindedness involves encouraging a willingness and ability to:

- **empathize with others:** to place oneself in the predicament of others or at least imagine issues from others' perspectives;
- **overcome bias:** to resist placing the interests or perspective of one's own group above those of others.

The ability to empathize requires solely that we try to understand in a vivid way what others think and how they feel. Empathy is not the same as open-mindedness, though it is related. Empathy presupposes openness to views different from our own, but it goes further: it requires that we "feel" the other person's state. The need to promote empathy arises because learning more about other people may not increase students' appreciation of what their lives are like. Empathizing with others is not synonymous with unqualified acceptance—a sensitive exposure to practices may legitimately redouble students' sense of another's oddness or unreasonableness. Neither is promoting empathy tantamount to encouraging moral relativism; students may still judge certain practices undesirable or unappealing. However, we shouldn't criticize others until we have walked a mile in their shoes.

Bias refers to unwarranted or unfair preference for one's own interests or affiliations. Bias was demonstrated in contrasting descriptions in the British press of British and Iraqi actions at the height of the Persian Gulf War in 1991. British forces were described as "cautious" and "loyal," and Iraqi troops as "cowardly" and "blindly obedient"; British sorties were "first strikes" and "pre-emptive" while Iraqi initiatives were "sneak missile attacks" and "without provocation" (*The Guardian* 1991). More recently, in the reporting of the aftermath of Hurricane Katrina in New Orleans, black residents were said to be "looting," while white residents were "finding" provisions (Raw Story 2005). These accounts are biased even if we agree that Iraq deserved condemnation for provoking the war and that New Orleans' residents were stealing property; identical actions were judged differently based solely on the identity of the group that performed them.

Three forms of bias are particularly relevant for multicultural and global education:

- **Ethnocentrism.** Believing that one's own cultural group is superior to others is known as enthnocentrism. It is not necessarily ethnocentric to prefer most features of North American life to those of

other cultures, but it is ethnocentric to judge them better simply because they are ours. Unless students are able to see the merits of other cultures, studying them will fuel the belief that "our ways are the best ways." As Jenness (1990, 412) remarked in his extensive review of social studies, some educators are concerned that "the world studies program may well turn out to be a fatter photo album, ethnocentrically selected and arranged." For example, people in North America typically bathe once a day, which is a socially acceptable level of cleanliness. In Japanese culture, bathing once a day may be regarded as unclean, while in some European cultures, bathing once a day may be regarded as indulgent and wasteful. An ethnocentric point of view interprets the actions of others as inappropriate—either deficient or excessive—rather than as socially defined adaptations.

- **National fanaticism.** A refusal to assess policies and events involving our own country impartially or to recognize that our national best interests should not always take precedence over the interests of other countries or people is known as national fanaticism.
- **Presentism.** Giving precedence to the interests of current generations at the expense of persons yet to be born is known as presentism. In other words, the felt urgency of our immediate needs and desires precludes fair-minded consideration of others' future needs. Concern with this form of bias underlies much of the criticism of the adequacy of environmental policies and contemporary consumer decisions.

To encourage fair-mindedness, regularly expect students to explore and defend positions from different points of view, especially from perspectives that differ from their own. For students who have difficulty in being fair-minded, teachers may challenge thinking in non-threatening ways by presenting opposing reasons and identifying inconsistencies in attitude. It is likely, however, that reasoning with students will not be sufficient. Students may benefit from exposure to evocative situations where they can "feel" for themselves the power and merit of other perspectives. There are at least three sources of these sorts of visceral experiences:

- **Vicarious experiences** where students come to live the lives of others through films and stories, or from guest speakers. There are many collections of films and stories about various countries and cultures that have been written or produced by people from those cultures.[2]

- **Simulated experiences** where students act out the predicament of others through role play or other simulation.
- **First-hand experiences** where students encounter the points of view of others in meaningful, "real-life" contexts—through field trips, exchanges, or social action projects.

No matter how they are brought about, experiences of other perspectives help to evoke students' sensitivities to points of view that they might otherwise downplay or ignore. The feature "What's Fair?" highlights an activity to help students develop empathy for people living in poverty.

Choose a resource dealing with a specific cultural group and review its teaching instructions. Look for evidence of how the suggested activities support or undermine the elements of a multicultural/global perspective:

- **Open-mindedness:** a willingness to entertain new ideas and alternative ways of looking at people, places, and events. It requires:
  - recognizing differences in points of view, and
  - entertaining various points of view.
- **Full-mindedness:** the inclination to make up one's mind on the basis of adequate understanding of the whole story. It requires:
  - anticipating complexity;
  - recognizing stereotyping; and
  - suspending judgment when warranted.
- **Fair-mindedness:** the inclination to give a fair hearing to alternative points of view; to judge matters on the basis of their own merits, rather than our own interests and preferences. It requires:
  - empathizing with others, and
  - overcoming bias.

Alter or design one or more activities to enhance a multicultural/global perspective on the featured cultural group.

Conclusion

The four objectives met in this chapter are:

- to illustrate the importance of helping students approach the study of their world from a more "global" and "diverse" perspective;
- to outline five main areas of the content or substantive dimension of a global perspective;
- to outline three key traits of the attitudinal or perceptual dimension; and
- to suggest ways to nurture multiple points of view—through direct instruction, teacher modelling, and "experiential" activities.

Although our focus is social studies, promoting a global/multicultural perspective should not be exclusive to this subject, nor should it be an occasional add-on within a designated unit. Rather, efforts to promote a global perspective can and should be embedded in much of what we teach each day.

ENDNOTES

1   In an earlier article, Case (1993) identified five interrelated elements of the point of view or perceptual dimension (open-mindedness, anticipation of complexity, resistance to stereotyping, inclination to empathize, and non-chauvinism). In a 1995 article intended for elementary teachers, these traits were collapsed into three more general categories: open-mindedness, full-mindedness, and fair-mindedness.

2   The Critical Thinking Consortium has various teaching resources and a comprehensive list of contemporary novels dealing with global development issues identified by country, issue, and reading level. See Investigating Realistic Stories at www.tc2.ca/cmsms/index.php?page=investigating-sources-online

REFERENCES

Banks, J.A., ed. 2004. *Diversity and citizenship education: Global perspectives.* San Francisco: Jossey-Bass.

Beckett, K. and L. Darling. 1988. The view of the world portrayed in social studies textbooks. Occasional paper #13. *Explorations in Development/Global Education.* Vancouver: Research and Development in Global Studies, University of British Columbia.

British Columbia Ministry of Education. 1983. *Social studies curriculum guide: Grade 1–grade 7.* Victoria, BC: Author.

Case, R. 1989. Global perspective or tunnel vision? The mandated view of the world in Canadian social studies curricula. Occasional paper #23. *Explorations in Development/Global Education.* Vancouver: Research and Development in Global Studies, University of British Columbia.

———. 1993. Key elements of a global perspective. *Social Education* 57 (6): 318–325.

———. 1995. Nurturing a global perspective in elementary students. In *Thinking Globally about Social Studies Education,* ed. R. Fowler and I. Wright, 19–34. Vancouver: Research and Development in Global Studies, University of British Columbia.

The Guardian. 1991. Mad dogs and Englishmen. February 22.

Hanvey, R.G. 1976. *An attainable global perspective.* New York: Global Perspectives in Education.

Jenness, D. 1990. *Making sense of social studies.* New York: Macmillan.

Johnson, C. 1997. Expressing a global perspective: Experiences in a Mexican classroom. Unpublished paper.

Kniep, W.M. 1986. Defining a global education by its content. *Social Education* 50: 437–446.

Newmann, F.M. 1991. Promoting higher order thinking in social studies: Overview of a study of 16 high school departments. *Theory and Research in Social Education* 19: 324–340.

Perinbaum, L. 1989. A new frontier for teachers. *Alberta Teachers' Association Magazine* 69: 23–25.

Raw Story. 2005. *Questions of racism in hurricane photo captions; Yahoo responds.* Accessed online at www.rawstory.com/news/2005/Blogs_raise_questions_of_racism_in_hurricane_photo_cap_0902.html.

Saarinen, T.F. 1973. Student views of the world. In *Images and environment: Cognitive mapping and spatial behavior,* ed. R.M. Downs and D. Stea, 148–161. Chicago: Aldine Publishing.

Schuncke, G.M. 1984. Global awareness and younger children: Beginning the process. *Social Studies* 75: 248–251.

Silverstein, B. 1989. Enemy images: The psychology of US attitudes and cognitions regarding the Soviet Union. *American Psychologist* 44 (6): 903–913.

Torney-Purta, J.V. 1983. Psychological perspectives on enhancing civic education through education of teachers. *Journal of Teacher Education* 34: 30–34.

Werner, W., B. Connors, T. Aoki, and J. Dahlie. 1977. *Whose culture? Whose heritage? Ethnicity within Canadian social studies curricula.* Vancouver: Centre for the Study of Curriculum and Instruction, University of British Columbia.

Zachariah, M. 1989. Linking global education with multicultural education. *Alberta Teachers' Association Magazine* 69: 48–51.

23

Teaching for Hope

Walt Werner

One cannot live in this media-rich culture without feeling some unease about the future. Weekly we encounter disturbing images of urgent proportions. A litany of enormous challenges—including poverty and famine, human rights abuses and repression, desertification and ecological stress, social chaos, and international debts—confronts our increasingly interdependent world. After Lebanon, Cambodia, and Ireland came Ethiopia, Sudan, Bosnia, and Rwanda [then Iraq, Afghanistan, and Darfur—Ed.], and we have come to expect that a list of similar place names will continue. Systemic interactions among diverse problems are overwhelming in their complexity and ambiguity, and this leads to uncertainties. According to the Club of Rome,

> Never in the course of history has humankind been faced with so many threats and dangers . . . the causes and consequences of which form an inextricable maze. . . . Individuals feel helpless, caught, as it were, between the rise of previously unknown perils on the one hand, and an incapacity to answer the complex problems in time and to attack the roots of evil, not just its consequences, on the other hand. (King and Schneider 1991, 127–128)

Even though this barrage of bad news leaves us psychologically fatigued, we still need to rationalize the realities of what we see and hear, because no matter what our politics, we want a better future (Kennedy 1993; Roche 1993).

For children, though, pictures of a broken world speak directly to their own future. Implied is their tomorrow. Whether this realization occurs in a dramatic moment of insight or slowly awakens as a vague awareness, the consequence can be uncertainty about the future or, even worse, some loss of hope.

Classrooms are unwitting partners in this loss. It begins when youth encounter texts and images that imply a deeply problematic future. Through classroom projects, print and online resources, and discussions of current events, students glean bits of information from which they construct their personal views, often of a crisis-ridden and confusing world created by adults who seem unwilling or unable to change it. "Youngsters piece together these fragments in a jumbled patchwork of mixed perceptions that make them anxious," observed Van Ornum (1984, 16). "The world is not safe. If adults are scared and helpless, what chance do kids have?" When unchecked, these feelings lead over time to insecurity or cynicism about the prospects for individual and collective futures.

Such outcomes, however, are educationally unacceptable because schools are in the business of strengthening realistic hope in the future. Let me illustrate with an event from a grade 10 social studies class. Groups were organized around research projects related to a number of global issues. I thought they were learning well to sort through controversial problems when a young woman quietly informed me that she would rather drop out of her study group and do an individual project on cowry shells. When asked what social or economic issues were represented by these natural artifacts, she replied that she was not aware of any issues nor was she interested. She simply wanted to study the shells, as she said, "because they're beautiful." I suddenly realized that here was a sixteen-year-old whose sense of future was threatened. The cumulative effect of my "ambulance chasing" pedagogy was a sense of helplessness, a feeling that the range and complexity of issues were too difficult to understand, let alone solve. My focus on problems left her with a deepening uncertainty.

Anyone who is a teacher is necessarily an optimist. Our working with young people represents a commitment to the future. We are teaching for hope. But what does it mean to have hope? Many years ago, Philip Phenix reminded educators that "Hope is the mainspring of human existence." This is no idle slogan, for, as he explained, "conscious life is a continual projection into the future. . . . Without hope, there is no incentive for learning, for the impulse to learn presupposed confidence in the possibility of improving one's existence" (1974, 123). Essential to hope is a knowledgeable and reflective confidence in the future and a willingness to engage it. The future, whether one's own or that of a larger group, is seen as open, having possibilities, rather than foreclosed or predetermined. This belief entails confidence that current problems and worrisome trends can be addressed in response to care and effort, that good planning and strategic action taken today can have significant consequences. In short, hope expresses itself as a "Yes" to tomorrow.

How can youth's sense of hope for the future be strengthened through classrooms? Part of the answer lies in the important roles that emotion, information, vision, and efficacy have in young people's coming to understand the problems and complexities of their larger world. Through a teacher's sensitive use of these four avenues, hope can be encouraged during discussions about global issues.

Select two current crises that are widely reported in the news. Arrange to discuss these crises with three or four students. Ask them what they feel about each crisis, what they know about them, whether they see the possibility of positive resolutions, and whether there is anything the students can do to help bring about a solution. Summarize their responses and draw several conclusions about the levels of hopefulness these students express.

Emotion

Honest treatment of subject matter, whether in the humanities or sciences, will at times give rise to emotionally loaded concerns and questions about the future. For decades, educators have known that harm to learning does not necessarily come from material that evokes emotion (Jones 1970, 69–86). Any learning that is memorable and important is also emotion-full. Expressions of feeling—such as surprise, anger, wonder, uncertainty, awe, consternation, commitment—engage the interest and imagination of students, extend their involvement with the subject matter, and imbue the curriculum with the kind of personal significance that impels rather than hinders learning.

There is an emotion, however, that is not a friend of learning: anxious students do not perform well. Anxiety about the future rests on feelings of helplessness and isolation in the face of threatening prospects (Jones 1970). And when children are unwilling to talk freely about topics that engender this sense of aloneness and hopelessness, their uninformed imaginations give rise to misperceptions of issues that can further reinforce anxiety (Stackhouse 1991).

How can the study of global problems and issues help youth feel less anxious about the future, less helpless about the prospects for change, and less alone in their imaginations? That students feel threatened by questions about the future needs to be dealt with rather than avoided. Classroom discussions, when sensitively directed by the teacher, can counter anxiety. For example:

- Watch for *signs of anxiety*, and seek ways to ameliorate this feeling and to promote a sense of community and efficacy. Indicators of a loss of hope can be varied. For example, off-hand comments or jokes during conversations about world problems may indicate fear, confusion, resignation, or anger; these refusals to discuss issues seriously may be masking deeper ambivalences. Expressions of apathy or lack of interest—such as protesting the topic, disengagement from discussion, or incomplete or poorly done projects—may also be attempts to protect oneself.
- Take seriously *the sentiments* about anxiety or hopelessness that children express during discussions of current events and issues. Help them articulate the reasons for these attitudes, and where appropriate, provide counter-examples and new information that challenges narrow or unsubstantiated beliefs.

- Focus discussions not only on the informational content of issues, but also on their *emotional content.* How do students feel about the issue? Emotions have to be shared—listened to and discussed—in order to be understood and harnessed for learning. As concerns are expressed, children realize that they are not alone in their imaginations about the future; there are broader communities of concern embracing people around the earth.

Information

Shielding children from global problems cannot be a solution to preserving their sense of hope. Purging the curriculum of topics that raise concerns for young people, or focussing discussion only on "safe" areas, are not options except for making classrooms more sterile places. As Van Ornum suggests, "Today's young people, for better or worse, are savvy and cynical. Old before their time, they know a dodge when they see one" (1984, 3). They already know from television that many people lead wretched lives because of environmental degradation, armed conflicts, and poverty, and that some adults are not hopeful about change (Kaplan 1994). But if children hear little acknowledgement of these realities, they conclude that educators either do not care or are not being honest; neither case instills confidence in learning about global issues. The perceived dark side of the world calls for information rather than silence.

Thoughtful discussion of information is essential, though, because a source of hopelessness can be misinformation, misunderstood information, or a lack of information about the nature and extent of a problem. Any defensible belief in the future has to include, among other things, an adequate knowledge—a realistic understanding and honest appraisal—of what the situation is. Herein lies a responsibility of educators to ensure that students have accurate and balanced input when discussing global issues, and to check whether the inferences drawn from classroom conversations and other texts are reasonable. Sketchy or inaccurate "facts," as well as hearsay, casual comments, and a neglect of context, can lead to unwarranted conclusions, overgeneralizations, or false impressions of what the future might be like (Jickling 1994).

If we want students to develop a reasoned hope in the future, then during classroom discussions:

- probe for *inferences* that children hold about the future. Are these inferences warranted by the best information at hand? Could their conclusions lead to unfounded fears or unrealistic expectations? Uninformed or misinformed fears and confidences both constitute naiveté.
- provide greater awareness of the broad range of *institutions* dedicated to gathering and disseminating reliable information about issues, and of the many groups that use this information to lobby governments for new policies or changed laws. This research and development work is premised on a strong confidence in the future.

Emphasis in the classroom upon inert information—often packaged as worksheets and end-of-chapter questions—only provides youth with disconnected "facts" about the state of their world. Unless meaningful connections among these isolated bits and pieces are forged, the picture of the larger world may make little sense beyond a bewildering array of problems. Hope falters when the content learned by students does not lead to better understanding.

Vision

Hope cannot rest only upon an understanding of what is or will be the case (information), but also upon imagined alternatives and how these may be achieved (vision). "Where there is no vision," says an ancient proverb, "people perish." It is not enough to want a "better world" without articulating what this might mean: What are one's priorities for an improved world, and how could they be achieved? Alternative futures are defined as we "name" them through goals, plans, and policies. Problem solving calls for a willingness to project outcomes and to choose from among competing scenarios. Rich imagination is the stuff of hope. But imagination withers whenever young people are treated as less than mindful agents through unimaginative pedagogy.

Children's hope is strengthened as their imaginations are engaged in understanding and "making" their world:

- Introduce *visionary concepts* that define alternatives for the future. Some examples are "sustainable environment," "respect for the rule of international law," "the commons," and "human rights." That these concepts may be controversial does not disqualify them from classrooms, but highlights the fact that they represent important values for envisioning the future.

- Discuss why the world community has forged institutions that embody and implement *collective visions* for the future. Examples include the world court and international law, as well as the many other agencies and covenants of the United Nations (Department of Foreign Affairs and International Trade, 1994).

- Give students opportunities to define and share *personal visions* for the future. Imagination is clarified and enlarged as it is challenged in a context of alternatives (Boulding 1995; Korten 1995). Not only do the visual and performing arts offer multiple modes for expressing doubts and hopes about the future, but also through "writing and sharing stories, creating images, and participating in role plays, we can simulate events as though we are already in the future. Our objective in such visualizations is not to predict the future, but to perceive potential futures in the here-and-now and to conceptualize what it will take to get there from here" (Bryant 1995, 40). Visions can be created and shared through various avenues, including poetry, music, drama, dance, story, drawing, and painting.

Hope is never fostered when students' own creative envisioning of desirable futures is disallowed, when information about the world is treated as a given to be received rather than re-imagined. Youth need to theorize about possibilities.

Efficacy

A concern that youth express when they begin to recognize the extent of world problems is why adults are not solving them. This query is not about more information on specific government policies and projects, but more deeply about how the world of adults works. It is an attempt to understand the kind of world in which they live: Is it a world in which adults do not care about problems that occur elsewhere? where adults do not know what to do? or where adults care more about present interests than consequences for the future? Some of children's deepest fears about abandonment are here tapped (Hevesi 1990). They seek assurances that adults can be trusted to protect the new generation's future. No wonder they become apprehensive.

Our goal is to encourage the development of those abilities and dispositions that allow young people to engage in appropriate personal, social, and political action. Hope is indistinguishable from a belief that individuals and groups influence and shape their futures through action. A strong sense of personal efficacy is a driving force behind any achievement. Without it, there is little open-mindedness to new ideas, willingness to reflect on one's own plans, or motivation and confidence in becoming proactive. To paraphrase Saul Alinsky, "There can be no darker or more devastating tragedy than the death of people's faith in themselves and in their power to direct their future. Denial of the opportunity for participation is the denial of human dignity...." Students need to understand why they are not powerless to make a contribution at some level.

Fostering efficacy is not an add-on to studies of global issues, but should be part and parcel of the ongoing discussions:

- Focus on the worldwide extent of *agencies, partnerships*, and *networks* engaged in problem solving. Young people are not aware of the range of groups—whether governments, international institutions, non-governmental organizations, grassroots community initiatives, or the private sector—committed to action and what they are doing. The important understanding here is that the difficulties facing our interdependent globe are being worked on by many people in various ways.

- Infuse *good news stories* about the successes that individuals, groups, and institutions are having in their actions. Elicit examples of actions that have been and are being taken to solve problems. Valuable experience and skills have been gained over the past decades, and considerable progress was achieved in areas such as health, agriculture, and social justice (Canadian International Development Agency 1987). The purpose for introducing positive examples is to provide a balanced and honest, not utopian, view of the gains that are made locally and internationally.

- Encourage discussion of *personal actions* that could be taken at home and in the school or community. The complexity of issues and problems does not preclude consideration of meaningful action: What can I personally do? Is there collective action that we should plan? Depending upon the age and circumstances of students, activities may involve letter-writing, changing one's consumer habits, attending a seminar for further information, joining the work of a community organization, or forming a school club. Appropriate action is not only a way to apply what is learned, but also a means for understanding issues better and strengthening efficacy.

Curricula and classrooms are largely organized around and for passivity. Often students are taught political incapacity rather than efficacy through the large amounts of inert knowledge they are given. They learn inadvertently that "doing school work" is not meant to be "real work" that has any direct impact on (or even relevance for) larger issues. This is why discussions about efficacy are so important for undercutting learned helplessness.

Conclusion

Classroom discussions of global issues may increase student anxieties about the future. This is why educators need to reflect on the roles that emotion, information, vision, and efficacy may have in shaping young people's beliefs about their tomorrow. I am not advocating that we put a light and happy face on the world. Youth already have a sense of dark crises on the horizon, but these realities need not imply despair. Hope requires a careful understanding of issues, and the development of reasoned visions and a realistic sense of efficacy. It is then that the sobering images on TV screens and the problems they imply can be seen with possibility.

Let me conclude with a personal anecdote. Late one night I heard my son, who was in grade 1 at the time, call from his room. I turned on the light and noticed that he had been crying. "When I grow up," he announced, "there will be no more wilderness." Whatever he meant by "wilderness" was not as important at this point as his expression of a threatened personal future. This loss of hope had started earlier in the day during a classroom discussion about stresses on ecosystems around the world, followed that evening by a television documentary on the loss of wilderness in western Canada. Because he lacked adequate information and the necessary conceptual tools to appraise the issues, what little understanding he gained from these two events led to a confused and anxious inference about his own future. I assured him that, although wilderness was indeed under serious threat in places, many groups of concerned people just like him were working to protect ecosystems through new policies and laws, and that there were things that he and I could do as well. Over the next few days, we sought new information, shared our visions, and explored ways to enhance efficacy.

Think of a contemporary local, national, or international issue or problem that you would want to explore with students. Use the author's four key ideas of emotion, information, vision, and efficacy to develop a list of a dozen activities or discussion points that you could use to build hope in students as they explore the issue.

ACKNOWLEDGMENT

This chapter appeared originally in 1995 in *Thinking globally about social studies*, ed. R. Fowler and I. Wright, 57–60. Vancouver: Research and Development in Global Studies, University of British Columbia.

REFERENCES

Boulding, E. 1995. Why imagine the future? *Context: A Journal of Hope, Sustainability, and Change* 40: 50.

Bryant, B. 1995. Rehearsing the future. *Context: A Journal of Hope, Sustainability, and Change* 40: 39–50.

Canadian International Development Agency. 1987. *Sharing our future: Canadian international development assistance*. Hull: Minister of Supply and Services Canada.

Department of Foreign Affairs and International Trade. 1994. *Canadian reference guide to the United Nations*. Hull: Minister of Supply and Services Canada.

Hevesi, D. 1990. NY children feel both fearful, guilty about the homeless. *Globe and Mail*, May 22.

Jickling, B. 1994. Studying sustainable development: Problems and possibilities. *Canadian Journal of Education* 19 (3): 231–240.

Jones, R. 1970. *Fantasy and feeling in education*. New York: Harper Colophon Books.

Kaplan, R. 1994. The coming anarchy. *Atlantic Monthly*, February, 44–76.

Kennedy, P. 1993. *Preparing for the twenty-first century*. New York: Random House.

King, A. and B. Schneider. 1991. *The first global revolution: A report by the Council of the Club of Rome*. New York: Pantheon.

Korten, D. 1995. A new day's coming in. *Context: A Journal of Hope, Sustainability, and Change* 40: 14–18.

Phenix, P. 1974. Transcendence and the curriculum. In E. Eisner and E. Vallence, eds., *Conflicting conceptions of curriculum* (117–132). Berkeley, CA: McCutchan.

Roche, D. 1993. The new world order: Justice in international relations. *Global Education* 1 (1): 31–38.

Stackhouse, J. 1991. There's method in the misery. *Globe and Mail*, October 18.

Van Ornum, W. 1984. *Talking to children about nuclear war*. New York: Continuum.

24 Cultivating Legally Aware and Empowered Citizens

Wanda Cassidy and Margaret Ferguson

"That's not fair!"

"She hit me!"

"Stop peeking at my answers!"

"He called me a bad name!"

"She owes me five dollars!"

"Hey, do you want to hear the new CD I burned from the net?"

"Teacher, Ronnie isn't following the rules!"

"Someone rifled through my desk!"

"You're a bully!"

"I feel left out and picked on!"

When asked whether they teach law, elementary teachers usually are surprised by the question, and respond in the negative. Yet, as suggested by the sample student comments listed above, every day in elementary classrooms and hallways and on school playgrounds, teachers and students grapple with law-related issues. They may not immediately identify them as legal, but the law has much to say about getting along with others, respecting people's property and their right to privacy, making fair decisions, keeping promises, and ensuring that rules are applied fairly. Inevitably, students learn about law through the policies and practices at school.

In addition, the social studies curriculum provides many opportunities for elementary students to learn about law. Topics in each grade are directly or indirectly related to law, for example, rights and responsibilities of family and community members, government and the Charter of Rights and Freedoms, the founding of Canada, First Nations issues, immigration and our multicultural mosaic, the environment, and Canada and its place in the world.

Law is foundational to social studies education and to cultivating informed and empowered citizens. In this chapter, we explain the purpose of law-related education and its importance to elementary social studies. We explore three approaches—conceptual, practical, and participatory—to addressing the law component in the formal and informal curriculum, and suggest instructional strategies for each.

What Is Law-Related Education?

The term "law-related education" or LRE was coined over forty years ago to describe the kind of education about law that is appropriate for students in public school. There is a tendency to think that studying law means learning the body of rules and procedures that lawyers acquire in law school or that adults learn in a piecemeal fashion as they proceed through life. This is not the recommended approach for elementary schools: most classroom teachers are ill-equipped to disseminate such information and the technical aspects of law are not the most appropriate law-related content to teach in public schools. For this reason, the term "law-related education" was coined to distinguish the teaching about law in the schools from the teaching of laws to lawyers and other legal professionals.

Rather than transmitting technical information about laws, LRE is more centrally concerned with promoting student understanding of the role that law plays in society and in their personal lives. Certainly, specific laws are studied from time to time, but the emphasis is on understanding why we have laws, the sources of law, legal institutions and structures, and other aspects of the foundations of law. The content of LRE is the ideas or concepts underlying the legal system—notions such as rights, responsibilities, authority, justice, and equality. LRE examines the values or beliefs embodied in our law, such as respect for property and human life. LRE involves developing basic citizenship attributes—such as critical thinking and conflict resolution—to help students participate effectively in a legally regulated world, and to effect change when the rules no longer reflect the kind of community we want. LRE encourages active learning and the use of community resources to gain a realistic look at the legal system in operation. Important LRE objectives include reducing cynicism, understanding the limitations of law, and assuming some responsibility for making the system responsive to people's needs.

LRE seeks to develop critically aware and socially responsible citizens who are willing and able to make a positive difference in their neighbourhood, community, and nation. These aims are intertwined with the goals of social studies education more broadly: preparing young people for citizenship, developing students' abilities to think critically about issues, and encouraging students to take action to make the world a better place (Marker and Mehlinger 1992, Newmann 1989). Law professor Hugh Kindred captures the value of law-related education in furthering social studies goals:

> In a participatory democracy, it is vital that students learn about their rights and duties as citizens. Knowledge of the institutions that control the society is a prerequisite to intelligent democratic action.... In addition, it is important that students know not only their civic responsibilities, but also their freedoms of action within the Canadian system of government. The measure of good citizenship is not inculcated conformity, but a healthy respect for the rights of others as well as one's own, and an allegiance to orderly processes, even in diversity. The character of law encourages such critical, yet constructive attitudes. Consequently its study will develop them in students, the next generation of Canadian citizen. (1979, 534)

As well, there is a profoundly practical reason for learning about the law. LRE is basic to survival in a world where law is pervasive. We marry, have families, travel, conduct business, worship, and even die according to law. Our written laws proliferate at a staggering rate. The federal government has enacted hundreds, if not thousands, of statutes and every province has approximately five hundred statutes in place. Thousands of regulations appended to these statutes contain the procedural "nuts and bolts" that affect how we act. Add municipal bylaws to this list and it is easy to appreciate that the long arm of the law reaches into almost every aspect of our lives. Without some appreciation of the nature and scope of this influence, students' ability to function in society is impaired. Furthermore, ignorance of the law is not considered a justifiable excuse when a law is not followed.

Efforts to infuse LRE into elementary schools are typically organized around three approaches (Starr 1989):

- **conceptual:** focussing on the core concepts and principles in law;
- **practical:** stressing the day-to-day implications of law; and
- **participatory:** involving students in the application of law-related procedures.

Most programs in Canadian social studies classes combine elements of all three approaches, depending on curriculum expectations, grade level, and teacher and student needs and interests.

THE CONCEPTUAL APPROACH

The conceptual approach examines central legal ideas such as liberty, justice, and equality—concepts that form the bedrock of a democratic society and which are lauded in school. Even primary students have strong notions about what is right or fair, and are intrigued by dilemmas that present opportunities to examine issues of power, authority, privacy, responsibility, and property. This approach to LRE focusses on broad principles and concepts, and emphasizes critical thinking.

One way to address concepts is through a case study. Cases can either be real (for example, historical events, actual court cases, or current events), based on stories from children's literature, or imagined dilemmas. In an article entitled "A Tale of Two Gates," James Lengel (1984) suggests how the story *Peter Rabbit* can involve students in analysis of abstract concepts such as punishment, justice (fairness), authority, and responsibility. In this classic tale, Peter Rabbit lived with Flopsy, Mopsy, Cotton-Tail, and his mother underneath the root of a very big fir tree. One morning old Mrs. Rabbit tells her children that they may go into the fields and down the lane, but they are not to go into Mr. McGregor's garden because their father had an "accident" there—he was put in a pie by Mrs. McGregor. Like most children's stories, *Peter Rabbit* sets out a problem of obedience and disobedience, of adventure and misadventure, of making and breaking rules. This realistic, close-to-home conflict raises the following important legal issues:

- Was the father's fate really an accident?
- Was it fair for Mr. McGregor to punish the father so harshly?
- What could have been a fairer punishment?
- Did Mrs. Rabbit have the authority to make the rule she did?
- Was it a good rule?

FIGURE 24.1   WHO HAS A RESPONSIBILITY?

		IS _____ ABLE TO HELP YOU?	IS IT FAIR TO EXPECT THAT _____ SHOULD HELP YOU?
Imagine you have been asked by your teacher to bring back to your classroom a big box of books that is too heavy for you to carry. You think of three people who might have a responsibility to help you.	A teacher who is standing beside the box	yes / no	yes / no
	Your friend who is sick at home	yes / no	yes / no
	A big boy who is very strong who has been sent with you by your teacher to help carry the box	yes / no	yes / no

		IS _____ ABLE TO HELP YOU?	IS IT FAIR TO EXPECT THAT _____ SHOULD HELP YOU?
Imagine you are in class working on an arithmetic problem that is too hard for you to do, but you must solve the problem before you go to recess. You think of three people who might have a responsibility to help you.	Your teacher who is standing beside you	yes / no	yes / no
	Your friend who is really good at arithmetic and sits next to you	yes / no	yes / no
	The person who lives next door to you, who is very good at arithmetic, but who has left town for a long trip	yes / no	yes / no

In case studies, students wrestle with the facts, issues, and arguments, and come to a reasoned decision that can be justified according to the evidence. There are no "pat" or "right" answers in a case study. Rather, the purpose is to teach students to distinguish relevant facts from irrelevant ones, synthesize issues into a key problem or question needing resolution, articulate perspectives from more than one side, reach a reasoned decision, and justify their conclusion with sound reasons (Bognar, Cassidy, and Clarke 1997). The featured text "Case Study Method" suggests a five-step structure for a case study.

Many topics in the elementary social studies curriculum have a legal angle. When examining the roles and responsibilities in a community, for example, teachers can invite students to consider why we need laws, how a law might be changed, whether we need police officers to keep the peace, what role each citizen has in improving the neighbourhood, whether children should have rights, and what penalties are appropriate when someone damages the environment. Similarly, immigration may be studied through the notions of diversity, inclusion, and multiculturalism. Topics such as government and politics invite examination of the rule of law, the role of the judiciary, and the importance of the Charter of Rights and Freedoms to articulating the values we espouse as Canadians.

Figure 24.1, "Who Has a Responsibility?" (adapted from McDermid, Abbott, and Case 2003), describes an activity to help primary students understand when someone has a responsibility to do something. In assessing responsibility in the two hypothetical scenarios, students would consider two factors: whether the persons are able to help, and whether it is fair to expect them to help. Building on this understanding, students would then examine responsibilities that other people in the community have and eventually responsibilities that students themselves have.

THE PRACTICAL APPROACH

The focus of the practical approach is law's impact on the daily lives and decisions of Canadians, including children. At the elementary level, students need to understand that law affects them each day in many ways, whether they are aware of it or not. A simple activity to sensitize students to the diverse ways in which laws touch their lives is to ask them to write a story describing who they are, where they live, and what they did from the time they got up in the morning to their arrival in the classroom. (Younger students can draw pictures representing the things they do each day.) After

discussing the stories, help students see that law regulates everything from the kinds of homes they live in, to the beds they sleep on, what is written on their breakfast cereal boxes, the type of fabric in their clothes, how parents treat them, bicycle safety, school hours, the type of playground equipment at school, what can be said in school textbooks, what they can or cannot say or do to a fellow student, and the air they breathe.

A related activity to increase upper elementary students' awareness of the scope of the law is to circulate sections of the local newspaper. Ask groups of students to identify any article, advertisement, or section that relates to law. Initially, students may find a few obvious examples (such as a crime committed, a lawsuit, or a police matter). However, with guidance, students can see that almost every part of the paper is connected to law—including the sports pages, advertisements, classified section, comics, entertainment section, and most headline articles. As the featured text "Law in Our Everyday Lives" suggests, law regulates and shapes almost everything we do on a daily basis.

Appreciating the practical implications of rights contained in documents such as the United Nations Convention on the Rights of the Child or the Canadian Charter of Rights and Freedoms requires that students understand that human rights exist to protect the most basic of human needs. Students learn the importance of these entitlements by examining the consequences that follow when these rights are not respected. Using Figure 24.2, "Drawing the Line on Our Right to Food" (adapted from Nicol and Kirk 2004), students might consider the point along a continuum from total absence to complete luxury at which meeting this basic need becomes a right. Students would decide this by considering the implications, on the one hand, of not meeting the need for a person's well-being and, on the other hand, of placing an unfair burden on the rest of society who would have a responsibility to see that this right is respected. The articulation of this point can be used to generate a statement of rights (for example, every child has a right to enough food so that . . .), which can be posted to a class charter, and eventually compared with the UN Convention on the Rights of the Child or Canadian Charter of Rights and Freedoms.

Select an important legal principle (such as equality, justice, personal responsibility, or the rule of law) and develop one or more activities to help students better understand the concept and to nurture their appreciation of its importance as a personal and social value.

LAW IN OUR EVERYDAY LIVES

- **Name.** Laws specify the surname a child can take. Everyone's name is registered on a legal document, the birth certificate. There is a legal procedure to follow for changing one's name.
- **Address.** Do students live in a village, city, or town? This designation is determined by law. Zoning laws specify the type of dwellings that can be built in an area. The procedures for numbering homes and naming streets in municipalities are regulated by law.
- **School.** Laws require children to attend school and these laws set the number of hours of instruction per day and per year. The law requires adults to pay taxes to support schools and sets out the rights and responsibilities of teachers and principals.
- **Pets.** Municipalities have laws that affect the type of pet one can have, and whether or not a pet requires a licence and a leash on public property. Cruelty to animals can be a criminal offence.
- **Family.** Laws specify how marriage must take place, how people come to assume the rights and responsibilities as a mother or father, under what conditions divorce can occur, how adoptions occur, who is entitled to inherit property when a family member dies, and so on.
- **Food.** Laws regulate the handling and packaging of food, what foods can be imported and exported, and what businesses must do before they can sell food.
- **Transportation.** Drivers and owners of vehicles have many laws to obey—licensing, insurance, and traffic laws. Bicycles, scooters, and skateboards are also regulated by laws.
- **Contracts.** Any time goods are bought or sold, we are entering into a contract. Consumer protection laws ensure that contracts are fair.
- **Money.** Laws establish what currency is legal tender in a country.
- **Businesses.** The formation and operation of businesses are governed by law, including the rights and responsibilities of employers and employees.

THE PARTICIPATORY APPROACH

Many LRE advocates stress a participatory approach to learning, where students engage directly with legal resources in the community and with real or realistic law-related problems. Judges, lawyers, legislators, human rights advocates, environmentalists, and others are invited into the classroom, and students interact with local law-related agencies. Courthouses are open to the public, and many courts (with prior permission) will allow classes to view a trial in session or conduct their own mock trial in a spare courtroom. Many law-related agencies are willing to share their knowledge with students (for example, immigrant services societies, Native friendship centres, human rights groups, mediation services, media watch, internet regulators, consumer protection agencies, animal rights groups, or multicultural groups). Exploring the roles that these agencies play in our society gives breadth to students' understanding of the richness of community resources, and complements their knowledge of more typical services like the police, firefighters, postal service, and recreational facilities. (See the Additional Resources section at the end of this chapter for contact information on public legal education agencies that have a mandate to support teachers in various provinces and territories.)

The participatory approach stresses that students learn about law by experiencing legal processes and decision-making in ways that simulate real life. This means that mock trials and role plays based on legal procedures are central to LRE pedagogy. Simple simulations or role plays may be developed based on neighbourhood or school issues, historical events, or stories from literature. For example, as described in the featured text "Resolving a Neighbourhood Conflict," students can experience the procedures of a small claims court by participating in a three-way role play involving two disputing parties and a judge.[1]

Mock trials, which involve more formal enactment of legal procedures than do role plays, have been used in elementary social studies classes to address historical and current events (Cassidy and Yates 1998, 2005; Norton 1992). In a mock trial, students put a character on trial and then enact the trial playing the roles of the accused, the witnesses, court personnel, and the media. Classes have examined a gold rush murder case tried by the infamous hanging judge, Matthew Bailey Begbie; charged a student in the case of a missing social studies exam; run a school Litter Court to try classmates accused of littering the school playground; and put on trial such fairytale characters as Goldilocks, Hansel and Gretel, Peter Pan, and Alice in Wonderland. Current events also provide engaging scenarios that can be used as the basis for mock trials.

Children's literature provides a rich source of material for mock trials or role plays involving law-related issues such as good and bad leadership, responsible and irresponsible behaviour, and freedom, equality, justice, and privacy. The case of Peter Rabbit, described earlier, illustrates

FIGURE 24.2 DRAWING THE LINE ON OUR RIGHT TO FOOD

What point along the continuum describes the amount of food that you believe every child has a right to expect?

| No Food | Just a little food to keep you from being hungry, not very nutritious | Some nutritious food every day but still hungry sometimes | Enough nutritious food every day and occasional treats | As much food as you want, all the time |

Rights statement: _____

Reasons why the line is not lower	Reasons why the line is not higher

this potential. Peter Rabbit could be put on trial for trespassing on Mr. McGregor's garden and for stealing Mr. McGregor's vegetables. The witnesses for the prosecution might include Mr. McGregor, Mrs. Mouse, the Scarecrow, and Constable Meadows. The witnesses for the defence might include Peter, Benjamin Bunny, Cotton-Tail, and old Mrs. Rabbit. Lawyers present the case with the help of a court clerk, court recorder, sheriff, and jury. Some students could assume media roles by preparing newspaper articles on the case or running a video camera. Unlike a scripted trial, students develop their roles based on the story, and the lawyers for the prosecution and defence prepare questions for their witnesses and to cross-examine the other side's witnesses. The prosecution presents the story and tries to prove that Peter is guilty of both charges beyond a reasonable doubt. The defence challenges the story, presents Peter's side, and calls witnesses to introduce doubt that Peter did the things as charged or that he intended to do them. The jury—classmates or another class in the school—determines the verdict.

In the additional resources listed at the end of this chapter, we provide annotations of other promising stories. Following is a list of stories for primary children organized by law-related themes (Doge 2004):

Rules
The Signmaker's Assistant, by Tedd Arnold
Aunt Chip and the Great Triple Creek Dam Affair, by Patricia Polacco

Honesty
Franklin Fibs, by Paulette Bourgeois and Brenda Clark
The Three Little Wolves and the Big Bad Pig, by Eugene Trivizas and Helen Oxenbury
John's Choice: A Story about Honesty, by Jane Belk Moncure

Pollution
The Tower, by Michael Twinn and Arlette Lavie
One World, by Michael Foreman
The World that Jack Built, by Ruth Brown

Vandalism
The Giants' Child, by Marcia K. Vaughan
Purple, Green and Yellow, by Robert Munsch and Hélène Desputeaux
Play Lady: La Señora Juguetona, by Eric Hoffman and Suzanne Tornquist

Street Safety
Traffic Safety, by Nancy Loewen and Penny Dann
Tin Lizzie, by Peter Spier
Curious George Rides a Bike, by H.A. Rey

Trespassing
Somebody and the Three Blairs, by Marilyn Tolhurst and Simone Abel
Deep in the Forest, by Brinton Turkle
Goldilocks Returns, by Lisa Campbell Ernst

RESOLVING A NEIGHBOURHOOD CONFLICT

Scenario

Between the Sámi yard and the Finn yard next door stood a beautiful, massive tree. The Finn ancestors planted the tree a century ago, and over the years the trunk of the tree expanded so that half the trunk and many of the branches extended over the property line into the Sámi yard. The four Sámi children loved to climb the tree and played in it for hours. The Finns didn't seem to mind when Jo Sámi, the oldest child, built a tree house in the branches and slept there with a friend on hot summer evenings. The Finns' children had left home long ago, so they liked to see children playing outside.

The Finns, however, were getting older and hated to rake up the leaves and prune the branches. They also wished for more daylight because the tree blocked out most of the sunshine on that side of their house where they had two picture windows. The Sámis, on the other hand, were grateful for the shade the tree provided.

One day, while the Sámis were away, Mr. and Mrs. Finn arranged for the tree to be chopped down. When the Sámi family arrived home, they were devastated. The younger children cried for days. When the Sámis tried to talk to the Finns about it, Mrs. Finn just said, "Well, it was our tree and we had a right to do with it what we wanted." Mr. Sámi said: "Well, I'm not so sure; it was also on our property too; you had no right! Besides, we've used it for years, and you didn't seem to mind!"

The Sámis want to plant another tree in the empty spot, but can't afford to buy a large one unless they are given money for their loss of the old tree. The Sámis decide to take the Finns to court for loss of enjoyment of the tree, and to seek damages of one thousand dollars to pay for a new large tree.

Role play

Divide the class into small groups of three students each. One student assumes the role of the plaintiff, the Sámis. The second student plays the defendant in the lawsuit, the Finns. The third student plays the role of judge who hears both sides of the issue, asks questions of each party, determines whether the Sámis have a legitimate case against the Finns and, if so, whether damages and court costs should be awarded.

Before the role play, each side should prepare its case and decide how best to present it to the judge. During the preparation time, the judge reads through the case and records questions to ask. The judge's options in deciding the issue include the following:

- rule in favour of the Sámis and make the Finns pay them one thousand dollars plus court costs;
- dismiss the claim against the Finns, which would require the Sámis to pay the court costs of both parties; or
- decide on a middle ground where both parties pay their own court costs, and the Finns pay a lesser amount to the Sámis, or to require that both parties come to a mutually agreeable size and type of tree and plant it in a spot on which they agree.

Once the judge in each trial has heard the case and made a decision, the judicial decisions and reasons for the decisions should be shared with the rest of the class. Discuss the following broader issues:

- Why were there different decisions?
- What were the most convincing arguments?
- What aspects of law would you have liked to know more about before you reached your decision?
- Is court the best place to resolve a problem like this one?

Law

A Small Lot, by Eros Keith

Old Henry, by Joan W. Blos and Stephen Gammell

Jonathan Cleaned Up—Then He Heard a Sound: or Blackberry Subway Jam, by Robert Munsch and Michael Martchenko

Annie Bananie and the People's Court, by Leah Komaiko

Carla Goes to Court, by Jo Beaudry and Lynne Ketchum

Parliament: Canada's Democracy and How It Works, by Maureen McTeer

Monkey Tales, by Laurel Dee Gugler and Vlasta van Kampen

Adjudicating actual classroom and school disagreements afford wonderful LRE opportunities. One such dispute resolution mechanism is mediation. In this method, parties work together with the help of a third party to come to a mutually agreeable decision. This involves give and take, with each side letting go of certain demands or moderating others in order to agree on a solution. This procedure may be simulated in class, with students learning listening and negotiating skills in the process. Students are presented with an issue, either from history or the current day, and then work in one of the disputant groups or in a mediator group to come to a solution.

Many schools have peer mediation programs where students involved in conflict learn to solve their differences with the assistance of trained student mediators and without the intervention of teachers. Student mediators might be coached to use the steps outlined in the featured text "Resolving a Neighbourhood Conflict" when assisting other students to resolve a dispute.

The growing interest in social responsibility and

ORGANIZING A MOCK TRIAL

Mock trials can be conducted informally in class or conducted with costumes and props in a local courthouse or other public place with actual members of the judiciary or legal profession presiding. There are three phases to a trial: the preparatory phase, the trial itself, and the post-trial discussion. The phases for a criminal mock trial suitable for primary and intermediate-level students are outlined below.

Preparatory phase

- Decide on the story or event for the trial, or choose one of the scripted or packaged mock trials available.[2]
- Help students understand the criminal charge, the facts of the case, and the key issues.
- Review basic information with students about the justice system (adversarial model, need for impartial decision, role of court personnel, innocent until proven guilty, concept of intent, reasonable doubt).
- Assign (or allow students to choose) their roles: the accused, witnesses, Crown prosecutors, defence lawyers, court clerk, court reporter, sheriffs, and media (court artist, newspaper reporters, television journalists). A lawyer or school principal should be asked to play the role of judge.
- Divide students into four small groups that will each prepare their case:
  - Crown prosecution and their witnesses;
  - defence lawyers, the accused, and their witnesses;
  - court personnel; and
  - the media.
- If following a script, emphasize that the case should be presented without notes as much as possible. For more complex trials involving role cards instead of a script, emphasize the development of arguments, writing good questions to be asked in court, and presenting one's evidence as convincingly as possible.
- Invite students to prepare costumes that represent their role.

Enacting the trial

- If the trial is conducted in the school gymnasium, library, or classroom, design the room to model a real courtroom, as illustrated in Figure 24.3 (adapted from Cassidy and Yates 2005).
- Once the trial begins, it should continue without interruption until the jury reaches a decision and the sentence is rendered (if guilty), or the accused is set free (if not guilty). The teacher's role is to take notes and comment following the trial, not to guide or interrupt the trial.

Post-trial discussion

- Immediately after the trial, debrief with students, allowing them to share their feelings and thoughts about the trial, and to come out of role.
- With the full class listening/contributing, address each group:
  - **Jury:** What evidence was most convincing? Which characters were most believable? Why did you decide the case as you did?
  - **Lawyers:** Which arguments were most persuasive? Would you have changed your presentation in any way?
  - **Witnesses:** What did you experience being in the witness box? Did any aspects of the trial surprise you?
  - **Court personnel:** Why is the role of court clerk and court reporter important? Did the sheriff feel any differently about the role after donning a costume?
  - **Media:** What parts of this trial are you going to write about or present to classmates? What role does the media play in real court cases?
  - **Whole class:** What did you learn about the law and court system as a result of participating in this trial?
- The days following the trial provide other opportunities for reflection, or more in-depth investigation of aspects of the justice system and conceptual issues such as the advantages and disadvantages of the adversarial model, whether judgment by peers in a jury system is the best method of determining guilt, whether there are better ways to resolve disputes than through the courts, and so on.

---

in restorative justice is also compatible with law-related education, particularly if the programs developed are respectful of individuals, give credence to due process, allow for diversity and reasonable dissent, seek to be just and fair, and work towards the good of all (Whitley 2002). It is important, too, that the whole school community be involved in these initiatives, working together to model and practise the values of responsibility or restoration, rather than expecting only the students to comply (Epstein 1999). Approaches that engage all stakeholders and become embedded in school culture

have a far greater impact on learning than programs that merely formalize the goals and do not implement them into all levels of practice.

Teachers would be remiss if they focussed exclusively on the formal curriculum of social studies education, yet failed to consider the law-related implications of the informal or "hidden" curriculum. What we do in the classroom—what is modelled and practised—has a powerful effect on children's learning (Jackson 1990; Jackson, Boostrom, and Hansen 1993). Establishing working principles for the classroom and a few rules

FIGURE 24.3 COURTROOM LAYOUT

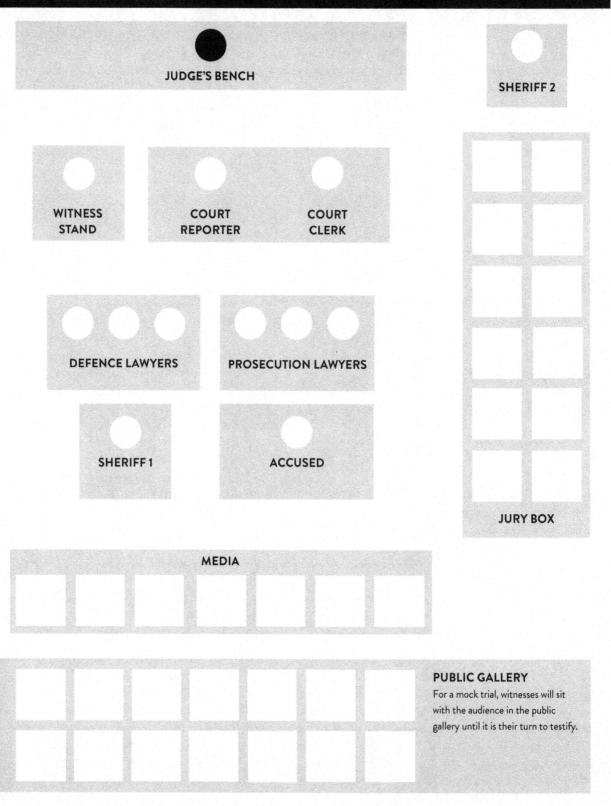

JUDGE'S BENCH

SHERIFF 2

WITNESS STAND

COURT REPORTER

COURT CLERK

DEFENCE LAWYERS

PROSECUTION LAWYERS

SHERIFF 1

ACCUSED

JURY BOX

MEDIA

PUBLIC GALLERY
For a mock trial, witnesses will sit with the audience in the public gallery until it is their turn to testify.

to support these principles helps to model for students the ideals of thoughtful law-making and citizen involvement. These conditions for a "democratic" classroom can be nurtured at the beginning of the school year by considering and, if appropriate, inviting students to consider the following kinds of questions:

- What are the shared values and beliefs that will form the basis of the classroom community?
- Will these values be reflected in classroom rules or procedures?
- Will students' views be solicited?
- How many rules are needed and how will these rules be established?
- To what extent will students be able to have input into the rule-making, and how will this be done?
- How will rules be enforced and who will judge whether a rule has been broken?
- Will the consequences for the breach of a rule be fair and flexible so that the context of the offence is considered?
- Is there a need to clarify or modify the rules as situations develop? How will this be done?
- How does one measure the fairness or appropriateness of a rule? (Should all students find the rules acceptable, or is it sufficient that the majority agree?)

Create a list of approximately ten basic principles embedded in our formal justice system (for example, the right to be heard, to be presumed innocent until proven guilty, freedom of expression, freedom of conscience). Develop a detailed plan for classroom operations that would model these values in ways that are appropriate and realistic for students at the grade level you teach.

Conclusion

The law dimension is an essential part of an adequate social studies education. The kind of education in law for which we advocate is not that of mini lawyers-in-training, but rather sensitizing children to the role that law plays in their lives and in a democratic society. We have illustrated a range of opportunities and strategies for incorporating law-related topics into the formal and informal curriculum. No single approach to LRE is required—you are encouraged to start small with an approach that best suits your purposes and resources. By doing this, you will join elementary teachers across North America who are advancing children's awareness

GUIDELINES FOR PEER MEDIATORS

- **Who is involved?** Make sure every person involved in the conflict is present. List their names, grades, and teachers.
- **What happened?** Each student should be given a chance to say what happened without being interrupted or corrected by the others who are involved. You decide the order of speaking. Use active listening skills and ask open-ended questions to make sure you get as many facts as possible. After everyone has spoken, summarize the facts as you understand them. Does everyone agree this is what happened?
- **What is the real problem?** Help the students identify the issue that is causing the problem. Identifying feelings is often a first step (for example, "I feel angry because…"). Each person has to listen very carefully to what the others are saying. The real issues are often hidden.
- **How can we fix the problem?** Encourage students to think of as many solutions as possible. Do not let them discard any solution until all the options are understood. What solution is acceptable to everyone? When an agreement is reached, make sure everyone understands it. Write down what was decided. The problem may happen again and the agreement may have to be changed.

of legal concepts and procedures and empowering them as effective and responsible members of their classroom, school, and neighbourhood communities.

ENDNOTES

1   This story is taken from Cassidy and Yates (2005). Additional examples are provided in this book, as well as a discussion on how to use contemporary children's stories and multicultural stories to address law-related issues. Other references are Ferguson (1998) and Gascoigne (1998).

2   For a list of trials, see the Justice Education Society of BC's website or consult www.lawcentralschools.ca/abc/default. aspx and www.lawconnection.ca.

REFERENCES

Bognar, C., W. Cassidy, and P. Clarke. 1997. *Social studies in British Columbia: Results of the 1996 Provincial Learning Assessment*. Victoria, BC: Province of British Columbia.

Cassidy, W. and R. Yates, eds. 1998. *Let's talk about law in elementary school*. Calgary: Detselig.

———. 2005. *Once upon a crime: Using stories, simulations and mock trials to explore justice and citizenship in elementary school*. Calgary: Detselig.

Doge, K. 2004. Books with law-related themes for primary students. In *Law in the Curriculum*, Education 448 Course Reader, W. Cassidy and R. Yates, Reading 5.4. Burnaby: Faculty of Education, Distance Education, Continuing Studies, Simon Fraser University.

Epstein, J. 1999. Creating school, family, and community partnerships. In *Contemporary issues in curriculum*, 2nd ed., ed. A. Ornstein and L.S. Behar-Horenstein, 422–441. Boston: Allyn & Bacon.

Ferguson, M. 1998. Learning law-related concepts through literature. In *Let's talk about law in elementary school*, ed. W. Cassidy and R. Yates, 89–116. Calgary: Detselig.

Gascoigne, H. 1998. Looking at law through story drama. In *Let's talk about law in elementary school*, ed. W. Cassidy and R. Yates, 71–88. Calgary: Detselig.

Jackson, P.W. 1990. *Life in classrooms*. New York: Teachers College Press.

Jackson, P.W., R. Boostrom, and D. Hansen. 1993. *The moral life of schools*. San Francisco: Jossey-Bass.

Kindred, H. 1979. Legal education in Canadian schools? *Dalhousie Law Journal* 5 (2): 534–542.

Lengel, J. 1984. A tale of two gates. *Update on Law-Related Education* (Fall): 27–28.

Marker, G. and H. Mehlinger. 1992. Social studies. In *Handbook of research on curriculum*, ed. P.W. Jackson. New York: Macmillan.

McDermid, M., M. Abbott, and R. Case, eds. 2003. *Rights, roles and responsibilities at school*. Richmond, BC: The Critical Thinking Consortium.

Newmann, F.M. 1989. *Education for citizen action: Challenge for secondary curriculum*. Berkeley, CA: McCutchan.

Nicol, J. and D. Kirk. 2004. *Caring for young people's rights*. Richmond, BC: The Critical Thinking Consortium.

Norton, J. 1992. The State v. the Big Bad Wolf: A study of the justice system in the elementary school. *Social Studies and the Young Learner* 5 (1): 5–9.

Starr, I. 1989. The law studies movement: A brief look at the past, the present and the future. In *Law vs. learning: Examination for discovery*, ed. W. Crawford, 11–15. Toronto: Canadian Law Information Council.

Whitley, C. 2002. Building citizenship, democracy and a community of learners within a context of a restorative justice model. Unpublished master's project. Burnaby, BC: Simon Fraser University.

SUPPLEMENTARY RESOURCES

WEBSITES SUITABLE FOR ELEMENTARY GRADES

Law*Central* Canada. Law*Central* Schools: Law Related Resources, Teachers' Tools, and Student Extras: www.lawcentralschools.ca/abc/default.aspx.

BC Civil Liberties Association. Citizenship teaching module: www.bccla.org/citizenship.

Justice Education Society of BC. Resources and programs for teachers: www.justiceeducation.ca/teachers-youth.

Centre for Education, Law and Society (CELS). Articles and lesson plans for classroom use: www.lawconnection.ca.

Public Legal Education Association of Saskatchewan (PLEA). Elementary and secondary school resources related to the law: www.plea.org.

United Nations Cyberschoolbus. Global legal issues from children's perspectives: www.un.org/pubs/cyberschoolbus.

STORIES WITH LAW-RELATED DIMENSIONS

Ering, Timothy Basil. 2003. *The Story of Frog Belly Rat Bone*. Cambridge, MA: Candlewick Press. Cementland is gray and ugly. One day, a boy finds a special and mysterious treasure that promises to change Cementland into an enjoyable place. When thieves steal the treasure, he must come up with a creative plan to thwart them and save the treasure.

Issues: Who does the treasure legally belong to? What punishment should the thieves face? What are the legal issues involved in the boy's plan to save the treasure? If the thieves have a change of heart, should the charges be dropped? What are the rights and responsibilities of the citizens of Cementland?

Levine, Arthur A. 1993. *Pearl Moscowitz's Last Stand*. Illustrated by Robert Roth. New York: Tambourine Books. The neighbourhood on Gingko Street has experienced many changes throughout the years. Friendships flourish as new families arrive from new cultures, but one by one, the cherished gingko trees have disappeared. When City Hall decides to remove the last tree, in the name of progress, Pearl Moscowitz gathers the community together to take a stand.

Issues: How can a community exercise democratic involvement and have a meaningful effect on civic decisions? Are there times when civil disobedience is the only option? Explore the issue of protection of the environment versus "progress."

Miller, William. 1998. *The Bus Ride.* Illustrated by John Ward. New York: Lee & Low Books. The story of an African-American girl and her mom who challenge an unjust law. Though they must sit at the back of the bus, one day the little girl moves up to the front—causing a huge discussion across the city. This story is loosely based on Rosa Parks' historic decision not to give up her seat to a white passenger on a bus in Montgomery, Alabama, in 1955.

Issues: This story examines discrimination, racism, individual rights, and changing laws.

Patron, Susan. 1991. *Burgoo Stew.* Illustrated by Mike Shenon. New York: Orchard Books. Five mean and hungry boys from a poor area go to their neighbour's house and demand that he make them some food, or else they will steal it. In the end, the neighbour teaches the boys to share and help.

Issues: This story looks at bullying, intimidation, theft, and sharing.

Wildsmith, Brian. 1993. *The Owl and the Woodpecker.* Oxford University Press. The animals in the forest hold a meeting to try to resolve a problem between two members of their community who are fighting. Woodpecker is creating a noise during the day when Owl is trying to sleep. Neither of them will move. The peaceful life of the forest is being destroyed.

Issues: How does a community resolve a problem between two members who both think they are right? Who has a legal right to stay? What legal obligations do the woodpecker and the owl have to preserve the peace? Explore the actions of each animal in relation to social responsibility, diversity, democratic rights and responsibilities, and solving problems.

PUBLIC LEGAL EDUCATION AGENCIES IN CANADA

There are a number of organizations and resources available to teachers who wish to enhance the program they offer in law-related education.

Alberta
Centre for Public Legal Education
#800, 10050 – 112 Street
Edmonton, AB T5N 2J1
Tel: 780-451-8764
Fax: 780-451-2341
www.cplea.ca

British Columbia
Centre for Education, Law and Society
Simon Fraser University
250 – 13450 – 102 Avenue
Surrey, BC V3T 0A3
Tel: 778-782-8045
cels.sfu.ca

Justice Education Society of BC
260 – 800 Hornby Street
Vancouver, BC V6Z 2C5
Tel: 604-660-9870
www.justiceeducation.ca/

Legal Services Society
400 – 510 Burrard Street
Vancouver, BC V6C 3A8
Tel: 604-601-6000
www.lss.bc.ca

People's Law School
150 – 900 Howe Street
Vancouver, BC V6Z 2M4
Tel: 604-331-5400
www.publiclegaled.bc.ca

Manitoba
Community Legal Education Association
205 – 414 Graham Avenue
Winnipeg, MB R3C 0L8
Tel: 204-943-2382
www.communitylegal.mb.ca

New Brunswick
Public Legal Education and Information Service of New Brunswick
P.O. Box 6000
Fredericton, NB E3B 5H1
Tel: 506 453-5369
www.legal-info-legale.nb.ca

Newfoundland
Public Legal Information of Newfoundland
31 Peet Street, Suite 227
St. John's, NL A1B 3W8
Tel: 709-722-2643
www.publiclegalinfo.com

Northwest Territories

Law Society of the Northwest Territories
4th Floor, Diamond Plaza
5204 – 50th Avenue
P.O. Box 1298
Yellowknife, NT   X1A 2N9
Tel: 867-873-3828
www.lawsociety.nt.ca

Nova Scotia

Legal Information Society of Nova Scotia
5523 B Young Street
Halifax, NS   B3K 1Z7
Tel: 902-454-2198
www.legalinfo.org

Ontario

Community Legal Education Ontario
119 Spadina Avenue, Suite 600
Toronto, ON   M5V 2L1
Tel: 416-408-4420
www.cleo.on.ca

Justice for Children and Youth
Canadian Foundation for Children, Youth and the Law
415 Yonge Street, Suite 1203
Toronto, ON   M5B 2E7
Tel: 416-920-1633
www.jfcy.org

Prince Edward Island

Community Legal Information Association of Prince Edward
    Island
P.O. Box 1207
1st Floor, Sullivan Building
Fitzroy Street
Charlottetown, PEI   C1A 7M8
Tel: 902-892-0853
www.cliapei.ca

Quebec

Barreau du Québec
445 boulevard Saint Laurent
Montréal, PQ   H2Y 3T8
Tel: 514-954-3459
www.barreau.qc.ca/en

Commission des Services Juridiques
2, Complexe Desjardins
Tour Est, Bureau 1404
C.P. 123, Succursale Desjardins
Montréal, PQ   H5B 1B3
Tel: 514-873-3562
www.csj.qc.ca/SiteComm/W2007English/Main_En_v3.asp

Ministère de la Justice du Québec
1200 route de l'Eglise, 6e étage
Québec, PQ   G1V 4M1
www.justice.gouv.qc.ca/English/accueil.asp

Saskatchewan

Public Legal Education Association of Saskatchewan
500 – 333 25th Street East
Saskatoon, SK   S7K 0L4
Tel: 306-653-1868
www.plea.org

Yukon

Yukon Public Legal Education Association
c/o Yukon College Library
P.O. Box 2799
Whitehorse, YK   Y1A 5K4
Tel: 867-668-5297
www.yplea.com

PART 6

Planning and Assessing for Instruction

25

Creating Course, Unit, and Lesson Plans for Elementary Social Studies

Roland Case

This chapter outlines a framework for teacher planning from the general aims for an entire course to the specific decisions about which method and resource to employ in a particular lesson. First, I offer four principles to guide deliberations: be purposeful, build thoughtfully, draw widely and wisely, and plan loosely. The principles parallel the practice of experienced hikers planning a long-distance wilderness trek through boundless, unfamiliar territory: an apt metaphor for the challenges of course, unit, and lesson planning.

Guiding Principles of Planning

Hikers must be clear about where they are starting and their final destination. Otherwise, they are likely to lose their bearings, particularly in confusing terrain. Without a clear sense of direction, hikers may get lost and fail to reach their destination, or at least waste considerable time and energy. Although the destination may not be in view until near the end of a trip, hikers always know the general direction to head. Typically, they plot their route in outline form. They anticipate change, but recognize the value of having a clear plan, even a provisional one. To keep themselves on track, hikers identify prominent features or landmarks in intermediate reach to serve as beacons. Of course, the bulk of hikers' time is spent attending to immediate objectives—getting up a ravine, checking resources, maintaining positive morale, and so on. Hikers look for easy routes or pre-established paths to expedite their travel, and they take detours when there is reason to. Hikers continually double-check, often

intuitively, that the choices they make are aligned with the more distant beacon.

The many insights about effective planning to be drawn from this analogy can be summarized in four general principles: be purposeful, build thoughtfully, draw widely and wisely, and plan loosely.

BE PURPOSEFUL

The principle that planning should be purposeful is my most significant recommendation. We need to decide where we want to take our students and to use that destination to orient everything we do. Without clear, conscious direction, our teaching is aimless—amounting to a string of activities leading nowhere in particular and serving no important purpose. Just as trekkers need to set and be guided by long-, intermediate-, and immediate-term destinations, so do teachers:

- Our ultimate destinations are our ideals or ultimate vision—for society and for our students.
- Our intermediate destinations (the beacons) are our goals for an individual unit and course.
- Our immediate destinations are our objectives for specific lessons.

The principle of being purposeful does not suppose a "teacher-driven" approach. There can be extensive student involvement in setting destinations, and individuals can be encouraged to strike out in different directions when feasible. It often makes sense for students of varying abilities and interests to follow different paths towards the same ultimate destination.

For purposeful planning, destinations should meet four criteria. They should be:

- **Clear and focussed.** Both in the long and short term, we should know what we hope to achieve with our students. Vaguely understood goals and objectives do not provide a sense of purpose, just as vague or vast landmarks, say a mountain range or an ocean, will not keep hikers on a consistent path.
- **Manageable.** We should not expect to do it all and if we try—in an entire course or in an individual lesson—we might end up doing a superficial job that makes no lasting difference.
- **Justifiable.** We cannot pursue our own preferred direction without seriously considering students' best interests, parents' rights, and other curricular and professional responsibilities.
- **Aligned.** Our long- and short-term destinations must be in alignment, so that we are continually working towards our ultimate destination. This requires that:
  - rationale inform our goals;
  - goals orient our objectives; and
  - objectives determine our day-to-day decisions about teaching methods, resources, and assessment.

BUILD THOUGHTFULLY

Building thoughtfully involves anticipating the intermediate steps and the resources and tools needed to achieve our ultimate goals. One of Chinese philosopher Lao Tzu's expressions is especially relevant: a journey of a thousand miles starts with a single step. It is not enough that we have a grand plan; we must also attend to how we will get there. Just as the trekker must decide what equipment is needed to cross a river and what supplies are necessary for survival, teachers must also consider what students need to reach the desired goals.

Effective implementation of the principle of thoughtful building depends on at least three considerations:

- **Nurture an environment conducive to learning.** We must work to develop the classroom and school environment that supports the desired learning. For example, if we want to develop student autonomy, we must establish a climate that encourages students to take risks and make up their own minds.

- **Provide meaningful contexts for learning.** A concern expressed by many teachers is that students do not perceive social studies to be relevant. We can help students better appreciate social studies by planning activities that will motivate them, and by framing our units and lessons in contexts that resonate with them.
- **Teach the prerequisites.** Just as it is unfair to expect someone to construct an elaborate house without having the tools to do the job, so is it unfair to expect significant student achievement without providing the intellectual tools needed for success. We must think through what students require for success at each step—for example, what knowledge, abilities, and attitudes students need to become good researchers. Then, we must plan how to assist students in acquiring these tools.

DRAW WIDELY AND WISELY

Preoccupation with a narrow theme and overreliance on a single method, such as lectures, or a single resource such as a textbook, are like staying on pre-established paths long after they cease to lead towards the destination. We must draw imaginatively from varied planning approaches, methods and resources in our quest for better ways to help students get where we want them to go.

Effective implementation of the principle of drawing widely and wisely involves:

- **Integrating the content of different disciplines and subjects.** We should make meaningful links among the disciplines within social studies, draw insights from other subjects, and connect what students study in school with their experiences and concerns.
- **Using diverse learning resources.** We should make effective use of diverse resources from computers to cartoons, textbooks to picture books, and feature films to guest speakers.
- **Using varied teaching methods.** We should plan a rich array of activities from teacher-directed to student-directed, written work to small-group conversation, and seat-work to fieldwork.

PLAN LOOSELY

The principle of planning loosely arises because there is no guaranteed path for all students for all times; planning is a messy and uncertain affair. Not only will one path not work for all students, but conditions change, our students change, and we change. We should be prepared to reformulate our plans to accommodate the countless unanticipated turns that arise halfway through the year or in the middle of a lesson. However, planning is not fanciful, but rather a deeply practical matter. Its point is to identify what is most worthwhile to teach and then to design a course, a unit, or a lesson that increases the likelihood of success.

Effective implementation of the principle of planning loosely involves the following:

- **Expect diversity.** Always expect and accommodate diversity in student interests and abilities as much as possible.
- **Allow for student choice.** Entrench opportunities for student choice and self-direction in our teaching.
- **Stay flexible.** Remain open to change. Instead of viewing a lesson or unit plan as the fixed menu for the day or month, we should look on planning as a vehicle for scrutinizing where our teaching is heading and deciding how to get there.

I believe these four principles should permeate all of our planning, from decisions about ultimate goals to our most immediate objectives. I offer a four-level framework for planning that embodies these principles:

- the vision for the year;
- a course plan;
- unit plans; and
- individual lesson plans.

These levels are akin to progressive snapshots of the Earth, beginning with a global view and zeroing in on a particular site. Each level has increasing detail of a progressively smaller area of instruction. Despite sequencing discussion of the model from the general to the specific, planning need not proceed this way. Those who like to begin with the concrete will find it more productive to start with particular lessons and resources, and work from there to the more general vision. Regardless of where we start, all of us will likely move back and forth between levels as our ideas become clearer. By the end of our planning deliberations, however, we will need to have thought through the issues raised at each level in a coherent way.

Realistically, the full set of plans outlined in this framework would take years of thinking and piloting to complete. Nevertheless, all of us, and especially new teachers, can benefit from a deeper understanding of the considerations of comprehensive planning. The framework is an ultimate destination—an invitation to strive for an ideal. Even if the ideal is never fully reached, we will get closer to where we want to be by attempting it.

Creating a Vision for the Year

The most general level of planning involves creating a vision for the entire year. In effect, it asks: "In a hundred words or less, what am I really attempting to achieve in social studies this year?" The point of planning at this level is to give focus to a course. Figure 25.1 is a form that might be used to articulate a vision for the year. There are three main components:

- **Rationale.** Our rationale should be a clear and defensible account of our educational ideals—the ultimate purpose of our efforts as educators.
- **Priority goals.** Our priority goals are the handful of educational goals that will be the major focus of attention for the year. We must have priorities because we cannot do everything well. If these goals are met, we will have moved students closer to the ideals set out in our rationale.
- **Classroom climate.** The classroom climate is the qualities and procedures that define a learning environment that promotes the priority goals and, ultimately, our rationale.

FORMULATING A RATIONALE

A rationale is a description of the ideal individual or society we hope to promote through education. Four broad categories of rationales for social studies may be positioned along two continua:

Social acceptance/social change continuum
- **Social initiation.** Transmitting the understandings, abilities, and values that students require to fit into, and be contributing members of, society.
- **Social reform.** Promoting the understandings, abilities, and values necessary to critique and improve society.

Student-centred/subject-centred continuum
- **Personal development.** Fostering the personal talents and character of each student so that they develop fully as individuals and social beings.
- **Intellectual development.** Developing understanding and appreciation of the knowledge and forms of inquiry in social science.

In the sample vision for the year, Figure 25.2, you will find elements from each of these four categories. Two questions should guide thinking about our rationale: Am I clear about the ideals I am striving for? Are these justifiable ideals?

FIGURE 25.1   VISION FOR THE YEAR

THEME FOR THE YEAR		GRADE
Rationale		
Priority Goals		**Classroom Climate**
Content knowledge	Personal and social values	
Critical thinking	Individual and collective action	
Information accessing and reporting	Other	

CLARITY OF FOCUS

Many of the ideals found in rationales for social studies—such as personal autonomy, critical thinking, productive citizenship, or tolerant society—are potentially vague. Unless we are clear in our own minds what we mean by such notions, they will not be useful guides to our planning. Does a tolerant society mean that we begrudgingly accept differences? What sorts of differences will we tolerate? Religious views? Alternative lifestyles? Perhaps we want to focus largely on racial, ethnic, and cultural differences. We may also want an embracing vision that is not about putting up with differences but welcoming and accepting people because of their cultural contributions. These are different emphases, and being clear about these particulars is useful when planning.

JUSTIFIED IDEALS

The following considerations should guide our decisions about whether or not our rationale is justifiable. Does it address:

- the broad needs of our students?
- the broad needs of the local community?
- the broad needs of society? and
- our own values as educators?

The value of a clear, justifiable rationale is that it helps us to recognize and stick to what really matters.

I remember getting bogged down in the minutiae of the curriculum and frustrated by the day's events while teaching an especially troubled group of grade 6/7 students. It was at these times that I reminded myself why I was there. Long before I called it my "rationale," I knew my reason for persisting was to help these students take personal responsibility for their lives. I had seen too many of their peers fall by the wayside, driven to self-destruction by a lack of trust of others and a lack of respect for themselves. I hoped I could teach them about literature and science along the way, but not if pursuing these goals interrupted my more pressing mission. My justification for this "personal development" rationale was that functional literacy, personal responsibility, and self-respect were what these students most needed in their lives and what their parents most hoped for them.

ESTABLISHING PRIORITY GOALS

Establishing priority goals is a step in implementing our rationale. Priority goals identify our key educational emphases for the year. If we could make a real difference in several areas, what would we hope to achieve? With the students described above, my priorities included teaching them to read at the level required to understand a newspaper; commit themselves to a task and complete it; treat each other with respect; and develop pride in themselves.

In deciding what to emphasize in a given year, it is useful to consider how our rationale could be advanced through the general goals of social studies. The

FIGURE 25.2 SAMPLE VISION FOR THE YEAR

THEME FOR THE YEAR Canada before and after Confederation	GRADE middle school

Rationale

My ideal citizen is:
- able to cope with a complex, uncertain world
- willing and trained to think things through rigorously
- knowledgeable about a wide range of issues
- committed and willing to work to make the world better for all
- emotionally mature and socially adept

Priority Goals		Classroom Climate
Content knowledge • understands the complexities and interrelations of many of the historical and contemporary problems in Canada • has knowledge of both the ennobling and regrettable events in Canada's past	**Personal and social values** • has empathy and respect for others • is committed to social justice • is respectful of different viewpoints • has tolerance for ambiguity • is independent-minded	• respectful, safe environment • students challenged in non-threatening ways • emphasis on self-directed learning—independent projects, peer and self-assessment • abundant opportunities for student choice • students expected to form personal opinions and support them with reasons
Critical thinking • can competently analyze controversial issues • sees issues from varying perspectives • possesses the tools of a good critical thinker	**Individual and collective action** • is able and willing to work co-operatively with others, even in difficult situations • can plan thoughtfully to solve demanding problems	
Information accessing and reporting • can plan and conduct independent research • can effectively use media and other local sources of information	**Other**	

following list represents the range of goals social studies typically seeks to promote:

- **content knowledge:** the breadth and depth of factual and conceptual knowledge students should possess about their world;
- **critical thinking:** the ability and inclination to assess what to believe and how to act competently;
- **information accessing and reporting:** the ability to identify information needs, extract information from varied sources, and represent this information in appropriate forms;
- **personal and social values:** the desired values about ourselves and others; and
- **individual and collective action:** the ability to analyze problems in our lives and in society, plan appropriate courses of action individually and in collaboration with others, put plans into action, and evaluate their effectiveness.

We need not be bound by these goals, and may prefer to use the terminology of the provincial curriculum or some other document. In an integrated course, we would include goals from other subjects as well as social studies. What is important is identifying a manageable number of priority goals. We will, of course, pursue many other goals; but our priorities are the most productive and pressing avenues to promote our ideals. Often our rationale overlaps with our priority goals because some of the ideals in our rationale are direct aims of social studies. Typically, however, our ideals are broader aspirations, and we emphasize only some aspect of them. For example, a "social reform" rationale might include the ideals of promoting a world without poverty, hunger, and war. In a given year, we might emphasize only a few goals that promote these ideals, for example, teaching students to treat one another respectfully and to use peer-mediation and other non-violent forms of interpersonal conflict resolution.

FIGURE 25.3 COURSE PLAN

UNIT DESCRIPTION	UNIT OBJECTIVES				
	Content knowledge	Critical thinking	Information accessing and reporting	Personal and social values	Individual and collective action
Unit 1 Synopsis Main goals					
Unit 2 Synopsis Main goals					
Unit 3 Synopsis Main goals					
Unit 4 Synopsis Main goals					
Unit 5 Synopsis Main goals					

In deciding our priority goals, we should consider:

- the needs and expressed wishes of our students;
- the provincial curriculum;
- the nature of social studies and the purposes it is expected to serve;
- the expressed wishes of parents and the community;
- the needs of society; and
- our own priorities and strengths as educators.

SHAPING THE CLASSROOM CLIMATE

Although classroom climate has not traditionally been seen as part of the defining vision of a course, it is increasingly obvious that this factor plays a significant role in supporting or impeding the achievement of social studies goals. Many of us will have been frustrated by a prevailing mood in the class that undermined students' thinking critically about issues or taking responsibility for their learning. We can identify and plan how to guide the conduct of our class to best serve our goals. As an example, consider the rationale of promoting students' ability to think things through with rigour. To take the risks involved in thinking for themselves, students need a classroom that is safe and respectful. Also, the "challenging" required to help students probe their thinking deeply must be non-threatening. These features are important operating principles for the classroom. See chapter 10, "Supporting a Community of Critical Inquiry," for more about nurturing classroom climate.

Developing a Course Plan

Although the vision for the year is our ultimate destination and should always be at the back of our minds, like trekkers, we will not have that vision constantly in our sights. Our conscious focus will be more immediate: deciding what we have to teach in September and November in

TYPES OF UNIT ORGANIZERS

Theme

The connection among elements in the unit is that they are in some way associated with a common theme. Some types of themes are:

- **Places.** For example: Egypt, our neighbourhood, deserts, the moon.
- **Events.** For example: building the pyramids, inventing the atomic bomb.
- **Eras.** For example: the Depression, pre-Copernican Europe.
- **Concepts.** For example: friendship, harmony, time, creativity.
- **Generalizations.** For example: humans are social animals, history repeats itself.
- **Phenomena.** For example: evolution, war, growing up.
- **Entities.** For example: bears, atoms, multinational companies.

Narrative

A narrative is a series of episodes that uses a familiar structure for connecting and building upon a unit's elements. Each element must fit the story being told. Some sample narratives are:

- developing story of a country, province, or city
- tale of a people, family, or person
- steps in a discovery or invention
- account of a quest or adventure

Issue

An issue is a question about what ought to be the case; it invites a value judgment. Entire units might focus on issues such as:

- Should students have a right to select their textbook?
- Are large families better than small families?

- Should further technological innovation be encouraged?
- Which innovation from ancient Greece has had the most influence on our lives?

Inquiry

An inquiry is a specific question inviting students to uncover how things were, are, or are likely to become. Entire units might be organized around inquiries such as:

- What motivated/drove famous people to greatness?
- How is "waste" dealt with in nature?
- What will my life be like thirty years from now?
- Is the United States more like ancient Sparta or Athens?

Problem

A problem is a specific question about a course of action. Instead of merely talking about what should or might occur, entire units could lead students to act on problems such as:

- Can we reduce the amount of paper wasted in school?
- How can our school be made more safe?
- What can we do to protect our parks and wildlife?
- What can we do to improve working conditions in developing countries?

Project

A project involves creation of a "product" of some kind. Entire units might focus on products such as:

- a model or replica
- a demonstration or performance
- a diorama or mural
- a written or audiovisual piece

order to get where we want to be in June. The purpose of the second level of the planning model—the course plan—is to set out the general sequence and structure of the pursuit of our goals. Just as a long trip is broken into phases, so too is the journey through the curriculum divided up into units of study—usually between three and five units over the course of a year. The course plan plots the objectives or outcomes to be promoted in each unit. Figure 25.3 is a form that might be used to lay out a course plan. It includes:

- choosing an appropriate focus for units;
- identifying specific objectives for each unit; and
- sequencing objectives across units.

DECIDING ON A UNIT FOCUS

Typically, planning a course begins with identifying the topic or unifying idea for each unit. These unit organizers provide the vehicle for promoting the goals; they are the shell within which the contents of a unit will develop. The most common type of unit organizer is a theme (for example, families, communities, our natural resources), but there are other types. The feature "Types of Unit Organizers" describes six types of unit organizers.

The type of organizer we use influences the shape or direction of a unit. For example, a unit organized around the theme of the explorer Simon Fraser provides a different orientation than a project-based unit organized around the tasks of researching, writing, and producing a play about Simon Fraser's travels, or an issue-based unit on judging Simon Fraser a hero or a rogue. Although there will be overlap in what is learned

TABLE 25.1   UNPACKING THE UNDERLYING IDEA OF A UNIT

UNIFYING IDEA/BROAD UNDERSTANDING	CURRICULAR OUTCOMES ADDRESSED (BC CURRICULUM 2006)	GUIDING QUESTIONS
Families care for each other and work together to meet each other's needs. (grade 1)	Describe basic human needs. Describe how families can be similar and different. Describe roles and responsibilities at home. Identify strategies to address a school-based problem.	How does my family help me? How can I best contribute to my family? What are the benefits of a small/big family? What are my most powerful family memories? How might we help this family?
A community is more than buildings and places; it is a network of interdependent people who work together. (grade 3)	Describe the importance of communities. Describe the roles and responsibilities of local government. Compare ways in which needs and wants are met in communities. Describe how personal roles, rights, and responsibilities can affect the well-being of the community. Gather information from a variety of sources. Formulate a response to a relevant issue or problem.	What people and places in my community are important to me? Who contributes to my quality of life? How can I contribute to my community? What are the different experiences of people in my community? What is community "spirit"? What makes a good community?

in all three units, there will also be important differences. Accordingly, we should select unit topics that best advance our goals.

Surprisingly, identifying a unit organizer need not define what will be taught in a unit. For example, a unit with the theme "ancient Egypt" might focus on any number of studies:

- the environment's significance in shaping human activity (for example, the impact of the Nile);
- the thinking behind religious and cultural practices of "foreign" groups (for example, studying the rationale for embalming, beliefs about reincarnation);
- the mathematical and engineering accomplishments of civilization (for example, building pyramids);
- the work of archaeologists in adding to our knowledge (for example, carrying out a simulated dig, reading about famous discoveries).

Various educators have stressed the power of unpacking these kinds of underlying ideas in a topic through "essential" or guiding questions (Erickson 1998, Wiggins and McTighe 2005) to guide students in "uncovering" the curriculum. The examples in Table 25.1 illustrate how underlying ideas, curricular outcomes, and guiding questions help create a focus for learning activities.

An important step in focussing a unit is to decide upon three or four goals to emphasize and use these goals to guide how the topic is best handled: as a theme or an issue? And what theme or issue in particular? The partial course plan in Figure 25.4 contains a synopsis, the main goals, and the objectives for the first unit in a year-long course of nineteenth-century

Canada. The main goals of this unit are to help students learn to work effectively together in groups, to teach them about conducting independent research, and to develop a broad understanding of key events leading up to Confederation. The unit organizer—a project to create a giant timeline of events during this period—was chosen because it is a good vehicle to serve these three goals.

IDENTIFYING SPECIFIC OBJECTIVES

As we think about our unit topic and main goals, we begin to identify specific objectives or learning outcomes for the unit, which need to be outlined more systematically. At this stage we are not concerned about teaching methods—what we will have students do—but rather what we hope students will learn. That said, many teachers prefer to begin with activities and then decide the objectives.

Objectives are simply more specific elements of a goal; objectives often take a lesson or two to cover, whereas goals are more general aims that may take an entire unit or longer to achieve. The key challenge in identifying specific objectives is to unpack what is involved in promoting the goals we have set for the unit and for the year. For example, in developing a sample unit plan, we want to think through what objectives are involved in promoting the goal of independent library research. What are the crucial tools students need in order to develop this ability and which of these are best taught in this unit? Should students learn to use library reference aids, the internet and other electronic research

FIGURE 25.4 SAMPLE COURSE PLAN

UNIT DESCRIPTION

Unit #1

Timeline: The lead-up to Confederation

Synopsis

The class is divided into five teams that are to research and prepare a giant illustrated timeline that will be posted around the classroom depicting the major social, political, cultural, and economic events and people in Canada from 1815 to Confederation. Each team is responsible for researching, documenting, and illustrating major landmarks and key figures for a ten-year period. Groups must decide by consensus, on the basis of agreed-upon criteria, the most significant events and persons of their time period. Students are expected to share their findings orally and prepare a background sheet to be handed out to the class. The unit will conclude with a student-created exam on events and people depicted in the timeline.

Main goals

- Learn to work effectively and co-operatively in groups.
- Learn to conduct independent library research.
- Develop a broad overview of events leading to Confederation.

UNIT OBJECTIVES

Content knowledge	Critical thinking	Information accessing and reporting	Personal and social values	Individual and collective action
• Understands the political, economic, social, and geographical factors leading to Confederation. • Has knowledge of key events and persons in the development of Canada from 1815 to 1867.	• Is able to assess appropriateness of information sources for a purpose. • Is able to use criteria to reach a reasoned decision.	• Uses library reference aids to locate sources (for example, bibliography, catalogue, electronic search engines). • Uses textual aids to locate information (for example, table of contents, index, glossary, keywords, headings, legend). • Summarizes ideas in his or her own words. • Uses graphics (for example, timelines, charts, graphs) to present information. • Communicates clearly and accurately both orally and visually.	• Takes pride in preparing quality work. • Respects opinions and is supportive of others. • Respects the rights of everyone in the group.	• Understands collaboration, co-operation, compromise, consensus. • Engages respectfully in group discussion. • Plans how to organize the group, divide up the tasks, and schedule and monitor the work plan. • Fulfills roles and responsibilities effectively and fairly.

tools? If students already know how to locate information sources, do they need help extracting information from these sources?

Although it is difficult to do, the best place to begin articulating objectives at this degree of specificity is during course planning, by examining the main goals of the unit and developing lists of more specific objectives for each. The curriculum guide or other teacher resources often provide detailed objectives for specific goals. We will not be able to do it all in any one unit; we must decide the most important objectives. As a general rule, we are well advised to do a smaller number of things very well, rather than attempt to do too many things and end up doing them poorly. If we focus on a few main goals, three or four perhaps, if time runs out, the key objectives of our main goals will not be sacrificed.

The following considerations are particularly relevant for deciding unit objectives:

- the overall rationale for the course and the main goals for the unit;
- students' interests and prior learning;
- the requirements of the provincial curriculum;
- our own teaching interests and competencies;
- the resources available in the school and district; and
- the possibilities for integration with other areas of study.

SEQUENCING OBJECTIVES ACROSS UNITS

The final task in developing a one-year overview is to decide on the scope and sequence of objectives from unit to unit. The prime consideration in the scope of objectives is to make sure the entire set of curricular objectives is addressed over the course of the year. When considering sequence, we must check that the order in which we plan to teach objectives is reasonable; for example, the objectives planned for early in a unit do not rely on objectives not yet taught. In many instances, the sequence of many objectives will not matter; for example, whether we teach students to interpret photographs or maps first. In other cases, the sequence may be crucial. For example, teaching basic procedures for using the internet, such as finding websites given an address, must be taught prior to introducing more sophisticated tools such as searching. There are no hard and fast rules about scope and sequence of objectives. Here are some suggestions for ways to proceed over the year:

- from simple to difficult;

- from concrete to abstract;
- from general to specific;
- in chronological order (especially relevant with content objectives);
- in reverse chronological order from present working back;
- from near to far; and
- from far to near.

Using the social studies curriculum for a particular grade level, develop a vision for the entire year including a brief outline of the focus and main objectives for three or four units. You may want to use the templates in this chapter ("Vision for the Year" and "Course Plan"). Systematically develop aspects of your priority goals for the year throughout the units.

Outlining Unit Plans

The next, and more specific, level of planning is developing the details of each unit in the course plan. As illustrated in Figure 25.5, unit plans typically consist of summary notes outlining the objectives for the lessons, the proposed methods or activities, the anticipated resources needed, and the suggested assessment strategy for each. A unit might contain anywhere from ten to twenty lessons. One procedure for developing a unit plan follows:

- Brainstorm teaching strategies and resources to promote the goals and objectives. Look for teaching resources in a school library, teacher's resource centre, or catalogues of print and multimedia resources to supplement your ideas. Talk to others who have taught the topic. Assemble as many ideas and resources as you can.
- Identify an introductory activity: first impressions are important. This same principle applies to introducing new units of study. The introductory lesson(s) to a unit:
  - arouses student interest and provokes questions;
  - provides background information and sets context for what is to follow;
  - provides diagnostic information about students' current knowledge, attitudes, and skills; and
  - helps teacher and students formulate a plan of action for study.

The feature "Ways to Introduce a Unit" offers suggestions for beginning new units of instruction in an engaging and effective manner.
- Identify a culminating activity to summarize or

FIGURE 25.5 UNIT PLAN

UNIT TOPIC		GRADE	UNIT #
Unit goals	1. 2. 3. 4.		

LESSON TITLE	SPECIFIC OBJECTIVES	METHODS/ ACTIVITIES	RESOURCES	ASSESSMENT STRATEGIES AND CRITERIA

draw attention to the main goals and provide an occasion to demonstrate students' learning. The culminating activity may refer back to the introduction or be used to "frame" the unit and be previewed at the beginning of the unit.

- Indicate the specific lessons and their order, and specify objectives for each lesson. Check the course plan to see that all relevant objectives for that unit are addressed. Select the teaching strategies, student activities, and learning resources from your brainstorming that will best serve each lesson's objective(s). Also specify your assessment strategy for the lesson's objectives, including what qualities, or criteria, you will look for in students' work (e.g., the report is well organized, shows evidence of empathy for the people described, and is historically accurate).
- Finally, review the draft unit plan with another person to ensure:
  - *Adequate emphasis on each goal.* Verify that the activities and objectives in the unit plan match the main goals in the course plan. If there is a shift,

either bring the unit back into line to promote the main goals, or change the unit's focus.
- *Appropriate sequence.* Check to see that lessons are ordered in a reasonable sequence with prerequisite objectives taught first, and that the unit builds towards a culminating activity with a sense of completion for students.
- *Reasonable flow.* Check if lessons are connected over the whole unit with adequate transitions. Although every lesson will not follow smoothly from one to the next, the better the flow, the less student confusion there will be.
- *Rich variety.* Review the proposed activities, resources, and assessment strategies for variety, rather than relying excessively on one or two types of activities (for example, answering questions from a textbook) or assessment strategies (for example, journal reflections).

Figure 25.6 is a sample of a partial unit plan.

FIGURE 25.6 SAMPLE UNIT PLAN

UNIT TOPIC: OUR SCHOOL COMMUNITY			GRADE 1	UNIT #
Unit goals	1. Develop students' ability to read simple maps. 2. Increase students' familiarity and comfort with the school setting and staff. 3. Develop students' appreciation of the contributions that others make to the school. 4. Develop students' ability to use criteria in thinking critically.			

LESSON TITLE	SPECIFIC OBJECTIVES	METHODS/ACTIVITIES	RESOURCES	ASSESSMENT STRATEGIES AND CRITERIA
Making school our home	• learn the layout of the school • learn the meaning of the concept "criteria" • learn to use criteria in making a decision	Read *Welcome Back to Pokeweed Public School*. Introduce map of our school and lead students on a tour of their school. Make a list of people and places encountered. Brainstorm what might be done to make the school more "homey" (for example, get to know everyone, learn where everything is). Introduce the concept of "criteria"—what something "looks like" or "sounds like" when it is done right. Assist students in generating criteria for sound actions (that is, realistic, safe, serves purpose). Discuss which options for making school more "homey" meet the criteria for sound action. Plan how the class might carry out some of these options.	• *Welcome Back to Pokeweed Public School* by John Bianchi	• assess whether students recognize when a possible option meets or does not meet the criteria
Learning to read maps	• learn to read symbols and locate sites on simple maps	Read *Mandy and the Flying Map* to introduce the idea of maps. Discuss the concept of a "bird's-eye" view. Walk students through a classroom map pointing out things on the map and in the classroom. Play a game where students think of things in the classroom and give clues on the map to help others guess the object.	• *Mandy and the Flying Map* by Ann Powell • overhead or poster-sized map of the classroom	• using a game format, assess whether students correctly move to places identified on the classroom map • assess whether students can correctly point on the map to classroom objects
Touring our school	• learn to follow simple maps and locate objects on the map	Working in small groups and accompanied by a parent or helper, students go on another tour of the school. They are to trace the route followed and add features to their maps as they come to key spots in the school.	• copies of a simple school map	• assess students' ability to correctly locate their location on the map and draw objects in the school on their maps
Who are the people in our school?	• learn who works in the school	Read *Who's Behind the Door at Our School?* Students list the people in their school and the position they have (that is, Ms. Smith is the principal; Mrs. Jones, the custodian; Mr. Chan, learning assistance teacher). Paste photographs of each person on a poster next to their name and position.	• *Who's Behind the Door at Our School?* by Michael Salmon • staff photographs	• using a game format, assess that students can correctly match the name, picture, and position of each staff member

FIGURE 25.6   SAMPLE UNIT PLAN (CONT.)

What do the people in our school do?	• learn the duties performed by each staff member	Brainstorm questions students might ask to learn more about each person and what they do. Discuss the criteria for a good question (clear, gives lots of information—not "yes" or "no," may be unexpected). As a class, decide upon a common set of questions to use to interview each staff member. Pairs of students interview a designated person. Students trace the route to the interview on their map.	• interview question and recording sheets for each pair of students	• assess whether students recognize when a question meets or does not meet the criteria • assess whether students correctly trace their route on the school map
Who's contributing the most?	• appreciate staff contributions to school • learn to support positions with a reason	Record information gathered from interviews on posters next to each person's picture. Discuss criteria for deciding who contributes most (protects safety, affects largest number of students). Students vote for the three people who are doing the most to make the school a positive place, providing a reason for each choice.	• "ballot" to vote for three most significant contributors	• using the "ballot," assess whether students offer a relevant reason for each choice • observe informally during class discussions to see if students show appreciation for staff contributions

Creating Lesson Plans

The most specific level of planning is the individual lesson. This is where we think through exactly what, when, and how each lesson will transpire. The more experienced we are, the less detailed our lesson plans need to be. There are many ways to plan a lesson; I recommend dividing the lesson plan into seven tasks, described below and outlined in Figure 25.7.

- **Formulate lesson objectives.** Objectives specify what we expect students to learn from the activities. These objectives will already be identified if a unit plan has been developed. Although there is no hard and fast rule, it may be unwise to have more than three objectives for any given lesson. Promoting one or two outcomes effectively is preferred to attempting many things less effectively. It is important not to confuse objectives with methods. This is a statement of method: "Students will debate an issue." Statements of objectives identify what students will learn by engaging in the debate. For example, "Students will learn to express their ideas clearly" or "Students will learn to develop persuasive arguments to support their position." "Students will experience what it is like to be discriminated against" is a statement of method, whereas "students will acquire greater sensitivity to the feelings of others" is a statement of objective.

- **Introduce the lesson.** The introduction should provide an engaging and illuminating launch that creates a "mindset" and focusses attention. Here are some suggestions:
  - Establish a connection with a previous lesson.
  - Explain the purpose and value of what is to be learned.
  - Provide an overview of what will take place.
  - Invite students to share what they know about the topic.
  - Involve students in an enjoyable activity or pose a question or dilemma to arouse curiosity and set the context.

- **Develop and sequence the body of the lesson.** The body of the lesson is both the teacher instructions and student activities that make up the bulk of the learning work. Here are some suggestions:
  - Break down each objective into teachable elements and think of how each can be taught.
  - Vary the activities so there is a change of pace.
  - Think about dividing the tasks into tightly orchestrated segments between ten and twenty minutes' duration to avoid students tiring.
  - Although not always appropriate, it is useful to think of six stages in the body of a lesson:
    - *Instructional input:* the teacher or students introduce new information or a new notion, through reading or viewing.

WAYS TO INTRODUCE A UNIT

- **Audiovisuals.** Viewing an audiovisual resource is motivating and provides information for students to build on. When choosing audiovisual material to introduce a unit, focus on stimulating interest rather than the amount of information provided.
- **Brainstorming.** Brainstorming is a useful way to pre-assess students' knowledge about a topic and help them organize their current knowledge. The teacher's role is to record all responses without criticism, help students expand on others' ideas, and stick to a time limit. Following a brainstorming session, the teacher helps students sort the ideas into categories using approaches such as webbing or data retrieval charts. Keep the framework until the end of the unit so students can see how much they have learned.
- **Discrepant event.** A discrepant event provokes student thought through something unusual. For example, tell students that a civilization began on the banks of a river that flooded regularly. A desert surrounded the civilization, which made the climate dry and hot. Ask them to predict the chances of this civilization surviving and ask for guesses of the civilization's identity. If students do not guess, tell them the civilization is ancient Egypt, which flourished on the banks of the Nile River in Africa for thousands of years. Ask students why the civilization of ancient Egypt was established there. They can then do research activities to verify or refute their ideas.
- **Displays.** A teacher-created display can arouse interest and provide initial information about a topic. The display should be set up a week or more prior to beginning the unit to give students time to interact with display items and discuss them. Alternatively, students can create, or help create, displays by bringing in relevant items, articles, and illustrations.
- **Field experience.** A field experience is often considered to be most effective at the end of a unit because students have greater understanding. However, such an experience can be useful at the beginning of a unit because it piques interest and provides a springboard to further information.

- **Guest speaker.** Invite a guest who has special knowledge about the unit topic to speak. Students' parents may be willing to speak about their occupations, countries of origin, or other areas of expertise. One way to find out if parents are willing to speak is to send a questionnaire home at the beginning of the school year. Other sources of speakers include retired people's organizations, consulates, government departments and agencies, and public relations departments of large companies.
- **Music.** Play a tape that is representative of a time, place, or topic. For instance, if studying a particular country, play traditional folk music from that culture. Songs from popular Canadian children's singers can illustrate topics such as friendship, family relationships, and roles and responsibilities of family members. "The Wreck of the Edmund Fitzgerald" by Gordon Lightfoot is an example of a song connected to Canada's transportation system.
- **Mystery box.** Show students a gift-wrapped box containing several objects related to the unit. Let each student handle the box. Have students use a "twenty questions" approach to figure out which objects are in the box; they are limited to twenty questions and must begin with general questions to eliminate as many possibilities as quickly as possible. Record the guesses on the blackboard. When twenty questions have been asked, open the box and explain each object.
- **Simulation.** A simulation can be an extremely motivating unit introduction. To begin a unit on industrialization, have students simulate an assembly line. A unit on local government could be introduced with a simulated city council meeting, in which members make a decision related to commercial versus recreational uses of land. Follow up with discussion about how the simulated experience relates to the unit.
- **Stories.** Stories can engage students and bring a unit to life. The book *Maxine's Tree* by Diane Leger-Haskell could begin a unit on the environment; a Greek myth could begin a unit on ancient Greece.

- *Modelling:* the teacher or students demonstrate what is to be done with this new knowledge.
- *Trial run:* students try one or two examples (or the first steps) on their own or in small groups to see if they have grasped the task.
- *Group feedback:* the class discusses issues and difficulties encountered during the trial run.
- *Application of knowledge:* students proceed with the main assignment.

- *Coaching:* the teacher or students (in pairs or in co-operative groups) provide individual advice as problems and questions arise during the course of work on the assignment.
- **Prepare resources.** Plan what instructional materials, activity sheets, readings, and questions will be used to support the lesson.
- **Draw closure.** Propose a means for debriefing and consolidating students' learning. Closure often involves the following:
  - Students summarize what they have learned.

FIGURE 25.7   LESSON PLAN

Lesson title	
Objectives	By the end of this lesson, students will: 1. 2. 3. 4.
Introduction	
Body of lesson	
Closure	
Assessment	
Extension	

- Students apply learning to a new situation.
- The teacher synthesizes key ideas and draws connections.
- **Assess student learning.** Assessment tells us how well the objective(s) have been met. Students should be provided a clear indication of assessment prior to completing an assignment, including:
  - the criteria to be used to assess student learning; and
  - the standards or levels of performance for each criteria (what does "very good" look like and how does it differ from "good"?).
- **Extend or follow up on the lesson.** The extension is a way to provide for students who finish early. Unless we plan educationally enriching activities for them, they will waste considerable class time. Extension activities are also useful when the lesson goes more quickly than planned, and they encourage students who may want to pursue ideas further.

The sample lesson plan in Figure 25.8 illustrates many of these suggestions. The lesson's focus is the concept of inference—interpreting and drawing conclusions from accepted facts. Students consider whether or not Simon Fraser is a hero by reading a historical account of his explorations and his dealings with First Nations people.

FIGURE 25.8 SAMPLE LESSON PLAN

Lesson title	Simon Fraser: Hero or Rogue?
Objectives	By the end of this lesson, students will: • understand the concepts of "directly observed fact" and "inference" and be able to identify inferences drawn by an author; • understand that different inferences may be drawn from the same event (and the most defensible inference is the one that is most plausible given the facts); • be able to generate and defend an interpretation of a historical event; and • know about Simon Fraser's experiences with the First Nations people.
Introduction	Tell students that Simon Fraser was a famous Canadian explorer; a major river and a university have been named after him. Suggest that there is reason to suspect that history has been too kind to him; it is possible he doesn't deserve his fame. The point of the lesson is to find out what sort of person he really was. Before doing that, students must learn how to interpret facts.
Body of lesson	1. **Teach about inferences** (the difference between directly observable/audible fact and an inference). With little or no prior explanation, perform these gestures and ask students to explain what you are doing: • Point your finger at a student and motion for him or her to come. • Put your finger to your mouth to indicate silence. • Pretend to be thinking. After students have answered, suggest that they have interpreted or drawn an inference from what you were doing. Ask them to tell you exactly what they saw. Use a chart like this one to record responses

DIRECTLY OBSERVABLE FACTS	INFERENCES
Directing index finger at student and curling it inward. Putting index finger to your lip. Looking upward pensively and saying "Well, I wonder…"	Teacher wants student to come to her. Teacher is trying to quiet class. Teacher is thinking about something.

2. **Reinforce understanding.** Ask the class to come up with a definition of: (a) a directly observable fact, and (b) an inference. Ask students for examples of directly observable facts and possible inferences to be drawn. Provide several examples and discuss the inferences implied in the statements (include some that are contentious).

3. **Model the assignment.** Direct students' attention to the first paragraph of the reading for this lesson "The Descent of the Fraser River." Invite students to identify directly observed facts and inferences. Ask students to speculate about other inferences that might be drawn from these events. For example, it is stated that "The route was so rough that a pair of moccasins was worn to shreds in one day of portaging." The wearing out of a pair of moccasins in one day is the directly observable fact. The author's inference seems to be that Fraser and his men were determined, persevering, and willing to endure great sacrifice.

4. **Apply learning.** Direct student attention to the Student Instructions sheet (for younger students present them orally) and the Data Recording Chart. Explain the tasks (which may be done individually or in small groups). Ask one-half of the class to focus on Simon Fraser and the other half of the class to focus on the First Nations people. Confirm that students understand what is expected before setting them to work.

5. **Share insights.** After students have had sufficient time to complete the assignment, invite them to share their findings. Begin by asking about the more interesting facts and inferences that students found. Then ask individuals to share their assessments of the character of Simon Fraser and the First Nations people. Encourage debate and ask students to defend and qualify their answers based on evidence in the text. Be careful to note that all First Nations people may not have the same character—some may be friendlier than others, and so on.

6. **Apply knowledge.** Based on their own deliberations and on class discussion, ask students to list five or six words or phrases they believe describe Simon Fraser's character fairly, and five or six words or phrases that describe the character of the First Nations people he encountered. Students must support character descriptions by referring to their interpretations of facts. Remind students that events may have several plausible interpretations, and their task is to decide which is the most defensible. Expect older students to defend their interpretations of specific events in light of other evidence in the text.

FIGURE 25.8 SAMPLE LESSON PLAN (CONT.)

Closure	• Discuss how finding out more about Simon Fraser from other sources could resolve differences of opinion about the sort of person he was (for example, Simon Fraser's diary; the diaries of some of his companions; what is known about Simon Fraser from his friends, employers, and competitors). • Consider the following question: What is the true nature of history: fact or inference? In your own words, explain what this question asks and support your position with examples from the report about Simon Fraser's trip and an account of the trip from a First Nations perspective.

Assessment	• Evaluate each student's character profile in light of the following criteria: adequacy of support for conclusion, sensitivity to alternative inferences, ability to support particular inferences with textual evidence.
	
	• Present students with a drawing of Simon Fraser and his crew. Pose the following questions:
	  • Which one of the men in the drawing is Simon Fraser? Explain the reasons for your choice.
	  • What impressions does this drawing give you about these explorers and the region they are travelling through?
	  • Draw your own picture of Simon Fraser and his men from a First Nations perspective. On the back of your picture explain the key differences between your picture and the drawing provided.
	
	• Use these criteria to assess students' picture study:
	  • Correctly identifies the middle person (in the front canoe) and recognizes that clothing, physical appearance, and lack of a paddle are key differences between this person and the rest.
	  • The number of plausible inferences suggested (e.g., the region is dangerous, uncivilized, and largely uninhabited, and the explorers are daring, afraid, and determined).
	  • Assess students' pictures (and explanations) in terms of the number and plausibility of inferences drawn from the First Nations perspective.
	  • Imaginativeness of inferences drawn might be another criterion.

Extension	• Ask students to write a two-page detailed account of Simon Fraser's trip from the perspective of one of the First Nations people that Simon Fraser would likely have encountered. Their account should be consistent with the directly observable facts in the attached historical report. (It is expected that students will draw different inferences from these facts.) Criteria for assessment: the plausibility of inferences drawn and sensitivity to alternative inferences when facts are seen from different perspectives. Other criteria might include: accuracy of chronological sequence, imaginativeness of inferences drawn, and completeness of account of all the major events. • Discuss factors that affect the credibility of reports, such as: Were the witnesses physically present? Do they have an obvious self-interest? Are they trustworthy sources? Why might Simon Fraser's diary not be completely credible? Why might he be motivated to distort the truth, consciously or unconsciously? You might also introduce the concepts of primary and secondary sources.

SIMON FRASER: HERO OR ROGUE?

Simon Fraser is a famous Canadian explorer; among other forms of recognition, a major river and a university have been named after him. Has history been too kind to Simon Fraser? Does he deserve this fame? What sort of person was he? What sort of people were the First Nations people that Simon Fraser encountered on his travels? Read the attached historical report, "The Descent of the Fraser River," and complete the following task(s).

Step 1

Circle all the statements in the attached report that provide obvious insight into the character (personality traits, personal strengths and weaknesses) of Simon Fraser and/or the First Nations people he encountered.

Step 2

Use the data recording chart to summarize what the report tells us about Simon Fraser and the First Nations people. In the left-hand column, describe what occurred; in the middle and right-hand column note character traits that the author and you attribute to the person(s). In many cases, the author does not present directly observed facts, but only his inferences. In these situations, indicate what you imagine the observed facts were. Examples have been provided on the data recording chart.

1. Simon Fraser's character: In the left-hand column, list any directly observable facts about the events and actions involving Simon Fraser. For each directly observable fact, indicate in the middle column what the author infers about his character from the facts, and in the right-hand column indicate what you infer from these facts.

2. Characteristics of First Nations people: In the left-hand column, list any directly observable facts about the events and actions involving First Nations people. For each directly observable fact, indicate in the middle column what the author infers about their character from the facts, and in the right-hand column indicate what you infer from these facts.

Step 3

1. List approximately five words or phrases to portray your assessment of Simon Fraser's character. Be prepared to defend your assessment.

2. List approximately five words or phrases to portray your assessment of the First Nations people's character. Be prepared to defend your assessment.

DATA RECORDING CHART

SIMON FRASER'S CHARACTERISTICS

Directly observable facts	Author's inferences	Your inferences
Example: The places where they had to carry their canoes were so rough that a pair of moccasins wore out in one day.	Simon Fraser is a very determined individual—nothing will stop him.	Fraser may be determined, but perhaps he just doesn't know how to walk in this kind of countryside.

FIRST NATIONS CHARACTERISTICS

Directly observable facts	Author's inferences	Your inferences
Example: The First Nations people said the river could not be canoed and Fraser believed them.	The First Nations people were truthful.	Perhaps the First Nations people were trying to scare Fraser.

THE DESCENT OF THE FRASER RIVER[1]

On May 28, 1808, Simon Fraser led twenty-three men on an expedition to find a route from the interior of British Columbia to the Pacific Ocean along the river that Fraser imagined was the Columbia River. Day after day, they encountered obstacles as they paddled. The river was a continual series of rapids and the carrying places were extremely dangerous or very long. The places where they had to carry their canoes to get around the rapids were so rough that a pair of moccasins was worn to shreds in one day. Fraser decided the First Nations people he had met were correct in saying that the river was not passable for canoes. So Fraser and his men set out on foot, carrying packs weighing eighty pounds each. In his diary, Fraser wrote that they experienced "a good deal of fatigue and disagreeable walking" but he and his men continued on their journey.

Soon they met First Nations people who told them that ten more days would bring them to the sea. One villager said that he had been to the sea and had seen "great canoes" and white men. When Fraser and his party proceeded, many of the locals walked with them. Two days later, at a large village near present-day Lillooet, First Nations people told them that the river was navigable from their village to the sea. Fraser bargained for two canoes. At another village (now Lytton), the people were so friendly that Fraser was called upon to shake hands with twelve hundred of them. In return, he and his men were well fed and were able to get two wooden canoes.

Despite what the First Nations people had said about the river being navigable, the explorers soon found their way blocked by numerous rapids. Two canoes were lost. More canoes were obtained from the Native people. During this time, the explorers toiled over the roughest country they had ever seen:

> We had to pass over huge rocks assisted by the Indians.... As for the road by land, we could scarcely make our way with even only our guns. I have been for a long period among the Rocky Mountains, but have never seen anything like this country. It is so wild that I cannot find words to describe our situation at times. We had to pass where no human being should venture; yet in those places there is a regular footpath impressed, or rather indented upon the very rocks by frequent travelling. Besides this, steps which are formed like a ladder ... furnish a safe and convenient passage to the Natives; but we, who had not the advantage of their education and experience, were often in imminent danger when obliged to follow their example. [extract from Fraser's journal]

At Spuzzum, Fraser was impressed by a number of totem poles, each fifteen feet high and "carved in a curious but rude manner, yet pretty well proportioned." Friendly First Nations living in large frame houses presented them with roast salmon. In a large village near where

Illustration by Charles W. Jefferys.

the town of Hope now stands, they were entertained inside a huge community house built of cedar planks. The First Nations people warned that the Natives of the coast were "wicked" and would attack them, but Fraser would not alter his plan. When these First Nations people refused to lend him a canoe, Fraser took one by force. For a while, people in canoes from the village followed them; they waved weapons and shouted war songs, but Fraser and his men ignored them. Soon after, another group came at them "howling like wolves" and swinging war clubs, but they did not attack Fraser's group. Fraser ordered his men to paddle farther along to a second village, but the behaviour of the First Nations people forced them to turn back. On July 2, near what is now New Westminster, Fraser decided to return up the river to find provisions before attempting to continue his trip to the ocean. This was the farthest point reached by the explorers. Fraser's reception by First Nations people on his return up the river was not friendly—one group seized a canoe and began to steal from the baggage. Fraser forced a canoe from them and left a blanket in return. For several days, hostile First Nations people followed them. They finally reached friendly villages and were guided over rough bridges and swaying ladders by Natives who "went up and down these wild places with the same agility as sailors do on board a ship."

Fraser finally arrived back at Fort George on August 6. Although he had not accomplished his goal of exploring the Columbia River, he had discovered the river that now bears his name. Because of his voyage, the confusion between the Fraser River and the Columbia River was cleared up.

Select two or three outcomes from the social studies curriculum and develop a detailed lesson plan using the template outlined in this chapter, or another of your choosing. Ensure that the lesson teaches and assesses the identified learning outcomes.

Closing Remarks

The challenges to thoughtful planning are a lot like trying to negotiate a wilderness; just as it is easy to lose one's way in the forest, so too is it easy to become disoriented when planning for instruction at any level. We are especially likely to stumble if we fail to articulate or lose sight of our important educational destinations. The multitude of choices about what and how to do it, and our desire to do it all, may result in plans that are scattered and superficial. Setting a modest number of challenging goals and doing them well may be the best course to follow.

Having just emphasized the importance of a strong guiding direction to one's teaching, let me also caution that we should not feel bound to follow a preordained set of steps and activities when circumstances change. We need to monitor student reactions as we go, changing plans in midstream when appropriate. In addition, as we learn more about teaching, we should revisit our plans from year to year.

ACKNOWLEDGMENTS

Thanks to Mary Abbott for developing the examples found in "Unpacking the Underlying Idea." Thanks also to Penney Clark for the list found in "Ways of Introducing a Unit."

ENDNOTE

1   This is a shortened version of "The descent of the Fraser River" by Malcolm G. Parks in *Discoverers and Explorers in Canada—1763–1911* (Portfolio II #4), illustrated by Charles W. Jefferys and published by Imperial Oil Ltd. Used with permission.

REFERENCES

Erickson, L.H. 1998. *Concept-based curriculum and instruction: Teaching beyond the facts.* Thousand Oaks, CA: Corwin Press.

Wiggins, G. and J. McTighe. 2005. *Understanding by design* (2nd ed.). Alexandria, VA: Association of Supervision and Curriculum Development.

SUPPLEMENTARY RESOURCES

Two detailed lesson plans, "Sample Primary Lesson: Passing Along Kindness" and "Sample Upper Elementary Lesson: Arctic Survival" are available for downloading at Pacific Educational Press's web page for *The Anthology of Social Studies*: www.pacific edpress.ca/?p=2687.

26 Embedding Authentic Assessment in Elementary Classrooms

Roland Case and Stefan Stipp

The common expression "what is counted counts" implies that the learning objectives we assess are the truly important ones. Student sensitivity to this maxim is echoed in their refrains: "Is this on the test?" and "Will it be for marks?" Consequently, if we value critical thinking or the ability to apply knowledge in new contexts, our assessment practices should reflect it. Unfortunately, most assignments and tests emphasize recall of information, which signals to students that remembering facts is what really matters.

This shortcoming will not be redressed by simply devoting more attention to assessing other goals. Ironically, many ways in which thinking abilities are currently assessed are self-defeating. The "timed" nature of tests and the "once-over and one-time nature" of many assignments do not invite student reflection. Advocates of "higher" standards typically call for raised expectations of student performance and for expanded testing, but it is not obvious that these steps enhance student learning. High-achieving students motivated by grades may already be trying their best, and may be distracted from genuine learning by heightened fears of poor grades. Lesser-motivated students may be doubly discouraged by raising the "educational bar" even further out of their reach and by constant reminders of their inferior performance (Assessment Reform Group 2002, 4). In addition, many important educational goals—such as student responsibility, real-life problem solving, reflection, and empathy—are rarely measured. Numerous research studies suggest that our system-wide and classroom-based assessment practices inhibit genuine learning.

Overcoming the negative effects of common assessment practices is the driving motive for "authentic assessment." The term "authentic" refers to measuring the real, actual, or genuine thing as opposed to a poor substitute. The aim is to supplement traditional assessment practices with "alternative" approaches that offer more meaningful and productive strategies (Gronlund and Cameron 2004, 10). There are three interrelated purposes of authentic assessment:

- **Greater "authenticity."** Advocates of assessment reform seek a closer fit between the attributes and abilities actually measured and our most valued educational goals. Too often we assess what is easiest and neglect what is more difficult to assess yet nonetheless important (for example, students' ability to think critically and solve realistic problems).
- **Supporting learning.** Advocates of assessment reform are committed to using evaluation to help students learn. Often assessment interrupts or discourages learning. We can enhance learning by making assessment tasks more meaningful, demystifying the process, and involving students.
- **Fairness to all students.** Advocates of alternative assessment are concerned that some students are penalized by current practices, not because these students know less, but because the methods and conditions of assessment mask their competency. For example, some students struggle to communicate what they know under the pressure of a single, timed written examination.

FIGURE 26.1   RESEARCH REPORT ASSESSMENT

1.	**Bibliography** (1 mark for each book)		/4
2.	**Notes** very good (3) good (2) satisfactory (1) poor (0)		/3
3.	**Charts, maps, drawings, etc.** #1 #2 #3 a) neat: b) accurate: c) relevant:		/9

4.	**Text**
	a) neatness: . . . . /2
	b) spelling, grammar, punctuation:
	      (1/2 mark off per error) . . . . /5
	c) coverage of major points:
	      all (5)
	      almost all (4)
	      most (3)
	      some (2)
	      few (1). . . . . /5
	d) well written:
	      good (2)
	      satisfactory (1)
	      poor (0) . . . . /2
			/14

5.	**Comments:**		
TOTAL			/30

This chapter first explores four principles for making assessment more authentic:

- Focus assessment on what really matters;
- Ensure assessments are valid indications of student competence;
- Use assessment to support student learning; and,
- Develop assessment practices that use teacher time efficiently.

Then, we suggest ways to develop and use assessment strategies to further these principles. A follow-up chapter focuses on nurturing student ownership of assessment. Before proceeding, I invite you to assess an assessment device from my own teaching.

Assessing My Assessment

Years ago, after graduating with my teaching certificate, I proudly developed a marking sheet for a student research project. I asked students to select an aspect of India they wished to independently research, such as climate or religion. I instructed them to consult several library resources and prepare a written report including several visuals, and to clearly connect these charts, graphs, maps, or other visuals to the text. To discourage copying of reports from published sources, students were to also submit research notes. Figure 26.1 is the assessment sheet I used to evaluate their work.

Make a written list of the strengths and weaknesses of my marking sheet. Decide the grade you would assign it based on the following scale:

outstanding	A+/A
very good	A–/B+
good	B/B–
satisfactory	C+/C
poor	C–/D
very poor	F

I have asked several hundred pre-service and practising teachers to assess this early evaluation effort of mine. The grades assigned it have ranged the entire spectrum with approximately 90 per cent of responses dividing evenly between "good," "satisfactory," and "poor." This variance is cause for concern: as professionals, how can we have confidence in our assessment practices if there is such latitude in our judgment of quality? The lack of agreement is especially disturbing since our assessment has potentially profound effects on our students. For example, if I was a secondary student and this assessment was typical, it could have the following consequences.

- "Outstanding" would qualify me for university scholarships.
- "Very good" would enable me to attend the university of my choice, but not on scholarship.
- "Good" would allow me to get into a university, but perhaps not my first choice.
- "Satisfactory" would mean I would be lucky to get into a community college.
- "Poor" would prevent me from directly continuing post-secondary studies.
- "Very poor" would require that I repeat the grade.

I do not wish to infer too much from my informal survey, but it does indicate inconsistency in our understanding of good assessment. I believe that better understanding and implementation of the four principles outlined above would improve this predicament.

The implicit message is that we should neither be satisfied with, nor confident in, our assessments of students' work until we have seriously scrutinized our own assessment practices. Just as we use criteria to assess our students' work, so too should we use the principles of authentic assessment to judge our assessments.

Focus on What Really Matters

The most significant question to ask when judging our assessment practices is whether or not we are assessing what really matters. Are the criteria we use to judge students' work reflective of the most important educational objectives? Since what teachers assess affects what students consider important and ultimately what they learn, our assessment practices should do justice to the breadth and complexity of the goals of social studies. Assessments that are skewed towards a limited range of desired outcomes, such as factual knowledge, fail to assess and possibly discourage student growth in other outcomes. This concern is at the root of much criticism of standardized testing, which often focusses on curriculum outcomes easily scored by machine. This leaves a considerable gap between the outcomes schools are expected to promote and the outcomes used to measure school performance. In a study from the University of Wisconsin, the overlap in one subject between the curriculum and the test was just five per cent (cited in Simmons 2004, 37). The author suggests this disparity undervalues some of the most important life skills such as critical thinking and problem solving.

When I first looked back at my research marking sheet, the most shocking realization was the imbalance in my assessment. One-third of the project mark dealt with mechanics—neatness, spelling, and punctuation. Although these are appropriate criteria, it strikes me as a mistake to give these twice as much weight as the content of the report. One consequence of this weighting is that students who knew a lot about their topic but did not write in standard English could fail the assignment. On the positive side, I did place some value on information gathering (the use of multiple references and competent note-taking) and on content knowledge (the need for students to cover the main points of the topic). Regrettably I did not attach any importance to

students' ability to think about the material they were researching.

Over the course of a unit or term (not necessarily on any given assignment), we should assess all relevant goals, and the relative emphasis assigned these goals in our assessment should reflect their importance. One strategy for checking that each goal is weighted appropriately within an overall assessment plan is a "table of specifications." At the end of a reporting period, list all the graded assignments and tests and record the amount of marks devoted to each goal in a table similar to Table 26.1. In this example, the five main goals are indicated in the left-hand column, and the different assessment strategies appear across the top of the chart. The right-hand column reports the percentage of marks assigned to each goal: for example, understanding of key concepts is worth 40 per cent of the total marks (160/400). Be prepared for a surprise when you discover the importance you actually attach to your goals. The weighting of marks should match the importance of these goals according to the curriculum and your own professional sense of what really matters, given the students you teach. Although not always possible, setting up a table of specifications before, or partway through, a term allows you to make adjustments.

Use Valid Indicators

A second consideration in authentic assessment is validity. In the context of authentic assessment, validity can be defined as a close fit between the kinds of attributes actually measured by an assessment device and the intended educational goals. An assessment strategy is valid if it assesses the outcomes it claims to assess.

My intention with the marking sheet on the research project was to assess students' ability to identify and use multiple sources of information. I now doubt that assigning a mark for each reference in the bibliography measures this ability. Students could score very well on this part of the assignment even if they did not actually use more than one of the books they listed. For that matter, I could not even be sure that students knew how to find the books—someone may have obtained the books for them. My reliance on the number of references in the bibliography was not a valid indicator of students' research abilities. If I wanted to assess the students' ability to locate and find appropriate sources, I should have created a task in the library where students were expected to retrieve and assess relevant sources. I could have measured their ability to make use of multiple

TABLE 26.1 SPECIFICATION OF GOALS ASSESSED

UNIT GOALS	ASSESSMENT STRATEGIES					Total marks	% of total mark
	Quizzes	Activity sheets	Group project	In-class observation	Research reports		
Critical thinking about issues	15	–	–	20	25	60	15
Information gathering	15	–	20	–	25	60	15
Recall of factual information	50	30	–	–	–	80	20
Understanding of key concepts	20	20	70	–	50	160	40
Co-operation with others	–	–	30	10	–	40	10
TOTAL	100	50	120	30	100	400	100

sources by assigning marks to students who cited several sources of relevant information in their final report. The outcome measured in the "coverage of the main points" section of my marking scheme is equally problematic. Students may have written on all the main points without understanding them. If I was serious about finding out if they had gained any understanding of the topic, it would have been better to ask students to orally tell me their findings in their own words.

The importance of validity was brought home to me when I asked my grade 6 students to determine how much money each would have to contribute for a picnic lunch on a daylong field trip. Even though we had practised detailed word problems for several weeks, my students were incapable of applying their knowledge to the authentic problem. They made no connection between the arithmetic we had been doing and the challenge before them. My assessment of their understanding was based on a quiz using word problems like the following:

> If there are thirty students in the class and students want an average of two sandwiches each, how many slices of bread do we need? How many loaves of bread do we need if there are twenty slices of bread in each loaf? If bread sells for $1.25 per loaf what will be the total cost? How much must each student contribute to cover the cost?

Even after the connection was explained, my students were unable to solve the problem. I had taught them to solve word problems on costing lunches, but I had not taught them how to cost the lunch. As Grant Wiggins (1989, 706) suggests, "school tests make the complex simple by dividing it into isolated and simplistic chores—as if the students need not practise the true test of performance, the test of putting all elements together." I would never have realized the gaps in their abilities, and addressed them, unless I had assigned a real-life assessment task. If we do not assess beyond isolated competencies in artificial situations, we are unlikely to know whether students are able to use their knowledge.

Another factor affecting validity is the conditions under which assessment occurs. The use of "surprise" tests and a failure to make the basis for judgment clear to students may impair students' abilities to show what they know. Instead, students may be rewarded for anticipating what the teacher wants. As well, traditional timed tests reward students who perform well in on-the-spot situations and discriminate against students who are equally knowledgeable but less able to perform under contrived conditions. A very common concern for validity, especially acute with students whose first language is not English, is that students' answers may be a function of their written fluency and not their understanding. Although this obstacle cannot be completely overcome, there are ways to mitigate it:

- Assignments and questions should be explained orally to students, the instructions translated, and visual aids and other low vocabulary prompts used frequently.
- Whenever feasible, allow students to represent their answers in graphic form, orally, in written point form, or perhaps even in their native tongue.
- Whenever appropriate, offer alternative assignments, reduced expectations, or additional assistance to offset language impediments.

We can also enhance validity by using several different devices to gather information about achievement. If, for example, the ability to solve real-life problems is important, we should not be satisfied with asking students to consider a hypothetical situation. An observation checklist or rating scale may be particularly effective in assessing student performance in group projects and class presentations. Having students keep a journal while participating in a project or simulation activity can provide rich information about student attitudes towards themselves and others. For example, while preparing for a class discussion or debate, students might reflect on expressing and defending their positions, or about working with others.

Use Assessment to Support Learning

Advocates of assessment reform are emphatic about using assessment to enhance learning. This is reflected in the distinction between the traditional phrase "assessment of learning" and "assessment for learning" (Assessment Reform Group 1999, 2). In their 2002 review, this same group concluded that students would be better motivated and learn more if assessment practices were more focussed on supporting learning than on measuring learning (10). More recently, educators are talking about "assessment as learning" to heighten awareness of assessment tasks as opportunities for learning, not simply for providing formative feedback (British Columbia Ministry of Education 2005, 23–24). Self-assessment is an example of an assessment task that is also a learning task as students examine their own work and think through its strengths and shortcomings.

Greater validity of assessment measures is in itself an attempt to use assessment to support learning. As suggested by the example about planning for the field trip lunch, if an assessment does not capture what it is we really value, then we are less likely to know when we have succeeded in reaching our objective. Assessment practices can support learning in at least four important ways:

- clearly communicate expectations;
- involve students in the assessment process;
- provide helpful feedback on learning; and
- provide opportunities and incentives for students to improve.

COMMUNICATE EXPECTATIONS

If students know clearly what is expected of them they are more likely to succeed. Students will be clearer about expectations if they are informed specifically about the criteria used to mark them, the importance assigned to each, and the standards for achievement of these criteria. The concepts of criteria and standards are often used interchangeably, but there is a clear distinction. Criteria are the features or attributes that provide the grounds for judging quality. Sample criteria include:

- historical accuracy
- originality of ideas
- use of several sources
- clarity of presentation
- depth of answer
- active participation in project
- openness to new ideas
- flow/structure of the paper
- neatness
- spelling accuracy

Standards are the benchmarks, performance levels, or degrees of achievement of a given criterion (that is, "high" and "low" standards). Standards can be binary (for example, correct/incorrect, pass/fail, satisfactory/unsatisfactory) or have multiple levels (for example, A+ to F, outstanding to very weak, well above expectations to not yet meeting expectations). Sample standards for three criteria are listed in Table 26.2.

My grade 6 students might have been better able to succeed at their research report had I clearly indicated all the criteria and standards for assessment. When assessing their notes I judged them as "very good," "good," and so on, without indicating the criteria I was using. Was it the neatness of the notes? Conciseness? Amount of notes? Or perhaps all of these? Even if students knew the criteria, they may still not know what distinguished a "good" from a "satisfactory" standard. And yet, if I wanted them to improve, this is precisely the understanding they required. Besides supporting learning, another powerful reason for clearly articulating standards is that it reduces inconsistency and arbitrariness in assessments. When I look at the standards I offered for "coverage of main points" I now wonder if there is any real difference between "almost all" and "most" points and between "some" and a "few" points. With no clear distinction between performance levels, I could not have reliably distinguished

TABLE 26.2 SAMPLE STANDARDS

CRITERION	STANDARDS	DESCRIPTIONS OF PERFORMANCE LEVELS
Historical accuracy	excellent	no factual inaccuracies
	good	at most, a few minor factual inaccuracies that do not affect the conclusion
	satisfactory	one major inaccuracy and several minor factual inaccuracies
	unsatisfactory	several or more major factual inaccuracies that completely undermine the conclusion
Depth of answer	in-depth	all main topics are analyzed in a probing and careful manner
	modest depth	although there is evidence of careful analysis, some aspects are not addressed in much depth
	superficial	for the most part, topics are addressed superficially
Spelling accuracy	excellent	zero errors
	very good	at most 2 errors
	good	between 3 and 5 errors
	satisfactory	between 6 and 9 errors
	poor	10 or more errors

between them. To model how we can support learning by clearly articulating standards for assessment criteria, Table 26.3 describes standards for each of the four principles as criteria for judging authentic assessments. Read my descriptions of each standard and decide if you recognize what each involves.

INVOLVE STUDENTS IN ASSESSMENT

Involving students directly in the assessment process is another way to support learning. Chapter 27 "Building Student Ownership of Assessment in Elementary Classrooms," provides more detail on each of the following areas for student involvement:

- **Setting criteria and standards.** Joint teacher and student negotiation of the criteria and standards for judgment increases student understanding and ultimately performance.
- **Creating assessment tasks.** Another way to involve students is by inviting them to assist in developing the assessment tasks.
- **Self- and peer assessment.** Involving students in self- and peer assessment can greatly enhance learning by reinforcing students' own understandings of what is expected.

PROVIDE FEEDBACK ON LEARNING

We can enhance learning by helping students see how they might improve. Providing students with useful feedback must go beyond assigning a mark or offering a brief comment. Although some students may be concerned exclusively with their mark, Paul Black and Dylan Wiliam (1998) have found that this leads to no improvement in student achievement—marks are about assessment of learning, not assessment for learning. In fact, Black and Wiliam conclude that grading and other forms of comparative feedback actually get in the way of learning and are especially demotivating for less accomplished students. Because of the negative effects of repeated failure, some educators recommend providing scores at the end of the grading period when it is necessary to prepare an evaluation report, and not before. According to the Assessment Reform Group (2002, 10), teachers should ideally assign marks only if students have a good chance of succeeding. In the interim, students should be provided with abundant feedback and encouragement.

If we want students to improve, our feedback must clearly communicate what has been successfully done, where improvement is needed, and what they might do to improve. A carefully prepared rubric can go a long

TABLE 26.3 ASSESSING THE ASSESSMENT

	HIGHLY EVIDENT	MOSTLY EVIDENT	PARTIALLY EVIDENT	COMPLETELY ABSENT
Focusses on the important goals	6 — The weighting of marks closely matches the important objectives of the assignment.	4 — The weighting of marks generally matches the important objectives of the assignment.	2 — The weighting of marks is out of balance with the important objectives of the assignment.	0 — The weighting of marks misses or seriously under-represents the important objectives of the assignment.
Provides valid indications of student ability	6 — The assignment and marking scheme directly measure student ability on all intended outcomes.	4 — The assignment and marking scheme measure in a fairly direct way student ability on important intended outcomes.	2 — The assignment and marking scheme are unlikely to measure student ability on the intended outcomes.	0 — The assignment and marking scheme measure student ability on the intended outcomes in a superficial, contrived, or distorted manner.
Supports student learning	6 — The device very clearly identifies the criteria and standards and provides helpful feedback for improvement. Has significant potential to reinforce and encourage important student learning.	4 — The device is generally clear about the criteria and standards and provides some helpful feedback for improvement. Has some potential to reinforce and encourage student learning.	2 — The device contains significant gaps or ambiguities in communicating the criteria and standards and offers little helpful feedback for improvement. Key aspects of the assessment fail to reinforce and encourage student learning.	0 — The device is very vague or confused about the criteria and standards, and offers no helpful feedback for improvement. Offers nothing to support, and may discourage, student learning.
Uses teacher time efficiently	3 — The assessment and feedback method very efficiently uses teacher time in providing significant information to students.	2 — The assessment and feedback method is somewhat efficient in its demands on teacher time relative to the rewards.	1 — The assessment and feedback method is somewhat inefficient in its demands on teacher time relative to the rewards.	0 — The assessment and feedback method requires very extensive teacher time relative to the rewards.

Outstanding (A+/A): 19–21
Very Good (A–/B+): 16–18
Good (B/B–): 12–15
Satisfactory (C+/C): 9–11
Poor (C–/D): 5–8

Total: /21

Grade:

way towards providing this feedback, both on how students have done and how they might improve. In my own experience, students benefit most from the use of rubrics when marks are not indicated. The lack of a summative judgment requires them to read the descriptors more carefully and encourages them to believe that it is not too late to improve. Other methods of providing effective feedback include:

- very specific written teacher comments;
- teacher conferences;
- comments by fellow students explaining areas for improvement;
- large and small group discussion of answers; and
- exemplars—samples of high-quality student work, so long as improvement requires more than simply copying the ideas in the exemplar.

PROVIDE OPPORTUNITIES AND INCENTIVES TO IMPROVE

Where feasible, use assessment to encourage students to learn on their own and to revise and rethink their work. Possible strategies include establishing a habit of assessing key objectives in subsequent units, and making it clear to students that certain abilities will be assessed routinely. Those students who make some effort to improve their understanding may be motivated by supplemental tests or makeup assignments. One of my most counterproductive assessment habits as a public school teacher was my penchant for "one-shot" efforts. Rarely did I ask students to seriously revise their work—if work was revisited it was only to tidy up typos or add a missing sentence or two. Now, in my university teaching, I no longer have one-time assignments. In my graduate class, for example, instead of writing three different papers, my students write the same paper three times. The first and second drafts are distributed to everyone in the class for critique. In the first draft, students show largely what they could do before the course. The significant improvement—the deeper, more insightful learning—occurs with the two subsequent revisions where students work through the ideas raised by their colleagues and by me.

Before inviting students to undertake serious revision, we should ensure that they have meaningful input as to how they did initially and what they might do to improve. Since elementary and secondary students may be less motivated to engage in subsequent revisions than students in graduate school, we must encourage them in this regard:

- Ask students to redo only a part of the original assignment (for example, the two worst [or preferred] answers, or the opening and closing paragraphs of an essay).
- Create additional incentives for revising a draft (for example, revised assignments might be exhibited in a fair, submitted to the newspaper, published in a book, or otherwise shared with adults or other students).
- Comment on but do not mark the initial draft. Establish that only the revised draft "counts" for marks.
- Weeks or months later ask students to revisit an earlier work to see how much they have progressed.

When encouraging students to learn from feedback, it is not simply a matter of them redoing completed assignments, but also formulating plans to use the lessons learned to improve upcoming projects. For example, we might ask students to identify a learning goal, anticipate an obstacle, and suggest how they might overcome it.

Using Teachers' Time Efficiently

The final, perhaps one might say the bottom-line, criterion of good assessment is efficient use of teacher time. Although efficiency has no direct relationship to authentic assessment, the incredible press on teachers' time means that changes, however desirable, are unlikely to occur if they are more time-consuming. Generally speaking, marking sheets, including the one I developed for the research project, are efficient assessment tools. Once familiar with the layout it is easy to complete the sheet quickly because it keeps the assessor focussed and saves having to repeatedly write out the same comments. Rubrics are great savers of marking time, but they require considerable up-front development time. For this reason, I am inclined to develop rubrics for major projects during the year—starting with the one that causes the biggest marking headache—and when I want students to undertake peer or self-assessment.

Clearly articulated criteria and standards, communicated beforehand, increase the likelihood of students providing what the teacher is looking for, and help focus the teacher's attention when marking. Clear expectations reduce the likelihood of protracted discussions with students who complain that they did not know what was required.

Student peer and self-assessment can save teacher time provided students are adequately trained. It saves time because it means that students are giving each other feedback that the teacher would otherwise give. Developing students' abilities to assess their work and that of their peers may be an efficient "learning" strategy. In my university teaching, I marvel at how much graduate students learn about, and improve, their writing from frequent opportunities to critique the work of fellow students. But perhaps the biggest efficiency arising from self-assessment comes from a shift in the perceived ownership of learning. The relationship between student and teacher changes once students realize that they, and not the teacher, have primary responsibility for their grades. There is less need for the teacher to chase after the students and drum the information into them. Students are more independent, self-reliant, and committed—and, as a result, more is learned.

Reflecting on Your Learning

Return to your initial assessment of my marking sheet. Consider the merits and oversights in your earlier thoughts about my device. Use the assessment rubric presented earlier to reassess my marking sheet. What grade do you now think it is worth? Even if your

TABLE 26.4 STRENGTHS AND SHORTCOMINGS OF COMMON ASSESSMENT STRATEGIES

	STRENGTHS	SHORTCOMINGS
Regular Written Assignments	• allow for ongoing feedback • involve no extra work to prepare since they are part of the instructional plan • can provide for in-depth work	• present difficulties for students who have difficulty writing or who are unable to write • may not build from one assignment to the next • penalize students who need practice time before they are ready to be assessed • may involve considerable ongoing marking
Quizzes and Tests	• may be quick to mark, especially if they are multiple choice • provide a summary snapshot of student learning • can assess for a breadth of information	• may focus largely on recall of factual information • difficult to address broad spectrum of curriculum outcomes • cause some students stress • tend to focus on short-term learning
In-class Observation	• may reveal insights that would not otherwise be identified • can assess abilities that are difficult to capture on paper • allow for immediate feedback • require no after-school marking	• hard to manage given time demands of a lesson • difficult to observe students equally • one-time efforts may not present a true picture of students' abilities
Essays and Research Reports	• allow for ongoing feedback • can provide for in-depth study of a topic	• may involve a lot of student homework • are typically time-consuming for teachers to mark
Projects and Culminating Tasks	• can be more fun, engaging, and worthwhile than other assessment tasks • can draw together learning over a unit • can assess for a breadth of knowledge and abilities • often further students' learning while they complete the task	• may require considerable in-class and out-of-class time relative to the educational benefits • students may become bored if tasks drag on or are seen as "make work" • it may be difficult to use common criteria to assess different student projects
Portfolios	• build student ownership in learning and assessment • track growth over time • encourage student goal-setting and self-monitoring	• can become the mere accumulation of "stuff" • may require a lot of time to review and evaluate

assessment is largely unchanged, do you have greater confidence in the grade you assigned? Is it a fairer, more valid assessment? Are you clearer about how you might help me improve my assessment practices? I hope the answer is yes to all these questions, and to one further question: Do you have a better understanding of principles to follow in making your own assessment practices more authentic?

Select an assessment device that you have developed or that is included in a teaching resource (for example, a quiz, end-of-unit project, observation checklist). Use the rubric "Assessing the Assessment" to evaluate this device. Based on what you have learned about the four principles, suggest ways to make the device more authentic.

Strategies for Authentic Student Assessment

To begin the discussion of how to choose assessment strategies that are valid measures of our teaching goals, it is helpful to distinguish between assessment *targets* and assessment *strategies*. An assessment target is the learning outcome we hope to assess (for example, understanding of key concepts, ability to think critically, ability to read maps). Authentic assessment targets the outcomes that really matter. The assessment strategy is the means by which we find out how well students have met the target. For example, we might assess students' ability to read a map using any number of strategies including in-class assignments, map-related questions on a quiz, in-class observations of group work, or a culminating project involving map reading. There is no single best assessment method. Each strategy has its merits and shortcomings depending on the target and context of the assessment. The ultimate decision about which strategy (or strategies) to use for a particular target depends on how well it meets the criteria for authentic assessment in the circumstances: validity of the measures, the support of student learning, and the efficient use of teacher time.

Six common strategies for student assessment are:

- regular written assignments
- quizzes and tests
- in-class observations
- essays and research reports
- projects or culminating tasks
- portfolios

Table 26.4 compares these strategies. They overlap in many respects, but it is useful for discussion to distinguish them.

Regular Written Assignments

The most frequent sources of evidence of student achievement are the activity sheets and written tasks completed by students each day. In some respects these are ideal assessment opportunities: they are frequent, provide tangible evidence of learning, and are a seamless part of instruction. Despite these advantages, there are concerns associated with regularly attaching marks to written assignments, one being that it is unfair to those students who need more time to learn.

FRAMING ASSIGNMENTS FOR NON-WRITERS

Written assignments can be framed for non-writers. One approach is to arrange for parent volunteers or older students to record non-writers' answers. Another is to use images. Figure 26.2 describes how students can communicate answers by sorting cards into piles. The teacher reads the description of a series of statements and students paste the images onto a sheet of paper under the appropriate column—"memory" or "not a memory." In the example in Figure 26.3, the teacher reads out clues one at a time and students circle all the objects identified by each clue.

MARKING REGULAR ASSIGNMENTS

There is little disagreement about the value of providing quality feedback (from teacher or students) on any assignment. But should every assignment be graded for reporting? For years it was commonly recommended that teachers assess students on a large number of assignments to avoid penalizing students for occasional poor performance. This practice is being questioned because of the unfairness of assessing students before they have had ample opportunity to learn what is expected of them. More recent thinking recommends that only students' best work be assessed. Since the primary purpose of classroom assignments is to help students learn, holding students accountable for their performance while they are still learning is analogous to a theatre critic reviewing a play midway through rehearsals. No doubt some actors will have their roles in good shape but many, including those with the finest performances on opening night, may still be exploring their character.

Imagine a situation where three assignments over the course of a unit are focussed on the same outcome, such as how to read maps. The following results are recorded for two students:

	Assignment 1	Assignment 2	Assignment 3	Average mark	Best result
Mindy	8	8	8	8 or B+	8 or B+
Chan	4	6	10	6.7 or B−	10 or A

When reporting on student achievement, it would be misleading and unfair to assign Mindy a "B+" and Chan "B−" since Chan's understanding is arguably superior to Mindy's. The averaging of marks can also have a discouraging effect; students who struggle to learn a topic will realize that their mark will be averaged down because of earlier poor performances even if they do very well in the end. These problems are behind the popular adage: assess often and mark rarely.

Ensuring that we assign marks to students' *best* efforts does not mean that only the *final* effort should be graded. On any given day, students may do poorly for reasons unrelated to their learning. It would be unfair to penalize students who did well all term simply because they were distracted during the final assignment. Another concern in relying exclusively on a final assignment is that assignments over a term might not stress identical outcomes. The solution is to provide opportunities to learn that are not graded and to only grade students on assignments that allow them to show what they have learned.

FIGURE 26.2 SORTING MEMORIES

I had such a great time at the beach
this summer.

My birthday is next week.

I am sitting on the floor.

When I was little I ate dog food once.

FIGURE 26.3 SOLVING THE MYSTERY

It is something to eat.

It comes warm.

It is long and skinny.

Quizzes and Tests

Another common strategy to test how well students have mastered the content is an end-of-unit quiz. This approach allows students to show what they have learned after they have studied the material. Research suggests that student learning may be better served by frequent short tests rather than infrequent long ones (Boston 2002, 3), and by providing quality feedback in addition to assigning a mark (Black and Wiliam 1998, 144).

The most significant factor influencing the value of a test is the quality of the questions. For ease of student completion and teacher marking, quizzes tend to consist of two kinds of questions: *closed-ended* questions such as multiple choice, true or false, labelling, and matching columns; or, *open-ended* questions requiring a few words or sentences to answer. Much could be said about developing quality test questions, but we want to emphasize two recommendations:

- design short-answer questions to assess beyond mere recall of information; and
- ensure the validity of questions in quizzes and tests.

ASSESSING BEYOND RECALL

A common criticism of test questions is that they only assess recall of information. This need not be so. Short-answer questions can also assess depth of understanding, critical thinking, social responsibility, and other important goals. For instance, open-ended short-answer questions can assess student reflection by inviting students to revisit initial ideas or opinions after they have had a chance to think about the matter. Figure 26.4 outlines students' pre- and post-unit reflections on a famous person. Post-unit responses can be assessed in terms of their accuracy and open-mindedness, and the insightfulness of reflection.

Figure 26.5 illustrates how closed-ended questions can be used to gather information about student attitudes. Margaret Chapman (1991, 69), a British Columbia primary teacher, developed this device to assess empathy for people in other countries. Before and after studying the needs of people in Chile, Margaret read the statements to her grade 1 students and they circled the appropriate face depending on whether they agreed (the "happy face"), were not sure (the "so-so face"), or disagreed (the "sad face").

There are, however, limits to what short-answer questions can assess. For example, multiple-choice questions can only measure students' abilities to select correctly from a set of supplied answers. Multiple-choice questions reduce complex learning outcomes to individual test items, whereas we may be concerned with students' abilities to integrate what they know in realistic situations. While these limitations provide powerful reasons for using "alternative" strategies, there is a role for tests beyond measuring information recall.

WATCHING FOR VALIDITY

In using short-answer questions, we may think we are measuring something we are not, so it is important to check that we actually measure our target outcomes. A common presumption is that we assess students' understanding of a concept by asking them to offer a definition. Understanding a concept is much broader than recalling the definition. For example, a discussion about "fairness" may lead some children to believe that fairness means everyone receives the same thing in an equal amount, such as everyone in the class receiving the same snack. Yet, this is not necessarily fair; some students may have an allergy to the ingredients, or a dislike for them.

Assessing conceptual understanding requires more than asking for a definition. Students need to provide fresh examples or explain why a given scenario is not illustrative. For example, to assess younger children's understanding of "fairness," we might ask them to explain whether or not it is fair to give everyone the same snack, taking into consideration allergies and likes and dislikes.

In-Class Observations

Another assessment strategy is to observe students' classroom behaviour and listen to their talk. In this approach, sometimes referred to as "naturalistic assessment," the teacher is a participant-observer who collects information about student learning while engaged in the duties of teaching. Teachers assess naturalistically in an ad hoc fashion every time they confirm students have understood a lesson, or check to see whether students have done their work, or ask students to indicate difficulties. With formal naturalistic assessment, information is collected systematically and records are kept for reporting.

In-class observations are particularly appropriate for assessing student abilities and attitudes not measured by traditional pen-and-paper assignments or isolated assessment tasks. In addition, extended observation is more likely to provide rich accounts of student learning and insight into factors influencing learning. There are various information-gathering strategies for formal in-class observations:

- anecdotal "field notes" of significant comments or incidents—for example, noting the strategies a student uses to solve a problem, or watching for students' growth in self-esteem or attitudes towards school work over a period of several months;
- student-teacher conferences to gather information about students while helping them learn;
- checklists or other devices to record the incidence of particular behaviour—such as completion of work, the number of books read, or students' co-operative participation in group assignments. Figure 26.6 is a checklist to record how well students use aids to locate information.

FIGURE 26.4   HERO OR CELEBRITY?

After studying famous people, students consider whether a particular personality (e.g., rock star, athlete, or politician) is a genuine hero. Students offer a preliminary response at the beginning of the unit and reconsider their conclusions at the end of the unit, based on their learning.

My first opinion was that _____ was ☐ a genuine hero
☐ not a genuine hero

because _____

_____

_____

I have   ☐ changed
☐ not changed

my opinion because   _____

_____

_____

FIGURE 26.5   ASSESSING FOR EMPATHY

1. I want all my friends to be like me.	 😊	 😐	 ☹
2. We should help other, poorer countries even if it means we have to give up things.	 😊	 😐	 ☹
3. We like learning about people who live in other countries.	 😊	 😐	 ☹
4. What happens to other people is only important to me if I know them.	 😊	 😐	 ☹

Often, like an anthropologist, a teacher will seek several sources of evidence to corroborate his or her judgments. For example, in assessing students' critical-thinking ability, a teacher might use information from peer and self-assessment of students' willingness to entertain alternative opinions, analyses of products for quality of reasoning, and observed students' comments about attitudes towards "thinking things through."

Peer observation and self-monitoring save teacher time and provide an important learning opportunity: an invitation for students to reflect on their learning as they work. Students may also have access to information that is not readily available to the teacher. Figure 26.7 is an example of a classroom observation device for students (or teachers) to assess co-operative group work.

Identify one or two curriculum outcomes to assess using the three strategies discussed thus far: regular written assignments, quizzes, and in-class observations. Briefly outline how you would use each strategy for the selected outcome(s).

Essays and Research Reports

Extended-answer questions such as essays, reports, and position papers are a common assessment strategy for upper elementary and secondary students. Generally, they supply a more holistic measure of learning than short-answer questions. There are, however, several limitations:

- essays are heavily dependent on students' writing fluency;
- students may be overwhelmed by the demands of large writing projects, particularly in younger grades; and,
- essays are time-consuming to mark.

For these reasons it is worth considering what prominence the traditional research paper merits in social studies classes. Many students dislike writing reports and may do little more than transcribe ideas directly from reference books. Students might learn more effectively from smaller, less daunting assignments that emphasize multiple revisions of their ideas. Certainly, we should expect students to think for themselves and not simply assemble ideas from other sources.

The merits of any given extended-answer assignment depend on the quality of the question or task. At the very least this requires providing students with explicit,

unambiguous direction. Questions can be posed with a focus on students' critical thinking rather than rehashing arguments found in books. We think it also helps to provide (or assist students to generate) a structure for organizing their report. For example, the question "Research and defend your personal position on establishing a world government" could be altered as follows:

Present and defend your personal position on establishing a world government using the following structure:

1. explain in your own words what this would involve;
2. identify and explain the major reasons in support of your position;
3. identify and explain the major reasons that opponents might offer against your position; and
4. justify your position by arguing why the supporting reasons are more convincing than the reasons against your position.

Projects or Culminating Tasks

A relatively recent alternative approach to assessment, often referred to as performance assessment, is to have students complete realistic tasks typically faced as a citizen, writer, businessperson, scientist, community leader, historian, and so on. These tasks may involve performing a feat or producing a product. Examples for both are given here:

Perform a feat
- perform a dramatic scene depicting a historical event
- hold a formal parliamentary debate on a controversial piece of legislation
- teach fellow students about family traditions
- organize and run a school fundraising event
- conduct a trial around a historical incident
- adjudicate between nominees for an award
- make a presentation to city council on a proposed change to local laws

Produce a product
- build a model of a logging site or ancient village
- make a film about promoting racial harmony
- create a set of exam questions and sample answers for an end-of-unit test
- prepare a "consultant's report" on a local pollution problem
- develop a foreign-language script for a radio play
- create "museum" displays depicting local history

FIGURE 26.6   LOCATING INFORMATION CHECKLIST

STUDENTS

Uses information-locating aids: ✗ = not at all ○ = somewhat ✓ = adeptly	Saul	Pam	Chan	Niam						
locate section in table of contents	○	✗	✓	✓						
locate page in index	✓	✗	✓	✓						
find word in glossary	✓	○	✓	✓						
find word in dictionary	✓	○	✓	✓						
skim paragraph to locate information										
use headings to locate information	✗	○	✓	✓						
...										

- create a web page on the history of the school
- publish a (contemporary or historical) class newspaper or journal

Because performance assessments usually involve realistic tasks, they are more likely than traditional methods to measure students' ability to apply a complex set of real-life abilities and understandings. The emphasis is on knowledge-in-use, as opposed to regurgitation. Such tasks also provide an important opportunity for learning: they enhance—not simply measure—student understanding. A performance task to plan a summer vacation (described in Heckley Kon and Martin-Kniep 1992) illustrates these features. In this assessment, pairs of students are given a map of California and a list of state parks with camping facilities, and are asked to plan a detailed itinerary for a family from the San Francisco area going on a camping trip to a state camping facility in northern California. Students must measure distances, calculate travelling time, describe particulars of the travel route, and develop a contingency plan in the event of a strike by workers on the Golden Gate and Bay bridges. As well, they have to negotiate with a partner the destination

and route that best accommodate the interests of all family members.

As this example suggests, performance assessments can be engaging, which solves the difficulties of assessing those students who do poorly on evaluations because they are unmotivated. If we want to assess what students are *capable* of doing, it is only fair that we provide opportunities where students are likely to want to do well.

Because performance tasks are complex, they provide opportunities to assess a variety of outcomes using many methods, including:

- interviewing students about their conclusions and their experiences during the project;
- analyzing students' preparatory materials for quality of research;
- analyzing group discussions for evidence of thoughtfulness in preparing products and making decisions;
- assessing students' written or oral reports for content knowledge and quality of language use and presentation; and
- assessing classroom discussions or debates for evidence of students' ability to engage in thoughtful dialogue.

FIGURE 26.7   CO-OPERATIVE DECISION-MAKING

Your name:_____ Group member's name: _____

Use a separate sheet for each person. Do not show or discuss your assessment with anyone else.

For each action or attitude circle the number that most accurately reflects this student's behaviour during group work.

Describe an actual incidence or example of behaviour as evidence to support your assessment.

	Rarely or never		About half the time		Consistently or nearly always	Not enough information to decide
1. Willing to reconsider position	1	2	3	4	5	no information
Supporting evidence:						
2. Willing to defend personal opinion	1	2	3	4	5	no information
Supporting evidence:						
3. Respects others who disagree	1	2	3	4	5	no information
Supporting evidence:						
4. Challenges others' thinking in responsible ways	1	2	3	4	5	no information
Supporting evidence:						
5. Works towards establishing agreement	1	2	3	4	5	no information
Supporting evidence:						

Key considerations of performance assessments are: choosing the task, setting the context, providing direction, and, when possible, arranging for an audience. To be fair, a performance task should integrate what students have been studying; it is novel in the drawing together of studied elements to solve a realistic problem. Setting a realistic context for the task provides students rich opportunity to think through the options.

An example of a performance task for primary students completing a unit on family is to create and present a memory box to celebrate family members (Abbott, Ford, and Case 2003). Throughout the unit, students recall memories associated with various relatives and decide on the most powerful positive memory for each member. Students identify various objects associated with their powerful memories and then select the best object for each. These items are placed in a memory box, which is shared at a "celebrating families" event. The rubric in Figure 26.8 assesses students' understanding of the concept of memory, ability to identify memories and memorable objects, and ability to judge the most powerful memory and memorable object for each family member.

Portfolios

Portfolio assessment, where students compile a collection of work completed over a period of time, is the final assessment strategy we will consider here. Portfolio assessment mirrors the practice of artists and designers who carefully assemble samples to represent key characteristics of their work to demonstrate competencies. Assessment portfolios are "a purposeful collection of student work that exhibits the student's efforts, progress, and achievements in one or more areas" (Paulson, Paulson, and Meyer 1991, 60).

Because portfolios are based on cross-sections of student work completed over time, they offer a richer

FIGURE 26.8   ASSESSING FAMILY MEMORIES

	SOPHISTICATED UNDERSTANDING	EXTENDED UNDERSTANDING	BASIC UNDERSTANDING	PARTIAL RECOGNITION	PRE-RECOGNITION
Understands concept of memory	Correctly distinguishes memories from non-memories when given simple examples, and correctly states in own words the difference between the two terms.	Correctly distinguishes memories from non-memories when given simple examples, and provides own example of both terms.	Correctly distinguishes memories from non-memories when given simple examples.	When provided with simple examples of memories and non-memories, can correctly identify some of them.	When provided with a simple example of a memory, cannot identify it as a "memory."
Recalls family memories	Recalls many family memories with considerable detail, including the feelings evoked.	Recalls three or four family memories with some detail, including the feelings evoked.	Recalls with modest detail one or two of the most obvious family memories.	Understands what is asked, but can just barely identify a family memory.	Does not understand what is asked when invited to identify or recall a family memory.
Identifies powerful memory	Offers a powerful memory and explains the feelings evoked.	Offers a powerful memory with a simple explanation.	Offers a rather predictable powerful memory without much explanation.	Offers a memory that is not very powerful.	Unable to identify a powerful memory.
Identifies memorable objects	Identifies several memorable objects associated with a story about a family member.	Identifies two memorable objects associated with a story about a family member.	Identifies the most obvious memorable object associated with a story about a family member.	Understands what is asked, but identifies an object that is unconnected to the memory or the family member.	Does not understand what is asked when invited to identify a memorable object.
Chooses a best memorable object	Chooses a best memorable object and explains the feelings evoked.	Chooses a best memorable object with a simple explanation.	Chooses a predictable best memorable object without offering any explanation.	Chooses a best object that is not very memorable.	Unable to choose a best memorable object.

portrait of a range of student achievements than an end-of-unit test. Also, unlike traditional forms of assessment, where assignments are marked and then forgotten, portfolios encourage both teacher and students to monitor growth over time. Typically, students are involved to varying degrees in selecting, analyzing, assessing, and reporting on the products in their portfolio. This involvement often results in greater ownership of their learning. These benefits are particularly likely when portfolios are used as the focus for conferences where students use their portfolio to explain their progress and levels of achievement to their parents or teacher. In fact, it has been suggested that portfolios be primarily "a reason for talking" (Murphy and Smith 1990, 1).

Portfolios may be general in focus, cover many subjects, or be subject or topic specific (e.g., social studies or the Inuit). Asking students to focus on one area can help them see that learning can be represented in different ways. When collecting samples of learning in social studies, students could web, list, write, videotape, draw, or brainstorm their understanding of concepts.

Portfolio assessment has five phases:

- **Accumulation of products**. At the beginning of the unit, establish procedures for collecting and storing student work. The date that work is completed should be indicated on every assignment. If a specific set of outcomes has been identified as the portfolio's theme, ensure students have varied opportunities during the term to produce work in these areas. Materials produced by students may include:
  - annotated bibliographies of books or documents read
  - artwork (preliminary sketches and final products)
  - audio recordings
  - book reports
  - charts and graphs

- drawings
- essays (drafts and final copies)
- evaluations of self and peers
- group reports
- interview results
- journals or diaries
- maps
- notes (classroom, laboratory, or field)
- peer evaluations
- photographs of projects, models, displays, or murals
- reading inventories
- tests and quizzes
- videotapes of presentations, debates, interviews, or simulations
- worksheets

- **Selection of portfolio pieces.** Near the end of a unit, discuss how students are to select a sampling for their portfolio from the array of products. Students should have some discretion in selecting portfolio contents. The selected products may represent the student's best efforts, or be indicative of typical performance. They may focus on a particular theme such as growth as a critical thinker, development of a global perspective, or appreciation of culture. It may be important to limit the number of pieces to include in a portfolio, since thoughtful analysis becomes unwieldy if too many pieces are included. A summary or checklist such as a table of contents may be helpful.

- **Reflection.** Alone or in collaboration with peers, each student reviews the portfolio contents to assess achievement or progress over the term. These reflections might involve identifying criteria and standards, analyzing patterns or key features, diagnosing strengths and problem areas, and setting personal plans and targets. Providing samples of other students' work at various performance levels may assist students in assessing their own work.

- **Reporting.** Students should be expected to report (orally or in writing) what they observe about their learning and to recommend a plan of action. Student-led conferences with the teacher, and often with parents, are common ways of student reporting. Alternatively, students might prepare audio-recorded analyses of their portfolios. It may be helpful for students to prepare and practise their oral reports with fellow students. For younger students reporting might be as simple as:

SUGGESTIONS FOR DEVELOPING CULMINATING PROJECTS

Identify the important outcomes for a unit:

- Think of real-life feats or products that could represent exemplary achievement of key outcomes.
- Determine the realistic scenario and the context of the performance assessment.
- Clearly articulate the requirements and parameters of the task orally or in writing.
- Consider what students must know to succeed. Ensure they have sufficient instruction; assessment tasks can be made easier by providing additional instruction.
- For each of the desired outcomes, determine the criteria to be used to assess students' products. Share the criteria with students prior to completion of the task.
- Determine how evidence for each criterion will be collected (e.g., through observation, conferencing, analysis of written products, etc.). Where appropriate, create rubrics, checklists, or other marking devices.
- After using the performance assessment, consider how to improve it next time. It may be helpful to ask students to comment to this end.

The topic for my portfolio is _____

_____

_____

The two pieces we selected that show my learning are:

1. _____

2. _____

Things we did well:

1. _____

2. _____

Things we might improve upon:

1. _____

2. _____

My plan for next time is _____

_____

_____

- **Feedback.** Feedback on two fronts can be given by the teacher (and parents): (1) student achievement or progress over the term, as evidenced in the portfolio; and (2) the quality of student analysis, personal accountability, and reporting represented by the portfolio itself. For young students the feedback might be as simple as "two stars and a wish"—noting two positive aspects and an area for improvement.

Portfolio creator _____

Two stars:

★ _____

★ _____

One wish:

→ _____

Identify four or five complementary outcomes from the curriculum. Using the three strategies discussed in the second half of this chapter (essays, culminating projects, and portfolios), briefly outline assessment of the selected curriculum outcomes using each of these three strategies.

Conclusion

In this chapter we have explored the principles of authentic assessment and applied them to the development of assessment strategies for the elementary classroom. Our objective is to encourage assessment practices that are valid, fair, and richly support student learning.

ACKNOWLEDGMENT

We wish to thank Robert Hogg of the Alberta Assessment Consortium and Rosemary Evans of Branksome Hall School for their helpful suggestions during revision of this chapter.

REFERENCES

Abbott, M., C. Ford, and R. Case. 2003. *Celebrating families.* Richmond, BC: The Critical Thinking Consortium.

Assessment Reform Group. 1999. *Assessment for learning: Beyond the black box.* Cambridge, UK: University of Cambridge.

———. 2002. *Testing, motivation and learning.* Cambridge, UK: University of Cambridge.

Black, P. and D. Wiliam. 1998. Inside the black box: Raising standards through classroom assessment. *Phi Delta Kappan* 80 (2): 139–148.

Boston, C. 2002. The concept of formative assessment. *Practical Assessment, Research and Evaluation* 8 (9): 1–5. Accessed online at PAREonline.net/getvn.asp?v=8&n=9.

British Columbia Ministry of Education. 2005. *Social Studies 10: Integrated Resource Package 2005* (Response Draft). Victoria, BC: Author.

Chapman, M. 1991. *Nurturing a global perspective among primary students, using Chilean arpilleras.* Unpublished Master of Education project, Simon Fraser University, Burnaby, BC.

Gronlund, N.E. and I.J. Cameron. 2004. *Assessment of student achievement* (Canadian edition). Toronto: Pearson Education Canada.

Heckley Kon, J. and G. Martin-Kniep. 1992. Students' geographic knowledge and skills in different kinds of tests: Multiple-choice versus performance assessment. *Social Education* 56 (2): 95–98.

Murphy, S. and M.A. Smith. 1990. Talking about portfolios. *The Quarterly* 12 (2): 1–3, 24–27.

Paulson, F.L., P.R. Paulson, and C.A. Meyer. 1991. What makes a portfolio a portfolio? *Educational Leadership* 48 (5): 60–63.

Simmons, N.E. 2004. (De)grading the standardized test. *Education Canada* 44 (3): 37–39.

Wiggins, G. 1989. A true test: Toward more authentic and equitable assessment. *Phi Delta Kappan* 70: 703–713.

27

Building Student Ownership of Assessment in Elementary Classrooms

Roland Case

Years ago, I read an article entitled "So, what did I get on my muffin?" The author (Emblem 1994), a home economics teacher, suggested that this was a common student response to returned assignments. This response suggests that students lack recognition that marks are earned. Rather, it seems students view teachers as random dispensers of marks. Students present teachers with a product and hope the teacher reciprocates by "giving" them good marks.

When students reveal a lack of personal responsibility for the marks they earn, we as teachers are failing to promote student ownership of assessment. In this chapter, I discuss the challenges to and strategies for building student ownership of assessment. In particular, I explore four areas:

- creating meaningful assessment tasks;
- setting criteria;
- establishing standards; and
- supporting peer and self-assessment.

Creating Meaningful Tasks

We will be hard pressed to build student ownership in assessment if students are turned off by the tasks and assignments being assessed. Students are less likely to take ownership if they don't care about the work. To avoid this, keep three principles in mind when devising assessment tasks:

- **Less is more.** Students are more likely to be drawn

into their work if they have more time to do it and if there is less of it—both in terms of the size of tasks and their frequency. For example, instead of a dozen test questions, reduce the number by half and encourage students to do a more thorough job. We might learn as much about students' knowledge of a topic by asking them to provide a detailed, labelled diagram than an extended written explanation. Rather than grading homework assignments every week or research projects every second month, reduce their frequency and devote more time to helping students learn to improve their performance.

- **Students can contribute.** Involving students in creating assessment tasks is another way to increase the likelihood of students buying in.
  - Ask students to draft test questions and sample answers for an end-of-unit test, and use them.
  - Provide students with a list of specific outcomes you wish to assess and invite them to propose feasible projects or activities to demonstrate their learning.
  - Invite students to develop "source materials" for use in an assessment. For example, students might prepare accounts of various events containing four or five deliberately placed errors that other students would be expected to detect, or students might construct profiles of mystery famous people or historical events for other students to identify.

- **Assessments don't have to be boring.** We can go a long way towards increasing student buy-in by

FIGURE 27.1 SAMPLE NOTES[1]

Below is a short passage on the Inuit's use of caribou and three sets of notes summarizing this text. Identify the strengths and weaknesses of each.

RESEARCH TOPIC: Inuit use caribou

Text: In the fall, the Inuit hunt caribou with bows and arrows. The caribou have spent the summer grazing and are now fat. As well, their coats are getting thicker to protect them during the long winter. Caribou are also hunted in the late spring as they migrate north for the summer. The caribou are very important to the Inuit. The Inuit kill many caribou because they need much food and many skins.

SAMPLE NOTES

#1	#2	#3
• bows and arrows • fall • coats • migrate north • important • kill • hides	• kill caribou in fall when they are fat • thick coats • also hunt in late spring • important for food and hides • many caribou needed	• Inuit hunt caribou with bows and arrows in fall • caribou have spent summer grazing • now they are fat • their coats are getting thicker • thick coats protect them during the long winter • Inuit also hunt caribou in late spring when caribou migrate north for summer • caribou very important to the Inuit • they kill many because they need much food and many skins
Strengths:	Strengths:	Strengths:
Weaknesses:	Weaknesses:	Weaknesses:

making assessment tasks interesting and relevant. Here are a few examples:

- Game-show-type contests can replace multiple-choice quizzes.
- Instead of a research essay on immigration, students might draft and send a formal brief to the minister responsible for immigration, or prepare and present an application for permanent residency in Canada to a mock immigration tribunal.
- Convert a biography of a famous person into a request for a candid letter of reference or for responses to a census or attitude questionnaire completed from that person's point of view.

Setting Criteria

Unless we are explicit about our criteria for judgment, our assessments may be misleading since different people may employ different criteria. This problem is even more acute if our assessments are based on narrow or inappropriate considerations. The problems of differing and, in some cases, dubious criteria may explain why some students have such vague ideas about what their work is worth.

Thus, the first challenge in building student ownership is to ensure that our assessments are based on *relevant*, *representative*, and *manageable* criteria that are *clear* to students. These four considerations are, in effect, the criteria for identifying and justifying assessment criteria. Understanding them will help to ensure that we set sound criteria. If we want students to set their own criteria, we will want them to recognize and be able to apply these four considerations as well.

RELEVANT CRITERIA

How do I know whether the criteria I select (or those that students generate) are the right ones? This is essentially a question about the relevance of criteria, which depends largely on the assignment's purpose. For the most part, the criteria for assessing any activity should relate to its particular objectives, which in turn should be connected to the more general goals or intended outcomes of social studies. For example, in social studies, it would not be relevant to evaluate a report or other piece of extended writing largely on the basis of grammar and punctuation. Emphasis on these criteria is more appropriate to language arts, where mastery of the technical aspects of writing is a main goal. In contrast,

TABLE 27.1 SAMPLE CRITERIA FOR ASSESSING ASSIGNMENTS

Justification for a conclusion	• Is the information factually accurate? • Does the answer reveal depth of understanding? • Are the reasons supported with evidence?
Oral presentation	• Is the presentation thoughtfully structured? • Is it clear? • Does it engage the audience?
Plan to solve a problem	• Is the solution doable? • Is it fair to all parties? • Will it solve the problem? • Is it safe?
Co-operative group work	• Did students apply themselves to the task? • Were students willing to take turns? • Did students show sensitivity to the feelings of others?

a piece of extended writing in social studies should emphasize criteria such as clarity of communication, ability to use information to support a position, accuracy of information, and depth of analysis. Two strategies to help identify relevant criteria are:

- **Consider the purpose.** Ask yourself the curricular intent of the learning activity. For example, two common purposes for writing a paragraph are to communicate ideas and to persuade people to accept a position. Any criteria that affect these purposes will be potentially relevant considerations (for example, clarity of expression, use of examples, organization of ideas, number and quality of arguments, amount and quality of supporting evidence).
- **Think of specific sample responses.** Thinking of very good and very poor sample answers is also effective in identifying criteria. For example, share with students a poorly written paragraph and an especially well-written paragraph. Ask them to identify what makes the outstanding paragraph so good and the inferior one poor. Poor examples are often more useful in identifying criteria. In Figure 27.1, "Sample Notes," students consider three sets of notes summarizing a short passage about the Inuit's use of caribou. By considering the strengths and weaknesses of each set of notes, students learn to identify the relevant criteria for good notes.

REPRESENTATIVE CRITERIA

Assessment criteria should include a representative range of the important considerations. For example, when deciding on the merits of a proposed solution to

a social problem, it would not be sufficient to consider only whether the solution was likely to be effective in addressing the problem. Other important considerations include fairness to all sides and feasibility. Articulating a representative range of criteria helps students recognize the full set of requirements for a particular curriculum expectation. Table 27.1 gives some relevant criteria that may be applied to a sampling of social studies assignments.

MANAGEABLE NUMBER OF CRITERIA

The number of criteria for any given assignment is another consideration. Obviously, younger students will be able to deal with fewer criteria than older students and very young students may be able to handle only one or two. For older students, it may be overwhelming to introduce many criteria at one time. No assignment need address the full range of criteria for a particular curriculum outcome as the broader range of relevant criteria can be assessed over the unit or term.

One way to avoid overburdening students with too many criteria is to frame them in broader, more general terms that subsume several specific criteria. For example, "effective presentation manner" instead of: "clarity and audibility of voice, posture, and eye contact." However, if the presentation is a major part of the assignment, it may not be wise to incorporate these more specific criteria into general terms.

CLEAR TO STUDENTS

A final consideration is the need for criteria to be clearly articulated. One confusing tendency is vaguely worded criteria such as "active listener" or "creative." Students must understand precisely what we mean in order for criteria-based assessment to be effective. We are better off substituting specific terms for ambiguous concepts such as "creativity" (for example, offers ideas that are not obvious or not mentioned in class) and "active listening" (for example, attends carefully to what others say, refers to other students' ideas during discussions).

Assessment criteria can be articulated in two ways—*descriptively* or *qualitatively*. How we specify criteria affects the quality of direction we provide students:

- **Descriptive criteria** specify the desired features in observable or immediately identifiable terms. The desired feature is present, or it is not. For example, descriptive criteria for assessing a paragraph may include:
  - Opens with a statement of position.
  - The body contains three reasons for the position.
  - Closes with a summary statement.
- **Qualitative criteria** specify the desired features in terms of attributes or qualities that characterize the effectiveness of each constituent part. Qualitative criteria are not present or absent, but rather exist within a range. For example, qualitative criteria for assessing a paragraph may include:
  - Opens with a *clear* and *accurate* statement of position.
  - The body of the paragraph contains *plausible* and *relevant* reasons for the position.
  - Closes with a *concise* and *powerful* summary statement.

Articulating criteria in descriptive terms is easier for students and teachers to recognize—for example, we simply look for the required number of sentences and reasons, and check that the closing sentence offers a summary. With younger students and in the early stages of students' work on a topic, it *may* be appropriate to specify criteria largely in descriptive terms—simply expecting students to come up with three reasons, or even one reason, for their position. The use of descriptive criteria makes most sense if our sole concern is that students understand a concept (for example, that they understand the concept of "a reason" or "a topic sentence").

The disadvantage of descriptive criteria is that they may not allow us to distinguish when the desired feature has been competently completed. For example, the three "reasons" provided may be largely irrelevant to the position taken, or the opening sentence may be confusing. With descriptive criteria, students may simply include the identified component without any attention to its quality. For this reason, we are better advised to assess knowledge of concepts such as "reason" or "topic sentence" prior to asking students to use them in a paragraph. We might do this by asking students to provide a definition, recognize examples and non-examples, and offer a sample of each. Once students show their understanding, we will want to teach them what is required for effective application of these concepts. After all, it is not just any three reasons that we seek, but three "plausible" and "relevant" reasons.

Qualitative criteria identify those qualities that indicate effective application of a concept. In applying qualitative criteria we must judge the extent to which the requirements have been met (for example, how "clear" is the synthesis or how "plausible" are the reasons). Of course, we need to help students recognize what is involved in satisfying qualitative requirements.

To foster students' understanding of assessment criteria:

- Provide students with clear indicators of what may be involved in satisfying a criterion. For example, "I know I am being *friendly* when I …
  - compliment others on their work;
  - offer to help others before they ask me to;
  - use friendly words and smile; and,
  - share my supplies and my ideas."
- Ask students to provide concrete indicators of each criterion: What does it look like? Sound like? Feel like? As suggested in the feature "Generating Criteria," students can be aided in making the transition from descriptive to qualitative criteria by adding the question: "What are the underlying qualities that make this effective?"
- Invite students to restate in their own words the criteria for an assignment.
- Provide student samples that meet and do not meet the assigned criteria and ask them to compare these samples (for example, "Which of the three examples of notes on Inuit use of seal and caribou meet the criteria for clear, comprehensive, and concise note-taking?").

DECIDING UPON CRITERIA

Before leaving the discussion of criteria, it is worth considering who should set the criteria. As with

GENERATING CRITERIA[2]

As a first step in generating criteria, ask students to brainstorm what success on a task looks and sounds like. The focus in the following example is harmonious group work. In two columns, record student suggestions about what harmonious groups look and sound like (typically these will be identified in terms of descriptive criteria). Ask students to look for the qualities underlying or implicit in these sights and sounds—these are likely to be qualitative criteria. For example, students nodding at each other or saying, "that's a good idea" are examples of supportive behaviour. After identifying the underlying qualities for all the suggested actions and words, ask students to review their list of criteria:

- Are all the suggestions relevant? (For example, it might have been suggested that the "look" of a harmonious group requires that everyone be sitting down.)
- Is the list representative of the important features of a harmonious group?
- Should some criteria be eliminated or combined to make the list more manageable?
- Is each criterion clearly stated? Does everyone know what each means?

HARMONIOUS GROUP WORK	
Looks like	**Sounds like**
students smile at each other students look at each other students nod to each other	"What do you think about this?" "That's an interesting idea." "Are you okay?"
Underlying qualities	
are supportive/encouraging of each other are interested in others' ideas are sensitive to each other's feelings	

virtually all educational decisions, the answer depends on the circumstances. Generally speaking, it may be desirable to involve students in establishing assessment criteria, but there are times when this is not feasible or worth the effort. For example, if students lack knowledge of the topic, they may be able to offer little until they learn more. For major assignments, student ownership is especially important and it may be worthwhile to devote the time needed to jointly set criteria; on other occasions, it may be sufficient to invite students to comment on or suggest additions to the criteria. In most situations, the class as a whole should be able to agree on criteria; however, it may sometimes be useful to allow individuals to add unique criteria of their own.

Imagine you have just asked students to create an information drawing or poster about a particular community or country. Identify, in terms clear to students, three or four relevant and representative criteria drawn from the curriculum outcomes for a particular grade. Explain how you would ensure that all students understand the learning objectives for the task.

Establishing Standards

Identifying assessment criteria is only the first step in building student ownership of assessment; we must then articulate the levels of achievement or standards for each criterion. Specifying standards involves deciding the degree to which each criterion has been met (for example, what would a "clear" position statement look like? How would this differ from a "very clear" position statement?). Articulating standards is important for three reasons:

- **Supports student learning.** There is immense educational value in helping students recognize when their work meets or fails to meet certain standards. Articulating standards helps students learn what "doing well" means and what doing even better requires.
- **Facilitates fair grading.** Articulating standards is necessary for translating performance on an assignment into a grade or other summative judgment. What does "at grade level" look like and how does this differ from "above" or "below" grade level? How good is 30 out of 35? Is it "outstanding," and warrants an A or an A+? Or is it "very good," and

warrants a B or B+? To share a common understanding of the basis for these performance levels, teachers and students need to be clear about the standards being used. This is especially true when students take part in peer and self-assessment. When a single teacher assesses a class set of assignments, there is some expectation that a common set of standards are applied even if not explicitly articulated. Consistent standards are unlikely when thirty different students are assessing themselves and others.

- **Builds student ownership.** Making the bases for our assessments more explicit assists in changing students' mindsets from "What grade did you *give* me?" to "Where along this scale does my work belong?" If the standards are well articulated and students are trained in making careful, fair-minded assessments of their own and their peers' work, the teacher's role becomes relegated increasingly to checking the soundness of students' assessments.

JUSTIFYING STANDARDS

The justification of standards is inevitable but should not be arbitrary. Whether in the form of letter grades or terms such as "excellent" and "poor," standards can be norm-referenced, based on the work of a normal population, or criterion-referenced, based on some external benchmark.

- **Norm-referenced standards** are about how well a product or performance matches the work of a normal or typical population (for example, Is this a "typical" performance for a grade 6 student? Would only about 30 per cent of the class meet this level? Would this be within the top 10 per cent of the province?). Some universities insist that not more than 20 per cent of students in a given class receive an "A." With norm-referenced standards, it is theoretically impossible for all students to get a top score—students are rated relative to how well others perform. To this extent, norm-referenced standards may discourage co-operation among students, because as students do better, the standard becomes higher for everyone.
- **Criterion-referenced standards** are determined by benchmarks not directly dependent on how well others in the population perform, but on an external reference (for example, what is needed in order to read the newspaper, or successfully meet an agreed-on goal). Criterion-referenced judgments are not based on expectations of what the average student is likely to achieve, but on an independent level of expectation. With criterion-referenced standards, it is theoretically possible for everyone to achieve a high rating.

Norm-referenced standards may be justified in terms of the places available in the next educational level or a "normal" distribution of the population (for example, the bell curve—the top 10 per cent get "excellent," the next 20 per cent get "good," and so on)—or a comparison with what "average" students have done in previous years. Criterion-referenced standards may be justified in terms of what would likely be required in order to be employable, or succeed at a task. For example, grade 3 students should be able to write a clear, four-sentence paragraph after completing the relevant unit.

Pre-established standards in certain areas are available from provincial ministries of education. For example, Table 27.2 summarizes performance standards for three aspects of social responsibility at various grade ranges, developed by the British Columbia Ministry of Education (2001, 19, 61, 139).

When setting standards for our assignments, we should be sensitive to both norm- and criterion-referenced considerations. There is little merit in adopting a criterion-based standard that no student can meet because it is too demanding or challenges no one because it is too easy. In other words, we should temper this standard with norm-referenced expectations. Conversely, it seems counterproductive to decide beforehand on norm-referenced grounds that only the top five students will be allowed to do "very well" and at least five students must do "poorly." Rather, we should rely on published guidelines, past experience, and our own professional intuition about what are fair and educationally realistic expectations. In justifying the standards articulated in Figure 27.2, I tempered my impression of a masterful essay to make allowances for the reasonably expected abilities of secondary students who should not be required to operate at the same level as graduate students. Just as with setting criteria, it is appropriate to ask for students' comment on the proposed standards. In some circumstances, we can help students set the standards themselves for "good" and "very good" performances on an assignment.

TABLE 27.2 SAMPLING OF STANDARDS FOR SOCIAL RESPONSIBILITY

ASPECT	EXCEEDS EXPECTATIONS	FULLY MEETS EXPECTATIONS	MEETS EXPECTATIONS (MINIMUM LEVEL)	NOT YET WITHIN EXPECTATIONS
Contributing to the classroom and school community (kindergarten–grade 3 expectations)	• Welcoming, friendly, kind, and helpful • Participates in and contributes to classroom and group activities; often takes on extra responsibilities	• Usually welcoming, friendly, kind, and helpful • Participates in and contributes to classroom and group activities	• Usually friendly and, if asked, will help or include others • May need prompting to participate in and contribute to classroom and group activities	• Often unfriendly or disrespectful of others • Generally reluctant to participate in and contribute to classroom and group activities
Solving problems in peaceful ways (grade 4–5 expectations)	• Considers others' views, and uses some effective strategies for resolving conflicts; takes responsibility and shows good judgment about when to get adult help • Can explain an increasing variety of problems or issues and generate and evaluate strategies	• Tries to manage anger, listen to others, and apply logical reasons to resolve conflicts; usually knows when to get adult help • Can explain simple problems or issues and generate and select simple, logical strategies	• Tries to state feelings and manage anger; often needs support to resolve conflicts, frequently overestimating or underestimating the need for adult help • Can identify simple problems or issues and generate some strategies; tends to rely on the same strategies for all problems	• Does not take responsibility or listen to another's views in a conflict situation; tends to blame and put down others • Has difficulty stating problems or issues, and may be unable to suggest or choose appropriate strategies
Valuing diversity and defending human rights (grade 8–10 expectations)	• Respectful and ethical; speaks out and takes action to support diversity and defend human rights, even when that may not be a popular stance	• Respectful and fair; increasingly willing to speak up or take action to support diversity and defend human rights	• Usually respectful; supports those who speak up or take action to support diversity and defend human rights	• Sometimes disrespectful; may stereotype or avoid those perceived as different in some way

COMMUNICATING STANDARDS

Assessment standards that are identified by a simple set of labels such as excellent, good, satisfactory, or poor offer little help to students. They identify the levels but don't explain or articulate what is required. The most common way to articulate standards is a rubric, which is a scale describing the criteria and standards for an assignment or test. Two types of scales are used in rubrics:

- **Holistic scales** cluster the description of standards for all criteria in one paragraph so that a single overall judgment is made about an assignment, which takes all the criteria into account at once. Figure 27.2 is a holistic scale rubric for judging which of five descriptions best characterizes the overall thoughtfulness of a report on a social issue.
- **Analytic scales** specify the standards for criteria separately, with a judgment made for each criterion. Figure 27.3 is an analytic scale used to self-assess students' performance in a decision-making simulation. There are four criteria judged separately—acting

effectively in role, contributing relevant ideas, sincerely supporting others, and sincerely seeking a "win-win" solution.

An advantage of holistic scales is that we need make one judgment only. This often reduces the time required to assess student work. The disadvantage of holistic scales is that students may overlook particular criteria embedded in the global descriptors. On the other hand, analytic scales focus students' attention on each aspect of an assignment. When self-assessing, it may be easier to begin with analytic scales so students can attend to one criterion at a time. Having said this, the difference between analytic and holistic scales may be a matter of degree: specific criteria can always be clustered into more general categories, so an analytic scale can be modified to closely resemble a holistic one. The social responsibility rubric shown earlier in Table 27.2 is a modified analytic scale; the British Columbia Ministry of Education has grouped several criteria within each of the three general categories of contributing to community, solving problems, and defending human rights.

FIGURE 27.2   HOLISTIC RUBRIC: THOUGHTFUL REPORT

SCORE	DESCRIPTION OF REPORT
4	**Accomplished and very thoughtful.** The report clearly identifies all the main ideas of the issue. The discussion explains the important points carefully and with lots of detail. Personal opinions are well explained and supported with convincing examples and believable reasons.
3	**Competent and thoughtful.** The report is generally clear about the main ideas of the issue. The discussion explains most of the important matters in a careful manner. Personal observations are generally supported with relevant examples and believable reasons.
2	**Somewhat thoughtful, but flawed.** The report identifies some of the main ideas of the issue, but misses other important ones. The discussion explains some important points, but often states the obvious or overlooks basic points. Personal opinions are supported with a few reasons and examples that are not always convincing.
1	**Little or no thoughtfulness.** The report does not clearly identify any of the main ideas of the issue. The discussion does very little to explain the important points. Personal opinions are not supported with relevant examples and believable reasons.
0	**Not done.** No report submitted.

Another variable in assessment rubrics is the level of detail in the descriptions of performance levels—rubrics can be fully articulated or skeletal in their detail (Mertler 2001):

- **Fully articulated rubrics.** The most elaborate rubrics richly describe each level of performance. These "fully articulated" rubrics are difficult to develop, and require numerous revisions before balanced and precise descriptions are produced. Unless the descriptions of standards are clear and mutually exclusive (i.e., no overlap between descriptors), the rubric is unreliable. Fully articulated rubrics may be worth the effort, especially for major projects involving student self- and peer assessment. The elaborate descriptions provide considerable guidance, clarity, and consistency, which are especially important when students adopt an assessor's role.
- **Skeletal rubrics.** On a more regular basis it may be advisable to use less elaborate rubrics in which the descriptions for each level are not articulated in detail. In most cases, standards can be delineated using a single word or phrase describing various levels of

performance, such as "always," "often," "occasionally," and "rarely." See Figure 27.3 for a rubric students can use to self-assess their role-playing efforts in a simulated town hall meeting. Where possible, use words that clearly communicate the basis for distinguishing between levels (for example, quantity of correct answers, degree of clarity, extent to which each criterion is present) rather than words such as "excellent" or "poor," which are vague.

Increasingly, educators are expressing concerns about the misuse and negative implications of rubrics. For example, Alfie Kohn (2006, 13) reports a teacher's observation that her students appear "unable to function unless every required item is spelled out for them in a grid and assigned a point value." Rather than building ownership in learning, for some students rubrics accentuate the focus on doing things simply for marks. These problems can be addressed by ensuring that assessment criteria reflect important curriculum outcomes and by articulating assessment standards in qualitative terms that reflect the intent of the assignment.

In addition to providing rubrics or involving

GUIDELINES FOR DEVELOPING FULLY ARTICULATED RUBRICS

- **Generate criteria.** Brainstorm criteria for assessing the assignment.
- **Prioritize criteria.** Select the most important and relevant criteria, justified in light of curriculum expectations and the assignment's purpose.
- **Consolidate criteria.** Cluster criteria around common themes; consider rephrasing some criteria more generally to reduce

the number of specific criteria. Organize criteria into categories (for example, presentation, content, research) and avoid vague terms such as "creativity" and "critical thinking." Where possible, use precise criteria (for example, goes beyond the obvious, questions the accuracy of the author's claims, offers evidence to support position).

(continued on next page)

- **Set levels**. Decide on the number of performance levels to specify—rubrics commonly articulate between three and five levels. With younger students, three levels may be most appropriate. It is always possible to assign a mark midway between two levels.
- **Select variables to distinguish performance levels.** Each level of performance can be distinguished in two ways:
  - Alter the extent and degree to which the criterion has been met. For example, performance levels for "clear explanations" may range from "*every important* idea has been *clearly* explained" through "the *most important* ideas are *generally clearly* explained" to "*no clear* explanations are provided." Some writers (Bennett and Mulgrew 2009, 7) believe that it is never appropriate to include any quantitative references in a rubric (for example, many, most, some); but most writers recommend that quantitative descriptors not be the sole basis for distinguishing different performance levels.
  - Add an additional condition at certain levels of performance. For example, the highest performance level for "clear explanations" may be distinguished by inclusion of an additional expectation ("every *main idea* has been *clearly explained* in the students' *own words*") that is not present in the other descriptors ("the main ideas are generally clearly explained" or "no clear explanations are provided."

Many rubrics are flawed in distinguishing between performance levels in two ways:
  - **Use of entirely descriptive standards.** For example, performance levels for "provides reasons" may range from "provides *three or more* reasons" through "provides *two* reasons" to "*no reasons provided*." However, is a student who provides three irrelevant and unsound reasons performing at a higher level than a student who provides only one irrelevant, unsound reason? Adding qualitative standards such as "provides relevant and sound reasons" solves this problem.
  - **Inconsistency across performance levels.** For example, it would be inappropriate to distinguish levels for "provides reasons" with descriptors that range from "provides several *plausible* reasons" through "provides a few *clear and relevant* reasons" to "reasons are *not supported with any examples*." The problem arises because different *kinds* of criteria (plausible, clear, relevant, supported with examples) are used at each level. Performance levels should vary only in the degree of achievement for a particular criterion.
- **Draft polar descriptors.** Begin by describing the standards at the very top and the very bottom of the scale: What would the best performance look like? What would the worst level of performance look like? Decide whether the performance is

better articulated in a single description (making it a holistic scale) or whether an analytic scale is easier to use and clearer to students. Because it is better to start with the best that students can achieve rather than the worst, many assessment experts recommend describing the highest performance level on the left-hand side of a rubric and the lowest level on the right-hand side.
- **Draft intermediate descriptors.** The most difficult task in creating a rubric is describing the in-between standards. It may be helpful to look at existing rubrics for ideas on the kinds of words to use to distinguish different gradations of performance. An advantage of using an odd number of performance levels (three or five levels) is that the intermediate levels can be distinguished by splitting the difference between the poles. For example, on a five-point scale, the third level would be exactly midway between the descriptions of a "one" and a "five," and the second level would then be midway between the descriptions of a "one" and a "three."
- **Refine draft.** After developing an initial version of the rubric, check that the descriptors are mutually exclusive and precise, and that the intervals between the levels are "approximately equivalent" (i.e., the amount of improvement between any two levels is roughly the same). This step is the most demanding and frustrating since it is difficult to find precise words to distinguish each performance level for each criterion. Very subtle changes in wording may make all the difference between a reliable rubric and one that provides little guidance. Be especially careful about the use of vague terms such as "good" or "successful," since the very point of articulating standards is to unpack these kinds of terms for students.
- **Finalize the performance levels.** Assign labels to each level and decide the weight to be attached to each criterion according to its importance. If appropriate, decide on the grade to be awarded for each range of marks by asking the following sorts of questions: "If a student received 15 out of 20 marks on this assignment, what grade does this mark deserve?" "What about a 10 out of 20?" Translating a mark to a grade requires deciding whether to use criterion- or norm-referenced standards. Will it be based on what percentage of the class will be allowed to receive an A, B, C, and so on, is there an independent benchmark to which we can refer, or should both considerations be balanced?
- **Pilot the rubric.** Before using a rubric in an actual assessment situation, score a sample of assignments to uncover unanticipated flaws. If this is not feasible, ask for critical feedback from someone else (for example, Based on these descriptions, would you know what a "good" or "fair" assessment requires? Does the weighting of marks seem reasonable? Are the levels clearly distinguished?).

FIGURE 27.3   SELF-ASSESSMENT OF ROLE PLAY

During the meetings I acted effectively in role … ❏ almost never ❏ about half the time ❏ all of the time	Evidence to support my evaluation:
During the meetings I contributed relevant ideas … ❏ almost never ❏ a few times ❏ whenever appropriate	Evidence to support my evaluation:
During the meetings I sincerely supported other people's ideas … ❏ almost never ❏ a few times ❏ whenever appropriate	Evidence to support my evaluation:
During the meetings I tried sincerely to find a "win-win" solution … ❏ not at all ❏ made an effort ❏ worked very hard	Evidence to support my evaluation:
I made my greatest contribution during the meetings when I …	

students in their development, we can help students understand assessment standards in several ways:

- Provide actual samples of previous students' work at each performance level;
- Provide a set of standards and ask students to assess their own work and identify what would be required to bring it up to the next level; and
- Ask students to prepare a sample answer to match each performance level on the scale; for example, students might write a "weak," "good," and "excellent" answer to a question.

Supporting Peer and Self-Assessment

It is essential when building ownership for learning that we involve students in assessing their own work and that of their peers. This can be as simple as inviting students to informally review an assignment in light of several identified criteria or as formal as assigning a mark based on a rubric.

The feature "Introducing Peer Critique" contains detailed suggestions for grooming students as self- and peer assessors. Here are a few general guidelines:

- Before asking students to put their work on the line, invite the class to critique something you have produced (for example, an essay you wrote as a student, a mock presentation you make). When it is time for peer critique, start with group assignments so the responsibility is shared among several students. Ensure that the early instances of critique are low risk, relatively easy to perform, and have an obvious benefit (for example, bonus marks).
- Emphasize peer and self-assessment as critique—seeing the positives, not just the negatives. In the early days of peer critique, do not allow negative comments, only positive ones. A good indication of when to allow comments about concerns/weaknesses is when students start asking each other what is "wrong" with their work.
- Establish, and model, a few simple guidelines for giving critique: perhaps students should (1) start with two (or more) positive comments before offering a (single) concern, and (2) phrase negative comments in the form of a query (for example, "I'm not sure I understand why you did it this way." Or, "Could you help me see what you had in mind?").
- Make sure students understand the criteria and standards to use in assessment. Because different students will apply inconsistent standards, it may be best to limit peer or self-assessment to informal critique unless there is a rubric for students to use.
- Until students demonstrate the ability and

	WELL DEVELOPED	COMPETENT	UNDERDEVELOPED
Justification for self-assessments	Offers clear and specific evidence to support each self-assessment and the evidence is highly consistent with the assigned rating.	Offers some evidence to support each self-assessment and the evidence is generally consistent with the assigned rating.	Offers no evidence to support any of the self-assessments or the evidence is clearly inconsistent with the assigned rating.
Reasonableness of personal ratings	Every one of the ratings seems completely deserved given the student's performance in the role play.	The ratings seem generally deserved given the student's performance in the role play.	The ratings seem completely undeserved given the student's performance in the role play.

INTRODUCING PEER CRITIQUE

When introducing students to peer critique, it is advisable to model the procedure initially in a whole class setting, with an assignment volunteered by a student(s) willing to undergo public scrutiny (alternatively, use a former student's assignment). Afterwards, students can repeat the process with their own assignments in small groups.

Review the criteria

Begin by reviewing two sets of criteria with students—the criteria related to the assignment and the criteria for peer critique.

- *Criteria for judging the assignment.* Review with students, perhaps with an overhead transparency or a handout, a handful of criteria that students are to consider. Limit the number of criteria to four or five, especially if students are new to the enterprise. You might also ask students to look for specific strategies that contributed or did not contribute to achievement (strategies for achieving clarity include using specific examples, supplementing oral comments with visual aids, and limiting the number of points made).

- *Criteria for peer critiques.* Explain to students that just as there are criteria for judging the merits of an assignment, so too are there criteria for successful critiques. Explain the following criteria:
  - *respectful*: comments should not be mean-spirited, insulting, or condescending (stress the importance of this criterion);
  - *relevant*: comments—whether positive or negative—should not be trivial or off-topic but connected to the criteria for a successful assignment;
  - *specific*: comments should identify particular aspects rather than vague (use an example to illustrate the value of specific compared to vague comments); and,
  - *constructive*: the primary purpose of critique is to improve performance—not to belittle or to criticize; advice on how to improve is preferable to comments that merely note areas of strength and weakness.

Examine the assignment

While examining the assignment to be critiqued, invite students to make written notes in light of the evaluation criteria. It may be sufficient for students to record comments in two columns— "Positive Features" and "Areas for Improvement." A more sophisticated approach is to subdivide the columns into rows, one for each criterion that students are to consider. Students then look explicitly for "positive features" and "areas for improvement" for each. In the following chart, students indicate the criteria they are considering for both "Strengths" and "Areas to think about."

Set the terms of the critique

Once the assignment has been reviewed, structure the sharing of the critique in the following manner:

- *Lead with the positives.* I firmly believe that critiques should always begin with "unqualified" comments on the "strengths" of the assignment. This reduces the anxiety all of us feel when we subject our work to scrutiny. Even when reminded about starting with the positives, students have a tendency to slip into partly negative comments. Politely interrupt whenever apparently positive comments take on negative tones. As well, students often have difficulty coming up with positive comments—not because strengths are absent but because we are prone to notice what is wrong. Prepare a list beforehand of positive comments to infuse into the discussion in the event that student-generated comments are not forthcoming. Remind students that the point is not to show off or to make others feel inadequate, but to help fellow students produce the best possible product.

- *Suggest areas for improvement.* Only after abundant expression of strengths should concerns or areas of improvement be expressed. Encourage students to provide specific suggestions about how the assignment might be improved.

Coach the recipient of the critique

Just prior to the critique, encourage the student (or group of students) receiving the critique to assume an active listening role—limiting comments to asking for clarification or elaboration, checking for understanding and whether or not ideas offered by individual commentators are shared by others in the class. Encourage recipients not to be defensive, and not to feel that they should defend what they have done. Their role is to hear what others have to say, and after the critique is over, to decide for themselves which, if any, of the comments are worth acting upon. Praise students for agreeing to subject their work to public scrutiny.

Debrief the critique

Close the activity by asking for student observations, beginning with the recipient(s) of the critique. The teacher's role throughout should be to acknowledge how difficult peer critique can be, especially for recipients, but to stress that the experience can be very fruitful when done well. Encourage students to integrate comments from the critique into their final product.

STRENGTHS

CRITERIA	NOTES

AREAS TO THINK ABOUT

CRITERIA	NOTES

commitment to assess conscientiously and fairly, it is ill-advised to use their assessments for assigning grades. Teachers have this ethical and legal responsibility, and reserve the right to veto any student-assigned mark that is clearly unwarranted.

- Provide feedback to students about the quality of their assessment judgments. To signal to students that peer and self-assessment are important, you may want to assess their assessments. The rubric in Figure 27.4 may be used to assess students' self-evaluation of their role play in a town hall meeting.[3]

Conclusion

There are, of course, many other factors to consider and issues to explore in learning to build student ownership of assessment. As well, there are many practical hurdles to overcome as we unpack the "black box" of assessment for our students. My own experiences have convinced me of the importance, for educational and ethical reasons, of ensuring that students clearly understand and have some ownership of assessment of their work. In fact, class discussions about previously vague

criteria and unarticulated standards have led to fruitful examination by me and my students about what it is that students need to learn. Being clear and committed to the criteria and standards for assessment can only lead to improved teaching and learning.

ACKNOWLEDGMENT

I am grateful to Robert Hogg of the Alberta Assessment Consortium and Rosemary Evans of Branksome Hall School for their helpful suggestions in preparing this chapter.

ENDNOTES

1   This example is adapted from Nichol and Case 2003.
2   This example was suggested by Tom Morton, a retired social studies teacher in Vancouver.
3   This rubric was adapted from Northey, Nicol and Case 2003.

REFERENCES

Bennett, S. and A. Mulgrew. 2009. *Building better rubrics.* Edmonton: Alberta Assessment Consortium.

British Columbia Ministry of Education. 2001. *BC performance standards: Social responsibility—A framework*. Victoria, BC: Ministry of Education, Student Assessment and Program Evaluation Branch, Province of British Columbia. Accessed online at www.bced.gov.bc.ca/perf_stands/social_resp.htm.

Emblem, S. 1994. So, what did I get on my muffin? *SnapShots 4* (2): 4–5.

Kohn, A. 2006. The trouble with rubrics. *English Journal* 95 (4): 12–15. Accessed online at www.csun.edu/~krowlands/ Content/Academic_Resources/Composition/Responding/ Kohn-Rubrics.pdf.

Mertler, C. 2001. Designing scoring rubrics for your classroom. *Practical Assessment, Research and Evaluation* 7 (25). Accessed online at pareonline.net/getvn.asp?v=7&n=25.

Nicol, J. and R. Case, eds. 2003. *The resourcefulness of the Inuit.* Vancouver, BC: The Critical Thinking Consortium.

Northey, D., J. Nicol, and R. Case, eds. 2003. *Brazilian rainforest.* Vancouver, BC: The Critical Thinking Consortium.

Acknowledgments

CHAPTER 2 "Social Studies is . . . A Poem" by Donna Robinson was originally cited in "Social Studies Poems," ed. John J. Chiodo, *Social Education* 54 (7): 467–468. © National Council of the Social Studies. Reprinted by permission.

Cartoon © John Anfin. Used by permission.

CHAPTER 4 The illustration of ancient Egypt, by Danna deGroot, is reproduced by permission of the publisher from David Scott, Cliff Falk, and Jenny Kierstead, *Legacies of Ancient Egypt* (Vancouver, BC: The Critical Thinking Consortium, 2002), 75. © 2002 Ministry of Education, Province of British Columbia.

CHAPTER 6 The icons for critical thinking tools are copyright The Critical Thinking Consortium. Used by permission.

Figure 6.1, Promoting Critical Thinking, is adapted by permission of the publisher from Mike Denos and Roland Case, *Teaching about Historical Thinking* (Vancouver, BC: The Critical Thinking Consortium, 2006), 75. © 2006 by The Critical Thinking Consortium.

Table 6.1, Thinking Critically about Logging Old-Growth Forests, is used by permission of the authors from Sharon Balin, Roland Case, Jerrold R. Coombs, and LeRoi Daniels, "Conceptualizing Critical Thinking," *Journal of Curriculum Studies* 31 (3): 285–302.

CHAPTER 7 "The 'Suburb of Happy Homes'" illustration, by Fraser Wilson, was first published in 1942 in the *Vancouver Sun* on the occasion of the fiftieth anniversary of Burnaby's incorporation.

CHAPTER 11 Figure 11.2, Evaluating Resources on Canadian Explorers, is adapted by permission of the publisher from John Harrison, Neil Smith, and Ian Wright, eds., *Selected Critical Challenges in Social Studies—Intermediate/Middle School* (Vancouver, BC: The Critical Thinking Consortium, 2004), 81. © 2004 The Critical Thinking Consortium.

Figure 11.3, Assessing Students' Notes, is adapted by permission of the publisher from Jan Nicol and Roland Case, eds., *The Resourcefulness of the Inuit* (Vancouver, BC: The Critical Thinking Consortium), 116. © 2002 Ministry of Education, Province of British Columbia.

"Summary of Emily's Talk" by Laura Brown is reproduced by permission of the author and that of her teacher, Vivian Brighten, and her mother, Wendy Pitt-Brooke.

CHAPTER 13 Figure 13.1, Consequences for Stakeholders, is adapted by permission of the publisher from Roland Case, Cliff Falk, Neil Smith, and Walt Werner, *Active Citizenship: Student Action Projects* (Vancouver, BC: The Critical Thinking Consortium), 55. © 2004 The Critical Thinking Consortium.

Figure 13.2, Action Plan, is adapted by permission of the publisher from Roland Case et al., *Active Citizenship: Student Action Projects* (Vancouver, BC: The Critical Thinking Consortium), 57. © 2004 The Critical Thinking Consortium.

Figure 13.3, Reflecting on Our Project, is adapted by permission of the publisher from Roland Case et al., *Active Citizenship: Student Action Projects* (Vancouver, BC: The Critical Thinking Consortium), 69. © 2004 The Critical Thinking Consortium.

CHAPTER 15 The photo "The shame of the city: Can we give our children no better playing space?" is reproduced courtesy of Library and Archives Canada (C-030947). Used by permission.

The photo "Fraser River Indians" is reproduced courtesy of Royal BC Museum, BC Archives (E-04419). Used by permission.

The photo "Hon. Donald A. Smith driving the last spike to complete the Canadian Pacific Railway," by Alexander Ross, is reproduced courtesy of Library and Archives Canada (C-003693).

The photo "The last spike C.P.R. staged by construction party that missed the official ceremony" is reproduced courtesy of Library and Archives Canada (C-014115).

The photo "Canoe manned by voyageurs passing a waterfall" by Frances Anne Hopkins (1836–1919) is reproduced courtesy of Library and Archives Canada (Acc. No. 1989-401-1).

The photo "Sharing a moment" is by Penney Clark. Used by permission.

The photo "Housing built for Chinese labourers working on the Canadian Pacific Railway" is reproduced courtesy of the Royal BC Museum, BC Archives (I-30869). Used by permission.

The photo "Ukrainian women cutting logs, Athabasca, Alberta, c. 1930" is reproduced courtesy of Library and Archives Canada/Canadian National Railway Company fonds (C-019134).

CHAPTER 16 "Globe-Trotting Teddies" is adapted by permission from author Penney Clark, "Listening to the Ambulance Sirens: Is this any way to teach?" *Canadian Social Studies* 34 (3): 38. © 2000 *Canadian Social Studies*, www.quasar.ualberta.ca/css.

Figure 16.2, Sample Interview Form, is adapted by permission from Mary Abbott, Carole Ford, and Roland Case, eds., *Contributing to Family and Community* (Vancouver, BC: The Critical Thinking Consortium), 119–120. © 2003 Ministry of Education, Province of British Columbia.

Figure 16.3, Note of Appreciation, is adapted with permission from Mary Abbott et al., eds., *Contributing to Family and Community* (Vancouver, BC: The Critical Thinking Consortium), 121. © 2003 Ministry of Education, Province of British Columbia.

CHAPTER 18 Figure 18.1, Documenting the Details, is adapted by permission of the publisher from David Scott et al., *Legacies of Ancient Egypt* (Vancouver, BC: The Critical Thinking Consortium). © 2002 Ministry of Education, Province of British Columbia.

CHAPTER 19 Clay liver picture is used courtesy of Susan Duncan.

CHAPTER 20 "The Eporuvians Come to Call": The Eporuvian role play was developed by Anne Hill, an elementary teacher in Terrace, BC. Used by permission.

CHAPTER 21 "The Road Less Travelled" cartoon is by Erica Ball, a librarian at Hazelton Secondary School, Hazelton, BC. Used by permission.

CHAPTER 22 "Believe It or Not" is reproduced by permission of the publisher from Jan Nicol and Roland Case, eds., *The Resourcefulness of the Inuit* (Vancouver, BC: The Critical Thinking Consortium), 95. © 2002 Ministry of Education, Province of British Columbia.

CHAPTER 23 This chapter is reproduced by permission of the authors from Robert Fowler and Ian Wright, eds., *Thinking Globally about Social Studies Education* (Vancouver, BC: Research and Development in Global Studies, University of British Columbia), 51–60. © 1995.

CHAPTER 24 Figure 24.1, Who Has a Responsibility?, is adapted by permission of the publisher from Maureen McDermid, Mary Abbott, and Roland Case, eds., *Rights, Roles, and Responsibilities at School* (Vancouver, BC: The Critical Thinking Consortium), 88–89. © 2003 Ministry of Education, Province of British Columbia.

Figure 24.2, Drawing the Line on Our Right to Food, is adapted by permission of the publisher from Jan Nicol and Dan Kirk, *Caring for Young People's Rights* (Vancouver, BC: The Critical Thinking Consortium), 79. © 2004 The Critical Thinking Consortium.

CHAPTER 25 Figure 25.6, Sample Unit Plan, is adapted by permission from a unit by primary teachers Janis Chappell, Robin Johnson, Kerrin McLeod, and Danielle Doucette.

"The Descent of the Fraser River" is a shortened version of "The Descent of the Fraser River" in M.G. Parks and C.W. Jefferys, illus., *Discoverers and Explorers in Canada—1763–1911*, Portfolio II #4 (Imperial Oil Ltd., n.d.). Reproduced by permission.

CHAPTER 26 Figure 26.1, Sorting Memories, is adapted by permission from Mary Abbott et al., eds., *Contributing to Family and Community* (Vancouver, BC: The Critical Thinking Consortium), 95. © 2003 Ministry of Education, Province of British Columbia.

Figure 26.2, Solving the Mystery, is adapted by permission from Mary Abbott et al., eds., *Contributing to Family and Community* (Vancouver, BC: The Critical Thinking Consortium), 83. © 2003 Ministry of Education, Province of British Columbia.

Figure 26.8, Assessing Family Memories, is adapted by permission from Mary Abbott et al., eds., *Contributing to Family and Community* (Vancouver, BC: The Critical Thinking Consortium), 98. © 2003 Ministry of Education, Province of British Columbia.

CHAPTER 27   Figure 27.1, Sample Notes, is adapted from Jan Nicol and Roland Case, eds., *The Resourcefulness of the Inuit* (Vancouver: The Critical Thinking Consortium), 110. © 2002 Ministry of Education, Province of British Columbia.

Figure 27.3, Self-Assessment of Role Play, is adapted by permission from Don Northey, Jan Nicol, and Roland Case, eds. *Brazilian Rain Forest* (Vancouver, BC: The Critical Thinking Consortium), 106. © 2003 Ministry of Education, Province of British Columbia.

Figure 27.4, Assessing Students' Self-Assessment of Their Role Play Performance, is adapted with permission from Don Northey et al., eds., *Brazilian Rain Forest* (Vancouver, BC: The Critical Thinking Consortium), 113. © 2003 Ministry of Education, Province of British Columbia.

Contributors

EDITORS

ROLAND CASE is executive director of The Critical Thinking Consortium (TC²)—a non-profit association of school districts and educational organizations across Canada. He is a retired professor of social studies education at Simon Fraser University in British Columbia. Roland has edited or authored over 100 published works. Notable among these is the award-winning series of TC² teaching resources entitled *Critical Challenges Across the Curriculum*. In addition to his public school and university teaching, Roland has worked with over 18,000 educators across Canada and in the United States, England, Israel, Russia, India, Finland, and Hong Kong to support the infusion of critical thinking. Roland was the 2006 recipient of the Distinguished Academics Career Achievement Award from the Confederation of University Faculty Associations of BC (CUFA).

PENNEY CLARK is a professor in the Department of Curriculum and Pedagogy at the University of British Columbia and the director of the History Education Network/Histoire et éducation en réseau (THEN/HiER). She was awarded the Killam Teaching Prize in 2005 for her teaching of social studies curriculum and instruction, history of curriculum, and politics of curriculum development courses at UBC. She co-authored three Canadian history textbooks and has published articles in the *Journal of Canadian Studies, Canadian Journal of Education, American Journal of Education, History of Education Quarterly,* and *Theory and Research in Social Education.* Her most recent publication is the edited volume, *New Possibilities for the Past: Shaping History Education in Canada* (UBC Press, 2011). For additional information, see: edcp.educ.ubc.ca/faculty/penney-clark

AUTHORS

MARY ABBOTT began her career as a primary teacher and later taught all of the elementary grades, special education, and also served as teacher-librarian. She retired from the Faculty of Education at Vancouver Island University in 2009. Her teaching areas have included social studies methods, language arts methods, literacy development, and assessment. As a member of the Critical Thinking Consortium, Mary is involved in the creation and editing of teaching resources and the facilitation of professional development for teachers.

PHILIP BALCAEN is a faculty member at the University of British Columbia's Okanagan campus, where he teaches mathematics, teaching methodology for science, and graduate courses in curriculum studies. Previously, he taught at Simon Fraser University and at the secondary level in the BC public education system. His research interests include school-university collaboration, critical thinking, environmental studies and education, and critically thoughtful e-learning.

WANDA CASSIDY is an associate professor in the Faculty of Education and director of the Centre for Education, Law and Society at Simon Fraser University in British Columbia. Her research primarily focuses on law-related education and its intersection with citizenship education and the civil society. She is interested in the relationship between law and societal values and beliefs, including the ethics of care, social responsibility, human rights, and social justice. Current research projects include an examination of legal literacy among students in grades 6 to 10 and cyberbullying in middle schools and at the post-secondary level.

LEROI DANIELS was a professor emeritus in the Faculty of Education at the University of British Columbia until his death in 2011. He was a founding member of the Critical Thinking Consortium and an author of the model of critical thinking that forms the conceptual foundation of the consortium's work. LeRoi wrote various articles on critical thinking and was co-editor of *Critical Challenges Across the Curriculum*, a series of teaching resources for critical thinking.

LINDA FARR DARLING is the Eleanor Rix Professor of Rural Teacher Education in the Faculty of Education at the University of British Columbia, a position dedicated to preparing, recruiting, and supporting rural teachers for British Columbia through research, teaching, and policy work. As part of her role, she oversees a UBC teacher education program located in the West Kootenays where she teaches courses on rural issues and the ethical dimensions of teaching and learning. Linda's current research focuses on place-conscious learning in K–12 classrooms and in teacher preparation. She is also studying the potential role of schooling in rural revitalization efforts. She is working with research partners in New South Wales to explore Australian initiatives in this area.

CHRISTINE EIDE emigrated from Holland to northern British Columbia when she was twelve years old. At age fifteen she got an after-school job working in a Hudson's Bay trading post. She began her teaching career in a one-room school, Upper Kispiox Rural School. Christine has taught a range of grade levels in various northern communities, and was a principal for nineteen years before retirement. She has been a faculty associate in Simon Fraser University's teacher education program and a practicum placement coordinator for the University of Northern British Columbia's B.Ed. program.

MARGARET FERGUSON is a teacher in northern British Columbia. She has a law degree from the University of Alberta and has published numerous articles on law-related education. For thirteen years, Margaret was the School Reorganizing Coordinator for the Legal Resource Centre in the Faculty of Extension at the University of Alberta.

SUSAN GIBSON began her career as a social studies teacher in the public school systems in both Alberta and Ontario, where she taught the elementary/middle years grades. She is now a professor in the Department of Elementary Education in the Faculty of Education at the University of Alberta. Since completing her PhD in Curriculum Studies at the University of British Columbia in 1995, Susan has taught undergraduate courses on social studies curriculum and graduate curriculum courses. Much of her research has focussed on how best to prepare pre-service and practising educators to teach social studies in a digital age. In 2009, she wrote *Teaching Elementary Social Studies: A Social Constructivist Approach* (Nelson Education). This book describes the problem-based inquiry approach to learning to teach social studies that Susan uses in her undergraduate teaching, for which she won both the Faculty of Education Undergraduate Teaching Award and the University of Alberta's Rutherford Award for Excellence in Undergraduate Teaching.

GARFIELD GINI-NEWMAN is a senior lecturer at the Ontario Institute for Studies in Education (OISE) at the University of Toronto and a senior national consultant with the Critical Thinking Consortium. Formerly, he was a curriculum consultant with the York Region District School Board and a classroom educator for fifteen years teaching a range of subjects, including history, philosophy, politics, and English. He has spoken across Canada and internationally on critical thinking, brain-compatible classrooms, curriculum design, and effective assessment practice. Garfield has also authored seven textbooks and has taught in the Faculty of Education at both York University and the University of British Columbia.

LAURA GINI-NEWMAN is currently an instructional resource teacher and a Math Gains coach for the Peel District School Board in Ontario. She is also a facilitator for the Critical Thinking Consortium. Laura has developed math resources for students at risk and has presented on the topic of "Critical Thinking in Mathematics," both in Ontario and the United States. She has been a consultant in Peel for nine years with returns to classroom practice. Her work ranges from writing textbooks and assessment handbooks to facilitating school improvement plans.

MICHAEL LING is a senior lecturer in the Faculty of Education at Simon Fraser University in British Columbia. He works primarily with in-service teachers in graduate diploma and degree programs. He is interested in what occurs at the intersection of culture, education, and the arts, and in the ways that these areas contribute to our collective and individual pursuit of meaning in the world and to a meaningful life.

ROBERTA MCKAY has been a professor in the Department of Elementary Education at the University of Alberta. She has authored social studies textbooks and teacher guides for use in elementary and secondary schools. She is currently the director of the Master of Education in Educational Studies program in the Faculty of Education at the University of Alberta. Her awards include the Rutherford Award for Excellence in Undergraduate Teaching from the University of Alberta, the Exemplary Dissertation Award from the National Council for the Social Studies, and the Educational Research Award from the Alberta Teachers' Association.

CATHY MORGAN began teaching primary grades in a small northern community in British Columbia in 1971, and she taught for many years at the elementary levels. For several years she was a faculty associate in Simon Fraser University's professional development program where she worked with aboriginal and non-aboriginal student teachers. For the past six years prior to retirement, Cathy served as the administrator of a small rural school.

TOM MORTON taught for over thirty years in Kabala, Sierra Leone; Montreal; and Vancouver at the high school and university levels. Over his career, Tom has received the British Columbia Social Studies Teacher of the Year Award, the Governor General's Award for Excellence in Teaching Canadian History, and the Kron Award for Excellence in Holocaust Education. He is one of the founders of the British Columbia Cooperative Learning Association and is the author of *Cooperative Learning and Social Studies: Towards Excellence and Equity* (Kagan). He co-authored *The Big Six Historical Thinking Concepts* (Nelson). Currently, he is the Provincial Coordinator of the BC Heritage Fairs Society.

JOHN MYERS is currently a curriculum instructor in elementary and secondary education at the Ontario Institute for Studies in Education (OISE), University of Toronto—after a four-decade teaching career in Canada and elsewhere. His interests include Canadian immigration history and policy, classroom assessment, and the thoughtful use of a repertoire of teaching strategies across the curriculum. At present, he is involved in a project with several American teachers on the use of co-operative learning to promote social and emotional development linked to academic achievement.

PAUL NEUFELD is an associate professor in the Faculty of Education at Simon Fraser University in British Columbia, where he teaches courses on reading and learning disabilities. His research is inspired by broad questions about how best to address the needs of students for whom school is often challenging—historically, schools have not supported these students well. More specifically, his research focuses on the reading development and instruction of students that struggle with print and on the historical emergence, practice, and ongoing development of the constructs of learning disabilities and attention-deficit/hyperactivity disorder in school contexts.

LYNN NEWBERY graduated from the University of Toronto in the mid-sixties, and moved to a coastal community in British Columbia where she first discovered the excitement of teaching about First Nations history and culture. She has held teaching or administrative positions in secondary and elementary schools, and been active in the communities in which she has lived. After retiring from the public school system, Lynn became a faculty associate with Simon Fraser University, working with student teachers. She is currently a school trustee with Coast Mountain School District.

ÖZLEM SENSOY is an associate professor in the Faculty of Education at Simon Fraser University in British Columbia. She conducts research on social justice education, critical media literacy, and cultural studies. Her research articles have appeared in such journals as *Gender and Education*, *Discourse: Studies in the Cultural Politics of Education*, and *Race Ethnicity and Education*. She is the co-editor of the award-winning books *Muslim Voices in School* (Sense Publishing, 2009) and *Rethinking Popular Culture and Education* (Rethinking Schools, 2011). Her most recent book, published by Teachers College Press, is called *Is Everyone Really Equal?* For additional information, see: www.educ.sfu.ca/research/sensoy.

NEIL SMITH has been an instructor of social studies curriculum and instruction courses at Vancouver Island University. He was a teaching scholar (2004–2009) with the Teaching and Learning Centre at that university and has also worked as a facilitator for "Appreciative Inquiry and Instructional Skills" workshops. He is currently working as an educational consultant with a focus on developing professional learning communities through inquiry learning.

STEFAN STIPP has taught humanities at secondary schools in Surrey, BC, for eighteen years and has also been a faculty associate in Simon Fraser University's teacher education program. Additional background about his work with portfolio assessment can be found in his Master's thesis, "Tilling the Soil: Making Portfolio Assessment Work in an Integrated High School Humanities Setting." He is currently developing a framework to help students become self-regulated learners.

AMY VON HEYKING is an associate professor in the Faculty of Education at the University of Lethbridge in Alberta. She is a member of the executive board of the History Education Network (THEN/HiER). Her areas of research include history teaching and learning, and the history of school curricula in Canada. She is the author of the teaching resource *Teaching with Dear Canada* (Scholastic Canada, 3 vols.), head author of the *Teaching Social Studies Through Literature* series (Scholastic Canada), and author of *Creating Citizens: History and Identity in Alberta's Schools* (University of Calgary Press, 2006).

WALTER WERNER is a retired faculty member who taught social studies education in the University of British Columbia's Department of Curriculum and Pedagogy. He has also taught graduate courses in curriculum issues and curriculum change and implementation, and has published widely in the areas of global education and visual literacy.

ANDREW YOUNG has taught in BC public schools for over twenty years. He completed an MA in Environmental Education and Communications from Royal Roads University. Andrew also spent three summers as an instructor for a geography methods class in the Faculty of Education at the University of British Columbia. In addition to teaching, Andrew served as the Canadian Council for Geographic Education (CCGE) representative for BC and the Yukon for the maximum term of six years and is now a member of the Royal Canadian Geographical Society College of Fellows. Andrew's enthusiastic commitment to geographic education extends beyond the classroom with field trips to Mount St. Helens, presenting workshops at social studies conferences, marking geography exams, and participating in Project Watershed.

Index

R

racism. *See* prejudice and racism

RAFT writing, 117–18

RallyRobin, RallyTable, RallyRead
  strategies, 130, *131*

Raths, Louis, 26, 233

rationales
  for citizenship education, 20–29
  in course planning, 279–80
  for social studies, 15–16
  in yearly vision, 281–82, *283*
  See also purpose, curricular

reader-response perspective, 198–201,
  199, *200–201*
  See also literature, in social studies

readers' theatre, 200–201

reading comprehension, 206–14, *212–13*
  during- and after-reading strategies,
    208–10
  overviewing strategy, *212–13*
  pre-reading strategies, 207–8
  teaching the strategies, 210–14, *212–13*
  as thinking, 206–7

Reading Teacher, The (journal), 195, *198*

reasoned judgment, 15, 68, 69, 70, 71–72
  See also judgments and decisions

reflection
  assessment and, 299
  in community classrooms, *105*
  in co-operative learning, 126, *126*,
    127–28, *129*, 129–30
  in critical inquiry, *91*, 93
  on field experiences, 6, 186
  on literature, *199*, *200–201*, 201
  on local expert interviews, *182*, 188
  on portfolios, 316
  on social action projects, 144, *145*
  See also closure and debriefing;
    culminating tasks

research projects. *See* student research

resources. *See* teaching resources

responsibility concepts, *266*

Review strategy, *131*

revising, *71*, 98, 305–6

Rindisbacher, Peter (painter), 161

Robinson, Donna
  "Social Studies is . . . A Poem," 9

Rogoff, Barbara, 100–101

role models, *241*
  See also teacher modelling

role-playing
  for current events, 262
  in global/multicultural education, 257
  for history studies, 42, 119, 164
  in literature studies, *199*, *200–201*
  "neighbourhood conflict" example,
    268–69, *270*
  self-assessment of, *327*, *328*
  for timelines, 119
  as tool for understanding, 70, 72, 84
  in values education, 232
  See also mock trials

root criticism, of knowledge, 25

Rosenblatt, Louise, 192, 193

"rotten rules" game, *85*

RoundRobin, Roundtable strategies, 130,
  131, 132

rubrics. *See under* assessment

Ruskin, John, 166

Ryerson, Egerton, 65, 67

S

Saarinen, Thomas, 250

Santayana, George, 22

Sarason, Seymour, 124

Saskatoon Public School Division, 134

scavenger hunts, *153*, 220

Schweitzer, Albert, 106

Seixas, Peter, 27, 35–36

self-assessment, 304, 306, 316, *327*,
  327–29, *328–29*
  See also assessment: student
    involvement and ownership

self-regulated reading comprehension
  strategies, 213–14

Seneca, 125

sequencing, in lesson planning, 291–
  92, *294*

sequencing and seriation concepts, 39–40,
  208, 209

Shermis, Samuel, 25, 27–28, 29n2

Shernoff, David, 89

Shields, Pat, 119

short-term vs. lasting differences
  example, 81, *82*

Siegel, Harvey, 56

Simon, Sidney, 26, 233

"Simon Fraser" lesson, *294–97*

simulations and modelling
  of archaeological digs, *21*, 72, *243*, 286

in conceptual understanding, 84, *85*

in global/multicultural education, 257

of political action, *184*

in unit plans, *292*

in values education, 232
  See also mock trials; role-playing

simultaneous interaction, in co-operative
  learning, 130

Singer, Marcus, 237

Slavin, Robert, 125

Smith, Elizabeth (teacher case study),
  113–14

social acceptance/social change spectrum,
  22, *22*, 23–25, 281

social and political action, 135–47
  "Calgary Zoo" example, *139*, 140
  child labour example, 141–42
  in citizenship education, 28, 135
  community appropriateness, 137–38
  community food programs
    example, 141
  complexity in, 140–43
  in course plans and vision, *283*, 283,
    284, 287
  in current events teaching, 263
  as curriculum goal, 12, 138
  environmental issues, 136, 137,
    140–41, *141*, 142
  evaluation of, 138–39, 144, *145*
  in global/multicultural education, 257
  implementation, 144
  literature and, *194*
  McDonald's example, 142
  motivation from, 137
  Nike boycott, 142–43
  planning for, 137–40, *143*
  project framework, *136*, 137–44
  Project Love, 136–37, 147
  resources for, 138, 147
  in social reform orientation, 25
  stakeholder consequences, *142*, 142–43
  street-naming example, 138, 140
  Terry Fox National School Run Day
    example, 136, 147
  types of, 135–37
  value development and, 231
  in yearly vision, 283, *283*

Social Education (journal), 195, *198*